PROSE FOR DISCUSSION

E.W. BUXTON

SECOND EDITION
Revised by
Bonnie Buxton

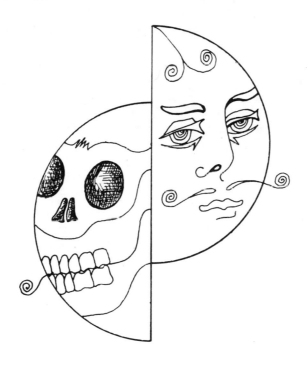

gage EDUCATIONAL PUBLISHING COMPANY
A DIVISION OF CANADA PUBLISHING CORPORATION
TORONTO ONTARIO CANADA

ACKNOWLEDGMENTS—We gratefully acknowledge the valuable assistance of Don Biamonte and teachers of the Edmonton Separate School Board who tested the selections added to the revised edition of this anthology; and of Patrick Drysdale, the publisher's editor, for his encouragement and suggestions. We are grateful also to the following individuals for their help in the two-year experimental period that preceded publication of the original edition in 1968: Madeleine Bailey, Don Biamonte, Melvin Coates, Dick Eldridge, Earle G. Hawkesworth, Sister Florence Leduc, Grace Mersereau, Margaret Molloy, J. Nelson Periera, Don Robertson, Father Sebastian.

To the various authors and publishers who have permitted the use of their work, and who are separately acknowledged on the first page of each selection, we express our appreciation. Every attempt has been made to reproduce exactly the text of the original of each selection; hence there will be discrepancies in spelling and punctuation, which vary with the times and depend also on the usage of the author's country of origin.

7 8 9 10 11   BP   91 90 89 88 87

ISBN 0-7715-2004-2

Contents

1 / Education and experience

2 / The measure of a man

3 / Man and society

4 / Science, technology, and the arts

Introduction

Most of the essays and short stories in this anthology were first tested in classrooms by the teachers whose names are listed in the acknowledgments. The most important criterion for selection was the suitability of the material for engaging student interest and thereby giving pleasure and promoting fruitful discussion.

It is recognized, of course, that interest and pleasure are general terms and that the level or kind of pleasure that an individual obtains from literature depends to a considerable extent upon his age and degree of maturity. For example, children in elementary school usually enjoy books and stories that make them laugh at ridiculous or slapstick situations, that carry them to other times or exotic places, or that enable them to identify with individuals who overcome giants and dragons, cross perilous seas and deserts, fight pirates and Indians, hunt wild animals, foil outlaws and capture criminals, or score the tie-breaking goal in the final seconds of the last period. In progressing through junior and senior high school, students should be acquiring new interests and developing abilities that will enable them to gain pleasure from literature which makes greater demands upon the reader, literature which offers insights into the complexities of human behavior.

Teachers in the high schools today have abundant evidence to show that their students are vitally concerned with contemporary problems. One of my colleagues has been asking hundreds of students about the topics they feel are most worthy of discussion in class and in written assignments. A high proportion of the topics suggested involve questions like: What are my goals? What is ambition? What is friendship? What causes racial prejudice? Can war ever be abolished? These questions indicate that young people are searching for some set of values, some reasonably clear guidelines for behavior, some tentative answers to a multitude of questions about themselves, their relationships with other people, and their place in a society whose mores and institutions they are expected to accept, but which is itself in a state of rapid change.

Obviously, certain aspects of human relationships can become meaningful only through direct experience, and many of the conflicts which disturb society today have so many hidden roots and twisting branches that our most intelligent leaders are baffled in their search for solutions. Literature must not be looked upon as *the* source of morals and precepts that will lead automatically to "the good life" and a utopian society.

Nevertheless, literature has the potential to assist students in their quest for a better understanding of themselves and their world. Although a writer may not provide definite answers to complex problems, he or she can bring to light many dimensions that may otherwise remain obscure. The effective writer can help his reader to view experience with an objectivity not always possible in real life, where the lapse of time and the distraction of concomitant or subsequent events may obscure the essential meaning of a situation before any analysis can be completed. This objectivity the good writer can provide by selecting from the complexity of human experience those elements which will enable him to present his vision with clarity and force. For example, in his brief but moving "Convocation Address,"

Hungarian-born poet George Faludy relates his experience in a Soviet concentration camp to the survival of the human spirit in the age of crisis. He describes how, in this work camp, a love of learning ensured the physical and spiritual survival of several hundred people, including himself. Those prisoners who were intent only on survival perished—victims Faludy compares to today's consumers "who seem obsessed with producing and consuming an ever-growing mountain of things to ensure comfort and survival; who have addicted themselves to energy as if to morphine and until they are ready to destroy all nature to increase the dosage . . . ."

Discussion of this comparatively simple essay may suggest that the pleasure and the insight which students gain from a selection will depend upon what they bring to their reading: their curiosity about human behavior, their ability to relate literature to their own experience, and their sensitivity to the meanings and implications that may underly the writer's statements. For example, students can enjoy "The Secret Life of Walter Mitty" when their experience with life and literature has been sufficiently broad to enable them to sense the humor inherent in the sharp contrasts between Mitty's ineffectual behavior in the real world and his nonchalant mastery of every emergency encountered in his secret life. The fun in the story has the same source as that in most jokes: it depends upon an unexpected change of direction that the audience cannot possibly foresee. However, some students will see that Thurber's story is something more than a series of anecdotes with unexpected endings. The adolescent who has at times created his own world of fantasy, for example, may respond empathetically to Mitty's need to create a secret life to which he can retire when reality becomes oppressive. Other students may see Mitty not only as akin to themselves but as representative of most of us who devise our own stratagems for defence against forces that threaten our dignity, our individuality, or our self-confidence—and the forces may include our own feelings of inadequacy as well as the domination of wives or husbands, employers, supervisors, administrators, and even high-school teachers.

When approaching more difficult selections, the student is justified in assuming that, because a good writer tries to eliminate from his material all non-essential elements, what he does retain must have some relevance to the experience that he is attempting to communicate. Proceeding from this assumption, the student can be encouraged to ask questions as to why the writer selected those elements that he has included in his narrative. Thus, in attempting to achieve a reasonably valid interpretation of "The Portable Phonograph," the student might raise such questions as the following: Why does Clark devote almost a quarter of his story to a detailed description of the setting? Why select four men and place them in a cave? Why indicate that the four men are intelligent, well educated, interested in the arts? Why allude to religious rituals at several points throughout the story? Why conclude with a piece of lead pipe, and why describe it as "comfortable"?

A second reasonably valid assumption the student can make is that most of the material in this book possesses universality. For example, the behavior of Walter Mitty or of Uncle Billy in "Willow Song," is representative of the behavior of individuals or groups of individuals around the globe. The implications of the behavior of the professor in "The Portable Phonograph" are disturbing in a world where, in spite of the threat posed by the hydrogen bomb, nearly all of the "civilized" nations are devoting a large proportion of their revenue to maintaining the forces that Clark may be symbolizing by the "comfortable piece of lead pipe." For other illustrations of the universality of literature, students might consider what we mean when we call a person a Scrooge, a Goliath, a Venus, a Hercules, a Cassandra, or a Paul Bunyan.

Related to the universality of a selection is the multiplicity of meaning that can be supported by references to the behavior of characters, to comments made by the author, or to objects, situations, or statements that may have a symbolic significance. In engaging in this exploration of possible meanings, students will be growing in their ability to read attentively and creatively, to think critically, to organize and present ideas in speech and writing, to listen with attention and respect to the ideas of their classmates, and to revise their conclusions in the light of new evidence. Discussions that foster the growth of these abilities will be most productive if each student develops the attitude that he is a member of a group engaged in a co-operative search for truth, not a competition for the "right" answer.

Sometimes the teacher may initiate the quest for meaning by having each member of the group read a selection quickly and then go through it again, jotting down a series of statements that seem to form a pattern and to suggest a possible interpretation. For example, during a preliminary reading of "The Giraffe," most students will sense that Mauro Senesi is telling his story to illuminate some aspect of life that has relevance far beyond the boundaries of a small Italian village. In their search for meaning, one group of students may note that several statements in the story emphasize the giraffe's vision. For example, "It must have seen . . . who knows how far . . ." "It was as if the giraffe were our periscope, to see from up above who knows what, who knows where." Students may observe that the giraffe was continually revealing or uncovering things that people wished to keep hidden from view. For example, it denuded "the trees that the Mayor had planted in a little square to camouflage it as a park." A third group may point out that while the giraffe was received first with perplexity and then with mounting suspicion and anger by the adults, the boys admired and respected it because it made them feel larger, more human. And when the giraffe died in spite of their heroic efforts to care for it, one of the group cursed the town "where giraffes can't live because there's room only for things that are already here." What does the giraffe stand for? Is Senesi's story related in any way to "The Doll's House," to "A Novelist's Allegory," or to "Convocation Address"? It is possible that members of a class, by exchanging, shaping, and reshaping ideas, can provide some interesting answers that neither their teacher nor the editor may have foreseen. Relating and comparing a selection with others can sometimes help students to gain insights that the study of the pieces in isolation does not provide. For example, "The Education of Hyman Kaplan" is revealed as something more than a comedy when the student sees that Mr. Parkhill's rigidity, his practicality, and his lack of sensitivity are similar to the qualities exhibited by Jody's father, Carl, in "The Leader of the People," by Big Simon in "Thus I Refute Beelzy," by Aunt Beryl in "The Doll's House," and the American writer in "On Living in a Cold Country." All five "teachers" fail to understand or to appreciate behavior that is spontaneous, genuine, imaginative, prompted by feeling rather than confined by rules or logic. Students might discuss whether all of these selections have something to say about the conflict between realism and romanticism. They might also wonder whether there are any implications for education.

The range of materials in the anthology should provide for a variety of teaching approaches and student activities. Thus, selections like "The Portable Phonograph," "Composition: Double Exposure," "Counterparts," and "The Door," invite close reading, considerable probing for meanings and implications, and lively discussion. Lighter selections, such as "Children Are Monsters," "The Grown-Up Problem," and "The Schartz-Metterklume Method," may introduce a comic interlude that permits rapid reading, a brief informal discussion, and the opportunity to chuckle at man's follies, idiosyncracies, and perversities. Some selections may suggest an oral reading by the teacher or by students who read well. The following are illustrative procedures that may contribute to understanding and appreciation:

During a discussion, a student reads aloud statements in the text that illustrate or defend his interpretation of a selection.

To introduce "The Door," the teacher reads aloud the first two or three paragraphs and then discusses the way that E. B. White exploits the resources of form and structure to reinforce his view of modern man vainly attempting to find some stability amid shifting forces in a society where "Everything . . . is something it isn't."

A selection like "Holiday Memory" almost demands effective oral interpretation if students are to appreciate the way that Dylan Thomas used word music—alliteration, assonance, and rhythmical patterns—to capture the gaiety, delightful confusion, and exuberance of the holiday experience. Students can learn much about the relationship between form and content in prose and poetry by listening to someone (perhaps Dylan Thomas himself in a recording) who can effectively read this selection—or "Fern Hill" or "A Child's Christmas in Wales." Selections like "The Secret Life of Walter Mitty" and "Buck Fanshaw's Funeral" might be read aloud by a group of students, with each student in the group playing the part of one of the speakers. We have observed a class having a hilarious time listening to an oral presentation of "Mr. Kaplan and Shakespeare," with one student acting as narrator, a second as Mr. Parkhill, two girls reading the halting contributions of Miss Caravello and Mrs. Yampolsky, and a boy with considerable talent for mimicry assuming Mr. Kaplan's role of defender of the bard and interpreter of the meditations of "Julius Scissors" in the "tant."

In addition to providing for varied reading activities, the selections in the text should offer interesting models, topics, and ideas for student writing. For example:

As a culmination to the discussion of such selections as "Father Opens My Mail" or "The Grown-Up Problem" or "Thus I Refute Beelzy," students may write a short theme describing what they consider a viable relationship between parents and offspring or between teachers and students.

Essayists like Machiavelli, Lin Yutang, Bruno Bettelheim, and Pierre Berton state that many of our long-praised virtues, including honesty, thrift, industry, patient acceptance of adversity, and obedience to authority may, under certain conditions, become vices. These writers seem to be challenging their readers either to join their camp or to defend an opposing position. Some students may wish to accept the challenge as the basis for an argumentative essay.

Occasionally, it may be worthwhile for students to imitate the form and style of a certain writer. For example, some members of the class may develop a Socratic dialogue, like that used in the selection from *The Republic*, to present their blueprint for high school education or for a better community. Other students may be interested in describing another imaginary adventure of Walter Mitty, imitating the style and technique used by James Thurber.

Students who spent the previous summer vacation working may be confident that they can write of situations just as harassing, or mentors just as demanding, as those encountered by Malvina Hoffman and Moss Hart. Others may feel more comfortable reminiscing about their own experiences, using simple words and short sentences, similar to the prose of Minnie Aodla Freeman in "Life Among the Qallunaat."

The problem confronting the young police officer in "Shooting an Elephant" is one that every young person will face from time to time throughout his life. It is the problem of deciding whether to respond to a critical situation in accordance with one's own convictions or to submit to the pressure imposed directly or indirectly by one's peers or by society. Students may wish to narrate a personal experience in which they faced this kind of crisis. As a more academic assignment, they may compare or contrast the individual-versus-group situation which confronted the young police officer in "Shooting an Elephant" with that facing Huck in Mark Twain's *Huckleberry Finn* or Dr. Stockman in Ibsen's *An Enemy of the People*.

In addition to fostering a range of writing activities, a number of the selections may introduce the student to a study of varieties of usage, regional dialects, etymology, and semantics. For example, some teachers have found that "Buck Fanshaw's Funeral" provides an amusing introduction to "functional varieties"; that is, the variations in speech that may result from differences in the education, occupation, or social and cultural environment of the speakers. In Twain's story the "varieties" fail to function because the wide divergence between the minister's grandiose statements and Scotty's colorful metaphors makes communication between the two speakers almost impossible—even though they are engaged in what might be termed a "life-and-death" conversation. Students might attempt to manipulate their language by imitating style, or by changing statements from one level or variety to another. For example, both the minister's oratorical expressions and Scotty's mining camp metaphors may be rewritten in clear, informal English. In "The Cask of Amontillado," Montresor's formal statement "When he ventured upon insult, I vowed revenge" can be revised to the informal, "When he insulted me, I decided to get even"; the slang, "When he called me a rat, I decided to flatten him"; and the non-standard, "When he done what he done, I seen that I'd have to get back at him somehow."

Some teachers and students may feel that an anthology that contains no editorial notes, comments, or discussion questions is incomplete—and perhaps with some justification. Undoubtedly, a series of questions following a selection may open fruitful areas for discussion and writing. However, our comments throughout this introduction indicate our belief that the most vigorous discussion may develop when students themselves formulate questions concerning the writer's intention, his selection and treatment of material, and what he appears to be saying or implying about man and society. The dialogue can become particularly stimulating when the selection being discussed is relevant to a current editorial, a magazine article, or a local, national, or international issue that is of immediate concern to the students. For these reasons, "student helps" designed by someone outside the classroom may diminish the leadership of teachers and students, and may make the exploration of the stories and essays in this text less spontaneous, more stereotyped, more mechanical than it might be if students and teachers are free to design their own instruments for analysis and evaluation.

These considerations relating to study helps in general may explain the omission of biographical sketches from the anthology. In a story or an essay the writer's theme, his point of view, his acceptance or rejection of conventional beliefs, and his treatment of the subject may challenge a student to find out when and where he lived and what educational and environmental conditions may have influenced his writing. Questions of this kind are probably best answered, not by a terse hundred-word biography, but by the student's referring to some of the more comprehensive biographical and critical material that is now available for almost all of the writers whose work is included in this book.

This use of materials to supplement selections in an anthology should be an essential feature of most English programs in the high schools today. The selections in this book should therefore be viewed as an introduction to the work of many writers rather than as a complete curriculum in literature. Thus, students who enjoy "The Cask of Amontillado," "The Leader of the People," "The Basement Room," "Two Soldiers," or "On Living in a Cold Country," may turn to other works by Poe, Steinbeck, Greene, Faulkner or MacLennan. Excellent collections of short stories by contemporary Canadian writers can now be purchased in very inexpensive editions and should be available in the school library or the English classroom. The essays in the anthology can be supplemented by other collections and by challenging articles and editorials from newspapers and from such periodicals as *The Saturday Review of Literature, Maclean's, Saturday Night, Harper's, The New Yorker*, and *The Atlantic*.

Throughout this introduction, we have emphasized the "processes" that the student may use in examining and interpreting literature. We have stressed independent reading and student formulation of questions and answers because we recognize that in all the years following his graduation from our educational institutions the student will have no editor, teacher, or parents to direct his reading. He will be largely dependent then on his own resources for interpretation and judgment. One of the aims of this book is to provide opportunities for developing these resources, to guide the student in his search for the meaning of literature and of life.

Education and experience

If we want to find out if a colt is nervous, we expose him to alarming
noises; so we must introduce our guardians when they are young to
fear, and by contrast, give them opportunities for pleasure, proving
them far more rigorously than we prove gold in a furnace. If they
bear themselves well and are not easily bamboozled, if they show
themselves self-reliant and maintain in all circumstances the principles
of balance and harmony they learned in their education, then they may
be expected to be of greatest service to the community as well as to
themselves.
— Plato

Do not think that youth has no force because he cannot speak to you
and me. Hark! In the next room who speaks so clear and emphatic?
Good Heavens! It is he! It is that very lump of bashfulness and
phlegm which for weeks has done nothing but eat when you were by,
and now rolls out these words like bell strokes. It seems he knows how
to speak to his contemporaries. Bashful or bold then, he will know
how to make us seniors very unnecessary.
— Ralph Waldo Emerson

O youth! The strength of it, the faith of it, the imagination of
it! . . . Youth! All youth! The silly, charming, beautiful youth.
— Joseph Conrad

All education is free in this sense; it cannot be shut up within walls.
To teach people to think, if only to make them more useful as soldiers
and mechanics, is to open all thoughts to them—a whole world of new
ideas.
— Arthur Joyce Cary

GREAT TEACHERS AND THEIR PUPILS

Gilbert Highet

In Western civilization there are two lines of teachers from whom all modern teaching stems: the Greek philosophers and the Hebrew prophets. Outside the Jewish community the influence of the Greeks is far wider, stronger, and more varied—with the exception of the teaching of Jesus himself. In this book we are not concerned with what is taught, but with *how* teaching is done; yet in content, also, our schools and our universities are much more Greek than Hebrew. The Greek teachers claimed to be following the movement of Reason. The Hebrew prophets knew they were uttering the voice of God. We admire both, but we are apt to think that while a group of men who are in touch with God can change the world by a rare and miraculous intervention, it needs the steady work of reason to keep the place going and to train the young.

Apart from elementary schoolmasters, instructors of scribes and the like, the first professional higher educators in the Western world were the group of brilliant talkers and keen thinkers who appeared in Greece during the fifth century B.C. They were called "sophists." (The word means something like "professional wise men," and, because of its implication that these men sold their brains for money, fell into disrepute. After Socrates, the intellectuals preferred to call themselves "philosophers," which means "lovers of wisdom for its own sake.") We are still talking about many of the ideas the sophists worked out: for instance, it was they who first discussed whether there were any absolute standards of morality, or merely artificial conventions; whether justice is a constant, or simply means the will of the ruling class; and so forth. As thinkers—particularly as destructive critics—they were dazzling. As teachers, they were superficial.

They were exclusively lecturers. All that we hear of them shows them as phenomenally graceful and subtle talkers, usually to fairly large audiences. In that they are the direct ancestors of the modern "authority" who tours the large cities giving a carefully prepared speech in which his own personal power or charm is combined with well-spaced jokes and memorable epigrams, the whole varying very little from one repetition to another. Like him, they were highly paid and widely advertised and welcomed by a reception committee and entertained by ambitious hosts. But unlike him, some of them professed to be authorities on *everything*. They said they could lecture on any subject under the sun. Often they were challenged to speak on odd and difficult topics, and accepted the dare. However, they did not usually pretend to know more facts than others, but rather to be able to think and talk better. In that, perhaps, they are the ancestors of the modern journalists who have the knack of turning out a bright and interesting article on any new subject, without using special or expert information. The perfect example of the modern sophist would be Bernard Shaw, if he had only spoken his inimitable prefaces with his inimitable charm instead of printing them. Like him, the sophists dazzled everyone without convincing anyone of anything positive. Like him, they argued unsystematically and unfairly, but painted over the gaps in their reasoning with glossy rhetoric. Like him, they had few constructive ideas, and won most applause by taking traditional notions and showing they were based on convention rather than logic. Like him, they demonstrated that almost anything could be proved by a fast talker—sometimes, as a stunt, they made a powerful speech on one side of a question in the morning and an equally powerful speech on the opposite side in the afternoon. And like him, they never allowed anyone else to get a word in edgewise.

The results of the sophists' method of teaching were both good and bad. They were a strong disruptive force in civilization, for they helped to blow up many sound traditional values, and often blinded their pupils by the temporary brilliance of the explosion, leaving them no help in rebuilding their individual and social lives. Yet they taught the Greeks what no other Mediterranean nation ever learnt, that thought alone is one of the strongest forces in human life. The respect for the thinker which they created has lasted, off and on, until this very day.

To some of his contemporaries Socrates looked like a sophist. But he distrusted and opposed the sophists wherever possible. They toured the whole Greek world: Socrates stayed in Athens, talking to his fellow-citizens. They made carefully prepared continuous speeches; he only asked questions. They took rich fees for their teaching; he refused regular payment, living and dying poor. They were elegantly dressed, turned out like filmstars on a personal-appearance tour, with secretaries and personal servants and elaborate advertising. Socrates wore the workingman's clothes, bare feet and a smock; in fact, he had been a stonemason and carver by trade, and came from a working-class family. They spoke in specially prepared lecture-halls; he talked to people at street-corners and in the gymnasium (like public baths and bathing-beaches nowadays), where every afternoon the young men exercised, and the old men talked, while they all sunbathed. He fitted in so well there that he sometimes compared himself to the athletic coach, who does not run or wrestle, but teaches others how to run and wrestle better: Socrates said he trained people to think. Lastly, the sophists said they knew everything and were ready to explain it. Socrates said he knew nothing and was trying to find out.

The sophists were the first lecturers. Socrates was the first tutor. His invention was more radical than theirs. Speeches such as they delivered could be heard elsewhere—in the new democratic law-courts, where clever orators tried to sway large juries by dozens of newly-developed oratorical tricks, and in the theatres, where tragic kings, queens, gods, and heroes accused and defied one another in immortal tirades, and in the assemblies of the people, where any citizen could speak on the destinies of Athens. And traveling virtuosi like the sophists were fairly common in other fields—touring musicians, painters, and sculptors, eminent poets like Simonides, were all welcome in Greek cities and at the rich courts of the "tyrants." It was not too hard, then, for the sophists to work out a performance of their own, as brilliant and sometimes as impermanent as a harpist's recital. The innovations Socrates made were to use ordinary conversation as a method of teaching, and to act on one society only, his own city of Athens, instead of detaching himself and traveling. He was not even a "brilliant conversationalist," in the style of Oscar Wilde and Madame du Deffand. He does not seem to have made memorable epigrams or thrown off eloquent paragraphs of improvisation like Coleridge. His talk was not "full of flowers and stars." He made the other fellow do most of the talking. He merely asked questions.

But anyone who has watched a cross-examination in court knows that this is more difficult than making a prepared speech. Socrates questioned all sorts and conditions, from schoolboys to elderly capitalists, from orthodox middle-of-the-road citizens to extremists, friends and enemies, critics and admirers, the famous and the obscure, prostitutes and politicians, artists and soldiers, average Athenians and famous visitors. It was incredibly difficult for him to adapt himself to so many different characters and outlooks, and yet we know that he did. (In this one of his truest descendants was St. Ignatius Loyola, founder of the Jesuits, who was different for every different person he talked to, and adapted his manner, indulgent or severe, gay or serious, to the character of the person he was interviewing.) Socrates looked ugly. He had good manners, but no aristocratic polish. Yet he was able to talk to the cleverest and the toughest minds of his age and to convince them that they knew no more than he did. His methods were, first, the modest declaration of his own ignorance—which imperceptibly flattered the other man and made him eager to explain to such an intelligent but naïve inquirer; second, his adaptability—which showed him the side on which each man could be best approached; and, third, his unfailing good humor—which allowed him always to keep the conversation going and at crises, when the other lost his temper, to dominate it. Some of the most delightful dramatic scenes in literature are those dialogues in which we see him confronted by a brilliant fanatic and drenched with a shower of words that would have silenced most others, and then emerging, with a humorous pretense of timidity, to shake off the rhetoric and pursue the truth, until at last, under his gently persistent questions, his opponent is—not forced, but led, to admit that he was wrong, and to fall into helpless silence.

We know he was a good teacher, because he had good pupils. The greatest was Plato, who founded a college, named Academy, to pursue the studies on which Socrates had launched him. As well as teaching and studying, Plato wrote books on philosophical problems all his life. Nearly every one is in the form of a conversation, and nearly every one is dominated by Socrates. There has rarely been a finer tribute to any master by any pupil. Plato's own character and his own philosophical ideas were strongly marked, but he seems to subordinate

himself entirely to the personality and method of Socrates in every book but his last. He never appears in any of his dialogues by name, and mentions himself only twice. The dialogues were apparently meant to reproduce Socrates' own method of teaching by conversation, with the very accents of his voice. They show him to us as a young man, tackling the highly publicized sophists on their own ground; at a gay party in the prime of his life, surrounded by the best minds of his time, rising poets and scientists and statesmen, helping to bring the best out of them all and dominating the whole interplay of eloquence and imagination; in the gymnasium chatting with young athletes and their fathers; in the streets questioning passersby; interviewing a touring celebrity; bringing geometrical proofs out of the mind of a little untrained slave-boy; speaking his own defense in his trial at the age of seventy, and still teaching the Athenians by the firmness with which he holds to his convictions; and, in the last hours before his execution, arguing for the immortality of the soul. In all these different situations he combines the steady unflinching aim, the pursuit of truth, with the most supple adaptability of approach to different people.

But the queerest thing about his teaching is that we do not exactly know what he taught. We know *how* he taught. We know that very well. But we do not know precisely what lessons his pupils and interlocutors drew from his questioning. His different pupils say he taught different things. Young Xenophon knew him before going out East to become a soldier of fortune, and wrote memoirs of him later. He shows Socrates as an inquisitive, pawky, charming but annoying eccentric, who inquired into everything and criticized everything more or less indiscriminately. Another of his pupils, Aristippus, thought he destroyed all moral traditions and all permanent spiritual values by his criticism, and encouraged men to live life without conventions, following only pleasure and the instincts. Plato himself began by writing conversations in which Socrates proved nothing except that no one knows anything; or, at most, that virtue must be knowledge. Then he went on to conversations where Socrates, after breaking down traditional theories, proceeded to build up elaborate theories of his own—still working on the question-and-answer principle, but reducing the other man to a mere stooge saying "Yes" and "No" and "Go on." Some of these theories are called Plato's by later writers. Were they Plato's, or did Socrates teach them?

Evidently the answer is "*both*." Socrates did not teach them in their fully explicit form, or his other pupils would have remembered them also. But Plato did not work them out entirely on his own. They were produced by the action of Socrates' teaching upon his mind. Also, we must remember that anyone who taught so well as Socrates and who used cross-examination as his method cannot have thrown out questions at random. He must have had some set of positive beliefs from which his questions flowed; and even if he did not explain them positively, his more brilliant pupils could reconstruct them. His teaching is therefore one of the great examples of the power of implication. What a teacher says outright sometimes goes unheard. What he stimulates his pupils to think out for themselves often has a far more potent influence upon them.

Plato himself taught more systematically and more exclusively than his master. More systematically, because he established a college instead of going about the streets: it had entrance examinations and disciplinary rules, and was apparently run rather like a monastery or a club of research workers. More exclusively, because instead of chatting with everybody he preferred specially selected pupils, and instead of falling into spontaneous conversations he gave lectures, which were sometimes very difficult to understand. But he was not a working man as Socrates had been. He was a nobleman, rich and gifted, a poet by his earliest inclinations and a mystic all his life, who felt it impossible to teach *everyone* and limited his efforts to highly-trained, carefully chosen listeners. He was the founder of the examination system. His teaching therefore had a strictly limited effect. He had one outstandingly bad pupil, the young prince Dionysius of Syracuse, whom he tried to make into a philosopher-king, and who became a tyrant; and one superlatively good one, Aristotle, probably the best and broadest single mind the human species has yet produced. But besides these he has made many hundreds of pupils through his books, which are supreme masterpieces of the teacher's art.

In them he shows his master Socrates proposing a problem to one of his friends or pupils. Questions are asked, gently and almost casually. As the answers are given, Socrates draws them together and asks further questions about their apparent inconsistencies. Under his patient interrogation, irrational judgments are thrown aside and shallow ideas are plumbed and discarded and objections are raised and countered and slowly, slowly, under the guidance of Reason alone, we are carried through the labyrinthine paths of learning until we arrive at a positive result, which we could by no means have foreseen when we started and could not have reached except by cool rational discussion. At least, that is the effect which Plato wishes to produce. Every step of the argument is exposed. There are no appeals to higher authority. During the discussion there is no escape into windy words or mystical ideas. If you, as you read, think that the writer or the speakers are cheating, you are not intimidated or dissuaded from doing so. You are like a stranger who has walked up to a little group which includes Socrates, and who listens to the conversation without joining in it. At any moment, at any word, you can turn away and decide, if you wish, that Socrates is a charlatan and that his pupils are stooges hypnotized into agreeing with him. Some do. Many do. All do when they go beyond Socrates to Plato and read *The Laws*, a sinister document which should stand on the same shelf as George Orwell's *Nineteen Eighty-*

Four but expresses admiration of the bad state Orwell exposes.

Obviously what Plato taught was—as far as politics are concerned—anti-democratic and narrow-minded and at the end both sad and bad. But *how* he taught it is what concerns us; and he taught it through these brilliantly seductive conversations in which the reader, since he cannot identify himself with Socrates, automatically identifies himself with the interlocutor, and so finds himself saying "Yes" and "Certainly" to propositions which he would never have thought of if he had been left alone. In politics this is highly dangerous. In metaphysics and logic and even in morality it is a very healthy and exercising method of teaching. And certainly it is one of the most powerful ever invented. As you begin to read a Socratic dialogue written by Plato, you relax under the charm of the surroundings and the gentleness of the initial exchanges, and before you know it you are still thinking, yet thinking along the lines suggested—not laid down, but suggested—by a teacher who died two thousand three hundred years ago.

There could not be a better example of the distinction between the subject-matter of teaching and the method of teaching. Few of us admire or believe the doctrines which Plato taught. All of us must admire the methods by which he taught them. From his master Socrates he had learnt that there is no possible way to educate people, to convert them and change them and convince them fully and lastingly, except by calm, cool reasoning. Ask the questions. Examine the answers. Go on discussing until the reason is satisfied with the result. As you think by yourself, all alone, you should converse with Reason almost as though Reason were another person, with claims to respect at least equal to your own. When you argue with someone else, the argument should not be a fight between you two, but a hunt after Reason, in which you both join, helping each other to detect and capture the truth you both desire. To read a dialogue in which Plato shows the work of his teacher is not necessarily to be convinced of the conclusions which are its end-product; but it always produces admiration of the men who could exhibit reasoned argument as the strongest and most permanent force in human affairs.

ꜰʀᴏᴍ THE REPUBLIC

Plato

. . . "We may assume then that our guardians need [certain] qualities. But how are they to be brought up and educated? If we try to answer this question, I wonder whether it will help us

— *excerpts from Plato's* The Republic, *edited by E. V. Rieu and published by Penguin Books, London; reprinted by permission*

at all in our main enquiry into the origin of justice and injustice? We do not want to leave out anything relevant, but we don't want to embark on a long digression."

To which Adeimantus replied, "I expect it will help us all right."

"Then, my dear Adeimantus, we must certainly pursue the question," I rejoined, "even though it proves a long business. So let us set about educating our guardians as if we had as much time on our hands as the traditional story-teller."

"Let us by all means."

"What kind of education shall we give them then? We shall find it difficult to improve on the time-honoured distinction between the training we give to the body and the training we give to the mind and character."

"True."

"And we shall begin with the mind and character, shall we not?"

"Of course."

"In this type of education you would include stories, would you not?"

"Yes."

"These are of two kinds, true stories and fiction. Our education must use both, and start with fiction."

"I don't understand you."

"But you know that we begin by telling children stories. These are, in general, fiction, though they contain some truth. And we tell children stories before we start them on physical training."

"That is so."

"That is what I meant by saying that we start to train the mind before the body. And the first step, as you know, is always what matters most, particularly when we are dealing with those who are young and tender. That is the time when they are taking shape and when any impression we choose to make leaves a permanent mark."

"That is certainly true."

"Shall we therefore allow our children to listen to any stories written by anyone, and to form opinions the opposite of those we think they should have when they grow up?"

"We certainly shall not."

"Then it seems that our first business is to supervise the production of stories, and choose only those we think suitable, and reject the rest. We shall persuade mothers and nurses to tell our chosen stories to their children and so mould their minds and characters rather than their bodies. The greater part of the stories current to-day we shall have to reject."

"Which are you thinking of?"

"We can take some of the major legends as typical. For all are cast in the same mould and have the same effect. Do you agree?"

"Yes: but I'm not sure which you refer to as major."

"The stories in Homer and Hesiod and the poets. For it is the poets who have always made up stories to tell to men."

"Which stories do you mean and what fault do you find in them?"

"The worst fault possible," I replied, "especially if the story is an ugly one."

"And what is that?"

"Misrepresenting gods and heroes, like a portrait painter who fails to catch a likeness."

"That is a fault which certainly deserves censure. But give me more details."

"Well, on the most important of subjects, there is first and foremost the foul story about Ouranos and the things Hesiod says he did, and the revenge Cronos took on him. While the story of what Cronos did, and what he suffered at the hands of his son, is not fit to be repeated as it is to the young and innocent, even if it were true; it would be best to say nothing about it, or if it must be told, tell it to a select few under oath of secrecy, at a rite which required, to restrict it still further, the sacrifice not of a mere pig but of something large and expensive."

"These certainly are awkward stories."

"And they shall not be repeated in our state, Adeimantus," I said. "Nor shall any young audience be told that anyone who commits horrible crimes, or punishes his father unmercifully, is doing nothing out of the ordinary but merely what the first and greatest of the gods have done before."

"I entirely agree," said Adeimantus, "that these stories are unsuitable."

"Nor can we permit stories of wars and plots and battles among the gods; they are quite untrue, and if we want our prospective guardians to believe that quarrelsomeness is one of the worst of evils, we must certainly not let them embroider robes with the story of the Battle of the Giants, or tell them the tales about the many and various quarrels between gods and heroes and their friends and relations. On the contrary, if we are to persuade them that no citizen ever quarrelled with any other, because it is sinful, our old men and women must tell children stories with this end in view from the first, and we must compel our poets to tell them similar stories when they grow up. But we can permit no stories about Hera being tied up by her son, or Hephaestus being flung out of Heaven by his father for trying to help his mother when she was getting a beating, or any of Homer's Battles of the Gods, whether their intention is allegorical or not. Children cannot distinguish between what is allegory and what isn't, and opinions formed at that age are usually difficult to eradicate or change; it is therefore of the utmost importance that the first stories they hear shall aim at producing the right moral effect."

"Your case is a good one," he agreed, "but if someone wanted details, and asked what stories we were thinking of, what should we say?"

To which I replied, "My dear Adeimantus, you and I are not writing stories but founding a state. And the founders of a state, though they must know the type of story the poet must produce, and reject any that do not conform to that type, need not write them themselves." . . .

"It is not only to the poets . . . that we must issue orders requiring them to represent good character in their poems or not to write at all; we must issue similar orders to all artists and prevent them portraying bad character, ill-discipline, meanness, or ugliness in painting, sculpture, architecture, or any work of art, and if they are unable to comply they must be forbidden to practise their art. We shall thus prevent our guardians being brought up among representations of what is evil, and so day by day and little by little, by feeding as it were in an unhealthy pasture, insensibly doing themselves grave psychological damage. Our artists and craftsmen must be capable of perceiving the real nature of what is beautiful, and then our young men, living as it were in a good climate, will benefit because all the works of art they see and hear influence them for good, like the breezes from some healthy country, insensibly moulding them into sympathy and conformity with what is rational and right."

"That would indeed be the best way to bring them up." . . .

"The next stage in the training of our young men will be physical education. And here again they must be carefully trained from childhood onwards. I have my own opinions about it: let me see if you agree. In my view physical excellence does not of itself produce good character: on the other hand, excellency of mind and character will make the best of the physique it is given. What do you think?"

"I agree."

"We should do well then to leave the elaboration of rules for physical training to minds that have been thoroughly educated; all we need do, for brevity's sake, is to give a rough outline."

"Yes."

"We have already forbidden drink. A guardian is the last person in the world to get drunk and not know where he is."

"It would be absurd," he replied, "for a guardian to need someone to look after him."

"What about diet? Our guardians, you will agree, are competing in the most important of all contests. Should they train like ordinary athletes?"

"Perhaps so."

"But the athlete in training is a sleepy creature and his health delicately balanced. Haven't you noticed how they sleep most of their time, and how the smallest deviation from their routine leads to serious illness?"

"Yes, I've noticed that."

"So we shall need a better adjusted form of training for our soldier-athletes. They must be as wakeful as watchdogs, their sight and hearing must be of the keenest, and their health must not be too delicate to endure the many changes of food and drink, and the varieties of temperature that campaigning entails."

"I agree."

"And do you not also agree that the best form of physical training would be one akin to the simple education we have just been describing?"

"What do you mean?"

"I mean a suitably simple physical training, concentrating particularly on training for war."

"In what way?"

"Even Homer can tell you that," I replied. "For you know that when his heroes are on campaign he does not give them fish to eat, although they are on the shore of the Hellespont, nor boiled meat, but only roast. That is what suits soldiers best, because it is, generally speaking, easier to cook something direct on the fire than carry round pots and pans for the purpose."

"Much easier."

"And Homer, I think, never mentions seasonings. Indeed, even the ordinary athlete knows that if he is to be fit he must keep off them."

"And he is quite right to do so."

"In that case I assume that you don't approve of the luxury of Syracusan and Sicilian cooking."

"I should think not."

"And what about Corinthian girl-friends? Do you disapprove of them for men who want to keep fit?"

"I certainly do."

"And Attic confectionery, which is supposed to be so good, must go too?"

"It must."

"We might, I think, with justice compare these luxurious ways of living and eating with the music and song which used a wide range of harmony and rhythm. Elaborate music, we found, produces indiscipline, and elaborate food produces disease. But simplicity in music produces discipline of character, and simplicity in physical education health of body."

"Very true."

"And the prevalence of indiscipline and dis-ease in a community leads, does it not, to the opening of law courts and surgeries in large numbers, and law and medicine begin to give themselves airs, especially when they are paid so much attention even by free men."

"That is bound to happen.". . .

On the education of doctors and judges . . . "The best way for a doctor to acquire skill is to have, in addition to his knowledge of medical science, as wide and as early an acquaintance as possible with serious illness; in addition he should have experienced all kinds of disease in his own person and not be of an altogether healthy constitution. For doctors don't use their bodies to cure other people—if so, they could not allow their health to be bad—they use their minds; and if they're defective mentally their treatment can't be good."

"True."

"But with a judge it's a matter of mind controlling mind. And the mind must not be brought up from its youth to associate with wickedness, or to run through a whole range of crimes in order to get first-hand experience on which to judge them in other people, as the doctor did with diseases of the body: on the contrary, the mind must, while it is still young, remain quite without experience or contact with bad characters, if its moral development is to be good and its moral judgement sound. That is why people of good character seem simple when they are young, and are easily taken in by dishonesty—because they have in themselves nothing to give them a sympathetic understanding of vice."

"That's a common experience," he agreed.

"Which is why a good judge must not be a young man," I replied, "but an old one to whom knowledge of wickedness has come late in life, not as a feature he perceives in his own character, but as an evil whose effects he has learned after long practice to discern in other people, something about which he knows but of which he has no personal experience."

"A man like that would be a real judge indeed." . . .

"These then are the kind of doctors and judges for whom you will legislate in your state. They will treat those of your citizens whose physical and psychological constitution is good; as for the others, they will leave the unhealthy to die, and those whose psychological constitution is incurably warped they will put to death."

"That seems to be the best thing both for the individuals concerned and for society."

"And so," I said, "your young men, so long as they maintain their simple form of education, which, as we have said, breeds discipline, will take care not to need judicial treatment."

"True."

"And if they successfully follow on the same track in their physical training, they will never need a doctor except in cases of necessity."

"I agree."

"It is, of course, to stimulate their energy and initiative that they undergo these severities in their training, not merely to make themselves tough, which is the object of the diet and exercises of the ordinary athlete. And that, my dear Glaucon," I went on, "is why I say that the purpose of the two established types of education (literary and physical) is not, as some suppose, to deal one with the mind and the other with the body."

"What is it then?" he asked.

"I think that perhaps in the main both aim at training the mind."

"And how do they do that?"

"Have you noticed," I asked, "how a life-long devotion to physical exercise, to the exclusion of anything else, produces a certain type of mind? Just as a neglect of it produces another type? One type tends to be tough and un-civilized, the other soft and over-sensitive, and ——"

"Yes, I have noticed that," he broke in; "excessive emphasis on athletics produces a pretty uncivilized type, while a purely literary and academic training leaves a man with less backbone than is decent."

"It is the energy and initiative in their nature that may make them uncivilized," I said; "if you treat it properly it should make them brave, but if you overstrain it it turns them tough and uncouth, as you would expect."

"I agree," he said.

"The philosophic temperament, on the other hand, is gentle; too much relaxation may produce an excessive softness, but if it is treated properly the result should be civilized and humane."

"That is so."

"Now we agreed that our Guardians must have both these elements in their nature, did we not?"

"Yes."

"And must not the two elements be combined to produce a mind that is civilized and brave, as opposed to cowardly and uncivilized?"

"That is so."

"So when a man surrenders to the charms of music and lets the sound of the sweet, soft, mournful strains we have described flood into his soul, and gives up all his time to the pleasures of song, the effect at first on his energy and initiative of mind, if he has any, is to soften it as iron is softened in a furnace, and made workable instead of hard and unworkable: but if he does not break the enchantment, the next stage is that it melts and runs, till the spirit has quite run out of him and his mental guts (if I may so put it) are entirely removed, and he has become what Homer calls 'a feeble fighter'." . . .

"On the other hand, there is the man who takes a lot of strenuous physical exercise and lives well, but has little acquaintance with literature or philosophy. The physical health that results from such a course first fills him with confidence and energy, and increases his courage. But if he devotes himself exclusively to it, and never opens a book, any capacity he may have for learning is weakened by being starved of instruction or enquiry and by never taking part in any intelligent discussion, and becomes deaf and blind, because its perceptions are never cleared and strengthened by use."

"That is what happens." . . .

"What I should say therefore is that these two methods of education seem to have been given by god to men to train our initiative and our reason. They are not intended, one to train body, the other mind, except incidentally, but to ensure a proper harmony between energy and initiative on the one hand and reason on the other, by turning each to the right pitch. And so we may venture to assert that anyone who can produce the best blend of the physical and intellectual sides of education and apply them to the training of character, is producing harmony in a far more important sense than any mere musician."

"A very reasonable assertion."

"We must therefore ensure, my dear Glaucon," I said, "that there is always someone like this in charge of education in our state, if its constitution is to be preserved."

"We most certainly must."

"That, then, is an outline of the way in which we should educate and bring up our Guardians. For we need not go into detail about their dramatic performances, field sports of various kinds, and athletic competitions on foot or horseback. The details follow naturally from what we have said, and should give no particular difficulty."

"Yes, I dare say they won't be particularly difficult," he agreed.

"Well," I continued, "what comes next? We shall have to decide, I suppose, which of our Guardians are to govern, and which to be governed."

"I suppose so."

"Well, it is obvious that the elder must have authority over the younger."

"That is obvious."

"And again that those who govern must be the best."

"That's equally obvious."

"And the best farmers are those who have the greatest skill at farming, are they not?"

"Yes."

"And so if we want to pick the best guardians, we must pick those who have the greatest skill in watching over the interests of the community."

"Yes."

"For that shan't we need men who, besides being intelligent and capable, really care for those interests?"

"True."

"But we care most for what we love."

"Inevitably."

"And the deepest affection is based on community of interest, when we feel that our own good and ill fortune is completely bound up with that of someone else."

"That is so."

"So we must choose from among our guardians those who appear to us, when we scrutinize their whole career, to be most completely devoted to what they judge to be the interests of the community, and never prepared to act against them."

"They are the men for our purpose."

"A close watch must be kept on them, then, at all ages, to see if they stick to this principle, and do not forget or throw overboard, under the influence of force or propaganda, the conviction that they must always do what is best for the community."

"What do you mean by throwing overboard?" he asked.

"I will explain," I said. "It seems to me that when any belief leaves us, the loss is either voluntary or involuntary. Voluntary when the belief is false and we learn better, involuntary whenever the belief is true."

"I understand what you mean by a voluntary loss, but I don't see how it happens involuntarily."

"But why? Surely you agree that men are always unwilling to lose a good thing, but willing enough to be rid of a bad one. And isn't it a bad thing to be deceived about the truth, and a good thing to know what the truth is? For I assume that by knowing the truth you mean knowing things as they really are."

"Yes, you are quite right," he conceded, "and I agree that men are unwilling to lose a belief that is true."

"So when it happens it must be due to theft or propaganda or force."

"Now I don't understand again," he said.

"I'm afraid I'm talking too theatrically," I answered. "By 'theft' I simply mean the insensible process by which we are argued out of our beliefs, or else simply forget them in the course of time. Now perhaps you understand."

"Yes."

"By 'force' I mean what happens when we change our beliefs under the influence of pain or suffering."

"This too I understand," he said.

"And I think that you too would call it 'propaganda' when people are enticed into a change of opinion by promises of pleasure, or terrified into it by threats."

"Yes, propaganda and deceit always go together."

"To go back to what I was saying, then," I continued, "we must look for the Guardians who will stick most firmly to the principle that they must always do what they think best for the community. We must watch them closely from their earliest years, and set them tasks in doing which they are most likely to forget or be led astray from this principle; and we must choose only those who don't forget and are not easily misled. Do you agree?"

"Yes."

"And with the same end in view we must see how they stand up to pain and suffering."

"We must."

"We must also watch their reactions to the third kind of test, propaganda. If we want to find out if a colt is nervous we expose him to alarming noises: so we must introduce our Guardians when they are young to fear and, by contrast, give them opportunities for pleasure, proving them far more rigorously than we prove gold in the furnace. If they bear themselves well and are not easily bamboozled, if they show themselves self-reliant and maintain in all circumstances the principles of balance and harmony they learned in their education, then they may be expected to be of the greatest service to the community as well as to themselves. And any Guardian who survives these continuous trials in childhood, youth, and manhood unscathed, shall be given authority in our state; he shall be honoured during his lifetime and when he is dead shall have the tribute of a public funeral and appropriate memorial.

"That in brief, and without going into details," I concluded, "is the way in which I would select the Guardians who are to be given authority as Rulers."

"And that's the way I think it should be done," he replied.

"Strictly speaking, then, it is for them that we should reserve the term Guardian in its fullest sense, their function being to see that friends at home shall not wish, nor foes abroad be able, to harm our state: while the young men whom we have been describing as Guardians should more strictly be called Auxiliaries, their function being to assist the Rulers in the execution of their decisions."

"I agree," he said. . . .

"It would be therefore reasonable to say that, besides being so educated, they should be housed and their material needs provided for in a way that will not prevent them being efficient Guardians, yet will not tempt them to pray upon the rest of the community."

"There is truth in that."

"Well then," I said, "if that is our object, I suggest that they should live and be housed as follows. First, they shall have no private property beyond the barest essentials. Second, none of them shall possess a dwelling-house or other property to which all have not the right of entry. Next, their food shall be provided by the other citizens in payment for the duties they perform as Guardians; it shall be suitable for men living under the rigours of military training and discipline, and in quantity enough to ensure that there is neither a surplus nor a deficit over the year. They shall eat together in messes and live together like soldiers in camp. They must be told that they have no need for mortal and material gold and silver, because they have in their hearts the heavenly gold and silver given them by the gods as a permanent possession, and it would be wicked to pollute the heavenly gold in their possession by mixing it with earthly, for theirs is without impurity, while that in currency among men is a common source of wickedness. They alone, therefore, of all the citizens are forbidden to touch or handle silver or gold; they must not come under the same roof as them, nor wear them as ornaments, nor drink from vessels made of them. Upon this their safety and that of the state depends. If they acquire private property in land, houses, or money, they will become farmers and men of business instead of Guardians, and harsh tyrants instead of partners in their dealings with their fellow citizens, with whom they will live on terms of mutual hatred and suspicion; they will be more afraid of internal revolt than external attack, and be heading fast for destruction that will overwhelm the whole community.

"These are the reasons why we should provide for the housing and other material needs of the Guardians in the way I have described. So shall we legislate accordingly?"

"Let us do so by all means," answered Glaucon.

"But look here, Socrates," interrupted Adeimantus, "how would you answer the objection that you aren't making your Guardians particularly happy? It's their own fault, of course, because the state is in their control, but they don't seem to get any good out of it. Other rulers possess lands and build themselves large houses and furnish them magnificently; they offer sacrifices to the gods at their own expense, they entertain visitors from abroad, and have plenty of the gold and silver you were just talking about, and everything else which is commonly thought of to make a man happy. But one might almost describe your Guardians as a set of hired mercenaries with nothing to do in the city but perpetual guard-duty." . . .

"I think," I said, "that we shall find our reply if we stick to the path we have been pursuing, and say that, though it would not in fact be in the least surprising if our Guardians were very happy indeed, our purpose in founding our state was not to promote the happiness of a single class, but, so far as possible, of the whole community. Our idea was that we were most likely to find justice in such a community, and similarly injustice in a really badly run community, and so be able to decide the question we are trying to answer. We are therefore at the moment trying to construct what we think is a happy community by securing the happiness not of a select minority, but of the whole. The opposite kind of community we will examine presently. Now if we were painting a statue and were met with the criticism that we were not using the most beautiful colours for the most beautiful parts of the body— for we had not coloured the eyes, the body's most precious feature, red, but black—we could, I think, reasonably reply as follows: 'It is absurd to expect us to represent the beauty of the eye in a way which does not make it look like an eye at all, and the same is true of the other parts of the body; you should look rather to see whether we have made the whole beautiful by giving each part its due. So, in the present case, don't make us give our Guardians the kind of happiness that will make them anything but Guardians. We could perfectly well clothe our farmers in royal robes and put crowns on their heads and tell them to cultivate the land at their pleasure, and we could sit our potters round the fire, and let them drink and enjoy themselves, putting their wheel at their side for them to work as they feel inclined; indeed, we could try to make the whole community happy by giving everyone else similar comforts. But you must not ask us to do so; for the result of such advice will be that our farmers are no longer farmers nor our potters potters, and that all the classes that make up our community lose their characteristic form. In some cases this does not matter much—the community suffers nothing very terrible if its cobblers are bad and become degenerate and pretentious; but if the Guardians of its laws and constitution, who alone have the opportunity to bring it good government and prosperity, become a mere sham, then clearly it is completely ruined."

"So if we are making genuine guardians, who will never harm the community, while our critic prefers idlers enjoying themselves in something more like a fun-fair than a city, then he is not thinking of a community at all. We must therefore decide whether our object in setting up the Guardian class is to make it as happy as we can, or whether happiness is a thing we should look for in the community as a whole. If it is, our Guardians and Auxiliaries must be compelled to act accordingly and be persuaded, as indeed must everyone else, that it is their business to perfect themselves in their own particular job; then our city will be built on the right basis, and, as it grows, we can leave each class to enjoy the degree of happiness its nature permits."

"That," he said, "seems to put it very fairly."

CLASSROOM WITHOUT WALLS

Marshall McLuhan

It's natural today to speak of "audio and visual aids" to teaching, for we still think of the book as norm, of other media as incidental. We also think of the new media—press, radio, movies, TV—as MASS MEDIA & think of the book as an individualistic form.

Individualistic because it isolated the reader in silence & helped create the Western "I." Yet it was the first product of mass production.

With it everybody could have the same books. It was impossible in medieval times for different students, different institutions, to have copies of the same book. Manuscripts, commentaries, were dictated. Students memorized.

Instruction was almost entirely oral, done in groups. Solitary study was reserved for the advanced scholar. The first printed books were "visual aids" to oral instruction.

Before the printing press, the young learned by listening, watching, doing. So, until recently, our own rural children learned the language & skills of their elders. Learning took place outside the classrooms. Only those aiming at professional careers went to school at all.

Today in our cities, most learning occurs outside the classroom. The sheer quantity of information conveyed by press-mags-film-TV-radio *far exceeds* the quantity of information conveyed by school instruction & texts. This challenge has destroyed the monopoly of the book as a teaching aid & cracked the very walls of the classroom, so suddenly, we're confused, baffled.

In this violently upsetting social situation, many teachers naturally view the offerings of the new media as entertainment, rather than education. *But this view carries no conviction to the student.*

Find a classic which wasn't first regarded as light entertainment. Nearly all vernacular works were so regarded until the 19th century.

Many movies are obviously handled with a degree of insight & maturity at least equal to the level permitted in today's textbooks. Olivier's *Henry V* & *Richard III* assemble a wealth of scholarly & artistic skill which reveal Shakespeare at a very high level, yet in a way easy for the young to enjoy.

The movie is to dramatic representation what the book was to the manuscript. It makes available to many & at many times & places what otherwise would be restricted to a few at few times & places. The movie, like the book, is a ditto device. TV shows to 50,000,000 simultaneously. Some feel that the value of experiencing a book is diminished by being extended to many minds. This notion is always implicit in the phrases "mass media," "mass entertainment"—useless phrases obscuring the fact THAT *English itself is a mass medium.* Today we're beginning to realize that the new media aren't just mechanical gimmicks for creating worlds of illusion, *but new languages with new & unique powers of expression.* Historically, the resources of English have been shaped & expressed in constantly new & changing ways. The printing press changed, not only the quantity of writing, but the character of language & the relations between author & public. Radio, film, TV pushed written English towards the spontaneous shifts & freedom of the spoken idiom. They aided us in the recovery of intense awareness of facial language & bodily gesture. If these "mass media" should serve only to weaken or corrupt previously achieved levels of verbal & pictorial culture, it won't be because there's anything inherently wrong with them. *It will be because we've failed to master them as new languages in time to assimilate them to our total cultural heritage.*

These new developments, under quiet analytic survey, point to a basic strategy of culture for the classroom. When the printed book first appeared, it threatened the oral procedures of teaching, and created the classroom as we now know it. Instead of making his own text, his own dictionary, his own grammar, the student started out with these tools. He could study, not one, but several languages. Today these new media threaten, instead of merely reinforce, the procedures of this traditional classroom. It's customary to answer this threat with denunciations of the unfortunate character & effect of movies & TV, just as the comicbook was feared & scorned & rejected from the classroom. Its good & bad features in form & content, when carefully set beside other kinds of art & narrative, could have become a major asset to the teacher.

Where student interest is already intensely focused is the natural point at which to be in the elucidation of other problems & interests. *The educational task is not only to provide basic tools of perception, but to develop judgement & discrimination with ordinary social experience.*

Few students ever acquire skill in analysis of newspapers. Fewer have any ability to discuss a movie intelligently. *To be articulate & discriminating about ordinary affairs & information is the mark of an educated man.*

It's misleading to suppose there's any basic difference between education & entertainment. *This distinction merely relieves people* of the responsibility of looking into the matter. *It's like setting up a distinction between* didactic & lyric poetry on the ground that one teaches, the other pleases. *However, it's always been true* that whatever pleases teaches more effectively.

THE SCHARTZ-METTERKLUME METHOD

Saki

Lady Carlotta stepped out on to the platform of the small wayside station and took a turn or two up and down its uninteresting length, to kill time till the train should be pleased to proceed on its way. Then, in the roadway beyond, she saw a horse struggling with a more than ample load, and a carter of the sort that seems to bear a sullen hatred against the animal that helps him to earn a living. Lady Carlotta promptly betook her to the roadway, and put rather a different complexion on the struggle. Certain of her acquaintances were wont to give her plentiful admonition as to the undesirability of interfering on behalf of a distressed animal, such interference being "none of her business." Only once had she put the doctrine of non-interference into practice, when one of its most eloquent exponents had been besieged for nearly three hours in a small and extremely uncomfortable maytree by an angry boar-pig, while Lady Carlotta, on the other side of the fence, had proceeded with the water-colour sketch she was engaged on, and refused to interfere between the boar and his prisoner. It is to be feared that she lost the friendship of the ultimately rescued lady. On this occasion she merely lost the train, which gave way to the first sign of impatience it had shown throughout the journey, and steamed off without her. She bore the desertion with philosophical indifference; her friends and relations were thoroughly well used to the fact of her luggage arriving without her. She wired a vague non-committal message to her destination to say that she was coming on "by another train." Before she had time to think what her next move might be she was confronted by an imposingly attired lady, who seemed to be taking a prolonged mental inventory of her clothes and looks.

"You must be Miss Hope, the governess I've come to meet," said the apparition, in a tone that admitted of very little argument.

"Very well, if I must I must," said Lady Carlotta to herself with dangerous meekness.

"I am Mrs. Quabarl," continued the lady; "and where, pray, is your luggage?"

"It's gone astray," said the alleged governess, falling in with the excellent rule of life that the absent are always to blame; the luggage had, in point of fact, behaved with perfect correctitude. "I've just telegraphed about it," she added, with a nearer approach to truth.

"How provoking," said Mrs. Quabarl; "these railway companies are so careless. However, my maid can lend you things for the night," and she led the way to her car.

During the drive to the Quabarl mansion Lady Carlotta was impressively introduced to the nature of the charge that had been thrust upon her; she learned that Claude and Wilfrid were delicate, sensitive young people, that Irene had the artistic temperament highly developed, and that Viola was something or other else of a mould equally commonplace among children of that class and type in the twentieth century.

"I wish them not only to be *taught*," said Mrs. Quabarl, "but *interested* in what they learn. In their history lessons, for instance, you must try to make them feel that they are being introduced to the life-stories of men and women who really lived, not merely committing a mass of names and dates to memory. French, of course, I shall expect you to talk at mealtimes several days in the week."

"I shall talk French four days of the week and Russian in the remaining three."

"Russian? My dear Miss Hope, no one in the house speaks or understands Russian."

"That will not embarrass me in the least," said Lady Carlotta coldly.

Mrs. Quabarl, to use a colloquial expression, was knocked off her perch. She was one of those imperfectly self-assured individuals who are magnificent and autocratic as long as they are not seriously opposed. The least show of unexpected resistance goes a long way towards rendering them cowed and apologetic. When the new governess failed to express wondering admiration of the large newly-purchased and expensive car, and lightly alluded to the superior advantages of one or two makes which had just been put on the market, the discomfiture of her patroness became almost abject. Her feelings were those which might have animated a general of ancient warfaring days, on beholding his heaviest battle-elephant ignominiously driven off the field by slingers and javelin throwers.

At dinner that evening, although reinforced by her husband, who usually duplicated her opinions and lent her moral support generally, Mrs. Quabarl regained none of her lost ground. The governess not only helped herself well and truly to wine, but held forth with considerable show of critical knowledge on various vintage matters, concerning which the Quabarls were in no wise able to pose as authorities. Previous governesses had limited their conversation on the wine topic to a respectful and doubtless sincere expression of a preference for water. When this one went as far as to recommend a wine firm in whose hands you could not go very far wrong Mrs. Quabarl thought it time to turn the conversation into more usual channels.

"We got very satisfactory references about you from Canon Teep," she observed; "a very estimable man, I should think."

"Drinks like a fish and beats his wife, otherwise a very lovable character," said the governess imperturbably.

"My *dear* Miss Hope! I trust you are exaggerating," exclaimed the Quabarls in unison.

"One must in justice admit that there is some provocation," continued the romancer. "Mrs. Teep is quite the most irritating bridge-player that I have ever sat down with; her leads and declarations would condone a certain amount of brutality in her partner, but to souse her with the contents of the only soda-water siphon in the house on a Sunday afternoon, when one couldn't get another, argues an indifference to the comfort of others which I cannot altogether overlook. You may think me hasty in my judgments, but it was practically on account of the siphon incident that I left."

"We will talk of this some other time," said Mrs. Quabarl hastily.

"I shall never allude to it again," said the governess with decision.

Mr. Quabarl made a welcome diversion by asking what studies the new instructress proposed to inaugurate on the morrow.

"History to begin with," she informed him.

"Ah, history," he observed sagely; "now in teaching them history you must take care to interest them in what they learn. You must make them feel that they are being introduced to the life-stories of men and women who really lived——"

"I've told her all that," interposed Mrs. Quabarl.

"I teach history on the Schartz-Metterklume method," said the governess loftily.

"Ah, yes," said her listeners, thinking it expedient to assume an acquaintance at least with the name.

"What are you children doing out here?" demanded Mrs. Quabarl the next morning, on finding Irene sitting rather glumly at the head of the stairs, while her sister was perched in an attitude of depressed discomfort on the window-seat behind her, with a wolf-skin rug almost covering her.

"We are having a history lesson," came the unexpected reply. "I am supposed to be Rome, and Viola up there is the she-wolf; not a real wolf, but the figure of one that the Romans used to set store by—I forget why. Claude and Wilfrid have gone to fetch the shabby women.

"The shabby women?"

"Yes, they've got to carry them off. They didn't want to, but Miss Hope got one of father's fives-bats and said she'd give them a number nine spanking if they didn't, so they've gone to do it."

A loud, angry screaming from the direction of the lawn drew Mrs. Quabarl thither in hot haste, fearful lest the threatened castigation might even now be in process of infliction. The outcry, however, came principally from the two small daughters of the lodge-keeper, who were being hauled and pushed towards the house by the panting and dishevelled Claude and Wilfrid, whose task was rendered even more arduous by the incessant, if not very effectual, attacks of the captured maidens' small brother. The governess, fives-bat in hand, sat negligently on the stone balustrade, presiding over the scene with the cold impartiality of a Goddess of Battles. A furious and repeated chorus of "I'll tell muvver" rose from the lodge children, but the lodge-mother, who was hard of hearing, was for the moment immersed in the preoccupation of her washtub. After an apprehensive glance in the direction of the lodge (the good woman was gifted with the highly militant temper which is sometimes the privilege of deafness) Mrs. Quabarl flew indignantly to the rescue of the struggling captives.

"Wilfrid! Claude! Let those children go at once. Miss Hope, what on earth is the meaning of this scene?"

"Early Roman history; the Sabine women, don't you know? It's the Schartz-Metterklume method to make children understand history by acting it themselves; fixes it in their memory, you know. Of course, if, thanks to your interference, your boys go through life thinking that the Sabine women ultimately escaped, I really cannot be held responsible."

"You may be very clever and modern, Miss Hope," said Mrs. Quabarl firmly, "but I should like you to leave here by the next train. Your luggage will be sent after you as soon as it arrives."

"I'm not certain exactly where I shall be for the next few days," said the dismissed instructress of youth; "you might keep my luggage till I wire my address. There are only a couple of trunks and some golf-clubs and a leopard cub."

"A leopard cub!" gasped Mrs. Quabarl. Even in her departure this extraordinary person seemed destined to leave a trail of embarrassment behind her.

"Well, it's rather left off being a cub; it's more than half-grown, you know. A fowl every day and a rabbit on Sundays is what it usually gets. Raw beef makes it too excitable. Don't trouble about getting the car for me, I'm rather inclined for a walk."

And Lady Carlotta strode out of the Quabarl horizon.

The advent of the genuine Miss Hope, who had made a mistake as to the day on which she was due to arrive, caused a turmoil which that good lady was quite unused to inspiring. Obviously the Quabarl family had been woefully befooled, but a certain amount of relief came with the knowledge.

"How tiresome for you, dear Carlotta," said her hostess, when the overdue guest ultimately arrived; "how very tiresome losing your train and having to stop overnight in a strange place."

"Oh, dear, no," said Lady Carlotta, "not at all tiresome—for me."

CANADA EXPLAINED

Eric Nicol

PREHISTORIC CANADA, SUCH AS IT WAS

Prehistoric Canada covers the period of everything before Bruce Hutchison.

Before the coming of man (and, more important, woman) Canada was a large area inhabited only by buffalo and ice ages. Later the buffalo found that they weren't actually buffalo at all but bison, whereupon they became extinct.

More recently the bison, or buffalo, have made a dramatic comeback, thanks to a rough training program and plenty of roadwork, so that they are now so plentiful they have to be shot. They may become extinct again.

The first humans to come to Canada were the Indians. There is some mystery as to where the Indians came from. Some experts say that they came from the same place as the Eskimo. This doesn't help much because nobody knows where the Eskimo came from either. (Except the Eskimo, and they aren't talking.)

Equally mysterious were the series of ice ages that covered Canada with giant glaciers, which in turn receded into the Arctic. Thus Canada was one of the first countries to have automatic defrosting.

The chief characteristic of an ice age was that the huge flux of ice ground down everything in its path and drove the inhabitants south. Today this feature of Canadian life is provided by income tax.

CANADA DISCOVERED AWKWARDLY

The first white explorer to reach Canada was

— *"Canada Explained" by Eric Nicol, reprinted from A Herd of Yaks by Eric Nicol, by permission of The Ryerson Press, Toronto*

Erik the Red. Other Scandinavians trying to sail across the Atlantic had failed, but Erik the Red was a Norse of a different colour.

It is sometimes asked how it was that Erik the Red landed in Canada. But with a name like that he had a fat chance of landing in the States.

Thanks to the description of Canada that Erik took home, nobody else tried to discover Canada for several hundred years.

The next wave of explorers was led by Christopher Columbus, who sailed west in an attempt to find a new route to the east. This was a typical government project.

When Columbus landed in America he assumed that it was India. Fortunately he was wrong, as this would have made Canada Tibet and discouraged pretty well all the tourists except Lowell Thomas.

After Columbus discovered America for Spain, the king of France (Louis Roy) ordered his explorers to go out and discover something. The thrones of France and Spain hated each other at the time because of inter-marriage.

The first French explorer to reach Canada was Jacques Cartier, later immortalized in "Frère Jacques," the Quebec national anthem.

All the French explorers landed at Gaspé, because it was so picturesque. They planted the flag of France and called it New Scotland.

The first English explorer to reach Canada was Jock Cabot, but he forgot to bring a flag. By the time he went back for it, he was too late to claim anything but his pension.

The next great English explorer was Henry Hudson, who was still looking for India. Hudson sailed into a large body of water and proved that it was a mistake. He gave his name to this bay, which became the name of a large Canadian retail store (advt.).

About this time Lloyd's of London, the great maritime insurance firm, anxious to encourage British shipping, conducted their "I Discovered a Continent" contest, with first prize of a free floater policy. Nobody took them up, however, till Captain Cook, who showed a good deal of originality by trying to find a route *back* from India.

Meanwhile the French explorer Champlain was working his way up the St. Lawrence, having had the typically French idea of starting a colony with the help of his wife (Madame Champlain). To help them the king sent ships with cargoes of brides. This was the Golden Age of Canadian longshoring.

The Frenchmen who took the brides were called "seigneurs" because they were too busy meeting the boats to do any work. The seigneurs became the ruling class and every spring had the privilege of falling through the ice first.

THE FRENCH VERSUS THE ENGLISH

Eventually the French fur traders paddling down-river started meeting the English fur traders paddling up-river, and both sides realized that there weren't enough gullible Indians to go 'round.

The result was that the French began a campaign of pillaging British forts. Where there was no fort for the French to pillage, the British built one.

This war went on for more years than anybody cares to remember owing to the long distances the armies had to march to meet defeat. However, the British at last outwitted the French by sending back to the Old Country for more men than the French had. As these men started arriving by ship, the war became a struggle between French arms and British bottoms.

The British troops were led by General Wolfe, who had been carefully trained in the British military art of losing every battle but the last one.

The commander of the French fortress of Quebec, General Montcalm, was too busy hauling wood to notice that the British were sneaking up the cliff the back way.

In the ensuing battle both the British and French generals were mortally wounded, but the British refused to admit that it was a draw. The French therefore went back to their farms swearing that they would have "la revanche du berceau," a French expression meaning the family allowance.

This campaign proved so popular that the British were sorry they'd won and granted the French freedom of religion, freedom of language and several other freedoms that the French hadn't even thought of.

The war ended with the Treaty of Paris, France.

THE REASON FOR OTTAWA

Noticing that the capital of Canada kept jumping back and forth from Quebec to Toronto every four years, Queen Victoria ordered that it should be nailed down at Ottawa.

The Queen did not notice of course that this site was close to a large match factory and therefore bound to burn down sooner or later, which it did.

However, the Canadian government accepted her decision since it was the only time Her Majesty had given Canada any capital without charging interest.

Also Ottawa combined the respectability of being in Ontario with the desirability of being able to get into Quebec before the pubs closed.

THE BIRTH OF A NOTION

Meanwhile, having become more charming than ever, Sir John A. Macdonald was leaning towards a confederation of Canada and the Maritime provinces. To persuade the different leaders that this was a good idea he arranged a series of conferences in different places such as Quebec, London and Charlotte Whitton.

These proceedings were nearly upset by the

tragic shooting, in the Yukon, of D'Arcy McGrew, a brilliant Irish-Canadian oracle.

However, Macdonald pressed his union suit with vigor. At last he had everybody around the same long table and informed them that, by the grace of Her Majesty, they were all fathers—the fathers of Confederation.

To celebrate the occasion all the new fathers crossed their legs and had their photo taken. The date of the historic occasion was July 1, 1867, which is the only date in Canadian history.

Still reeking charm, Macdonald went to London and helped the Queen choose a name for the newborn country, settling on "Canada" because that was what it was called.

They also chose the motto, A mari usque ad mare, or "A little water with that whisky."

One by one the other colonies of Canada joined the Confederation, just as soon as they could see their way clear to getting more out of it than they were putting into it.

THE REVOLTING COLONIES

Around this time, whatever it was, the British colonies became restless and dumped a shipload of tea into Boston harbour. This led to the American Revolution and also explains how Americans make tea.

Before the colonies had been restless very long, under George Washington, they noticed that Canada was closer for attack than the Mother Country and the going was drier under foot. They therefore dispatched several expeditions of small troops (minute men) specially chosen for their ability to march all winter without soles on their boots.

These revolting Americans attacked Canada unfairly, hitting below the border where possible. The governor of Canada, a guy named Carleton, was obliged to leave his college and offer resistance. He called upon the French habitants, but they weren't home.

As usual, the red coats were a better target than the green mountain boys from Vermont, so that once again the British were obliged to advance backwards until the fleet arrived.

The Americans did in fact capture Montreal, where they were warmly welcomed by the English residents. This so confused the Americans that Carleton had time to call upon the French habitants again. They were still out to lunch.

Since this was longer than Carleton could wait, he decided to retire boldly to Quebec. Fortunately many of the Americans had signed on to fight for one year only, so that the Canadian garrison was able to take an impressive toll of expired contracts.

Backed by the British fleet, Carleton chased the Americans back across the border and became the hero who had saved Canada from independence.

However, he had been very disappointed with the way the French habitants had failed to take advantage of the privilege of having been conquered by the British, refusing to sell food to the Americans only after the Americans ran out of cash and tried to pass cheques. Carleton went home to England in a huff, the favourite means of transportation of British governors at that time.

According to the Treaty of Paris (France), both sides in the war agreed on a border between the two countries drawn so that, no matter where train or bus passengers crossed it, the immigration men would be able to wake them up in the middle of the night.

THE WAR OF 1812, '13, '14, ETC.

The War of 1812 was caused by land-hungry Americans, who looked west and saw the savage Indians, looked north and saw the peaceful Canadians, and agreed that Canada was ripe for emancipation.

Since Britain was busy fighting a war with Napoleon, the Americans also had reason to believe that the Canadians' only successful strategy in war, the arrival of the British fleet, was weakened.

They therefore set out to shoot Canada free.

A few Canadians and Indians under General Brock—later known as "the Brockbusters"—chose to fight for continued tyranny, which proved a nasty shock for those members of the American force who had been promised only a military parade through attractive countryside, with French girls throwing kisses and a favourable rate of exchange for their dollar.

Before the Americans could rally, the War of 1812 had been held over to 1813. For the Americans 1813 was one of the worst years of the War of 1812, though not as bad as the following year (1814). An expeditionary force attempted to surprise the Canadians at the Beaver Dams, but the Canadians had been warned of their approach by Laura Secord, who knew the beavers personally, and made her way alone through 20 miles of pathless forest and past American sentries.

But for this courageous action by Laura Secord, Canadians today would be eating Martha Washington's chocolates.

By 1814 the British had defeated Napoleon and the inevitable British fleet arrived in Canada. With their shipping and trade cut off, and Washington burning, the Americans gave up their attempt to liberate Canada.

The war ended with the signing of the Treaty of Paris, France.

RETURN OF LOUIS RIEL

Saskatchewan, which hadn't had its rebellion yet and was resentful, now broke out in hostile halfbreeds. The halfbreeds were self-conscious about losing their land and not being baptized. They therefore sent for Louis Riel, who was making a comeback in the States.

After being hanged, Riel had been elected to parliament but was disqualified on the grounds that, being deceased, he was only eligible for the Senate. This left Riel bitter towards the government, and he seized the opportunity to lead a rebel force in a running retreat from law and order.

Riel was caught again and hanged at Regina.

This time it took. He never ran for public office again.

QUEBEC: PART OF CANADA?

During recent years there have been signs of less bitterness between French Canada and English Canada. In fact the Treaty of 1763 was not actually ratified till the retirement of Rocket Richard.

It was the Rocket who led most French-Canadians to accept the theory that Montcalm could have won if his men had attacked with regulation hockey sticks instead of rifles. When the Rocket retired, so died the last hope of a comeback on the Plains of Abraham.

Canadian unity has also been forged by Grey Cup Day, the annual autumnal ceremony of sacrificing a pig, inflating its skin with air and casting this into a sea of mud where 24 armoured men fight for possession of the bladder. The vast audience of worshippers share vicariously in the pig's experience by killing a bottle and getting a skin full.

Opinion varies as to whether the Grey Cup orgy represents a badly-timed fertility rite or an attempt to propitiate the Corn Mother (Mrs. Seagram).

Whatever it is, this event brings together, from different parts of the country, Canadians who distrust each other for no good reason, and sends them home, after 48 hours of association, with any number of excellent reasons to distrust each other.

THE ARTS IN CANADA

The arts have been flourishing in Canada, a glorious explosion of talent of which this present volume is only one of the more obvious examples.

The Group of Seven has been succeeded by the Group of Eleven, a 57% increase in less than a generation. For the first time Canadian artists have something in the bank: a mural.

Despite the temporary set-back of Canadian verse when the CNR repainted the walls of its washrooms, poetry in the country continues to thrive. Poetry is not only being written, by Reaney, Macpherson, Dudek and Klein, but it is being read, by Klein, Dudek, Macpherson and Reaney.

As for the theatre, huge new temples of Thespis have been erected in Toronto, Edmonton, Calgary and Vancouver, as well as Stratford. These have opened the Golden Age of Souvenir Programmes. As never before, Canadians are anxious to be seen at the theatre. Some of them even go inside, where the seats are, and watch whatever it is that the management has chosen as a conversation piece for Intermission. Other countries are producing better plays, but Canada is second to none in distinguished intermissions.

CANADA—EVER GROWING, AND GROWING, AND . . .

Canada is growing. This country has the highest birth-rate of all the industrialized nations. Either that or it has the lowest birth-rate of all the backward nations. Whichever way we look at it, this is the land of *opportunity*.

THE EDUCATION OF WOMEN

Daniel Defoe

I have often thought of it as one of the most barbarous customs in the world, considering us as a civilized and a Christian country, that we deny the advantages of learning to women. We reproach the sex every day with folly and impertinence; while I am confident, had they the advantages of education equal to us, they would be guilty of less than ourselves.

One would wonder, indeed, how it should happen that women are conversible at all; since they are only beholden to natural parts, for all their knowledge. Their youth is spent to teach them to stitch and sew or make baubles. They are taught to read, indeed, and perhaps to write their names, or so; and that is the height of a woman's education. And I would but ask

---

— "*The Education of Women*" by Daniel Defoe, *reprinted from English Essays, Harvard Classics, vol. 27, published by P. F. Collier & Son Company, New York, 1910; this material reproduced with the permission of Crowell Collier and Macmillan, Inc.*

any who slight the sex for their understanding, what is a man (a gentleman, I mean) good for, that is taught no more? I need not give instances, or examine the character of a gentleman, with a good estate, or a good family, and with tolerable parts; and examine what figure he makes for want of education.

The soul is placed in the body like a rough diamond; and must be polished, or the lustre of it will never appear. And 'tis manifest, that as the rational soul distinguishes us from brutes; so education carries on the distinction, and makes some less brutish than others. This is too evident to need any demonstration. But why then should women be denied the benefit of instruction? If knowledge and understanding had been useless additions to the sex, GOD Almighty would never have given them capacities; for he made nothing needless. Besides, I would ask such, What they can see in ignorance, that they should think it a necessary ornament to a woman? or how much worse is a wise woman than a fool? or what has the woman done to forfeit the privilege of being taught? Does she plague us with her pride and impertinence? Why did we not let her learn, that she might have had more wit? Shall we upbraid women with folly, when 'tis only the error of this inhuman custom, that hindered them from being made wiser?

The capacities of women are supposed to be greater, and their senses quicker than those of the men; and what they might be capable of being bred to, is plain from some instances of female wit, which this age is not without. Which upbraids us with Injustice, and looks as if we denied women the advantages of education, for fear they should *vie* with the men in their improvements. . . .

[They] should be taught all sorts of breeding suitable both to their genius and quality. And in particular, Music and Dancing; which it would be cruelty to bar the sex of, because they are their darlings. But besides this, they should be taught languages, as particularly French and Italian: and I would venture the injury of giving a woman more tongues than one. They should, as a particular study, be taught all the graces of speech, and all the necessary air of conversation; which our common education is so defective in, that I need not expose it. They should be brought to read books, and especially history; and so to read as to make them understand the world, and be able to know and judge of things when they hear of them.

To such whose genius would lead them to it, I would deny no sort of learning; but the chief thing, in general, is to cultivate the understandings of the sex, that they may be capable of all sorts of conversation; that their parts and judgements being improved, they may be as profitable in their conversation as they are pleasant.

Women, in my observation, have little or no difference in them, but as they are or are not distinguished by education. Tempers, indeed, may in some degree influence them, but the main distinguishing part is their Breeding.

The whole sex are generally quick and sharp.

I believe, I may be allowed to say, generally so: for you rarely see them lumpish and heavy, when they are children; as boys will often be. If a woman be well bred, and taught the proper management of her natural wit; she proves generally very sensible and retentive.

And, without partiality, a woman of sense and manners is the finest and most delicate part of GOD's Creation, the glory of Her Maker, and the great instance of His singular regard to man, His darling creature: to whom He gave the best gift either GOD could bestow or man receive. And 'tis the sordidest piece of folly and ingratitude in the world, to withhold from the sex the due lustre which the advantages of education gives to the natural beauty of their minds.

A woman well bred and well taught, furnished with the additional accomplishments of knowledge and behaviour, is a creature *without comparison*. Her society is the emblem of sublimer enjoyments, her person is angelic, and her conversation heavenly. She is all softness and sweetness, peace, love, wit, and delight. She is every way suitable to the sublimest wish, and the man that has such a one to his portion, has nothing to do but to rejoice in her, and be thankful.

On the other hand, Suppose her to be the *very same* woman, and rob her of the benefit of education, and it follows—

If her temper be good, want of education makes her soft and easy.
Her wit, for want of teaching, makes her impertinent and talkative.
Her knowledge, for want of judgement and experience, makes her fanciful and whimsical.
If her temper be bad, want of breeding makes her worse; and she grows haughty, insolent, and loud.
If she be passionate, want of manners makes her a termagant and a scold, *which is much at one with Lunatic.*
If she be proud, want of discretion (which still is breeding) makes her conceited, fantastic, and ridiculous.
And from these she degenerates to be turbulent, clamorous, noisy, nasty, the devil! . . .

The great distinguishing difference, which is seen in the world between men and women, is in their education; and this is manifested by comparing it with the difference between one man or woman, and another.

And herein it is that I take upon me to make such a bold assertion, That all the world are mistaken in their practice about women. For I cannot think that GOD Almighty ever made them so delicate, so glorious creatures; and furnished them with such charms, so agreeable and so delightful to mankind; with souls capable of the same accomplishments with men: and all, to be only Stewards of our Houses, Cooks, and Slaves.

Not that I am for exalting the female government in the least: but, in short, *I would have men take women for companions, and educate them to be fit for it.* A woman of sense and breeding will scorn as much to encroach upon the prerogative of man, as a man of sense will scorn to oppress the weakness of the woman. But if the women's souls were refined and improved by teaching, that word would be lost. To say, the *weakness* of the sex, as to judgement, would be nonsense; for ignorance and folly would be no more to be found among women than men.

I remember a passage, which I heard from a very fine woman. She had wit and capacity enough, an extraordinary shape and face, and a great fortune: but had been cloistered up all her time; and for fear of being stolen, had not had the liberty of being taught the common necessary knowledge of women's affairs. And when she came to converse in the world, her natural wit made her so sensible of the want of education, that she gave this short reflection on herself: "I am ashamed to talk with my very maids," says she, "for I don't know when they do right or wrong. I had more need go to school, than be married."

I need not enlarge on the loss the defect of education is to the sex; nor argue the benefit of the contrary practice. 'Tis a thing will be more easily granted than remedied. This chapter is but an Essay at the thing: and I refer the Practice to those Happy Days (if ever they shall be) when men shall be wise enough to mend it.

LETTER TO HIS SON

Lord Chesterfield

London, September 5, O.S. 1748

Dear Boy: I have received yours, with the enclosed German letter to Mr. Grevenkop,

— *reprinted from The Letters of The Earl of Chesterfield to his Son, vol. I, edited with an introduction by Charles Strachey, and with notes by Annette Calthrop, published by Methuen & Co. Ltd., London, 1901, second edition 1924*

which he assures me is extremely well written, considering the little time that you have applied yourself to that language. As you have now got over the most difficult part, pray go on diligently, and make yourself absolutely master of the rest. Whoever does not entirely possess a language, will never appear to advantage, or even equal to himself, either in speaking or writing it. His ideas are fettered, and seem imperfect or confused, if he is not master of all the words and phrases necessary to express them. I therefore desire, that you will not fail writing a German letter once every fortnight to Mr. Grevenkop; which will make the writing of that language familiar to you; and moreover, when you shall have left Germany, and be arrived at Turin, I shall require you to write even to me in German; that you may not forget with ease, what you have with difficulty learned. I likewise desire, that while you are in Germany, you will take all opportunities of conversing in German, which is the only way of knowing that, or any other language accurately. You will also desire your German master to teach you the proper titles and superscriptions to be used to people of all ranks; which is a point so material, in Germany, that I have known many a letter returned unopened, because one title in twenty has been omitted in the direction.

St. Thomas's Day now draws near, when you are to leave Saxony and go to Berlin; and I take it for granted, that if anything is yet wanting to complete your knowledge of the state of that Electorate, you will not fail to procure it before you go away. I do not mean, as you will easily believe, the number of churches, parishes, or towns; but I mean the constitution, the revenues, the troops, and the trade of that Electorate. A few questions sensibly asked, of sensible people, will produce you the necessary informations; which I desire you will enter in your little book. Berlin will be entirely a new scene to you, and I look upon it, in a manner, as your first step into the great world; take care that step be not a false one, and that you do not stumble at the threshold. You will be there in more company than you have yet been; Manners and Attentions will therefore be more necessary. Pleasing in company is the only way of being pleased in it yourself. Sense and knowledge are the first and necessary foundations for pleasing in company; but they will by no means do alone, and they will never be perfectly welcome, if they are not accompanied with Manners and Attentions. You will best acquire these by frequenting the companies of people of fashion; but then you must resolve to acquire them, in those companies, by proper care and observation; for I have known people who, though they have frequented good company all their lifetime, have done it in so inattentive and unobserving a manner, as to be never the better for it, and to remain as disagreeable, as awkward, and as vulgar, as if they had never seen any person of fashion. When you go into good company (by good company is meant the people of the first fashion of the place) observe carefully their turn, their manners, their address; and conform your own to them. But this is not all neither; go deeper still; observe their characters, and pry, as far as you can, into both their hearts and their heads. Seek for their particular merit, their predominant passion, or their prevailing weakness; and you will then know what to bait your hook with to catch them. Man is a composition of so many, and such various ingredients, that it requires both time and care to analyse him: for though we have all the same ingredients in our general composition, as reason, will, passions, and appetites; yet the different proportions and combinations of them in each individual, produce that infinite variety of characters which, in some particular or other, distinguishes every individual from another. Reason ought to direct the whole, but seldom does. And he who addresses himself singly to another man's reason, without endeavouring to engage his heart in his interest also, is no more likely to succeed, than a man who should apply only to a king's nominal minister, and neglect his favourite. I will recommend to your attentive perusal, now that you are going into the world, two books, which will let you as much into the characters of men, as books can do; I mean, *Les Réflexions Morales de Monsieur de la Rochefoucault*,[1] and *Les Caractères*

---

[1] [The well-known François, Duc de la Rochefoucault, Prince de Marsillac, was born 1613, and died 1680. The book to which Lord Chesterfield refers is: *Réflexions ou Sentences et Maximes Morales, avec un discours sur les Réflexions* (attributed to Segrais) *et un avis au lecteur*. The *discours* and the *avis* disappeared in subsequent editions. The first edition was published in 1665.]

de La Bruyère:[2] but remember, at the same time, that I only recommend them to you as the best general maps, to assist you in your journey, and not as marking out every particular turning and winding that you will meet with. There your own sagacity and observation must come to their aid. La Rochefoucault is, I know, blamed, but I think without reason, for deriving all our actions from the source of self-love. For my own part, I see a great deal of truth, and no harm at all, in that opinion. It is certain, that we seek our own happiness in everything we do; and it is as certain, that we can only find it in doing well, and in conforming all our actions to the rule of right reason, which is the great law of nature. It is only a mistaken self-love that is a blamable motive, when we take the immediate and indiscriminate gratification of a passion, or appetite, for real happiness. But am I blamable, if I do a good action, upon account of the happiness which that honest consciousness will give me? Surely not. On the contrary, that pleasing consciousness is a proof of my virtue. The reflection, which is the most censured in Monsieur de la Rochefoucault's book, as a very ill-natured one, is this, *On trouve dans le malheur de son meilleur ami, quelque chose qui ne déplaît pas.* And why not? Why may I not feel a very tender and real concern for the misfortune of my friend, and yet at the same time feel a pleasing consciousness at having discharged my duty to him, by comforting and assisting him to the utmost of my power in that misfortune? Give me but virtuous actions, and I will not quibble and chicane about the motives. And I will give anybody their choice of these two truths, which amount to the same thing: He who loves himself best is the honestest man; or, The honestest man loves himself best.

The characters of La Bruyère are pictures from the life; most of them finely drawn, and highly coloured. Furnish your mind with them first, and when you meet with their likeness, as you will every day, they will strike you the more. You will compare every feature with the original; and both will reciprocally help you to discover the beauties and the blemishes.

As women are a considerable, or at least a pretty numerous part of company; and as their suffrages go a great way towards establishing a man's character in the fashionable part of the world (which is of great importance to the fortune and figure he proposes to make in it), it is necessary to please them. I will therefore, upon this subject, let you into certain *Arcana*, that will be very useful for you to know, but which you must, with the utmost care, conceal; and never seem to know. Women, then, are only children of a larger growth;[3] they have an entertaining tattle, and sometimes wit; but for solid reasoning, good sense, I never knew in my life one that had it, or who reasoned or acted consequentially for four and twenty hours together. Some little passion or humour always breaks in upon their best resolutions. Their beauty neglected or controverted, their age increased or their supposed understandings depreciated, instantly kindles their little passions, and overturns any system of consequential conduct, that in their most reasonable moments they might have been capable of forming. A man of sense only trifles with them, plays them, humours and flatters them, as he does with a sprightly, forward child; but he neither consults them about, nor trusts them with serious matters; though he often makes them believe that he

---

[2] [Jean de la Bruyère was born in 1639, 1640, or 1641 (all these dates have been given by different biographers) in a French village near the town of Dourdan. As a young man he had an office in the collection of the revenue at Caen, Normandy. But his literary talents becoming known, he was appointed by Bossuet tutor to one of the royal children of France. In 1693 La Bruyère was, by express command of Louis the Fourteenth, elected one of the forty members of the Academy of France. La Bruyère's Dialogues on Quietism were finished after his death by the Abbé Dupin, and published in 1699.]

---

[3] [Men are but children of a larger growth. — Dryden. *All for love,* iv., I.]

does both; which is the thing in the world that they are proud of; for they love mightily to be dabbling in business (which, by the way, they always spoil); and being justly distrustful, that men in general look upon them in a trifling light, they almost adore that man who talks more seriously to them, and who seems to consult and trust them; I say, who seems; for weak men really do, but wise ones only seem to do it. No flattery is either too high or too low for them. They will greedily swallow the highest, and gratefully accept of the lowest; and you may safely flatter any woman, from her understanding down to the exquisite taste of her fan. Women who are either indisputably beautiful, or indisputably ugly, are best flattered upon the score of their understandings: but those who are in a state of mediocrity, are best flattered upon their beauty, or at least their graces; for every woman, who is not absolutely ugly, thinks herself handsome; but not hearing often that she is so, is the more grateful, and the more obliged to the few who tell her so: whereas a decided and conscious beauty looks upon every tribute paid to her beauty only as her due: but wants to shine, and to be considered on the side of her understanding; and a woman who is ugly enough to know that she is so, knows that she has nothing left for it but her understanding, which is consequently (and probably in more senses than one) her weak side. But these are secrets, which you must keep inviolably, if you would not, like Orpheus, be torn to pieces by the whole sex: on the contrary, a man who thinks of living in the great world, must be gallant, polite and attentive to please the women. They have, from the weakness of men, more or less influence in all courts; they absolutely stamp every man's character in the *beau monde*, and make it either current, or cry it down, and stop it in payments. It is, therefore, absolutely necessary to manage, please and flatter them:

and never to discover the least mark of contempt, which is what they never forgive; but in this they are not singular, for it is the same with men; who will much sooner forgive an injustice than an insult. Every man is not ambitious, or covetous, or passionate; but every man has pride enough in his composition to feel and resent the least slight and contempt. Remember, therefore, most carefully to conceal your contempt, however just, wherever you would not make an implacable enemy. Men are much more unwilling to have their weaknesses and their imperfections known, than their crimes; and if you hint to a man that you think him silly, ignorant, or even ill bred or awkward, he will hate you more and longer, than if you tell him plainly, that you think him a rogue. Never yield to that temptation, which to most young men is very strong, of exposing other people's weaknesses and infirmities, for the sake either of diverting the company, or showing your own superiority. You may get the laugh on your side by it for the present; but you will make enemies by it for ever; and even those who laugh with you then, will, upon reflection fear, and consequently hate you: besides that it is ill natured, and a good heart desires rather to conceal than expose other people's weaknesses or misfortunes. If you have wit, use it to please, and not to hurt: you may shine, like the sun in the temperate zones, without scorching. Here it is wished for; under the Line it is dreaded.

These are some of the hints which my long experience in the great world enables me to give you; and which, if you attend to them, may prove useful to you, in your journey through it. I wish it may be a prosperous one; at least, I am sure that it must be your own fault if it is not.

Make my compliments to Mr. Harte, who I am very sorry to hear, is not well. I hope by this time he is recovered. Adieu!

FATHER OPENS MY MAIL

Clarence Day

There was a time in my boyhood when I felt that Father had handicapped me severely in life by naming me after him, "Clarence." All literature, so far as I could see, was thronged with objectionable persons named Clarence. Percy was bad enough, but there had been some good fighters named Percy. The only Clarence in history was a duke who did something dirty at Tewkesbury, and who died a ridiculous death afterwards in a barrel of malmsey.

As for the Clarences in the fiction I read, they were horrible. In one story, for instance, there were two brothers, Clarence and Frank. Clarence was a "vain, disagreeable little fellow," who was proud of his curly hair and fine clothes, while Frank was a "rollicking boy who was ready to play games with anybody." Clarence didn't like to play games, of course. He just minced around looking on.

One day when the mother of these boys had gone out, this story went on, Clarence "tempted" Frank to disobey her and fly their kite on the roof. Frank didn't want to, but Clarence kept taunting him and daring him until Frank was stung into doing it. After the two boys went up to the roof, Frank got good and dirty, running up and down and stumbling over scuttles, while Clarence sat there, giving him orders, and kept his natty clothes tidy. To my horror, he even spread out his handkerchief on the trapdoor to sit on. And to crown all, this sneak told on Frank as soon as their mother came in.

— *"Father Opens My Mail"* by Clarence Day, from *Life With Father* by Clarence Day, published by *Alfred A. Knopf, Inc., New York, 1935; copyright 1935 by Clarence Day; reprinted by permission*

This wasn't an exceptionally mean Clarence, either. He was just run-of-the-mill. Some were worse.

So far as I could ever learn, however, Father had never heard of these stories, and had never dreamed of there being anything objectionable in his name. Quite the contrary. And yet as a boy he had lived a good rough-and-tumble boy's life. He had played and fought on the city streets, and kept a dog in Grandpa's stable, and stolen rides to Greenpoint Ferry on the high, lurching bus. In the summer he had gone to West Springfield and had run down Shad Lane through the trees to the house where Grandpa was born, and had gone barefoot and driven the cows home just as though he had been named Tom or Bill.

He had the same character as a boy, I suppose, that he had as a man, and he was too independent to care if people thought his name fancy. He paid no attention to the prejudices of others, except to disapprove of them. He had plenty of prejudices himself, of course, but they were his own. He was humorous and confident and level-headed, and I imagine that if any boy had tried to make fun of him for being named Clarence, Father would simply have laughed and told him he didn't know what he was talking about.

I asked Mother how this name had ever happened to spring up in our family. She explained that my great-great-grandfather was Benjamin Day, and my great-grandfather was Henry, and consequently my grandfather had been named Benjamin Henry. He in turn had named his eldest son Henry and his second son Benjamin. The result was that when Father was born there was no family name left. The privilege of choosing a name for Father had thereupon been given to Grandma, and unluckily for the

Day family she had been reading a novel, the hero of which was named Clarence.

I knew that Grandma, though very like Grandpa in some respects, had a dreamy side which he hadn't, a side that she usually kept to herself, in her serene, quiet way. Her romantic choice of this name probably made Grandpa smile, but he was a detached sort of man who didn't take small matters seriously, and who drew a good deal of private amusement from the happenings of everyday life. Besides, he was partly to blame in this case, because that novel was one he had published himself in his magazine.

I asked Mother, when she had finished, why I had been named Clarence too.

It hadn't been her choice, Mother said. She had suggested all sorts of names to Father, but there seemed to be something wrong with each one. When she had at last spoken of naming me after him, however, he had said at once that that was the best suggestion yet—he said it sounded just right.

Father and I would have had plenty of friction in any case. This identity of names made things worse. Every time that I had been more of a fool than he liked, Father would try to impress on me my responsibilities as his eldest son, and above all as the son to whom he had given his name, as he put it. A great deal was expected, it seemed to me, of a boy who was named after his father. I used to envy my brothers, who didn't have anything expected of them on this score at all.

I envied them still more after I was old enough to begin getting letters. I then discovered that when Father "gave" me his name he had also, not unnaturally, I had to admit, retained it himself, and when anything came for Clarence S. Day he opened it, though it was sometimes for me.

He also opened everything that came addressed to Clarence S. Day, Jr. He didn't do this intentionally, but unless the "Jr." was clearly written, it looked like "Esq.," and anyhow Father was too accustomed to open all Clarence

Day letters to remember about looking carefully every time for a "Jr." So far as mail and express went, I had no name at all of my own.

For the most part nobody wrote to me when I was a small boy except firms whose advertisements I had read in the *Youth's Companion* and to whom I had written requesting them to send me their circulars. These circulars described remarkable bargains in magicians' card outfits, stamps and coins, pocket knives, trick spiders, and imitation fried eggs, and they seemed interesting and valuable to me when I got them. The trouble was that Father usually got them and at once tore them up. I then had to write for such circulars again, and if Father got the second one too, he would sometimes explode with annoyance. He became particularly indignant one year, I remember, when he was repeatedly urged to take advantage of a special bargain sale of false whiskers. He said that he couldn't understand why these offerings kept pouring in. I knew why, in this case, but at other times I was often surprised myself at the number he got, not realizing that as a result of my postcard request my or our name had been automatically put on several large general mailing lists.

During this period I got more of my mail out of Father's wastebasket than I did from the postman.

At the age of twelve or thirteen, I stopped writing for these childish things and turned to a new field. Father and I, whichever of us got at the mail first, then began to receive not merely circulars but personal letters beginning:

Dear Friend Day:

In reply to your valued request for one of our Mammoth Agents' Outfits, kindly forward post-office order for $1.49 to cover cost of postage and packing, and we will put you in a position to earn a large income in your spare time with absolutely no labor on your part, by taking subscriptions for *The Secret Handbook of Mesmerism*, and our *Tales of Blood* series.

And one spring, I remember, as the result of what I had intended to be a secret application on my part, Father was assigned "the exclusive rights for Staten Island and Hoboken of selling the Gem Home Popper for Pop Corn. Housewives buy it at sight."

After Father had stormily endured these afflictions for a while, he and I began to get letters from girls. Fortunately for our feelings, these were rare, but they were ordeals for both of us. Father had forgotten, if he ever knew, how silly young girls can sound, and I got my first lesson in how unsystematic they were. No matter how private and playful they meant their letters to be, they forgot to put "Jr." on the envelope every once in so often. When Father opened these letters, he read them all the way through, sometimes twice, muttering to himself over and over: "This is very peculiar. I don't understand this at all. Here's a letter to me from some person I never heard of. I can't see what it's about." By the time it had occurred to him that possibly the letter might be for me, I was red and embarrassed and even angrier at the girl than at Father. And on days when he had read some of the phrases aloud to the family, it nearly killed me to claim it.

Lots of fellows whom I knew had been named after their fathers without having such troubles. But although Father couldn't have been kinder-hearted or had any better intentions, when he saw his name on a package or envelope it never dawned on him that it might not be for him. He was too active in his habits to wait until I had a chance to get at it. And as he was also single-minded and prompt to attend to unfinished business, he opened everything automatically and then did his best to dispose of it.

This went on even after I grew up, until I had a home of my own. Father was always perfectly decent about it, but he never changed. When he saw I felt sulky, he was genuinely sorry and said so, but he couldn't see why all this should annoy me, and he was surprised and amused that it did. I used to get angry once in a while when something came for me which I particularly hadn't wished him to see and which I would find lying, opened, on the hall table marked "For Jr.?" when I came in; but nobody could stay angry with Father—he was too utterly guiltless of having meant to offend.

He often got angry himself, but it was mostly at things, not at persons, and he didn't mind a bit (as a rule) when persons got angry at him. He even declared, when I got back from college, feeling dignified, and told him that I wished he'd be more careful, that he suffered from these mistakes more than I did. It wasn't *his* fault, he pointed out, if my stupid correspondents couldn't remember my name, and it wasn't any pleasure to him to be upset at his breakfast by finding that a damned lunatic company in Battle Creek had sent him a box of dry bread crumbs, with a letter asserting that this rubbish would be good for his stomach. "I admit I threw it into the fireplace, Clarence, but what else could I do? If you valued this preposterous concoction, my dear boy, I'm sorry. I'll buy another box for you today, if you'll tell me where I can get it. Don't feel badly! I'll buy you a barrel. Only I hope you won't eat it."

In the days when Mrs. Pankhurst and her friends were chaining themselves to lamp-posts in London, in their campaign for the vote, a letter came from Frances Hand trustfully asking "Dear Clarence" to do something to help Woman Suffrage—speak at a meeting, I think. Father got red in the face. "Speak at one of their meetings!" he roared at Mother. "I'd like nothing better! You can tell Mrs. Hand that it would give me great pleasure to inform all those crackpots in petticoats exactly what I think of their antics."

"Now, Clare," Mother said, "you musn't talk that way. I like that nice Mrs. Hand, and anyhow this letter must be for Clarence."

One time I asked Father for his opinion of a low-priced stock I'd been watching. His opinion was that it was not worth a damn. I thought this over, but I still wished to buy it, so I placed a scale order with another firm instead of with Father's office, and said nothing about it. At the end of the month this other firm sent me a statement, setting forth each of my little transactions in full, and of course they forgot to put the "Jr." at the end of my name. When Father opened the envelope, he thought at first in his excitement that this firm had actually opened an account for him without being asked. I found him telling Mother that he'd like to wring their damned necks.

"That must be for me, Father," I said, when I took in what had happened.

We looked at each other.

"You bought this stuff?" he said incredulously. "After all I said about it?"

"Yes, Father."

He handed over the statement and walked out of the room.

Both he and I felt offended and angry. We stayed so for several days, too, but we then made it up.

Once in a while when I got a letter that I had no time to answer I used to address an envelope to the sender and then put anything in it that happened to be lying around on my desk—a circular about books, a piece of newspaper, an old laundry bill—anything at all, just to be amiable, and yet at the same time to save myself the trouble of writing. I happened to tell several people about this private habit of mine at a dinner one night—a dinner at which Alice Duer Miller and one or two other writers were present. A little later she wrote me a criticism of Henry James and ended by saying that I needn't send her any of my old laundry bills because she wouldn't stand it. And she forgot to put on the "Jr."

"In the name of God," Father said bleakly, "this is the worst yet. Here's a woman who says I'd better not read *The Golden Bowl*, which I have no intention whatever of doing, and she also warns me for some unknown reason not to send her my laundry bills."

The good part of all these experiences, as I realize now, was that in the end they drew Father and me closer together. My brothers had only chance battles with him. I had a war. Neither he nor I relished its clashes, but they made us surprisingly intimate.

THE GROWN-UP PROBLEM

Art Buchwald

There has been so much discussion about teenage problems that the grown-up problem is practically being ignored. And yet if you pick up a newspaper, you realize grown-ups are responsible for some of the most serious prob-

lems this country has ever faced.

For example, 60 percent of all crime in the United States is committed by grown-ups.

The birth rate among grown-up women is four times that of teen-agers.

The divorce rate is double.

The purchasing power of grown-ups almost exceeds that of teen-agers.

Grown-ups are responsible for more daytime accidents than any other age group.

The source of these statistics is sociology Prof. Heinrich Applebaum, B.A., M.S., LL.D.,

Y.E.H., Y.E.H., Y.E.H., who told me in an exclusive interview that his studies showed grown-ups were drifting farther away from society all the time.

"The average grown-up," Prof. Applebaum said, "feels his children don't understand him. The more time he spends with them, the less they communicate with him. So the adult feels isolated, insecure, and misunderstood. In defense he seeks out other grown-ups who feel the same way he does. Pretty soon they form gangs, go to the theater together, hold cocktail parties and dances, and before you know it you have a complete breakdown of the family."

"Why do you think grown-ups are constantly rebelling against their children, Professor?"

"I guess it's an age-old old-age problem. You have parents wanting to break away and yet not having the nerve to cut the ties completely. Grown-ups are afraid to stand up to their children, so they rebel against society instead."

"Do you think teen-agers could in some way be responsible for the behavior of their parents?"

"I definitely do," the Professor said. "Grown-ups try to emulate teen-agers. They want to do exactly what teen-agers do, which is to drink, smoke, and drive fast cars. If teen-agers didn't do these things, their parents wouldn't. For every bad adult in America, I'm sure you'll find a bad teen-ager somewhere in the background."

"Where do you think the trouble starts?"

"In the home. Teen-agers are too rough on their parents. They're always criticizing them for listening to Frank Sinatra records and reading *Holiday* magazine. Teen-agers don't have any patience with their mothers and fathers. They can't understand why their parents like Doris Day and Rock Hudson movies or what they see in Cary Grant. If teen-agers spent more time with grown-ups and tried to understand them, I don't think you'd have half the trouble that you have in the United States today."

"Do you mean teen-agers should spend more time at home with their parents?"

"Of course. Grown-ups need security. They want to know where their children are. They want the feeling they belong. Only teen-agers can give grown-ups this feeling."

"Professor, have you found any homes where grown-ups are leading healthy, normal, secure lives, thanks to the attention they've received from their loving teen-age children?"

"We haven't yet. But we've been looking only a year. These surveys take time."

CHILDREN ARE MONSTERS

Robert Thomas Allen

Whenever I tell my friends that I write at home, they imply that I'm lucky to be able to work in peace and quiet, completely free of distractions.

Actually, each morning as I sit with my fingers poised over my typewriter looking out onto a deceptively quiet street I find myself the lone spectator of a nether world of mayhem, treachery and propaganda that often keeps me absorbed for hours.

— *"Children are Monsters" by Robert Thomas Allen, reprinted by permission of the author from Maclean's Magazine, August 1, 1954*

As each man leaves the house for downtown, preschool-age children are turned outdoors, one by one, their little faces wiped clean of toast crumbs and their souls full of diabolical plans. They pass my window all day long, in thin-column formation, in a perpetual state of spine-chilling, dead-pan, passionless war. They wear hunting caps, long pink night-gowns, their mother's shoes and lace curtains. Sometimes they move by on wheels, sometimes on foot, but they all have one objective: to frame one another.

By lunchtime things have become so snarled that it's impossible to tell who is telling the truth. Right and wrong are so balled up in one gumbo mixture of bubble gum and tricycles that none of the mothers could sort them out, even if they wanted to. They just don't worry about it.

The other day I watched two little boys with shaved heads ride around a tree on their tri-cycles, slowly and aimlessly, from eight in the morning till suppertime, telling one another in agitated voices that they'd break one another's tricycles, that they'd climb up onto lamp posts and drop rocks on one another's heads, that they'd put one another in jail. Around eleven o'clock, one of them got off his trike, went over and hit the other in the mouth, then went home hollering, "Mummy! Pete hit me."

His mother came out, looked at him sharply, said, "Pull your pants up," and went back in.

Two strange little boys meeting for the first time will stand looking into one another's faces for a moment, then start conscientiously kicking one another until one starts howling and goes home.

Little tots with legs like noodles toddle off each morning in pigtails, bows, pocket-size dresses, on their way to play a day-long game, the object of which is to try to get somebody else spanked. When they score, they all stand around sucking their popsicles watching. They don't laugh or gloat or show any excitement. Their faces are completely expressionless.

Every other minute they go and tell their mothers. If they haven't anything to tell them, they tell them anything. Sometimes they tell their own mothers, sometimes they tell the other kid's mother. If they can't find either mother they tell the breadman. It's a peculiar world where the idea seems to be if you can stay with it until everyone is grown up it will all sort itself out.

The other day a little girl with a head of white curls let out a nerve-shattering scream that brought six mothers racing from their doors, three of them in curlers.

"Doris! What *is* it!" gasped one of them.

Doris put her hand on her flat little chest, looked across a geranium hedge at another little girl, and said in a hoarse stage whisper, "Gail looked at me!"

"It's time you came in for lunch anyway," her mother said.

One afternoon three little girls were playing. Suddenly two of them pushed the third off the veranda, then picked up her doll and threw it at her, breaking its head. I was almost ready to leap up from my typewriter and cross the road to lecture them on the rudiments of justice, sports-manship and the Geneva Conference. The little girl who had been shoved off the veranda screamed. The other two screamed back at her. The woman of the house came out.

"They broke my doll's head," the little girl wailed.

"Why did you break Susan's doll?" the woman asked, mechanically retying a bow.

"We were through playing with her," one of them said.

"Pull up your socks," the woman said, "and don't get dirty."

One time I listened to one youngster ask in a flat monotone, at intervals all morning, if the other would let her play with her doll carriage.

"Can I have your carriage?" she'd say.

"No."

At noon the mother of the kid with the carriage put her head out the door and called her daughter in for lunch. The youngster put the top of the carriage up and started for home, and fell down the veranda steps. She lay on her back, reaching for a sound proportionate to the fall. I could hear the scream coming like water working its way up to the nozzle of a garden hose. Just before it arrived the other kid who stood looking down at her like a little Richard Widmark in pigtails, evidently figuring that she was going to die, said, "Can I have your carriage now?"

Mercy seems something that begins to show itself around voting age. My own youngest daughter, who, although going to school, is still young enough to retain the preschool spirit, will chatter away at lunch.

"There's a boy in our class named Johnny," she'll say, industriously spooning chicken-noodle soup into herself. "He talks all the time."

"M-hm," I say.

"This morning the teacher said, 'Well I'm going to put you between two good little girls, Martha and Mary.'"

(Mary is my daughter.)

"So?" I say.

"'And if you talk' she said, 'I'm going to ask Martha and Mary to tell me and I'm going to send you to the office.' We had great fun."

"How do you mean?"

"We tried to get him to talk so we could tell the teacher."

"You *what!*" I bring her into focus. It's just beginning to dawn on me what she said.

"We tried to see how we could get him to talk," she says, getting up to get some more soup.

My wife says, "Oh, Mary, you shouldn't!"

"Shouldn't what?" Mary says, in surprise.

"Shouldn't take more soup," my wife says.

In the world of women and children, promises and systems of ethics are held together lightly by a thin coating of orange juice and hair fix and an occasional safety pin. It often leaves me wishing that I were back downtown amid the jolly cut-throat atmosphere of big business. There, people do one another in according to firm principles. Back home, nobody would recognize a principle if they found it in their shredded wheat.

It amounts to the same thing, probably, but it's easier on the nerves when it doesn't take place on a quiet sunny street.

THUS I REFUTE BEELZY

John Collier

"There goes the tea bell," said Mrs. Carter. "I hope Simon hears it."

They looked out from the window of the drawing-room. The long garden, agreeably neglected, ended in a waste plot. Here a little

— *"Thus I Refute Beelzy"* by *John Collier, from Presenting Moonshine by John Collier; copyright 1960 by John Collier; reprinted by permission of The Harold Matson Company Inc.*

summer-house was passing close by beauty on its way to complete decay. This was Simon's retreat: it was almost completely screened by the tangled branches of the apple tree and the pear tree, planted too close together, as they always are in suburban gardens. They caught a glimpse of him now and then, as he strutted up and down, mouthing and gesticulating, performing all the solemn mumbo-jumbo of small boys who spend long afternoons at the forgotten ends of long gardens.

"There he is, bless him," said Betty.

"Playing his game," said Mrs. Carter. "He won't play with the other children any more. And if I go down there—the temper! And comes in tired out."

"He doesn't have his sleep in the afternoons?" asked Betty.

"You know what Big Simon's ideas are," said Mrs. Carter. "'Let him choose for himself,' he says. That's what he chooses, and he comes in as white as a sheet."

"Look. He's heard the bell," said Betty. The expression was justified, though the bell had ceased ringing a full minute ago. Small Simon stopped in his parade exactly as if its tinny dingle had at that moment reached his ear. They watched him perform certain ritual sweeps and scratchings with his little stick, and come lagging over the hot and flaggy grass towards the house.

Mrs. Carter led the way down to the play-room, or garden-room, which was also the tea-room for hot days. It had been the huge scullery of this tall Georgian house. Now the walls were cream-washed, there was coarse blue net in the windows, canvas-covered armchairs on the stone floor, and a reproduction of Van Gogh's *Sun-flowers* over the mantelpiece.

Small Simon came drifting in, and accorded Betty a perfunctory greeting. His face was an almost perfect triangle, pointed at the chin, and he was paler than he should have been. "The little elf-child!" cried Betty.

Simon looked at her. "No," said he.

At that moment the door opened, and Mr. Carter came in, rubbing his hands. He was a dentist, and washed them before and after everything he did. "You!" said his wife. "Home already!"

"Not unwelcome, I hope," said Mr. Carter, nodding to Betty. "Two people cancelled their appointments: I decided to come home. I said, I hope I am not unwelcome."

"Silly!" said his wife. "Of course not."

"Small Simon seems doubtful," continued Mr. Carter. "Small Simon, are you sorry to see me at tea with you?"

"No, Daddy."

"No, what?"

"No, Big Simon."

"That's right. Big Simon and Small Simon. That sounds more like friends, doesn't it? At one time little boys had to call their father 'sir.' If they forgot—a good spanking. On the bottom, Small Simon! On the bottom!" said Mr. Carter, washing his hands once more with his invisible soap and water.

The little boy turned crimson with shame or rage.

"But now, you see," said Betty, to help, "you can call your father whatever you like."

"And what," asked Mr. Carter, "has Small Simon been doing this afternoon? While Big Simon has been at work."

"Nothing," muttered his son.

"Then you have been bored," said Mr. Carter. "Learn from experience, Small Simon. Tomorrow, do something amusing, and you will not be bored. I want him to learn from experience, Betty. That is my way, the new way."

"I have learned," said the boy, speaking like an old, tired man, as little boys so often do.

"It would hardly seem so," said Mr. Carter, "if you sit on your behind all the afternoon, doing nothing. Had *my* father caught me doing nothing, I should not have sat very comfortably."

"He played," said Mrs. Carter.

"A bit," said the boy, shifting on his chair.

"Too much," said Mrs. Carter. "He comes in all nervy and dazed. He ought to have his rest."

"He is six," said her husband. "He is a reasonable being. He must choose for himself. But what game is this, Small Simon, that is worth getting nervy and dazed over? There are very few games as good as all that."

"It's nothing," said the boy.

"Oh, come," said his father. "We are friends, are we not? You can tell me. I was a Small Simon once, just like you, and played the same games you play. Of course there were no aeroplanes in those days. With whom do you

36

play this fine game? Come on, we must all answer civil questions, or the world would never go round. With whom do you play?"

"Mr. Beelzy," said the boy, unable to resist.

"Mr. Beelzy?" said his father, raising his eyebrows inquiringly at his wife.

"It's a game he makes up," said she.

"Not makes up!" cried the boy. "Fool!"

"That is telling stories," said his mother. "And rude as well. We had better talk of something different."

"No wonder he is rude," said Mr. Carter, "If you say he tells lies, and then insist on changing the subject. He tells you his fantasy: you implant a guilt feeling. What can you expect? A defence mechanism. Then you get a real lie."

"Like in *These Three*," said Betty. "Only different, of course. *She* was an unblushing little liar."

"I would have made her blush," said Mr. Carter, "in the proper part of her anatomy. But Small Simon is in the fantasy stage. Are you not, Small Simon? You just make things up."

"No, I don't," said the boy.

"You do," said his father. "And because you do, it is not too late to reason with you. There is no harm in a fantasy, old chap. There is no harm in a bit of make-believe. Only you have to know the difference between day dreams and real things, or your brain will never grow. It will never be the brain of a Big Simon. So come on. Let us hear about this Mr. Beelzy of yours. Come on. What is he like?"

"He isn't like anything," said the boy.

"Like nothing on earth?" said his father. "That's a terrible fellow."

"I'm not frightened of him," said the child, smiling. "Not a bit."

"I should hope not," said his father. "If you were, you would be frightening yourself. I am always telling people, older people than you are, that they are just frightening themselves. Is he a funny man? Is he a giant?"

"Sometimes he is," said the little boy.

"Sometimes one thing, sometimes another," said his father. "Sounds pretty vague. Why can't you tell us just what he's like?"

"I love him," said the small boy. "He loves me."

"That's a big word," said Mr. Carter. "That might be better kept for real things, like Big Simon and Small Simon."

"He is real," said the boy, passionately. "He's not a fool. He's real."

"Listen," said his father. "When you go down the garden there's nobody there. Is there?"

"No," said the boy.

"Then you think of him, inside your head, and he comes."

"No," said Small Simon. "I have to do something with my stick."

"That doesn't matter."

"Yes, it does."

"Small Simon, you are being obstinate," said Mr. Carter. "I am trying to explain something to you. I have been longer in the world than you have, so naturally I am older and wiser. I am explaining that Mr. Beelzy is a fantasy of yours. Do you hear? Do you understand?"

"Yes, Daddy."

"He is a game. He is a let's-pretend."

The little boy looked down at his plate, smiling resignedly.

"I hope you are listening to me," said his father. "All you have to do is to say, 'I have been playing a game of let's-pretend. With someone I make up, called Mr. Beelzy.' Then no one will say you tell lies, and you will know the difference between dreams and reality. Mr. Beelzy is a day dream."

The little boy still stared at his plate.

"He is sometimes there and sometimes not there," pursued Mr. Carter. "Sometimes he's like one thing, sometimes another. You can't really see him. Not as you see me. I am real. You can't touch him. You can touch me. I can touch you." Mr. Carter stretched out his big, white, dentist's hand, and took his little son by the shoulder. He stopped speaking for a moment and tightened his hand. The little boy sank his head still lower.

"Now you know the difference," said Mr. Carter, "between a pretend and a real thing. You and I are one thing; he is another. Which is the pretend? Come on. Answer me. Which is the pretend?"

"Big Simon and Small Simon," said the little boy.

"Don't!" cried Betty, and at once put her hand over her mouth, for why should a visitor cry "Don't!" when a father is explaining things in a scientific and modern way?

"Well, my boy," said Mr. Carter, "I have said you must be allowed to learn from experience. Go upstairs. Right up to your room. You shall learn whether it is better to reason, or to be perverse and obstinate. Go up. I shall follow you."

"You are not going to beat the child?" cried Mrs. Carter.

"No," said the little boy. "Mr. Beelzy won't let him."

"Go on up with you!" shouted his father.

Small Simon stopped at the door. "He said he wouldn't let anyone hurt me," he whimpered. "He said he'd come like a lion, with wings on, and eat them up."

"You'll learn how real he is!" shouted his father after him. "If you can't learn it at one end, you shall learn it at the other. I'll have your breeches down. I shall finish my cup of tea first, however," said he to the two women.

Neither of them spoke. Mr. Carter finished his tea, and unhurriedly left the room, washing his hands with his invisible soap and water.

Mrs. Carter said nothing. Betty could think of nothing to say. She wanted to be talking: she was afraid of what they might hear.

Suddenly it came. It seemed to tear the air apart. "Good God!" she cried. "What was that? He's hurt him." She sprang out of her chair, her silly eyes flashing behind her glasses. "I'm going up there!" she cried, trembling.

"Yes, let us go up," said Mrs. Carter. "Let us go up. That was not Small Simon."

It was on the second-floor landing that they found the shoe, with the man's foot still in it, like that last morsel of a mouse which sometimes falls from the jaws of a hasty cat.

PENNY IN THE DUST

Ernest Buckler

My sister and I were walking through the old sun-still fields the evening before the funeral, recalling this or that thing which had happened in this or that place, turning over memories after the fashion of families who gather again in the place where they were born—trying to disclose and identify themselves with the strange children

— *"Penny in the Dust" by Ernest Buckler; reprinted by permission of the author*

they must have been.

"Do you remember the afternoon we thought you were lost?" my sister said. I did. That was as long ago as the day I was seven.

"We searched everywhere," she said, "up in the meetinghouse, back in the blueberry barrens —we even looked in the well. I think it's the only time I ever saw Father really upset. He didn't even stop to tie up the horse's reins. He raced right through the chopping where Tom Reeve was burning brush, looking for you—

right through the flames almost. They couldn't do a thing with him. And you up in your bed, sound asleep!

"It was all over losing a penny or something, wasn't it?" she went on, when I didn't answer. It was. She laughed indulgently. "You were a crazy kid, weren't you?"

I was. But there was more to it than that. I had never seen a brand-new penny before. I thought they were all black. This one was bright as gold. And my father had given it to me.

You would have to understand about my father and that is the hard thing to tell. If I say that he worked all day long, but I had never seen him hurry, that would make him sound like a stupid man. If I say that he never held me on his knee and that I never heard him laugh out loud in his life, it would make him sound humorless and severe. If I said that whenever I'd be telling mother some of my fancy plans and he'd come into the kitchen I'd stop, like someone hiding the pages of a foolish book, you'd think that he was distant and that in some kind of way I was afraid of him. None of that would be true.

There's no way you can tell it to make it sound like anything more than an inarticulate man a little at sea with an imaginative child. You'll have to take my word for it that there was more to it than that. It was as if his sure-footed way in the fields forsook him the instant he came near the door of my child's world and that he must wipe off his feet before he stood inside, awkward and conscious of trespass; and that I, sensing that but not understanding it, felt, at the sound of his solid step outside, my world's foolish fragility.

He would fix the small spot where I planted beans and other quick-sprouting seeds before he prepared the big garden, even if the spring was late; but he wouldn't ask me how many rows I wanted and, if he made three tiny rows and I wanted four, I couldn't ask him to change them. If I walked behind the load of hay, longing to ride, and he walked ahead of the oxen, I couldn't ask him to put me up and he wouldn't make any move to do so, until he saw me trying to grasp

the binder.

He, my father, had just given me a new penny, bright as gold.

He took it from his pocket several times, pretending to examine the date on it, waiting for me to notice it. He couldn't offer me *anything* until I had shown some sign that the gift would be welcome.

"You can have it if you want it, Dan," he said at last.

I said, "Oh, thanks." Nothing more.

I started with it to the store. For a penny you could buy the magic cylinder of "Long Tom" popcorn, with Heaven knows what colored jewel on the ring inside. But the more I thought of my bright penny disappearing forever into the black drawstring pouch the Assyrian merchant kept his money in, the slower my steps lagged as the store came nearer and nearer. I sat down in the road.

It was that time of magic suspension in an August afternoon. The lifting smells of leaves and cut clover hung still in the sun. The sun drowsed, like a kitten curled upon my shoulder. The deep flour-fine dust in the road puffed about my bare ankles, warm and soft as sleep. A swallow-tailed butterfly clung to the road, its bright-banded wings spreading and converging like the movements of breathing. The sound of the cowbells came sharp and hollow from the cool swamp.

I began to play with the penny, postponing the decision. I would close my eyes and bury it deep in the sand and then, with my eyes still closed, get up and walk around and then come back to search for it, tantalizing myself each time with the thrill of discovering afresh its bright shining edge. I did that again and again. Alas, once too often.

It was almost dark when their excited talking in the room woke me. It was mother who had found me. I suppose when it came dusk she thought of me in the bed other nights and I suppose she looked there without any reasonable hope, but as you do when the search has become desperate, in every place where the thing lost has ever lain before. And now suddenly she was crying.

"Danny!" she cried, with the pointlessness of sudden relief, "*where* have you been!"

"I lost my penny," I said.

"You lost your penny—? But what made you come up here and hide?"

If my father hadn't been there, I might have told her. But when I looked up at my father, standing there like the shape of everything sound and straight, it was like daylight shredding the memory of a foolish dream. How could I bear the shame of repeating before him the soft twisting visions I had built in my head in the magic August afternoon when almost anything could be made to seem real, as I buried the penny and dug it up again? How could I explain that pit-of-the-stomach sickness which struck through the whole day when I had to believe, at last, that it was really lost? How could I explain that I wasn't really hiding from *them?* How, with the words and the understanding I had then, that the only possible place to run from that awful feeling of loss was the soft, absorbing, dark safeness of bed? That I had cried myself asleep?

"I lost my penny," I said. I looked at father and turned my face into the pillow. "I want to go to sleep."

"Danny," my mother said, "it's almost nine o'clock. You haven't had a bite of supper. Do you know you almost scared the *life* out of us!"

"You better git some supper," my father said. It was the only time he had spoken.

I knew mother would talk about it and talk about it, but I never dreamed of father ever mentioning it again. But the next morning when we had the forks in our hands, ready to toss out the hay, he seemed to hold up the moment of actually leaving for the field. He stuck his fork in the ground and brought in another pail of water, though the kettle was chock-full. He took out the shingle nail that held his broken brace together and put it back in exactly the same hole. He went into the shop to see if the pigs had cleaned up all their breakfast.

"Ain't you got no idea where you lost your penny?" he said suddenly.

"Yes," I said, "I know just about."

"Let's see if we can't find it," he said.

We walked down the road together, stiff with awareness. He didn't hold my hand.

"It's right here somewheres," I said. "I was playin' with it in the dust." He looked at me, questioningly but he didn't ask me what game anyone could possibly play with a penny in the dust.

I might have known he would find it. In making a whistle he could tap alder bark with his jackknife just exactly hard enough so it wouldn't break but so it would twist free from the wood beneath, though I couldn't believe he had ever made a whistle for himself when he was a child. His great fingers could trace loose the hopeless snarl of a fishing line that I could only succeed in tangling tighter and tighter. If I broke the handle of my wheelbarrow ragged beyond sight of any possible repair, he could take it and bring it back to me so you could hardly see the place if you weren't looking for it.

He got down on his knees and drew his fingers carefully through the dust, like a harrow; not clawing it frantically in heaps as I had done, covering even while I uncovered. He found the penny almost at once.

He held it in his hand, as if the moment of passing it to me were a deadline for something he dreaded to say, but must. Something that could not be postponed any longer if it were to be spoken at all.

"Dan," he said, "You needn'ta hid. I wouldn'ta beat you."

"*Beat* me: Oh, Father! You didn't think *that* was the reason—?" I felt almost sick.

Do you know how I felt then? I felt as if I had beaten *him*. His face looked like I had seen it of an evening when mother wasn't speaking and he would pick up a schoolbook or a paper and follow the lines patiently, though he never read any other time at all. I had to tell him the truth then. Because only the truth, no matter how foolish it was, would have the unmistakable sound of truth, to scatter that awful idea out of his head.

"I wasn't hidin', father," I said, "honest— I was—I was buryin' my penny and makin' out I was diggin' up treasure. I was makin' out I was findin' gold. I didn't know what to *do* when I lost it, I just didn't know where to *go*—" His head was bent forward, like mere listening. I had to make it truer still.

"I made out it was gold," I said desperately, "and I—I was makin' out I bought you a mowin' machine so's you could get your work done early every day so's you and I could go into town in the big automobile I made out I bought and everyone'd turn around and look at us drivin' down the streets—" His head was perfectly still, as if he were only waiting with patience for me to finish.

"—*laughin'* and *talkin'*—" I said, louder, smiling intensely, compelling him, by the absolute conviction of some true particular, to believe me.—

He looked up then. It was the only time I had ever seen tears in his eyes.

I wondered, though, why he hesitated and then put the penny back in his own pocket.

Yesterday I knew. I never found any fortune and we never had a car to ride in together. But I think he knew what that would be like, just the same. I found the penny again yesterday, when we were getting out his good clothes—in an upper vest pocket where no one ever carries change. It was still shining. He must have kept it polished.

I left it there.

BROTHER DEATH

Sherwood Anderson

There were the two oak stumps, knee high to a not-too-tall man and cut quite squarely across. They became to the two children objects of wonder. They had seen the two trees cut but had run away just as the trees fell. They hadn't thought of the two stumps, to be left standing there; hadn't even looked at them. Afterward Ted said to his sister Mary, speaking of the stumps: "I wonder if they bled, like legs, when a surgeon cuts a man's leg off." He had been hearing war stories. A man came to the farm one day to visit one of the farm hands, a man who had been in the World War and had

— "*Brother Death*" *by Sherwood Anderson, from* Sherwood Anderson: Short Stories, *Hill and Wang, New York, 1962; by permission of Harold Ober Associates Inc.; copyright © 1933 by Sherwood Anderson, renewed 1961 by Eleanor Copenhaver Anderson*

lost an arm. He stood in one of the barns talking. When Ted said that, Mary spoke up at once. She hadn't been lucky enough to be at the barn when the one-armed man was there talking, and was jealous. "Why not a woman's or a girl's leg?" she said, but Ted said the idea was silly. "Women and girls don't get their legs and arms cut off," he declared. "Why not? I'd just like to know why not?" Mary kept saying.

It would have been something if they had stayed, that day the trees were cut. "We might have gone and touched the places," Ted said. He meant the stumps. Would they have been warm? Would they have bled? They did go and touch the places afterward, but it was a cold day and the stumps were cold. Ted stuck to his point that only men's arms and legs were cut off, but Mary thought of automobile accidents. "You can't think just about wars. There might be an automobile accident," she declared, but Ted wouldn't be convinced.

They were both children, but something had made them both in an odd way old. Mary was fourteen and Ted eleven, but Ted wasn't strong and that rather evened things up. They were the children of a well-to-do Virginia farmer named John Grey in the Blue Ridge country in southwestern Virginia. There was a wide valley called the "Rich Valley," with a railroad and a small river running through it and high mountains in sight, to the north and south. Ted had some kind of heart disease, a lesion, something of the sort, the result of a severe attack of diphtheria when he was a child of eight. He was thin and not strong, but curiously alive. The doctor said he might die at any moment, might just drop down dead. The fact had drawn him peculiarly close to his sister Mary. It had awakened a strong and determined maternalism in her.

The whole family, the neighbors, on neighboring farms in the valley, and even the other children at the schoolhouse where they went to school recognized something as existing between the two children. "Look at them going along there," people said. "They do seem to have good times together, but they are so serious. For such young children they are too serious. Still, I suppose, under the circumstances, it's natural." Of course, everyone knew about Ted. It had done something to Mary. At fourteen she was both a child and a grown woman. The woman side of her kept popping out at unexpected moments.

She had sensed something concerning her brother Ted. It was because he was as he was, having that kind of a heart, a heart likely at any moment to stop beating, leaving him dead, cut down like a young tree. The others in the Grey family, that is to say, the older ones, the mother and father and an older brother, Don, who was eighteen now, recognized something as belonging to the two children, being, as it were, between them, but the recognition wasn't very definite. People in your own family are likely at any moment to do strange, sometimes hurtful things to you. You have to watch them. Ted and Mary had both found that out.

The brother Don was like the father, already at eighteen almost a grown man. He was that sort, the kind people speak of, saying, "He's a good man. He'll make a good solid dependable man." The father, when he was a young man, never drank, never went chasing the girls, was never wild. There had been enough wild young ones in the Rich Valley when he was a lad. Some of them had inherited big farms and had lost them, gambling, drinking, fooling with fast horses and chasing after the women. It had been almost a Virginia tradition, but John Grey was a land man. All the Greys were. There were other large cattle farms owned by Greys up and down the valley.

John Grey, everyone said, was a natural cattle man. He knew beef cattle, of the big so-called export type, how to pick and feed them to make beef. He knew how and where to get the right kind of young stock to turn into his fields. It was blue-grass country. Big beef cattle went directly off the pastures to market. The Grey farm contained over twelve hundred acres, most of it in blue grass.

The father was a land man, land hungry. He had begun, as a cattle farmer, with a small place inherited from his father, some two hundred acres, lying next to what was then the big Aspinwahl place and, after he began, he never stopped getting more land. He kept cutting in on the Aspinwahls, who were a rather horsey, fast lot. They thought of themselves as Virginia aristocrats, having, as they weren't so modest about pointing out, a family going back and back, family tradition, guests always being entertained, fast horses kept, money being bet on fast horses. John Grey getting their land, now twenty acres, then thirty, then fifty, until at last he got the old Aspinwahl house, with one of the Aspinwahl girls, not a young one, not one of the best-looking ones, as wife. The Aspinwahl place was down, by that time, to less than a hundred acres, but he went on, year after year, always being careful and shrewd, making every penny count, never wasting a cent, adding and adding to what was now the Grey place. The former Aspinwahl house was a large old brick house with fireplaces in all the rooms and was very comfortable.

People wondered why Louise Aspinwahl had married John Grey, but when they were wondering they smiled. The Aspinwahl girls were all well educated, had all been away to college, but Louise wasn't so pretty. She got nicer after marriage, suddenly almost beautiful. The Aspinwahls were, as everyone knew, naturally sensitive, really first class, but the men couldn't hang onto land and the Greys could. In all that section of Virginia, people gave John Grey credit for being what he was. They respected him. "He's on the level," they said, "as honest as a horse. He has cattle sense, that's it." He could run his big hand down over the flank of a steer and say, almost to the pound, what he would weigh on the scales or he could look at a calf or a yearling and say, "He'll do," and he would do. A steer is a steer. He isn't supposed to do anything but make beef.

There was Don, the oldest son of the Grey family. He was so evidently destined to be a Grey, to be another like his father. He had long been a star in the 4-H Club of the Virginia county and, even as a lad of nine and ten, had won prizes at steer judging. At twelve he had produced, no one helping him, doing all the work himself, more bushels of corn on an acre of land than any other boy in the state.

It was all a little amazing, even a bit queer to Mary Grey, being as she was a girl peculiarly conscious, so old and young, so aware. There was Don, the older brother, big and strong of body like the father, and there was the young brother Ted. Ordinarily, in the ordinary course of life, she being what she was—female—it would have been quite natural and right for her to have given her young-girl's admiration to Don, but she didn't. For some reason, Don barely existed for her. He was outside, not in it, while, for her, Ted, the seemingly weak one of the family, was everything.

Still there Don was, so big of body, so quiet, so apparently sure of himself. The father had begun, as a young cattle man, with the two hundred acres, and now he had the twelve hundred. What would Don Grey do when he started? Already he knew, although he didn't say anything, that he wanted to start. He wanted to run things, be his own boss. His father had offered to send him away to college, to an agricultural college, but he wouldn't go. "No. I can learn more here," he said.

Already there was a contest, always kept under the surface, between the father and son. It concerned ways of doing things, decisions to be made. As yet, the son always surrendered.

It is like that in a family, little isolated groups formed within the larger group, jealousies, concealed hatreds, silent battles secretly going on—among the Greys, Mary and Ted, Don and his father, the mother and the two younger children, Gladys, a girl child of six now, who adored her brother Don, and Harry, a boy child of two.

As for Mary and Ted, they lived within their own world, but their own world had not been established without a struggle. The point was that Ted, having the heart that might at any moment stop beating, was always being treated tenderly by the others. Only Mary understood that—how it infuriated and hurt him.

"No, Ted, I wouldn't do that."

"Now, Ted, do be careful."

Sometimes Ted went white and trembling with anger—Don, the father, the mother, all keeping at him like that. It didn't matter what he wanted to do, learn to drive one of the two family cars, climb a tree to find a bird's nest, run a race with Mary. Naturally, being on a farm, he wanted to try his hand at breaking a colt, beginning with him, getting a saddle on, having it out with him. "No, Ted. You can't." He had learned to swear, picking it up from the farm hands and from boys at the country school. "Hell! Goddam!" he said to Mary. Only Mary understood how he felt, and she had not put the matter very definitely into words, not even to herself. It was one of the things that made her old when she was so young. It made her stand aside from the others of the family, aroused in her a curious determination. "They shall not." She caught herself saying the words to herself. "They shall not.

"If he is to have but a few years of life, they shall not spoil what he is to have. Why should they make him die, over and over, day after day?" The thoughts in her did not become so definite. She had resentment against the others. She was like a soldier, standing guard over Ted.

The two children drew more and more away, into their own world, and only once did what Mary felt come to the surface. That was with the mother.

It was on an early summer day and Ted and Mary were playing in the rain. They were on a side porch of the house, where the water came pouring down from the eaves. At a corner of the porch there was a great stream, and first Ted and then Mary dashed through it, returning to the porch with clothes soaked and water running in streams from soaked hair. There was something joyous, the feel of the cold water on the body, under clothes, and they were shrieking with laughter when the mother came to the door. She looked at Ted. There was fear and anxiety in her voice. "Oh, Ted, you know you mustn't, you mustn't." Just that. All the rest implied. Nothing said to Mary. There it was. "Oh, Ted, you mustn't. You mustn't run hard, climb trees, ride horses. The least shock to you may do it." It was the old story again, and, of course, Ted understood. He went white and trembled. Why couldn't the rest understand that was a hundred times worse for him? On that day, without answering his mother, he ran off the porch and through the rain toward the barns. He wanted to go hide himself from everyone. Mary knew how he felt.

She got suddenly very old and very angry. The mother and daughter stood looking at each other, the woman nearing fifty and the child of fourteen. It was getting everything in the family reversed. Mary felt that, but felt she had

to do something. "You should have more sense, Mother," she said seriously. She also had gone white. Her lips trembled. "You mustn't do it any more. Don't you ever do it again."

"What, child?" There was astonishment and half anger in the mother's voice. "Always making him think of it," Mary said. She wanted to cry, but didn't.

The mother understood. There was a queer tense moment before Mary also walked off, toward the barns, in the rain. It wasn't all so clear. The mother wanted to fly at the child, perhaps shake her for daring to be so impudent. A child like that to decide things—to dare to reprove her mother. There was so much implied—even that Ted be allowed to die, quickly, suddenly, rather than that death, danger of sudden death, be brought again and again to his attention. There were values in life, implied by a child's words: "Life, what is it worth? Is death the most terrible thing?" The mother turned and went silently into the house, while Mary, going to the barns, presently found Ted. He was in an empty horse stall, standing with his back to the wall, staring. There were no explanations. "Well," Ted said presently; and "Come on, Ted," Mary replied. It was necessary to do something, even perhaps more risky than playing in the rain. The rain was already passing. "Let's take off our shoes," Mary said. Going barefoot was one of the things forbidden Ted. They took their shoes off and, leaving them in the barn, went into an orchard. There was a small creek below the orchard, a creek that went down to the river and now it would be in flood. They went into it and once Mary got swept off her feet so that Ted had to pull her out. She spoke then. "I told Mother," she said, looking serious.

"What?" Ted said. "Gee, I guess maybe I saved you from drowning," he added.

"Sure you did," said Mary. "I told her to let you alone." She grew suddenly fierce. "They've all got to—they've got to let you alone," she said.

There was a bond. Ted did his share. He

was imaginative and could think of plenty of risky things to do. Perhaps the mother spoke to the father and to Don, the older brother. There was a new inclination in the family to keep hands off the pair, and the fact seemed to give the two children new room in life. Something seemed to open out. There was a little inner world created, always, every day, being re-created, and in it there was a kind of new security. It seemed to the two children—they could not have put their feeling into words— that, being in their own created world, feeling a new security there, they could suddenly look out at the outside world and see, in a new way, what was going on out there in the world that belonged also to others.

It was a world to be thought about, looked at, a world of drama too, the drama of human relations, outside their own world, in a family, on a farm, in a farmhouse. —— On a farm, calves and yearling steers arriving to be fattened, great heavy steers going off to market, colts being broken to work or to saddle, lambs born in the late winter. The human side of life was more difficult, to a child often incomprehensible, but after the speech to the mother, on the porch of the house that day when it rained, it seemed to Mary almost as though she and Ted had set up a new family. Everything about the farm, house and the barns got nicer. There was a new freedom. The two children walked along a country road, returning to the farm from school in the late afternoon. There were other children in the road but they managed to fall behind or they got ahead. There were plans made. "I'm going to be a nurse when I grow up," Mary said. She may have remembered dimly the woman nurse, from the county-seat town, who had come to stay in the house when Ted was so ill. Ted said that as soon as he could—it would be when he was younger yet than Don was now— he intended to leave and go out West —— far out, he said. He wanted to be a cowboy or a broncobuster or something, and, that failing, he thought he would be a railroad engineer. The railroad that went down through the Rich Valley crossed a corner of the Grey farm, and from the road in the afternoon they could sometimes see trains, quite far away, the smoke rolling up. There was a faint rumbling noise, and, on clear days they could see the flying piston rods of the engines.

As for the two stumps in the field near the house, they were what was left of two oak trees. The children had known the trees. They were cut one day in the early fall.

There was a back porch to the Grey house— the house that had once been the seat of the Aspinwahl family—and from the porch steps a path led down to a stone spring house. A spring came out of the ground just there, and there was a tiny stream that went along the edge of a field, past two large barns and out across a meadow to a creek—called a "branch," in Virginia, and the two trees stood close together beyond the spring house and the fence.

They were lusty trees, their roots down in the rich, always damp soil, and one of them had a great limb that came down near the ground, so that Ted and Mary could climb into it and out another limb into its brother tree, and in the fall, when other trees, at the front and side of the house, had shed their leaves, blood-red leaves still clung to the two oaks. They were like dry blood on gray days, but on other days, when the sun came out, the trees flamed against distant hills. The leaves clung, whispering and talking when the wind blew, so that the trees themselves seemed carrying on a conversation.

John Grey had decided he would have the trees cut. At first it was not a very definite decision. "I think I'll have them cut," he announced.

"But why?" his wife asked. The trees meant a good deal to her. They had been planted, just in that spot, by her grandfather, she said, having in mind just a certain effect. "You see how in the fall, when you stand on the back porch, they are so nice against the hills." She spoke of the trees, already quite large, having been brought from a distant woods. Her mother had often spoken of it. The man, her grandfather, had a special feeling for trees. "An Aspinwahl would do that," John Grey said. "There is enough yard, here about the house, and enough trees. They do not shade the house or the yard. An Aspinwahl would go to all that trouble for trees and then plant them where grass might be growing." He had suddenly determined, a half-formed determination in him suddenly hardening. He had perhaps heard too much of the Aspinwahls and their ways. The conversation regarding the trees took place at the table, at the noon hour, and Mary and Ted heard it all.

It began at the table and was carried on afterward out of doors, in the yard back of the house. The wife had followed her husband out. He always left the table suddenly and silently, getting quickly up and going out heavily, shutting doors with a bang as he went. "Don't, John," the wife said, standing on the porch and calling to her husband. It was a cold day, but the sun was out and the trees were like great bonfires against gray distant fields and hills. The older son of the family, young Don, the one so physically like the father and apparently so like him in every way, had come out of the house with the mother, followed by the two children, Ted and Mary, and at first Don said nothing, but, when the father did not answer the mother's protest but started toward the barn, he also spoke. What he said was obviously the determining thing, hardening the father.

To the two other children—they had walked a little aside and stood together watching and listening—there was something. There was their own child's world. "Let us alone and we'll let you alone." It wasn't as definite as that. Most of the definite thoughts about what happened in the yard that afternoon came to Mary Grey long afterward, when she was a grown woman. At the moment, there was merely a sudden sharpening of the feeling of isolation, a wall between herself and Ted and the others. The father, even then perhaps, seen in a new light, Don and the mother seen in a new light.

There was something, a driving destructive thing in life, in all relationships between people. All of this felt dimly that day—she always believed both by herself and Ted—but only thought out long afterward, after Ted was dead. There was the farm her father had won from the Aspinwahls—greater persistence, greater shrewdness. In a family, little remarks dropped from time to time, an impression slowly built up. The father, John Grey, was a successful man. He had acquired. He owned. He was the commander, the one having power to do his will. And the power had run out and covered not only other human lives, impulses in others, wishes, hungers in others—he himself might not have, might not even understand—but it went far out beyond that. It was, curiously, the power also of life and death. Did Mary Grey think such thoughts at that moment —— ? She couldn't have. —— Still, there was her own peculiar situation, her relationship with her brother Ted, who was to die.

Ownership that gave curious rights, dominances—fathers over children, men and women over lands, houses, factories in cities, fields. "I will have the trees in that orchard cut. They produce apples but not of the right sort. There is no money in apples of that sort any more."

"But, sir —— you see —— look —— the trees there against that hill, against the sky."

"Nonsense. Sentimentality."

Confusion.

It would have been such nonsense to think of the father of Mary Grey as a man without feeling. He had struggled hard all his life, perhaps, as a young man, gone without things wanted, deeply hungered for. Someone has to manage things in this life. Possessions mean power, the right to say, "Do this" or "Do that." If you struggle long and hard for a thing it becomes infinitely sweet to you.

Was there a kind of hatred between the father and the older son of the Grey family? "You are one also who has this thing—the impulse to power, so like my own. Now you are young and

I am growing old." Admiration mixed with fear. If you would retain power it will not do to admit fear.

The young Don was so curiously like the father. There were the same lines about the jaws, the same eyes. They were both heavy men. Already the young man walked like the father, slammed doors as did the father. There was the same curious lack of delicacy of thought and touch—the heaviness that plows through, gets things done. When John Grey had married Louise Aspinwahl he was already a mature man, on his way to success. Such men do not marry young and recklessly. Now he was nearing sixty and there was the son—so like himself, having the same kind of strength.

Both land lovers, possession lovers. "It is my farm, my house, my horses, cattle, sheep." Soon now, another ten years, fifteen at the most, and the father would be ready for death. "See, already my hand slips a little. All of this to go out of my grasp." He, John Grey, had not got all of these possessions so easily. It had taken much patience, much persistence. No one but himself would ever quite know. Five, ten, fifteen years of work and saving, getting the Aspinwahl farm piece by piece. "The fools!" They had liked to think of themselves as aristocrats, throwing the land away, now twenty acres, now thirty, now fifty.

Raising horses that could never plow an acre of land.

And they had robbed the land too, had never put anything back, doing nothing to enrich it, build it up. Such a one thinking: "I'm an Aspinwahl, a gentleman. I do not soil my hands at the plow."

"Fools who do not know the meaning of land owned, possessions, money—responsibility. It is they who are second-rate men."

He had got an Aspinwahl for a wife and, as it had turned out, she was the best, the smartest and, in the end, the best-looking one of the lot. And now there was his son, standing at the moment near the mother. They had both come down off the porch. It would be natural and right for this one—he being what he already was, what he would become—for him, in his turn, to come into possession, to take command.

There would be, of course, the rights of the other children. If you have the stuff in you (John Grey felt that his son Don had) there is a way to manage. You buy the others out, make arrangements. There was Ted—he wouldn't be alive—and Mary and the two younger children. "The better for you if you have to struggle."

All of this, the implication of the moment of sudden struggle between father and son, coming slowly afterward to the man's daughter, as yet little more than a child. Does the drama take place when the seed is put into the ground or afterward when the plant has pushed out of the ground and the bud breaks open, or still later, when the fruit ripens? There were the Greys with their ability—slow, saving, able, determined, patient. Why had they superseded the Aspinwahls in the Rich Valley? Aspinwahl blood also in the two children, Mary and Ted.

There was an Aspinwahl man—called "Uncle Fred," a brother to Louise Grey—who came sometimes to the farm. He was a rather striking-looking, tall old man with a gray Vandyke beard and a mustache, somewhat shabbily dressed but always with an indefinable air of class. He came from the county-seat town, where he lived now with a daughter who had married a merchant, a polite, courtly old man who always froze into a queer silence in the presence of his sister's husband.

The son Don was standing near the mother on the day in the fall, and the two children, Mary and Ted, stood apart.

"Don't, John," Louise Grey said again. The father, who had started away toward the barns, stopped.

"Well, I guess I will."

"No, you won't," said young Don, speaking suddenly. There was a queer fixed look in his eyes. It had flashed into life—something that was between the two men: "I possess —— I will possess." The father wheeled and looked sharply at the son and then ignored him.

For a moment the mother continued pleading. "But why, why?"

"They make too much shade. The grass does **not** grow."

"But there is so much grass, so many acres of grass."

John Grey was answering his wife, but now again he looked at his son. There were unspoken words flying back and forth.

"I possess. I am in command here. What do you mean by telling me that I won't?"

"Ha! So! You possess now, but soon I will possess."

"I'll see you in hell first."

"You fool! Not yet! Not yet!"

None of the words, set down above, was spoken at the moment, and afterward the daughter Mary never did remember the exact words that had passed between the two men. There was a sudden quick flash of determination in Don—even perhaps sudden determination to stand by the mother—even perhaps something else—a feeling in the young Don out of the Aspinwahl blood in him—for the moment tree love superseding grass love—grass that would fatten steers. ——

Winner of 4-H Club prizes, champion young corn-raiser, judge of steers, land lover, possession lover.

"You won't," Don said again.

"Won't what?"

"Won't cut those trees."

The father said nothing more at the moment but walked away from the little group toward the barns. The sun was still shining brightly. There was a sharp cold little wind. The two trees were like bonfires lighted against distant hills.

It was the noon hour and there were two men, both young, employees on the farm, who lived in a small tenant house beyond the barns. One of them, a man with a harelip, was married and the other a rather handsome silent young man, boarded with him. They had just come from the midday meal and were going toward one of the barns. It was the beginning of the fall corn-cutting time and they would be going together to a distant field to cut corn.

The father went to the barn and returned with the two men. They brought axes and a long crosscut saw. "I want you to cut those two trees." There was something, a blind, even stupid determination in the man, John Grey. And at that moment his wife, the mother of his children —— There was no way any of the children could ever know how many moments of the sort she had been through. She had married John Grey. He was her man.

"If you do, Father—" Don Grey said coldly.

"Do as I tell you! Cut those two trees!" This addressed to the two workmen. The one who had a harelip laughed. His laughter was like the bray of a donkey.

"Don't," said Louise Grey, but she was not addressing her husband this time. She stepped to her son and put a hand on his arm.

"Don't."

"Don't cross him. Don't cross my man." Could a child like Mary Grey comprehend? It takes time to understand things that happen in life. Life unfolds slowly to the mind. Mary was standing with Ted, whose young face was white and tense. Death at his elbow. At any moment. At any moment.

"I have been through this a hundred times. That is the way this man I married has succeeded. Nothing stops him. I married him; I have had my children by him.

"We women choose to submit.

"This is my affair, more than yours, Don, my son."

A woman hanging onto her thing—the family, created about her.

The son not seeing things with her eyes. He shook off his mother's hand lying on his arm. Louise Grey was younger than her husband, but, if he was now nearing sixty, she was drawing near fifty. At the moment she looked very delicate and fragile. There was something, at the moment, in her bearing— Was there, after all, something in blood, the Aspinwahl blood?

In a dim way perhaps, at the moment, the

48

child Mary did comprehend. Women and their men. For her then, at that time, there was but one male, the child Ted. Afterward she remembered how he looked at that moment, the curiously serious old look on his young face. There was even, she thought later, a kind of contempt for both the father and brother, as though he might have been saying to himself— he couldn't really have been saying it; he was too young— "Well, we'll see. This is something. These foolish ones—my father and my brother. I myself haven't long to live. I'll see what I can while I do live."

The brother Don stepped over near to where his father stood.

"If you do, Father—" he said again.

"Well?"

"I'll walk off this farm and I'll never come back."

"All right. Go then."

The father began directing the two men who had begun cutting the trees, each man taking a tree. The young man with the harelip kept laughing, the laughter like the bray of a donkey. "Stop that," the father said sharply, and the sound ceased abruptly. The son Don walked away, going rather aimlessly toward the barn. He approached one of the barns and then stopped. The mother, white now, half ran into the house.

The son returned toward the house, passing the two younger children without looking at them, but did not enter. The father did not look at him. He went hesitatingly along a path at the front of the house and through a gate and into a road. The road ran for several miles down through the valley and then, turning, went over a mountain to the county-seat town.

As it happened, only Mary saw the son Don when he returned to the farm. There were three or four tense days. Perhaps, all the time, the mother and son had been secretly in touch. There was a telephone in the house. The father stayed all day in the fields and when he was in the house was silent.

Mary was in one of the barns on the day when Don came back and when the father and son met. It was an odd meeting.

The son came, Mary always afterward thought, rather sheepishly. The father came out of a horse's stall. He had been throwing corn to work horses. Neither the father nor the son saw Mary. There was a car parked in the barn and she had crawled into the driver's seat, her hands on the steering wheel, pretending she was driving.

"Well," the father said. If he felt triumphant, he did not show his feeling.

"Well," said the son, "I have come back."

"Yes, I see," the father said. "They are cutting corn." He walked toward the barn door and then stopped. "It will be yours soon now," he said. "You can be boss then."

He said no more and both men went away, the father toward the distant fields and the son toward the house. Mary was afterwards quite sure that nothing more was ever said.

What had the father meant?

"When it is yours you can be boss." It was too much for the child. Knowledge comes slowly. It meant:

"You will be in command, and for you, in your turn, it will be necessary to assert.

"Such men as we are cannot fool with delicate stuff. Some men are meant to command and others must obey. You can make them obey in your turn.

"There is a kind of death.

"Something in you must die before you can possess and command."

There was, so obviously, more than one kind of death. For Don Grey one kind and for the younger brother Ted, soon now perhaps, another.

Mary ran out of the barn that day, wanting eagerly to get out into the light, and afterward, for a long time, she did not try to think her way through what had happened. She and her brother Ted did, however, afterward, before he died, discuss quite often the two trees. They went on a cold day and put their fingers on the stumps, but the stumps were cold. Ted kept asserting that only men got their legs and arms cut off, and she protested. They continued doing things that had been forbidden Ted to do, but no one protested, and, a year or two later, when he died, he died during the night in his bed.

But while he lived, there was always, Mary afterward thought, a curious sense of freedom, something that belonged to him that made it good, a great happiness, to be with him. It was, she finally thought, because having to die his kind of death, he never had to make the surrender his brother had made—to be sure of possessions, success, his time to command—would never have to face the more subtle and terrible death that had come to his older brother.

BUTCHER BIRD

Wallace Stegner

That summer the boy was alone on the farm except for his parents. His brother was working at Orullian's Grocery in town, and there was no one to run the trap line with or swim with in the dark, weed-smelling reservoir where garter snakes made straight rapid lines in the water and the skaters rowed close to shore. So every excursion was an adventure, even if it was only a trip across the three miles of prairie to Larsen's to get mail or groceries. He was excited at the visit to Garfield's as he was excited by everything unusual. The hot midsummer afternoon was still and breathless, the air harder to breathe than usual. He knew there was a change in weather coming because the gingersnaps in their tall cardboard box were soft and bendable when he snitched two to stick in his pocket. He could tell too by his father's grumpiness accumulated through two weeks of drought, his habit of looking off into the southwest, from which either rain or hot winds might come, that something was brewing. If it was rain every-thing would be fine, his father would hum under his breath getting breakfast, maybe let him drive the stoneboat or ride the mare down to Larsen's for mail. If it was hot wind they'd have to walk soft and speak softer, and it wouldn't be any fun.

They didn't know the Garfields, who had moved in only the fall before; but people said they had a good big house and a bigger barn and that Mr. Garfield was an Englishman and a little funny talking about scientific farming and making the desert blossom like the rose. The boy's father hadn't wanted to go, but his mother thought it was unneighborly not to call at least once in a whole year when people lived only four miles away. She was, the boy knew, as anxious for a change, as eager to get out of that atmosphere of waiting to see what the weather would do—that tense and teeth-gritting expectancy—as he was.

He found more than he looked for at Garfield's. Mr. Garfield was tall and bald with a big nose, and talked very softly and politely. The boy's father was determined not to like him right from the start.

When Mr. Garfield said, "Dear, I think we might have a glass of lemonade, don't you?", the boy saw his parents look at each other, saw

— *"Butcher Bird" by Wallace Stegner, reprinted by permission from* Harper's Magazine, *No. 182, January, 1941*

the beginning of a contemptuous smile on his father's face, saw his mother purse her lips and shake her head ever so little. And when Mrs. Garfield, prim and spectacled, with a habit of tucking her head back and to one side while she listened to anyone talk, brought in the lemonade, the boy saw his father taste his and make a little face behind the glass. He hated any summer drink without ice in it, and had spent two whole weeks digging a dugout icehouse just so that he could have ice water and cold beer when the hot weather came.

But Mr. and Mrs. Garfield were nice people. They sat down in their new parlor and showed the boy's mother the rug and the gramophone. When the boy came up curiously to inspect the little box with the petunia-shaped horn and the little china dog with "His Master's Voice" on it, and the Garfields found that he had never seen or heard a gramophone, they put on a cylinder like a big spool of tightly wound black thread and lowered a needle on it, and out came a man's voice singing in Scotch brogue, and his mother smiled and nodded and said, "My land, Harry Lauder! I heard him once a long time ago. Isn't it wonderful, Sonny?"

It was wonderful all right. He inspected it, reached out his fingers to touch things, wiggled the big horn to see if it was loose or screwed in. His father warned him sharply to keep his hands off, but then Mr. Garfield smiled and said, "Oh, he can't hurt it. Let's play something else," and found a record about the saucy little bird on Nelly's hat that had them all laughing. They let him wind the machine and play the record over again, all by himself, and he was very careful. It was a fine machine. He wished he had one.

About the time he had finished playing his sixth or seventh record, and George M. Cohan was singing "She's a grand old rag, she's a high-flying flag, and forever in peace may she wave," he glanced at his father and discovered that he was grouchy about something. He wasn't taking any part in the conversation but was sitting with his chin in his hand staring out

of the window. Mr. Garfield was looking at him a little helplessly. His eyes met the boy's and he motioned him over.

"What do you find to do all summer? Only child, are you?"

"No, sir. My brother's in Whitemud. He's twelve. He's got a job."

"So you come out on the farm to help," said Mr. Garfield. He had his hand on the boy's shoulder and his voice was so kind that the boy lost his shyness and felt no embarrassment at all in being out there in the middle of the parlor with all of them watching.

"I don't help much," he said. "I'm too little to do anything but drive the stoneboat, Pa says. When I'm twelve he's going to get me a gun and then I can go hunting."

"Hunting?" Mr. Garfield said. "What do you hunt?"

"Oh, gophers and weasels. I got a pet weasel. His name's Lucifer."

"Well," said Mr. Garfield. "You seem to be a pretty manly little chap. What do you feed your weasel?"

"Gophers." The boy thought it best not to say that the gophers were live ones he threw into the weasel's cage. He thought probably Mr. Garfield would be a little shocked at that.

Mr. Garfield straightened up and looked round at the grown folks. "Isn't it a shame," he said, "that there are so many predatory animals and pests in this country that we have to spend our time destroying them? I hate killing things."

"I hate weasels," the boy said. "I'm just saving this one till he turns into an ermine, and then I'm going to skin him. Once I speared a weasel with the pitchfork in the chicken coop and he dropped right off the tine and ran up my leg and bit me after he was speared clean through."

He finished breathlessly, and his mother smiled at him, motioning him not to talk so much. But Mr. Garfield was still looking at him kindly. "So you want to make war on the cruel things, the weasels and hawks," he said.

"Yes, sir," the boy said. He looked at his

mother and it was all right. He hadn't spoiled anything by telling about the weasels.

"Now that reminds me," Mr. Garfield said, rising. "Maybe I've got something you'd find useful."

He went into another room and came back with a .22 in his hand. "Could you use this?"

"I —— yes, *sir!*" the boy said. He had almost, in his excitement, said "I hope to whisk in your piskers," because that was what his father always said when he meant anything real hard.

"If your parents want you to have it," Mr. Garfield said and raised his eyebrows at the boy's mother. He didn't look at the father, but the boy did.

"Can I, Pa?"

"I guess so," his father said. "Sure."

"Thank Mr. Garfield nicely," said his mother.

"Gee," the boy breathed. "Thanks, Mr. Garfield, ever so much."

"There's a promise goes with it," Mr. Garfield said. "I'd like you to promise never to shoot anything with it but the bloodthirsty animals— the cruel ones like weasels and hawks. Never anything like birds or prairie dogs."

"How about butcher birds?"

"Butcher birds?" Mr. Garfield said.

"Shrikes," said the boy's mother. "We've got some over by our place. They kill all sorts of things, snakes and gophers and other birds. They're worse than the hawks because they just kill for the fun of it."

"By all means," said Mr. Garfield. "Shoot all the shrikes you see. A thing that kills for the fun of it ——" He shook his head and his voice got solemn, almost like the voice of Mr. McGregor, the Sunday School Superintendent in town, when he was asking the benediction. "There's something about the way the war drags on, or maybe just this country," he said, "that makes me hate killing. I just can't bear to shoot anything any more, even a weasel."

The boy's father turned cold eyes away from Mr. Garfield and looked out of the window. One big brown hand, a little dirty from the wheel of the car, rubbed against the day-old

bristles on his jaws. Then he stood up and stretched. "Well, we got to be going," he said.

"Oh, stay a little while," Mr. Garfield said. "You just came. I wanted to show you my trees."

The boy's mother stared at him. "Trees?"

He smiled. "Sounds a bit odd out here, doesn't it? But I think trees will grow. I've made some plantings down below."

"I'd love to see them," she said. "Sometimes I'd give almost anything to get into a good deep shady woods. Just to smell it, and feel how cool ——"

"There's a little story connected with these," Mr. Garfield said. He spoke to the mother alone, warmly. "When we first decided to come out here I said to Martha that if trees wouldn't grow we shouldn't stick it. That's just what I said, 'If trees won't grow we shan't stick it.' Trees are almost the breath of life to me."

The boy's father was shaken by a sudden spell of coughing, and the mother shot a quick look at him and looked back at Mr. Garfield with a light flush on her cheekbones. "I'd love to see them," she said. "I was raised in Minnesota, and I never will get used to a place as barren as this."

"When I think of the beeches back home in England," Mr. Garfield said, and shook his head with a puckering smile round his eyes.

The father lifted himself heavily out of his chair and followed the rest of them out to the coulee edge. Below them willows grew profusely along the almost-dry creek, and farther back from the water there was a grove of perhaps twenty trees about a dozen feet high.

"I'm trying cottonwoods first because they can stand dry weather," Mr. Garfield said.

The mother was looking down with all her longings suddenly plain and naked in her eyes. "It's wonderful," she said. "I'd give almost anything to have some on our place."

"I found the willows close by here," said Mr. Garfield. "Just at the south end of the hills they call Old-Man-on-His-Back, where the stream comes down."

"Stream?" the boy's father said. "You mean that trickle?"

"It's not much of a stream," Mr. Garfield said apologetically. "But ——"

"Are there any more there?" the mother said.

"Oh, yes. You could get some. Cut them diagonally and push them into any damp ground. They'll grow."

"They'll grow about six feet high," the father said.

"Yes," said Mr. Garfield. "They're not, properly speaking, trees. Still —— "

"It's getting pretty smothery," the father said rather loudly. "We better be getting on."

This time Mr. Garfield didn't object, and they went back to the car exchanging promises of visits. The father jerked the crank and climbed into the Ford, where the boy was sighting along his gun. "Put that down," his father said. "Don't you know any better than to point a gun around people?"

"It isn't loaded."

"They never are," his father said. "Put it down now."

The Garfields were standing with their arms round each other's waists, waiting to wave good-by. Mr. Garfield reached over and picked something from his wife's dress.

"What was it, Alfred?" she said peering.

"Nothing. Just a bit of fluff."

The boy's father coughed violently and the car started with a jerk. With his head down almost to the wheel, still coughing, he waved, and the mother and the boy waved as they went down along the badly set cedar posts of the pasture fence. They were almost a quarter of a mile away before the boy, with a last wave of the gun, turned round again and saw that his father was purple with laughter. He rocked the car with his joy, and when his wife said, "Oh, Harry, you big fool," he pointed helplessly to his shoulder. "Would you mind," he said. "Would you mind brushing that bit o' fluff off me showldah?" He roared again, pounding the wheel. "I shawn't stick it," he said. "I bloody well shawn't stick it, you knaow!"

"It isn't fair to laugh at him," she said. "He can't help being English."

"He can't help being a sanctimonious old mudhen either, braying about his luv-ly luv-ly trees. They'll freeze out the first winter."

"How do you know? Maybe it's like he says— if they get a start they'll grow here as well as anywhere."

"Maybe there's a gold mine in our back yard too, but I'm not gonna dig to see. I couldn't stick it."

"Oh, you're just being stubborn," she said. "Just because you didn't like Mr. Garfield ——"

He turned on her in heavy amazement. "Well, my God! Did you?"

"I thought he was very nice," she said, and sat straighter in the back seat, speaking loudly above the creak of the springs and cough of the motor. "They're trying to make a home, not just a wheat crop. I liked them."

"Uh, huh." He was not laughing any more now. Sitting beside him, the boy could see that his face had hardened and the cold look had come into his eye again. "So I should start talking like I had a mouthful of bran, and planting trees around the house that'll look like clothesline poles in two months."

"I didn't say that."

"You thought it though." He looked irritably at the sky, misted with the same delusive film of cloud that had fooled him for three days, and spat at the roadside. "You thought it all the time we were there. 'Why aren't you more like Mr. Garfield, he's such a nice man'." With mincing savagery he swung round and mocked her. "Shall I make it a walnut grove? Or a big maple sugar bush? Or maybe you'd like an orange orchard."

The boy was looking down at his gun, trying not to hear them quarrel, but he knew what his mother's face would be like—hurt and a little flushed, her chin trembling into stubbornness. "I don't suppose you could bear to have a rug on the floor, or a gramophone?" she said.

He smacked the wheel hard. "Of course I could bear it if we could afford it. But I sure as hell would rather do without than be like that old sandhill crane."

"I don't suppose you'd like to take me over to the Old-Man-on-His-Back some day to get some willow slips either."

"What for?"

"To plant down in the coulee, by the dam."

"That dam dries up every August. Your willows wouldn't live till snow flies."

"Well, would it do any harm to try?"

"Oh, shut up!" he said. "Just thinking about that guy and his fluff and his trees gives me the pleefer."

The topless Ford lurched, one wheel at a time, through the deep burnout by their pasture corner, and the boy clambered out with his gun in his hand to slip the loop from the three-strand gate. It was then that he saw the snake, a striped limp ribbon, dangling on the fence, and a moment later the sparrow, neatly butchered and hung by the throat from the barbed wire. He pointed the gun at them. "Lookit!" he said. "Lookit what the butcher bird's been doing."

His father's violent hand waved at him from the seat. "Come on! Get the wire out of the way!"

The boy dragged the gate through the dust, and the Ford went through and up behind the house, perched on the bare edge of the coulee in the midst of its baked yard and framed by the dark fireguard overgrown with Russian thistle. Walking across that yard a few minutes later, the boy felt its hard heat under his sneakers. There was hardly a spear of grass within the fireguard. It was one of his father's prides that the dooryard should be like cement. "Pour your wash water out long enough," he said, "and you'll have a surface so hard it won't even make mud." Religiously he threw his water out three times a day, carrying it sometimes a dozen steps to dump it on a dusty or grassy spot.

The mother had objected at first, asking why they had to live in the middle of an alkali flat, and why they couldn't let grass grow up to the door. But he snorted her down. Everything round the house ought to be bare as a bone. Get a good prairie fire going and it'd jump that guard like nothing, and if they had grass to the door where'd they be? She said why not plow a wider fireguard then, one a fire couldn't jump, but he said he had other things to do besides plowing fifty-foot fireguards.

They were arguing inside when the boy came up on the step to sit down and aim his empty .22 at a fencepost. Apparently his mother had been persistent, and persistence when he was not in a mood for it angered the father worse than anything else. Their talk came vaguely through his concentration, but he shut his ears on it. If that spot on the fencepost was a coyote now, and he held the sight steady, right on it, and pulled the trigger, that old coyote would jump about eighty feet in the air and come down dead as a mackerel, and he could tack his hide on the barn the way Mr. Larsen had one, only the dogs had jumped and torn the tail and hind legs off Mr. Larsen's pelt, and he wouldn't get more than the three-dollar bounty out of it. But then Mr. Larsen had shot his with a shotgun anyway, and the hide wasn't worth much even before the dogs tore it. ——

"I can't for the life of me see why not," his mother said inside. "We could do it now. We're not doing anything else."

"I tell you they wouldn't grow!" said his father with emphasis on every word. "Why should we run our tongues out doing everything that mealy-mouthed fool does?"

"I don't want anything but the willows. They're easy."

He made his special sound of contempt, half-snort, half-grunt. After a silence she tried again. "They might even have pussies on them in the spring. Mr. Garfield thinks they'd grow, and he used to work in a greenhouse, his wife told me."

"This isn't a greenhouse, for Chris-sake."

"Oh, let it go," she said. "I've stood it this long without any green things around. I guess I can stand it some more."

The boy, aiming now toward the gate where the butcher bird, coming back to his prey, would in just a minute fly right into Deadeye's unerring bullet, heard his father stand up suddenly.

"Abused, aren't you?" he said.

The mother's voice rose. "No, I'm not abused! Only I can't see why it would be so awful to get some willows. Just because Mr. Garfield gave me the idea, and you didn't like him ———"

"You're right I didn't like Mr. Garfield," the father said. "He gave me a pain right under the crupper."

"Because," the mother's voice said bitterly, "he calls his wife 'dear' and puts his arm around her and likes trees. It wouldn't occur to you to put your arm around your wife, would it?"

The boy aimed and held his breath. His mother ought to keep still, because if she didn't she'd get him real mad and then they'd both have to tiptoe around the rest of the day. He heard his father's breath whistle through his teeth, and his voice, mincing, nasty. "Would you like me to kiss you now, *dear?*"

"I wouldn't let you touch me with a ten-foot pole," his mother said. She sounded just as mad as he did, and it wasn't often she let herself get that way. The boy squirmed over when he heard the quick hard steps come up behind him and pause. Then his father's big hand, brown and meaty and felted with fine black hair, reached down over his shoulder and took the .22.

"Let's see this cannon old Scissor-bill gave you," he said.

It was a single-shot, bolt-action Savage, a little rusty on the barrel, the bolt sticky with hardened grease when the father removed it. Sighting up through the barrel, he grunted. "Takes care of a gun like he takes care of his farm. Probably used it to cultivate his luv-ly trees."

He went out into the sleeping porch, and after a minute came back with a rag and a can of machine oil. Hunching the boy over on the step, he sat down and began rubbing the bolt with the oil-soaked rag.

"I just can't bear to shoot anything any more," he said, and laughed suddenly. "I just

cawn't stick it, little man." He leered at the boy, who grinned back uncertainly. Squinting through the barrel again, the father breathed through his nose and clamped his lips together, shaking his head.

The sun lay heavy on the baked yard. Out over the corner of the pasture a soaring hawk caught wind and sun at the same time, so that his light breast feathers flashed as he banked and rose. Just wait, the boy thought. Wait till I get my gun working and I'll fix you, you hen-robber. He thought of the three chicks a hawk had struck earlier in the summer, the three balls of yellow with the barred mature plumage just coming through. Two of them dead when he got there and chased the hawk away, the other gasping with its crop slashed wide open and the wheat spilling from it on the ground. His mother had sewed up the crop, and the chicken had lived, but it always looked droopy, like a plant in drought time, and sometimes it would stand and work its bill as if it were choking.

By golly, he thought, I'll shoot every hawk and butcher bird in twenty miles. I'll ———

"Rustle around and find me a piece of baling wire," his father said. "This barrel looks like a henroost."

Behind the house he found a piece of rusty wire, brought it back and watched his father straighten it, wind a bit of rag round the end, ram it up and down through the barrel, and peer through again. "He's leaded her so you can hardly see the grooves," he said. "But maybe she'll shoot. We'll fill her with vinegar and cork her up to-night."

The mother was behind them, leaning against the jamb and watching. She reached down and rumpled the father's black hair. "The minute you get a gun in your hand you start feeling better," she said. "It's just a shame you weren't born fifty years sooner."

"A gun's a good tool," he said. "It hadn't ought to be misused. Gun like this is enough to make a guy cry."

"Well, you've got to admit it was nice of

Mr. Garfield to give it to Sonny," she said. It was the wrong thing to say. The boy had a feeling somehow that she knew it was the wrong thing to say, that she said it just to have one tiny triumph over him. He knew it would make him boiling mad again, even before he heard his father's answer.

"Oh, sure, Mr. Garfield's a fine man. He can preach a better sermon than any homesteader in Saskatchewan. God Almighty! everything he does is better than what I do. All right. All right, *all right!* Why the hell don't you move over there if you like it so well?"

"If you weren't so blind ——!"

He rose with the .22 in his hand and pushed past her into the house. "I'm not so blind," he said heavily in passing. "You've been throwing that bastard up to me for two hours. It don't take very good eyes to see what that means."

His mother started to say, "All because I want a few little ——" but the boy cut in on her, anxious to help the situation somehow. "Will it shoot now?" he said.

His father said nothing. His mother looked down at him, shrugged, sighed, smiled bleakly with a tight mouth. She moved aside when the father came back with a box of cartridges in his hand. He ignored his wife, speaking to the boy alone in the particular half-jocular tone he always used with him or the dog when he wasn't mad or exasperated.

"Thought I had these around," he said. "Now we'll see what this smoke-pole will do."

He slipped a cartridge in and locked the bolt, looking round for something to shoot at. Behind him the mother's feet moved on the floor, and her voice came purposefully. "I can't see why you have to act this way," she said. "I'm going over and get some slips myself."

There was a long silence. The angled shade lay sharp as a knife across the baked front yard. The father's cheek was pressed against the stock of the gun, his arms and hands as steady as stone.

"How'll you get there?" he said, whispering down the barrel.

"I'll walk."

"Five miles and back."

"Yes, five miles and back. Or fifty miles and back. If there was any earthly reason why you should mind ——"

"I don't mind," he said, and his voice was soft as silk. "Go ahead."

Close to his mother's long skirts in the doorway, the boy felt her stiffen as if she had been slapped. He squirmed anxiously, but his desperation could find only the question he had asked before. His voice squeaked on it: "Will it shoot now?"

"See that sparrow out there?" his father said, still whispering. "Right out by that cactus?"

"Harry!" the mother said. "If you shoot that harmless little bird!"

Fascinated, the boy watched his father's dark face against the rifle stock, the locked, immovable left arm, the thick finger crooked inside the trigger guard almost too small to hold it. He saw the sparrow, gray, white-breasted, hopping obliviously in search of bugs, fifty feet out on the gray earth. "I just —— can't —— bear —— to —— shoot —— anything," the father said, his face like dark stone, his lips hardly moving. "I just —— can't —— stick it!"

"Harry!" his wife screamed.

The boy's mouth opened, a dark wash of terror shadowed his vision of the baked yard cut by its sharp angle of shade.

"Don't, pa!"

The rocklike figure of his father never moved. The thick finger squeezed slowly down on the trigger, there was a thin, sharp report, and the sparrow jerked and collapsed into a shapeless wad on the ground. It was as if, in the instant of the shot, all its clean outlines vanished. Head, feet, the white breast, the perceptible outlines of the folded wings, disappeared all at once, were crumpled together and lost, and the boy sat beside his father on the step with the echo of the shot still in his ears.

He did not look at either of his parents. He looked only at the crumpled sparrow. Step by step, unable to keep away, he went to it, stooped, and picked it up. Blood stained his fingers, and he held the bird by the tail while he wiped the smeared hand on his overalls. He heard the click as the bolt was shot and the empty cartridge ejected, and he saw his mother come swiftly out of the house past his father, who sat still on the step. Her hands were clenched, and she walked with her head down, as if fighting tears.

"Ma!" the boy said dully. "Ma, what'll I do with it?"

She stopped and turned, and for a moment they faced each other. He saw the dead pallor of her face, the burning eyes, the not-quite-controllable quiver of her lips. But her words, when they came, were flat and level, almost casual.

"Leave it right there," she said. "After a while your father will want to hang it on the barbed wire."

THE BASEMENT ROOM

Graham Greene

1

When the front door had shut them out and the butler Baines had turned back into the dark heavy hall, Philip began to live. He stood in front of the nursery door, listening until he heard the engine of the taxi die out along the street. His parents were gone for a fortnight's holiday; he was "between nurses," one dismissed and the other not arrived; he was alone in the great Belgravia house with Baines and Mrs. Baines.

He could go anywhere, even through the green baize door to the pantry or down the stairs to the basement living-room. He felt a stranger in his home because he could go into any room and all the rooms were empty.

You could only guess who had once occupied them: the rack of pipes in the smoking-room beside the elephant tusks, the carved wood

tobacco jar; in the bedroom the pink hangings and pale perfumes and the three-quarter finished jars of cream which Mrs. Baines had not yet cleared away; the high glaze on the never-opened piano in the drawing-room, the china clock, the silly little tables and the silver: but here Mrs. Baines was already busy, pulling down the curtains, covering the chairs in dust-sheets.

"Be off out of here, Master Philip," and she looked at him with her hateful peevish eyes, while she moved round, getting everything in order, meticulous and loveless and doing her duty.

Philip Lane went downstairs and pushed at the baize door; he looked into the pantry, but Baines was not there, then he set foot for the first time on the stairs to the basement. Again he had the sense: this is life. All his seven nursery years vibrated with the strange, the new experience. His crowded busy brain was like a city which feels the earth tremble at a distant earthquake shock. He was apprehensive, but he was happier than he had ever been. Everything was more important than before.

Baines was reading a newspaper in his shirt-sleeves. He said, "Come in, Phil, and make

— "*The Basement Room*" by Graham Greene, from *Twenty-One Stories* by Graham Greene, published by *William Heinemann Limited, London, Melbourne, Toronto, 1954*

yourself at home. Wait a moment and I'll do the honours," and going to a white cleaned cupboard he brought out a bottle of ginger-beer and half a Dundee cake. "Half-past eleven in the morning," Baines said. "It's opening time, my boy," and he cut the cake and poured out the ginger-beer. He was more genial than Philip had ever known him, more at his ease, a man in his own home.

"Shall I call Mrs. Baines?" Philip asked, and he was glad when Baines said no. She was busy. She liked to be busy, so why interfere with her pleasure?

"A spot of drink at half-past eleven," Baines said, pouring himself out a glass of ginger-beer, "gives an appetite for chop and does no man any harm."

"A chop?" Philip asked.

"Old Coasters," Baines said, "call all food chop."

"But it's not a chop?"

"Well, it might be, you know, cooked with palm oil. And then some paw-paw to follow."

Philip looked out of the basement window at the dry stone yard, the ash-can and the legs going up and down beyond the railings.

"Was it hot there?"

"Ah, you never felt such heat. Not a nice heat, mind, like you get in the park on a day like this. Wet," Baines said, "corruption." He cut himself a slice of cake. "Smelling of rot," Baines said, rolling his eyes round the small basement room, from clean cupboard to clean cupboard, the sense of bareness, of nowhere to hide a man's secrets. With an air of regret for something lost he took a long draught of ginger-beer.

"Why did father live out there?"

"It was his job," Baines said, "same as this is mine now. And it was mine then too. It was a man's job. You wouldn't believe it now, but I've had forty niggers under me, doing what I told them to."

"Why did you leave?"

"I married Mrs. Baines."

Philip took the slice of Dundee cake in his hand and munched it round the room. He felt very old, independent and judicial; he was aware that Baines was talking to him as man to man. He never called him Master Philip as Mrs. Baines did, who was servile when she was not authoritative.

Baines had seen the world; he had seen beyond the railings, beyond the tired legs of typists, the Pimlico parade to and from Victoria. He sat there over his ginger pop with the resigned dignity of an exile; Baines didn't complain; he had chosen his fate, and if his fate was Mrs. Baines he had only himself to blame.

But to-day, because the house was almost empty and Mrs. Baines was upstairs and there was nothing to do, he allowed himself a little acidity.

"I'd go back to-morrow if I had the chance."

"Did you ever shoot a nigger?"

"I never had any call to shoot," Baines said. "Of course I carried a gun. But you didn't need to treat them bad. That just made them stupid. Why," Baines said, bowing his thin grey hair with embarrassment over the ginger pop, "I loved some of those damned niggers. I couldn't help loving them. There they'd be laughing, holding hands; they liked to touch each other; it made them feel fine to know the other fellow was round. It didn't mean anything we could understand; two of them would go about all day without loosing hold, grown men; but it wasn't love; it didn't mean anything we could understand."

"Eating between meals," Mrs. Baines said. "What would your mother say, Master Philip?"

She came down the steep stairs to the basement, her hands full of pots of cream and salve, tubes of grease and paste. "You oughtn't to encourage him, Baines," she said, sitting down in a wicker armchair and screwing up her small ill-humoured eyes at the Coty lipstick, Pond's cream, the Leichner rouge and Cyclax powder and Elizabeth Arden astringent.

She threw them one by one into the waste-paper basket. She saved only the cold cream. "Telling the boy stories," she said. "Go along to the nursery, Master Philip, while I get lunch."

Philip climbed the stairs to the baize door. He heard Mrs. Baines's voice like the voice in a nightmare when the small Price light has guttered in the saucer and the curtains move; it was sharp and shrill and full of malice, louder than people ought to speak, exposed.

"Sick to death of your ways, Baines, spoiling the boy. Time you did some work about the house," but he couldn't hear what Baines said in reply. He pushed open the baize door, came up like a small earth animal in his grey flannel shorts into a wash of sunlight on a parquet floor, the gleam of mirrors dusted and polished and beautified by Mrs. Baines.

Something broke downstairs, and Philip sadly mounted the stairs to the nursery. He pitied Baines; it occurred to him how happily they could live together in the empty house if Mrs. Baines were called away. He didn't want to play with his Meccano sets; he wouldn't take out his train or his soldiers; he sat at the table with his chin on his hands: this is life; and suddenly he felt responsible for Baines, as if he were the master of the house and Baines an ageing servant who deserved to be cared for. There was not much one could do; he decided at least to be good.

He was not surprised when Mrs. Baines was agreeable at lunch; he was used to her changes. Now it was "another helping of meat, Master Philip," or "Master Philip, a little more of this nice pudding." It was a pudding he liked, Queen's pudding with a perfect meringue, but he wouldn't eat a second helping lest she might count that a victory. She was the kind of woman who thought that any injustice could be counterbalanced by something good to eat.

She was sour, but she liked making sweet things; one never had to complain of a lack of jam or plums; she ate well herself and added soft sugar to the meringue and the strawberry jam. The half light through the basement window set the motes moving above her pale hair like dust as she sifted the sugar, and Baines crouched over his plate saying nothing.

Again Philip felt responsibility. Baines had looked forward to this, and Baines was disappointed: everything was being spoilt. The sensation of disappointment was one which Philip could share; knowing nothing of love or jealousy or passion he could understand better than anyone this grief, something hoped for not happening, something promised not fulfilled, something exciting turning dull. "Baines," he said, "will you take me for a walk this afternoon?"

"No," Mrs. Baines said, "no. That he won't. Not with all the silver to clean."

"There's a fortnight to do it in," Baines said.

"Work first, pleasure afterwards." Mrs. Baines helped herself to some more meringue.

Baines suddenly put down his spoon and fork and pushed his plate away. "Blast," he said.

"Temper," Mrs. Baines said softly, "temper. Don't you go breaking any more things, Baines, and I won't have you swearing in front of the boy. Master Philip, if you've finished you can get down." She skinned the rest of the meringue off the pudding.

"I want to go for a walk," Philip said.

"You'll go and have a rest."

"I will go for a walk."

"Master Philip," Mrs. Baines said. She got up from the table leaving her meringue unfinished, and came towards him, thin, menacing, dusty in the basement room. "Master Philip, you do as you're told." She took him by the arm and squeezed it gently; she watched him with a joyless passionate glitter and above her head the feet of the typists trudged back to the Victoria offices after the lunch interval.

"Why shouldn't I go for a walk?" But he weakened; he was scared and ashamed of being scared. This was life; a strange passion he couldn't understand moving in the basement room. He saw a small pile of broken glass swept into a corner by the waste-paper basket. He looked to Baines for help and only intercepted hate; the sad hopeless hate of something behind bars.

"Why shouldn't I?" he repeated.

"Master Philip," Mrs. Baines said, "you've got to do as you're told. You mustn't think just because your father's away there's nobody here to ——"

"You wouldn't dare," Philip cried, and was startled by Baines's low interjection:

"There's nothing she wouldn't dare."

"I hate you," Philip said to Mrs. Baines. He pulled away from her and ran to the door, but she was there before him; she was old, but she was quick.

"Master Philip," she said, "you'll say you're sorry." She stood in front of the door quivering with excitement. "What would your father do if he heard you say that?"

She put a hand out to seize him, dry and white with constant soda, the nails cut to the quick, but he backed away and put the table between them, and suddenly to his surprise she smiled; she became again as servile as she had been arrogant. "Get along with you, Master Philip," she said with glee, "I see I'm going to have my hands full till your father and mother come back."

She left the door unguarded and when he passed her she slapped him playfully. "I've got too much to do today to trouble about you. I haven't covered half the chairs," and suddenly even the upper part of the house became unbearable to him as he thought of Mrs. Baines moving round shrouding the sofas, laying out the dust-sheets.

So he wouldn't go upstairs to get his cap but walked straight out across the shining hall into the street, and again, as he looked this way and looked that way, it was life he was in the middle of.

2

It was the pink sugar cakes in the window on a paper doily, the ham, the slab of mauve sausage, the wasps driving like small torpedoes across the pane that caught Philip's attention. His feet were tired by pavements; he had been afraid to cross the road, had simply walked first in one direction, then in the other. He was nearly home now; the square was at the end of the street; this was a shabby outpost of Pimlico, and he smudged the pane with his nose looking for sweets, and saw between the cakes and ham a different Baines. He hardly recognised the bulbous eyes, the bald forehead. It was a happy, bold and buccaneering Baines, even though it was, when you looked closer, a desperate Baines.

Philip had never seen the girl. He remembered Baines had a niece and he thought that this might be her. She was thin and drawn, and she wore a white mackintosh; she meant nothing to Philip; she belonged to a world about which he knew nothing at all. He couldn't make up stories about her, as he could make them up about withered Sir Hubert Reed, the Permanent Secretary, about Mrs. Wince-Dudley who came up once a year from Penstanley in Suffolk with a green umbrella and an enormous black handbag, as he could make them up about the upper servants in all the houses where he went to tea and games. She just didn't belong; he thought of mermaids and Undine; but she didn't belong there either, nor to the adventures of Emil, nor to the Bastables. She sat there looking at an iced pink cake in the detachment and mystery of the completely disinherited, looking at the half-used pots of powder which Baines had set out on the marble-topped table between them.

Baines was urging, hoping, entreating, commanding, and the girl looked at the tea and the china pots and cried. Baines passed his handkerchief across the table, but she wouldn't wipe her eyes; she screwed it in her palm and let the tears run down, wouldn't do anything, wouldn't speak, would only put up a silent despairing resistance to what she dreaded and wanted and refused to listen to at any price. The two brains battled over the tea-cups loving each other, and there came to Philip outside, beyond the ham and wasps and dusty Pimlico pane, a confused indication of the struggle.

He was inquisitive and he didn't understand and he wanted to know. He went and stood in the doorway to see better, he was less sheltered than he had ever been; other people's lives for the first time touched and pressed and moulded.

He would never escape that scene. In a week he had forgotten it, but it conditioned his career, the long austerity of his life; when he was dying he said: "Who is she?"

Baines had won; he was cocky and the girl was happy. She wiped her face, she opened a pot of powder, and their fingers touched across the table. It occurred to Philip that it would be amusing to imitate Mrs. Baines's voice and call "Baines" to him from the door.

It shrivelled them; you couldn't describe it in any other way, it made them smaller, they weren't happy any more and they weren't bold. Baines was the first to recover and trace the voice, but that didn't make things as they were. The sawdust was spilled out of the afternoon; nothing you did could mend it, and Philip was scared. "I didn't mean——" He wanted to say that he loved Baines, that he had only wanted to laugh at Mrs. Baines. But he had discovered that you couldn't laugh at Mrs. Baines. She wasn't Sir Hubert Reed, who used steel nibs and carried a pen-wiper in his pocket; she wasn't Mrs. Wince-Dudley; she was darkness when the night-light went out in a draught; she was the frozen blocks of earth he had seen one winter in a graveyard when someone said, "They need an electric drill"; she was the flowers gone bad and smelling in the little closet room at Penstanley. There was nothing to laugh about. You had to endure her when she was there and forget about her quickly when she was away, suppress the thought of her, ram it down deep.

Baines said, "It's only Phil," beckoned him in and gave him the pink iced cake the girl hadn't eaten, but the afternoon was broken, the cake was like dry bread in the throat. The girl left them at once; she even forgot to take the powder; like a small blunt icicle in her white mackintosh she stood in the doorway with her back to them, then melted into the afternoon.

"Who is she?" Philip asked. "Is she your niece?"

"Oh, yes," Baines said, "that's who she is; she's my niece," and poured the last drops of water on to the coarse black leaves in the teapot.

"May as well have another cup," Baines said.

"The cup that cheers," he said hopelessly, watching the bitter black fluid drain out of the spout.

"Have a glass of ginger pop, Phil?"

"I'm sorry. I'm sorry, Baines."

"It's not your fault, Phil. Why, I could believe it wasn't you at all, but her. She creeps in everywhere." He fished two leaves out of his cup and laid them on the back of his hand, a thin soft flake and a hard stalk. He beat them with his hand: "To-day," and the stalk detached itself, "to-morrow, Wednesday, Thursday, Friday, Saturday, Sunday," but the flake wouldn't come, stayed where it was, drying under his blows, with a resistance you wouldn't believe it to possess. "The tough one wins," Baines said.

He got up and paid the bill and out they went into the street. Baines said, "I don't ask you to say what isn't true. But you needn't mention to Mrs. Baines you met us here."

"Of course not," Philip said, and catching something of Sir Hubert Reed's manner, "I understand, Baines." But he didn't understand a thing; he was caught up in other people's darkness.

"It was stupid," Baines said. "So near home, but I hadn't time to think, you see. I'd got to see her."

"Of course, Baines."

"I haven't time to spare," Baines said. "I'm not young. I've got to see that she's all right."

"Of course you have, Baines."

"Mrs. Baines will get it out of you if she can."

"You can trust me, Baines," Philip said in a dry important Reed voice; and then, "Look out. She's at the window watching." And there indeed she was, looking up at them, between the lace curtains, from the basement room, speculating. "Need we go in, Baines?" Philip asked, cold lying heavy on his stomach like too much pudding; he clutched Baines's arm.

"Careful," Baines said softly, "careful."

"But need we go in, Baines? It's early. Take me for a walk in the park."

"Better not."

"But I'm frightened, Baines."

"You haven't any cause," Baines said. "Nothing's going to hurt you. You just run along upstairs to the nursery. I'll go down by the area and talk to Mrs. Baines." But even he stood hesitating at the top of the stone steps pretending not to see her, where she watched between the curtains. "In at the front door, Phil, and up the stairs."

Philip didn't linger in the hall; he ran, slithering on the parquet Mrs. Baines had polished, to the stairs. Through the drawing-room doorway on the first floor he saw the draped chairs; even the china clock on the mantel was covered like a canary's cage; as he passed it, it chimed the hour, muffled and secret under the duster. On the nursery table he found his supper laid out: a glass of milk and piece of bread and butter, a sweet biscuit, and a little cold Queen's pudding without the meringue. He had no appetite; he strained his ears for Mrs. Baines's coming, for the sound of voices, but the basement held its secrets; the green baize door shut off that world. He drank the milk and ate the biscuit, but he didn't touch the rest, and presently he could hear the soft precise footfalls of Mrs. Baines on the stairs: she was a good servant, she walked softly; she was a determined woman, she walked precisely.

But she wasn't angry when she came in; she was ingratiating as she opened the night nursery door—"Did you have a good walk, Master Philip?"—pulled down the blinds, laid out his pyjamas, came back to clear his supper. "I'm glad Baines found you. Your mother wouldn't have liked your being out alone." She examined the tray. "Not much appetite, have you, Master Philip? Why don't you try a little of this nice pudding? I'll bring you up some more jam for it."

"No, no, thank you, Mrs. Baines," Philip said.

"You ought to eat more," Mrs. Baines said. She sniffed round the room like a dog. "You didn't take any pots out of the waste-paper basket in the kitchen, did you, Master Philip?"

"No," Philip said.

"Of course you wouldn't. I just wanted to make sure." She patted his shoulder and her fingers flashed to his lapel; she picked off a tiny crumb of pink sugar. "Oh, Master Philip," she said, "that's why you haven't any appetite. You've been buying sweet cakes. That's not what your pocket money's for."

"But I didn't," Philip said. "I didn't."

She tasted the sugar with the tip of her tongue.

"Don't tell lies to me, Master Philip. I won't stand for it any more than your father would."

"I didn't, I didn't," Philip said. "They gave it me. I mean Baines," but she had pounced on the word "they." She had got what she wanted; there was no doubt about that, even when you didn't know what it was she wanted. Philip was angry and miserable and disappointed because he hadn't kept Baines's secret. Baines oughtn't to have trusted him; grown-up people should keep their own secrets, and yet here was Mrs. Baines immediately entrusting him with another.

"Let me tickle your palm and see if you can keep a secret." But he put his hand behind him; he wouldn't be touched. "It's a secret between us, Master Philip, that I know all about them. I suppose she was having tea with him," she speculated.

"Why shouldn't she?" he said, the responsibility for Baines weighing on his spirit, the idea that he had got to keep her secret when he hadn't kept Baines's making him miserable with the unfairness of life. "She was nice."

"She was nice, was she?" Mrs. Baines said in a bitter voice he wasn't used to.

"And she's his niece."

"So that's what he said," Mrs. Baines struck softly back at him like the clock under the duster. She tried to be jocular. "The old scoundrel. Don't you tell him I know, Master Philip." She stood very still between the table and the door, thinking very hard, planning something. "Promise you won't tell. I'll give you that Meccano set, Master Philip——"

He turned his back on her; he wouldn't promise, but he wouldn't tell. He would have nothing to do with their secrets, the responsibilities they were determined to lay on him. He was only anxious to forget. He had received already a larger dose of life than he had bargained for, and he was scared. "A 2A Meccano set, Master Philip." He never opened his Meccano set again, never built anything, never created anything, died, the old dilettante, sixty years later with nothing to show rather than preserve the memory of Mrs. Baines's malicious voice saying good night, her soft determined footfalls on the stairs to the basement, going down, going down.

3

The sun poured in between the curtains and Baines was beating a tattoo on the water-can. "Glory, glory," Baines said. He sat down on the end of the bed and said, "I beg to announce that Mrs. Baines has been called away. Her mother's dying. She won't be back till to-morrow."

"Why did you wake me up so early?" Philip said. He watched Baines with uneasiness; he wasn't going to be drawn in; he'd learnt his lesson. It wasn't right for a man of Baines's age to be so merry. It made a grown person human in the same way that you were human. For if a grown-up could behave so childishly, you were liable too to find yourself in their world. It was enough that it came at you in dreams: the witch at the corner, the man with a knife. So "It's very early," he complained, even though he loved Baines, even though he couldn't help being glad that Baines was happy. He was divided by the fear and the attraction of life.

"I want to make this a long day," Baines said. "This is the best time." He pulled the curtains back. "It's a bit misty. The cat's been out all night. There she is, sniffing round the area. They haven't taken in any milk at 59. Emma's shaking out the mats at 63." He said: "This was what I used to think about on the Coast: somebody shaking mats and the cat coming home. I can see it to-day," Baines said, "just as if I was still in Africa. Most days you don't notice what you've got. It's a good life if you don't weaken."

He put a penny on the washstand. When you've dressed, Phil, run and get a *Mail* from the barrow at the corner. I'll be cooking the sausages."

"Sausages?"

"Sausages," Baines said. "We're going to celebrate to-day. A fair bust." He celebrated at breakfast, restless, cracking jokes, unaccountably merry and nervous. It was going to be a long, long day, he kept on coming back to that: for years he had waited for a long day, he had sweated in the damp Coast heat, changed shirts, gone down with fever, lain between the blankets and sweated, all in the hope of this long day, that cat sniffing round the area, a bit of mist, the mats beaten at 63. He propped the *Mail* in front of the coffee-pot and read pieces aloud. He said, "Cora Down's been married for the fourth time." He was amused, but it wasn't his idea of a long day. His long day was the Park, watching the riders in the Row, seeing Sir Arthur Stillwater pass beyond the rails ("He dined with us once in Bo; up from Freetown; he was governor there"), lunch at the Corner House for Philip's sake (he'd have preferred himself a glass of stout and some oysters at the York bar), the Zoo, the long bus ride home in the last summer light: the leaves in the Green Park were beginning to turn and the motors nuzzled out of Berkeley Street with the low sun gently glowing on their wind-screens. Baines envied no one, not Cora Down, or Sir Arthur Stillwater, or Lord Sandale, who came out on to the steps of the Army and Navy and then went back again because he hadn't got anything to do and might as well look at another paper. "I said don't let me see you touch that black again." Baines had led a man's life; everyone on top of the bus pricked their ears when he told Philip all about it.

"Would you have shot him?" Philip asked, and Baines put his head back and tilted his dark respectable manservant's hat to a better angle as the bus swerved round the artillery memorial.

"I wouldn't have thought twice about it. I'd have shot to kill," he boasted, and the bowed figure went by, the steel helmet, the heavy cloak, the down-turned rifle and the folded hands.

"Have you got the revolver?"

"Of course I've got it," Baines said. "Don't I need it with all the burglaries there've been?" This was the Baines whom Philip loved: not Baines singing and carefree, but Baines responsible, Baines behind barriers, living his man's life.

All the buses streamed out from Victoria like a convoy of aeroplanes to bring Baines home with honour. "Forty blacks under me," and there waiting near the area steps was the proper conventional reward, love at lighting-up time.

"It's your niece," Philip said, recognising the white mackintosh, but not the happy sleepy face. She frightened him like an unlucky number; he nearly told Baines what Mrs. Baines had said; but he didn't want to bother, he wanted to leave things alone.

"Why, so it is," Baines said. "I shouldn't wonder if she was going to have a bit of supper with us." But he said they'd play a game, pretend they didn't know her, slip down the area steps, "and here," Baines said, "we are," lay the table, put out the cold sausages, a bottle of beer, a bottle of ginger pop, a flagon of harvest burgundy. "Everyone his own drink," Baines said. "Run upstairs, Phil, and see if there's been a post."

Philip didn't like the empty house at dusk before the lights went on. He hurried. He wanted to be back with Baines. The hall lay there in quiet and shadow prepared to show him something he didn't want to see. Some letters rustled down, and someone knocked. "Open in the name of the Republic." The tumbrils rolled, the head bobbed in the bloody basket. Knock, knock, and the postman's footsteps going away. Philip gathered the letters. The slit in the door was like the grating in a jeweller's window. He remembered the policeman he had seen peer through. He had said to his nurse, "What's he doing?" and when she said, "He's seeing if everything's all right," his brain immediately filled with images of all that might be wrong. He ran to the baize door and the stairs. The girl was already there and Baines was kissing her. She

leant breathless against the dresser. "This is Emmy, Phil."

"There's a letter for you, Baines."

"Emmy," Baines said, "it's from her." But he wouldn't open it. "You bet she's coming back."

"We'll have supper, anyway, "Emmy said. "She can't harm that."

"You don't know her," Baines said. "Nothing's safe. Damn it," he said, "I was a man once," and he opened the letter.

"Can I start?" Philip asked, but Baines didn't hear; he presented in his stillness and attention an example of the importance grown-up people attached to the written word: you had to write your thanks, not wait and speak them, as if letters couldn't lie. But Philip knew better than that, sprawling his thanks across a page to Aunt Alice who had given him a doll he was too old for. Letters could lie all right, but they made the lie permanent; they lay as evidence against you: they made you meaner than the spoken word.

"She's not coming back till to-morrow night," Baines said. He opened the bottles, he pulled up the chairs, he kissed Emmy again against the dresser.

"You oughtn't to," Emmy said, "with the boy here."

"He's got to learn," Baines said, "like the rest of us," and he helped Philip to three sausages. He only took one himself; he said he wasn't hungry; but when Emmy said she wasn't hungry either he stood over her and made her eat. He was timid and rough with her; he made her drink the harvest burgundy because he said she needed building up; he wouldn't take no for an answer, but when he touched her his hands were light and clumsy too, as if he was afraid to damage something delicate and didn't know how to handle anything so light.

"This is better than milk and biscuits, eh?"

"Yes," Philip said, but he was scared, scared for Baines as much as for himself. He couldn't help wondering at every bite, at every draught of the ginger pop, what Mrs. Baines would say if she ever learnt of this meal; he couldn't imagine it, there was a depth of bitterness and rage in Mrs. Baines you couldn't sound. He said, "She won't be coming back to-night?" but you could tell by the way they immediately understood him that she wasn't really away at all; she was there in the basement with them, driving them to longer drinks and louder talk, biding her time for the right cutting word. Baines wasn't really happy; he was only watching happiness from close to instead of from far away.

"No," he said, "she'll not be back till to-morrow." He couldn't keep his eyes off happiness; he'd played around as much as other men, he kept on reverting to the Coast as if to excuse himself for his innocence; he wouldn't have been so innocent if he'd lived his life in London, so innocent when it came to tenderness. "If it was you, Emmy," he said, looking at the white dresser, the scrubbed chairs, "this'd be like a home." Already the room was not quite so harsh; there was a little dust in corners, the silver needed a final polish, the morning's paper lay untidily on a chair. "You'd better go to bed, Phil; it's been a long day."

They didn't leave him to find his own way up through the dark shrouded house; they went with him, turning on lights, touching each other's fingers on the switches; floor after floor they drove the night back; they spoke softly among the covered chairs; they watched him undress, they didn't make him wash or clean his teeth, they saw him into bed and lit his night-light and left his door ajar. He could hear their voices on the stairs, friendly like the guests he heard at dinner-parties when they moved down to the hall, saying good night. They belonged; wherever they were they made a home. He heard a door open and a clock strike, he heard their voices for a long while, so that he felt they were not far away and he was safe. The voices didn't dwindle, they simply went out, and he could be sure that they were still somewhere not far from him, silent together in one of the many empty rooms, growing sleepy together as he grew sleepy after the long day.

He just had time to sigh faintly with satis-faction, because this too perhaps had been life, before he slept and the inevitable terrors of sleep came round him: a man with a tricolour hat beat at the door on His Majesty's service, a bleeding head lay on the kitchen table in a basket, and the Siberian wolves crept closer. He was bound hand and foot and couldn't move; they leapt round him breathing heavily; he opened his eyes and Mrs. Baines was there, her grey untidy hair in threads over his face, her black hat askew. A loose hair-pin fell on the pillow and one musty thread brushed his mouth. "Where are they?" she whispered. "Where are they?"

4

Philip watched her in terror. Mrs. Baines was out of breath as if she had been searching all the empty rooms, looking under loose covers.

With her untidy grey hair and her black dress buttoned to her throat, her gloves of black cotton, she was so like the witches of his dreams that he didn't dare to speak. There was a stale smell in her breath.

"She's here," Mrs. Baines said; "you can't deny she's here." Her face was simultaneously marked with cruelty and misery; she wanted to "do things" to people, but she suffered all the time. It would have done her good to scream, but she daren't do that: it would warn them. She came ingratiatingly back to the bed where Philip lay rigid on his back and whispered, "I haven't forgotten the Meccano set. You shall have it to-morrow, Master Philip. We've got secrets together, haven't we? Just tell me where they are."

He couldn't speak. Fear held him as firmly as any nightmare. She said, "Tell Mrs. Baines, Master Philip. You love your Mrs. Baines, don't you?" That was too much; he couldn't speak, but he could move his mouth in terri-fied denial, wince away from her dusty image.

She whispered, coming closer to him, "Such deceit. I'll tell your father. I'll settle with you myself when I've found them. You'll smart; I'll see you smart." Then immediately she was still, listening. A board had creaked on the floor below, and a moment later, while she stooped listening above his bed, there came the whispers of two people who were happy and sleepy together after a long day. The night-light stood beside the mirror and Mrs. Baines could see bitterly there her own reflection, misery and cruelty wavering in the glass, age and dust and nothing to hope for. She sobbed without tears, a dry, breathless sound; but her cruelty was a kind of pride which kept her going; it was her best quality, she would have been merely pitiable without it. She went out of the door on tiptoe, feeling her way across the landing, going so softly down the stairs that no one behind a shut door could hear her. Then there was complete silence again; Philip could move; he raised his knees; he sat up in bed; he wanted to die. It wasn't fair, the walls were down again between his world and theirs; but this time it was something worse than merriment that the grown people made him share; a passion moved in the house he recognised but could not understand.

It wasn't fair, but he owed Baines everything: the Zoo, the ginger pop, the bus ride home. Even the supper called on his loyalty. But he was frightened; he was touching something he touched in dreams: the bleeding head, the wolves, the knock, knock, knock. Life fell on him with savagery: you couldn't blame him if he never faced it again in sixty years. He got out of bed, carefully from habit put on his bedroom slippers, and tiptoed to the door: it wasn't quite dark on the landing below because the curtains had been taken down for the cleaners and the light from the street came in through the tall windows. Mrs. Baines had her hand on the glass door-knob; she was very carefully turning it; he screamed: "Baines, Baines."

Mrs. Baines turned and saw him cowering in his pyjamas by the banisters; he was helpless, more helpless even than Baines, and cruelty grew at the sight of him and drove her up the stairs. The nightmare was on him again and he couldn't move; he hadn't any more courage left for ever; he'd spent it all, had been allowed no

time to let it grow, no years of gradual hardening; he couldn't even scream.

But the first cry had brought Baines out of the best spare bedroom and he moved quicker than Mrs. Baines. She hadn't reached the top of the stairs before he'd caught her round the waist. She drove her black cotton gloves at his face and he bit her hand. He hadn't time to think, he fought her savagely like a stranger, but she fought back with knowledgeable hate. She was going to teach them all and it didn't really matter whom she began with; they had all deceived her; but the old image in the glass was by her side, telling her she must be dignified, she wasn't young enough to yield her dignity; she could beat his face, but she mustn't bite; she could push, but she mustn't kick.

Age and dust and nothing to hope for were her handicaps. She went over the banisters in a flurry of black clothes and fell into the hall; she lay before the front door like a sack of coals which should have gone down the area into the basement. Philip saw; Emmy saw; she sat down suddenly in the doorway of the best spare bedroom with her eyes open as if she were too tired to stand any longer. Baines went slowly down into the hall.

It wasn't hard for Philip to escape; they'd forgotten him completely; he went down the back, the servants' stairs because Mrs. Baines was in the hall; he didn't understand what she was doing lying there; like the startling pictures in a book no one had read to him, the things he didn't understand terrified him. The whole house had been turned over to the grown-up world; he wasn't safe in the night nursery; their passions had flooded it. The only thing he could do was to get away, by the back stair, and up through the area, and never come back. You didn't think of the cold, of the need of food and sleep; for an hour it would seem quite possible to escape from people for ever.

He was wearing pyjamas and bedroom slippers when he came up into the square, but there was no one to see him. It was that hour of the evening in a residential district when everyone is at the theatre or at home. He climbed over the iron railings into the little garden: the plane-trees spread their large pale palms between him and the sky. It might have been an illimitable forest into which he had escaped. He crouched behind a trunk and the wolves retreated; it seemed to him between the little iron seat and the tree-trunk that no one would ever find him again. A kind of embittered happiness and self-pity made him cry; he was lost; there wouldn't be any more secrets to keep; he surrendered responsibility once and for all. Let grown-up people keep to their world and he would keep to his, safe in the small garden between the plane-trees. "In the lost childhood of Judas, Christ was betrayed"; you could almost see the small unformed face hardening into the deep dilettante selfishness of age.

Presently the door of 48 opened and Baines looked this way and that; then he signalled with his hand and Emmy came; it was as if they were only just in time for a train, they hadn't a chance of saying good-bye; she went quickly by like a face at a window swept past the platform, pale and unhappy and not wanting to go. Baines went in again and shut the door; the light was lit in the basement, and a policeman walked round the square, looking into the areas. You could tell how many families were at home by the lights behind the first-floor curtains.

Philip explored the garden: it didn't take long: a twenty-yard square of bushes and plane-trees, two iron seats and a gravel path, a padlocked gate at either end, a scuffle of old leaves. But he couldn't stay: something stirred in the bushes and two illuminated eyes peered out at him like a Siberian wolf, and he thought how terrible it would be if Mrs. Baines found him there. He'd have no time to climb the railings; she'd seize him from behind.

He left the square at the unfashionable end and was immediately among the fish-and-chip shops, the little stationers selling Bagatelle, among the accommodation addresses and the dingy hotels with open doors. There were few people about because the pubs were open, but a blowsy woman carrying a parcel called out to him across the street and the commissionaire outside a cinema would have stopped him if he hadn't crossed the road. He went deeper: you could go farther and lose yourself more completely here than among the plane-trees. On the fringe of the square he was in danger of being stopped and taken back: it was obvious where he belonged: but as he went deeper he lost the marks of his origin. It was a warm night: any child in those free-living parts might be expected to play truant from bed. He found a kind of camaraderie even among grown-up people; he might have been a neighbour's child as he went quickly by, but they weren't going to tell on him, they'd been young once themselves. He picked up a protective coating of dust from the pavements, of smuts from the trains which passed along the backs in a spray of fire. Once he was caught in a knot of children running away from something or somebody, laughing as they ran; he was whirled with them round a turning and abandoned, with a sticky fruit-drop in his hand.

He couldn't have been more lost; but he hadn't the stamina to keep on. At first he feared that someone would stop him; after an hour he hoped that someone would. He couldn't find his way back, and in any case he was afraid of arriving home alone; he was afraid of Mrs. Baines, more afraid than he had ever been. Baines was his friend, but something had happened which gave Mrs. Baines all the power. He began to loiter on purpose to be noticed, but no one noticed him. Families were having a last breather on the doorsteps, the refuse bins had been put out and bits of cabbage stalks soiled his slippers. The air was full of voices, but he was cut off; these people were strangers and would always now be strangers; they were marked by Mrs. Baines and he shied away from them into a deep class-consciousness. He had been afraid of policemen, but now he wanted one to take him home; even Mrs. Baines could do nothing against a policeman. He sidled past a constable who was directing traffic, but he was too busy to pay him any attention. Philip sat down against a wall and cried.

It hadn't occurred to him that that was the easiest way, that all you had to do was to surrender, to show you were beaten and accept kindness. —— It was lavished on him at once by two women and a pawnbroker. Another policeman appeared, a young man with a sharp incredulous face. He looked as if he noted everything he saw in pocket-books and drew conclusions. A woman offered to see Philip home, but he didn't trust her: she wasn't a match for Mrs. Baines immobile in the hall. He wouldn't give his address; he said he was afraid to go home. He had his way; he got his protection. "I'll take him to the station," the policeman said, and holding him awkwardly by the hand (he wasn't married; he had his career to make) he led him round the corner, up the stone stairs into the little bare over-heated room where Justice waited.

5

Justice waited behind a wooden counter on a high stool; it wore a heavy moustache; it was kindly and had six children ("three of them nippers like yourself"); it wasn't really interested in Philip, but it pretended to be, it wrote the address down and sent a constable to fetch a glass of milk. But the young constable was interested; he had a nose for things.

"Your home's on the telephone, I suppose," Justice said. "We'll ring them up and say you are safe. They'll fetch you very soon. What's your name, sonny?"

"Philip."

"Your other name?"

"I haven't got another name." He didn't want to be fetched; he wanted to be taken home by someone who would impress even Mrs. Baines. The constable watched him, watched the way he drank the milk, watched him when he winced away from questions.

"What made you run away? Playing truant, eh?"

"I don't know."

"You oughtn't to do it, young fellow. Think how anxious your father and mother will be."

"They are away."

"Well, your nurse."

"I haven't got one."

"Who looks after you, then?" That question went home. Philip saw Mrs. Baines coming up the stairs at him, the heap of black cotton in the hall. He began to cry.

"Now, now, now," the sergeant said. He didn't know what to do; he wished his wife were with him; even a policewoman might have been useful.

"Don't you think it's funny," the constable said, "that there hasn't been an inquiry?"

"They think he's tucked up in bed."

"You are scared, aren't you?" the constable said. "What scared you?"

"I don't know."

"Somebody hurt you?"

"No."

"He's had bad dreams," the sergeant said. "Thought the house was on fire, I expect. I've brought up six of them. Rose is due back. She'll take him home."

"I want to go home with you," Philip said; he tried to smile at the constable, but the deceit was immature and unsuccessful.

"I'd better go," the constable said. "There may be something wrong."

"Nonsense," the sergeant said. "It's a woman's job. Tact is what you need. Here's Rose. Pull up your stockings, Rose. You're a disgrace to the Force. I've got a job of work for you." Rose shambled in: black cotton stockings drooping over her boots, a gawky Girl Guide manner, a hoarse hostile voice. "More tarts, I suppose."

"No, you've got to see this young man home." She looked at him owlishly.

"I won't go with her," Philip said. He began to cry again. "I don't like her."

"More of that womanly charm, Rose," the sergeant said. The telephone rang on his desk. He lifted the receiver. "What? What's that?" he said. "Number 48? You've got a doctor?"

He put his hand over the telephone mouth. "No wonder this nipper wasn't reported," he said. "They've been too busy. An accident. Woman slipped on the stairs."

"Serious?" the constable asked. The sergeant mouthed at him; you didn't mention the word death before a child (didn't he know? he had six of them), you made noises in the throat, you grimaced, a complicated shorthand for a word of only five letters anyway.

"You'd better go, after all," he said, "and make a report. The doctor's there."

Rose shambled from the stove; pink apply-dapply cheeks, loose stockings. She stuck her hands behind her. Her large morgue-like mouth was full of blackened teeth. "You told me to take him and now just because something inter-esting —— I don't expect justice from a man ——"

"Who's at the house?" the constable asked.

"The butler."

"You don't think," the constable said, "he saw ——"

"Trust me," the sergeant said. "I've brought up six. I know 'em through and through. You can't teach me anything about children."

"He seemed scared about something."

"Dreams," the sergeant said.

"What name?"

"Baines."

"This Mr. Baines," the constable said to Philip, "you like him, eh? He's good to you?" They were trying to get something out of him; he was suspicious of the whole roomful of them; he said "yes" without conviction because he was afraid at any moment of more responsibilities, more secrets.

"And Mrs. Baines?"

"Yes."

They consulted together by the desk: Rose was hoarsely aggrieved; she was like a female imper-sonator, she bore her womanhood with an un-natural emphasis even while she scorned it in her creased stockings and her weather-exposed face. The charcoal shifted in the stove; the room was over-heated in the mild late summer eve-ning. A notice on the wall described a body found in the Thames, or rather the body's clothes: wool vest, wool pants, wool shirt with blue stripes, size ten boots, blue serge suit worn at the elbows, fifteen and a half celluloid collar. They couldn't find anything to say about the body, except its measurements, it was just an ordinary body.

"Come along," the constable said. He was interested, he was glad to be going, but he couldn't help being embarrassed by his company, a small boy in pyjamas. His nose smelt some-thing, he didn't know what, but he smarted at the sight of the amusement they caused: the pubs had closed and the streets were full again of men making as long a day of it as they could. He hurried through the less frequented streets, chose the darker pavements, wouldn't loiter, and Philip wanted more and more to loiter, pulling at his hand, dragging with his feet. He dreaded the sight of Mrs. Baines waiting in the hall: he knew now that she was dead. The sergeant's mouthings had conveyed that; but she wasn't buried, she wasn't out of sight; he was going to see a dead person in the hall when the door opened.

The light was on in the basement, and to his relief the constable made for the area steps. Per-haps he wouldn't have to see Mrs. Baines at all. The constable knocked on the door because it was too dark to see the bell, and Baines an-swered. He stood there in the doorway of the neat bright basement room and you could see the sad complacent plausible sentence he had prepared wither at the sight of Philip; he hadn't expected Philip to return like that in the police-man's company. He had to begin thinking all over again; he wasn't a deceptive man; if it hadn't been for Emmy he would have been quite ready to let the truth lead him where it would.

"Mr. Baines?" the constable asked.

He nodded; he hadn't found the right words; he was daunted by the shrewd knowing face, the sudden appearance of Philip there.

"This little boy from here?"

"Yes," Baines said. Philip could tell that there was a message he was trying to convey, but he shut his mind to it. He loved Baines, but Baines had involved him in secrets, in fears he didn't understand. The glowing morning thought "This is life" had become under Baines's tuition the repugnant memory, "That was life": the musty hair across the mouth, the breathless cruel tortured inquiry "Where are they," the heap of black cotton tipped into the hall. That was what happened when you loved: you got involved; and Philip extricated himself from life, from love, from Baines with a merciless egotism.

There had been things between them, but he laid them low, as a retreating army cuts the wires, destroys the bridges. In the abandoned country you may leave much that is dear—a morning in the Park, an ice at a corner house, sausages for supper—but more is concerned in the retreat than temporary losses. There are old people who, as the tractors wheel away, implore to be taken, but you can't risk the rearguard for their sake: a whole prolonged retreat from life, from care, from human relationships is involved.

"The doctor's here," Baines said. He nodded at the door, moistened his mouth, kept his eyes on Philip, begging for something like a dog you can't understand. "There's nothing to be done. She slipped on these stone basement stairs. I was in here. I heard her fall." He wouldn't look at the notebook, at the constable's spidery writing which got a terrible lot on one page.

"Did the boy see anything?"

"He can't have done. I thought he was in bed. Hadn't he better go up? It's a shocking thing. O," Baines said, losing control, "it's a shocking thing for a child."

"She's through there?" the constable asked.

"I haven't moved her an inch," Baines said.

"He'd better then ——"

"Go up the area and through the hall," Baines said, and again he begged dumbly like a dog: one more secret, keep this secret, do this for old Baines, he won't ask another.

"Come along," the constable said. "I'll see you up to bed. You're a gentleman; you must come in the proper way through the front door like the master should. Or will you go along with him, Mr. Baines, while I see the doctor?"

"Yes," Baines said, "I'll go." He came across the room to Philip, begging, begging, all the way with his soft old stupid expression: this is Baines, the old Coaster; what about a palm-oil chop, eh?; a man's life; forty niggers; never used a gun; I tell you I couldn't help loving them: it wasn't what we call love, nothing we could understand. The messages flickered out from the last posts at the border, imploring, beseeching, reminding: this is your old friend Baines; what about an eleven's; a glass of ginger-pop won't do you any harm; sausages; a long day. But the wires were cut, the messages just faded out into the enormous vacancy of the neat scrubbed room in which there had never been a place where a man could hide his secrets.

"Come along, Phil, it's bedtime. We'll just go up the steps——" Tap, tap, tap, at the telegraph; you may get through, you can't tell, somebody may mend the right wire. "And in at the front door."

"No," Philip said, "no. I won't go. You can't make me go. I'll fight. I won't see her."

The constable turned on them quickly. "What's that? Why won't you go?"

"She's in the hall," Philip said. "I know she's in the hall. And she's dead. I won't see her."

"You moved her then?" the constable said to Baines. "All the way down here? You've been lying, eh? That means you had to tidy up ——. Were you alone?"

"Emmy," Philip said, "Emmy." He wasn't going to keep any more secrets: he was going to finish once and for all with everything, with Baines and Mrs. Baines and the grown-up life beyond him; it wasn't his business and never, never again, he decided, would he share their confidences and companionship. "It was all Emmy's fault," he protested with a quaver which reminded Baines that after all he was only a child; it had been hopeless to expect help there; he was a child; he didn't understand what it all meant; he couldn't read this shorthand of terror;

he'd had a long day and he was tired out. You could see him dropping asleep where he stood against the dresser, dropping back into the comfortable nursery peace. You couldn't blame him. When he woke in the morning, he'd hardly remember a thing.

"Out with it," the constable said, addressing Baines with professional ferocity, "who is she?" just as the old man sixty years later startled his secretary, his only watcher, asking "Who is she? Who is she?" dropping lower and lower into death, passing on the way perhaps the image of Baines: Baines hopeless, Baines letting his head drop, Baines "coming clean."

THE DOLL'S HOUSE

Katherine Mansfield

When dear old Mrs. Hay went back to town after staying with the Burnells she sent the children a doll's house. It was so big that the carter and Pat carried it into the courtyard, and there it stayed, propped up on two wooden boxes beside the feed-room door. No harm could come to it; it was summer. And perhaps the smell of paint would have gone off by the time it had to be taken in. For, really, the smell of paint coming from that doll's house ("Sweet of old Mrs. Hay, of course; most sweet and generous!")—but the smell of paint was quite enough to make anyone seriously ill, in Aunt Beryl's opinion. Even before the sacking was taken off. And when it was——

There stood the doll's house, a dark, oily, spinach green, picked out with bright yellow. Its two solid little chimneys, glued onto the roof, were painted red and white, and the door, gleaming with yellow varnish, was like a little slab of toffee. Four windows, real windows, were divided into panes by a broad streak of green. There was actually a tiny porch, too, painted yellow, with big lumps of congealed paint hanging along the edge.

But perfect, perfect little house! Who could possibly mind the smell? It was part of the joy, part of the newness.

"Open it quickly, someone!"

The hook at the side was stuck fast. Pat pried it open with his penknife, and the whole house-front swung back, and—there you were, gazing at one and the same moment into the drawing-room and dining-room, the kitchen and two bedrooms. That is the way for a house to open! Why don't all houses open like that? How much more exciting than peering through the slit of a door into a mean little hall with a hatstand and two umbrellas! That is—isn't it?—what you long to know about a house when you put your hand on the knocker. Perhaps it is the way God opens houses at dead of night when He is taking a quiet turn with an angel.——

"O-oh!" The Burnell children sounded as though they were in despair. It was too marvelous; it was too much for them. They had never seen anything like it in their lives. All the rooms were papered. There were pictures on the walls, painted on the paper, with gold frames complete. Red carpet covered all the floors

---

— *"The Doll's House"* by Katherine Mansfield, from *The Dove's Nest and other stories*, published by Alfred A. Knopf, Inc., New York, 1923; reprinted by permission of The Society of Authors, literary representative of the estate of the late Katherine Mansfield

except the kitchen; red plush chairs in the drawing-room, green in the dining-room; tables, beds with real bedclothes, a cradle, a stove, a dresser with tiny plates and one big jug. But what Kezia liked more than anything, what she liked frightfully, was the lamp. It stood in the middle of the dining-room table, an exquisite little amber lamp with a white globe. It was even filled all ready for lighting, though, of course, you couldn't light it. But there was something inside that looked like oil, and that moved when you shook it.

The father and mother dolls, who sprawled very stiff as though they had fainted in the drawing-room, and their two little children asleep upstairs, were really too big for the doll's house. They didn't look as though they belonged. But the lamp was perfect. It seemed to smile at Kezia, to say: "I live here." The lamp was real.

The Burnell children could hardly walk to school fast enough the next morning. They burned to tell everybody, to describe, to—well—to boast about their doll's house before the school-bell rang.

"I'm to tell," said Isabel, "because I'm the eldest. And you two can join in after. But I'm to tell first."

There was nothing to answer. Isabel was bossy, but she was always right, and Lottie and Kezia knew too well the powers that went with being eldest. They brushed through the thick buttercups at the road edge and said nothing.

"And I'm to choose who's to come and see it first. Mother said I might."

For it had been arranged that while the doll's house stood in the courtyard they might ask the girls at school, two at a time, to come and look. Not to stay to tea, of course, or to come traipsing through the house. But just to stand quietly in the courtyard while Isabel pointed out the beauties, and Lottie and Kezia looked pleased.——

But hurry as they might, by the time they had reached the tarred palings of the boys' playground the bell had begun to jangle. They only just had time to whip off their hats and fall into line before the roll was called. Never mind.

Isabel tried to make up for it by looking very important and mysterious and by whispering behind her hand to the girls near her: "Got something to tell you at playtime."

Playtime came and Isabel was surrounded. The girls of her class nearly fought to put their arms round her, to walk away with her, to beam flatteringly, to be her special friend. She held quite a court under the huge pine trees at the side of the playground. Nudging, giggling together, the little girls pressed up close. And the only two who stayed outside the ring were the two who were always outside, the little Kelveys. They knew better than to come anywhere near the Burnells.

For the fact was the school the Burnell children went to was not at all the kind of place their parents would have chosen if there had been any choice. But there was none. It was the only school for miles. And the consequence was all the children in the neighborhood, the Judge's little girls, the doctor's daughters, the store-keeper's children, the milkman's, were forced to mix together. Not to speak of there being an equal number of rude, rough little boys as well. But the line had to be drawn somewhere. It was drawn at the Kelveys. Many of the children, including the Burnells, were not allowed even to speak to them. They walked past the Kelveys with their heads in the air, and as they set the fashion in all matters of behavior, the Kelveys were shunned by everybody. Even the teacher had a special voice for them, and a special smile for the other children when Lil Kelvey came up to her desk with a bunch of dreadfully common-looking flowers.

They were the daughters of a spry, hard-working little washerwoman, who went about from house to house by the day. This was awful enough. But where was Mr. Kelvey? Nobody knew for certain. But everybody said he was in prison. So they were the daughters of a washerwoman and a jailbird. Very nice company for other people's children! And they looked it. Why Mrs. Kelvey made them so conspicuous was hard to understand. The truth was they

72

were dressed in "bits" given to her by the people for whom she worked. Lil, for instance, who was a stout, plain child, with big freckles, came to school in a dress made from a green art-serge tablecloth of the Burnells', with red plush sleeves from the Logans' curtains. Her hat, perched on top of her high forehead, was a grown-up woman's hat, once the property of Miss Lecky, the postmistress. It was turned up at the back and trimmed with a large scarlet quill. What a little guy she looked! It was impossible not to laugh. And her little sister, our Else, wore a long white dress, rather like a nightgown, and a pair of little boy's boots. But whatever our Else wore, she would have looked strange. She was a tiny wishbone of a child, with cropped hair and enormous solemn eyes—a little white owl. Nobody had ever seen her smile; she scarcely ever spoke. She went through life holding on to Lil, with a piece of Lil's skirt screwed up in her hand. Where Lil went our Else followed. In the playground, on the road going to and from school, there was Lil marching in front and our Else holding on behind. Only when she wanted anything, or when she was out of breath, our Else gave Lil a tug, a twitch, and Lil stopped and turned round. The Kelveys never failed to understand each other.

Now they hovered at the edge; you couldn't stop them listening. When the little girls turned round and sneered, Lil, as usual, gave her silly, shamefaced smile, but our Else only looked.

And Isabel's voice, so very proud, went on telling. The carpet made a great sensation, but so did the beds with real bedclothes, and the stove with an oven door.

When she finished, Kezia broke in. "You've forgotten the lamp, Isabel."

"Oh, yes," said Isabel, "and there's a teeny little lamp, all made of yellow glass, with a white globe, that stands on the dining-room table. You couldn't tell it from a real one."

"The lamp's best of all," cried Kezia. She thought Isabel wasn't making half enough of the little lamp. But nobody paid any attention. Isabel was choosing the two who were to come back with them that afternoon and see it. She chose Emmie Cole and Lena Logan. But when the others knew they were all to have a chance, they couldn't be nice enough to Isabel. One by one they put their arms round Isabel's waist and walked her off. They had something to whisper to her, a secret. "Isabel's *my* friend."

Only the little Kelveys moved away forgotten; there was nothing more for them to hear.

Days passed, and as more children saw the doll's house, the fame of it spread. It became the one subject, the rage. The one question was: "Have you seen Burnells' doll's house? Oh, ain't it lovely!" "Haven't you seen it? Oh, I say!"

Even the dinner hour was given up to talking about it. The little girls sat under the pines eating their thick mutton sandwiches and big slabs of johnny-cake spread with butter. While always, as near as they could get, sat the Kelveys, our Else holding on to Lil, listening too, while they chewed their jam sandwiches out of a newspaper soaked with large red blobs. ——

"Mother," said Kezia, "can't I ask the Kelveys just once?"

"Certainly not, Kezia."

"But why not?"

"Run away, Kezia; you know quite well why not."

At last everybody had seen it except them. On that day the subject rather flagged. It was the dinner hour. The children stood together under the pine trees, and suddenly, as they looked at the Kelveys eating out of their paper, always by themselves, always listening, they wanted to be horrid to them. Emmie Cole started the whisper.

"Lil Kelvey's going to be a servant when she grows up."

"O-oh, how awful!" said Isabel Burnell, and she made eyes at Emmie.

Emmie swallowed in a very meaning way and nodded to Isabel as she'd seen her mother do on those occasions.

"It's true—it's true—it's true," she said.

Then Lena Logan's little eyes snapped. "Shall I ask her?" she whispered.

"Bet you don't," said Jessie May.

"Pooh, I'm not frightened," said Lena. Suddenly she gave a little squeal and danced in front of the other girls. "Watch! Watch me! Watch me now!" said Lena. And sliding, gliding, dragging one foot, giggling behind her hand, Lena went over to the Kelveys.

Lil looked up from her dinner. She wrapped the rest quickly away. Our Else stopped chewing. What was coming now?

"Is it true you're going to be a servant when you grow up, Lil Kelvey?" shrilled Lena.

Dead silence. But instead of answering, Lil only gave her silly, shamefaced smile. She didn't seem to mind the question at all. What a sell for Lena! The girls began to titter.

Lena couldn't stand that. She put her hands on her hips; she shot forward. "Yah, yer father's in prison!" she hissed, spitefully.

This was such a marvellous thing to have said that the little girls rushed away in a body, deeply, deeply excited, wild with joy. Someone found a long rope, and they began skipping. And never did they skip so high, run in and out so fast, or do such daring things as on that morning.

In the afternoon Pat called for the Burnell children with the buggy and they drove home. There were visitors. Isabel and Lottie, who liked visitors, went upstairs to change their pinafores. But Kezia thieved out at the back. Nobody was about; she began to swing on the big white gates of the courtyard. Presently, looking along the road, she saw two little dots. They grew bigger, they were coming towards her. Now she could see that one was in front and one close behind. Now she could see that they were the Kelveys. Kezia stopped swinging. She slipped off the gate as if she was going to run away. Then she hesitated. The Kelveys came nearer, and beside them walked their shadows, very long, stretching right across the road with their heads in the buttercups. Kezia clambered back on the gate; she had made up her mind; she swung out.

"Hullo," she said to the passing Kelveys.

They were so astounded that they stopped.

Lil gave her silly smile. Our Else stared.

"You can come and see our doll's house if you want to," said Kezia, and she dragged one toe on the ground. But at that Lil turned red and shook her head quickly.

"Why not?" asked Kezia.

Lil gasped, then she said: "Your ma told our ma you wasn't to speak to us."

"Oh, well," said Kezia. She didn't know what to reply. "It doesn't matter. You can come and see our doll's house all the same. Come on. Nobody's looking."

But Lil shook her head still harder.

"Don't you want to?" asked Kezia.

Suddenly there was a twitch, a tug at Lil's skirt. She turned round. Our Else was looking at her with big, imploring eyes; she was frowning; she wanted to go. For a moment Lil looked at our Else very doubtfully. But then our Else twitched her skirt again. She started forward. Kezia led the way. Like two little stray cats they followed across the courtyard to where the doll's house stood.

"There it is," said Kezia.

There was a pause. Lil breathed loudly, almost snorted; our Else was still as a stone.

"I'll open it for you," said Kezia kindly. She undid the hook and they looked inside.

"There's the drawing-room and the dining-room, and that's the——"

"Kezia!"

Oh, what a start they gave!

"Kezia!"

It was Aunt Beryl's voice. They turned round. At the back door stood Aunt Beryl, staring as if she couldn't believe what she saw.

"How dare you ask the little Kelveys into the courtyard?" said her cold, furious voice. "You know as well as I do you're not allowed to talk to them. Run away, children, run away at once. And don't come back again," said Aunt Beryl. And she stepped into the yard and shooed them out as if they were chickens.

"Off you go immediately!" she called, cold and proud.

They did not need telling twice. Burning with

74

angelic

shame, shrinking together, Lil huddling along like her mother, our Else dazed, somehow they crossed the big courtyard and squeezed through the white gate.

"Wicked, disobedient little girl!" said Aunt Beryl bitterly to Kezia, and she slammed the doll's house to.

The afternoon had been awful. A letter had come from Willie Brent, a terrifying, threatening letter, saying if she did not meet him that evening in Pulman's Bush, he'd come to the front door and ask the reason why! But now that she had frightened those little rats of Kelveys and given Kezia a good scolding, her heart felt lighter. That ghastly pressure was gone. She went back to the house humming.

When the Kelveys were well out of sight of Burnells', they sat down to rest on a big red drainpipe by the side of the road. Lil's cheeks were still burning; she took off the hat with the quill and held it on her knee. Dreamily they looked over the hay paddocks, past the creek, to the group of wattles where Logan's cows stood waiting to be milked. What were their thoughts?

Presently our Else nudged up close to her sister. But now she had forgotten the cross lady. She put out a finger and stroked her sister's quill; she smiled her rare smile.

"I seen the little lamp," she said, softly.

Then both were silent once more.

CONVOCATION ADDRESS

George Faludy

Some years ago in Hungary I found myself, for the second time in my life, in a concentration camp. There were some thirteen hundred inmates: democrats, Catholics, liberals, socialists and people without any political preferences, most sentenced to hard labor on trumped-up charges, though a few were there without having been sentenced or even charged. We could neither write nor receive letters or parcels; we had no books, newspapers, radios, or visitors. We cut stones from dawn to dusk 365 days a year, except for May Day. We did this on a diet of 1200 calories a day. Our situation was thus better than in a Nazi concentration camp, but much worse than in the present-day Soviet camps recently described by Bukovsky and others.

At first we returned to the barracks at night deadly tired, with no strength even to pull off our army boots and fall asleep on the rotten straw sacks. Our lives seemed not to differ from those of the slaves that built the pyramids, and our futures seemed equally bleak. But already on the day of my arrest, in the Black Maria that took me away, I had met young friends who had been denied a university education because of the war. Their faces had lit up: "You can lecture us in the camp," they said, "and we'll get our university education that way." After about a week in the camp two of them approached me and insisted that I start my lectures immediately after lights-out. We were by then even more exhausted than on the day of our arrival. At first four men sat beside my pallet, and we were jeered at by the others. Eventually twelve prisoners gathered beside my straw sack every night for an hour or two. We recited poems,

———*from an address by Dr. Faludy to University of Toronto Convocation, November 29, 1978; by permission of the author*

Hungarian poems, and foreign poems in translation. Among the English ones the "Ode to the West Wind" became the favorite. Then I would speak on literature, history or philosophy and my lecture would be discussed by all.

I was by no means the only prisoner to deliver such lectures. A former member of the short-lived democratic government knew *Hamlet* and *A Midsummer Night's Dream* by heart, and recited both to an enthusiastic audience. There were lectures on Roman Law, on the history of the Crusades, narrations of large parts of *War and Peace*, courses in mathematics and astronomy avidly listened to, sometimes by men who had never entered a secondary school. There was even a former staff colonel who whistled entire operas. Those of us who lectured ransacked our memories to keep alive a civilization from which we were hopelessly—and, it seemed, permanently—cut off.

There were prisoners who looked on all this with disgust, maintaining that we were insane to spend our sleeping time in lectures when we were all going to die anyway. These men, intent on survival, retreated into themselves, becoming lonely, merciless with others, shutting out thought and even speech.

By the second winter of our imprisonment it began to happen when we were at work that once, twice or even three times in the course of a day a prisoner would suddenly stop work and stagger off through the deep snow. After twenty or thirty yards of running he would collapse. In each case the man would die a day or two later, usually without regaining consciousness. Those who died in this way were always the men who had been most determined to survive, those who had concentrated on nothing but food, sleep and warmth. For my part, owing perhaps to large doses of pragmatism and positivism in my youth I was reluctant to admit the obvious: that delighting in a good poem or discussing Plato's Socratic dialogue could somehow arm the spirit to the point that it could prevent the body's collapse.

But then I was presented with proof. While I was washing myself in the snow before the barracks one evening, one of my pupils, a former government official, a strong young man, came up to tell me that he would not attend the lecture that night, nor indeed any other night. He wanted to survive and was going to sleep rather than talk; he was going, he said, to live the life of a tree or a vegetable. He waited before me as if expecting my objection. I was indescribably tired, and closing my eyes I saw scenes from my childhood, the sort of hallucinations one has in a state of semi-starvation. Suddenly it occurred to me that I must dissuade the man. But he was already gone. He slept perhaps twenty yards from me, but I never summoned the strength to argue with him. Five days later we saw him stop work, begin to run towards the trees, and then collapse in the snow. His death has been on my conscience ever since. But without exception all those who lectured, and all those who listened, survived.

It does not seem to me far-fetched to apply this lesson in the infinitely more pleasant society of this country. It justifies, I think, the Platonic view that man as given by nature owes it to himself to obey the dictates of his higher nature to rise above evil and mindlessness. Those in the camp who attempted this, survived; although physical survival had not been their aim. And those who for the sake of physical survival vegetated, perished in large numbers. It seems to me that the mentality of these latter is, *mutatis mutandis*, analogous to the mentality of the consumer societies of the world, of those who seem obsessed with producing and consuming an ever-growing mountain of things to ensure comfort and survival; who have addicted themselves to energy as if to morphine until they are ready to destroy all nature to increase the dosage; who have, indeed, increased our life span but have failed to mention that the brain requires jogging even more than the heart if that life span is to mean anything.

The other conclusion I have drawn from my camp experience, and have tried to embody in my own poetry, is that our whole fragile tradition of art and thought is neither an amusement nor a yoke. For those who steep themselves in it, it provides both a guide and a goal for surpassing all the half-baked ideologies that have blown up at our feet in this century like landmines. Sitting comfortably in the present and looking forward to longevity in an unknown future does nothing to ensure our survival nor even to make it desirable. In any case we do not live in the future; we live in the present, and all we have to guide us in this present is the accumulated thought and experience of those who have lived before us.

For all the deficiency of my own learning, then, this is what I have attempted to voice in my work, and at this point in my life I feel safe in echoing the words of Petronius: *Pervixi: neque enim fortuna malignior umquam eripiet nobis quod prior hora dedit*—I have lived, and no evil fate can ever take away from us what the past has given. I believe we will do ourselves a favor if we extend the meaning of the author of the *Satyricon* to include the past of all humanity.

THE FIFTY-YARD DASH

William Saroyan

After a certain letter came to me from New York the year I was twelve, I made up my mind to become the most powerful man in my neighborhood. The letter was from my friend Lionel Strongfort. I had clipped a coupon from *Argosy*

— *"The Fifty-Yard Dash" by William Saroyan; copyright 1938, 1966, by William Saroyan; reprinted from My Name is Aram by permission of Harcourt Brace & World, Inc.*

All-Story Magazine, signed it, placed it in an envelope, and mailed it to him. He had written back promptly, with an enthusiasm bordering on pure delight, saying I was undoubtedly a man of uncommon intelligence, potentially a giant, and—unlike the average run-of-the-mill people of the world who were, in a manner of speaking, dreamwalkers and daydreamers—a person who would some day be somebody.

His opinion of me was very much like my own. It was pleasant, however, to have the opinion so emphatically corroborated, particularly by a man in New York—and a man with the greatest chest expansion in the world. With the letter came several photographic reproductions of Mr. Strongfort wearing nothing but a little bit of leopard skin. He was a tremendous man and claimed that at one time he had been puny. He was loaded all over with muscle and appeared to be somebody who could lift a 1920 Ford roadster and tip it over.

It was an honor to have him for a friend.

The only trouble was—I didn't have the money. I forget how much the exact figure was at the beginning of our acquaintanceship, but I haven't forgotten that it was an amount completely out of the question. While I was eager to be grateful to Mr. Strongfort for his enthusiasm, I didn't seem to be able to find words with which to explain about not having the money, without immediately appearing to be a dreamwalker and a daydreamer myself. So, while waiting from one day to another, looking everywhere for words that would not blight our friendship and degrade me to commonness, I talked the matter over with my uncle Gyko, who was studying Oriental philosophy at the time. He was amazed at my curious ambition, but quite pleased. He said the secret of greatness, according to Yoga, was the releasing within one's self of those mysterious vital forces which are in all men.

These strength, he said in English which he liked to affect when speaking to me, ease from God. I tell you, Aram, eat ease wonderful.

I told him I couldn't begin to become the powerful man I had decided to become until I sent Mr. Strongfort some money.

Mohney! my uncle said with contempt. I tell you, Aram, mohney is nawthing. You cannot bribe God.

Although my uncle Gyko wasn't exactly a puny man, he was certainly not the man Lionel Strongfort was. In a wrestling match I felt certain Mr. Strongfort would get a headlock or a half-nelson or a toe-hold on my uncle and either make him give up or squeeze him to death. And then again, on the other hand, I wondered. My uncle was nowhere near as big as Mr. Strongfort, but neither was Mr. Strongfort as dynamically furious as my uncle. It seemed to me that, at best, Mr. Strongfort, in a match with my uncle, would have a great deal of unfamiliar trouble—I mean with the mysterious vital forces that were always getting released in my uncle, so that very often a swift glance from him would make a big man quail and turn away, or, if he had been speaking, stop quickly.

Long before I had discovered words with which to explain to Mr. Strongfort about the money, another letter came from him. It was as cordial as the first, and as a matter of fact, if anything, a little more cordial. I was delighted and ran about, releasing mysterious vital forces, turning handsprings, scrambling up trees, rolling somersaults, trying to tip over 1920 Ford roadsters, challenging all comers to wrestle, and in many other ways alarming my relatives and irritating the neighbors.

Not only was Mr. Strongfort not sore at me, he had reduced the cost of the course. Even so, the money necessary was still more than I could get hold of. I was selling papers every day, but *that* money was for bread and stuff like that. For a while I got up very early every morning and went around town looking for a small satchel full of money. During six days of this adventuring I found a nickel and two pennies. I found also a woman's purse containing several foul-smelling cosmetic items, no money, and a slip of paper on which was written in an ignorant hand: Steve Hertwig, 3764 Ventura Avenue.

Three days after the arrival of Mr. Strongfort's second letter, his third letter came. From this time on our correspondence became onesided. In fact, I didn't write at all. Mr. Strongfort's communications were overpowering and not at all easy to answer, without money. There was, in fact, almost nothing to say.

It was wintertime when the first letter came, and it was then that I made up my mind to become the most powerful man in my neighborhood and ultimately, for all I knew, one of the most powerful men in the world. I had ideas of my own as to how to go about getting that way, but I had also the warm friendship and high regard of Mr. Strongfort in New York, and the mystical and furious guardianship of my uncle Gyko, at home.

The letters from Mr. Strongfort continued to arrive every two or three days all winter and on into springtime. I remember, the day apricots were ripe enough to steal, the arrival of a most charming letter from my friend in New York. It was a hymn to newness on earth, the arrival of springtime, the time of youth in the heart, of renewal, fresh strength, fresh determination, and many other things. It was truly a beautiful epistle, probably as fine as any to the Romans or anybody else. It was full of the legend-quality, the world-feeling, and the dignity-of-strength-feeling so characteristic of Biblical days. The last paragraph of the lovely hymn brought up, apologetically, the coarse theme of money. The sum was six or seven times as little as it had been originally, and a new element had come into Mr. Strongfort's program of changing me over from a nobody to a giant of tremendous strength, and extreme attractiveness to women. Mr. Strongfort had decided, he said, to teach me everything in one fell swoop, or one sweep fall, or something of that sort. At any rate, for three dollars, he said, he would send me all his precious secrets in one envelope and the rest would be up to me.

I took the matter up with my uncle Gyko, who by this time had reached the stage of fasting, meditating, walking for hours, and vibrating. We had had discussions two or three times a week all winter and he had told me in his own unique broken-English way all the secrets *he* had been learning from Yoga.

I tell you, Aram, I can do *anything*. Eat ease wonderful.

I believed him, too, even though he had lost a lot of weight, couldn't sleep, and had a strange dynamic blaze in his eyes. He was very scornful of the world that year and was full of pity for the dumb beautiful animals that man was mistreating, killing, eating, domesticating, and teaching to do tricks.

I tell you, Aram, eat ease creaminal to make the horses work. To keal the cows. To teach the dogs to jump, and the monkeys to smoke pipes.

I told him about the letter from Mr. Strongfort.

Mohney! he said. Always he wants mohney. I do not like heem.

My uncle was getting all his dope free from the theosophy-philosophy-astrology-and-miscellaneous shelf at the Public Library. He believed, however, that he was getting it straight from God. Before he took up Yoga he had been one of the boys around town and a good drinker of *rakhi*, but after the light began to come to him he gave up drinking. He said he was drinking liquor finer than *rakhi* or anything else.

What's that? I asked him.

Aram, he said, eat ease weasdom.

Anyhow, he had little use for Mr. Strongfort and regarded the man as a charlatan.

He's all right, I told him.

But my uncle became furious, releasing mysterious vital forces, and said, I wheel break hease head, fooling all you leatle keads.

He ain't fooling, I said. He says he'll give me all his secrets for three dollars.

I tell you, Aram, he does not know any seacrets. He ease a liar.

I don't know about that. I'd like to try that stuff.

Eat ease creaminal, my uncle Gyko said, but I wheal geave you tree dollar.

He gave me the necessary three dollars and I sent them along to Mr. Strongfort. The envelope came from New York, full of Mr. Strongfort's secrets. They were strangely simple. It was all stuff I had known anyhow but had been too lazy to pay any attention to. The idea was to get up early in the morning and for an hour or so to do various kinds of acrobatic exercises, which were illustrated. Also to drink plenty of water, get plenty of fresh air, eat good wholesome food, and keep it up until you were a giant.

I felt a little let down and sent Mr. Strongfort a short polite note saying so. He ignored the note and I never heard from him again. In the meantime, I had been following the rules and growing more powerful every day. When I say *in the meantime*, I mean for four days I followed the rules. On the fifth day I decided to sleep instead of getting up and filling the house with noise and getting my grandmother sore. She used to wake up in the darkness of early morning and shout that I was an impractical fool and would never be rich. She would go back to sleep for five minutes, wake up, and then shout that I would never buy and sell for a profit. She would sleep a little more, waken, and shout that there were once three sons of a king; one was wise like his father; the other was crazy about girls; and the third had less brains than a bird. Then she would get out of bed, and, shouting steadily, tell me the whole story while I did my exercises.

The story would usually warn me to be sensible and not go around waking her up before daybreak all the time. That would always be the moral, more or less, although the story itself would be about three sons of some king, or three brothers, each of them very wealthy and usually very greedy, or three daughters, or three proverbs, or three roads, or something else like that.

She was wasting her breath, though, because I wasn't enjoying the early-morning acrobatics any more than she was. In fact, I was beginning to feel that it was a lot of nonsense, and that my uncle Gyko had been right about Mr. Strongfort in the first place.

So I gave up Mr. Strongfort's program and returned to my own, which was more or less as follows: to take it easy and grow to be the most powerful man in the neighborhood without any trouble or exercise. Which is what I did.

That spring Longfellow School announced that a track meet was to be held, one school to compete against another; *everybody* to participate.

Here, I believed, was my chance. In my opinion I would be first in every event.

Somehow or other, however, continuous meditation on the theme of athletics had the effect of growing into a fury of anticipation that continued all day and all night, so that before the day of the track meet I had run the fifty-yard dash any number of hundreds of times, had jumped the running broad jump, the standing broad jump, and the high jump, and in each event had made my competitors look like weaklings.

This tremendous inner activity, which was strictly Yoga, changed on the day of the track meet into fever.

The time came at last for me and three other athletes, one of them a Greek, to go to our marks, get set, and go; and I did, in a blind rush of speed which I knew had never before occurred in the history of athletics.

It seemed to me that never before had any living man moved so swiftly. Within myself I ran the fifty yards fifty times before I so much as opened my eyes to find out how far back I had left the other runners. I was very much amazed at what I saw.

Three boys were four yards ahead of me and going away.

It was incredible. It was unbelievable, but it was obviously the truth. There ought to be some mistake, but there wasn't. There they were, ahead of me, going away.

Well, it simply meant that I would have to overtake them, with my eyes open, and win the race. This I proceeded to do. They continued, incredibly, however, to go away, in spite of my intention. I became irritated and decided to put them in their places for the impertinence, and began releasing all the mysterious vital forces within myself that I had. Somehow or other, however, not even this seemed to bring me any closer to them and I felt that in some strange way I was being betrayed. If so, I decided, I would shame my betrayer by winning the race in spite of the betrayal, and once again I threw fresh life and energy into my running. There wasn't a great distance still to go, but I knew I would be able to do it.

Then I knew I wouldn't.

The race was over.

I was last, by ten yards.

Without the slightest hesitation I protested and challenged the runners to another race, same distance, back. They refused to consider the proposal, which proved, I knew, that they were afraid to race me. I told them they knew very well I could beat them.

It was very much the same in all the other events.

When I got home I was in high fever and very angry. I was delirious all night and sick three days. My grandmother took very good care of me and probably was responsible for my not dying. When my uncle Gyko came to visit me he was no longer hollow-cheeked. It seems he had finished his fast, which had been a long one—forty days or so; and nights too, I believe. He had stopped meditating, too, because he had practically exhausted the subject. He was again one of the boys around town, drinking, staying up all hours, and following the women.

I tell you, Aram, he said, we are a great family. We can do *anything*.

TWO SOLDIERS

William Faulkner

Me and Pete would go down to Old Man Killegrew's and listen to his radio. We would wait until after supper, after dark, and we would stand outside Old Man Killegrew's parlor window, and we could hear it because Old Man Killegrew's wife was deaf, and so he run the radio as loud as it would run, and so me and Pete could hear it plain as Old Man Killegrew's wife could, I reckon, even standing outside with the window closed.

And that night I said, "What? Japanese? What's a pearl harbor?" and Pete said, "Hush."

— *"Two Soldiers" by William Faulkner, from Collected Stories of William Faulkner, published by Random House, Inc., New York, 1950 (originally in the Saturday Evening Post, March 2, 1942); copyright © 1954 by William Faulkner; reprinted by permission

And so we stood there, it was cold, listening to the fellow in the radio talking, only I couldn't make no heads nor tails neither out of it. Then the fellow said that would be all for a while, and me and Pete walked back up the road to home, and Pete told me what it was. Because he was nigh twenty and he had done finished the Consolidated last June and he knowed a heap: about them Japanese dropping bombs on Pearl Harbor and that Pearl Harbor was across the water.

"Across what water?" I said. "Across that Government reservoy up at Oxford?"

"Naw," Pete said. "Across the big water. The Pacific Ocean."

We went home. Maw and pap was already asleep, and me and Pete laid in the bed, and I still couldn't understand where it was, and Pete told me again—the Pacific Ocean.

"What's the matter with you?" Pete said.

"You're going on nine years old. You been in school now ever since September. Ain't you learned nothing yet?"

"I reckon we ain't got as fer as the Pacific Ocean yet," I said.

We was still sowing the vetch then that ought to been all finished by the fifteenth of November, because pap was still behind, just like he had been ever since me and Pete had knowed him. And we had firewood to git in, too, but every night me and Pete would go down to Old Man Killegrew's and stand outside his parlor window in the cold and listen to his radio; then we would come back home and lay in the bed and Pete would tell me what it was. That is, he would tell me for a while. Then he wouldn't tell me. It was like he didn't want to talk about it no more. He would tell me to shut up because he wanted to go to sleep, but he never wanted to go to sleep.

He would lay there, a heap stiller than if he was asleep, and it would be something, I could feel it coming out of him, like he was mad at me even, only I knowed he wasn't thinking about me, or like he was worried about something, and it wasn't that neither, because he never had nothing to worry about. He never got behind like pap, let alone stayed behind. Pap give him ten acres when he graduated from the Consolidated, and me and Pete both reckoned pap was durn glad to get shut of at least ten acres, less to have to worry with himself; and Pete had them ten acres all sowed to vetch and busted out and bedded for the winter, and so it wasn't that. But it was something. And still we would go down to Old Man Killegrew's every night and listen to his radio, and they was at it in the Philippines now, but General MacArthur was holding um. Then we would come back home and lay in the bed, and Pete wouldn't tell me nothing or talk at all. He would just lay there still as a ambush and when I would touch him, his side or his leg would feel hard and still as iron, until after a while I would go to sleep.

Then one night—it was the first time he had

said nothing to me except to jump on me about not chopping enough wood at the wood tree where we was cutting—he said, "I got to go."

"Go where?" I said.

"To that war," Pete said.

"Before we even finish gettin' in the firewood?"

"Firewood, hell," Pete said.

"All right," I said. "When we going to start?"

But he wasn't even listening. He laid there, hard and still as iron in the dark. "I got to go," he said. "I jest ain't going to put up with no folks treating the Unity States that way."

"Yes," I said. "Firewood or no firewood, I reckon we got to go."

This time he heard me. He laid still again, but it was a different kind of still.

"You?" he said. "To a war?"

"You'll whup the big uns and I'll whup the little uns," I said.

Then he told me I couldn't go. At first I thought he just never wanted me tagging after him, like he wouldn't leave me go with him when he went sparking them girls of Tull's. Then he told me the Army wouldn't leave me go because I was too little, and then I knowed he really meant it and that I couldn't go nohow noways. And somehow I hadn't believed until then that he was going himself, but now I knowed he was and that he wasn't going to leave me go with him a-tall.

"I'll chop the wood and tote the water for you-all then!" I said. "You got to have wood and water!"

Anyway, he was listening to me now. He wasn't like iron now.

He turned onto his side and put his hand on my chest because it was me that was laying straight and hard on my back now.

"No," he said. "You got to stay here and help pap."

"Help him what?" I said. "He ain't never caught up nohow. He can't get no further behind. He can sholy take care of this little shirttail of a farm while me and you are whupping them Japanese. I got to go too. If you got to go, then so have I."

"No," Pete said. "Hush now. Hush." And he meant it, and I knowed he did. Only I made sho from his own mouth. I quit.

"So I just can't go then," I said.

"No," Pete said. "You just can't go. You're too little, in the first place, and in the second place ——"

"All right," I said. "Then shut up and leave me go to sleep."

So he hushed then and laid back. And I laid there like I was already asleep, and pretty soon he was asleep and I knowed it was the wanting to go to the war that had worried him and kept him awake, and now that he had decided to go, he wasn't worried any more.

The next morning he told maw and pap. Maw was all right. She cried.

"No," she said, crying, "I don't want him to go. I would rather go myself in his place, if I could. I don't want to save the country. Them Japanese could take it and keep it, so long as they left me and my family and my children alone. But I remember my brother Marsh in that other war. He had to go to that one when he wasn't but nineteen, and our mother couldn't understand it then any more than I can now. But she told Marsh if he had to go, he had to go. And so, if Pete's got to go to this one, he's got to go to it. Jest don't ask me to understand why."

But pap was the one. He was the feller. "To the war?" he said. "Why, I just don't see a bit of use in that. You ain't old enough for the draft, and the country ain't being invaded. Our President in Washington, D.C., is watching the conditions and he will notify us. Besides, in that other war your ma just mentioned, I was drafted and sent clean to Texas and was held there nigh eight months until they finally quit fighting. It seems to me that, along with your Uncle Marsh who received a actual wound on the battlefields of France, is enough for me and mine to have to do to protect the country, at least in my lifetime. Besides, what'll

I do for help on the farm with you gone? It seems to me I'll get mighty far behind."

"You been behind as long as I can remember," Pete said. "Anyway, I'm going. I got to."

"Of course he's got to go," I said. "Them Japanese ——"

"You hush your mouth!" maw said, crying. "Nobody's talking to you! Go and get me a armful of wood! That's what you can do!"

So I got the wood. And all the next day, while me and Pete and pap was getting in as much wood as we could in that time because Pete said how pap's idea of plenty of wood was one more stick laying against the wall that maw ain't put on the fire yet, Maw was getting Pete ready to go. She washed and mended his clothes and cooked him a shoe box of vittles. And that night me and Pete laid in the bed and listened to her packing his grip and crying, until after a while Pete got up in his nightshirt and went back there, and I could hear them talking, until at last maw said, "You got to go, and so I want you to go. But I don't understand it, and I won't never, and so don't expect me to." And Pete come back and got into the bed again and laid again still and hard as iron on his back, and then he said, and he wasn't talking to me, he wasn't talking to nobody: "I got to go. I just got to."

"Sho you got to," I said. "Them Japanese ——" He turned over hard, he kind of surged over onto his side, looking at me in the dark.

"Anyway, you're all right," he said. "I expected to have more trouble with you than with all the rest of them put together."

"I reckon I can't help it neither," I said. "But maybe it will run a few years longer and I can get there. Maybe someday I will jest walk in on you."

"I hope not," Pete said. "Folks don't go to wars for fun. A man don't leave his maw crying just for fun."

"Then why are you going?" I said.

"I got to," he said. "I just got to. Now you go on to sleep. I got to ketch that early bus in the morning."

"All right," I said. "I hear tell Memphis is a big place. How will you find where the Army's at?"

"I'll ask somebody where to go to join it," Pete said. "Go on to sleep now."

"Is that what you'll ask for? Where to join the Army?" I said.

"Yes," Pete said. He turned onto his back again. "Shut up and go to sleep."

We went to sleep. The next morning we et breakfast by lamplight because the bus would pass at six o'clock. Maw wasn't crying now. She jest looked grim and busy, putting breakfast on the table while we et it. Then she finished packing Pete's grip, except he never wanted to take no grip to the war, but maw said decent folks never went nowhere, not even to a war, without a change of clothes and something to tote them in. She put in the shoe box of fried chicken and biscuits and she put the Bible in, too, and then it was time to go. We didn't know until then that maw wasn't going to the bus. She jest brought Pete's cap and overcoat, and still she didn't cry no more, she jest stood with her hands on Pete's shoulders and she didn't move, but somehow, and just holding Pete's shoulders, she looked as hard and fierce as when Pete had turned toward me in the bed last night and tole me that anyway I was all right.

"They could take the country and keep the country, so long as they never bothered me and mine," she said. Then she said, "Don't never forget who you are. You ain't rich and the rest of the world outside of Frenchman's Bend never heard of you. But your blood is good as any blood anywhere, and don't you never forget it."

Then she kissed him, and then we was out of the house, with pap toting Pete's grip whether Pete wanted him to or not. There wasn't no dawn even yet, not even after we had stood on the highway by the mailbox, a while. Then we seen the lights of the bus coming and I was watching the bus until it come up and Pete flagged it, and then, sho enough, there was

daylight—it had started while I wasn't watching. And now me and Pete expected pap to say something else foolish, like he done before, about how Uncle Marsh getting wounded in France and that trip to Texas pap taken in 1918 ought to be enough to save the Unity States in 1942, but he never. He done all right too. He jest said, "Good-by, son. Always remember what your ma told you and write her whenever you find the time." Then he shaken Pete's hand, and Pete looked at me a minute and put his hand on my head and rubbed my head durn nigh hard enough to wring my neck off and jumped into the bus, and the feller wound the door shut and the bus began to hum; then it was moving, humming and grinding and whining louder and louder; it was going fast, with two little red lights behind it that never seemed to get no littler, but just seemed to be running together until pretty soon they would touch and jest be one light. But they never did, and then the bus was gone, and even like it was, I could have pretty nigh busted out crying, nigh to nine years old and all.

Me and pap went back to the house. All that day we worked at the wood tree, and so I never had no good chance until about middle of the afternoon. Then I taken my slingshot and I would have liked to took all my bird eggs, too, because Pete had give me his collection and he holp me with mine, and he would like to git the box out and look at them as good as I would, even if he was nigh twenty years old. But the box was too big to tote a long ways and have to worry with, so I just taken the shikepoke egg, because it was the best un, and wropped it up good into a matchbox and hid it and the slingshot under the corner of the barn. Then we et supper and went to bed, and I thought then how if I would 'a' had to stayed in that room and that bed like that even for one more night, I jest couldn't 'a' stood it. Then I could hear pap snoring, but I never heard no sound from maw, whether she was asleep or not, and I don't reckon she was. So I taken my shoes and drapped them out the window, and then I clumb out like I used to watch Pete do when he was still jest seventeen and pap held that he was too young yet to be tomcatting around at night, and wouldn't leave him out, and I put on my shoes and went to the barn and got the slingshot and the shikepoke egg and went to the highway.

It wasn't cold, it was jest durn confounded dark and that highway stretched on in front of me like, without nobody using it, it had stretched out half again as fer just like a man does when he lays down, so that for a time it looked like full sun was going to ketch me before I had finished them twenty-two miles to Jefferson. But it didn't. Daybreak was jest starting when I walked up the hill into town. I could smell breakfast cooking in the cabins and I wished I had thought to brought me a cold biscuit, but that was too late now. And Pete had told me Memphis was a piece beyond Jefferson, but I never knowed it was no eighty miles. So I stood there on that empty square, with daylight coming and coming and the street lights still burning and that Law looking down at me, and me still eighty miles from Memphis, and it had took me all night to walk jest twenty-two miles, and so, by the time I got to Memphis at that rate, Pete would 'a' done already started for Pearl Harbor.

"Where do you come from?" the Law said.

And I told him again. "I got to get to Memphis. My brother's there."

"You mean you ain't got any folks around here?" the Law said. "Nobody but that brother? What are you doing way off down here and your brother in Memphis?"

And I told him again, "I got to get to Memphis. I ain't got no time to waste talking about it and I ain't got time to walk it. I got to git there today."

"Come on here," the Law said.

We went down another street. And there was the bus, just like when Pete got into it yestiddy morning, except there wasn't no lights on it now and it was empty. There was a regular bus dee-po like a railroad dee-po, with a ticket counter and a feller behind it, and the Law said, "Set down over there," and I set down on the bench, and the Law said, "I want to use your telephone," and he talked in the telephone a minute and put it down and said to the feller behind the ticket counter, "Keep your eye on him. I'll be back as soon as Mrs. Habersham can arrange to get herself up and dressed." He went out. I got up and went to the ticket counter.

"I want to go to Memphis," I said.

"You bet," the feller said. "You set down on the bench now. Mr. Foote will be back in a minute."

"I don't know no Mr. Foote," I said. "I want to ride that bus to Memphis."

"You got some money?" he said. "It'll cost you seventy-two cents."

I taken out the matchbox and unwropped the shikepoke egg. "I'll swap you this for a ticket to Memphis," I said.

"What's that?" he said.

"It's a shikepoke egg," I said. "You never seen one before. It's worth a dollar. I'll take seventy-two cents fer it."

"No," he said, "the fellers that own that bus insist on a cash basis. If I started swapping tickets for bird eggs and livestock and such, they would fire me. You go and set down on the bench now, like Mr. Foote ——"

I started for the door, but he caught me, he put one hand on the ticket counter and jumped over it and caught up with me and reached his hand out to ketch my shirt. I whupped out my pocketknife and snapped it open.

"You put a hand on me and I'll cut it off," I said.

I tried to dodge him and run at the door, but he could move quicker than any grown man I ever see, quick as Pete almost. He cut me off and stood with his back against the door and one foot raised a little, and there wasn't no other way to get out. "Get back on that bench and stay there," he said.

And there wasn't no other way out. And he stood there with his back against the door. So

I went back to the bench. And then it seemed like to me that dee-po was full of folks. There was that Law again, and there was two ladies in fur coats and their faces already painted. But they still looked like they had got up in a hurry and they still never liked it, a old one and a young one, looking down at me.

"He hasn't got a overcoat!" the old one said. "How in the world did he ever get down here by himself?"

"I ask you," the Law said. "I couldn't get nothing out of him except his brother is in Memphis and he wants to get back up there."

"That's right," I said. "I got to git to Memphis today."

"Of course you must," the old one said. "Are you sure you can find your brother when you get to Memphis?"

"I reckon I can," I said. "I ain't got but one and I have knowed him all my life. I reckon I will know him again when I see him."

The old one looked at me. "Somehow he doesn't look like he lives in Memphis," she said.

"He probably don't," the Law said. "You can't tell though. He might live anywhere, overhalls or not. This day and time they get scattered overnight from he—— hope to breakfast; boys and girls, too, almost before they can walk good. He might have been in Missouri or Texas either yestiddy, for all we know. But he don't seem to have any doubt his brother is in Memphis. All I know to do is send him up there and leave him look."

"Yes," the old one said.

The young one set down on the bench by me and opened a hand satchel and taken out a artermatic writing pen and some papers.

"Now, honey," the old one said, "we're going to see that you find your brother, but we must have a case history for our files first. We want to know your name and your brother's name and where you were born and when your parents died."

"I don't need no case history neither," I said. "All I want is to get to Memphis. I got to get there today."

"You see?" the Law said. He said it almost like he enjoyed it. "That's what I told you."

"You're lucky, at that, Mrs. Habersham," the bus feller said. "I don't think he's got a gun on him, but he can open that knife da—— I mean, fast enough to suit any man."

But the old one just stood there looking at me.

"Well," she said. "Well. I really don't know what to do."

"I do," the bus feller said. "I'm going to give him a ticket out of my own pocket, as a measure of protecting the company against riot and bloodshed. And when Mr. Foote tells the city board about it, it will be a civic matter and they will not only reimburse me, they will give me a medal too. Hey, Mr. Foote?"

But never nobody paid him no mind. The old one still stood looking down at me. She said "Well," again. Then she taken a dollar from her purse and give it to the bus feller. "I suppose he will travel on a child's ticket, won't he?"

"Wellum," the bus feller said, "I just don't know what the regulations would be. Likely I will be fired for not crating him and marking the crate Poison. But I'll risk it."

Then they were gone. Then the Law come back with a sandwich and give it to me.

"You're sure you can find that brother?" he said.

"I ain't convinced why not," I said. "If I don't see Pete first, he'll see me. He knows me too."

Then the Law went out for good, too, and I et the sandwich. Then more folks come in and bought tickets, and then the bus feller said it was time to go, and I got into the bus just like Pete done, and we was gone.

I seen all the towns. I seen all of them. When the bus got to going good, I found out I was jest about wore out for sleep. But there was too much I hadn't never saw before. We run out of Jefferson and run past fields and woods, then we would run into another town and out of that un and past fields and woods again, and then into another town with stores and gins and water tanks, and we run along by the railroad for a spell and I seen the signal arm move, and then I seen the train and then some more towns, and I was jest about plumb wore out for sleep, but I couldn't resk it. Then Memphis begun. It seemed like, to me, it went on for miles. We would pass a patch of stores and I would think that was sholy it and the bus would even stop. But it wouldn't be Memphis yet and we would go on again past water tanks and smokestacks on top of the mills, and if they was gins and sawmills, I never knowed there was that many and I never seen any that big, and where they got enough cotton and logs to run um I don't know.

Then I see Memphis. I knowed I was right this time. It was standing up into the air. It looked like about a dozen whole towns bigger than Jefferson was set up on one edge in a field, standing up into the air higher than ara hill in all Yoknapatawpha County. Then we was in it, with the bus stopping ever' few feet, it seemed like to me, and cars rushing past on both sides of it and the street crowded with folks from ever'where in town that day, until I didn't see how there could 'a' been nobody left in Mis'sippi a-tall to even sell me a bus ticket, let alone write out no case histories. Then the bus stopped. It was another bus dee-po, a heap bigger than the one in Jefferson. And I said, "All right. Where do folks join the Army?"

"What?" the bus feller said.

And I said it again, "Where do folks join the Army?"

"Oh," he said. Then he told me how to get there. I was afraid at first I wouldn't ketch on how to do in a town big as Memphis. But I caught on all right. I never had to ask but twice more. Then I was there, and I was durn glad to git out of all them rushing cars and shoving folks and all that racket for a spell, and I thought, It won't be long now, and I thought how if there was any kind of a crowd there that had done already joined the Army, too, Pete would likely see me before I seen him. And

so I walked into the room. And Pete wasn't there.

He wasn't even there. There was a soldier with a big arrerhead on his sleeve, writing, and two fellers standing in front of him, and there was some more folks there, I reckon. It seems to me I remember some more folks there.

I went to the table where the soldier was writing, and I said, "Where's Pete?" and he looked up and I said, "My brother. Pete Grier. Where is he?"

"What?" the soldier said. "Who?"

And I told him again. "He joined the Army yestiddy. He's going to Pearl Harbor. So am I. I want to ketch him. Where you all got him?" Now they were all looking at me, but I never paid them no mind. "Come on," I said. "Where is he?"

The soldier had quit writing. He had both hands spraddled out on the table. "Oh," he said. "You're going, too, hah?"

"Yes," I said. "They got to have wood and water. I can chop it and tote it. Come on. Where's Pete?"

The soldier stood up. "Who let you in here?" he said. "Go on. Beat it."

"Durn that," I said. "You tell me where Pete ——"

I be dog if he couldn't move faster than the bus feller even. He never come over the table, he come around it, he was on me almost before I knowed it, so that I jest had time to jump back and whup out my pocket-knife and snap it open and hit one lick, and he hollered and jumped back and grabbed one hand with the other and stood there cussing and hollering.

One of the other fellers grabbed me from behind, and I hit at him with the knife, but I couldn't reach him.

Then both of the fellers had me from behind, and then another soldier come out of a door at the back. He had on a belt with a britching strop over one shoulder.

"What the hell is this?" he said.

"That little son cut me with a knife!" the first soldier hollered. When he said that I tried to get at him again, but both them fellers was holding me, two against one, and the soldier with the backing strop said, "Here, here. Put your knife up, feller. None of us are armed. A man don't knife-fight folks that are barehanded." I could begin to hear him then. He sounded jest like Pete talked to me. "Let him go," he said. They let me go. "Now what's all the trouble about?" And I told him. "I see," he said. "And you come up to see if he was all right before he left."

"No," I said. "I came to ——"

But he had already turned to where the first soldier was wropping a handkerchief around his hand.

"Have you got him?" he said. The first soldier went back to the table and looked at some papers.

"Here he is," he said. "He enlisted yestiddy. He's in a detachment leaving this morning for Little Rock." He had a watch stropped on his arm. He looked at it. "The train leaves in about fifty minutes. If I know country boys, they're probably all down there at the station right now."

"Get him up here," the one with the backing strop said. "Phone the station. Tell the porter to get him a cab. And you come with me," he said.

It was another office behind that un, with jest a table and some chairs. We set there while the soldier smoked, and it wasn't long; I knowed Pete's feet soon as I heard them. Then the first soldier opened the door and Pete come in. He never had no soldier clothes on. He looked jest like he did when he got on the bus yestiddy morning, except it seemed to me like it was at least a week, so much had happened, and I had done had to do so much traveling. He come in and there he was, looking at me like he hadn't never left home, except that here we was in Memphis, on the way to Pearl Harbor.

"What in durnation are you doing here?" he said.

And I told him, "You got to have wood and water to cook with. I can chop it and tote it for you-all."

"No," Pete said. "You're going back home."

"No, Pete," I said. "I got to go too. I got to. It hurts my heart, Pete."

"No," Pete said. He looked at the soldier. "I jest don't know what could have happened to him, lootenant," he said. "He never drawed a knife on anybody before in his life." He looked at me. "What did you do it for?"

"I don't know," I said. "I jest had to. I jest had to git here. I jest had to find you."

"Well, don't you never do it again, you hear?" Pete said. "You put that knife in your pocket and you keep it there. If I ever again hear of you drawing it on anybody, I'm coming back from wherever I am at and whup the fire out of you. You hear me?"

"I would pure cut a throat if it would bring you back to stay," I said. "Pete," I said. "Pete."

"No," Pete said. Now his voice wasn't hard and quick no more, it was almost quiet, and I knowed now I wouldn't never change him. "You must go home. You must look after maw, and I am depending on you to look after my ten acres. I want you to go back home. Today. Do you hear?"

"I hear," I said.

"Can he get back home by himself?" the soldier said.

"He come up here by himself," Pete said.

"I can get back, I reckon," I said. "I don't live in but one place. I don't reckon it's moved."

Pete taken a dollar out of his pocket and give it to me. "That'll buy your bus ticket right to our mailbox," he said. "I want you to mind the lootenant. He'll send you to the bus. And you go back home and you take care of maw and look after my ten acres and keep that durn knife in your pocket. You hear me?"

"Yes, Pete," I said.

"All right," Pete said. "Now I got to go." He put his hand on my head again. But this time he never wrung my neck. He just laid his hand on my head a minute. And then I be dog if he didn't lean down and kiss me, and I heard his feet and then the door, and I never looked up and that was all, me setting there, rubbing the place where Pete kissed me and the soldier throwed back in his chair, looking out the window and coughing. He reached into his pocket and handed something to me without looking around. It was a piece of chewing gum.

"Much obliged," I said. "Well, I reckon I might as well start back. I got a right fer piece to go."

"Wait," the soldier said. Then he telephoned again and I said again I better start back, and he said again, "Wait. Remember what Pete told you."

So we waited, and then another lady come in, old, too, in a fur coat, too, but she smelled all right, she never had no artermatic writing pen nor no case history neither. She come in and the soldier got up, and she looked around quick until she saw me, and come and put her hand on my shoulder light and quick and easy as maw herself might 'a' done it.

"Come on," she said. "Let's go home to dinner."

"Nome," I said. "I got to ketch the bus to Jefferson."

"I know. There's plenty of time. We'll go home and eat dinner first."

She had a car. And now we was right down in the middle of all them other cars. We was almost under the busses, and all them crowds of people on the street close enough to where I could have talked to them if I had knowed who they was. After a while she stopped the car. "Here we are," she said, and I looked at it, and if all that was her house, she sho had a big family. But all of it wasn't. We crossed a hall with trees growing in it and went into a little room without nothing in it but a nigger dressed up in a uniform a heap shinier than them soldiers had, and the nigger shut the door, and then I hollered, "Look out!" and grabbed, but it was all right; that whole little room jest went right on up and stopped and the door opened and we was in another hall, and the

lady unlocked a door and we went in, and there was another soldier, a old feller, with a britching strop, too, and a silver-colored bird on each shoulder.

"Here we are," the lady said. "This is Colonel McKellogg. Now, what would you like for dinner?"

"I reckon I'll jest have some ham and eggs and coffee," I said.

She had done started to pick up the telephone. She stopped. "Coffee?" she said. "When did you start drinking coffee?"

"I don't know," I said. "I reckon it was before I could remember."

"You're about eight, aren't you?" she said.

"Nome," I said. "I'm eight and ten months. Going on eleven months."

She telephoned then. Then we set there and I told them how Pete had jest left that morning for Pearl Harbor and I had aimed to go with him, but I would have to go back home to take care of maw and look after Pete's ten acres, and she said how they had a little boy about my size, too, in a school in the East. Then a nigger, another one, in a short kind of shirttail coat, rolled a kind of wheelbarrer in. It had my ham and eggs and a glass of milk and a piece of pie, too, and I thought I was hungry. But when I taken the first bite I found out I couldn't swallow it, and I got up quick.

"I got to go," I said.

"Wait," she said.

"I got to go," I said.

"Just a minute," she said. "I've already telephoned for the car. It won't be but a minute now. Can't you drink the milk even? Or maybe some of your coffee?"

"Nome," I said. "I ain't hungry. I'll eat when I git home." Then the telephone rang. She never even answered it.

"There," she said. "There's the car." And we went back down in that 'ere little moving room with the dressed-up nigger. This time it was a big car with a soldier driving it. I got into the front with him. She give the soldier a dollar. "He might get hungry," she said. "Try to find a decent place for him."

"O.K., Mrs. McKellogg," the soldier said.

Then we was gone again. And now I could see Memphis good, bright in the sunshine, while we was swinging around it. And first thing I knowed, we was back on the same highway the bus run on this morning—the patches of stores and them big gins and sawmills, and Memphis running on for miles, it seemed like to me, before it begun to give out. Then we was running again between the fields and woods, running fast now, and except for that soldier, it was like I hadn't never been to Memphis a-tall. We was going fast now. At this rate, before I knowed it we would be home again, and I thought about me riding up to Frenchman's Bend in this big car with a soldier running it, and all of a sudden I begun to cry. I never knowed I was fixing to, and I couldn't stop it. I set there by that soldier, crying. We was going fast.

THE LEADER OF THE PEOPLE

John Steinbeck

On Saturday afternoon Billy Buck, the ranch-hand, raked together the last of the old year's haystack and pitched small forkfuls over the wire fence to a few mildly interested cattle. High in the air small clouds like puffs of cannon smoke were driven eastward by the March wind. The wind could be heard whishing in the brush on the ridge crests, but no breath of it penetrated down into the ranch cup.

The little boy, Jody, emerged from the house eating a thick piece of buttered bread. He saw Billy working on the last of the haystack. Jody tramped down scuffing his shoes in a way he had been told was destructive to good shoe-leather. A flock of white pigeons flew out of the black cypress tree as Jody passed, and circled the tree and landed again. A half-grown tortoise-shell cat leaped from the bunkhouse porch, galloped on stiff legs across the road, whirled and galloped back again. Jody picked up a stone to help the game along, but he was too late, for the cat was under the porch before the stone could be discharged. He threw the stone into the cypress tree and started the white pigeons on another whirling flight.

Arriving at the used-up haystack, the boy leaned against the barbed wire fence. "Will that be all of it, do you think?" he asked.

The middle-aged ranch-hand stopped his careful raking and stuck his fork into the ground. He took off his black hat and smoothed down his hair. "Nothing left to it that isn't soggy from ground moisture," he said. He replaced his hat and rubbed his dry leathery hands together.

"Ought to be plenty mice," Jody suggested.

"Lousy with them," said Billy. "Just crawling with mice."

"Well, maybe, when you get all through, I could call the dogs and hunt the mice."

"Sure, I guess you could," said Billy Buck. He lifted a forkful of the damp ground-hay and threw it into the air. Instantly three mice leaped out and burrowed frantically under the hay again.

Jody sighed with satisfaction. Those plump,

sleek, arrogant mice were doomed. For eight months they had lived and multiplied in the haystack. They had been immune from cats, from traps, from poison and from Jody. They had grown smug in their security, overbearing and fat. Now the time of disaster had come; they would not survive another day.

Billy looked up at the top of the hills that surrounded the ranch. "Maybe you better ask your father before you do it," he suggested.

"Well, where is he? I'll ask him now."

"He rode up to the ridge ranch after dinner. He'll be back pretty soon."

Jody slumped against the fence post. "I don't think he'd care."

As Billy went back to his work he said ominously, "You'd better ask him anyway. You know how he is."

Jody did know. His father, Carl Tiflin, insisted upon giving permission for anything that was done on the ranch, whether it was important or not. Jody sagged farther against the post until he was sitting on the ground. He looked up at the little puffs of wind-driven cloud. "Is it like to rain, Billy?"

"It might. The wind's good for it, but not strong enough."

"Well, I hope it don't rain until after I kill those damn mice." He looked over his shoulder to see whether Billy had noticed the mature profanity. Billy worked on without comment.

Jody turned back and looked at the side-hill where the road from the outside world came down. The hill was washed with lean March sunshine. Silver thistles, blue lupins and a few poppies bloomed among the sage bushes. Halfway up the hill Jody could see Doubletree Mutt, the black dog, digging in a squirrel hole. He paddled for a while and then paused to kick bursts of dirt out between his hind legs, and he dug with an earnestness which belied the knowledge he must have had that no dog had ever caught a squirrel by digging in a hole.

Suddenly, while Jody watched, the black dog stiffened, and backed out of the hole and looked up the hill toward the cleft in the ridge where the road came through. Jody looked up too. For a moment Carl Tiflin on horseback stood out against the pale sky and then he moved down the road toward the house. He carried something white in his hand.

The boy started to his feet. "He's got a letter," Jody cried. He trotted away toward the ranch house, for the letter would probably be read aloud and he wanted to be there. He reached the house before his father did, and ran in. He heard Carl dismount from his creaking saddle and slap the horse on the side to send it to the barn where Billy would unsaddle it and turn it out.

Jody ran into the kitchen. "We got a letter!" he cried.

His mother looked up from a pan of beans. "Who has?"

"Father has. I saw it in his hand."

Carl strode into the kitchen then, and Jody's mother asked, "Who's the letter from, Carl?"

He frowned quickly. "How did you know there was a letter?"

She nodded her head in the boy's direction. "Big-Britches Jody told me."

Jody was embarrassed.

His father looked down at him contemptuously. "He is getting to be a Big-Britches," Carl said. "He's minding everybody's business but his own. Got his big nose into everything."

Mrs. Tiflin relented a little. "Well, he hasn't enough to keep him busy. Who's the letter from?"

Carl frowned on Jody. "I'll keep him busy if he isn't careful." He held out a sealed letter. "I guess it's from your father."

Mrs. Tiflin took a hairpin from her head and slit open the flap. Her lips pursed judiciously. Jody saw her eyes snap back and forth over the lines. "He says," she translated, "he says he's going to drive out Saturday to stay for a little while. Why, this is Saturday. The letter must have been delayed." She looked at the postmark. "This was mailed day before yesterday. It should have been here yesterday." She looked up questioningly at her husband, and then her face darkened angrily. "Now what have you got that look on you for? He doesn't come often."

Carl turned his eyes away from her anger. He could be stern with her most of the time, but when occasionally her temper arose, he could not combat it.

"What's the matter with you?" she demanded again.

In his explanation there was a tone of apology Jody himself might have used. "It's just that he talks," Carl said lamely. "Just talks."

"Well, what of it? You talk yourself."

"Sure I do. But your father only talks about one thing."

"Indians!" Jody broke in excitedly. "Indians and crossing the plains!"

Carl turned fiercely on him. "You get out, Mr. Big-Britches! Go on, now! Get out!"

Jody went miserably out the back door and closed the screen with elaborate quietness. Under the kitchen window his shamed, downcast eyes fell upon a curiously shaped stone, a stone of such fascination that he squatted down and picked it up and turned it over in his hands.

The voices came clearly to him through the open kitchen window. "Jody's damn well right," he heard his father say. "Just Indians and crossing the plains. I've heard that story about how the horses got driven off about a thousand times. He just goes on and on, and he never changes a word in the things he tells."

When Mrs. Tiflin answered her tone was so changed that Jody, outside the window, looked up from his study of the stone. Her voice had become soft and explanatory. Jody knew how her face would have changed to match the tone. She said quietly, "Look at it this way, Carl. That was the big thing in my father's life. He led a wagon train clear across the plains to the coast, and when it was finished, his life was done. It was a big thing to do, but it didn't last long enough. Look!" she continued, "it's as though he was born to do that, and after he finished it, there wasn't anything more for him to do but think about it and talk about it. If there'd been any farther west to go, he'd have gone. He's

told me so himself. But at last there was the ocean. He lives right by the ocean where he had to stop."

She had caught Carl, caught him and entangled him in her soft tone.

"I've seen him," he agreed quietly. "He goes down and stares off west over the ocean." His voice sharpened a little. "And then he goes up to the Horseshoe Club in Pacific Grove, and he tells people how the Indians drove off the horses."

She tried to catch him again. "Well, it's everything to him. You might be patient with him and pretend to listen."

Carl turned impatiently away. "Well, if it gets too bad, I can always go down to the bunkhouse and sit with Billy," he said irritably. He walked through the house and slammed the front door after him.

Jody ran to his chores. He dumped the grain to the chickens without chasing any of them. He gathered the eggs from the nests. He trotted into the house with the wood and interlaced it so carefully in the wood-box that two armloads seemed to fill it to overflowing.

His mother had finished the beans by now. She stirred up the fire and brushed off the stove-top with a turkey wing. Jody peered cautiously at her to see whether any rancor toward him remained. "Is he coming today?" Jody asked.

"That's what his letter said."

"Maybe I better walk up the road to meet him."

Mrs. Tiflin clanged the stove-lid shut. "That would be nice," she said. "He'd probably like to be met."

"I guess I'll just do it then."

Outside, Jody whistled shrilly to the dogs. "Come on up the hill," he commanded. The two dogs waved their tails and ran ahead. Along the roadside the sage had tender new tips. Jody tore off some pieces and rubbed them on his hands until the air was filled with the sharp wild smell. With a rush the dogs leaped from the road and yapped into the brush after a rabbit. That was the last Jody saw of them, for when they failed to catch the rabbit, they went back home.

Jody plodded on up the hill toward the ridge top. When he reached the little cleft where the road came through, the afternoon wind struck him and blew up his hair and ruffled his shirt. He looked down on the little hills and ridges below and then out at the huge green Salinas Valley. He could see the white town of Salinas far out in the flat and the flash of its windows under the waning sun. Directly below him, in an oak tree, a crow congress had convened. The tree was black with crows all cawing at once.

Then Jody's eyes followed the wagon road down from the ridge where he stood, and lost it behind a hill, and picked it up again on the other side. On that distant stretch he saw a cart slowly pulled by a bay horse. It disappeared behind the hill. Jody sat down on the ground and watched the place where the cart would re-appear again. The wind sang on the hilltops and the puff-ball clouds hurried eastward.

Then the cart came into sight and stopped. A man dressed in black dismounted from the seat and walked to the horse's head. Although it was so far away, Jody knew he had unhooked the check-rein, for the horse's head dropped forward. The horse moved on, and the man walked slowly up the hill beside it. Jody gave a glad cry and ran down the road toward them. The squirrels bumped along off the road, and a roadrunner flirted its tail and raced over the edge of the hill and sailed out like a glider.

Jody tried to leap into the middle of his shadow at every step. A stone rolled under his foot and he went down. Around a little bend he raced, and there, a short distance ahead, were his grandfather and the cart. The boy dropped from his unseemly running and approached at a dignified walk.

The horse plodded stumble-footedly up the hill and the old man walked beside it. In the lowering sun their giant shadows flickered darkly behind them. The grandfather was dressed in a black broadcloth suit and he wore kid congress gaiters and a black tie on a short, hard collar. He carried his black slouch hat in his hand. His white beard was cropped close and his white eyebrows overhung his eyes like moustaches. The blue eyes were sternly merry. About the whole face and figure there was a granite dignity, so that every motion seemed an impossible thing. Once at rest, it seemed the old man would be stone, would never move again. His steps were slow and certain. Once made, no step could ever be retraced; once headed in a direction, the path would never bend nor the pace increase nor slow.

When Jody appeared around the bend, Grandfather waved his hat slowly in welcome, and he called, "Why, Jody! Come down to meet me, have you?"

Jody sidled near and turned and matched his step to the old man's step and stiffened his body and dragged his heels a little. "Yes, sir," he said. "We got your letter only today."

"Should have been here yesterday," said Grandfather. "It certainly should. How are all the folks?"

"They're fine, sir." He hesitated and then suggested shyly, "Would you like to come on a mouse hunt tomorrow, sir?"

"Mouse hunt, Jody?" Grandfather chuckled. "Have the people of this generation come down to hunting mice? They aren't very strong, the new people, but I hardly thought mice would be game for them."

"No, sir. It's just play. The haystack's gone. I'm going to drive out the mice to the dogs. And you can watch, or even beat the hay a little."

The stern, merry eyes turned down on him. "I see. You don't eat them, then. You haven't come to that yet."

Jody explained. "The dogs eat them, sir. It wouldn't be much like hunting Indians, I guess."

"No, not much—but then later, when the troops were hunting Indians and shooting children and burning teepees, it wasn't much different from your mouse hunt."

They topped the rise and started down into the ranch cup, and they lost the sun from their shoulders. "You've grown," Grandfather said.

"Nearly an inch, I should say."

"More," Jody boasted. "Where they mark me on the door, I'm up more than an inch since Thanksgiving even."

Grandfather's rich throaty voice said, "Maybe you're getting too much water and turning to pith and stalk. Wait until you head out, and then we'll see."

Jody looked quickly into the old man's face to see whether his feelings should be hurt, but there was no will to injure, no punishing nor putting-in-your-place light in the keen blue eyes. "We might kill a pig," Jody suggested.

"Oh, no! I couldn't let you do that. You're just humoring me. It isn't the time and you know it."

"You know Riley, the big boar, sir?"

"Yes, I remember Riley well."

"Well, Riley ate a hole into that same hay-stack, and it fell down on him and smothered him."

"Pigs do that when they can," said Grandfather.

"Riley was a nice pig, for a boar, sir. I rode him sometimes, and he didn't mind."

A door slammed at the house below them, and they saw Jody's mother standing on the porch waving her apron in welcome. And they saw Carl Tiflin walking up from the barn to be at the house for the arrival.

The sun had disappeared from the hills by now. The blue smoke from the house chimney hung in flat layers in the purpling ranch cup. The puff-ball clouds, dropped by the falling wind, hung listlessly in the sky.

Billy Buck came out of the bunkhouse and flung a wash basin of soapy water on the ground. He had been shaving in mid-week, for Billy held Grandfather in reverence, and Grandfather said that Billy was one of the few men of the new generation who had not gone soft. Although Billy was in middle age, Grandfather considered him a boy. Now Billy was hurrying toward the house too.

When Jody and Grandfather arrived, the three were waiting for them in front of the yard gate.

Carl said, "Hello, sir. We've been looking for you."

Mrs. Tiflin kissed Grandfather on the side of his beard, and stood still while his big hand patted her shoulder. Billy shook hands solemnly, grinning under his straw moustache. "I'll put up your horse," said Billy, and he led the rig away.

Grandfather watched him go, and then, turning back to the group, he said as he had said a hundred times before, "There's a good boy. I knew his father, old Mule-tail Buck. I never knew why they called him Mule-tail except he packed mules."

Mrs. Tiflin turned and led the way into the house. "How long are you going to stay, Father? Your letter didn't say."

"Well, I don't know. I thought I'd stay about two weeks. But I never stay as long as I think I'm going to."

In a short while they were sitting at the white oilcloth table eating their supper. The lamp with the tin reflector hung over the table. Outside the dining-room windows the big moths battered softly against the glass.

Grandfather cut his steak into tiny pieces and chewed slowly. "I'm hungry," he said. "Driving out here got my appetite up. It's like when we were crossing. We all got so hungry every night we could hardly wait to let the meat get done. I could eat about five pounds of buffalo meat every night."

"It's moving around does it," said Billy. "My father was a government packer. I helped him when I was a kid. Just the two of us could about clean up a deer's ham."

"I knew your father, Billy," said Grandfather. "A fine man he was. They called him Mule-tail Buck. I don't know why except he packed mules."

"That was it," Billy agreed. "He packed mules."

Grandfather put down his knife and fork and looked around the table. "I remember one time we ran out of meat——" His voice dropped to a curious low sing-song, dropped into a tonal groove the story had worn for itself. "There was no buffalo, no antelope, not even rabbits. The hunters couldn't even shoot a coyote. That was the time for the leader to be on the watch. I was the leader, and I kept my eyes open. Know why? Well, just the minute the people began to get hungry they'd start slaughtering the team oxen. Do you believe that? I've heard of parties that just ate up their draft cattle. Started from the middle and worked toward the ends. Finally they'd eat the lead pair, and then the wheelers. The leader of a party had to keep them from doing that."

In some manner a big moth got into the room and circled the hanging kerosene lamp. Billy got up and tried to clap it between his hands. Carl struck with a cupped palm and caught the moth and broke it. He walked to the window and dropped it out.

"As I was saying," Grandfather began again, but Carl interrupted him. "You'd better eat some more meat. All the rest of us are ready for our pudding."

Jody saw a flash of anger in his mother's eyes. Grandfather picked up his knife and fork. "I'm pretty hungry, all right," he said. "I'll tell you about that later."

When supper was over, when the family and Billy Buck sat in front of the fireplace in the other room, Jody anxiously watched Grandfather. He saw the signs he knew. The bearded head leaned forward; the eyes lost their sternness and looked wonderingly into the fire; the big lean fingers laced themselves on the black knees. "I wonder," he began, "I just wonder whether I ever told you how those thieving Piutes drove off thirty-five of our horses."

"I think you did," Carl interrupted. "Wasn't it just before you went up into the Tahoe country?"

Grandfather turned quickly toward his son-in-law. "That's right. I guess I must have told you that story."

"Lots of times," Carl said cruelly, and he avoided his wife's eyes. But he felt the angry eyes on him, and he said, "'Course I'd like to hear it again."

Grandfather looked back at the fire. His fingers unlaced and laced again. Jody knew how he felt, how his insides were collapsed and empty. Hadn't Jody been called a Big-Britches that very afternoon? He rose to heroism and opened himself to the term Big-Britches again. "Tell about Indians," he said softly.

Grandfather's eyes grew stern again. "Boys always want to hear about Indians. It was a job for men, but boys want to hear about it. Well, let's see. Did I ever tell you how I wanted each wagon to carry a long iron plate?"

Everyone but Jody remained silent. Jody said, "No. You didn't."

"Well, when the Indians attacked, we always put the wagons in a circle and fought from between the wheels. I thought that if every wagon carried a long plate with rifle holes, the men could stand the plates on the outside of the wheels when the wagons were in the circle and they would be protected. It would save lives and that would make up for the extra weight of the iron. But of course the party wouldn't do it. No party had done it before and they couldn't see why they should go to the expense. They lived to regret it, too."

Jody looked at his mother, and knew from her expression that she was not listening at all. Carl picked at a callus on his thumb and Billy Buck watched a spider crawling up the wall.

Grandfather's tone dropped into its narrative groove again. Jody knew in advance exactly what words would fall. The story droned on, speeded up for the attack, grew sad over the wounds, struck a dirge at the burials on the great plains. Jody sat quietly watching Grandfather. The stern blue eyes were detached. He looked as though he were not very interested in the story himself.

When it was finished, when the pause had been politely respected as the frontier of the story, Billy Buck stood up and stretched and hitched his trousers. "I guess I'll turn in," he said. Then he faced Grandfather. "I've got an old powder horn and a cap and ball pistol down to the bunkhouse. Did I ever show them to you?"

Grandfather nodded slowly. "Yes, I think you did, Billy. Reminds me of a pistol I had when I was leading the people across." Billy stood politely until the little story was done, and then he said, "Good night," and went out of the house.

Carl Tiflin tried to turn the conversation then. "How's the country between here and Monterey? I've heard it's pretty dry."

"It is dry," said Grandfather. "There's not a drop of water in the Laguna Seca. But it's a long pull from '87. The whole country was powder then, and in '61 I believe all the coyotes starved to death. We had fifteen inches of rain this year."

"Yes, but it all came too early. We could do with some now." Carl's eye fell on Jody. "Hadn't you better be getting to bed?"

Jody stood up obediently. "Can I kill the mice in the old haystack, sir?"

"Mice? Oh! Sure, kill them all off. Billy said there isn't any good hay left."

Jody exchanged a secret and satisfying look with Grandfather. "I'll kill every one tomorrow," he promised.

Jody lay in his bed and thought of the impossible world of Indians and buffaloes, a world that had ceased to be forever. He wished he could have been living in the heroic time, but he knew he was not of heroic timber. No one living now, save possibly Billy Buck, was worthy to do the things that had been done. A race of giants had lived then, fearless men, men of a staunchness unknown in this day. Jody thought of the wide plains and of the wagons moving across like centipedes. He thought of Grandfather on a huge white horse, marshaling the people. Across his mind marched the great phantoms and they marched off the earth and they were gone.

He came back to the ranch for a moment, then. He heard the dull rushing sound that space and silence make. He heard one of the dogs, out in the doghouse, scratching a flea and bumping his elbow against the floor with every

stroke. Then the wind arose again and the black cypress groaned and Jody went to sleep.

He was up half an hour before the triangle sounded for breakfast. His mother was rattling the stove to make the flames roar when Jody went through the kitchen. "You're up early," she said. "Where are you going?"

"Out to get a good stick. We're going to kill the mice today."

"Who is 'we'?"

"Why, Grandfather and I."

"So you've got him in it. You always like to have someone in with you in case there's blame to share."

"I'll be right back," said Jody. "I just want to have a good stick ready for after breakfast."

He closed the screen door after him and went out into the cool blue morning. The birds were noisy in the dawn and the ranch cats came down from the hill like blunt snakes. They had been hunting gophers in the dark, and although the four cats were full of gopher meat, they sat in a semi-circle at the back door and mewed piteously for milk. Doubletree Mutt and Smasher moved sniffing along the edge of the brush, performing the duty with rigid ceremony, but when Jody whistled, their heads jerked up and their tails waved. They plunged down to him wriggling their skins and yawning. Jody patted their heads seriously, and moved on to the weathered scrap pile. He selected an old broom handle and a short piece of inch-square scrap wood. From his pocket he took a shoelace and tied the ends of the sticks loosely together to make a flail. He whistled his new weapon through the air and struck the ground experimentally, while the dogs leaped aside and whined with apprehension.

Jody turned and started down past the house toward the old haystack ground to look over the field of slaughter, but Billy Buck, sitting patiently on the back steps, called to him, "You better come back. It's only a couple of minutes till breakfast."

Jody changed his course and moved toward the house. He leaned his flail against the steps. "That's to drive the mice out," he said. "I'll bet they're fat. I'll bet they don't know what's going to happen to them today."

"No, nor you either," Billy remarked philosophically, "nor me, nor anyone."

Jody was staggered by this thought. He knew it was true. His imagination twitched away from the mouse hunt. Then his mother came out on the back porch and struck the triangle, and all thoughts fell in a heap.

Grandfather hadn't appeared at the table when they sat down. Billy nodded at his empty chair. "He's all right? He isn't sick?"

"He takes a long time to dress," said Mrs. Tiflin. "He combs his whiskers and rubs up his shoes and brushes his clothes."

Carl scattered sugar on his mush. "A man that's led a wagon train across the plains has got to be pretty careful how he dresses."

Mrs. Tiflin turned on him. "Don't do that, Carl! Please don't!" There was more of threat than of request in her tone. And the threat irritated Carl.

"Well, how many times do I have to listen to the story of the iron plates, and the thirty-five horses? That time's done. Why can't he forget it, now it's done?" He grew angrier while he talked, and his voice rose. "Why does he have to tell them over and over? He came across the plains. All right! Now it's finished. Nobody wants to hear about it over and over."

The door into the kitchen closed softly. The four at the table sat frozen. Carl laid his mush spoon on the table and touched his chin with his fingers.

Then the kitchen door opened and Grandfather walked in. His mouth smiled tightly and his eyes were squinted.

"Good morning," he said, and he sat down and looked at his mush dish.

Carl could not leave it there. "Did—did you hear what I said?"

Grandfather jerked a little nod.

"I don't know what got into me, sir. I didn't mean it. I was just being funny."

Jody glanced in shame at his mother, and he saw that she was looking at Carl, and that she

wasn't breathing. It was an awful thing that he was doing. He was tearing himself to pieces to talk like that. It was a terrible thing to him to retract a word, but to retract it in shame was infinitely worse.

Grandfather looked sidewise. "I'm trying to get right side up," he said gently. "I'm not being mad. I don't mind what you said, but it might be true, and I would mind that."

"It isn't true," said Carl. "I'm not feeling well this morning. I'm sorry I said it."

"Don't be sorry, Carl. An old man doesn't see things sometimes. Maybe you're right. The crossing is finished. Maybe it should be forgotten, now it's done."

Carl got up from the table. "I've had enough to eat. I'm going to work. Take your time, Billy!" He walked quickly out of the dining-room. Billy gulped the rest of his food and followed soon after. But Jody could not leave his chair.

"Won't you tell any more stories?" Jody asked.

"Why, sure I'll tell them, but only when—I'm sure people want to hear them."

"I like to hear them, sir."

"Oh! Of course you do, but you're a little boy. It was a job for men, but only little boys like to hear about it."

Jody got up from his place. "I'll wait outside for you, sir. I've got a good stick for those mice."

He waited by the gate until the old man came out on the porch. "Let's go down and kill the mice now," Jody called.

"I think I'll just sit in the sun, Jody. You go kill the mice."

"You can use my stick if you like."

"No, I'll just sit here a while."

Jody turned disconsolately away, and walked down toward the old haystack. He tried to whip up his enthusiasm with thoughts of the fat juicy mice. He beat the ground with his flail. The dogs coaxed and whined about him, but he could not go. Back at the house he could see Grandfather sitting on the porch, looking small and thin and black.

Jody gave up and went to sit on the steps at

the old man's feet.

"Back already? Did you kill the mice?"

"No, sir. I'll kill them some other day."

The morning flies buzzed close to the ground and the ants dashed about in front of the steps. The heavy smell of sage slipped down the hill. The porch boards grew warm in the sunshine.

Jody hardly knew when Grandfather started to talk. "I shouldn't stay here, feeling the way I do." He examined his strong old hands. "I feel as though the crossing wasn't worth doing." His eyes moved up the side-hill and stopped on a motionless hawk perched on a dead limb. "I tell those old stories, but they're not what I want to tell. I only know how I want people to feel when I tell them.

"It wasn't Indians that were important, nor adventures, nor even getting out here. It was a whole bunch of people made into one big crawling beast. And I was the head. It was westering and westering. Every man wanted something for himself, but the big beast that was all of them wanted only westering. I was the leader, but if I hadn't been there, someone else would have been the head. The thing had to have a head.

"Under the little bushes the shadows were black at white noonday. When we saw the mountains at last, we cried—all of us. But it wasn't getting here that mattered, it was movement and westering.

"We carried life out here and set it down the way those ants carry eggs. And I was the leader. The westering was as big as God, and the slow steps that made the movement piled up and piled up until the continent was crossed.

"Then we came down to the sea, and it was done." He stopped and wiped his eyes until the rims were red. "That's what I should be telling instead of stories."

When Jody spoke, Grandfather started and looked down at him. "Maybe I could lead the people some day," Jody said.

The old man smiled. "There's no place to go. There's the ocean to stop you. There's a line of old men along the shore hating the ocean because it stopped them."

"In boats I might, sir."

"No place to go, Jody. Every place is taken. But that's not the worst—no, not the worst. Westering has died out of the people. Westering isn't a hunger any more. It's all done. Your father is right. It is finished." He laced his fingers on his knee and looked at them.

Jody felt very sad. "If you'd like a glass of lemonade I could make it for you."

Grandfather was about to refuse, and then he saw Jody's face "That would be nice," he said. "Yes, it would be nice to drink a lemonade."

Jody ran into the kitchen where his mother was wiping the last of the breakfast dishes. "Can I have a lemon to make a lemonade for Grandfather?"

His mother mimicked—"And another lemon to make a lemonade for you."

"No, ma'am. I don't want one."

"Jody! You're sick!" Then she stopped suddenly. "Take a lemon out of the cooler," she said softly. "Here, I'll reach the squeezer down to you."

The measure of a man

. . . We get that terrible spate of novels now current in which man is seen specifically and insistently as an ironic biological accident, inadequate, aimless,· meaningless, isolated, inherently evil, thwarted, self-corrupting, morally answerable to no one, clasped in the vise of determinisms economic or biological. . . . A concept of man that views him as not possessing the elements of freedom and self-determination is a concept of something less than man, essentially sub-human—the unman.
— Edmund Fuller

At the base of personality, sheer animal faith in life makes us affirm life. There is always a pistol or a bottle of sleeping pills, but we vote to wake tomorrow and cultivate our garden. Indeed, the affirmation is deeper than personality, for the body has a wisdom that resides in the nerves, the muscles, the very cells. They go on performing their function till death comes. Their function is the maintenance and renewal of human life. So is ours.
— Bernard DeVoto

Dr. Stockman: It means, my dear, that we are all alone . . . and the strong must learn to be lonely.
— Henrik Ibsen

HOBO

Carl Sandburg

I had my bitter and lonely hours moving out of boy years into a grown young man. I can remember a winter when the thought came often that it might be best to step out of it all. The second thought came, "What would be the best way?"

I had read in detective stories how prussic acid gives death in an eyeblink but I didn't know a doctor who would give me a prescription for it. "Rough on Rats" and carbolic acid were the only poisons I could think of and they would mean you wriggled and moaned with the pains and twists of dying. A revolver bullet through the head, that was clumsy to think about. To hang myself I would have to get a strong rope, find a place to fasten it, fix a box to stand on, kick the box loose and then drop. And it might be that while strangling my tongue would slide over my underlip and when they found me I would be too ugly a sight to think about. You have to work at several chores to hang yourself. It is more bother than any other way of killing yourself. I could throw myself into Lake George but I couldn't be sure but that I would swim to the bank and live on. The handiest way of all, I decided, would be what as kids we had talked of when there had been that suicide on Berrien Street—to stand in front of the Q. Fast Mail train and the *Evening Mail* would have a headline "Sandburg Boy Killed by Train" and it would look like an accident and no disgrace to the family.

After thinking about these different ways of doing away with myself, I would come out actually feeling a little cheerful. The idea came to me like a dawning, "If death is what you want all you have to do is to live on and it will come to you like a nice surprise you never imagined."

After that winter the bitter and lonely hours still kept coming at times, but I had been moving in a slow way to see that to all the best men and women I had known in my life and especially all the great ones that I had read about, life wasn't easy, life had often its bitter and lonely hours, and when you grow with new strengths of body and mind it is by struggle. I was through with *Tom the Bootblack*, *From Rags to Riches*, and all the books by Horatio Alger. Every one of his heroes had a streak of luck. There was a runaway horse and the hero saved a rich man's daughter by risking *his* life to grab the reins and save *her* life. He married the daughter and from then on life was peaches and cream for him.

There was such a thing as luck in life but if the luck didn't come your way it was up to you to step into struggle and like it. I was beginning to see some light. I read Ouida's *Under Two Flags*. The hero lost everything he had except a horse, lived a dirty and bloody life as a fighting man, with never a whimper. I read Olive Schreiner's *The Story of an African Farm*, sad lives on nearly every page, and yet a low music of singing stars and love too deep to ever be lost. I believed there were lives far more bitter and lonely than mine and they had fixed stars, dreams and moonsheens, hopes and mysteries, worth looking at during their struggles. I was groping. I was to go on groping. I read a definition that had won a prize: "Pluck is fighting with the scabbard when the sword is gone." I couldn't see it as a prize-winner. I preferred the hero who cried, "We'll fight till hell freezes over and then we'll fight on the ice!" That, if it didn't make sense, at least gave you a laugh.

I was nineteen years old, weighed one hundred and forty-two pounds, nearly a grown man. And I was restless. The jobs I had worked at all seemed dead-end with no future that called to me. Other boys were handy with girls and I had never found a "steady." Among the boys I could hold my own. With the girls I was bashful and couldn't think of what to say till after I left them, and then wasn't sure.

I read about the Spanish General Weyler and his cruelties with the people of Cuba who wanted independence and a republic. I read about Gomez, Garcia, the Maceos, with their scrabbling little armies fighting against Weyler. They became heroes to me. I tried to figure a way to get down there and join one of those armies. I would have signed up with any recruiting agent who could have got me down there. I believed I would have made a fair soldier in one of their armies. Nothing came of this hope.

What came over me in those years 1896 and 1897 wouldn't be easy to tell. I hated my home town and yet I loved it. And I hated and loved myself about the same as I did the town and the people. I knew then as I know now that it was a pretty good home town to grow up in. I came to see that my trouble was inside of myself more than it was in the town and the people.

I decided in June of 1897 to head west and work in the Kansas wheat harvest. I would beat my way on the railroads and see what happened. I would be a hobo and a "gaycat." I had talked with hoboes enough to know there is the professional tramp who never works and the gaycat who hunts work and hopes to go on and get a job that suits him. I would take my chances on breaking away from my home town where I knew every street and people in every block and farmers on every edge of the town.

. . . I would take to The Road, see rivers and mountains, every day meeting strangers to whom I was one more young stranger. The family didn't like the idea. Papa scowled. Mama kissed me and her eyes had tears after dinner

one noon when I walked out of the house with my hands free, no bag or bundle, wearing a black-sateen shirt, coat, vest, and pants, a slouch hat, good shoes and socks, no underwear, in my pockets a small bar of soap, a razor, a comb, a pocket mirror, two handkerchiefs, a piece of string, needles and thread, a Waterbury watch, a knife, a pipe and a sack of tobacco, three dollars and twenty-five cents in cash.

It was the last week in June, an afternoon bright and cool. A little west of the Santa Fe station stood a freight train waiting for orders. The conductor came out of the station and waved a yellow flimsy in his hand. As the train started I ran along and jumped into a boxcar. From then on I stood at the open side door, watched the running miles of young corn, reading such station names as Cameron and Stronghurst, names of villages and towns I had heard a thousand times and had never had sight of. Crossing the long bridge over the Mississippi my eyes swept over it with a sharp hunger that the grand old river satisfied. Except for my father, when riding to Kansas to buy land, no one of our family had seen the Father of Waters. As the train slowed down in Fort Madison, I jumped out and walked along saying, "Now I am in Iowa, the Hawkeye State, my first time off the soil of Illinois, the Sucker State." Never having seen a penitentiary, inside or out, I walked for a look at it, saw the guards in their towers, saw the high stone walls blank and dumb except for saying, "Here we hold, where they can't get away, the thieves and murderers caught in Iowa."

I bought a nickel's worth of cheese and crackers and sat eating and looking across the Father of Waters. The captain of a small steamboat said I could work passage to Keokuk unloading kegs of nails. I slept on the boat, had breakfast, sailed down the river watching fields and towns go by, at Burlington, Quincy, and Keokuk shouldering kegs of nails to the wharves. At Keokuk I spread newspapers on green grass near a canal, and with coat over shoulders, slept in the open with my left arm for a pillow.

I washed face and hands at the canal, using soap from my pocket and drying with a handkerchief. Then I met a fellow who said, "On the road?" I said "Yes." He led me to where he had been eating bread and meat unwrapped from a newspaper. "I got three lumps last night," he said, and handed me a lump for myself. A lump was what they handed you if they wanted to give you something to eat at a house where you asked for it. My new friend said, "I got a sitdown before I got the lumps." At one house he had been asked to sit at the kitchen table and eat. That was a sitdown. Then because he wanted to spend this day free to look at the canal and the blue sky, he went from house to house for lumps, hiding them under wooden sidewalks so his hands were empty. "At the last house," he said, "they offered me a sitdown and I couldn't tell them my belly was full but would they please wrap it up."

The lump he gave me had four slices of buttered bread and two thick cuts of roast beef. "This is breakfast and dinner for me," I said. "You're a good sport." He said, "I'm hoppin a freight for St. Louis tonight. I always feed good there."

He was long-boned. His flesh seemed to hang on his bones, his cheeks loose and his wide mouth loose-lipped. His face and hands were pudgy as though your fingers would sink into them if you touched them. "I'm a Noo Yawkah," he said. He had come out of a Brooklyn orphan asylum, had taken to The Road, and said he had never done a day's work in his life. He was proud he had never worked and had found a way to live without working. "The real tramp can't even think about work," he said, "and it gives him a pain in the ass to talk about it." He named Cincinnati Slim and Chicago Red and other professional tramps he had traveled with, mentioning them as though they were big names known to all tramps and I must have heard of them. He named towns where the jail food was good and how in the winter he would get a two or three months' sentence for vagrancy in those jails. "Or I might go South

for the cold weather," he said, "keeping away from the towns where they're horstyle." So now I had learned that where they are hostile they are "horstyle" in tramp talk and it has nothing to do with horses. . . .

Two policemen on Main Street looked me over from hat to shoes and I felt safe. During a heavy rainstorm that night I slept in the dry cellar of a house the carpenters hadn't finished and I was up and out before they came to work. I had a fifteen-cent breakfast, found an old tomato can, bought a cheap brush, had the can filled with asphaltum for a few nickels. Then I went from house to house in several blocks and got three jobs that day blacking stoves that were rusty, getting me seventy-five cents, and two jobs where my pay was dinner and supper. I slept again in the house the carpenters hadn't finished and the next day went from house to house and got no jobs with pay brushing asphaltum on rusty stoves, though I did get breakfast, dinner, and supper for three jobs. The next day I bought a refill of asphaltum, earned three meals and twenty-five cents. The next day was the same as the day before. I found that the housewives were much like those for whom I had poured milk in Galesburg. I found too that if I said I was hoping to earn money to go to college they were more ready to help me. The trouble was there were not enough rusty stoves.

The next day was the Fourth of July, with crowds pouring into Keokuk. I saw a sign "Waiter Wanted" in a small lunch counter near the end of Main Street. The owner was running the place by himself. He said I could make myself useful at fifty cents a day and meals. He showed me the eggs, lard, and frying pan, the buns and ham for sandwiches, the doughnuts and the coffeepot. Soon he went out, telling me I was in charge of the place and to be polite serving customers. This was ten o'clock in the morning. Three or four people drifted in before eleven-thirty, when he came back, feeling good, he said, and he would help through the noon rush. Five or six customers came in the next two hours and he sat in a quiet corner taking a sleep while I handled the trade. There were not more than two customers at any one time and I flourished around, got them what they called for on our plain and simple bill of fare. I felt important. Maybe after a while I might work up to be a partner in the business. I ate a ham sandwich with two fried eggs and coffee.

The owner woke up and went out saying he would be back soon. Three o'clock and he came in feeling better than the last time he came in. He had forgotten to eat at noon and there being no customers around, I offered to fix him two fried eggs, which I served him with a bun and coffee. He went out saying he would be back soon. I served two customers while he was gone. Five o'clock and he came back "stewed to the gills," slumped himself in a corner on the floor, and went to sleep. I fried myself three eggs and ate them with two buns and coffee. I fixed two sandwiches with thick cuts of ham, put them in my coat pockets along with two doughnuts, opened the money drawer and took out a half-dollar. With my coat on one arm, I closed the front door softly, and that night slept in a boxcar that took me halfway across the State of Missouri. For a poor boy seeking his fortune I hadn't done so bad for one day. And the next two weeks I wouldn't do so good in any one day.

Next was the railroad section gang at Bean Lake, Missouri. My Irish boss, Fay Connors, hired me at a dollar and twenty-five cents a day and I was to pay him three dollars a week for board and room in his four-room one-story house thirty feet from the railroad tracks. There were five of us in the gang and you would have known Connors was the boss. He liked his voice and his authority. At no time did he get mad and bawl out a man, but he had a frozen-faced way of letting men know he was once a section *hand* and was now a section *boss*. The one time I saw a tool in his hand was when he wasn't satisfied with the way another man showed me how to tamp a tie. He took the pick and swung it clean and straight, tamping the gravel or rock under

the tie so the bottom under the tie would be tight and not loose. I tamped ties several days from seven till noon, from one till six in the evening. I hadn't trained for it and my muscles ached at night like when I worked in the ice harvest at Galesburg. Then came weed-cutting. We swung our scythes along the right of way, the same motions hour after hour, ten hours a day. So I had to train a new set of muscles and *they* ached at night. On Sunday I washed my shirt and socks.

At morning, noon, and evening, the meals at the table in the Connors house were the same, fried side pork, fried potatoes, and coffee. Connors seemed to like it. So did his wife and the three small children. I hoped for some greens, for pork chops instead of side pork, for an egg or two, for one change to beef or lamb stew. At the end of two weeks, on a Sunday morning, I hopped a freight for Kansas City and left Boss Connors to collect for my board and room out of my paycheck. The rest of the pay was still owing and was never collected. If Connors did get it he couldn't have sent it to me, as he didn't know my address and I wasn't expecting to have any address for weeks or months.

In Kansas City Mrs. Mullin had a sign in the window of her restaurant on Armour Avenue, "Dishwasher Wanted." She took the sign out when the Swede boy from Illinois made himself at home in the kitchen with the mulatto chef and the one waiter, also a mulatto. I had good times in that kitchen. The chef was fat, jolly, always cheerful. The waiter was handsome, brown-faced, gay, and he could sing. Noontime was the rush hour of the workers from the meat-packing plants near by. It was a fight in that dish trough to get enough dirty dishes cleaned for serving the customers. I swept the eating room morning and afternoon and mopped it on Saturday.

My sleeping place was the end of a hallway with my cot curtained off, and I washed and shaved, using my pocket mirror, at a sink and faucet in the hall. I was tired one morning when I said to the chef, "I don't care whether school keeps or not." I remember the laugh of the chef as he told the waiter, "Gus says he don't care whether school keeps or not," and George the waiter laughed. I was going by the name of Gus Sandburg. Why I changed from Charlie to Gus I don't know. George could sing either old-time songs or late hits. One afternoon he sang a sad song that had me melting. I said, "That's pretty fine, George. It sure gets me." He said, "I'll sing that for a sweet girl tonight and she'll give me anything I ask her for." I believed him. Only a woman with a heart of stone wouldn't soften to the way George sang, I believed. He took a liking to me and would sing again special songs I called for.

I was up at six in the morning and had the eating room swept for customers who began coming in at six-thirty when we opened. I worked every weekday till eight o'clock at night except for an hour or two in the afternoon. I had three good meals a day. The chef would ask me what I wanted and fix it for me as though he was an uncle of mine and nothing was too good for me. I had Sunday off and walked miles around Kansas City comparing it to Galesburg, Peoria, Keokuk, and Chicago.

In a week or so the wheat harvest in western Kansas would be ready. Mrs. Mullin paid me my second week's pay of one dollar and fifty cents. I thanked her and said good-by and saw the sign "Dishwasher Wanted" whisked back into the street window. Shaking hands with George and the chef and saying good-by wasn't so easy. They were goodhearted men who had made everything easier and brighter for me.

I slept two nights in a fifteen-cent second-floor flophouse. Here were forty men all in one room, each with a cot about an arm's length apart from the cots on each side. At any time a near neighbor might be snoring, "sawing wood," and at two or three in the morning there might be a scream from a fellow waking out of a bad dream. I heard one man cursing, whether asleep or awake, cursing people and conditions. Worst of all were the flat brown creepers who could bite into your skin so you were awake on

the instant. They had homes in our blankets. We had no sheets.

I was tempted to spend ten cents for a dish of ice cream. The temptation got the best of me. I ate it in a big place full of gold chairs and mirrors. A diarrhea began. An abscess in the palm of the right hand ached and pained. It had probably started from handling the pick and scythe on the section job. I went to George and the chef at Mrs. Mullin's and told them I couldn't stand a doctor's bill. They sent me to a Catholic hospital. There, with few questions, a doctor had me lay my right hand on the table. He cut in with a knife, took out what was inside the swelling, and I fell to the floor in the first faint of my life. I came to in a second and he washed the hand, bandaged it, and said it would soon be well. I told him the diarrhea had weakened me. A nurse in nun's dress took me to another room, gave me a large spoonful of brown liquid that tasted good and gave me a bottle of it to take away. I guessed she was Spanish from the way she said, "Theez eez varry gooood fawr the di-oh-ree-ah." With her good voice and good heart I could have said, "You are an angel," but I was bashful.

Hopping freight trains on my way west I had one bad afternoon. A shack (hobo for brakeman) had ordered me off an open coal car where I was crouched hiding. When the train started I got on the same car again. The train was running full speed when he climbed down from the car ahead and another shack followed him. He put his face close to mine. "I told you to stay off this train. Now you'll come through with two bits or you'll take what you get." It was my first time with a shack of that kind. I took it that I might owe the railroad money for fare but he wasn't a passenger-fare collector. So I didn't come through with two bits. He outweighed me by forty pounds and when his right fist landed on my left jaw and his left fist slammed into my mouth I went to the floor. I slowly sat up and looked up toward him. He was snarling, "Stay where you are or you'll get more." Then as he and his partner turned to go he gave me a last look and laughed, "You can ride, you've earned it." He was the kind of shack who was surprised at a later time when the I.W.W. Wobblies took over trains, ganged up on him, and gave him the kind of bleeding mouth he handed me. I met brakemen who were not small-time grafters. One who spotted me in a boxcar corner said, "If you're goin to ride, keep out of sight."

I stood up and watched the passing land. The trees were few, no such timbers as in Illinois and Missouri. I had come to the Great Plains. I was traveling, though my handkerchief was splotched red from putting it to my mouth. When the train slowed down I got off and found myself at a hobo jungle, two men leaving to catch the train I had quit, two more washing their shirts in a shallow creek shaded by three cottonwood trees. I washed my shirt, socks, and handkerchief. The two men were gaycats, said they had spent their last nickel for a loaf of bread and a half-pound of Java and could I scrape the nickels for a few weenies? I said fair enough and went for the weenies and we ate well. I caught a freight that night that had me in Emporia, where I walked past the office of the *Emporia Gazette* but didn't have the nerve to step in and ask the editor, William Allen White, how he came to write "What's the Matter with Kansas?" I didn't agree with it but I liked his style. After a big two-bit meal I went to the city park, where I lay on the grass for a sleep and then talked with two men who got me to singing for them. It turned out they were professional tramps. They wanted me to go along with them. They were sure I could make money singing in saloons. They had the idea we would all share in the money so made. It seemed a little queer to me.

That night a bright full moon was up in a clear sky and out past the Santa Fe water tank waiting their chances to catch a freight train west was a gay bunch of eight men. One of them, a big husky, had a black eye from a fight with a shack and he was sure he had blacked the shack's eye. We told stories. The best-dressed man in the bunch had a bundle under one arm and had a laugh that said he could take care of himself. He told about a hobo at a back door asking a hatchet-faced woman for something to eat because he hadn't had a bite of food for two days. The woman said she would get him something. He waited. The door opened and the woman's skinny hand went toward him with a thin dry crust of bread in it as she said, "I give you this not for your sake nor for my sake but for Christ's sake." As he took the crust of bread and looked at it he turned his face toward her face and said, "Lady, listen to me. I beg of you not for my sake nor for your sake but for Christ's sake, put some butter on it!" Another of the bunch told about a Missouri boy who hadn't had much bringing-up. A woman at a back door had a pan of fresh doughnuts. She said, "Would you like a couple of these?" as she handed him two, and he busted out, "Missus, I could eat a thousand of them goddam things!" They seemed to be a keen and clean lot of travelers in the moonlight there that night, most of them heading toward the wheat harvest.

In a windy rain I jumped out of a boxcar and found a sleeping place under a loading platform for stock cars. About seven o'clock in the morning I read the station sign and learned I was in Hutchinson, Kansas. I had heard it was better not to hit the houses near the railroad. They had been hit too often by 'boes. I walked eight or ten blocks and hit two houses. "Have you got any work I can do for breakfast?" They took one look at me and shut the door. At the third house a woman sent her daughter to get me a saw, showed me a woodpile and a sawbuck. For an hour I kept the saw going, piled the wood, and went to the house. The smiling mother and daughter led me to the family table, set fried ham and potatoes, apple sauce, bread and coffee, before me. After I had eaten they handed me a large lump. I thanked them forty ways, walked Main Street to see what Hutchinson was like, and went on to my loading platform. Unwrapping the lump, I found fried chicken and bread that would make dinner and supper, along with two pocketfuls of apples that had come down in the wind and rain the night before.

I tried to get acquainted with a fellow I had seen at the other end of the platform in the early morning. What few words I could get out of him were German. He seemed about sixty years old, hump-shouldered, with a gray scraggly beard. He sat cross-legged for hours looking straight ahead of him. He had a neat bundle at his side and would put his hand on it once in a while to make sure it was there. His clothes were neat and clean. I asked him, "Which way you going?" and "How long you been here?" At each question he turned his head and gave me a slow look in the eye and turned his head back to go on looking at nothing straight ahead of him. At noon he slowly opened his bundle and took out a loaf of rye bread, cheese, and baloney. He slowly munched, looking straight ahead at nothing in particular. I held toward him a small piece of fried chicken and the look he gave me was as though the chicken might be poisoned.

He took out a New Testament in German type and read for a time while I smoked a pipe and read the two newspapers I had picked up on Main Street. There was plenty to talk about but I couldn't get him started. It could have been that he had secret sorrows and he was nursing them as he sat looking straight ahead. He couldn't have been sick or he wouldn't have chewed, smacked, and enjoyed his rye bread, cheese, and baloney. When I brought him a can of water from the station pump and drank of it before his very eyes, he did reach out and give himself a drink of it, but not a word from him nor a look of the eye saying thanks, it was good water I brought him. When I caught a late-afternoon freight he didn't return my wave to him from the train. He still sat on that loading platform looking straight ahead of him, a human sphinx shrouded in his personal secret sorrows. I did my imagining about what loves, hates, or murders might have made him crawl into an impregnable silence where he defied any shafts of laughter to break through his armor.

Lindsborg, Kansas, was Swedish, and Pastor Swenson, the head of Bethany College there, was a Lutheran Synod leader I had heard preach in Galesburg. It was either hay or broomcorn harvest I worked in with other Swedes on a farm near Lindsborg. I stayed three days at a dollar a day and meals, sleeping in a barn hayloft. On my third and last morning I had been awake a few minutes when I heard voices down below. One voice came clear to me, a Swede saying, "Is that *bum* up yet?" I said to myself, "Am I a bum?" And I answered, "Yes, I am a bum." I had bummed my way to Lindsborg. I had no baggage nor bundle and I expected to bum my way on a train out of Lindsborg. The first time in my life that I heard myself referred to as a bum was among Swedes I had made a detour to see. I wouldn't have expected him to say, "Is that young stranger up yet?" but he could have said, "Is that Swede from Illinois up yet?" To him I was a bum and he was giving me no such hand of fellowship as George or the chef in the Kansas City Kitchen.

Newspapers said the country was pulling out of the Hard Times, more factory chimneys smoking, the full dinner pail and the promised McKinley prosperity on the way. Yet there were still many men out of work, many men who had left their homes hoping for jobs somewhere. You could see these men riding the boxcars and sitting around the jungle hangouts. Some had learned hobo slang. Some didn't care for it. There was always a small fraternity who knew each other at once by their slang. They were professional tramps, who divided into panhandlers and petty thieves. I heard panhandlers talk about "how to work Main Street," what kind of faces to ask for a dime or a quarter. "Never mooch a goof wearing a red necktie," I heard. Panhandlers would argue about the best story to melt the heart of the citizen you walked along with on Main Street.

"I'm lookin for work and haven't had anything to eat for two days, and I've just had a letter my wife and two children are sick at home," takes longer and makes the citizen more suspicious than if you say, "I have to eat, could you spare a dime for a cup of coffee?" The longer you make your story, the more is the danger of the citizen asking you questions and while you are answering maybe a cop comes along "and he sees you're a vag and jugs you."

The petty thieves did less talking. The only one who got confidential with me wore a good brown suit, a brown shirt with a brown necktie. His face and mustache were like the pictures of the hero in the *Family Story Paper*. His quiet words to me were, "I'm a second-story man. I could use you." He would have me stand on his shoulders and climb up on a porch, go through a window, and search for money and jewels we would split. He hadn't been doing so well lately but he had seen many good times and they would come again. He would find girls to travel with us, he had a way with women, he said. He had a soft voice. He was polite, I told him I would think about it. I managed to get away from him without telling him what I thought about it. . . .

I was meeting fellow travelers and fellow Americans. What they were doing to my heart and mind, my personality, I couldn't say then nor later and be certain. I was getting a deeper self-respect that I had had in Galesburg, so much I knew. I was getting to be a better storyteller. You can be loose and easy when from day to day you meet strangers you will know only an hour or a day or two. What girls I was meeting on a job or at a sitdown usually wanted to know where I was from, where I was going, what kind of a home and folks I had, and I was working out of my bashfulness. Sometimes I spread it on a little thick about what a good home and education I had. They liked it when I said I would yet be going to college, though in my own mind I hadn't the slightest idea of how, where, and when I would go to college. But if a young stranger mentioned that he wanted to go to college, it gave the girls and women a higher opinion of the young stranger in their midst.

On one boxcar ride there was a young farm hand from Indiana of my own age. He had a face and a way of talking I liked so much that I asked him how it would be for the two of us to travel together and share and share alike for a few weeks. He said he would shake hands on that if I would go with him to the Klondike. The gold rush was on and he was heading for Alaska. He had expected to stop for the Kansas wheat harvest and earn money he needed but now he figured that might make him a little late in getting to the Chilkoot Pass and the gold waiting for the early ones. We were sorry to part. He reminded me of my brother Emil. He is one of those misty figures in memory that have you saying, "I wonder what ever became of him."

In one jungle was a little fellow in his middle forties who said that every summer he would break away from Chicago and take to the road, working now and then. "What I like," he said, "is to sleep under the stars. Do yuh know the stars is a great study? I never read a book about the stars but I never get tired of lookin at 'em and watchin how they move and change. The stars make me feel that whatever is wrong with the world or with me sometime is going to be made right. The stars is the only book I read." He had a question he said kept bothering his brain: "Why does God make it rain on the ocean where there is plenty of water and not on the desert where the rain is needed?" He wanted more light on that. "I like to watch the workins of my own mind," he said. "The longer I live my mind gets to be more of a mystery to me."

"Along next October you'll need a benny," I heard in one jungle and learned that a "benny" is an overcoat. "I think I'll try the goat in this town," said one and I learned the goat in a town is the Catholic priest. One fellow saying, "I had a good snooze in a knowledge box last night," meant he had slept in a country schoolhouse. "Have you scoffed?" or "Have you had your scoffins today?" meant "Have you eaten?" or "Have you had your eating today?"

I had bought for a nickel in an old bookshop in Kansas City a small *Cyclopaedia of Useful Information*. Many a time it came in handy to pass the time rambling through facts and figures. On one page there was a poem it said was a favorite of President Abraham Lincoln. As the days passed I learned by heart half the verses, finding that to say them made loneliness less lonely, such verses as:

Oh, why should the spirit of mortal be proud?
Like a swift fleeting meteor, a fast-flying cloud,
A flash of the lightning, a break of the wave,
He passes from life to his rest in the grave. . . .

At Larned, Pawnee County, Kansas, I refused to regard myself as a hobo. My father had owned one quarter section of land in that county which he sold and then bought another quarter section which he sold. My father had set foot in this town when he came to look at the land he bought. I had written for my father the letters sending tax payments to the county treasurer of Pawnee County. When I walked past the courthouse I felt like an important, respectable citizen, even though I was sleeping in empty boxcars that stood on the Santa Fe tracks waiting to be loaded with wheat. You could walk the few blocks of Main Street in about three minutes. You could see empty houses here and there. People had moved away because of conditions, Hard Times. On one corner stood a big ghost hotel empty of travelers, no business, and here and there on Main Street a place where they once were open for customers and now spiders and cobwebs had taken over. The weekly paper was worth reading if only for its name, the *Tillers and Toilers Journal*.

Having promised Vic Lundgren that I would look up his father, I did so, and wrote back to Vic that his father was suspicious of me and didn't care to send back any word to his wife, son, and daughter in Galesburg. I worked at

seventy-five cents a day helping a carpenter for three days. I worked five days with a crew threshing wheat—three days on one farm and two days on another—pitchforking bundles of wheat onto the tables of the thresher. It was hard work but the crew was jolly, the meals and cooking good, the barns clean where four of us slept on hay, the pay a dollar and twenty-five cents a day and board. Then there was to be no more work till five days later. I decided to head west to Lakin, where I heard there was more doing. . . .

At Lakin, Kansas, I noticed on a timetable that I was six hundred and eighty-four miles from Galesburg on the Santa Fe. I figured what with detours I had traveled a thousand miles since I left home. I worked with a threshing crew some three weeks around Lakin. The job finished on one farm, we moved to another farm with a different farmer and family. The work came easier with getting used to it. The dust in your nose and eyes, the chaff sliding down your sweating back, you got used to. One evening at six o'clock the boss said there was only two hours of threshing left and a full moon would be up. We ate supper, at seven went on threshing by the light of a bright full moon, and finished at nine o'clock. At ten o'clock the crew and thresher moved to another farm where we started in at seven in the morning.

A shack put me off the bumpers of a fast freight I caught out of Lakin. When you ride the bumpers you stand on the couplers between two cars and keep a good hold on a brake rod. The shack had leaned down and called, "You get off at the next stop or there'll be trouble." A minute after I got off, who was there but my blue-eyed friend I had chummed with at Larned. It was near midnight. We went to a lunch counter and he insisted on paying. He had a roll of bills. He said, "I'm flush," and he was. I told him I was catching the next freight out if there was an empty boxcar I could sleep in. He walked with me to the water tank, where he pulled from his hip pocket the same revolver he had shown me at Larned. He said, "This gat comes in handy, boy. It saves you a lot of hard work." Then it came out. He was sticking up harvest hands for their money. Once at a water tank and once in a boxcar he had pulled his gat and, "I pushed the gat into his guts and told him to come through with every dollar on him or I'd pull the trigger, and he came through." I had thirty-odd dollars on me and was wondering why he didn't push the gat into my guts. I think I would have come through with my last dollar. I think he still hoped I might buy a gat and go along with him as a partner, something like that. I forget the town where I left him when a freight came along. He said, "I expect some nice pickings here the next two or three days. Maybe I'll be seeing you in Rocky Ford on Melon Day.

Thousands poured into Rocky Ford for the Melon Day celebration. Watermelon and cantaloupe were handed out free to everybody. I rode a crowded passenger train that evening—sitting on a small board over the rods of a truck between the wheels of the train. I changed for a freight train where I had a boxcar sleep and got off in the morning not knowing where I was. I didn't bother to go back and read the station sign. I ate a sandwich as I walked west on the railroad track. The day was sunny and cool. My eyes caught high rises of tumbling land I had never met before. "Jesus," I said, "those are the Rocky Mountains." I hadn't planned it but there they were, rolling formations of rock and pine lifted away high. "There's the Hand of God," I said. I couldn't think of anything before in my life that had me using that phrase, "the Hand of God."

I walked on to Canyon City, took a look at the outside of the state penitentiary and felt good that I wasn't inside. I picked pears, earned meals and a few half-dollars, went on to Salida, where I spent two days. Then I took a Colorado Midland train heading back east aiming for Denver. It was night. There wasn't an empty boxcar on the train, and for the first time I was riding the bumpers late at night. I didn't

know what a stupid reckless fool I was. My feet were on those bumpers and there was no danger in that. My hands were on the brake rod so in case my feet should slip I could hold on and not go under the wheels. Suddenly I was saying to myself, "You damn fool, you've been asleep." My numb brain was saying that when you go to sleep on the bumpers you're in luck if your hands don't loosen and topple you down under the moving train. I would watch myself and not go to sleep again. We had been running along maybe an hour when again I caught myself coming out of a sleep. From then on I wouldn't trust myself to be still for even a second. I kept changing my position. I kept moving my feet and hands. I beat the sides of my head with my fists. I kicked one leg against the other. An hour of that and the train stopped and I got off and thanked God and the everlasting stars over the Rockies. Many a time later I said that the Angel of Death hovered over that train that night and saw me standing and sleeping and brushed past me with soft wing tips saying, "Not yet for this boy. He's young yet. Let him live."

I saw Pikes Peak so I could say I saw it. At the Windsor, a first-class hotel in Denver, I washed dishes two weeks, collected a dollar and fifty cents a week, a cubbyhole for a room and meals as good as were served to the silk-hat guests. Then came the question whether I should head for the West coast or east to Galesburg. I admitted I was a little homesick for the faces and streets of Galesburg. Where a passenger train was on slow speed out of the yards I hopped on the steps of a Pullman vestibule. A conductor and porter ordered me off. I got off and saw the train slow to a stop. I climbed on top of a Pullman car, lay with my head toward the engine, swore a solemn oath I wouldn't go to sleep. The car rocked and shook going around curves and my hands held tight so I wouldn't slide off the roof of the car. It was a cool September night and the train speed made it cold. I still had no underwear. I buttoned my coat, turned the collar up and tied a handkerchief around my neck. I went to sleep twice and coming out of it kept hitting and kicking myself to stay awake.

Daybreak came. An early farmer waved to me and laughed. I saw we were pulling in to a division point, McCook, Nebraska. I climbed down and started to walk out of the yards. A one-eyed man in plain clothes with a club and a star stood in my way. "Where did you come from?" His tone was horstyle. "I just got off that train," I said. He gave me my orders in a more horstyle tone: "We don't want the likes of you in this town. You get back on that train." There were no trainmen in sight as I climbed back to where I had been riding. I had a daylight view of the Nebraska landscape from McCook for thirty miles to the next stop at Oxford. No one was waiting for me at Oxford. I went to a lunch counter, where they let me into the kitchen to wash the cinders and soot out of my head, hair, ears, and neck. Then I ordered a monster breakfast of ham and eggs, fried potatoes, bread, coffee, and two pieces of pie, paying thirty-five cents in cash.

Heading east I stopped three days in a jungle with five good fellows. Shirt, socks, and handkerchiefs got washed. We had several meals of corn we picked from fields near by to roast or boil. One fellow was short and slim with a stoop to his shoulders and thick calluses on his hands. He could talk about hard work he had done, husking corn ten hours a day, driving a coal wagon and unloading the coal with a shovel, driving a team at spring plowing with the leather reins scraping his hands. He said the police took him for questioning in an Iowa city where there had been a burglary. They asked where he had been, where he was going, and "What do you do for a living?" He said, "Any hard work I can get," and showed them the tough leathery insides of his hands. One policeman said, "You can't be much of a thief with those hands," and they let him go.

He was in his middle thirties, had silky red hair, and a freckled face that brightened with crinkles when he talked. He said, "My mother had ten kids, six boys and four girls. The girls turned out good, married and have big families, all the girls but one. She has ways with men, went to Kansas City, paints her face, likes fancy clothes on her back, and we've lost hope of her. The boys turned out good steady workers, only one ever in jail and he broke out and they haven't caught him yet. My mother's father had eight kids and when his wife died at eighty-eight he waited til he was ninety and then had three kids by a half-breed Indian woman he married." The early September night stars were out and the six of us sat around a fire talking after our roast-corn supper. I believed the talk of this horny-handed, freckle-faced redhead. It seemed to me he was remembering the big main points of his family and folks and he talked it as he remembered it. He did more talking about his brothers and their jobs and troubles, about his sisters and their children. He went on remembering and talking what he remembered but only part of it stayed with me.

I was sorry to leave that friendly jungle. I caught a freight that landed me in Nebraska City. I chopped wood and picked apples for two sitdowns. At a large brick house where I chopped wood, the man of the house, a lawyer, seeing my suit of clothes somewhat ragged, asked me if I would like an old suit of his. He brought it out, an iron-gray all-wool suit, better than any I had had in my life. I got into it, thanked him, and offered to chop more wood but he laughed and said I'd better be on my way home. I found myself that night in a boxcar with four others. We spread our newspapers under us, threw our coats over our shoulders, and tried for sleep. The night was clear, cold and frosty. After two hours we were saying, "It's too cold to sleep here tonight." The five of us marched to the city calaboose and asked the marshal to let us in. The cells had the expected stink, but we spread our newspapers on the stone floor, slept warm, and on leaving were told to get out of town that same day.

I caught a freight for Omaha. For years I had been curious about Omaha. And of all interesting city names, is any more musical than Oh-mah-haw? I found Omaha merely smaller than Chicago and bigger than Galesburg. In Omaha, as in Kansas City and Denver, I stood before the United States Army recruiting office and lingered and read many times the pay and the conditions Uncle Sam offers his Regular Army boys. I was interested and came near enlisting. One year of service I could see, or maybe two years, but the required three years had me backing out. I would make my decision, walk away, and come back and read the pay and conditions again the next day and then make the same decision that three years was too long. I had met a Kansas harvest hand who had had three years of it and he said he spent most of his time in the Regular Army cleaning the same horse stables and mowing the same garrison lawns and it got monotonous. "I expected to get to travel," he said, "but about all the travelin I done was with a lawn mower." I thought of him too when I read on the boards the pay and conditions, and walked away.

The Hotel Mercer took me on as dishwasher at a dollar and fifty cents a week. It was a little queer how standard was the wage rate for a dishwasher. It never went as low as a dollar and twenty-five cents a week nor as high as a dollar and seventy-five cents a week. The pastry cook was a sweet Creole girl from New Orleans. The vegetable man, a fast potato-peeler, was John Whitney, and I hope he did well after what came to happen. The hotel was leased and run by a fancily dressed tall man who slid and slunk rather than walked around the place. He was known as Wink Taylor. I didn't notice him wink at any time but he probably had the name because he was quick as a wink. At the end of the first week I didn't get my standard pay of a dollar and fifty cents nor likewise at the end of the second week. Then came the word that the Hotel Mercer was closed, gone up the spout, foreclosed, and Wink Taylor vanished. He owed me three dollars that never got paid. He owed the chambermaids, the dining-room and kitchen hands, what they had

coming, which they never got.

I had one last sleep in the Mercer, crossed over to Council Bluffs and had a breakfast of one pork chop, fried potatoes, and bread and coffee for five cents. Then I caught one freight train after another till I came in sight of Galesburg the afternoon of October fifteenth. I had timed it so that I wouldn't feel on my head the crashing club of the night policeman Richardson, known far and wide as "that goddam nigger bull in Galesburg."

I walked along Berrien Street till I came to the only house in the United States where I could open a door without knocking and walk in for a kiss from the woman of the house. They gave me a sitdown and as they had had only two or three letters from me, they asked me where I had been and I told them the half of it. When I showed my father fifteen dollars and a few nickels, he said the money would come in handy and I should watch it. The clean bed sheets that night were not so bad. Mart was suspicious of my fine suit of clothes the next day. I'll bet you didn't buy it new. If you bought it, it was a hockshop." So I told him. Mart said that along in August he had read in a newspaper about a hobo riding the bumpers in western Kansas who fell off the bumpers and was mangled to death. The folks hadn't read it and he didn't tell them. "But I was afraid, Cully, that maybe it was you." Then I told him about how in Colorado it could have been me and I was a fool.

What had the trip done to me? I couldn't say. It had changed me. I was easier about looking people in the eye. When questions came I was quicker at answering them or turning them off. I had been a young stranger meeting many odd strangers and I had practised at having answers. At home and among my old chums of the Dirty Dozen they knew I had changed but they could no more tell how than I. Away deep in my heart now I had hope as never before. Struggles lay ahead, I was sure, but whatever they were I would not be afraid of them. . . .

THE LAMP AT NOON

Sinclair Ross

A little before noon she lit the lamp. Demented wind fled keening past the house: a wail through the eaves that died every minute or two. Three days now without respite it had held. The dust was thickening to an impenetrable fog.

She lit the lamp, then for a long time stood at the window motionless. In dim, fitful outline the stable and oat granary still were visible; beyond, obscuring fields and landmarks, the lower of dust clouds made the farmyard seem an isolated acre, poised aloft above a sombre void. At each blast of wind it shook, as if to topple and spin hurtling with the dust-reel into space.

From the window she went to the door, opening it a little, and peering toward the stable again. He was not coming yet. As she watched there was a sudden rift overhead, and for a moment through the tattered clouds the sun raced like a wizened orange. It shed a soft, diffused light, dim and yellow as if it were the light from the lamp reaching out through the open door.

She closed the door, and going to the stove tried the potatoes with a fork. Her eyes all the while were fixed and wide with a curious immobility. It was the window. Standing at it, she had let her forehead press against the pane until the eyes were strained apart and rigid. Wide like that they had looked out to the deepening ruin of the storm. Now she could not close them.

The baby started to cry. He was lying in a homemade crib over which she had arranged a tent of muslin. Careful not to disturb the folds of it, she knelt and tried to still him, whispering huskily in a singsong voice that he must hush and go to sleep again. She would have liked to rock him, to feel the comfort of his little body in her arms, but a fear had obsessed her that in the dust-filled air he might contract pneumonia. There was dust sifting everywhere. Her own throat was parched with it. The table had been set less than ten minutes, and already a film was gathering on the dishes. The little cry continued, and with wincing, frightened lips she glanced around as if to find a corner where the air was less oppressive. But while the lips winced the eyes maintained their wide, immobile stare. "Sleep," she whispered again. "It's too soon for you to be hungry. Daddy's coming for his dinner."

He seemed a long time. Even the clock, still a few minutes off noon, could not dispel a foreboding sense that he was longer than he should be. She went to the door again—and then recoiled slowly to stand white and breathless in the middle of the room. She mustn't. He would only despise her if she ran to the stable looking for him. There was too much grim endurance in his nature ever to let him understand the fear and weakness of a woman. She must stay quiet and wait. Nothing was wrong. At noon he would come—and perhaps after dinner stay with her awhile.

Yesterday, and again at breakfast this morning, they had quarrelled bitterly. She wanted him now, the assurance of his strength and nearness, but he would stand aloof, wary, remembering the words she had flung at him in her anger, unable to understand it was only the dust and wind that had driven her.

Tense, she fixed her eyes upon the clock, listening. There were two winds: the wind in flight, and the wind that pursued. The one sought refuge in the eaves, whimpering in fear;

— *"The Lamp at Noon" by Sinclair Ross, from The Lamp at Noon and other stories by Sinclair Ross, McClelland and Stewart, 1967 (originally in the Queen's Quarterly); by permission of the author*

the other assailed it there, and shook the eaves apart to make it flee again. Once as she listened this first wind sprang inside the room, distraught like a bird that has felt the graze of talons on its wing; while furious the other wind shook the walls, and thudded tumbleweeds against the window till its quarry glanced away again in fright. But only to return—to return and quake among the feeble eaves, as if in all this dust-mad wilderness it knew no other sanctuary.

Then Paul came. At his step she hurried to the stove, intent upon the pots and frying-pan. "The worst wind yet," he ventured, hanging up his cap and smock. "I had to light the lantern in the tool shed, too."

They looked at each other, then away. She wanted to go to him, to feel his arms supporting her, to cry a little just that he might soothe her, but because his presence made the menace of the wind seem less, she gripped herself and thought, "I'm in the right. I won't give in. For his sake, too, I won't."

He washed, hurriedly, so that a few dark welts of dust remained to indent upon his face a haggard strength. It was all she could see as she wiped the dishes and set the food before him: the strength, the grimness, the young Paul growing old and hard, buckled against a desert even grimmer than his will. "Hungry?" she asked, touched to a twinge of pity she had not intended. "There's dust in everything. It keeps coming faster than I can clean it up."

He nodded. "Tonight, though, you'll see it go down. This is the third day."

She looked at him in silence a moment, and then as if to herself muttered broodingly, "Until the next time. Until it starts again."

There was a dark resentment in her voice now that boded another quarrel. He waited, his eyes on her dubiously as she mashed a potato with her fork. The lamp between them threw strong lights and shadows on their faces. Dust and drought, earth that betrayed alike his labour and his faith, to him the struggle had given sternness, an impassive courage. Beneath the whip of sand his youth had been effaced. Youth,

zest, exuberance—there remained only a harsh and clenched virility that yet became him, that seemed at the cost of more engaging qualities to be fulfilment of his inmost and essential nature. Whereas to her the same debts and poverty had brought a plaintive indignation, a nervous dread of what was still to come. The eyes were hollowed, the lips pinched dry and colourless. It was the face of a woman that had aged without maturing, that had loved the little vanities of life, and lost them wistfully.

"I'm afraid, Paul," she said suddenly. "I can't stand it any longer. He cries all the time. You will go, Paul—say you will. We aren't living here—not really living—"

The pleading in her voice now, after its shrill bitterness yesterday, made him think that this was only another way to persuade him. He answered evenly, "I told you this morning, Ellen; we keep on right where we are. At least I do. It's yourself you're thinking about, not the baby."

This morning such an accusation would have stung her to rage; now, her voice swift and panting, she pressed on, "Listen, Paul—I'm thinking of all of us—you, too. Look at the sky—what's happening. Are you blind? Thistles and tumbleweeds—it's a desert. You won't have a straw this fall. You won't be able to feed a cow or a chicken. Please, Paul, say we'll go away—"

"Go where?" His voice as he answered was still remote and even, inflexibly in unison with the narrowed eyes and the great hunch of muscle-knotted shoulder. "Even as a desert it's better than sweeping out your father's store and running his errands. That's all I've got ahead of me if I do what you want."

"And here—" she faltered. "What's ahead of you here? At least we'll get enough to eat and wear when you're sweeping out his store. Look at it—look at it, you fool. Desert—the lamp lit at noon—"

"You'll see it come back." "There's good wheat in it yet."

"But in the meantime—year after year—can't you understand, Paul? We'll never get them back—"

He put down his knife and fork and leaned toward her across the table. "I can't go, Ellen. Living off your people—charity—stop and think of it. This is where I belong. I can't do anything else."

"Charity!" she repeated him, letting her voice rise in derision. "And this—you call this independence! Borrowed money you can't even pay the interest on, seed from the government—grocery bills—doctor bills—"

"We'll have crops again," he persisted. "Good crops—the land will come back. It's worth waiting for."

"And while we're waiting, Paul!" It was not anger now, but a kind of sob. "Think of me—and him. It's not fair. We have our lives, too, to live."

"And you think that going home to your family—taking your husband with you—"

"I don't care—anything would be better than this. Look at the air he's breathing. He cries all the time. For his sake, Paul. What's ahead of him here, even if you do get crops?"

He clenched his lips a minute, then, with his eyes hard and contemptuous, struck back, "As much as in town, growing up a pauper. You're the one who wants to go, it's not for his sake. You think that in town you'd have a better time—not so much work—more clothes—"

"Maybe—" She dropped her head defencelessly. "I'm young still. I like pretty things."

There was silence now—a deep fastness of it enclosed by rushing wind and creaking walls. It seemed the yellow lamplight cast a hush upon them. Through the haze of dusty air the walls receded, dimmed, and came again. At last she raised her head and said listlessly, "Go on—your dinner's getting cold. Don't sit and stare at me. I've said it all."

The spent quietness in her voice was even harder to endure than her anger. It reproached him, against his will insisted that he see and understand her lot. To justify himself he tried, "I was a poor man when you married me. You said you didn't mind. Farming's never been

easy, and never will be."

"I wouldn't mind the work or the skimping if there was something to look forward to. It's the hopelessness—going on—watching the land blow away."

"The land's all right," he repeated. "The dry years won't last forever."

"But it's not just dry years, Paul!" The little sob in her voice gave way suddenly to a ring of exasperation. "Will you never see? It's the land itself—the soil. You've plowed and harrowed it until there's not a root or fibre left to hold it down. That's why the soil drifts—that's why in a year or two there'll be nothing left but the bare clay. If in the first place you farmers had taken care of your land—if you hadn't been so greedy for wheat every year—"

She had taught school before she married him, and of late in her anger there had been a kind of disdain, an attitude almost of condescension, as if she no longer looked upon the farmers as her equals. He sat still, his eyes fixed on the yellow lamp flame, and seeming to know how her words had hurt him, she went on softly, "I want to help you, Paul. That's why I won't sit quiet while you go on wasting your life. You're only thirty—you owe it to yourself as well as me."

He sat staring at the lamp without answering, his mouth sullen. It seemed indifference now, as if he were ignoring her, and stung to anger again she cried, "Do you ever think what my life is? Two rooms to live in—once a month to town, and nothing to spend when I get there. I'm still young—I wasn't brought up this way."

"You're a farmer's wife now. It doesn't matter what you used to be, or how you were brought up. You get enough to eat and wear. Just now that's all I can do. I'm not to blame that we've been dried out five years."

"Enough to eat!" she laughed back shrilly. "Enough salt pork—enough potatoes and eggs. And look—" Springing to the middle of the room she thrust out a foot for him to see the scuffed old slipper. "When they're completely gone I suppose you'll tell me I can go barefoot —that I'm a farmer's wife—that it's not your fault we're dried out—"

"And what about these?" He pushed his chair away from the table now to let her see what he was wearing. "Cowhide—hard as boards—but my feet are so calloused I don't feel them any more."

Then he stood up, ashamed of having tried to match her hardships with his own. But frightened now as he reached for his smock she pressed close to him. "Don't go yet. I brood and worry when I'm left alone. Please, Paul— you can't work on the land anyway."

"And keep on like this? You start before I'm through the door. Week in and week out— I've troubles enough of my own."

"Paul—please stay—" The eyes were glazed now, distended a little as if with the intensity of her dread and pleading. "We won't quarrel any more. Hear it! I can't work—I just stand still and listen—"

The eyes frightened him, but responding to a kind of instinct that he must withstand her, that it was his self-respect and manhood against the fretful weakness of a woman, he answered unfeelingly, "In here safe and quiet—you don't know how well off you are. If you were out in it—fighting it—swallowing it—"

"Sometimes, Paul, I wish I was. I'm so caged—if I could only break away and run. See—I stand like this all day. I can't relax. My throat's so tight it aches—"

With a jerk he freed his smock from her clutch. "If I stay we'll only keep on all afternoon. Wait till tomorrow—we'll talk things over when the wind goes down."

Then without meeting her eyes again he swung outside, and doubled low against the buffets of the wind, fought his way slowly toward the stable. There was a deep hollow calm within, a vast darkness engulfed beneath the tides of moaning wind. He stood breathless a moment, hushed almost to a stupor by the sudden extinction of the storm and the stillness that enfolded him. It was a long, far-reaching still-

ness. The first dim stalls and rafters led the way into cavern-like obscurity, into vaults and recesses that extended far beyond the stable walls. Nor in these first quiet moments did he forbid the illusion, the sense of release from a harsh, familiar world into one of peace and darkness. The contentious mood that his stand against Ellen had roused him to, his tenacity and clenched despair before the ravages of wind, it was ebbing now, losing itself in the cover of darkness. Ellen and the wheat seemed remote, unimportant. At a whinny from the bay mare, Bess, he went forward and into her stall. She seemed grateful for his presence, and thrust her nose deep between his arm and body. They stood a long time motionless, comforting and assuring each other.

For soon again the first deep sense of quiet and peace was shrunken to the battered shelter of the stable. Instead of release or escape from the assaulting wind, the walls were but a feeble stand against it. They creaked and sawed as if the fingers of a giant hand were tightening to collapse them; the empty loft sustained a pipe-like cry that rose and fell but never ended. He saw the dust-black sky again, and his fields blown smooth with drifted soil.

But always, even while listening to the storm outside, he could feel the tense and apprehensive stillness of the stable. There was not a hoof that clumped or shifted, not a rub of halter against manger. And yet, though it had been a strange stable, he would have known, despite the darkness, that every stall was filled. They, too, were all listening.

From Bess he went to the big grey gelding, Prince. Prince was twenty years old, with rib-grooved sides, and high, protruding hipbones. Paul ran his hand over the ribs, and felt a sudden shame, a sting of fear that Ellen might be right in what she said. For wasn't it true—nine years a farmer now on his own land, and still he couldn't even feed his horses? What, then, could he hope to do for his wife and son?

There was much he planned. And so vivid was the future of his planning, so real and constant, that often the actual present was but half felt, but half endured. Its difficulties were lessened by a confidence in what lay beyond them. A new house—land for the boy—land and still more land—or education, whatever he might want.

But all the time was he only a blind and stubborn fool? Was Ellen right? Was he trampling on her life, and throwing away his own? The five years since he married her, were they to go on repeating themselves, five, ten, twenty, until all the brave future he looked forward to was but a stark and futile past?

She looked forward to no future. She had no faith or dream with which to make the dust and poverty less real. He understood suddenly. He saw her face again as only a few minutes ago it had begged him not to leave her. The darkness round him now was as a slate on which her lonely terror limned itself. He went from Prince to the other horses, combing their manes and forelocks with his fingers, but always it was her face before him, its staring eyes and twisted suffering. "See Paul—I stand like this all day. I just stand still—My throat's so tight it aches—"

And always the wind, the creak of walls, the wild lipless wailing through the loft. Until at last as he stood there, staring into the livid face before him, it seemed that this scream of wind was a cry from her parched and frantic lips. He knew it couldn't be, he knew that she was safe within the house, but still the wind persisted as a woman's cry. The cry of a woman with eyes like those that watched him through the dark. Eyes that were mad now—lips that even as they cried still pleaded, "See, Paul—I stand like this all day. I just stand still—so caged! If I could only run!"

He saw her running, pulled and driven headlong by the wind, but when at last he returned to the house, compelled by his anxiety, she was walking quietly back and forth with the baby in her arms. Careful, despite his concern, not to reveal a fear or weakness that she might think capitulation to her wishes, he watched a moment through the window, and then went off to the tool shed to mend harness. All afternoon he stitched and riveted. It was easier with the lantern lit and his hands occupied. There was a wind whining high past the tool shed too, but it was only wind. He remembered the arguments with which Ellen had tried to persuade him away from the farm, and one by one he defeated them. There would be rain again— next year, or the next. Maybe in his ignorance he had farmed his land the wrong way, seeding wheat every year, working the soil till it was lifeless dust—but he would do better now. He would plant clover and alfalfa, breed cattle, acre by acre and year by year restore to his land its fibre and fertility. That was something to work for, a way to prove himself. It was ruthless wind, blackening the sky with his earth, but it was not his master. Out of his land it had made a wilderness. He now, out of the wilderness, would make a farm and home again.

Tonight he must talk with Ellen. Patiently, when the wind was down, and they were both quiet again. It was she who had told him to grow fibrous crops, who had called him an ignorant fool because he kept on with summer fallow and wheat. Now she might be gratified to find him acknowledging her wisdom. Perhaps she would begin to feel the power and steadfastness of the land, to take a pride in it, to understand that he was not a fool, but working for her future and their son's.

And already the wind was slackening. At four o'clock he could sense a lull. At five, straining his eyes from the tool shed doorway, he could make out a neighbour's buildings half a mile away. It was over—three days of blight and havoc like a scourge—three days so bitter and so long that for a moment he stood still, unseeing, his senses idle with a numbness of relief.

But only for a moment. Suddenly he emerged from the numbness; suddenly the fields before him struck his eyes to comprehension. They lay black, naked. Beaten and mounded smooth with dust as if a sea in gentle swell had turned to stone. And though he had tried to prepare himself for such a scene, though he had known since yesterday that not a blade would last the storm, still now, before the utter waste confronting him, he sickened and stood cold. Suddenly like the fields he was naked. Everything that had sheathed him a little from the realities of existence: vision and purpose, faith in the land, in the future, in himself—it was all rent now, stripped away. "Desert," he heard her voice begin to sob. "Desert, you fool—the lamp lit at noon!"

In the stable again, measuring out their feed to the horses, he wondered what he would say to her tonight. For so deep were his instincts of loyalty to the land that still, even with the images of his betrayal stark upon his mind, his concern was how to withstand her, how to go on again and justify himself. It had not occurred to him yet that he might or should abandon the land. He had lived with it too long. Rather was his impulse still to defend it—as a man defends against the scorn of strangers even his most worthless kin.

He fed his horses, then waited. She too would be waiting, ready to cry at him, "Look now—that crop that was to feed and clothe us! And you'll still keep on! You'll still say 'Next year—there'll be rain next year'!"

But she was gone when he reached the house. The door was open, the lamp blown out, the crib empty. The dishes from their meal at noon were still on the table. She had perhaps begun to sweep, for the broom was lying in the middle of the floor. He tried to call, but a terror clamped upon his throat. In the wan, returning light it seemed that even the deserted kitchen was straining to whisper what it had seen. The tatters of the storm still whimpered through the eaves, and in their moaning told the desolation of the miles they had traversed. On tiptoe at last he crossed to the adjoining room; then at the threshold, without even a glance inside to satisfy himself that she was really gone, he wheeled again and plunged outside.

He ran a long time—distraught and headlong as a few hours ago he had seemed to watch her run—around the farmyard, a little distance into the pasture, back again blindly to the house to see whether she had returned—and then at a stumble down the road for help.

They joined him in the search, rode away for others, spread calling across the fields in the direction she might have been carried by the wind—but nearly two hours later it was himself who came upon her. Crouched down against a drift of sand as if for shelter, her hair in matted strands around her neck and face, the child clasped tightly in her arms.

The child was quite cold. It had been her arms, perhaps, too frantic to protect him, or the smother of dust upon his throat and lungs. "Hold him," she said as he knelt beside her. "So—with his face away from the wind. Hold him until I tidy my hair."

Her eyes were still wide in an immobile stare, but with her lips she smiled at him. For a long time he knelt transfixed, trying to speak to her, touching fearfully with his fingertips the dust-grimed cheeks and eyelids of the child. At last she said, "I'll take him again. Such clumsy hands—you don't know how to hold a baby yet. See how his head falls forward on your arm."

Yet it all seemed familiar—a confirmation of what he had known since noon. He gave her the child, then, gathering them up in his arms, struggled to his feet, and turned towards home.

It was evening now. Across the fields a few spent clouds of dust still shook and fled. Beyond, as if through smoke, the sunset smouldered like a distant fire.

He walked with a long dull stride, his eyes before him, heedless of her weight. Once he glanced down and with her eyes she still was smiling. "Such strong arms, Paul—and I was so tired just carrying him. ——"

He tried to answer, but it seemed that now the dusk was drawn apart in breathless waiting, a finger on its lips until they passed. "You were right, Paul. ——" Her voice came whispering, as if she too could feel the hush. "You said tonight we'd see the storm go down. So still now, and a red sky—it means tomorrow will be fine."

WILLOW SONG

Merna Summers

When I was eight years old I had a favourite place and a favourite person. My favourite place was the old Hadley farm, a house where nobody lived. It was the only empty house I'd ever seen—abandoned farm houses were not so common then as they were to become later—and I liked to hear my footsteps in its hollow rooms, to take note by changes of wallpaper colours the places where pictures had once hung, to calculate by depth of painted borders the size of congoleum rugs long since removed. In one bedroom, a room I considered mine, there was an airy yellow paper on the walls. In an inner corner the paper had peeled back. What was revealed was first a pink paper decorated with blue flowers, and then a dull beige paper decorated with brown and grey flowers.

I explored the leavings of the Hadleys like an archaeologist, seeking meaning in the broken pickle crock I found in the bushes behind the house, the still-thriving rhubarb at the edge of what had once been their garden, the frayed and rotted lengths of rope that stirred in the wind between poles that had supported their children's swing. They were people I'd never seen, not even in photographs, but I felt I knew them better than I knew my own family, who in any case were a mass of contradictions.

Once, coming to the Hadley place in June, I saw that the tall green shrubs that lined the driveway were lilacs. Purple blossoms— thousands and thousands and thousands of them—had appeared on the bushes, overcoming the air with their sweetness. I walked among them in something like distress. All that blooming, and for whom? Not for me, for I had come to them only by chance. And yet if I hadn't happened along, there would have been no-one to see their glory. I wept for the lilacs and for Mrs. Hadley who had planted them. I wanted to make it up to her that I was there and she was not. I tried to see with her eyes and smell with her nostrils.

But I didn't tell anyone nearer at hand about the lilacs. I didn't say, "Come, see." The Hadley place was mine. I never went there except alone. That was necessary.

The only person I wanted to show it to, in any case, was Mrs. Hadley. No. Mr. Hadley too. Mr. Hadley and Mrs. Hadley, one at a time. I saw myself walking along the drive with Mr. Hadley. "Lilacs break the heart," he would say, and I would nod sadly. Then he would thank me for loving his lilacs when there was no-one else to do it. I saw myself helping Mrs. Hadley make pickles, chopping cucumbers ever so carefully. Above all else I wanted to please the Hadleys, to devote myself utterly to serving them. Their house was my favourite place.

My favourite person? Well, beginning with the spring I was eight, my favourite person was my uncle, Billy Becker. Uncle Billy, who was nineteen the year I was eight, was my father's youngest brother, the youngest of a large family. Everyone adored him. It was the fact that he was unmarried and still living at home that made my grandparents' house my favourite place-to-stay.

By the time I was eight, I had an insider's knowledge of a good many houses. Both my mother and my father were members of large

———"Willow Song" by Merna Summers is reprinted from *The Skating Party*, by permission of Oberon Press

families, and in both families it was the custom for children to spend school holidays on the road, as it were, visiting with uncles, aunts and grandparents. We didn't see this visiting as any special treat. We "packed our turkey," as the family saying was, as happily, but as casually, as children in other families might search out a rope to skip.

Older children in our two families—my mother's and my father's—might be sent out when help was needed: when an aunt was under the weather or an uncle hard-pressed with field work. But if younger children were also kept on the move—and we were—it must simply have been a family inclination to share each other's children.

"It'll give us a rest," parents said as their children left them, and no doubt it did. If it imposed a corresponding week or ten days of unrest on the uncles, aunts or grandparents who took us off their hands, I was never aware of it. Perhaps the older members of the families didn't think about our visits one way or the other, any more than we did ourselves. Fathers plowed, mothers cooked and gardened, children circulated.

Visiting a Becker house was a very different experience from visiting a Stinson house. My father was a Becker. So was I. And so, I thought, was my mother. It was my mother's family who were Stinsons.

In Becker houses, children were made much of. "Hello, Sunshine," my Uncle Billy would greet me, picking me up and lifting me up to his own eye level. "How's my girl today?"

In my father's family, people were always asking me things like that. "Whose girl are you, Barbara?" they would ask, or, "Are you my girl?" In my mother's family, no one was anybody's girl.

I wasn't very old before I realized that the two families expected very different sorts of things from me. In my mother's family, after I'd put in a long and tiring day of trying to behave for company, nobody ever said, "You were a good girl." You were expected to be good, and no nonsense about it.

With my father's family, on the other hand,

goodness was regarded as an accomplishment. "You should have *seen* her!" they would cry. It was almost as if you'd brought off a miracle.

The two families were different in just about every way there is to be different. They had a different idea of celebration. A Becker wedding was a feast. There was roast beef and roast chicken and raisin pie and people. The people sat in a hall and passed heavy bowls and platters around long tables.

To the Stinsons, there was something painful about all that plenty. At their weddings, the tables were shorter and so was the food. People sat around individual card tables nibbling at what my father called "Stinson sandwiches," multi-layered concoctions held together by unlikely fillings.

"You don't go to a wedding to *eat*," my grandmother Stinson said firmly.

On the other hand, Stinson houses had a quiet comfort undreamed of by Beckers. Sunday dinner was a reassuring ritual, with a good deal of fussing about the quality of the Yorkshires, and as much ceremony in the service as my aunts could muster. None of them had complete sets of silver or bone china, but each aunt had a pattern she was collecting. Each also had some special sugar shell or pickle fork or berry spoon that had come, in some unexplained way, "from England." Once my grandmother Stinson showed me two gold-lined silver spoons in a velvet case. They were to be mine when I was old enough, she said. I looked forward to having them without impatience.

To me, attending church was one of the great pleasures of visiting a Stinson house, for my mother and father followed the Becker practice of staying away. The Stinsons worshipped God in the Church of England. "Naturally," I want to say about this, for all their predilections were English. On trips to the city, Stinsons stocked up on Ridgeway's tea and Peak Frean biscuits and ginger beer. When they felt that alcohol was called for, they drank sherry. Only my grandparents had ever actually seen England, but all my aunts gloried in tea cosies and toast racks and tea strainers. They went in for candlewick crochet and cutwork embroidery. They decorated their walls with pictures of country cottages surrounded by lupins, or brown-toned prints of decomposing abbeys. They wore sweaters that looked as if they'd been boiled, and they called their washcloths "flannels."

When it came to being English, they were, as my father said, "terrible as an army with banners." But what really irritated him was their unvoiced assumption that the rest of the world, if it had had any say in the matter, would have chosen to share their origins. Englishness was a trump card, and trump takes Ace.

Once, driven past prudence by some English smugness of my grandmother's, my father felt called upon to remind her that it was the Jews, not the English, who were God's chosen people.

"Be fair, Stanley," he claimed she said. "There weren't any English people around when He was making the choice."

It's because of my Stinson aunts that I still find it hard to believe that not all Englishwomen are fanatically clean housekeepers. Becker housekeeping was catch-as-catch-can. "Nobody's house is clean all the time," my Becker aunts told each other, but they were wrong. Stinson houses were. In a Stinson house, even the slop pail never smelled bad.

I liked that, but I liked the haphazard Becker houses too. The Stinsons had a passion for things that matched—matching forks, matching chairs, Blue Boy and Pink Lady in matching frames. In Becker houses the only things that ever matched were the five-pound coffee jars that were used to store rolled oats and brown sugar.

"If you want to have nice things you've got to take care of them," my grandmother Stinson said. My grandmother Becker might show you how to play the Jew's harp or mouth organ, or join you in teaching the dog to jump over the broom handle, but she never talked Dutch cleanser or furniture polish. She had no time for that.

When I was very young I was totally confused by the differences in the two families. Then, in

church one day with a Stinson aunt, I heard the text: "I am come that they might have life, and that they might have it more abundantly." I saw then that the differences in their two ways of life were probably divinely ordained. The Stinsons, who went to church, had abundantly furnished houses. The Beckers, no church-goers, had no such abundance of things.

There were other differences that I expected to have made clear to me in time. Why was it, for instance, that Stinsons reproved you for drawing attention to yourself, while Beckers applauded the same sort of behaviour?

My mother contended that my father's family paid more attention to me than was good for me. If that was true, my Uncle Billy Becker must have been the worst for me of them all.

When I stayed with my grandparents I rode beside Uncle Billy all day on the stoneboat, and he pointed out and identified kinds of birds, kinds of stones, kinds of clouds. At night he took me for rides on his bicycle. Our first bicycle ride together, I gripped the handlebars nervously and, with no clear idea of their purpose, succeeded in steering us into the ditch. As we picked ourselves up, I didn't know whether to laugh or cry.

"Never mind, Sunshine," Uncle Billy said. "You've just had your first spill off a bicycle." He made it sound like an event, something I ought to remember.

If Billy had a gift for living, and he did, it centred around his extraordinary sense of occasion. He understood that everyone longs to have life present him with some occasions worth remembering. If an old farmer sold out and moved to town, if a young couple were married and shivareed, if a local girl topped the province in her grade nine exams, it might be someone else who did the work of putting on a party, but it would be Uncle Billy who made it different from all other parties. He might write a funny poem, or paint a banner that said "Welcome Home, Mr. Forsyth," or organize a chorus to commemorate the event in song. Billy wasn't one to do things by halves.

120

The Stinsons, planning a bridal shower or a christening tea, worried about doing things right. Billy worried about giving people something to remember.

Billy also had a taste for practical jokes, some of which I now think could not have brought delight to anyone, but I'm sure nobody then ever censured him for it. Billy made people feel as if something was happening in their lives, and anyone who can do that is forgiven a lot.

He was as quick of temper as he was of generous impulse, but if you liked him, you forgot the first and remembered the second. Most people liked him. It would have been hard not to; he was so full of enthusiasms. Billy wanted to do everything there was. He wanted to be able to identify the stars, to call the flowers by their names, to collect rock samples. He wanted to re-cane chairs, to build stone wishing wells, to take up taxidermy. When my grandmother discovered that Billy was enrolled in three correspondence courses at once, "You're biting off more than you can chew," she warned him.

"Too many people worry about that," Billy said. "The thing to do is take as big a bite as you can, and then chew like crazy."

My grandmother had no answer for that. Like all Beckers, she was no meagre biter herself.

The spring I was eight the schools were closed by a scarlet fever epidemic and I was spending the unexpected holiday with Grandpa and Grandma Becker. With me was my brother, Vernon, who was five.

Billy's enthusiasm that spring was for egg-mounting. Not egg-*collecting*, or at least not especially egg collecting. He'd been collecting birds' eggs for years. He had the big ones stored in tissue-filled shoe boxes and the small ones stored, one to a box, in the little wooden containers in which cousin Lotta got her vials of insulin. These boxes were of smooth white wood and were beautifully built with dovetailed corners and slide-in lids. They'd suited Billy's purpose very well as long as his purpose was storage. Now he'd decided that the time had come to put his collec-

tion on display, and he had begun to build cases he intended to hang on the wall.

Billy didn't have many tools to work with. It was wonderful to see what he could do with a fret saw and a keyhole saw and a bag of finishing nails. When I got there, he had only one showcase finished, the one that was to hold his hawk eggs. These eggs, compared to the ones in the insulin boxes, were large. Each had its own four little walls to enclose it, and its own name neatly lettered on a white card beneath it.

"Billy's got about every egg there is," my grandmother said, but even I knew that wasn't true. He had left empty spaces in the case for hawk eggs he didn't have yet but hoped to get.

Looking over his shoulder one night, "What's a pigeon hawk, Uncle Billy?" I asked. I was reading the name lettered beneath one of the empty compartments.

"A hawk that eats pigeons," he said. "It's not just an ordinary hawk when you come right down to it. It's a kind of falcon. And it lays its eggs in a magpie's nest."

"Are they rare?" I asked. I knew that being rare made an egg special.

"Anything's rare if you haven't got it," Billy said.

My grandmother was standing at the cupboard baking a Dutch apple cake. Vernon was sitting on the floor, sliding the lid of an empty insulin box in and out.

"I know where I could get a pigeon hawk's egg," Billy said. He lettered another white card before he answered my unspoken question. "The trouble is, it's in a nest on a branch that wouldn't hold my weight."

My grandmother turned away from the cupboard, instantly alert. "I don't want you talking the children into climbing any trees, Billy," she said. "I mean that."

And to us, "You're not to go after that egg, mind," she said. "I don't care what Billy offers you to do it."

"Now, Ma," Billy said, grinning. "You know I wouldn't do a thing like that."

"You!" my grandmother said. "You! I'm surprised you haven't sweet-talked the hawk into bringing you the egg himself." She didn't sound cross. If Uncle Billy was the kind of boy no-one could resist, I saw that she liked him that way.

"I mean it just the same," she said again, and went back to her baking.

After a while Billy took me on his knee and began to tell me about the eggs that made up his collection. His voice when he spoke to me seemed to pay me honour. It made me feel as if I amounted to more than I'd supposed. I was intensely aware of Billy's arm around my shoulder, his fingers on my bare arm, as he talked.

It seemed as if each egg had its own story. Collecting birds' eggs, I saw, was no cut-and-dried business, but a chancy pursuit filled with hazards. Listening, I loved Uncle Billy for the dangers he had passed through.

The next morning Billy took Vernon and me with him out to the field to haul in some bundles left behind by the threshers. The hayrack was empty as we set out, and wheat kernels skipped on the bare floorboards like drops of water on a hot frying pan. We had to wrap ourselves around the rack front to keep from doing the same.

"The hawk's nest is in a big Balm of Gilead down in the valley," Billy said when we stopped for a gate at the top of a hill.

"Grandma said we weren't supposed to go after it," Vernon said. He was that kind of kid when he was five.

"And nobody asked you to, did they kid?" Uncle Billy said.

The next day Vernon went to town with my grandparents. I stayed home to cook Uncle Billy's dinner. As I was slicing cold potatoes into the frying pan, "Vernon's afraid to climb that tree," I announced. "He's scared of falling."

"But you're not scared, are you Sunshine?" Uncle Billy said.

"I climb trees all the time," I said, which was a lie. "I'll bet I could climb that big old Balm like nothing."

I was expecting Billy would refuse to let me try.

"You probably could," he said. "Tree-climbing's only dangerous if you're scared.

I put the lid on the potatoes and got out the sealer of meat my grandmother had left for us.

"If you were a different kind of girl," Billy said, "I'd offer you a quarter to climb that tree." He went to the basin in the corner, poured some water into it, and began to wash up. "But unless I miss my guess," he said, "you're the kind of girl, if she did it at all, would do it for love, not money."

I was pleased at how well my uncle Billy understood me.

Would I climb the tree? Would I, in years to come, be able to hear Uncle Billy tell people, "I'd never have been able to complete my collection without the help of my niece, Barbara Becker"?

"Where is the nest exactly?" I asked.

"I'll show you this afternoon," Uncle Billy said.

Billy had a drawstring bag fitted out with a padded case that he used to keep eggs from breaking while he was collecting them. We took it with us as we set out on our walk down to the valley.

The day was glorious. The spring hills were yellow with buffalo bean, the soddy clearings bristled with buckbrush, and reefs of silver willow zig-zagged down the side of rain-washed gullies. Overhead, big cumulous clouds were hightailing it across the sky toward Saskatchewan.

We entered the horse pasture by a rich-soiled hollow. I saw that there'd been a sprinkle of rain the night before, and the ground had covered with puffballs. Below us was the valley of the Wandering River. It had been a wet spring, and the river had overrun its banks and flooded the bottom lands. Close by the river's willow-hung edges, two white horses stood knee deep in their pasture. Blue above and blue below and, as far as we could see, the blue of hills behind the river.

I stood in my high pasture, princess among the puffballs, and went from seeing the valley to *becoming* it. The hills were mine and the river was mine and so were the white horses.

The pigeon hawk had chosen for her brooding a magpie's nest in the marshy lowlands where my grandfather's hay lands reached the Wandering

River. Here grew cow parsnip and Heal-All, Indian pipe and smartweed. The trees were red willow and poplar and Balm of Gilead.

Even if Billy hadn't know where the nest was, we would have had no difficulty finding it, for, as we came near, the two parent birds flew up protesting loudly against our intrusion and trying to drive us away. They were small birds, not much bigger than jays, but I knew they were fierce. I couldn't see their curved talons and falcon beaks, but I knew they were there. They circled above the nesting tree, their wings beating rapidly.

"They won't attack me, will they?" I asked.

"I don't think so," Uncle Billy said. "I never yet met the hawk would tangle with a man."

The tree, valley big, was rough of bark and shiny of leaf. Wisps of spring cotton still clung to its branches. Cotton lifted from the ground when we moved. The ground was pungent and sticky with the cast-off husks of the tree's leafing out. They stuck to our shoes like dates.

"I could boost you up to the first branch," Uncle Billy said. "You'd have to shinny up by yourself from there."

I looked up. The nest, a ramshackle dome of broken sticks, was black against the sky. It was out on a limb, all right, and it was pretty high up.

"I'm not sure if I should let you do it," Uncle Billy said.

"But I *want* to," I said. The evening before, sitting on his knee, I'd understood the expression, "She's soft on him." I had felt soft all over, soft and without any will of my own. But I had a will now.

"I'll get you the egg," I said, "I can climb this easy."

Billy was wearing a ball jacket, gold satin with maroon cotton banding at the neck and bottom. He gave it to me to protect my arms. It was still warm from his body when I put it on. I zipped it up and took the egg bag from him and hung it around my neck. Then I began to climb.

What was it like, pulling myself up that tree? I don't really remember. Later, when I was on the ground again, I saw that the inside of my knees had been scraped raw by the rough bark. I didn't

feel it as it was happening. Nor do I know how my arms and legs managed to pull me from foothold to foothold. I wasn't a tomboy, and I didn't have the strength of the habitual tree-climber. To climb so tall a tree should have been impossible for me. Yet I did it, without feeling pain or even—once I'd begun—fear.

I reached the limb that held the nest and inched my way outward. Then I saw what I hadn't realized before: that it wasn't possible to rise above it and look in. The nest was tall, perhaps three feet in depth. I didn't know how to proceed. Nor could I call down to Uncle Billy. One eight-year-old girl might balance on this limb, but not one eight-year-old girl plus her voice.

Billy, watching from below, realized the problem. "There should be holes in the side," he called. "Try to stick your arm in that way."

I felt around, found an opening, and nudged my way in. What I found there seemed to be a nest within a nest, a hard mud kernel in the middle of the pile of deadwood. By groping, I found the eggs, still warm from their parents' bodies, and I took one. It was quite a trick to keep the hold on one hand easy, so as not to break the egg, while the other hand and the rest of the body were hanging on for dear life, but somehow I did it. Then, either at the nest or at the branch's fork with the main tree, I managed to get the egg into the padding in the bag. I hung the bag backwards around my neck and began to come down.

As soon as I got to the bottom Uncle Billy opened the bag. "Boy, oh Boy!" he said. "You got it here all in one piece. I don't know how you did it, but you did it."

The egg was reddish brown with dark brown markings. I touched it. Then I lifted it to my face. It smelled warm.

I looked at Uncle Billy and we both smiled. I was through with pickle crocks and peeling wallpaper. It was living stuff I was dealing in now.

"Does the egg belong to you?" I asked him. What I wanted him to say was that it belonged to us both: him and me together.

"I guess so," he said. "Sure I don't know as the

hawk would want it back with our smell on it."

I wanted to keep my climb a secret, not out of fear of punishment, but because it would be better that way. But Billy said that Grandma would have to be told.

"Don't worry, Sunshine," he said. "Your grandma's bark is worse than her bite."

He was right about that anyway. My grandmother had quite a lot to say as she put salve on my legs, but what most of it added up to was that it was no use to cry over spilled milk; what was done couldn't be undone, and forgive and forget was her motto. I thought once more how different she was from the Stinsons. They didn't either forgive or forget. What would they have said to me under similar circumstances? To Billy? A broken promise was a serious thing with them, and when anyone failed to live up to their standards, they remembered it. The offender was in their bad books for good.

I was glad that my grandmother Becker was forgiving, for her house that spring was the best of all possible places to be. Every night I helped Billy with his egg-mounting. I was an initiate now, a partner. Touching a finger to an egg I would feel myself in the presence of fast-beating hearts and feathery down. Nest-building was locked in those eggs, and homing flight at day's end, and bird song.

I didn't realize then that a collected life is a doomed life. To me the eggs were merely in a period of waiting. When the time was right, they would get on with their becoming.

Billy was important to me, but I was important to him too. "Billy thinks that Barbara's 'just it,'" I heard my grandmother tell someone one day. I knew that Billy didn't feel the same way about Vernon, but that was all right with me too.

One night, when I was coming down the stairs with a bottle of India ink to write labels for Billy, I heard his voice from the kitchen, quick with anger.

"Look what you made me do," Billy said.

I came into the room and saw him facing Vernon. Vernon was cowering, uncertain whether to cry or call Grandma or run away.

"I didn't do anything," Vernon said.

"You were standing too close to my elbow," Billy said. "How do you expect me to get anything done with a kid pushing up against me all the time?"

There was a small, buff-coloured egg lying broken at their feet. Vernon bent down and tried to pick up the pieces of shell.

"Was it an important one, Uncle Billy?" I asked. What I meant was: was it a kind hard to come by?

"It could have been for all he cares," Billy said.

I could tell by his voice that I was included in his anger, but I forgave him.

"Now clear out, both of you, before I lose my temper," he said.

Vernon held it against Billy that he had hollered at us. I was ashamed of my brother. You had to take things into account with Billy. What he said Tuesday, meaning it, he no longer meant on Wednesday. You were expected to know that and consider it unsaid.

"Don't be an old woman, Vernon," Billy said when the third day came and Vernon was still sulking. Billy and I did not like boys who were old women.

After Vernon and I went back to our own house, life seemed very humdrum to me. It wasn't just novelty I craved, I think, but meaning as well. I had always had a hankering for a religious life. It persisted, even though I knew that, as a Becker, I ought to be above all that. Beckers saw religion as something other people went in for, something not in very good taste. Beckers even took it as an insult when anyone sent them a religious Christmas card.

Just the same, I envied children who, at bedtime, were asked, "Did you say your prayers?" instead of "Did you wash your feet?" My need to worship, wherever it came from, did not come from without. Perhaps every human being feels it, whether or not there is anybody there.

One day, flipping through an old National Geographic, I came across a picture that moved me profoundly. It was of a lone hawk, riding the air on motionless wings. I knew enough about birds to be pretty sure that the hawk was an osprey, but I pretended to myself that it was a pigeon hawk. I cut it out and found a frame for it. Then I got out my fountain pen and on the cardboard backing wrote an inscription.

"To my favourite girl with all my love," I wrote. I signed it, "Uncle Billy."

I put the picture in the frame and hung it on my bedroom wall, over a piece of furniture that we called a chiffonier.

All that summer I picked little bouquets and placed them in front of it. When fall came and the garden froze, I took to moving the hawk's picture from over the chiffonier to the dressing table and back again. I wanted to come into the room thinking of something else and have it surprise me.

Curiously, when Uncle Billy started to go around with Emily Patmore, what I felt was not jealousy but rather a deep delight. Emily was dark-haired and beautiful. It was as if she'd been specially selected to serve in my stead. *I* might have to go to school and gather eggs and carry in nightwood, but Emily—if she married Billy—could be with him all day, every day.

During the months they were going out together, when I washed dishes, I was not Barbara washing dishes for Mama, but Emily washing dishes for Billy. If on Saturday I helped Mama make pies, the hands that sliced the apples or rolled the piecrust were not my own hands, nor were the pies constructed to fill any ordinary hunger.

About a month before their wedding, I came home from school one day to find Billy and Emily in the living room. They'd been making the rounds of the relatives, and they were talking about their wedding plans.

Catching sight of me, "Hey, why don't we dress the kid up and let her pass the cake or something?" Billy said. And so I did that.

In our family not even newlyweds held themselves aloof from the visits of circulating children. At least Billy and Emily didn't. They asked me to come and stay with them a couple of months after the wedding.

"How's my girl?" Billy asked the old question when my father delivered me to their door. He had a different way of saying it than the other uncles, a way that made it seem like he was saying a good deal more.

I loved Billy and Emily's house. Everything in it might have been planned with me in mind. Some rooms have a quality of light that sets them apart from other rooms. My room in the Hadley house had had it; so did the room that was prepared for me here. There was a pale yellow paper on the walls, and dotted sheer curtains at the windows. The dresser drawers smelled of Camay soap.

Some nights Uncle Wallace and Aunt Margaret walked over; they only lived a half mile away. Then we would all gather around the radio and listen to *The Great Gildersleeve* or *Fibber McGee and Molly*.

The nights the three of us were alone together were made of different stuff altogether. "Go and get your hair brush," Billy would say to Emily, and she would get it. Then she would sit down on the floor in front of him and he would brush her hair, slowly and without words. When I went to bed, I couldn't sleep. I would lie there aching with the wonder of it. Would I ever be grown up?

By the time the next summer came, I was old enough to be expected to be of some use in the world. I had my own jobs to do at home, and I had the confidence that comes from never having failed at anything important. When I heard that Emily wasn't well, that one of the older girls would have to go over to take care of her, I hoped that I might be the one to be chosen.

My mother, when she told me that I had been, didn't say what was the matter with Emily. There had been a flu going around, and I supposed she had it. Perhaps my mother even hinted that that was the problem.

Emily vomited all the time. I held her head and then emptied the basin. She wasn't supposed to leave her bed except to use the chamber pot, so I took over the rest of the house as well. It was easy to forget that I was only ten, easy for me and maybe even easy for Billy, who was twenty-one, and Emily, who was a year younger.

Emily usually felt a little brighter in the evenings. Billy and I would go in and sit by her bedside, and Billy would tell us about the new chicken house he had started to build: how he was going to use sunlight and proper ventilation to prevent poultry disease, how he had designed the roosts for easy cleaning, how a chicken house so well-lit and draught-free would affect the egg production of any flock fortunate enough to be under its roof. Billy wasn't going to have barred rocks or leghorns like everyone else, but a breed new to Willow Bunch called Rhode Island Reds. We gathered that they were the most wonderful hens that ever pecked or scratched.

Billy had spent a great deal of time on his plans, and his farm work had got rather behindhand as a result. He ran from one thing to another, harrowing a few rounds on his summerfallow, seeding an acre or two of brome grass, weeding a row of Emily's garden. And of course every day he had to milk cows and separate milk.

I cooked Billy's meals and cleaned Billy's house and tried to help him with the garden and separating. Billy harrowed and hammered. Emily vomited. She wasn't as pretty as she had been before, and there was a sour smell in her room that no amount of cleaning and airing ever quite removed.

One morning, when I'd got the fire going in the cook stove and was starting to cook breakfast, Billy came in looking worried.

"Your Aunt Emily's not feeling very good today," he said. "I want you to keep a close eye on her and call me right away if anything goes wrong."

I didn't know what I was watching for, but I hovered over her all morning. She looked about the same to me. Billy was a little late coming in at noon—he had been putting together a gable vent and had forgotten about the time—and he went at once to Emily's room.

"You okay?" he asked from the door.

Emily smiled weakly. "If you can call this okay," she said. She had vomited three times that morning.

"You're sure you don't want to go to the hospital?" he asked. "I could phone and tell them I'm bringing you in." There wasn't a telephone in Billy and Emily's house. They used Uncle Wallace's.

"The doctor said it wouldn't make much difference one way or the other," Emily said. "He said it would be touch and go either way." She had a swallow of water from a glass by her bed. "I don't know if there's anything he could do," she said. "He sounded as if he thought the sooner I got it over with, the better." She sounded tired and uncertain, as if she wanted someone else to make the decision for her.

Billy thought the decision had been made. He didn't want her to go to the hospital, and so he supposed that she didn't want to go.

"What you need is a good nap," he said. "A nap and then a nice cup of tea."

His prescription may or may not have reassured Emily. It reassured me. "Don't you worry about a thing, Uncle Billy," I told him. "I'll take care of her."

"Billy, I'm scared." It was Emily who said it, but Billy who looked it. His face, just for a moment, was desperate.

Then, "What kind of talk is that?" he demanded. "You're going to be just fine." He talked a little more, persuading himself.

"I'm leaving you in good hands," he said. Then, I suppose to give Emily courage, he extracted a promise from me. "You won't leave the house even for a minute, will you Sunshine?" he asked.

I promised that I would not.

"Just call if you need me," Billy told me as he went back to his work. "I'll be right here."

I washed the dinner dishes and set the kitchen to rights. Then I went to see if Emily needed anything.

Usually I helped Emily out of bed when she needed to use the chamber pot, left her alone, and then came back to help her in again. After the first few days I had got used to seeing her in her nightgown, and she had got used to being seen. But when I went in that afternoon I saw that she had already been up. She was sitting on the edge of the bed, a blanket wrapped around her so that her nightgown was almost hidden. She was pale, and there were beads of perspiration on her upper lip.

"Are you cold?" I asked, because of the blanket. "Would you like me to close the window?"

"The window!" she said. "The window!

"For the love of God, Barbara, I'm bleeding to death."

I realized then there was a new smell in the sick room. Warm blood. It lay in a pool on the floor near her bed where, I supposed, Emily had vomited it. I had heard of people vomiting blood before. All of them had died.

"What shall I do?" I asked.

"Call your Uncle Billy," she said. Then she lay down, still wrapped in her blanket. "I want my mother," I heard her say as I ran out of the house.

In the yard, "Uncle Billy," I called. "Uncle Billy."

But he wasn't there. There was no answer, not from the chicken house, nor from the summerfallow, nor from the field of brome. I ran first toward one and then toward another, all the time calling.

I couldn't leave Aunt Emily. I had promised I would stay with her. But if I didn't get help she would die.

At last I gave up calling and began to run down the road toward Uncle Wallace's. It wasn't far, but it was too far for running. Aunt Margaret, at work in her garden, saw me coming and ran out to meet me.

"Aunt Emily is dying," I told her.

"You hush that kind of talk," Aunt Margaret said fiercely. "Nobody's dying around here." Then she went into the house to phone the doctor.

By the time she got through, I had regained my breath. We climbed into Uncle Wallace's car—Aunt Margaret knew how to drive—and we returned to Billy's house.

"The doctor will be here in half an hour," Aunt Margaret told Emily briskly. "Now how much blood have you lost?"

Emily indicated the pool on the floor. "That's most of it, I think," she said, "But I'm still losing it."

"Barbara, you get a mop and. . . ." Aunt Margaret stopped herself. "You shouldn't be in here at all," she said. "I'll clean it up before Billy comes in and sees it."

I went out and sat in the kitchen. It didn't seem odd to me that I—who had held Emily's head over the basin and emptied her chamber pot—should be shooed away now. Some time or other I must have realized that her trouble was not the flu.

When Billy came in, "Aunt Emily's not well," I told him. Now that I knew where it came from, it was unthinkable to tell him about the blood. "The doctor's coming. Aunt Margaret's with her."

I suppose Billy knew what happened. "Damn it all, kid," he said. "Why didn't you call me?"

"I didn't know where you were," I said.

"And you damn well didn't look very hard, did you?" he said. It took my brain a moment to register the words.

"I thought you were going to take care of her," he said.

His voice was hot with accusation. I remember some of the things he said after that, though not the order he said them in. He accused me of not wanting Emily to get well. He called me useless. He said he'd only been away a moment and I hadn't half tried. But it wasn't what he said that hurt the most. It was that he spoke as if I, Barbara, scarcely existed. I might never have existed at all.

He didn't stop until Aunt Margaret came out and told him to get ahold of himself. "You're upsetting Emily," she said.

"Just get this kid out of my sight, that's all," Billy said. "If she's still here when I come back in, I won't be responsible for what I do."

Then he went out to the road to watch for the doctor. Aunt Margaret sent me home to her place across the fields.

"Billy was beside himself," I heard Aunt Margaret tell my mother later.

"She'll get over it," my mother said. In a way she was right. Nothing hurts forever. In any case, there are some kinds of hurts you can get only once, like smallpox.

After that, I stopped circulating among relatives on my school holidays. "She's getting to be that age," my mother explained when my relatives asked about it.

One day, pulled by an impulse I didn't try to analyze, I walked over to the old Hadley place again. I found it different. Pickle crock, peeling wallpaper, frayed swing ropes—all were still in place, but they'd lost their power to move me. There was no reason to go there any more.

I didn't want to see Billy and I found it surprisingly easy to avoid him. Girl cousins, at family parties, often congregated in a bedroom. I had always scorned these feminine huddles, but I joined them now. By this and other means I was able to keep a certain distance between us for nearly two years.

To an adult, a year or two is no time at all. Children, I think, have the truer perception of time. In the two years since I had been banished from Billy's house, Emily had got pregnant again and had had a baby. Vernon had started school and passed into grade two. Grandma Becker had started to lose her hearing. Nothing was as it had been.

As for me, different things gave me pleasure now. I pored over magazine articles on table-setting and interior decoration. I was learning twelve different ways to fold a table napkin. My grandmother Stinson was teaching me to do candlewick crochet, and I had picked my own patterns in Royal Albert and Community Plate.

The spring I was twelve the Beckers gathered at my grandparents' house to celebrate their fif-tieth wedding anniversary. I knew I would see Billy, but I planned to keep the usual distance between us. Except for an accident of timing, I might have succeeded.

Uncle Wallace had brought a bottle of rum, and the men were down in the cellar having a drink. I was at the stove, filling bowls with vegetables. Just as I turned to carry a bowl of turnips to the table, the cellar door opened and there stood Billy, his face slightly flushed from the rum, not two feet away from me. We were face to face.

Perhaps Billy didn't know what to do about me any more than I knew what to do about him. Perhaps he thought if he made enough noise it would cover over all that had been, and put us on a new footing. Whatever the reason, his voice when he spoke was inordinately loud.

"Well, how's my girl?" he asked. He didn't wait for an answer.

"This little lady and I used to be pretty good friends, didn't we Sweetheart?" he said. "How've you been anyway?"

"Fine," I said. It would have been unthinkable not to answer at all.

"We've missed you," he said. "You ought to come over and see us some time."

Then a new thought struck him and his face lit up. "There's a sparrow hawk nesting in a tree at the edge of my hay quarter," he said.

He turned to the rest of them. "That'll fetch her if anything will," he said.

He probably thought it was the truth he spoke.

I said the bowl of turnips was hot: I'd have to put it on the table. . . and that was the end.

I felt old, a thousand years older than this boy with all his enthusiasms. There was no reason to tell him that the only hawk that would ever mean anything to me had been ripped up and consigned to the flames a long, long time ago.

THE INHERITOR

Frank Roberts

The man and the ewe and the dingo and a few crows wheeling above were the only visible living creatures in all that desolation.

They were on the only high land for miles around, a peaked hill known as Lone Pine because it had one tree on it. The tree was a very ordinary eucalypt but the words Lone Pine have such an historic association, even now, half a century afterward that any hill with one tree on it is apt to be known locally by that name.

This tree had suffered intense dry heat in its summers and withering dry cold in its winters and now, dead, its bare and gnarled and twisted branches made as good a monument as any to inland life, which is a longer war.

But the man saw it with a practical eye merely as the marker to a final refuge from the flood. The ewe and the dingo had no feelings at all about the tree, but the crows had. It was their natural roost and they had been there, conscious of the ewe cropping grass below them, and of the flood, and always prepared to wait patiently for the main chance when the dingo had appeared slinking along a low ridge, equally afraid of the rising water and of being silhouetted so plainly.

The dog scouted around the shrinking perimeter of Lone Pine, returned to the point where ridge met hillside, and stood sniffing the wind and waiting for a flash of instinct. It had come, and then he had walked up to the highest point of the hill and settled down near the tree to watch and wait.

He had seen the ewe but was not in a killing mood just then. And the crows flapped away from the tree, wheeled back to it, perched, and flapped away again. They were restless but not afraid of the dingo. He was a good provider.

But when the man appeared, walking along the ridge-top with the floodwater soaking his boots and running through the eroded dip where the ridge came to the hill, the crows left the tree and wheeled continuously.

The man had leaped from the ridge to the hillside and walked up the hill. He didn't see the earth-colored dog until it snarled. Then he saw its white teeth and blazing eyes. He looked down at the ridge and then up at the branches of the tree which he could reach with a good jump. But could he pull himself up quickly enough—or would the dingo prop at the sudden movement and slash at his legs? The essential habits of dingos were not in his experience, and the flood was another factor.

Then the ewe scented the wild dog. It was unlikely that she saw him. But she turned to run downhill and found the flood in front of her and bleated and ran around the hill, and the dingo crawled a few inches, watching her.

The man felt relieved. Presently the dog would attack the ewe, and he would hoist himself into the tree. He had only to remain still, and not divert the dingo from its instinctive passion for the ewe's throat.

The sheep ran about until it lost the dog scent, and then it noticed a new patch of grass and resumed cropping, moving on and up as the flood nudged its hoofs. It was stupid, even as sheep went.

The man stayed very still, watching the dingo stir an inch every time the ewe moved, hackles up and the skin along its spine quivering.

And then, God help him, the man began to feel pity for the sheep.

He was sure that the dingo had forgotten him, closed him out, but any simple movement would restore him. That might save the ewe.

He reasoned that the dog would not attack one creature while conscious of another that might attack it. Dingo had become a vernacular for a coward, but the wild dogs had survived from an age earlier than man by caution and cunning. Courage was a last resource.

He reasoned further that the ewe was unimportant, born to be killed by dog or man, but another thought came obliquely across this reasoning. If their isolation on the hill encouraged the dingo to have its anticipation to the full, letting the flood bring the ewe to it, he might be unable to hold his motionless pose and movement might turn the impassioned dog to him. He reasoned that this was unlikely and the idea false to his interests, but it persisted.

He knew it was compassion seeking to force him into foolish action by perversion of logic, suggesting that he divert the dingo now, before its exquisite desire became madness.

All this worrying to save a sheep? Damn the sheep and damn the dingo, let them continue the drama according to their natures, and let him get into that tree.

Then he knew that he could not. It was in his nature, too, to come down from trees and be master on the ground. He felt that if he should abandon the ewe and leap to safety he would diminish his own kind on the face of the earth. He must stay on the ground while ground remained.

Besides, the only low branch was too directly above the dingo.

He realized that this kind of thinking was more than foolish, it could be fatal. Soon their island would be so small that he and the dingo inevitably would be at one another's throats.

That image needed correcting. It was too dramatic. The dingo could only attack with its jaws and its weight, probably much less than his. He had defensive and offensive power in his hands, arms, legs and booted feet. So the dog had more to fear from him. He was afraid because it was wild, alien, capable of savagery, vicious, indomitable.

In a tight corner it might attack him and then it would fight to the death, and he would be lacerated terribly. This was really what he feared. It was still a question of the sheep or him.

The water was rising quickly and soon all three would be forced into a propinquity in which anything might happen. Unfortunately, while he could attract the dog's attention and perhaps save the ewe, he could not take the opposite line and disengage from the danger. He must act or submit to chance. This was the choice he faced.

Now he could feel pity for the ewe again, because he had made it reasonable. He felt sorry for the two inimical animals and himself, thrown together on this curious island in the flood. Only the wheeling crows were above pity. They were infinitely patient, nerveless, secure.

He realized that he had moved.

He had inclined his head and now the dingo's furious eyes were turned on him. He felt his heart respond to alarm. Then as if dismissing him as a potential danger, the dog turned back to the ewe, and he felt this was the moment. The sheep caught it, too, and stood bleating.

Even as the dog prepared for its charge to knock the ewe down and expose its throat to incisors, the man jumped and shouted. He knew it was wrong, that the whole argument had been opened again, when he had been free to jump for safety. But he was beyond reason and doing what he must.

The dingo hit the sheep and it fell over but the man was in reach before the teeth went in and booted the dog aside. It seemed to go with the kick, turning once in the air and landing on stiffened legs, facing him and snarling.

He heard the sheep scramble up and run away, and each wild bleat drew a response from the dog, a snap and snarl at the man.

He was going to kick again if it sprang at him, and he was more afraid of a dash at his legs. But suddenly the dingo swung away and ran up to the tree where it turned, hackled and

130

savage and in command of the high ground.

Now the man knew he was where he deserved to be, with the sheep. Gradually the water would force them up toward the dog, who held all the advantages and who now recognized his prime enemy.

The man walked around the little island, looking for a stick or a stone, even searching the flood for debris, but there was nothing of the slightest value.

"A man can be a fool," he said.

His voice sounded loud and made him realize how silent everything was, particularly their common menace, the flood.

"Just a stone," he asked of the stoneless ground.

He walked around the island again, moving slowly, watching both the ground and the ewe, which might be panicked into dashing straight to the tree and its death. Now that the issue had been made, he had to protect that animal or forever be a fool.

He looked at the squatting dingo, and the tree and the crows, and the ochre flood that covered the land. He was hoping for boats, but there were none in sight and sight extended for many miles from the top of Lone Pine.

No, there were no boats. And even if there were, even if some miracle brought one, the men in it would see what against the sky? A dead tree with some crows on it and a dingo sitting under it, and they would turn away.

The man knew that he could not let the dingo maintain control of the high ground for too long. But he also knew that if he approached it now it would almost certainly fight. In a while it might become more conscious of the flood, and afraid or at least troubled enough to accept if not welcome company. He had heard or read that animals so threatened forgot all other instincts. He decided to follow his reasoning this time, and be patient.

As the flood consumed the remaining ground, the man tried to stay close to the ewe without alarming it. By moving slowly and carefully

he managed to drive it around the island and keep it more aware of him than of the dog. He felt this roundabout way was better than gradual direct approach to the dingo. But nothing was better or best with this wild thing.

Stiff-legged and snarling, it turned as the man and the ewe circled, always with its hind to the tree. And as the distance between them shortened its fury increased and it snapped and snarled at both man and the ewe.

Now the sheep began to make short dashes up and down the slope, afraid of the water, terrified of the dingo, and inevitably about to sacrifice itself to one death or the other. The man was unable to stay between the two animals without danger and at any time now the dog would jump straight out at his throat.

And he had to make this happen so that he would not be surprised.

He stood in front of the dingo, almost eye to eye with it. He remained quite still, and then suddenly threw up his hands and shouted.

And the dog sprang and the man dropped to his hands and knees and sprang up again, meeting the expected midair turn and descent with the broad of his back.

He heard ground impact when he had hoped for a splash, and the dingo was back and had torn his leg while he was still turning downhill.

He kicked at it with the other foot but it danced out of his reach and in again for another slash, then aside when he kicked ahead, and in again for a tear at his flank.

And then the crazed ewe blundered into them and the dingo rolled over and the man fell on it and got both hands around its neck, lying on the dog while he strangled it.

It gagged and frothed and tried to get his wrists and dug and writhed and howled once and his hands and arms ached and his mind was torn and outraged by the act of murder. But he maintained his grim purpose.

When he stood up, perhaps a long time later, his forearms and wrists were bleeding freely and there were many gashes on his stomach and chest from the dog's paws. Both legs and one hip were badly gashed, but he had saved his hands and face.

The sheep stood a few feet away, cropping a tuft of grass under the dead tree.

It shied away when he put a hand out toward it, and ran around to the other side of the tree.

The man sat down and tore two long strips from his trouser leg. He strung them on his belt and went around one side of the tree and then doubled back quickly and caught the ewe before it could turn again. He threw it on its side and tied its legs. Now he had only to find some way of getting it up into the tree.

He did that by going up and breaking off part of one of the gaunt limbs and using it to dig the earth around the tree, making a mound on which he was able to stand and heave the trussed ewe across the lowest fork. She struggled, bleating terribly, and nearly fell before he could clamber on to the branch and hold her in place. But once he was in the tree it was all right.

He was sighted from an Army helicopter next morning, a bloodied, injured and demented man who refused to be taken off unless he could bring a trussed sheep with him.

"I can't do that, it's too risky, but I'll send one of the ducks to you," the pilot told him. "Can you hang on a while longer?"

"I'll hang on all right," the man said.

As they climbed away the pilot laughed and shook his head.

"That beats everything I've seen," he said to one of the rescued in the cabin. "He must be crazy about sheep."

His passenger looked down at the desolation and said, "It gets some like that, out here. That must be the only live sheep anywhere in all this."

The pilot could see that, although it had no special impact on him. He had seen all kinds of desolation. And he said, "Oh, well, I suppose that gives it some value. I guess it makes sense from his point of view."

But he couldn't help smiling again at the memory of that wild-looking man sitting astride a high branch, with his feet in the flood, and hanging on to that trussed sheep with both hands as though it had a golden fleece.

AN OCCURRENCE AT OWL CREEK BRIDGE

Ambrose Bierce

I

A man stood upon a railroad bridge in Northern Alabama, looking down into the swift waters twenty feet below. The man's hands were behind his back, the wrists bound with a cord. A rope loosely encircled his neck. It was attached to a stout cross-timber above his head, and the slack fell to the level of his knees. Some loose boards laid upon the sleepers supporting the metals of the railway supplied a footing for him and his executioners—two private soldiers of the Federal army, directed by a sergeant, who in civil life may have been a deputy sheriff. At a short remove upon the same temporary platform was an officer in the uniform of his rank, armed. He was a captain. A sentinel at each end of the bridge stood with his rifle in the position known as "Support," that is to say, vertical in front of the left shoulder, the hammer resting on the forearm thrown straight across the chest—a formal and unnatural position, enforcing an erect carriage of the body. It did not appear to be the duty of these two men to know what was occurring at the centre of the bridge; they merely blockaded the two ends of the foot plank which traversed it.

Beyond one of the sentinels nobody was in sight; the railroad ran straight away into a forest for a hundred yards, then, curving, was lost to view. Doubtless there was an outpost further along. The other bank of the stream was open ground—a gentle acclivity crowned with a stockade of vertical tree trunks, loop-holed for rifles, with a single embrasure through which protruded the muzzle of a brass cannon commanding the bridge. Midway of the slope between bridge and fort were the spectators—a single company of infantry in line, at "parade rest," the butts of the rifles on the ground, the barrels inclining slightly backward against the right shoulder, the hands crossed upon the stock. A lieutenant stood at the right of the line, the point of his sword upon the ground, his left hand resting upon his right. Excepting the group of four at the centre of the bridge not a man moved. The company faced the bridge, staring stonily, motionless. The sentinels, facing the banks of the stream, might have been statues to adorn the bridge. The captain stood with folded arms, silent, observing the work of his subordinates but making no sign. Death is a dignitary who, when he comes announced, is to be received with formal manifestations of respect, even by those most familiar with him. In the code of military etiquette silence and fixity are forms of deference.

The man who was engaged in being hanged was apparently about thirty-five years of age. He was a civilian, if one might judge from his dress, which was that of a planter. His features were good—a straight nose, firm mouth, broad forehead, from which his long, dark hair was combed straight back, falling behind his ears to the collar of his well-fitting frock coat. He wore a moustache and pointed beard, but no whiskers; his eyes were large and dark grey and had a kindly expression which one would hardly have expected in one whose neck was in the hemp. Evidently this was no vulgar assassin. The liberal military code makes provision for hanging many kinds of people, and gentlemen are not excluded.

The preparations being complete, the two

— "*An Occurrence at Owl Creek Bridge*" by Ambrose Bierce; reprinted from *In the Midst of Life* by Ambrose Bierce, published by Chatto and Windus, London, 1964, (first edition, 1892); also Clarke, Irwin and Company Limited, Toronto, 1964

private soldiers stepped aside and each drew away the plank upon which he had been standing. The sergeant turned to the captain, saluted and placed himself immediately behind that officer, who in turn moved apart one pace. These movements left the condemned man and the sergeant standing on the two ends of the same plank, which spanned three of the cross-ties of the bridge. The end upon which the civilian stood almost, but not quite, reached a fourth. This plank had been held in place by the weight of the captain; it was now held by that of the sergeant. At a signal from the former, the latter would step aside, the plank would tilt and the condemned man go down between two ties. The arrangement commended itself to his judgment as simple and effective. His face had not been covered nor his eyes bandaged. He looked a moment at his "unsteadfast footing," then let his gaze wander to the swirling water of the stream racing madly beneath his feet. A piece of dancing driftwood caught his attention and his eyes followed it down the current. How slowly it appeared to move! What a sluggish stream!

He closed his eyes in order to fix his last thoughts upon his wife and children. The water, touched to gold by the early sun, the brooding mists under the banks at some distance down the stream, the fort, the soldiers, the piece of drift— all had distracted him. And now he became conscious of a new disturbance. Striking through the thought of his dear ones was a sound which he could neither ignore nor understand, a sharp, distinct, metallic percussion like the stroke of a blacksmith's hammer upon the anvil; it had the same ringing quality. He wondered what it was, and whether immeasurably distant or near by— it seemed both. Its recurrence was regular, but as slow as the tolling of a death knell. He awaited each stroke with impatience and—he knew not why—apprehension. The intervals of silence grew progressively longer; the delays became maddening. With their greater in-frequency the sounds increased in strength and sharpness. They hurt his ear like the thrust of a

knife; he feared he would shriek. What he heard was the ticking of his watch.

He unclosed his eyes and saw again the water below him. "If I could free my hands," he thought, "I might throw off the noose and spring into the stream. By diving I could evade the bullets, and, swimming vigorously, reach the bank, take to the woods, and get away home. My home, thank God, is as yet outside their lines; my wife and little ones are still beyond the invader's farthest advance."

As these thoughts, which have here to be set down in words, were flashed into the doomed man's brain rather than evolved from it, the captain nodded to the sergeant. The sergeant stepped aside.

II

Peyton Farquhar was a well-to-do planter, of an old and highly-respected Alabama family. Being a slave owner, and, like other slave owners, a politician, he was naturally an original secession-ist and ardently devoted to the Southern cause. Circumstances of an imperious nature which it is unnecessary to relate here, had prevented him from taking service with the gallant army which had fought the disastrous campaigns ending with the fall of Corinth, and he chafed under the in-glorious restraint, longing for the release of his energies, the larger life of the soldier, the oppor-tunity for distinction. That opportunity, he felt, would come, as it comes to all in war time. Meanwhile he did what he could. No service was too humble for him to perform in aid of the South, no adventure too perilous for him to undertake if consistent with the character of a civilian who was at heart a soldier, and who in good faith and without too much qualification assented to at least a part of the frankly villainous dictum that all is fair in love and war.

One evening while Farquhar and his wife were sitting on a rustic bench near the entrance to his grounds, a grey-clad soldier rode up to the gate and asked for a drink of water. Mrs. Farquhar was only too happy to serve him with her own white hands. *slave owners.* While she was gone to fetch the water, her husband approached the dusty horseman and inquired eagerly for news from the front.

"The Yanks are repairing the railroads," said the man, "and are getting ready for another advance. They have reached the Owl Creek bridge, put it in order, and built a stockade on the other bank. The commandant has issued an order, which is posted everywhere, declaring that any civilian caught interfering with the railroad, its bridges, tunnels, or trains, will be summarily hanged. I saw the order."

"How far is it to the Owl Creek bridge?" Farquhar asked.

"About thirty miles."

"Is there no force on this side the creek?"

"Only a picket post half a mile out, on the railroad, and a single sentinel at this end of the bridge."

"Suppose a man—a civilian and student of hanging—should elude the picket post and perhaps get the better of the sentinel," said Farquhar, smiling, "what could he accomplish?"

The soldier reflected. "I was there a month ago," he replied. "I observed that the flood of last winter had lodged a great quantity of driftwood against the wooden pier at this end of the bridge. It is now dry and would burn like tow."

The lady had now brought the water, which the soldier drank. He thanked her ceremoniously, bowed to her husband, and rode away. An hour later, after nightfall, he repassed the plantation, going northward in the direction from which he had come. He was a Federal scout.

III

As Peyton Farquhar fell straight downward through the bridge, he lost consciousness and was as one already dead. From this state he was awakened—ages later, it seemed to him—by the pain of a sharp pressure upon his throat, followed by a sense of suffocation. Keen, poignant agonies seemed to shoot from his neck downward through every fibre of his body and limbs. These pains appeared to flash along well-defined lines of ramification, and to beat with an inconceivably rapid periodicity. They seemed like streams of pulsating fire heating him to an intolerable temperature. As to his head, he was conscious of nothing but a feeling of fullness—of congestion. These sensations were unaccompanied by thought. The intellectual part of his nature was already effaced; he had power only to feel, and feeling was torment. He was conscious of motion. Encompassed in a luminous cloud, of which he was now merely the fiery heart, without material substance, he swung through unthinkable arcs of oscillation, like a vast pendulum. Then all at once, with terrible suddenness, the light about him shot upward with the noise of a loud plash; a frightful roaring was in his ears, and all was cold and dark. The power of thought was restored; he knew that the rope had broken and he had fallen into the stream. There was no additional strangulation; the noose about his neck was already suffocating him, and kept the water from his lungs. To die of hanging at the bottom of a river!—the idea seemed to him ludicrous. He opened his eyes in the blackness and saw above him a gleam of light, but how distant, how inaccessible! He was still sinking, for the light became fainter and fainter until it was a mere glimmer. Then it began to grow and brighten, and he knew that he was rising toward the surface—knew it with reluctance, for he was now very comfortable. "To be hanged and drowned," he thought, "that is not so bad; but I do not wish to be shot. No; I will not be shot; that is not fair."

He was not conscious of an effort, but a sharp pain in his wrists apprised him that he was trying to free his hands. He gave the struggle his attention, as an idler might observe the feat of a juggler, without interest in the outcome. What splendid effort!—what magnificent, what superhuman strength! Ah, that was a fine endeavour! Bravo! The cord fell away; his arms parted and floated upward, the hands dimly seen on each side in the growing light. He watched them with a new interest as first one and then the other pounced upon the noose at his neck. They tore it away and thrust it fiercely aside, its undulations resembling those of a water-snake. "Put it back, put it back!" He thought he shouted these words to his hands, for the undoing of the noose had been succeeded by the direst pang which he had yet experienced. His neck ached horribly; his brain was on fire; his heart, which had been fluttering faintly, gave a great leap, trying to force itself out at his mouth. His whole body was racked and wrenched with an insupportable anguish! But his disobedient hands gave no heed to the command. They beat the water vigorously with quick, downward strokes, forcing him to the surface. He felt his head emerge; his eyes were blinded by the sunlight; his chest expanded convulsively, and with a supreme and crowning agony his lungs engulfed a great draught of air, which instantly he expelled in a shriek!

He was now in full possession of his physical senses. They were, indeed, preternaturally keen and alert. Something in the awful disturbance of his organic system had so exalted and refined them that they made record of things never before perceived. He felt the ripples upon his face and heard their separate sounds as they struck. He looked at the forest on the bank of the stream, saw the individual trees, the leaves and the veining of each leaf—saw the very insects upon them, the locusts, the brilliant-bodied flies, the grey spiders stretching their webs from twig to twig. He noted the prismatic colours in all the dewdrops upon a million blades of grass. The humming of the gnats that danced above the eddies of the stream, the beating of the dragonflies' wings, the strokes of the water spiders' legs, like oars which had lifted their boat—all these made audible music. A fish slid along beneath his eyes and he heard the rush of its body parting the water.

He had come to the surface facing down the stream; in a moment the visible world seemed to wheel slowly round, himself the pivotal point, and he saw the bridge, the fort, the soldiers upon the bridge, the captain, the sergeant, the two privates, his executioners. They were in silhouette against the blue sky. They shouted and gesticulated, pointing at him; the captain had drawn his pistol, but did not fire; the others were unarmed. Their movements were grotesque and horrible, their forms gigantic.

Suddenly he heard a sharp report and something struck the water smartly within a few inches of his head, spattering his face with spray. He heard a second report, and saw one of the sentinels with his rifle at his shoulder, a light cloud of blue smoke rising from the muzzle. The man in the water saw the eye of the man on the bridge gazing into his own through the sights of the rifle. He observed that it was a grey eye, and remembered having read that grey eyes were keenest and that all famous marksmen had them. Nevertheless, this one had missed.

A counter swirl had caught Farquhar and turned him half round; he was again looking into the forest on the bank opposite the fort. The sound of a clear, high voice in a monotonous singsong now rang out behind him and came across the water with a distinctness that pierced and subdued all other sounds, even the beating of the ripples in his ears. Although no soldier, he had frequented camps enough to know the dread significance of that deliberate, drawling, aspirated chant; the lieutenant on shore was taking a part in the morning's work. How coldly and pitilessly—with what an even, calm intonation, presaging and enforcing tranquility in the men—with what accurately-measured intervals fell those cruel words:

"Attention, company. —— Shoulder arms. —— Ready. —— Aim. —— Fire."

Farquhar dived—dived as deeply as he could. The water roared in his ears like the voice of Niagara, yet he heard the dulled thunder of the volley, and rising again toward the surface, met shining bits of metal, singularly flattened, oscillating slowly downward. Some of them touched him on the face and hands, then fell away, continuing their descent. One lodged between his collar and neck; it was uncomfortably warm, and he snatched it out.

As he rose to the surface, gasping for breath, he saw that he had been a long time under water; he was perceptibly farther down stream—nearer to safety. The soldiers had almost finished reloading; the metal ramrods flashed all at once in the sunshine as they were drawn from the barrels, turned in the air, and thrust into their sockets. The two sentinels fired again, independently and ineffectually.

The hunted man saw all this over his shoulder; he was now swimming vigorously with the current. His brain was as energetic as his arms and legs; he thought with the rapidity of lightning.

"The officer," he reasoned, "will not make that martinet's error a second time. It is as easy to dodge a volley as a single shot. He has probably already given the command to fire at will. God help me, I cannot dodge them all!"

An appalling plash within two yards of him, followed by a loud rushing sound, *diminuendo*, which seemed to travel back through the air to the fort and died in an explosion which stirred the very river to its deeps! A rising sheet of water, which curved over him, fell down upon him, blinded him, strangled him! The cannon had taken a hand in the game. As he shook his head free from the commotion of the smitten water, he heard the deflected shot humming through the air ahead, and in an instant it was cracking and smashing the branches in the forest beyond.

"They will not do that again," he thought; "the next time they will use a charge of grape. I must keep my eye upon the gun; the smoke will apprise me—the report arrives too late; it lags behind the missile. It is a good gun."

Suddenly he felt himself whirled round and round—spinning like a top. The water, the banks, the forest, the now distant bridge, fort and men—all were commingled and blurred. Objects were represented by their colours only; circular horizontal streaks of colour—that was

all he saw. He had been caught in a vortex and was being whirled on with a velocity of advance and gyration which made him giddy and sick. In a few moments he was flung upon the gravel at the foot of the left bank of the stream—the southern bank—and behind a projecting point which concealed him from his enemies. The sudden arrest of his motion, the abrasion of one of his hands on the gravel, restored him and he wept with delight. He dug his fingers into the sand, threw it over himself in handfuls and audibly blessed it. It looked like gold, like diamonds, rubies, emeralds; he could think of nothing beautiful which it did not resemble. The trees upon the bank were giant garden plants; he noted a definite order in their arrangement, inhaled the fragrance of their blooms. A strange, roseate light shone through the spaces among their trunks, and the wind made in their branches the music of aeolian harps. He had no wish to perfect his escape, was content to remain in that enchanting spot until retaken.

A whizz and rattle of grapeshot among the branches high above his head roused him from his dream. The baffled cannoneer had fired him a random farewell. He sprang to his feet, rushed up the sloping bank, and plunged into the forest.

All that day he travelled, laying his course by the rounding sun. The forest seemed interminable; nowhere did he discover a break in it, not even a woodsman's road. He had not known that he lived in so wild a region. There was something uncanny in the revelation.

By nightfall he was fatigued, footsore, famishing. The thought of his wife and children urged him on. At last he found a road which led him in what he knew to be the right direction. It was as wide and straight as a city street, yet it seemed untravelled. No fields bordered it, no dwelling anywhere. Not so much as the barking of a dog suggested human habitation. The black bodies of the great trees formed a straight wall on both sides, terminating on the horizon in a point, like a diagram in a lesson in perspective. Overhead, as he looked up through this rift in the wood, shone great golden stars looking unfamiliar and grouped in strange constellations. He was sure they were arranged in some order which had a secret and malign significance. The wood on either side was full of singular noises, among which—once, twice, and again—he distinctly heard whispers in an unknown tongue.

His neck was in pain, and, lifting his hand to it, he found it horribly swollen. He knew that it had a circle of black where the rope had bruised it. His eyes felt congested; he could no longer close them. His tongue was swollen with thirst; he relieved its fever by thrusting it forward from between his teeth into the cool air. How softly the turf had carpeted the untravelled avenue! He could no longer feel the roadway beneath his feet!

Doubtless, despite his suffering, he fell asleep while walking, for now he sees another scene—

perhaps he has merely recovered from a delirium. He stands at the gate of his own home. All is as he left it, and all bright and beautiful in the morning sunshine. He must have travelled the entire night. As he pushes open the gate and passes up the wide white walk, he sees a flutter of female garments; his wife, looking fresh and cool and sweet, steps down from the verandah to meet him. At the bottom of the steps she stands waiting, with a smile of ineffable joy, an attitude of matchless grace and dignity. Ah, how beautiful she is! He springs forward with extended arms. As he is about to clasp her, he feels a stunning blow upon the back of the neck; a blinding white light blazes all about him, with a sound like the shock of a cannon—then all is darkness and silence!

Peyton Farquhar was dead; his body, with a broken neck, swung gently from side to side beneath the timbers of the Owl Creek bridge.

FLIGHT

John Steinbeck

About fifteen miles below Monterey, on the wild coast, the Torres family had their farm, a few sloping acres above a cliff that dropped to the brown reefs and to the hissing white waters of the ocean. Behind the farm the stone mountains stood up against the sky. The farm buildings huddled like little clinging aphids on the mountain skirts, crouched low to the ground as though the wind might blow them into the

sea. The little shack, the rattling, rotting barn were gray-bitten with sea salt, beaten by the damp wind until they had taken on the color of the granite hills. Two horses, a red cow and a red calf, half a dozen pigs and a flock of lean, multicolored chickens stocked the place. A little corn was raised on the sterile slope, and it grew short and thick under the wind, and all the cobs formed on the landward sides of the stalks.

Mama Torres, a lean, dry woman with ancient eyes, had ruled the farm for ten years, ever since her husband tripped over a stone in the field one day and fell full length on a rattlesnake. When one is bitten on the chest there is not much that can be done.

Mama Torres had three children, two under-

— *"Flight" by John Steinbeck, from The Long Valley by John Steinbeck; copyright 1938, © 1966 by John Steinbeck; reprinted by permission of The Viking Press, Inc.*

sized black ones of twelve and fourteen, Emilio and Rosy, whom Mama kept fishing on the rocks below the farm when the sea was kind and when the truant officer was in some distant part of Monterey County. And there was Pepé, the tall smiling son of nineteen, a gentle, affectionate boy, but very lazy. Pepé had a tall head, pointed at the top, and from its peak, coarse black hair grew down like a thatch all around. Over his smiling little eyes Mama cut a straight bang so he could see. Pepé had sharp Indian cheek bones and an eagle nose, but his mouth was as sweet and shapely as a girl's mouth, and his chin was fragile and chiseled. He was loose and gangling, all legs and feet and wrists, and he was very lazy. Mama thought him fine and brave, but she never told him so. She said, "Some lazy cow must have got into thy father's family, else how could I have a son like thee." And she said, "When I carried thee, a sneaking lazy coyote came out of the brush and looked at me one day. That must have made thee so."

Pepé smiled sheepishly and stabbed at the ground with his knife to keep the blade sharp and free from rust. It was his inheritance, that knife, his father's knife. The long heavy blade folded back into the black handle. There was a button on the handle. When Pepé pressed the button, the blade leaped out ready for use. The knife was with Pepé always, for it had been his father's knife.

One sunny morning when the sea below the cliff was glinting and blue and the white surf creamed on the reef, when even the stone mountains looked kindly, Mama Torres called out the door of the shack, "Pepé, I have a labor for thee."

There was no answer. Mama listened. From behind the barn she heard a burst of laughter. She lifted her full long skirt and walked in the direction of the noise.

Pepé was sitting on the ground with his back against a box. His white teeth glistened. On either side of him stood the two black ones, tense and expectant. Fifteen feet away a redwood post was set in the ground. Pepé's right hand lay limply in his lap, and in the palm the big black knife rested. The blade was closed back into the handle. Pepé looked smiling at the sky.

Suddenly Emilio cried, "Ya!"

Pepé's wrist flicked like the head of a snake. The blade seemed to fly open in mid-air, and with a thump the point dug into the redwood post, and the black handle quivered. The three burst into excited laughter. Rosy ran to the post and pulled out the knife and brought it back to Pepé. He closed the blade and settled the knife carefully in his listless palm again. He grinned self-consciously at the sky.

"Ya!"

The heavy knife lanced out and sank into the post again. Mama moved forward like a ship and scattered the play.

"All day you do foolish things with the knife, like a toy-baby," she stormed. "Get up on thy huge feet that eat up shoes. Get up!" She took him by one loose shoulder and hoisted at him. Pepé grinned sheepishly and came half-heartedly to his feet. "Look!" Mama cried. "Big lazy, you must catch the horse and put on him thy father's saddle. You must ride to Monterey. The medicine bottle is empty. There is no salt. Go thou now, Peanut! Catch the horse."

A revolution took place in the relaxed figure of Pepé. "To Monterey, me? Alone? Sí, Mama."

She scowled at him. "Do not think, big sheep, that you will buy candy. No, I will give you only enough for the medicine and the salt."

Pepé smiled. "Mama, you will put the hat-band on the hat?"

She relented then. "Yes, Pepé. You may wear the hatband."

His voice grew insinuating. "And the green handkerchief, Mama?"

"Yes, if you go quickly and return with no trouble, the silk green handkerchief will go. If you make sure to take off the handkerchief when you eat so no spot may fall on it. ——"

"Sí, Mama. I will be careful. I am a man."

"Thou? A man? Thou art a peanut."

He went into the rickety barn and brought out a rope, and he walked agilely enough up the hill to catch the horse.

When he was ready and mounted before the door, mounted on his father's saddle that was so old that the oaken frame showed through torn leather in many places, then Mama brought out the round black hat with the tooled leather band, and she reached up and knotted the green silk handkerchief about his neck. Pepé's blue denim coat was much darker than his jeans, for it had been washed much less often.

Mama handed up the big medicine bottle and the silver coins. "That for the medicine," she said, "and that for the salt. That for a candle to burn for the papa. That for *dulces* for the little ones. Our friend Mrs. Rodriguez will give you dinner and maybe a bed for the night. When you go to the church say only ten Paternosters and only twenty-five Ave Marias. Oh! I know, big coyote. You would sit there flapping your mouth over Aves all day while you looked at the candles and the holy pictures. That is not good devotion to stare at the pretty things."

The black hat, covering the high pointed head and black thatched hair of Pepé, gave him dignity and age. He sat the rangy horse well. Mama thought how handsome he was, dark and lean and tall. "I would not send thee now alone, thou little one, except for the medicine," she said softly. "It is not good to have no medicine, for who knows when the toothache will come, or the sadness of the stomach. These things are."

"Adios, Mama," Pepé cried. "I will come back soon. You may send me often alone. I am a man."

"Thou art a foolish chicken."

He straightened his shoulders, flipped the reins against the horse's shoulder and rode away. He turned once and saw that they still watched him, Emilio and Rosy and Mama. Pepé grinned with pride and gladness and lifted the rough buckskin horse to a trot.

When he had dropped out of sight over a little dip in the road, Mama turned to the black ones, but she spoke to herself. "He is nearly a man now," she said. "It will be a nice thing to have a man in the house again." Her eyes sharpened on the children. "Go to the rocks now. The tide is going out. There will be abalones to be found." She put the iron hooks into their hands and saw them down the steep trail to the reefs. She brought the smooth stone *metate* to the doorway and sat grinding her corn to flour and looking occasionally at the road over which Pepé had gone. The noonday came and then the afternoon, when the little ones beat the abalones on a rock to make them tender and Mama patted the tortillas to make them thin. They ate their dinner as the red sun was plunging down toward the ocean. They sat on the doorsteps and watched the big white moon come over the mountain tops.

Mama said, "He is now at the house of our friend Mrs. Rodriguez. She will give him nice things to eat and maybe a present."

Emilio said, "Some day I too will ride to Monterey for medicine. Did Pepé come to be a man today?"

Mama said wisely, "A boy gets to be a man when a man is needed. Remember this thing. I have known boys forty years old because there was no need for a man."

Soon afterwards they retired, Mama in her big oak bed on one side of the room, Emilio and Rosy in their boxes full of straw and sheepskins on the other side of the room.

The moon went over the sky and the surf roared on the rocks. The roosters crowed the first call. The surf subsided to a whispering surge against the reef. The moon dropped toward the sea. The roosters crowed again.

The moon was near down to the water when Pepé rode on a winded horse to his home flat. His dog bounced out and circled the horse yelping with pleasure. Pepé slid off the saddle to the ground. The weathered little shack was silver in the moonlight and the square shadow of it was black to the north and east. Against the east the piling mountains were misty with light; their tops melted into the sky.

Pepé walked wearily up the three steps and into the house. It was dark inside. There was a rustle in the corner.

Mama cried out from her bed. "Who comes? Pepé, is it thou?"

"*Sí*, Mama."

"Did you get the medicine?"

"*Sí*, Mama."

"Well, go to sleep, then. I thought you would be sleeping at the house of Mrs. Rodriguez." Pepé stood silently in the dark room. "Why do you stand there, Pepé? Did you drink wine?"

"*Sí*, Mama."

"Well go to bed then and sleep out the wine."

His voice was tired and patient, but very firm. "Light the candle, Mama. I must go away into the mountains."

"What is this, Pepé? You are crazy." Mama struck a sulphur match and held the little blue burr until the flame spread up the stick. She set light to the candle on the floor beside her bed. "Now, Pepé, what is this you say?" She looked anxiously into his face.

He was changed. The fragile quality seemed to have gone from his chin. His mouth was less full than it had been, the lines of the lips were straighter, but in his eyes the greatest change had taken place. There was no laughter in them anymore, nor any bashfulness. They were sharp and bright and purposeful.

He told her in a tired monotone, told her everything just as it had happened. A few people came into the kitchen of Mrs. Rodriguez. There was wine to drink. Pepé drank wine. The little quarrel—the man started toward Pepé and then the knife—it went almost by itself. It flew, it darted before Pepé knew it. As he talked, Mama's face grew stern, and it seemed to grow more lean. Pepé finished. "I am a man now, Mama. The man said names to me I could not allow."

Mama nodded. "Yes, thou art a man, my poor little Pepé. Thou art a man. I have seen it coming on thee. I have watched you throwing

the knife into the post, and I have been afraid." For a moment her face had softened, but now it grew stern again. "Come! We must get you ready. Go. Awaken Emilio and Rosy. Go quickly."

Pepé stepped over to the corner where his brother and sister slept among the sheepskins. He leaned down and shook them gently. "Come, Rosy! Come, Emilio! The mama says you must arise."

The little black ones sat up and rubbed their eyes in the candlelight. Mama was out of bed now, her long black skirt over her nightgown. "Emilio," she cried. "Go up and catch the other horse for Pepé. Quickly, now! Quickly." Emilio put his legs in his overalls and stumbled sleepily out the door.

"You heard no one behind you on the road?" Mama demanded.

"No, Mama. I listened carefully. No one was on the road."

Mama darted like a bird about the room. From a nail on the wall she took a canvas water bag and threw it on the floor. She stripped a blanket from her bed and rolled it into a tight tube and tied the ends with string. From a box beside the stove she lifted a flour sack half full of black stringy jerky. "Your father's black coat, Pepé. Here, put it on."

Pepé stood in the middle of the floor watching her activity. She reached behind the door and brought out the rifle, a long 38-56, worn shiny the whole length of the barrel. Pepé took it from her and held it in the crook of his elbow. Mama brought a little leather bag and counted the cartridges into his hand. "Only ten left," she warned. "You must not waste them."

Emilio put his head in the door. " *'Qui 'st 'l caballo*, Mama."

"Put on the saddle from the other horse. Tie on the blanket. Here, tie the jerky to the saddle horn."

Still Pepé stood silently watching his mother's frantic activity. His chin looked hard, and his sweet mouth was drawn and thin. His little eyes followed Mama about the room almost suspiciously.

Rosy asked softly, "Where goes Pepé?"

Mama's eyes were fierce. "Pepé goes on a journey. Pepé is a man now. He has a man's thing to do."

Pepé straightened his shoulders. His mouth changed until he looked very much like Mama.

At last the preparation was finished. The loaded horse stood outside the door. The water bag dripped a line of moisture down the bay shoulder.

The moonlight was being thinned by the dawn and the big white moon was near down to the sea. The family stood by the shack. Mama confronted Pepé. "Look, my son! Do not stop until it is dark again. Do not sleep even though you are tired. Take care of the horse in order that he may not stop of weariness. Remember to be careful with the bullets—there are only ten. Do not fill thy stomach with jerky or it will make thee sick. Eat a little jerky and fill thy stomach with grass. When thou comest to the high mountains, if thou seest any of the dark watching men, go not near to them nor try to speak to them. And forget not thy prayers." She put her lean hands on Pepé's shoulders, stood on her toes and kissed him formally on both cheeks, and Pepé kissed her on both cheeks. Then he went to Emilio and Rosy and kissed both of their cheeks.

Pepé turned back to Mama. He seemed to look for a little softness, a little weakness in her. His eyes were searching, but Mama's face remained fierce. "Go now," she said. "Do not wait to be caught like a chicken."

Pepé pulled himself into the saddle. "I am a man," he said.

It was the first dawn when he rode up the hill toward the little canyon which let a trail into the mountains. Moonlight and daylight fought with each other, and the two warring qualities made it difficult to see. Before Pepé had gone a hundred yards, the outlines of his figure were misty; and long before he entered the canyon, he had become a gray, indefinite shadow.

Mama stood stiffly in front of her doorstep, and on either side of her stood Emilio and Rosy. They cast furtive glances at Mama now and then.

When the gray shape of Pepé melted into the hillside and disappeared, Mama relaxed. She began the high, whining keen of the death wail. "Our beautiful—our brave," she cried. "Our protector, our son is gone." Emilio and Rosy moaned beside her. "Our beautiful—our brave, he is gone." It was the formal wail. It rose to a high piercing whine and subsided to a moan. Mama raised it three times and then she turned and went into the house and shut the door.

Emilio and Rosy stood wondering in the dawn. They heard Mama whimpering in the house. They went out to sit on the cliff above the ocean. They touched shoulders. "When did Pepé come to be a man?" Emilio asked.

"Last night," said Rosy. "Last night in Monterey." The ocean clouds turned red with the sun that was behind the mountains.

"We will have no breakfast," said Emilio. "Mama will not want to cook." Rosy did not answer him. "Where is Pepé gone?" he asked.

Rosy looked around at him. She drew her knowledge from the quiet air. "He has gone on a journey. He will never come back."

"Is he dead? Do you think he is dead?"

Rosy looked back at the ocean again. A little steamer, drawing a line of smoke, sat on the edge of the horizon. "He is not dead," Rosy explained. "Not yet."

Pepé rested the big rifle across the saddle in front of him. He let the horse walk up the hill and he didn't look back. The stony slope took on a coat of short brush so that Pepé found the entrance to a trail and entered it.

When he came to the canyon opening, he swung once in his saddle and looked back, but the houses were swallowed in the misty light. Pepé jerked forward again. The high shoulder of the canyon closed in on him. His horse stretched out its neck and sighed and settled to the trail.

It was a well-worn path, dark soft leaf-mould earth strewn with broken pieces of sandstone. The trail rounded the shoulder of the canyon and dropped steeply into the bed of the stream. In the shallows the water ran smoothly, glinting in the first morning sun. Small round stones on the bottom were as brown as rust with sun moss. In the sand along the edges of the stream the tall, rich wild mint grew, while in the water itself the cress, old and tough, had gone to heavy seed.

The path went into the stream and emerged on the other side. The horse sloshed into the water and stopped. Pepé dropped his bridle and let the beast drink of the running water.

Soon the canyon sides became steep and the first giant sentinel redwoods guarded the trail, great round red trunks bearing foliage as green and lacy as ferns. Once Pepé was among the trees, the sun was lost. A perfumed and purple light lay in the pale green of the underbrush. Gooseberry bushes and blackberries and tall ferns lined the stream, and overhead the branches of the redwoods met and cut off the sky.

Pepé drank from the water bag, and he reached into the flour sack and brought out a black string of jerky. His white teeth gnawed at the string until the tough meat parted. He chewed slowly and drank occasionally from the water bag. His little eyes were slumberous and tired, but the muscles of his face were hard set. The earth of the trail was black now. It gave up a hollow sound under the walking hoofbeats.

The stream fell more sharply. Little waterfalls splashed on the stones. Five-fingered ferns hung over the water and dripped spray from their fingertips. Pepé rode half over in his saddle, dangling one leg loosely. He picked a bay leaf from a tree beside the way and put it into his mouth for a moment to flavor the dry jerky. He held the gun loosely across the pommel.

Suddenly he squared in his saddle, swung the horse from the trail and kicked it hurriedly up behind a big redwood tree. He pulled up the reins tight against the bit to keep the horse from whinnying. His face was intent and his nostrils quivered a little.

A hollow pounding came down the trail, and a horseman rode by, a fat man with red cheeks and a white stubble beard. His horse put down its head and blubbered at the trail when it came to the place where Pepé had turned off. "Hold up!" said the man and he pulled up his horse's head.

When the last sound of the hoofs died away, Pepé came back into the trail again. He did not relax in the saddle any more. He lifted the big rifle and swung the lever to throw a shell into the chamber, and then he let down the hammer to half cock.

The trail grew very steep. Now the redwood trees were smaller and their tops were dead, bitten dead where the wind reached them. The horse plodded on; the sun went slowly overhead and started down toward the afternoon.

Where the stream came out of a side canyon, the trail left it. Pepé dismounted and watered his horse and filled up his water bag. As soon as the trail had parted from the stream, the trees were gone and only the thick brittle sage and manzanita and chaparral edged the trail. And the soft black earth was gone, too, leaving only the light tan broken rock for the trail bed. Lizards scampered away into the brush as the horse rattled over the little stones.

Pepé turned in his saddle and looked back. He was in the open now: he could be seen from a distance. As he ascended the trail the country grew more rough and terrible and dry. The way wound about the bases of great square rocks. Little gray rabbits skittered in the brush. A bird made a monotonous high creaking. Eastward the bare rock mountaintops were pale and powder-dry under the dropping sun. The horse plodded up and up the trail toward a little V in the ridge which was the pass.

Pepé looked suspiciously back every minute or so, and his eyes sought the tops of the ridges ahead. Once, on a white barren spur, he saw a black figure for a moment, but he looked quickly away, for it was one of the dark watchers. No one knew who the watchers were, nor where they lived, but it was better to ignore them and never to show interest in them. They did not bother one who stayed on the trail and minded his own business.

The air was parched and full of light dust blown by the breeze from the eroding mountains. Pepé drank sparingly from his bag and corked it tightly and hung it on the horn again. The trail moved up the dry shale hillside, avoiding rocks, dropping under clefts, climbing in and out of old water scars. When he arrived at the little pass he stopped and looked back for a long time. No dark watchers were to be seen now. The trail behind was empty. Only the high tops of the redwoods indicated where the stream flowed.

Pepé rode on through the pass. His little eyes were nearly closed with weariness, but his face was stern, relentless and manly. The high mountain wind coasted sighing through the pass and whistled on the edges of the big blocks of broken granite. In the air, a red-tailed hawk sailed over close to the ridge and screamed angrily. Pepé went slowly through the broken jagged pass and looked down on the other side.

The trail dropped quickly, staggering among broken rock. At the bottom of the slope there was a dark crease, thick with brush, and on the other side of the crease a little flat, in which a grove of oak trees grew. A scar of green grass cut across the flat. And behind the flat another mountain rose, desolate with dead rocks and starving little black bushes. Pepé drank from the bag again for the air was so dry that it encrusted his nostrils and burned his lips. He put the horse down the trail. The hooves slipped and struggled on the steep way, starting little stones that rolled off into the brush. The sun was gone behind the westward mountain now, but still it glowed brilliantly on the oaks and on the grassy flat. The rocks and the hillsides still sent up waves of the heat they had gathered from the day's sun.

Pepé looked up to the top of the next dry withered ridge. He saw a dark form against the sky, a man's figure standing on top of a rock, and he glanced away quickly not to appear curious. When a moment later he looked up again, the figure was gone.

Downward the trail was quickly covered. Sometimes the horse floundered for footing, sometimes set his feet and slid a little way. They came at last to the bottom where the dark chaparral was higher than Pepé's head. He held up his rifle on one side and his arm on the other to shield his face from the sharp brittle fingers of the brush.

Up and out of the crease he rode, and up a little cliff. The grassy flat was before him, and the round comfortable oaks. For a moment he studied the trail down which he had come, but there was no movement and no sound from it. Finally he rode out over the flat, to the green streak, and at the upper end of the damp he found a little spring welling out of the earth and dropping into a dug basin before it seeped out over the flat.

Pepé filled his bag first, and then he let the thirsty horse drink out of the pool. He led the horse to the clump of oaks, and in the middle of the grove, fairly protected from sight on all sides, he took off the saddle and the bridle and laid them on the ground. The horse stretched his jaws sideways and yawned. Pepé knotted the lead rope about the horse's neck and tied him to a sapling among the oaks, where he could graze in a fairly large circle.

When the horse was gnawing hungrily at the dry grass, Pepé went to the saddle and took a black string of jerky from the sack and strolled to an oak tree on the edge of the grove, from under which he could watch the trail. He sat down in the crisp dry oak leaves and automatically felt for his big black knife to cut the jerky, but he had no knife. He leaned back on his elbow and gnawed at the tough strong meat. His face was blank, but it was a man's face.

The bright evening light washed the eastern

ridge, but the valley was darkening. Doves flew down from the hills to the spring, and the quail came running out of the brush and joined them, calling clearly to one another.

Out of the corner of his eye Pepé saw a shadow grow out of the bushy crease. He turned his head slowly. A big spotted wildcat was creeping towards the spring, belly to the ground, moving like thought.

Pepé cocked his rifle and edged the muzzle slowly around. Then he looked apprehensively up the trail and dropped the hammer again. From the ground beside him he picked an oak twig and threw it toward the spring. The quail flew up with a roar and the doves whistled away. The big cat stood up: for a long moment he looked at Pepé with cold yellow eyes, and then fearlessly walked back into the gulch.

The dusk gathered quickly in the deep valley. Pepé muttered his prayers, put his head down on his arm and went instantly to sleep.

The moon came up and filled the valley with cold blue light, and the wind swept rustling down from the peaks. The owls worked up and down the slopes looking for rabbits. Down in the brush of the gulch a coyote gabbled. The oak trees whispered softly in the night breeze.

Pepé started up, listening. His horse had whinnied. The moon was just slipping behind the western ridge, leaving the valley in darkness behind it. Pepé sat tensely gripping his rifle. From far up the trail he heard an answering whinny and the crash of shod hooves on the broken rock. He jumped to his feet, ran to his horse and led it under the trees. He threw on the saddle and cinched it tight for the steep trail, caught the unwilling head and forced the bit into the mouth. He felt the saddle to make sure the water bag and the sack of jerky were there. Then he mounted and turned up the hill.

It was velvet dark. The horse found the entrance to the trail where it left the flat, and started up, stumbling and slipping on the rocks. Pepé's hand rose up to his head. His hat was gone. He had left it under the oak tree.

The horse had struggled far up the trail when the first change of dawn came into the air, a steel grayness as light mixed thoroughly with dark. Gradually the sharp snaggled edge of the ridge stood out above them, rotten granite tortured and eaten by the winds of time. Pepé had dropped his reins on the horn, leaving direction to the horse. The brush grabbed at his legs in the dark until one knee of his jeans was ripped.

Gradually the light flowed down over the ridge. The starved brush and rocks stood out in the half light, strange and lonely in high perspective. Then there came warmth into the light. Pepé drew up and looked back, but he could see nothing in the darker valley below. The sky turned blue over the coming sun. In the waste of the mountainside, the poor dry brush grew only three feet high. Here and there, big outcroppings of unrotted granite stood up like mouldering houses. Pepé relaxed a little. He drank from his water bag and bit off a piece of jerky. A single eagle flew over, high in the light.

Without warning Pepé's horse screamed and fell on its side. He was almost down before the rifle crash echoed up from the valley. From a hole behind the struggling shoulder, a stream of bright crimson blood pumped and stopped. The hooves threshed on the ground. Pepé lay half stunned beside the horse. He looked slowly down the hill. A piece of sage clipped off beside his head and another crash echoed up from side to side of the canyon. Pepé flung himself frantically behind a bush.

He crawled up the hill on his knees and one hand. His right hand held the rifle up off the ground and pushed it ahead of him. He moved with the instinctive care of an animal. Rapidly he wormed his way toward one of the big outcroppings of granite on the hill above him. Where the brush was high he doubled up and ran, but where the cover was slight he wriggled forward on his stomach, pushing the rifle ahead of him. In the last little distance there was no cover at all. Pepé poised and then he darted across the space and flashed around the corner of the rock.

He leaned panting against the stone. When his breath came easier he moved along behind the big rock until he came to a narrow split that offered a thin section of vision down the hill. Pepé lay on his stomach and pushed the rifle barrel through the slit and waited.

The sun reddened the western ridges now. Already the buzzards were settling down toward the place where the horse lay. A small brown bird scratched in the dead sage leaves directly in front of the rifle muzzle. The coasting eagle flew back toward the rising sun.

Pepé saw a little movement in the brush far below. His grip tightened on the gun. A little brown doe stepped daintily out on the trail and crossed it and disappeared into the brush again. For a long time Pepé waited. Far below he could see the little flat and the oak trees and the slash of green. Suddenly his eyes flashed back at the trail again. A quarter of a mile down there had been a quick movement in the chaparral. The rifle swung over. The front sight nestled in the V of the rear sight. Pepé studied for a moment and then raised the rear sight a notch. The little movement in the brush came again. The sight settled on it. Pepé squeezed the trigger. The explosion crashed down the mountain and up the other side, and came rattling back. The whole side of the slope grew still. No more movement. And then a white streak cut into the granite of the slit and a bullet whined away and a crash sounded up from below. Pepé felt a sharp pain in his right hand. A sliver of granite was sticking out from between his first and second knuckles and the point protruded from his palm. Carefully he pulled out the sliver of stone. The wound bled evenly and gently. No vein nor artery was cut.

Pepé looked into a little dusty cave in the rock and gathered a handful of spider web, and he pressed the mass into the cut, plastering the soft web into the blood. The flow stopped almost at once.

The rifle was on the ground. Pepé picked it up, levered a new shell into the chamber. And then he slid into the brush on his stomach. Far to the right he crawled, and then up the hill, moving slowly and carefully, crawling to cover and resting and then crawling again.

In the mountains the sun is high in its arc before it penetrates the gorges. The hot face looked over the hill and brought instant heat with it. The white light beat on the rocks and reflected from them and rose up quivering from the earth again, and the rocks and bushes seemed to quiver behind the air.

Pepé crawled in the general direction of the ridge peak, zig-zagging for cover. The deep cut between his knuckles began to throb. He crawled close to a rattlesnake before he saw it, and when it raised its dry head and made a soft beginning whirr, he backed up and took another way. The quick gray lizards flashed in front of him, raising a tiny line of dust. He found another mass of spider web and pressed it against his throbbing hand.

Pepé was pushing the rifle with his left hand now. Little drops of sweat ran to the ends of his coarse black hair and rolled down his cheeks. His lips and tongue were growing thick and heavy. His lips writhed to draw saliva into his mouth. His little dark eyes were uneasy and suspicious. Once when a gray lizard paused in front of him on the parched ground and turned its head sideways he crushed it flat with a stone.

When the sun slid past noon he had not gone a mile. He crawled exhaustedly a last hundred yards to a patch of high sharp manzanita, and crawled desperately, and when the patch was reached he wriggled in among the tough gnarly trunks and dropped his head on his left arm. There was little shade in the meager brush, but there was cover and safety. Pepé went to sleep as he lay and the sun beat on his back. A few little birds hopped close to him and peered and hopped away. Pepé squirmed in his sleep and he raised and dropped his wounded hand again and again.

The sun went down behind the peaks and

the cool evening came, and then the dark. A coyote yelled from the hillside, Pepé started awake and looked about with misty eyes. His hand was swollen and heavy; a little thread of pain ran up the inside of his arm and settled in a pocket in his armpit. He peered about and then stood up, for the mountains were black and the moon had not yet risen. Pepé stood up in the dark. The coat of his father pressed on his arm. His tongue was swollen until it nearly filled his mouth. He wriggled out of the coat and dropped it in the brush, and then he struggled up the hill, falling over rocks and tearing his way through the brush. The rifle knocked against stones as he went. Little dry avalanches of gravel and shattered stone went whispering down the hill behind him.

After a while the old moon came up and showed the jagged ridge top ahead of him. By moonlight Pepé traveled more easily. He bent forward so that his throbbing arm hung away from his body. The journey uphill was made in dashes and rests, a frantic rush up a few yards and then a rest. The wind coasted down the slope rattling the dry stems of the bushes.

The moon was at meridian when Pepé came at last to the sharp backbone of the ridge top. On the last hundred yards of the rise no soil had clung under the wearing winds. The way was on solid rock. He clambered to the top and looked down on the other side. There was a draw like the last below him, misty with moonlight, brushed with dry struggling sage and chaparral. On the other side the hill rose up sharply and at the top the jagged rotten teeth of the mountain showed against the sky. At the bottom of the cut the brush was thick and dark.

Pepé stumbled down the hill. His throat was almost closed with thirst. At first he tried to run, but immediately he fell and rolled. After that he went more carefully. The moon was just disappearing behind the mountains when he came to the bottom. He crawled into the heavy brush feeling with his fingers for water.

There was no water in the bed of the stream, only damp earth. Pepé laid his gun down and scooped up a handful of mud and put it in his mouth, and then he spluttered and scraped the earth from his tongue with his finger, for the mud drew at his mouth like a poultice. He dug a hole in the stream bed with his fingers, dug a little basin to catch water; but before it was very deep his head fell forward on the damp ground and he slept.

The dawn came and the heat of the day fell on the earth, and still Pepé slept. Late in the afternoon his head jerked up. He looked slowly around. His eyes were slits of wariness. Twenty feet away in the heavy brush a big tawny mountain lion stood looking at him. Its long thick tail waved gracefully, its ears were erect with interest, not laid back dangerously. The lion squatted down on its stomach and watched him.

Pepé looked at the hole he had dug in the earth. A half inch of muddy water had collected in the bottom. He tore the sleeve from his hurt arm, with his teeth ripped out a little square, soaked it in the water and put it in his mouth. Over and over he filled the cloth and sucked it.

Still the lion sat and watched him. The evening came down but there was no movement on the hills. No birds visited the dry bottom of the cut. Pepé looked occasionally at the lion. The eyes of the yellow beast drooped as though he were about to sleep. He yawned and his long thin red tongue curled out. Suddenly his head jerked around and his nostrils quivered. His big tail lashed. He stood up and slunk like a tawny shadow into the thick brush.

A moment later Pepé heard the sound, the faint far crash of horses' hooves on gravel. And he heard something else, a high whining yelp of a dog.

Pepé took his rifle in his left hand and he glided into the brush almost as quietly as the lion had. In the darkening evening he crouched up the hill toward the next ridge. Only when the dark came did he stand up. His energy was short. Once it was dark he fell over the rocks and slipped to his knees on the steep slope, but he moved on and on up the hill, climbing and scrabbling over the broken hillside.

When he was far up toward the top, he lay down and slept for a little while. The withered moon, shining on his face, awakened him. He stood up and moved up the hill. Fifty yards away he stopped and turned back, for he had forgotten his rifle. He walked heavily down and poked about in the brush, but he could not find his gun. At last he lay down to rest. The pocket of pain in his armpit had grown more sharp. His arm seemed to swell out and fall with every heartbeat. There was no position lying down where the heavy arm did not press against his armpit.

With the effort of a hurt beast, Pepé got up and moved again toward the top of the ridge. He held his swollen arm away from his body with his left hand. Up the steep hill he dragged himself, a few steps and a rest, and a few more steps. At last he was nearing the top. The moon showed the uneven sharp back of it against the sky.

Pepé's brain spun in a big spiral up and away from him. He slumped to the ground and lay still. The rock ridge top was only a hundred feet above him.

The moon moved over the sky. Pepé half turned on his back. His tongue tried to make words, but only a thick hissing came from between his lips.

When the dawn came, Pepé pulled himself up. His eyes were sane again. He drew his great puffed arm in front of him and looked at the angry wound. The black line ran up from his wrist to his armpit. Automatically he reached in his pocket for the big black knife, but it was not there. His eyes searched the ground. He picked up a sharp blade of stone and scraped at the wound, sawed at the proud flesh and then squeezed the green juice out in big drops. Instantly he threw back his head and whined like a dog. His whole right side shuddered at the pain, but the pain cleared his head.

In the gray light he struggled up the last slope to the ridge and crawled over and lay down behind a line of rocks. Below him lay a deep canyon exactly like the last, waterless and desolate. There was no flat, no oak trees, not even heavy brush in the bottom of it. And on the other side a sharp ridge stood up, thinly brushed with starving sage, littered with broken granite. Strewn over the hill there were giant outcroppings, and on the top the granite teeth stood out against the sky.

The new day was light now. The flame of the sun came over the ridge and fell on Pepé where he lay on the ground. His coarse black hair was littered with twigs and bits of spider web. His eyes had retreated back into his head. Between his lips the tip of his black tongue showed.

He sat up and dragged his great arm into his lap and nursed it, rocking his body and moaning in his throat. He threw back his head and looked up into the pale sky. A big black bird circled nearly out of sight, and far to the left another was sailing near.

He lifted his head to listen, for a familiar sound had come to him from the valley he had climbed out of; it was the crying yelp of hounds, excited and feverish, on a trail.

Pepé bowed his head quickly. He tried to speak rapid words but only a thick hiss came from his lips. He drew a shaky cross on his breast with his left hand. It was a long struggle to get to his feet. He crawled slowly and mechanically to the top of a big rock on the ridge peak. Once there, he rose slowly, swaying to his feet, and stood erect. Far below he could see the dark brush where he had slept. He braced his feet and stood there, black against the morning sky.

There came a ripping sound at his feet. A piece of stone flew up and a bullet droned off into the next gorge. The hollow crash echoed up from below. Pepé looked down for a moment and then pulled himself straight again.

His body jarred back. His left hand fluttered helplessly toward his breast. The second crash sounded from below. Pepé swung forward and toppled from the rock. His body struck and rolled over and over, starting a little avalanche.

And when at last he stopped against a bush, the avalanche slid slowly down and covered up his head.

BEHAVIOR IN EXTERMINATION CAMPS

Bruno Bettelheim

The analysis of behavior inside the extermination camps, while more horrid, offers less of psychological interest [than the study of behavior in the work camps], since prisoners there had no time or occasion to change much psychologically.

The only psychological phenomenon that seems pertinent in this report is the fact that these prisoners knew they were destined to die and still made almost no effort to revolt. The few exceptions, less than a handful among millions, I shall ignore for the moment, since they represent the behavior of such a tiny minority.

On occasions, only one or two German guards would be escorting up to four hundred prisoners toward the extermination camps over lonesome roads. There was every chance that the four hundred could have overpowered their armed guards.[1] Even if some prisoners had been killed in the process, the majority would have been free to join partisan groups. At the very least they could have enjoyed a temporary revenge without loss to themselves, since they were slated for death anyway.

A nonpsychological analysis of the behavior of these prisoners does not seem adequate for explaining such docility. In order to understand the phenomenon of men not fighting back, although certain death awaited them,[2] it must be realized that the most active individuals had long ago made their efforts to fight National Socialism and were now either dead or exhausted. The Polish and Jewish prisoners who formed a majority in the extermination camps were mostly persons who for some reason had failed to escape and were not fighting back.

Their feeling of defeat does not imply they felt no strong hostility toward their oppressors. Weakness and submission are often charged with greater hostility than open counter-aggression. In counter-aggression, as for instance in the partisan or resistance movements, the opponents of German fascism found outlets for some of their hostilities through offensive action. But within the oppressed person who did not resist lay accumulating hostilities he was unable to discharge in action. Not even the mild relief of verbal aggression was open to him, because even that, he was afraid, would bring destruction by the SS.

The more hostility accumulated, the more

---

[1] Even Hoess, in his memoirs, wondered why the prisoners did not revolt since they could often have done it with ease, given their vast numbers.

— *Reprinted with permission of The Macmillan Company from The Informed Heart: Autonomy in a Mass Age by Bruno Bettelheim; ©by the Free Press of Glencoe 1960*

---

[2] This knowledge of certain death made their case different from those other prisoners who could still hope for eventual liberation.

terrified the prisoner became that it might break through in an explosive act spelling destruction for him. To prevent this, he felt he must at all times remain convinced of the extremely dangerous character of the aggressor; in that way his own fear would restrain him more effectively. So for his own protection he invested the SS with those features most threatening to himself. These, in turn, increased his anxiety, frustration, and hostility, and to keep them all under control, the SS had to be seen as even more murderous.[3]

The twin process of repressing all hostility and inflating the terrible image of the SS devoured almost all his emotional energy. If anything was left, it was soon used up by the fight against depression due to loss of status, separation from family, exhaustion due to malnutrition and disease, and the absolute hopelessness of the situation.

In the concentration camps some hostility could be discharged in the fight among prisoner factions. While the battles lasted the hope still lived that one's own party might win, bringing better conditions for oneself. "Moslems" of course no longer fought, did not belong to factions, did not discharge hostility but turned it against the self, like the prisoners in the extermination camps. And like them, they died. In the extermination camps the prisoners were also deprived of anything that might have restored self respect or the will to live, while the pent-up hostility grew uninterruptedly.

All this may explain the docility of prisoners who walked to the gas chambers or who dug their own graves and then lined up before them so that, shot down, they would fall into the graves. It may be assumed that most of these prisoners were by then suicidal. Walking to the gas chamber was committing suicide in a way that asked for none of the energy usually needed for deciding and planning to kill oneself.

Psychologically speaking, most prisoners in the extermination camps committed suicide by submitting to death without resistance.

If this speculation is correct, then one may say that in the extermination camps the goals of the SS found their ultimate realization. Through the use of terror the SS succeeded in forcing its opponents to do, out of their own will, what it wished them to do. Millions of people submitted to extermination because SS methods had forced them to see it not as a way out, but as the only way to put an end to conditions in which they could no longer live as human beings.

Since these remarks may seem far fetched, it should be added that the process just described is similar to what can be observed in some psychotic patients. The assumption that these prisoners developed states of mind similar to those observed in psychotic persons seems borne out by the behavior of former prisoners of extermination camps after their liberation. Their symptoms depended, of course, on initial personality assets and what the individual experienced after liberation. In some persons the symptoms appeared more severe, in others less so; some showed that their symptoms were reversible, others not.

Immediately after liberation nearly all prisoners engaged in asocial behavior that could only be explained by far reaching disintegration of their former personality structures. A few former inmates of extermination camps have been studied. Their grip on reality was extremely tenuous. Some were still suffering from delusions of persecution, others suffered from delusions of grandeur. The latter were the counterpart of guilt feelings for having been spared while parents or siblings had all perished. They were trying to justify and explain their own survival by delusionally inflating their importance. It also enabled them to compensate for the extreme damage done to their narcissism by the experience they had undergone.

---

[3]This mechanism differs only in degree from the widespread use of projection as a psychological defense in the "ordinary" concentration camps.

Business as usual

A few words about the world's reaction to the concentration camps: the terrors committed in them were experienced as uncanny by most civilized persons. It came as a shock to their pride that supposedly civilized nations could stoop to such inhuman acts. The implication that modern man has such inadequate control over his cruelty was felt as a threat. Three different psychological mechanisms were most frequently used for dealing with the phenomenon of the concentration camp: (a) its applicability to man in general was denied by asserting (contrary to available evidence) that the acts of torture were committed by a small group of insane or perverted persons; (b) the truth of the reports was denied by ascribing them to deliberate propaganda. This method was favored by the German government which called all reports on terror in the camps horror propaganda (*Greuelpropaganda*); (c) the reports were believed, but the knowledge of the terror was repressed as soon as possible.

All three mechanisms could be seen at work after liberation. At first, after the "discovery" of the camps, a wave of extreme outrage swept the Allied nations. It was soon followed by a general repression of the discovery. It may be that this reaction of the general public was due to something more than the shock dealt their narcissism by the fact that cruelty is still rampant among men. It may also be that the memory of the tortures was repressed out of some dim realization that the modern state now has available the means for changing personality. To have to accept that one's personality may be changed against one's will is the greatest threat to one's self respect. It must therefore be dealt with by action, or by repression.

The universal success of the *Diary of Anne Frank* suggests how much the tendency to deny is still with us, while her story itself demonstrates how such denial can hasten our own destruction. It is an onerous task to take apart such a human and moving story, arousing so much compassion for gentle Anne Frank. But I believe that its world-wide acclaim cannot be explained unless we recognize our wish to forget the gas chambers and to glorify attitudes of extreme privatization, of continuing to hold on to attitudes as usual even in a holocaust. Exactly because their going on with private life as usual brought destruction did it have to be glorified; in that way we could overlook the essential fact of how destructive it can be under extreme social circumstances.

While the Franks were making their preparations for going passively into hiding, thousands of other Jews in Holland and elsewhere in Europe were trying to escape to the free world, the better to survive or to be able to fight their executioners. Others who could not do so went underground—not simply to hide from the SS, waiting passively, without preparation for fight, for the day when they would be caught—but to fight the Germans, and with it for humanity. All the Franks wanted was to go on with life as nearly as possible in the usual fashion.

Little Anne, too, wanted only to go on with life as usual, and nobody can blame her. But hers was certainly not a necessary fate, much less a heroic one; it was a senseless fate. The Franks could have faced the facts and survived, as did many Jews living in Holland. Anne could have had a good chance to survive, as did many Jewish children in Holland. But for that she would have had to be separated from her parents and gone to live with a Dutch family as their own child.

Everybody who recognized the obvious knew that the hardest way to go underground was to do it as a family; that to hide as a family made detection by the SS most likely. The Franks, with their excellent connections among gentile Dutch families should have had an easy time hiding out singly, each with a different family. But instead of planning for this, the main principle of their planning was to continue as much as possible with the kind of family life they were accustomed to. Any other course would have meant not merely giving up the beloved family life, but also accepting as reality man's inhumanity to man. Most of all it would have forced them to accept that going on with life as usual was not an absolute value, but can sometimes be the most destructive of all attitudes.

There is little doubt that the Franks, who were able to provide themselves with so much, could have provided themselves with a gun or two had they wished. They could have shot down at least one or two of the "green police" who came for them. There was no surplus of such police. The loss of an SS with every Jew arrested would have noticeably hindered the functioning of the police state. The fate of the Franks wouldn't have been any different, because they all died anyway except for Anne's father, though he hardly meant to pay for his survival with the extermination of his whole family. But they could have sold their lives dearly instead of walking to their death.

There is good reason why the so successful play ends with Anne stating her belief in the good in all men. What is denied is the importance of accepting the gas chambers as real so that never again will they exist. If all men are basically good, if going on with intimate family living no matter what else is what is to be most admired, then indeed we can all go on with life as usual and forget about Auschwitz. Except that Anne Frank died because her parents could not get themselves to believe in Auschwitz. And her story found wide acclaim because for us too, it denies implicitly that Auschwitz ever existed. If all men are good, there was never an Auschwitz.

High time

At various places in this book I have mentioned how submitting to the total state leads to a disintegration of what once seemed a well integrated personality, plus a return to many infantile attitudes. At this point perhaps a theoretical speculation may be helpful. Years ago Freud postulated two opposite tendencies:

the life instincts, which he called eros or sex, and the destructive tendencies, which he named the death instinct. The more mature the person becomes, the more he should be able to "fuse" these two opposing tendencies, making the resultant "ego" energy available for the task of meeting and shaping reality.

The more immature the person, the more these tendencies are apt to push the total personality, at one moment in one direction, at the next moment in the other. Thus the so-called childlike friendliness of some primitive people, followed in the next moment by extreme "thoughtless" cruelty. But the disintegration, or perhaps one should better say the "defusion" of ego energy under extreme stress—at one moment into pure destructive tendencies ("Let it be over, no matter how"), at the next moment into irrational life tendencies ("Let's get something to eat now, even if it means death in short order")[4]—was only one aspect of man's primitivization in the total state. Another was engaging in infantile thought processes such as wishful thinking in place of a more mature evaluation of reality, and an infantile disregard for the possibility of death. These led many to think that they of all others would be spared and survive, and many more to simply disbelieve in the possibility of their own death. Not believing in its possibility, they did not prepare for it, including no preparation for how to defend their lives even when death became inescapable. Defending their lives before such time might have hastened their death. So up to a point, this "rolling with the punches" that the enemy dealt out was protective of life. But beyond that point it was destructive of both one's own life and that of others whose survival might be more certain too if one risked one's

---

[4]For example, those prisoners who ate the whole day's ration the moment they got it had nothing left for their faltering energies toward the end of the working day. Those who divided the little food they had and saved some for the moment when exhaustion threatened them most, fared much better in the long run.

own life. The trouble is that the longer one "rolls" with the punches, the more likely it becomes that one will no longer have the strength to resist when death becomes imminent, particularly if this yielding to the enemy is accompanied not by an inner strengthening of the personality (which it would require) but an inner disintegration.[5]

Those who did not deny validity to death, who neither denied nor repressed its possibility, who embraced no childish belief in their indestructibility, were those who prepared for it in time as a real possibility. It meant risking one's life for a self chosen purpose and in doing so, saving one's own life or that of others, or both. When Jews in Germany were restricted to their homes, those who did not allow inertia to take over used the imposing of such restrictions as a warning that it was high time to go underground, join the resistance movement, provide themselves with forged papers, etc., if they had not done so long ago. Most of them survived.

An example out of the lives of some distant relatives of mine may further illustrate. Early in the war, a young man living in a small Hungarian town banded together with a number of other Jews and they prepared themselves for what to do when the Germans invaded. As soon as the Nazis imposed curfews on the Jews, his group left for Budapest since the bigger the city, the better the chances for escaping detection. There, similar groups from other towns converged and joined those of Budapest. From among them they selected typically "Aryan" looking men who, equipped with false papers, immediately joined the Hungarian SS so as to be able to warn of impending actions, to report in advance when a particular district would be searched, etc.

This worked so well that most of the groups survived intact. But they had also equipped themselves with small arms, so that when detected they could put up enough of a fight for the majority to escape while a few would die fighting to gain time for the escape.[6] A few of the Jews who had joined the SS were discovered and immediately shot, probably a death preferable to one in the gas chambers. But even among their special group the majority survived, hiding within the SS up to the last moment.

My young relative was unable to convince some members of his family to go with him when he left. Three times, at tremendous risk to himself he returned, pointing out first the growing persecution of the Jews, later the fact that their transport to the gas chambers had already begun. He could not convince them to move out of their homes, to leave their possessions. On each visit he pleaded more desperately, on each visit he found them less willing or able to listen to him, much less able to take action. It was as if each time they were more on their way to the crematoria where they all in fact died.

On each visit his family clung more desperately to the old living arrangements, the possessions they had accumulated over a lifetime. It was like a parallel process in which their life energies were drained away while their possessions seemed to give them a pseudosecurity to replace the real assurance that no longer came from planning for their lives. Again like children, they preferred to cling desperately to some objects in which they had invested all the

<hr>

[5]This, too, could be observed in the story of the Franks, who bickered with each other over trifles, instead of supporting each other's desire to resist the demoralizing impact of their living conditions.

[6]Compare this to the Franks' selection of a hiding place that was basically a trap without an outlet, and that in all their months there no emergency escape route was constructed through which some of their group could at least have tried to escape while one or two of the men blocked and defended one of the small entrances with a homemade barricade. Compare also, Mr. Frank's teaching typically academic high school subjects to the youngsters, rather than how to make a getaway: a token of the same inability to face the possibility of death.

meaning they could no longer find in their lives. As they withdrew from the fight for survival, their lives began to reside more and more in these dead objects and the persons in them died piece by piece, little object by little object.

In Buchenwald, I talked to hundreds of German Jewish prisoners who were brought there in the fall of 1938. I asked them why they had not left Germany because of the utterly degrading conditions they were subjected to. Their answer was: How could we leave? It would have meant giving up our homes, our places of business. Their earthly possessions had so taken possession of them that they could not move; instead of using them, they were run by them.[7]

How the investing of possessions with one's life energy made people die piece by piece is also evident in the course of the Nazi attitude toward Jews. At the time of the first boycott of Jewish stores the whole external goal of the Nazis was the possessions of the Jews. They even let Jews take some of them out of the country if they would just go, leaving the bulk of their possessions behind. For a long time the intention of the Nazis, and of their first discriminatory laws, was to force undesirable minorities, including Jews, into emigration. Only when this did not work was the extermination policy instituted, though it also followed the inner logic of the Nazi racial ideology. But one wonders if the notion that millions of Jews (and later foreign nationals) would submit to extermination did not also result from seeing how much degradation they would accept without fighting back. The persecution of the Jews worsened, slow step by slow step, when no violent resistance occurred. It may have been Jewish acceptance, without fight, of ever harsher discrimination and degradation that first gave the SS the idea that they could be gotten to the point where they would walk to the gas chambers on their own.

Most Jews in Poland who did not believe in business as usual survived the second World War. As the Germans approached, they left everything behind and fled to Russia, much as many of them distrusted the Soviet system. But there, while perhaps citizens of a second order, they were at least accepted as human beings. Those who stayed on to continue business as usual moved toward their own destruction and perished. Thus in the deepest sense the walk to the gas chamber was only the last consequence of a philosophy of business as usual; a last step in no longer defying the death instinct, which might also be called the principle of inertia. Because the first step was taken long before one entered the death camp.

True, the same suicidal behavior has another meaning. It means that man can be pushed so far and no further; that beyond a certain point he chooses death to an inhuman existence. But the initial step toward this terrible choice was inertia.

Those who give in to it, who have withdrawn all vital energy from the world, can no longer act with initiative, and are threatened by it in others. They can no longer accept reality for what it is; having grown infantile, they see it only in the infantile perspective of a wishful denial of what is too unpleasant, of a wishful belief in their personal immortality. All this is dramatically illustrated in an experience of Lengyel's.[8] She reports that although she and her fellow prisoners lived just a few hundred yards from the crematoria and the gas chambers and knew what they were all about, yet after months most prisoners denied knowledge of them.[9] Realization of their true situation

---

[7]The Franks, too, postponed going into hiding because they wished first to transfer more of their possessions to their hideout. They postponed it so long that it was nearly too late for Anne's sister, who was called to the SS.

[8]Lengyel, O., *Five Chimneys,* The Story of Auschwitz, Chicago: Ziff Davis, 1947, pp. 54-55.
[9]German gentile civilians denied the gas chambers, too, but the same denial in them did not have the same meaning. By that time, civilians who faced facts and rebelled, invited death. Prisoners at Auschwitz were already doomed.

might have helped them to save either the life they were going to lose anyway, or the lives of others. But that realization they could not afford. When Lengyel and many other prisoners were selected to be sent to the gas chambers, they did not try to break away, as she successfully did. Worse, the first time she tried it, some of the fellow prisoners selected with her for the gas chambers called the supervisors, telling them she was trying to get away. Lengyel desperately asks the question: How was it possible that people denied the existence of the gas chambers when all day long they saw the crematoria burning and smelled the odor of burning flesh? How come they preferred not to believe in the extermination just to prevent themselves from fighting for their very own lives? She offers no explanation except that they begrudged anyone who might save himself from the common fate, because they lacked enough courage to risk action themselves. I believe they did it because they had given up their will to live, had permitted their death tendencies to flood them. As a result they now identified more closely with the SS who were devoting themselves to destruction, than with those fellow prisoners who still had a grip on life and hence managed to escape death.

Human competence for what?

When prisoners began to serve their executioners, to help them speed the death of their own kind, things had gone beyond simple inertia. By then, death instinct running rampant had been added to inertia. Those who tried to serve their executioners in what were once their civilian capacities were merely continuing if not business, then life as usual. Whereby they opened the door to their death.

Lengyel speaks of a Dr. Mengele, SS physician at Auschwitz, in a typical example of the "business as usual" attitude that enabled some prisoners, and certainly the SS, to retain whatever inner balance they could despite what they were doing. She describes how Dr. Mengele took

all correct medical precautions during childbirth, rigorously observing all aseptic principles, cutting the umbilical cord with greatest care, etc. But only half an hour later he sent mother and infant to be burned in the crematorium.[10]

Still, having made his choice, Dr. Mengele and others like him had, after all, to delude themselves at times to be able to live with themselves and their experience. Only one personal document on the subject has come to my attention, that of Dr. Nyiszli, a prisoner serving as "research physician" at Auschwitz.[11] How Dr. Nyiszli fooled himself can be seen, for example, in his repeatedly referring to himself as a doctor, though he worked as the assistant of a criminal. He speaks of the Institute for Race, Biological, and Anthropological Investigation as "one of the most qualified medical centers of the Third Reich" though it was devoted to proving falsehoods. That Nyiszli was a doctor didn't at all change the fact that he, like any of the prisoner officials who served the SS better than some SS were willing to serve it, was a participant, an accessory to the crimes of the SS. How then could he do it and survive?

The answer was: by taking pride in his professional skills, irrespective of what purpose they were used for. Again and again this pride in his professional skill permeates his story of his own and other prisoners' sufferings. The important issue here is that Dr. Nyiszli, Dr. Mengele, and hundreds of other far more prominent physicians, men trained long before the advent of Hitler to power, were participants in these human experiments and in the pseudoscientific investigations that went with them.[12] It is this

---

[10] *Op. cit.,* p. 147.
[11] Nyiszli, Dr. Miklos, *Auschwitz: A Doctor's Eyewitness Account,* New York: Frederick Fell, Inc., 1960.
[12] Among the heads of clinics or chairmen of departments who participated knowingly in the experiments were Professors Sauerbruch of the University of Munich and Eppinger of the University of Vienna—teachers of whole generations of physicians before Hitler. Dr. Gebhardt, the

pride in professional skill and knowledge, irrespective of moral implications, that is so dangerous. As a feature of modern society oriented toward technological competence it is still with us, though the concentration camps and the crematoria are no longer here. Auschwitz is gone, but as long as this attitude remains with us we shall not be safe from the indifference to life at its core.

It is easy to see that achieving a subtle balance between extremes may be an ideal way of life. It is harder to accept that this holds true even in a holocaust. But even in extreme conditions, to give way only to the heart or only to the mind is neither a good way to live, nor the way to survive. Living only to keep his family intact, even all Mr. Frank's love did not keep them alive, as a better informed heart might have done. Dr. Nyiszli, carried away by his high level training as a pathologist, and against the prompting of the heart, lent himself to such debasement of his deepest pride, his medical science, that one wonders what can have survived except his body.

I have met many Jews, as well as gentile anti-Nazis, who survived in Germany and in the occupied countries, like the group in Hungary described earlier. But they were all people who realized that when a world goes to pieces, when inhumanity reigns supreme, man cannot go on with business as usual. One then has to radically re-evaluate all of what one has done, believed in, stood for. In short, one has to take a stand on the new reality, a firm stand, and not one of retirement into even greater privatization.

If today, Negroes in Africa march against the guns of a police that defends *apartheid*—even if hundreds of them will be shot down and tens of thousands rounded up in concentration camps —their march, their fight, will sooner or later assure them of a chance for liberty and equality. Millions of the Jews of Europe who did not or could not escape in time or go underground as many thousands did, could at least have marched as free men against the SS, rather than to first grovel, then wait to be rounded up for their own extermination, and finally walk themselves to the gas chambers.

Yet the story of the extermination camps shows that even in such an overpowering environment, certain defenses do offer some protection, most important of which is understanding what goes on in oneself, and why. With enough understanding, the individual does not fool himself into believing that with every adjustment he makes he is protecting himself. He is able to recognize that much that on the surface seems protective, is actually self destructive. A most extreme example were those prisoners who volunteered to work in the gas chambers hoping it would somehow save their lives. All of them were killed after a short time. But many of them died sooner, and after weeks of a more horrible life, than might have been true if they had not volunteered.

Fighting back

Did no one of those destined to die fight back? Did none of them wish to die not by giving in but by asserting themselves in attacking the SS? A very few did. One of them was the twelfth *Sonderkommando*, prisoners working in the gas chambers.[13] Now all these *Kommandos* knew their fate since the first task of every new *Sonderkommando* was to cremate the corpses of the preceding *Kommando*, exterminated just a few hours before.

---

president of the German Red Cross, was also among them. (Mitscherlich, A., and Mielke, F., *Doctors of Infamy*, New York: Henry Schuman, Inc., 1949.)

[13]Nyiszli, *op. cit.* Scattered revolts in the death camps (Treblinka, etc.) are mentioned elsewhere in the literature, though I have not myself seen witnessed reports. Civilian uprisings began to occur with the turn of the war tide against Germany, but as in the case of the Warsaw uprising, the hour was far too late for the millions already dead.

In this single revolt of the twelfth *Sonderkommando*, seventy SS were killed, including one commissioned officer and seventeen noncommissioned officers; one of the crematoria was totally destroyed and another severely damaged. True, all eight hundred and fifty-three prisoners of the *Kommando* died. But this proves that a position in the *Sonderkommando* gave prisoners a chance of about ten to one to destroy the SS, a higher ratio than in the ordinary concentration camp.

The one *Sonderkommando* that revolted and took such a heavy toll of the enemy did not die much differently than all other *Sonderkommandos*. Why, then—and this is the question that haunts all who study the extermination camps—why then did millions walk quietly, without resistance, to their death when right before them were examples such as this *Kommando* that managed to destroy and damage part of their own chambers of death and kill almost 10 per cent of their number in SS? Why did so few of the millions of prisoners die like men, as did the men of only one of these *Kommandos*? Why did the rest of these *Kommandos* not revolt, but march themselves willingly to their death? Or what did it take for the exception to do so?

Perhaps another rare instance, an example of supreme self assertion, can shed light on the question. Once, a group of naked prisoners about to enter the gas chamber stood lined up in front of it. In some way the commanding SS officer learned that one of the women prisoners had been a dancer. So he ordered her to dance for him. She did, and as she danced, she approached him, seized his gun, and shot him down. She too was immediately shot to death.

But isn't it probable that despite the grotesque setting in which she danced, dancing made her once again a person? Dancing, she was singled out as an individual, asked to perform in what had once been her chosen vocation. No longer was she a number, a nameless, depersonalized prisoner, but the dancer she used to be. Transformed, however momentarily, she responded like her old self, destroying the enemy bent on her destruction, even if she had to die in the process.

Despite the hundreds of thousands of living dead men who moved quietly to their graves, this one example, and there were several like her, shows that in an instant the old personality can be regained, its destruction undone, once we decide on our own that we wish to cease being units in a system. Exercising the last freedom that not even the concentration camp could take away—to decide how one wishes to think and feel about the conditions of one's life— this dancer threw off her real prison. This she could do because she was willing to risk her life to achieve autonomy once more. If we do that, then if we cannot live, at least we die as men.

A MYSTERY OF HEROISM

Stephen Crane

The dark uniforms of the men were so coated with dust from the incessant wrestling of the two armies that the regiment almost seemed a part of the clay bank which shielded them from the shells. On the top of the hill a battery was arguing in tremendous roars with some other guns, and to the eye of the infantry the artillerymen, the guns, the caissons, the horses, were distinctly outlined upon the blue sky. When a piece was fired, a red streak as round as a log flashed low in the heavens, like a monstrous bolt of lightning. The men of the battery wore white duck trousers, which somehow emphasized their legs; and when they ran and crowded in little groups at the bidding of the shouting officers, it was more impressive than usual to the infantry.

Fred Collins, of A Company, was saying: "Thunder! I wisht I had a drink. Ain't there any water round here?" Then somebody yelled: "There goes th' bugler!"

As the eyes of half the regiment swept in one machinelike movement, there was an instant's picture of a horse in a great convulsive leap of a death wound and a rider leaning back with a crooked arm and spread fingers before his face. On the ground was the crimson terror of an exploding shell, with fibres of flame that seemed like lances. A glittering bugle swung clear of the rider's back as fell headlong the horse and the man. In the air was an odor as from a conflagration.

Sometimes they of the infantry looked down at a fair little meadow which spread at their feet. Its long green grass was rippling gently in a breeze. Beyond it was the gray form of a house half torn to pieces by shells and by the busy axes of soldiers who had pursued firewood. The line of an old fence was now dimly marked by long weeds and by an occasional post. A shell had blown the well-house to fragments. Little lines of gray smoke ribboning upward from some embers indicated the place where had stood the barn.

From beyond a curtain of green woods there came the sound of some stupendous scuffle, as if two animals of the size of islands were fighting. At a distance there were occasional appearances of swift-moving men, horses, batteries, flags, and with the crashing of infantry volleys were heard, often, wild and frenzied cheers. In the midst of it all Smith and Ferguson, two privates of A Company, were engaged in a heated discussion which involved the greatest questions of the national existence.

The battery on the hill presently engaged in a frightful duel. The white legs of the gunners scampered this way and that way, and the officers redoubled their shouts. The guns, with their demeanors of stolidity and courage, were typical of something infinitely self-possessed in this clamor of death that swirled around the hill.

One of a "swing" team was suddenly smitten quivering to the ground, and his maddened brethren dragged his torn body in their struggle to escape from this turmoil and danger. A young soldier astride one of the leaders swore and fumed in his saddle and furiously jerked at the bridle. An officer screamed out an order so violently that his voice broke and ended the sentence in a falsetto shriek.

— "*A Mystery of Heroism*" *by Stephen Crane, from* *The Complete Short Stories and Sketches of Stephen Crane*, *edited by Thomas A. Gullason and published by Doubleday & Company, Inc., Garden City, New York, 1963; copyright © 1963, Doubleday & Company, Inc.*

The leading company of the infantry regiment was somewhat exposed, and the colonel ordered it moved more fully under the shelter of the hill. There was the clank of steel against steel.

A lieutenant of the battery rode down and passed them, holding his right arm carefully in his left hand. And it was as if this arm was not at all a part of him, but belonged to another man. His sober and reflective charger went slowly. The officer's face was grimy and perspiring, and his uniform was tousled as if he had been in direct grapple with an enemy. He smiled grimly when the men stared at him. He turned his horse toward the meadow.

Collins, of A Company, said: "I wisht I had a drink. I bet there's water in that there ol' well yonder!"

"Yes, but how you goin' to git it?"

For the little meadow which intervened was now suffering a terrible onslaught of shells. Its green and beautiful calm had vanished utterly. Brown earth was being flung in monstrous handfuls. And there was a massacre of the young blades of grass. They were being torn, burned, obliterated. Some curious fortune of the battle had made this gentle little meadow the object of the red hate of the shells, and each one as it exploded seemed like an imprecation in the face of a maiden.

The wounded officer who was riding across this expanse said to himself: "Why, they couldn't shoot any harder if the whole army was massed here!"

A shell struck the gray ruins of the house, and as, after the roar, the shattered wall fell in fragments, there was a noise which resembled the flapping of shutters during a wild gale of winter. Indeed, the infantry paused in the shelter of the bank appeared as men standing upon a shore contemplating a madness of the sea. The angel of calamity had under its glance the battery upon the hill. Fewer white-legged men labored about the guns. A shell had smitten one of the pieces, and after the flare, the smoke, the dust, the wrath of this blow were gone, it

was possible to see white legs stretched horizontally upon the ground. And at that interval to the rear where it is the business of battery horses to stand with their noses to the fight, awaiting the command to drag their guns out of the destruction, or into it, or wheresoever these incomprehensible humans demanded·with whip and spur—in this line of passive and dumb spectators, whose fluttering hearts yet would not let them forget the iron laws of man's control of them—in this rank of brute soldiers there had been relentless and hideous carnage. From the ruck of bleeding and prostrate horses, the men of the infantry could see one animal raising its stricken body with its forelegs and turning its nose with mystic and profound eloquence toward the sky.

Some comrades joked Collins about his thirst. "Well, if yeh want a drink so bad, why don't yeh go git it?"

"Well, I will in a minnet, if yeh don't shut up!"

A lieutenant of artillery floundered his horse straight down the hill with as little concern as if it were level ground. As he galloped past the colonel of the infantry, he threw up his hand in swift salute. "We've got to get out of that," he roared angrily. He was a black-bearded officer, and his eyes, which resembled beads, sparkled like those of an insane man. His jumping horse sped along the column of infantry.

The fat major, standing carelessly with his sword held horizontally behind him and with his legs far apart, looked after the receding horseman and laughed. "He wants to get back with orders pretty quick, or there'll be no batt'ry left," he observed.

The wise young captain of the second company hazarded to the lieutenant colonel that the enemy's infantry would probably soon attack the hill, and the lieutenant colonel snubbed him.

A private in one of the rear companies looked out over the meadow, and then turned to a companion and said, "Look there, Jim!" It was the wounded officer from the battery, who some time before had started to ride across the meadow, supporting his right arm carefully with his left hand. This man had encountered a shell apparently at a time when no one perceived him, and he could now be seen lying face downward with a stirruped foot stretched across the body of his dead horse. A leg of the charger extended slantingly upward, precisely as stiff as a stake. Around this motionless pair the shells still howled.

There was a quarrel in A Company. Collins was shaking his fist in the faces of some laughing comrades. "Dern yeh! I ain't afraid t' go. If yeh say much, I will go!"

"Of course, yeh will! You'll run through that there medder, won't yeh?"

Collins said, in a terrible voice: "You see now!" At this ominous threat his comrades broke into renewed jeers.

Collins gave them a dark scowl, and went to find his captain. The latter was conversing with the colonel of the regiment.

"Captain," said Collins, saluting and standing at attention—in those days all trousers bagged at the knees—"Captain, I want t' git permission to go git some water from that there well over yonder!"

The colonel and the captain swung about simultaneously and stared across the meadow. The captain laughed. "You must be pretty thirsty, Collins?"

"Yes, sir, I am."

"Well—ah," said the captain. After a moment, he asked, "Can't you wait?"

"No, sir."

The colonel was watching Collins's face. "Look here, my lad," he said, in a pious sort of voice—"Look here, my lad"—Collins was not a lad—"don't you think that's taking pretty big risks for a little drink of water?"

"I dunno," said Collins uncomfortably. Some of the resentment toward his companions, which perhaps had forced him into this affair, was beginning to fade. "I dunno wether 'tis."

The colonel and the captain contemplated him for a time.

"Well," said the captain finally.

"Well," said the colonel, "if you want to go, why, go."

Collins saluted. "Much obliged t'yeh."

As he moved away the colonel called after him. "Take some of the other boys' canteens with you, an' hurry back now."

"Yes, sir, I will."

The colonel and the captain looked at each other then, for it had suddenly occurred that they could not for the life of them tell whether Collins wanted to go or whether he did not.

They turned to regard Collins, and as they perceived him surrounded by gesticulating comrades, the colonel said: "Well, by thunder! I guess he's going."

Collins appeared as a man dreaming. In the midst of the questions, the advice, the warnings, all the excited talk of his company mates, he maintained a curious silence.

They were very busy in preparing him for his ordeal. When they inspected him carefully, it was somewhat like the examination that grooms give a horse before a race; and they were amazed, staggered, by the whole affair. Their astonishment found vent in strange repetitions.

"Are yeh sure a-goin'?" they demanded again and again.

"Certainly I am," cried Collins at last, furiously.

He strode sullenly away from them. He was swinging five or six canteens by their cords. It seemed that his cap would not remain firmly on his head, and often he reached and pulled it down over his brow.

There was a general movement in the compact column. The long animal-like thing moved slightly. Its four hundred eyes were turned upon the figure of Collins.

"Well, sir, if that ain't th' derndest thing! I never thought Fred Collins had the blood in him for that kind of business."

"What's he goin' to do, anyhow?"

"He's goin' to that well there after water."

"We ain't dyin' of thirst, are we? That's foolishness."

"Well, somebody put him up to it, an' he's doin' it."

"Say, he must be a desperate cuss."

When Collins faced the meadow and walked away from the regiment, he was vaguely conscious that a chasm, the deep valley of all prides, was suddenly between him and his comrades. It was provisional, but the provision was that he return as a victor. He had blindly been led by quaint emotions, and laid himself under an obligation to walk squarely up to the face of death.

But he was not sure that he wished to make a retraction, even if he could do so without shame. As a matter of truth, he was sure of very little. He was mainly surprised.

It seemed to him supernaturally strange that he had allowed his mind to maneuver his body into such a situation. He understood that it might be called dramatically great.

However, he had no full appreciation of anything, excepting that he was actually conscious of being dazed. He could feel his dulled mind groping after the form and color of this incident. He wondered why he did not feel some keen agony of fear cutting his sense like a knife. He wondered at this, because human expression had said loudly for centuries that men should feel afraid of certain things, and that all men who did not feel this fear were phenomena— heroes.

He was, then, a hero. He suffered that disappointment which we would all have if we discovered that we were ourselves capable of those deeds which we most admire in history and legend. This, then, was a hero. After all, heroes were not much.

No, it could not be true. He was not a hero. Heroes had no shames in their lives, and, as for him, he remembered borrowing fifteen dollars from a friend and promising to pay it back the next day, and then avoiding that friend for ten months. When, at home, his mother had aroused him for the early labor of his life on the farm, it had often been his fashion to be irritable, childish, diabolical; and his mother had died since he had come to the war.

He saw that, in this matter of the well, the canteens, the shells, he was an intruder in the land of fine deeds.

He was now about thirty paces from his comrades. The regiment had just turned its many faces toward him.

From the forest of terrific noises there suddenly emerged a little uneven line of men. They fired fiercely and rapidly at distant foliage on which appeared little puffs of white smoke. The spatter of skirmish firing was added to the thunder of the guns on the hill. The little line of men ran forward. A color sergeant fell flat with his flag as if he had slipped on ice. There was hoarse cheering from this distant field.

Collins suddenly felt that two demon fingers were pressed into his ears. He could see nothing but flying arrows, flaming red. He lurched from the shock of this explosion, but he made a mad rush for the house, which he viewed as a man submerged to the neck in a boiling surf might view the shore. In the air little pieces of shell howled, and the earthquake explosions drove him insane with the menace of their roar. As he ran the canteens knocked together with a rhythmical tinkling.

As he neared the house, each detail of the scene became vivid to him. He was aware of some bricks of the vanished chimney lying on the sod. There was a door which hung by one hinge.

Rifle bullets called forth by the insistent skirmishers came from the far-off bank of foliage. They mingled with the shells and the pieces of shells until the air was torn in all directions by hootings, yells, howls. The sky was full of fiends who directed all their wild rage at his head.

When he came to the well, he flung himself face downward and peered into its darkness. There were furtive silver glintings some feet from the surface. He grabbed one of the canteens and, unfastening its cap, swung it down by the cord. The water flowed slowly in with an indolent gurgle.

And now, as he lay with his face turned away,

he was suddenly smitten with the terror. It came upon his heart like the grasp of claws. All the power faded from his muscles. For an instant he was no more than a dead man.

The canteen filled with a maddening slowness, in the manner of all bottles. Presently he recovered his strength and addressed a screaming oath to it. He leaned over until it seemed as if he intended to try to push water into it with his hands. His eyes as he gazed down into the well shone like two pieces of metal, and in their expression was a great appeal and a great curse. The stupid water derided him.

There was the blaring thunder of a shell. Crimson light shone through the swift-boiling smoke, and made a pink reflection on part of the wall of the well. Collins jerked out his arm and canteen with the same motion that a man would use in withdrawing his head from a furnace.

He scrambled erect and glared and hesitated. On the ground near him lay the old well bucket, with a length of rusty chain. He lowered it swiftly into the well. The bucket struck the water and then, turning lazily over, sank. When, with hand reaching tremblingly over hand, he hauled it out, it knocked often against the walls of the well and spilled some of its contents.

In running with a filled bucket, a man can adopt but one kind of gait. So, through this terrible field over which screamed practical angels of death, Collins ran in the manner of a farmer chased out of a dairy by a bull.

His face went staring white with anticipation—anticipation of a blow that would whirl him around and down. He would fall as he had seen other men fall, the life knocked out of them so suddenly that their knees were no more quick to touch the ground than their heads. He saw the long blue line of the regiment, but his comrades were standing looking at him from the edge of an impossible star. He was aware of some deep wheelruts and hoofprints in the sod beneath his feet.

The artillery officer who had fallen in this meadow had been making groans in the teeth of the tempest of sound. These futile cries, wrenched from him by his agony, were heard only by shells, bullets. When wild-eyed Collins came running, this officer raised himself. His face contorted and blanched from pain, he was about to utter some great beseeching cry. But suddenly his face straightened, and he called: "Say, young man, give me a drink of water, will you?"

Collins had no room amid his emotions for surprise. He was mad from the threats of destruction.

"I can't!" he screamed, and in his reply was a full description of his quaking apprehension. His cap was gone and his hair was riotous. His clothes made it appear that he had been dragged over the ground by the heels. He ran on.

The officer's head sank down, and one elbow crooked. His foot in its brass-bound stirrup still stretched over the body of his horse, and the other leg was under the steed.

But Collins turned. He came dashing back. His face had now turned gray, and in his eyes was all terror. "Here it is! here it is!"

The officer was as a man gone in drink. His arm bent like a twig. His head drooped as if his neck were of willow. He was sinking to the ground, to lie face downward.

Collins grabbed him by the shoulder. "Here it is. Here's your drink. Turn over. Turn over, man, for God's sake!"

With Collins hauling at his shoulder, the officer twisted his body and fell with his face turned toward that region where lived the unspeakable noises of the swirling missiles. There was the faintest shadow of a smile on his lips as he looked at Collins. He gave a sigh, a little primitive breath like that from a child.

Collins tried to hold the bucket steadily, but his shaking hands caused the water to splash all over the face of the dying man. Then he jerked it away and ran on.

The regiment gave him a welcoming roar. The grimed faces were wrinkled in laughter.

His captain waved the bucket away. "Give

it to the men!"

The two genial, skylarking young lieutenants were the first to gain possession of it. They played over it in their fashion.

When one tried to drink, the other teasingly knocked his elbow. "Don't Billie! You'll make me spill it," said the one. The other laughed.

Suddenly there was an oath, the thud of wood on the ground, and a swift murmur of astonishment among the ranks. The two lieutenants glared at each other. The bucket lay on the ground empty.

SHOOTING AN ELEPHANT

George Orwell

In Moulmein, in Lower Burma, I was hated by large numbers of people—the only time in my life that I have been important enough for this to happen to me. I was sub-divisional police officer of the town, and in an aimless, petty kind of way anti-European feeling was very bitter. No one had the guts to raise a riot, but if a European woman went through the bazaars alone somebody would probably spit betel juice over her dress. As a police officer I was an obvious target and was baited whenever it seemed safe to do so. When a nimble Burman tripped me up on the football field and the referee (another Burman) looked the other way, the crowd yelled with hideous laughter. This happened more than once. In the end the sneering yellow faces of young men that met me everywhere, the insults hooted after me when I was at a safe distance, got badly on my nerves. The young Buddhist priests were the worst of all. There were several thousands of them in the town and none of them seemed to have anything to do except stand on street corners and jeer at Europeans.

All this was perplexing and upsetting. For at that time I had already made up my mind that imperialism was an evil thing and the sooner I chucked up my job and got out of it the better. Theoretically—and secretly, of course—I was all for the Burmese and all against their oppressors, the British. As for the job I was doing, I hated it more bitterly than I can perhaps make clear. In a job like that you see the dirty work of Empire at close quarters. The wretched prisoners huddling in the stinking cages of the lock-ups, the grey, cowed faces of the long-term convicts, the scarred buttocks of the men who had been flogged with bamboos—all these oppressed me with an intolerable sense of guilt. But I could get nothing into perspective. I was young and ill-educated and I had had to think out my problems in the utter silence that is imposed on every Englishman in the East. I did not even know that the British Empire is dying, still less did I know that it is a great deal better than the younger empires that are going to supplant it. All I knew was that I was stuck between my hatred of the empire I served and my rage against the evil-spirited little beasts who tried to make my job impossible. With one part of my mind I thought of the British Raj

— *"Shooting an Elephant"* by George Orwell, from *Shooting an Elephant and other stories*, published by *Martin Secker and Warburg Limited, London, 1950; reprinted by permission of Miss Sonia Brownell*

as an unbreakable tyranny, as something clamped down, in *sæcula sæculorum*, upon the will of prostrate peoples; with another part I thought that the greatest joy in the world would be to drive a bayonet into a Buddhist priest's guts. Feelings like these are the normal by-products of imperialism; ask any Anglo-Indian official, if you can catch him off duty.

One day something happened which in a roundabout way was enlightening. It was a tiny incident in itself, but it gave me a better glimpse than I had had before of the real nature of imperialism—the real motives for which despotic governments act. Early one morning the sub-inspector at a police station the other end of the town rang me up on the 'phone and said that an elephant was ravaging the bazaar. Would I please come and do something about it? I did not know what I could do, but I wanted to see what was happening and I got on to a pony and started out. I took my rifle, an old .44 Winchester and much too small to kill an elephant, but I thought the noise might be useful *in terrorem*. Various Burmans stopped me on the way and told me about the elephant's doings. It was not, of course, a wild elephant, but a tame one which had gone "must." It had been chained up, as tame elephants always are when their attack of "must" is due, but on the previous night it had broken its chain and escaped. Its mahout, the only person who could manage it when it was in that state, had set out in pursuit, but had taken the wrong direction and was now twelve hours' journey away, and in the morning the elephant had suddenly reappeared in the town. The Burmese population had no weapons and were quite helpless against it. It had already destroyed somebody's bamboo hut, killed a cow and raided some fruit-stalls and devoured the stock; also it had met the municipal rubbish van, and, when the driver jumped out and took to his heels, had turned the van over and inflicted violences upon it.

The Burmese sub-inspector and some Indian constables were waiting for me in the quarter where the elephant had been seen. It was a very poor quarter, a labyrinth of squalid bamboo huts, thatched with palm-leaf, winding all over a steep hillside. I remember that it was a cloudy, stuffy morning at the beginning of the rains. We began questioning the people as to where the elephant had gone, and, as usual, failed to get any definite information. That is invariably the case in the East; a story always sounds clear enough at a distance, but the nearer you get to the scene of events the vaguer it becomes. Some of the people said that the elephant had gone in one direction, some said that he had gone in another, some professed not even to have heard of any elephant. I had almost made up my mind that the whole story was a pack of lies, when we heard yells a little distance away. There was a loud, scandalized cry of "Go away, child! Go away this instant!" and an old woman with a switch in her hand came round the corner of a hut, violently shooing away a crowd of naked children. Some more women followed, clicking their tongues and exclaiming; evidently there was something that the children ought not to have seen. I rounded the hut and saw a man's dead body sprawling in the mud. He was an Indian, a black Dravidian coolie, almost naked, and he could not have been dead many minutes. The people said that the elephant had come suddenly upon him round the corner of the hut, caught him with its trunk, put its foot on his back and ground him into the earth. This was the rainy season and the ground was soft, and his face had scored a trench a foot deep and a couple of yards long. He was lying on his belly with arms crucified and head sharply twisted to one side. His face was coated with mud, the eyes wide open, the teeth bared and grinning with an expression of unendurable agony. (Never tell me, by the way, that the dead look peaceful. Most of the corpses I have seen looked devilish.) The friction of the great beast's foot had stripped the skin from his back as neatly as one skins a rabbit. As soon as I saw the dead man I sent an orderly to a friend's house nearby to borrow an elephant rifle. I had already sent back the pony, not wanting it to go mad with fright and throw me if it smelt the elephant.

The orderly came back in a few minutes with a rifle and five cartridges, and meanwhile some Burmans had arrived and told us that the elephant was in the paddy fields below, only a few hundred yards away. As I started forward practically the whole population of the quarter flocked out of the houses and followed me. They had seen the rifle and were all shouting excitedly that I was going to shoot the elephant. They had not shown much interest in the elephant when he was merely ravaging their homes, but it was different now that he was going to be shot. It was a bit of fun to them, as it would be to an English crowd; besides they wanted the meat. It made me vaguely uneasy. I had no intention of shooting the elephant—I had merely sent for the rifle to defend myself if necessary—and it is always unnerving to have a crowd following you. I marched down the hill, looking and feeling a fool, with the rifle over my shoulder and an ever-growing army of people jostling at my heels. At the bottom, when you got away from the huts, there was a metalled road and beyond that a miry waste of paddy fields a thousand yards across, not yet ploughed but soggy from the first rains and dotted with coarse grass. The elephant was standing eight yards from the road, his left side towards us. He took not the slightest notice of the crowd's approach. He was tearing up bunches of grass, beating them against his knees to clean them and stuffing them into his mouth.

I had halted on the road. As soon as I saw the elephant I knew with perfect certainty that I ought not to shoot him. It is a serious matter to shoot a working elephant—it is comparable to destroying a huge and costly piece of machinery—and obviously one ought not to do it if it can possibly be avoided. And at that distance, peacefully eating, the elephant looked no more dangerous than a cow. I thought then and I think now that his attack of "must" was already passing off; in which case he would merely wander harmlessly about until the mahout came back and caught him. Moreover, I did not in the least want to shoot him. I decided that I would watch him for a little while to make sure that he did not turn savage again, and then go home.

But at that moment I glanced round at the crowd that had followed me. It was an immense crowd, two thousand at the least and growing every minute. It blocked the road for a long distance on either side. I looked at the sea of yellow faces above the garish clothes—faces all happy and excited over this bit of fun, all certain that the elephant was going to be shot. They were watching me as they would watch a conjurer about to perform a trick. They did not like me, but with the magical rifle in my hands I was momentarily worth watching. And suddenly I realized that I should have to shoot the elephant after all. The people expected it of me and I had got to do it; I could feel their two thousand wills pressing me forward, irresistibly. And it was at this moment, as I stood there with the rifle in my hands, that I first grasped the hollowness, the futility of the white man's dominion in the East. Here was I, the white man with his gun, standing in front of the unarmed native crowd—seemingly the leading actor of the piece; but in reality I was only an absurd puppet pushed to and fro by the will of those yellow faces behind. I perceived in this moment that when the white man turns tyrant it is his own freedom that he destroys. He becomes a sort of hollow, posing dummy, the conventionalized figure of a sahib. For it is the condition of his rule that he shall spend his life in trying to impress the "natives," and so in every crisis he has got to do what the "natives" expect of him. He wears a mask, and his face grows to fit it. I had got to shoot the elephant. I had committed myself to doing it when I sent for the rifle. A sahib has got to act like a sahib; he has got to appear resolute, to know his own mind and do definite things. To come all that way, rifle in hand, with two thousand people marching at my heels, and then to trail feebly away, having done nothing—no, that was impossible. The crowd would laugh at me. And my whole life, every white man's life in the East, was one long struggle not to be laughed at.

But I did not want to shoot the elephant. I watched him beating his bunch of grass against his knees, with that preoccupied grandmotherly air that elephants have. It seemed to me that it would be murder to shoot him. At that age I was not squeamish about killing animals, but I had never shot an elephant and never wanted to. (Somehow it always seems worse to kill a *large* animal.) Besides, there was the beast's owner to be considered. Alive, the elephant was worth at least a hundred pounds; dead, he would only be worth the value of his tusks, five pounds, possibly. But I had got to act quickly. I turned to some experienced-looking Burmans who had been there when we arrived, and asked them how the elephant had been behaving. They all said the same thing; he took no notice of you if you left him alone, but he might charge if you went too close to him.

It was perfectly clear to me what I ought to do. I ought to walk up to within, say, twenty-five yards of the elephant and test his behaviour. If he charged I could shoot, if he took no notice of me it would be safe to leave him until the mahout came back. But also I knew that I was going to do no such thing. I was a poor shot with a rifle and the ground was soft mud into which one would sink at every step. If the elephant charged and I missed him, I should have about as much chance as a toad under a steam-roller. But even then I was not thinking particularly of my own skin, only of the watchful yellow faces behind. For at that moment, with the crowd watching me, I was not afraid in the ordinary sense, as I would have been if I had been alone. A white man mustn't be frightened in front of "natives"; and so, in general, he isn't frightened. The sole thought in my mind was that if anything went wrong those two thousand Burmans would see me pursued, caught, trampled on and reduced to a grinning corpse like that Indian up the hill. And if that happened it was quite probable that some of them would laugh. That would never do. There was only one alternative. I shoved the cartridges into the magazine and lay down on the road to get a better aim.

The crowd grew very still, and a deep, low, happy sigh, as of people who see the theatre curtain go up at last, breathed from innumerable throats. They were going to have their bit of fun after all. The rifle was a beautiful German thing with cross-hair sights. I did not then know that in shooting an elephant one would shoot to cut an imaginary bar running from ear-hole to ear-hole. I ought, therefore, as the elephant was sideways on, to have aimed straight at his ear-hole; actually I aimed several inches in front of this, thinking the brain would be further forward.

When I pulled the trigger I did not hear the bang or feel the kick—one never does when a shot goes home—but I heard the devilish roar of glee that went up from the crowd. In that instant, in too short a time, one would have thought, even for the bullet to get there, a mysterious, terrible change had come over the elephant. He neither stirred nor fell, but every line of his body had altered. He looked suddenly stricken, shrunken, immensely old, as though the frightful impact of the bullet had paralysed him without knocking him down. At last, after what seemed a long time—it might have been five seconds, I dare say—he sagged flabbily to his knees. His mouth slobbered. An enormous senility seemed to have settled upon him. One could have imagined him thousands of years old. I fired again into the same spot. At the second shot he did not collapse but climbed with desperate slowness to his feet and stood weakly upright, with legs sagging and head drooping. I fired a third time. That was the shot that did for him. You could see the agony of it jolt his whole body and knock the last remnant of strength from his legs. But in falling he seemed for a moment to rise, for as his hind legs collapsed beneath him he seemed to tower upwards like a huge rock toppling, his trunk reaching skywards like a tree. He trumpeted, for the first and only time. And then down he came, his belly towards me, with a crash that seemed to shake the ground even where I lay.

I got up. The Burmans were already racing past me across the mud. It was obvious that the elephant would never rise again, but he was not dead. He was breathing very rhythmically with long rattling gasps, his great mound of a side painfully rising and falling. His mouth was wide open—I could see far down into caverns of pale pink throat. I waited a long time for him to die, but his breathing did not weaken. Finally I fired my two remaining shots into the spot where I thought his heart must be. The thick blood welled out of him like red velvet, but still he did not die. His body did not even jerk when the shots hit him, the tortured breathing continued without a pause. He was dying, very slowly and in great agony, but in some world remote from me where not even a bullet could damage him further. I felt that I had got to put an end to that dreadful noise. It seemed dreadful to see the great beast lying there, powerless to move and yet powerless to die, and not even to be able to finish him. I sent back for my small rifle and poured shot after shot into his heart and down his throat. They seemed to make no impression. The tortured gasps continued as steadily as the ticking of a clock.

In the end I could not stand it any longer and went away. I heard later that it took him half an hour to die. Burmans were bringing dahs and baskets even before I left, and I was told they had stripped his body almost to the bones by the afternoon.

Afterwards, of course, there were endless discussions about the shooting of the elephant. The owner was furious, but he was only an Indian and could do nothing. Besides, legally I had done the right thing, for a mad elephant has to be killed, like a mad dog, if its owner fails to control it. Among the Europeans opinion was divided. The older men said I was right, the younger men said it was a damn shame to shoot an elephant for killing a coolie, because an elephant was worth more than any damn Coringhee coolie. And afterwards I was very glad that the coolie had been killed; it put me legally in the right and it gave me a sufficient pretext for shooting the elephant. I often wondered whether any of the others grasped that I had done it solely to avoid looking a fool.

THE PLEASURES OF HOCKEY

Hugh Hood

I guess the best part is the skating. The highest praise you can give a hockey player is to say that he's skating all the time. I used to think this was a

———"The Pleasures of Hockey" by Hugh Hood is reprinted from <u>The Governor's Bridge is Closed</u> by permission of Oberon Press

metaphor meaning "he works hard" or "he's got a lot of competitive spirit" but it isn't. To play the game right you've got to keep moving all the time you're on the ice, at a steady three-quarters, say, of your top speed. When the time comes to make your play, you go hard. But you've got to be moving constantly. Watch the best players, even at a faceoff, and you'll see them moving in little circles, edging back and forth, flexing their knees. Or go out to watch a bantam practice, and you'll notice there's this one kid who never stops. He'll be the best player on the ice.

You could easily diagram the pattern that a left wing skates. He positions himself by the boards, 30 feet out from the net, takes the pass from the defenceman, lays the puck up to the centre and goes for the opposing blueline. If the play comes back to him, he breaks into top speed to get away from his check and make his move on the defenceman. When possession changes hands, he makes a wide turn, often going behind the opposing net, and comes back across the ice, heading for the left boards just about centre ice, where he'll have an angle on the winger he's covering. And he'll skate this same pattern over and over, maybe three times a shift, four shifts a period. When a sportswriter talks about "patrolling the boards," it's a cliché, but it's also true. Skate, skate, skate, avoid sudden stops and starts, pace yourself and keep moving, stay with your check when he's got the puck, and be ready to break when it comes to you. Move!

I'm only playing in an organized league once a week nowadays. I'd play two nights if I could get the time, but it's impossible, so to try and keep my skating somewhere near a decent standard, I'll go out to a pleasure rink near where I live two or three afternoons a week, to loosen up my legs and help my wind. I follow a set routine. When I come on the ice, I skate counter-clockwise around the rink at a good pace, but not as fast as possible, for as long as I can go without stopping to rest. Take the long stride, bend over, push with that big skating muscle along the thigh at the back of the leg, that's where the power comes from; get as much forward glide as possible from each leg movement. I don't try to skate like a sprinter, with a quick knee action, but more like a long-distance runner, pacing myself. By mid-winter I can go pretty fast for fifteen, twenty minutes, always counter-clockwise to start with, because that's my bad turn.

Perhaps because of the predominance of one half of the brain over the other, every skater has one side that's easy for him to turn on, one side

that's clumsy. I turn easily from left to right, lifting the left leg and cross it over the right, and using the right edge of the blades to dig into the ice. Going from right to left is much harder for me, so that's what I work on. If I want to turn around to skate backwards, it's much easier for me to put the left foot forward and swing my weight around on the left leg. A good hockey player can turn almost equally well to either side, but he'll favour one side slightly, right into the NHL, which is why it's hard for a defenceman, for example, to switch sides.

Out on a rink, around 2.30 on a weekday afternoon, I'll be alone most of the time; the kids are still in school. Sometimes a young mother brings her three-year-old along; usually the rink attendant is around somewhere. But that lovely smooth grey sheet of ice will be almost empty, and when I've warmed up for 40 minutes, first counter-clockwise, then clockwise, then some stops and starts, I'll play an imaginary game of hockey. Skate up to the opposition goal, forecheck the man coming out from behind the net, turn and go back, turn around and skate backwards, stop in front of my goal, line up for a faceoff, make a quick break to one side or the other. This looks strange to an onlooker, I suppose, but anybody who knows hockey will see immediately what I'm doing. I remember once I was going through this routine and a boy of fifteen watched me for a while, then said, "Way to forecheck," which pleased me a lot.

A side effect of this solitary skating that gives me a terrific charge is the way the light changes as you go from January through February. By mid-February the sun will be high in the sky at 3 in the afternoon, and you can see the edges of the rink soften, and water appear between the ice and the boards. It's like holding an hourglass on winter.

I'm 39, which means it takes me most of a winter to get skating so I can make the occasional good move in a game. In October and November, I can see what I ought to be doing. I can even get fairly close to the play, but I won't execute it right. Once or twice a season, usually down toward the beginning of March, I'll hit a point where my skating comes together. There is no physical feeling I know of that's quite like that, and only one that's better. When my skating finally comes right, it isn't a short intense pleasure, it's a long slow one, spread over my whole body, a sense of great health and well-being. My legs seem to be swinging loose from the hip in a long stride that eats up rink space, and my breathing is close to what it would be if I had the guts to quit smoking. This is when you start to make the plays the way you should. One of the most frequent plays that comes up for a right defenceman (my position) is the one where the opposing right defenceman, diagonally across the ice surface, dumps the puck around the boards behind the net to your side. You have to decide whether to move into the corner for that loose puck, or to start going back. If you can beat the wing into the corner, you can make a centering pass. One night a couple of weeks ago this situation came up twice, and I had to make that instant decision. Both times I went for the puck (by skating all out for about thirty feet, really flying, boy) and got to it in time to lay a smooth flat perfect pass right across the goalmouth.

I got the same kind of sensation that a golfer gets from a perfect long wood shot, that click and follow through where the rhythm is exactly right. You can't plan this; you don't make a conscious choice. The play comes up and you do or you don't, but you can't take time to think. The game is too fast, even a game like ours where not more than three or four good players are involved.

That's why hockey is so much less loaded down with fake science than pro football, for example. The basic plays and strategy are obvious and simple in hockey, and they're repeated endlessly, but never exactly the same way. I saw Jean Béliveau get a break from centre ice against the Hawks last week, and he was giving Jack Norris fakes from the blueline in, but fast fast fast, the head, the eyes, the knees. In the end he pulled him out of the net, went left, and put the puck in there, but Norris *didn't know* he was going to do that because Béliveau never does it the same way

twice. Even some very good players will repeat their favourite moves. Béliveau never does it the same twice in a row, and that's the best kind of hockey. You can anticipate play up to a point, know pretty well what your teammates will do, but in the actual situation things are never precisely the same as the last time. I've got a couple of patterns I'm painfully aware of, that I'll repeat over and over, so that the other club knows exactly what I'm going to do. No matter how many times I tell myself before the game not to use them, in the given situation I'll make the same play. If I'm lying back, and the puck comes to me at our blueline, or even inside our zone, I'll get rid of it in a hurry, usually by passing it to our left defenceman who's a much better player than me. I'm afraid to wait, look up, and go to my right, maybe because I'm left-handed and don't move the puck too well on the right side.

That's what I ought to do—make a move on the man who's checking me, but nine times out of ten I'll pass the puck to Hank. The other team knows this, and they'll play for that pass. A few times I've put the puck right on somebody's stick, which gives him a clean break. Pow! Maybe if I play another ten years I'll learn not to do that, anyway I keep trying. And there's one good thing about repeating your plays; the men on your own club know pretty well where you'll be and what you'll do. When you've played together for a while, your passing gets very precise, considering the speed of the game. Last night I trapped the puck just inside their blueline and moved it in front of their net fast. Brian Rossy was right there and all he had to do was take the shot. Goal. Bang, just like that, a play that worked just right, completely uncalculated.

There's a guy who plays against us, a centre, fast and smart and a much better skater than I am and yet for some reason when he comes into our zone on my side I'll tangle him up eight times out of ten. There doesn't seem to be any reason for it, but he seems to be sort of fatally attracted to where I am. After the game he'll be standing around the coffee counter growling at me, "You're impossible to get around," and the thing is, I'm not that good. We seem to be repeating a pattern over and over, with the minute variations that make the game so fascinating.

Then there's the locker-room kidding, the sense of intimate companionship and the friendliness that goes with it. Your dime-store psychiatrist is always on about team sports, and how they're the escape from sexual responsibility of the North American male. He gets away from his adult relationship with his wife, regresses to adolescence and appeases his latent homosexuality by getting together with the gang in that good old sweaty, semi-nude locker-room association. Lot of horse manure, if you ask me. There are plenty of unalloyed pleasures in life that have no sinister undertones—are simply what they seem—and this is one of them. I don't deny that team sports are a useful surrogate for hostility and aggression; better that than murder and war. But it's wiser to take the team association for what it seems, rather than analyzing the pleasure out of it. I come out of that locker-room on Friday nights with a splendid feeling of tiredness without mental exhaustion, something you just can't buy these days, and I wouldn't exchange it for anything.

I even like the dirty old equipment I've got. Three or four years ago, when I joined this league after not having played hockey for fifteen years, I was looking around for equipment and picked up stuff mostly on sale, a bit at a time till I had the essentials. I got a pair of hockey pants from a sporting-goods store that was going out of business, retail price $9.98, and I got them for $4.50 and let's face it, they're nothing special though they give the necessary protection. I've worn them in a hundred games and they're filthy and torn and beginning to come apart in places. I figured when I got them I'd just use them till I saw whether I could play in this league, then pick up some decent stuff.

I wouldn't replace them now for the world.

You get so damned attached to these things. There's a slash in the thumb of my right glove, where somebody skated over it one night. The glove kept me from losing my thumb, near as I

can figure, and I'm not going to throw it away, holes or no holes; same with my helmet. Four times this season I've taken a rap on the head from somebody's stick, or the puck, and each time the helmet protected me perfectly. I've got kind of attached to it.

It's these attachments and associations and traditions that hold you. As a rule we play our game Friday night with maybe 30 people in the stands, kids from the previous game or men coming in for the *Ligue Stanislas* game that usually follows ours, the arena staff. Some of our guys bring their wives now and then. Might be 40 people on a big night. But two weeks ago the arena scheduled a playoff game in the Metropolitan Junior A League to follow ours at 8.30. We were supposed to be off the ice by 8.15. The Laval Saints in the Junior league use this arena as their home ice, and they've got quite a following, so when we came on at 6.45 there were already a couple of hundred people sitting around in the stands, not taking any special notice of us.

I'd brought my son John with me to have a little skate before the game. He came out and took a couple of turns around the ice—the first time he'd ever been allowed to stay up to watch Daddy play. Then the game began and he sat at the timer's bench with one of the player's wives keeping an eye on him, to see he didn't get hit by a flying puck or something.

We played better than usual, a tight, low-score game, with a fair amount of hitting. And all the time more and more people kept coming into the arena to get good seats for the Saints' playoff. By the time the second period was half over the arena was filling up. I guess it seats just under 3000.

People kept coming and coming and, would you believe it, they began to follow our game. We don't play great hockey as a rule, but damned if the big crowd didn't get to the guys. Everybody started to play way over his head, and the crowd began to applaud the occasional good play. We'd got behind two-one and were pressing all the way through the second period. At the end of that period I went over to the timer's bench and lifted John onto the ice for one last skate. There was plenty of chuckling and a little ripple of applause for him from the crowd. I think he'll remember the occasion for a long time.

I'd never played before any kind of a crowd before. By 8 o'clock there must have been close to 2000 people in the place. Out on the ice we were all skating around with maximum grace and *élan*. Once our goalie made a sensational glove save off a hard shot from the blueline; he hadn't made a save like that all year, a real reflex grab. The puck would probably have gone over the net if he'd let it go, but he sure as hell looked great. The crowd oooh-ed and ahh-ed.

With about eight minutes to play we got the tying goal, and there was actually a cheer from the stands for the underdogs. Everybody kept digging and hustling; there were a few flare-ups and some shoving. When we got the goal that put us ahead three to two, the crowd didn't exactly go wild, but they made a lot of noise. I wouldn't have believed the difference a crowd makes, and I'm glad to have experienced it—the kind of thing everybody should experience once in a lifetime. Both teams really came on like the pros, and it ended three-two, a surprisingly low score for a league like ours. Everybody who watched saw an interesting, evenly-played game: even hockey like ours is fascinating to play and to watch.

And now I can't quite decide whether to explain to John that his Dad doesn't play before thousands every time out. Somehow I don't think I will.

COUNTERPARTS

James Joyce

The bell rang furiously and, when Miss Parker went to the tube, a furious voice called out in a piercing North of Ireland accent:

"Send Farrington here!"

Miss Parker returned to her machine, saying to a man who was writing at a desk:

"Mr Alleyne wants you upstairs."

The man muttered "*Blast* him!" under his breath and pushed back his chair to stand up. When he stood up he was tall and of great bulk. He had a hanging face, dark wine-coloured, with fair eyebrows and moustache: his eyes bulged forward slightly and the whites of them were dirty. He lifted up the counter and, passing by the clients, went out of the office with a heavy step.

He went heavily upstairs until he came to the second landing, where a door bore a brass plate with the inscription *Mr Alleyne*. Here he halted, puffing with labour and vexation, and knocked. The shrill voice cried:

"Come in!"

The man entered Mr Alleyne's room. Simultaneously Mr Alleyne, a little man wearing gold-rimmed glasses on a clean-shaven face, shot his head up over a pile of documents. The head itself was so pink and hairless it seemed like a large egg reposing on the papers. Mr Alleyne did not lose a moment:

"Farrington? What is the meaning of this? Why have I always to complain of you? May I

— "*Counterparts*" by *James Joyce, from Dubliners by James Joyce; originally published by B. W. Huebsch, Inc., 1916; all rights reserved; reprinted by permission of The Viking Press, Inc.*

ask you why you haven't made a copy of that contract between Bodley and Kirwan? I told you it must be ready by four o'clock."

"But Mr Shelly said, sir ——"

"*Mr Shelly said, sir* —— Kindly attend to what I say and not to what *Mr Shelly says, sir*. You have always some excuse or another for shirking work. Let me tell you that if the contract is not copied before this evening I'll lay the matter before Mr Crosbie —— Do you hear me now?"

"Yes, sir."

"Do you hear me now? —— Ay and another little matter! I might as well be talking to the wall as talking to you. Understand once for all that you get a half an hour for your lunch and not an hour and a half. How many courses do you want? I'd like to know —— Do you mind me now?"

"Yes, sir."

Mr Alleyne bent his head again upon his pile of papers. The man stared fixedly at the polished skull which directed the affairs of Crosbie & Alleyne, gauging its fragility. A spasm of rage gripped his throat for a few moments and then passed, leaving after it a sharp sensation of thirst. The man recognized the sensation and felt that he must have a good night's drinking. The middle of the month was passed and, if he could get the copy done in time, Mr Alleyne might give him an order on the cashier. He stood still, gazing fixedly at the head upon the pile of papers. Suddenly Mr Alleyne began to upset all the papers, searching for something. Then, as if he had been unaware of the man's presence till that moment, he shot up his head again, saying:

"Eh? Are you going to stand there all day? Upon my word, Farrington, you take things easy!"

"I was waiting to see ——"

"Very good, you needn't wait to see. Go downstairs and do your work."

The man walked heavily towards the door and, as he went out of the room, he heard Mr Alleyne cry after him that if the contract was not copied by evening Mr Crosbie would hear of the matter.

He returned to his desk in the lower office and counted the sheets which remained to be copied. He took up his pen and dipped it in the ink, but he continued to stare stupidly at the last words he had written: *In no case shall the said Bernard Bodley be* —— The evening was falling and in a few minutes they would be lighting the gas: then he could write. He felt that he must slake the thirst in his throat. He stood up from his desk and, lifting the counter as before, passed out of the office. As he was passing out the chief clerk looked at him inquiringly.

"It's all right, Mr Shelly," said the man, pointing with his finger to indicate the objective of his journey.

The chief clerk glanced at the hat-rack, but, seeing the row complete, offered no remark. As soon as he was on the landing the man pulled a shepherd's plaid cap out of his pocket, put it on his head and ran quickly down the rickety stairs. From the street door he walked on furtively on the inner side of the path towards the corner and all at once dived into a doorway. He was now safe in the dark snug of O'Neill's shop, and, filling up the little window that looked into the bar with his inflamed face, the colour of dark wine or dark meat, he called out:

"Here, Pat, give us a g.p., like a good fellow."

The curate brought him a glass of plain porter. The man drank it at a gulp and asked for a caraway seed. He put his penny on the counter and, leaving the curate to grope for it in the gloom, retreated out of the snug as furtively as he had entered it.

Darkness, accompanied by a thick fog, was gaining upon the dusk of February and the lamps in Eustace Street had been lit. The man went up by the houses until he reached the door of the office, wondering whether he could finish his copy in time. On the stairs a moist pungent odour of perfumes saluted his nose: evidently Miss Delacour had come while he was out in O'Neill's. He crammed his cap back again into his pocket and re-entered the office, assuming an air of absent-mindedness.

"Mr Alleyne has been calling for you," said

the chief clerk severely. "Where were you?"

The man glanced at the two clients who were standing at the counter as if to intimate that their presence prevented him from answering. As the clients were both male the chief clerk allowed himself a laugh.

"I know that game," he said. "Five times in one day is a little bit —— Well, you better look sharp and get a copy of our correspondence in the Delacour case for Mr Alleyne."

This address in the presence of the public, his run upstairs, and the porter he had gulped down so hastily confused the man and, as he sat down at his desk to get what was required, he realized how hopeless was the task of finishing his copy of the contract before half past five. The dark damp night was coming and he longed to spend it in the bars, drinking with his friends amid the glare of gas and the clatter of glasses. He got out the Delacour correspondence and passed out of the office. He hoped Mr Alleyne would not discover that the last two letters were missing.

The moist pungent perfume lay all the way up to Mr Alleyne's room. Miss Delacour was a middle-aged woman of Jewish appearance. Mr Alleyne was said to be sweet on her or on her money. She came to the office often and stayed a long time when she came. She was sitting beside his desk now in an aroma of perfumes, smoothing the handle of her umbrella and nodding the great black feather in her hat. Mr Alleyne had swivelled his chair round to face her and thrown his right foot jauntily upon his left knee. The man put the correspondence on the desk and bowed respectfully, but neither Mr Alleyne nor Miss Delacour took any notice of his bow. Mr Alleyne tapped a finger on the correspondence and then flicked it towards him as if to say: "*That's all right, you can go.*"

The man returned to the lower office and sat down again at his desk. He stared intently at the incomplete phrase: *In no case shall the said Bernard Bodley be* —— and thought how strange it was that the last three words began with the same letter. The chief clerk began to hurry Miss Parker, saying she would never have the letters typed in time for post. The man listened to the clicking of the machine for a few minutes and then set to work to finish his copy. But his head was not clear and his mind wandered away to the glare and rattle of the public-house. It was a night for hot punches. He struggled on with his copy, but when the clock struck five he had still fourteen pages to write. Blast it! He couldn't finish it in time. He longed to execrate aloud, to bring his fist down on something violently. He was so enraged that he wrote *Bernard Bernard* instead of *Bernard Bodley* and had to begin again on a clean sheet.

He felt strong enough to clear out the whole office single-handed. His body ached to do something, to rush out and revel in violence. All the indignities of his life enraged him. — Could he ask the cashier privately for an advance? No, the cashier was no good, no damn good: he wouldn't give an advance —— He knew where he would meet the boys: Leonard and O'Halloran and Nosey Flynn. The barometer of his emotional nature was set for a spell of riot.

His imagination had so abstracted him that his name was called twice before he answered. Mr Alleyne and Miss Delacour were standing outside the counter and all the clerks had turned round in anticipation of something. The man got up from his desk. Mr Alleyne began a tirade of abuse, saying that two letters were missing. The man answered that he knew nothing about them, that he had made a faithful copy. The tirade continued: it was so bitter and violent that the man could hardly restrain his fist from descending upon the head of the manikin before him.

"I know nothing about any other two letters," he said stupidly.

"*You* —— *know* —— *nothing*. Of course you know nothing," said Mr Alleyne. "Tell me," he added, glancing first for approval to the lady beside him, "do you take me for a fool? Do you think me an utter fool?"

The man glanced from the lady's face to the little egg-shaped head and back again; and almost before he was aware of it, his tongue had found a felicitous moment:

"I don't think, sir," he said, "that that's a fair question to put to me."

There was a pause in the very breathing of the clerks. Everyone was astounded (the author of the witticism no less than his neighbours) and Miss Delacour, who was a stout amiable person, began to smile broadly. Mr Alleyne flushed to the hue of a wild rose and his mouth twitched with a dwarf's passion. He shook his fist in the man's face till it seemed to vibrate like the knob of some electric machine:

"You impertinent ruffian! You impertinent ruffian! I'll make short work of you! Wait till you see! You'll apologize to me for your impertinence or you'll quit the office instanter! You'll quit this, I'm telling you, or you'll apologize to me!"

He stood in a doorway opposite the office, watching to see if the cashier would come out alone. All the clerks passed out and finally the cashier came out with the chief clerk. It was no use trying to say a word to him when he was with the chief clerk. The man felt that his position was bad enough. He had been obliged to offer an abject apology to Mr Alleyne for his impertinence, but he knew what a hornet's nest the office would be for him. He could remember the way in which Mr Alleyne had hounded little Peake out of the office in order to make room for his own nephew. He felt savage and thirsty and revengeful, annoyed with himself and with everyone else. Mr Alleyne would never give him an hour's rest; his life would be a hell to him. He had made a proper fool of himself this time. Could he not keep his tongue in his cheek? But they had never pulled together from the first, he and Mr Alleyne, ever since the day Mr Alleyne had overheard him mimicking his North of Ireland accent to amuse Higgins and Miss Parker; that had been the beginning of it. He might have tried Higgins for the money, but sure Higgins never had anything for himself. A man with two establishments to keep up, of course he couldn't ——

He felt his great body again aching for the comfort of the public-house. The fog had begun to chill him and he wondered could he touch Pat in O'Neill's. He could not touch him for more than a bob —— and a bob was no use. Yet he must get money somewhere or other: he had spent his last penny for the g.p. and soon it would be too late for getting money anywhere. Suddenly, as he was fingering his watch chain, he thought of Terry Kelly's pawn-office in Fleet Street. That was the dart! Why didn't he think of it sooner?

He went through the narrow alley of Temple Bar quickly, muttering to himself that they could all go to hell, because he was going to have a good night of it. The clerk in Terry Kelly's said *A crown!* but the consignor held out for six shillings; and in the end the six shillings was allowed him literally. He came out of the pawn-office joyfully, making a little cylinder of the coins between his thumb and fingers. In Westmoreland Street the footpaths were crowded with young men and women returning from business, and ragged urchins ran here and there yelling out the names of the evening editions. The man passed through the crowd, looking on the spectacle generally with proud satisfaction and staring masterfully at the office-girls. His head was full of the noises of tram-gongs and swishing trolleys and his nose already sniffed the curling fumes of punch. As he walked on he preconsidered the terms in which he would narrate the incident to the boys:

"So, I just looked at him —— coolly, you know, and looked at her. Then I looked back at him again —— taking my time you know. 'I don't think that's a fair question to put to me,' says I."

Nosey Flynn was sitting up in his usual corner of Davy Byrne's and, when he heard the story, he stood Farrington a half-one, saying it was as smart a thing as ever he heard. Farrington stood a drink in his turn. After a while O'Halloran and Paddy Leonard came in and the story was repeated to them. O'Halloran stood tailors of malt, hot, all round and told the story of the retort he had made to the chief clerk when he was in Callan's of Fownes's Street; but, as the retort was after the manner of the liberal shepherds in the eclogues, he had to admit that it was not as clever as Farrington's retort. At this Farrington told the boys to polish off that and have another.

Just as they were naming their poisons who should come in but Higgins! Of course he had to join with the others. The men asked him to give his version of it, and he did so with great vivacity, for the sight of five small hot whiskies was very exhilarating. Everyone roared laughing when he showed the way in which Mr Alleyne shook his fist in Farrington's face. Then he imitated Farrington, saying, "*And here was my nabs, as cool as you please,*" while Farrington looked at the company out of his heavy dirty eyes, smiling and at times drawing forth stray drops of liquor from his moustache with the aid of his lower lip.

When that round was over there was a pause. O'Halloran had money, but neither of the other two seemed to have any; so the whole party left the shop somewhat regretfully. At the corner of Duke Street Higgins and Nosey Flynn bevelled off to the left, while the other three turned back towards the city. Rain was drizzling down on the cold streets and, when they reached the Ballast Office, Farrington suggested the Scotch House. The bar was full of men and loud with the noise of tongues and glasses. The three men pushed past the whining match-sellers at the door and formed a little party at the corner of the counter. They began to exchange stories. Leonard introduced them to a young fellow named Weathers who was performing at the Tivoli as an acrobat and knockabout *artiste*. Farrington stood a drink all round. Weathers said he would take a small Irish and Apollinaris. Farrington, who had definite notions of what was what, asked the boys would they have an Apollinaris too; but the boys told Tim to make theirs hot. The talk became theatrical. O'Halloran stood a round and then Farrington stood another round, Weathers protesting that the hospitality was too Irish. He promised to get them in behind the scenes and introduce them to some nice girls. O'Halloran said that he and Leonard would go, but that Farrington wouldn't go because he was a married man; and Farrington's heavy dirty eyes leered at the company in token that he understood he was being chaffed. Weathers made them all have just one little tincture at his expense and promised to meet them later on at Mulligan's in Poolbeg Street.

When the Scotch House closed they went round to Mulligan's. They went into the parlour at the back and O'Halloran ordered small hot specials all round. They were all beginning to feel mellow. Farrington was just standing another round when Weathers came back. Much to Farrington's relief he drank a glass of bitter this time. Funds were getting low, but they had enough to keep them going. Presently two young women with big hats and a young man in a check suit came in and sat at a table close by. Weathers saluted them and told the company that they were out of the Tivoli. Farrington's eyes wandered at every moment in the direction of one of the young women. There was something striking in her appearance. An immense scarf of peacock-blue muslin was wound round her hat and knotted in a great bow under her chin; and she wore bright yellow gloves, reaching to the elbow. Farrington gazed admiringly at the plump arm which she moved very often and with much grace; and when, after a little time, she answered his gaze he admired still more her large dark brown eyes. The oblique staring expression in them fascinated him. She glanced at him once or twice and, when the party was leaving the room, she brushed against his chair and said "*O, pardon!*" in a London accent. He watched her leave the room in the hope that she would look back at him, but he was disappointed. He cursed his want of money and cursed all the rounds he had stood, particularly all the whiskies and Apollinaris which he had stood to Weathers. If there was one thing that he hated it was a sponge. He was so angry that he lost count of the conversation of his friends.

When Paddy Leonard called him he found that they were talking about feats of strength. Weathers was showing his biceps muscle to the company and boasting so much that the other two had called on Farrington to uphold the national honour. Farrington pulled up his sleeve accordingly and showed his biceps muscle to the company. The two arms were examined and compared and finally it was agreed to have a trial of strength. The table was cleared and the two men rested their elbows on it, clasping hands. When Paddy Leonard said "*Go!*" each was to try to bring down the other's hand on to the table. Farrington looked very serious and determined.

The trial began. After about thirty seconds Weathers brought his opponent's hand slowly down on to the table. Farrington's dark wine-coloured face flushed darker still with anger and humiliation at having been defeated by such a stripling.

"You're not to put the weight of your body behind it. Play fair," he said.

"Who's not playing fair?" said the other.

"Come on again. The two best out of three."

The trial began again. The veins stood out on Farrington's forehead, and the pallor of Weathers' complexion changed to peony. Their hands and arms trembled under the stress. After a long struggle Weathers again brought his opponent's hand slowly on to the table. There was a murmur of applause from the spectators. The curate, who was standing beside the table, nodded his red head towards the victor and said with stupid familiarity:

"Ah! that's the knack!"

"What the hell do you know about it?" said Farrington fiercely, turning on the man. "What do you put in your gab for?"

"Sh, sh!" said O'Halloran, observing the violent expression of Farrington's face. "Pony up, boys. We'll have just one little smahan more and then we'll be off."

A very sullen-faced man stood at the corner of O'Connell Bridge waiting for the little Sandy-mount tram to take him home. He was full of smouldering anger and revengefulness. He felt humiliated and discontented; he did not even feel drunk; and he had only twopence in his pocket. He cursed everything. He had done for himself in the office, pawned his watch, spent all his money; and he had not even got drunk. He began to feel thirsty again and he longed to be back again in the hot, reeking public-house. He had lost his reputation as a strong man, having been defeated twice by a mere boy. His heart swelled with fury and, when he thought of the woman in the big hat who had brushed against him and said *Pardon!* his fury nearly choked him.

His tram let him down at Shelbourne Road and he steered his great body along in the shadow of the wall of the barracks. He loathed returning to his home. When he went in by the side-door he found the kitchen empty and the kitchen fire nearly out. He bawled upstairs:

"Ada! Ada!"

His wife was a little sharp-faced woman who bullied her husband when he was sober and was bullied by him when he was drunk. They had five children. A little boy came running down the stairs.

"Who is that?" said the man, peering through the darkness.

"Me, pa."

"Who are you? Charlie?"

"No, pa. Tom."

"Where's your mother?"

"She's out at the chapel."

"That's right —— Did she think of leaving any dinner for me?"

"Yes, pa. I ——"

"Light the lamp. What do you mean by having the place in darkness? Are the other children in bed?"

The man sat down heavily on one of the chairs while the little boy lit the lamp. He began to mimic his son's flat accent, saying half to himself: "*At the chapel. At the chapel, if you please!*" When the lamp was lit he banged his fist on the table and shouted:

"What's for my dinner?"

"I'm going —— to cook it, pa," said the little boy.

The man jumped up furiously and pointed to the fire.

"On that fire! You let the fire out! By God, I'll teach you to do that again!"

He took a step to the door and seized the walking-stick which was standing behind it.

"I'll teach you to let the fire out!" he said, rolling up his sleeve in order to give his arm free play.

The little boy cried "*O, pa!*" and ran whimpering round the table, but the man followed him and caught him by the coat. The little boy looked about him wildly but, seeing no way of escape, fell upon his knees.

"Now, you'll let the fire out the next time!" said the man, striking at him vigorously with the stick. "Take that, you little whelp!"

The boy uttered a squeal of pain as the stick cut his thigh. He clasped his hands together in the air and his voice shook with fright.

"O, pa!" he cried. "Don't beat me, pa! And I'll —— I'll say a *Hail Mary* for you —— I'll say a *Hail Mary* for you, pa, if you don't beat me —— I'll say a *Hail Mary* ——"

THE SECRET LIFE OF WALTER MITTY

James Thurber

"We're going through!" The Commander's voice was like thin ice breaking. He wore his full-dress uniform, with the heavily braided white cap pulled down rakishly over one cold gray eye. "We can't make it, sir. It's spoiling for a hurricane, if you ask me." "I'm not asking you, Lieutenant Berg," said the Commander. "Throw on the power lights! Rev her up to 8,500! We're going through!" The pounding of the cylinders increased: ta-pocketa-pocketa-pocketa-*pocketa-pocketa*. The Commander stared at the ice forming on the pilot window. He walked over and twisted a row of complicated dials. "Switch on No. 8 auxiliary!" he shouted. "Switch on No. 8 auxiliary!" repeated Lieutenant Berg. "Full strength in No. 3 turret!" shouted the Commander. "Full strength in No. 3 turret!" The crew, bending to their various tasks in the huge, hurtling eight-engined Navy hydroplane, looked at each other and grinned.

— "*The Secret Life of Walter Mitty*" by *James Thurber; copyright © 1942 James Thurber, from My World—and Welcome to It, Harcourt Brace & World, New York; first printed in The New Yorker*

"The Old Man'll get us through," they said to one another. "The Old Man ain't afraid of Hell!"——

"Not so fast! You're driving too fast!" said Mrs. Mitty. "What are you driving so fast for?"

"Hmm?" said Walter Mitty. He looked at his wife, in the seat beside him, with shocked astonishment. She seemed grossly unfamiliar, like a strange woman who had yelled at him in a crowd. "You were up to fifty-five," she said. "You know I don't like to go more than forty. You were up to fifty-five." Walter Mitty drove on toward Waterbury in silence, the roaring of the SN202 through the worst storm in twenty years of Navy flying fading in the remote, intimate airways of his mind. "You're tensed up again," said Mrs. Mitty. "It's one of your days. I wish you'd let Dr. Renshaw look you over."

Walter Mitty stopped the car in front of the building where his wife went to have her hair done. "Remember to get those overshoes while I'm having my hair done," she said. "I don't need overshoes," said Mitty. She put her mirror back into her bag. "We've been all through that," she said, getting out of the car. "You're not a young man any longer." He raced the engine a little. "Why don't you wear gloves? Have you lost your gloves?" Walter Mitty reached in a pocket and brought out the gloves. He put them on, but after she had turned and gone into the building and he had driven on to a red light, he took them off again. "Pick it up, brother!" snapped a cop as the light changed, and Mitty hastily pulled on his gloves and lurched ahead. He drove around the streets aimlessly for a time, and then he drove past the hospital on his way to the parking lot.

——"It's the millionaire banker, Wellington McMillan," said the pretty nurse. "Yes?" said Walter Mitty, removing his gloves slowly. "Who has the case?" "Dr. Renshaw and Dr. Benbow, but there are two specialists here, Dr. Remington from New York and Mr. Pritchard-Mitford from London. He flew over." A door opened down a long, cool corridor and Dr. Renshaw came out. He looked distraught and haggard. "Hello, Mitty," he said. "We're having the devil's own time with McMillan, the millionaire banker and close personal friend of Roosevelt. Obstreosis of the ductal tract. Tertiary. Wish you'd take a look at him." "Glad to," said Mitty.

In the operating room there were whispered introductions: "Dr. Remington, Dr. Mitty, Mr. Pritchard-Mitford, Dr. Mitty." "I've read your book on streptothricosis," said Pritchard-Mitford, shaking hands. "A brilliant performance, sir." "Thank you," said Walter Mitty. "Didn't know you were in the States, Mitty," grumbled Remington. "Coals to Newcastle, bringing Mitford and me up here for a tertiary." "You are very kind," said Mitty. A huge, complicated machine, connected to the operating table, with many tubes and wires, began at this moment to go pocketa-pocketa-pocketa. "The new anaesthetizer is giving way!" shouted an interne. "There is no one in the East who knows how to fix it!" "Quiet, man!" said Mitty, in a low, cool voice. He sprang to the machine, which was now going pocketa-pocketa-queep-pocketa-queep. He began fingering delicately a row of glistening dials. "Give me a fountain pen!" he

snapped. Someone handed him a fountain pen. He pulled a faulty piston out of the machine and inserted the pen in its place. "That will hold for ten minutes," he said. "Get on with the operation." A nurse hurried over and whispered to Renshaw, and Mitty saw the man turn pale. "Coreopsis has set in," said Renshaw nervously. "If you would take over, Mitty?" Mitty looked at him and at the craven figure of Benbow, who drank, and at the grave, uncertain faces of the two great specialists. "If you wish," he said. They slipped a white gown on him; he adjusted a mask and drew on thin gloves; nurses handed him shining ——

"Back it up, Mac! Look out for that Buick!" Walter Mitty jammed on the brakes. "Wrong lane, Mac," said the parking-lot attendant, looking at Mitty closely. "Gee. Yeh," muttered Mitty. He began cautiously to back out of the lane marked "Exit Only." "Leave her sit there," said the attendant. "I'll put her away." Mitty got out of the car. "Hey, better leave the key." "Oh," said Mitty, handing the man the ignition key. The attendant vaulted into the car, backed it up with insolent skill, and put it where it belonged.

They're so damn cocky, thought Mitty, walking along Main Street; they think they know everything. Once he had tried to take his chains off, outside New Milford, and he had got them wound around the axles. A man had had to come out in a wrecking car and unwind them, a young, grinning garageman. Since then Mrs. Mitty always made him drive to a garage to have the chains taken off. The next time, he thought, I'll wear my right arm in a sling; they won't grin at me then. I'll have my right arm in a sling and they'll see I couldn't possibly take the chains off myself. He kicked at the slush on the sidewalk. "Overshoes," he said to himself, and he began looking for a shoe store.

When he came out into the street again, with the overshoes in a box under his arm, Walter Mitty began to wonder what the other thing was his wife had told him to get. She had told him twice, before they set out from their house for Waterbury. In a way he hated these weekly trips to town—he was always getting something wrong. Kleenex, he thought, Squibb's, razor blades? No, toothpaste, toothbrush, bicarbonate, carborundum, initiative and referendum? He gave it up. But she would remember it. "Where's the what's-its-name?" she would ask. "Don't tell me you forgot the what's-it's-name." A newsboy went by shouting something about the Waterbury trial.

——"Perhaps this will refresh your memory." The District Attorney suddenly thrust a heavy automatic at the quiet figure on the witness stand. "Have you ever seen this before?" Walter Mitty took the gun and examined it expertly. "This is my Webley-Vickers 50.80," he said calmly. An excited buzz ran around the courtroom. The Judge rapped for order. "You are a crack shot with any sort of firearms, I believe?" said the District Attorney, insinuatingly. "Objection!" shouted Mitty's attorney. "We have shown that the defendant could not have fired the shot. We have shown that he wore his right arm in a sling on the night of the fourteenth of July." Walter Mitty raised his hand briefly and the bickering attorneys were stilled. "With any known make of gun," he said evenly, "I could have killed Gregory Fitzhurst at three hundred feet *with my left hand*." Pandemonium broke loose in the courtroom. A woman's scream rose above the bedlam and suddenly a lovely, dark-haired girl was in Walter Mitty's arms. The District Attorney struck at her savagely. Without rising from his chair, Mitty let the man have it on the point of the chin. "You miserable cur!" ——

"Puppy biscuit," said Walter Mitty. He stopped walking and the buildings of Waterbury rose up out of the misty courtroom and surrounded him again. A woman who was passing laughed. "He said 'Puppy biscuit'," she said to her companion. "That man said 'Puppy biscuit' to himself." Walter Mitty hurried on. He went into an A. & P., not the first one he came to but a smaller one farther up the street. "I want some biscuit for small, young dogs," he said to the clerk. "Any special brand, sir?" The greatest pistol shot in the world thought a moment. "It says 'Puppies Bark for It' on the box," said Walter Mitty.

His wife would be through at the hairdresser's in fifteen minutes, Mitty saw in looking at his watch, unless they had trouble drying it; sometimes they had trouble drying it. She didn't like to get to the hotel first; she would want him to be there waiting for her as usual. He found a big leather chair in the lobby, facing a window, and he put the overshoes and the puppy biscuit on the floor beside it. He picked up an old copy of *Liberty* and sank down in the chair. "Can Germany Conquer the World Through the Air?" Walter Mitty looked at the pictures of bombing planes and of ruined streets.

—— "The cannonading has got the wind up in young Raleigh, sir," said the sergeant. Captain Mitty looked up at him through tousled hair. "Get him to bed," he said wearily. "With the others. I'll fly alone." "But you can't, sir," said the sergeant anxiously. "It takes two men to handle that bomber and the Archies are pounding hell out of the air. Von Richtman's circus is between here and Saulier." "Somebody's got to get that ammunition dump," said Mitty. "I'm going over. Spot of brandy?" He poured a drink for the sergeant and one for himself. War thundered and whined around the dugout and battered at the door. There was a rending of wood, and splinters flew through the room. "A bit of a near thing," said Captain Mitty carelessly. "The box barrage is closing in," said the sergeant. "We only live once, Sergeant," said Mitty, with his faint, fleeting smile. "Or do we?" He poured another brandy and tossed it off. "I never see a man could hold his brandy like you, sir," said the sergeant. "Begging your pardon, sir." Captain Mitty stood up and strapped on his huge Webley-Vickers automatic. "It's forty kilometers through hell, sir," said the sergeant. Mitty finished one last brandy. "After all," he said softly, "what isn't?" The pounding of the cannon increased;

there was the rat-tat-tatting of machine guns, and from somewhere came the menacing pocketa-pocketa-pocketa of the new flame-throwers. Walter Mitty walked to the door of the dugout humming "Auprès de Ma Blonde." He turned and waved to the sergeant. "Cheerio!" he said.——

Something struck his shoulder. "I've been looking all over this hotel for you," said Mrs. Mitty. "Why do you have to hide in this old chair? How did you expect me to find you?" "Things close in," said Walter Mitty vaguely. "What?" Mrs. Mitty said. "Did you get the what's-its-name? The puppy biscuit? What's in that box?" "Overshoes," said Mitty. "Couldn't you have put them on in the store?" "I was thinking," said Walter Mitty. "Does it ever occur to you that I am sometimes thinking?" She looked at him. "I'm going to take your temperature when I get you home," she said.

They went out through the revolving doors that made a faintly derisive whistling sound when you pushed them. It was two blocks to the parking lot. At the drugstore on the corner she said, "Wait here for me. I forgot something. I won't be a minute." She was more than a minute. Walter Mitty lighted a cigarette. It began to rain, rain with sleet in it. He stood up against the wall of the drugstore, smoking.—— He put his shoulders back and his heels together. "To hell with the handkerchief," said Walter Mitty scornfully. He took one last drag on his cigarette and snapped it away. Then, with that faint, fleeting smile playing about his lips, he faced the firing squad; erect and motionless, proud and disdainful, Walter Mitty the Undefeated, inscrutable to the last.

THE COP AND THE ANTHEM

O. Henry

On his bench in Madison Square Soapy moved uneasily. When wild geese honk high of nights, and when women without sealskin coats grow kind to their husbands, and when Soapy moves uneasily on his bench in the park, you may know that winter is near at hand.

A dead leaf fell in Soapy's lap. That was Jack Frost's card. Jack is kind to the regular denizens of Madison Square, and gives fair warning of his annual call. At the corners of four streets he hands his pasteboard to the North Wind, footman of the mansion of All Outdoors, so that the inhabitants thereof may make ready.

Soapy's mind became cognizant of the fact that the time had come for him to resolve himself into a singular Committee of Ways and Means to provide against the coming rigor. And therefore he moved uneasily on his bench.

The hibernatorial ambitions of Soapy were not of the highest. In them were no considerations of Mediterranean cruises, of soporific Southern skies or drifting in the Vesuvian Bay. Three months on the Island was what his soul craved. Three months of assured board and bed and congenial company, safe from Boreas and bluecoats, seemed to Soapy the essence of things desirable.

For years the hospitable Blackwell's had been his winter quarters. Just as his more fortunate fellow New Yorkers had bought their tickets to Palm Beach and the Riviera each winter, so Soapy had made his humble arrangements for

— "*The Cop and the Anthem*" by O. Henry, from *The Complete Works of O. Henry;* copyright © 1953 by *Doubleday & Company, Inc., New York; reprinted by permission*

his annual hegira to the Island. And now the time was come. On the previous night three Sabbath newspapers, distributed beneath his coat, about his ankles and over his lap, had failed to repulse the cold as he slept on his bench near the spurting fountain in the ancient square. So the Island loomed big and timely in Soapy's mind. He scorned the provisions made in the name of charity for the city's dependents. In Soapy's opinion the Law was more benign than Philanthropy. There was an endless round of institutions, municipal and eleemosynary, on which he might set out and receive lodging and food accordant with the simple life. But to one of Soapy's proud spirit the gifts of charity are encumbered. If not in coin you must pay in humiliation of spirit for every benefit received at the hands of philanthropy. As Caesar had his Brutus, every bed of charity must have its toll of a bath, every loaf of bread its compensation of a private and personal inquisition. Wherefore it is better to be a guest of the law, which, though conducted by rules, does not meddle unduly with a gentleman's private affairs.

Soapy, having decided to go to the Island, at once set about accomplishing his desire. There were many easy ways of doing this. The pleasantest was to dine luxuriously at some expensive restaurant; and then, after declaring insolvency, be handed over quietly and without uproar to a policeman. An accommodating magistrate would do the rest.

Soapy left his bench and strolled out of the square and across the level sea of asphalt, where Broadway and Fifth Avenue flow together. Up Broadway he turned, and halted at a glittering café, where are gathered together nightly the choicest products of the grape, the silkworm, and the protoplasm.

Soapy had confidence in himself from the lowest button of his vest upward. He was shaven, and his coat was decent and his neat black, ready-tied four-in-hand had been presented to him by a lady missionary on Thanksgiving Day. If he could reach a table in the restaurant unsuspected, success would be his. The portion of him that would show above the table would raise no doubt in the waiter's mind. A roasted mallard duck, thought Soapy, would be about the thing—with a bottle of Chablis, and then Camembert, a demi-tasse, and a cigar. One dollar for the cigar would be enough. The total would not be so high as to call forth any supreme manifestation of revenge from the café management; and yet the meat would leave him filled and happy for the journey to his winter refuge.

But as Soapy set foot inside the restaurant door the head waiter's eye fell upon his frayed trousers and decadent shoes. Strong and ready hands turned him about and conveyed him in silence and haste to the sidewalk and averted the ignoble fate of the menaced mallard.

Soapy turned off Broadway. It seemed that his route to the coveted Island was not to be an epicurean one. Some other way of entering limbo must be thought of.

At a corner of Sixth Avenue electric lights and cunningly displayed wares behind plate glass made a shop window conspicuous. Soapy took a cobblestone and dashed it through the glass. People came running around the corner, a policeman in the lead. Soapy stood still, with his hands in his pockets, and smiled at the sight of brass buttons.

"Where's the man that done that?" inquired the officer, excitedly.

"Don't you figure out that I might have had something to do with it?" said Soapy, not without sarcasm, but friendly, as one greets good fortune.

The policeman's mind refused to accept Soapy even as a clue. Men who smash windows do not remain to parley with the law's minions. They take to their heels. The policeman saw a man, halfway down the block running to catch a car. With drawn club he joined in the pursuit. Soapy, with disgust in his heart, loafed along, twice unsuccessful.

On the opposite side of the street was a restaurant of no great pretensions. It catered to large appetites and modest purses. Its crockery and atmosphere were thick; its soup and napery thin. Into this place Soapy took his accusive shoes and telltale trousers without challenge. At a table he sat and consumed beefsteak, flapjacks, doughnuts, and pie. And then to the waiter he betrayed the fact that the minutest coin and himself were strangers.

"Now, get busy and call a cop," said Soapy. "And don't keep a gentleman waiting."

"No cop for youse," said the waiter, with a voice like butter cakes and an eye like the cherry in a Manhattan cocktail. "Hey, Con!"

Neatly upon his left ear on the callous pavement two waiters pitched Soapy. He arose joint by joint, as a carpenter's rule opens, and beat the dust from his clothes. Arrest seemed but a rosy dream. The Island seemed very far away. A policeman who stood before a drugstore two doors away laughed and walked down the street.

Five blocks Soapy travelled before his courage permitted him to woo capture again. This time the opportunity presented what he fatuously termed to himself a "cinch." A young woman of a modest and pleasing guise was standing before a show window gazing with sprightly interest at its display of shaving mugs and inkstands, and two yards from the window a large policeman of severe demeanor leaned against a water plug.

It was Soapy's design to assume the rôle of the despicable and execrated "masher." The refined and elegant appearance of his victim and the contiguity of the conscientious cop encouraged him to believe that he would soon feel the pleasant official clutch upon his arm that would insure his winter quarters on the right little, tight little isle.

Soapy straightened the lady missionary's ready-made tie, dragged his shrinking cuffs into the open, set his hat at a killing cant, and sidled toward the young woman. He made eyes at her, was taken with sudden coughs and "hems," smiled, smirked and went brazenly through the impudent and contemptible litany of the "ma-

sher." With half an eye Soapy saw that the policeman was watching him fixedly. The young woman moved away a few steps, and again bestowed her absorbed attention upon the shaving mugs. Soapy followed, boldly stepping to her side, raised his hat and said:

"Ah there, Bedelia! Don't you want to come and play in my yard?"

The policeman was still looking. The persecuted young woman had but to beckon a finger and Soapy would be practically en route for his insular haven. Already he imagined he could feel the cozy warmth of the station-house. The young woman faced him and, stretching out a hand, caught Soapy's coat sleeve.

"Sure, Mike," she said, joyfully, "if you'll blow me to a pail of suds. I'd have spoke to you sooner, but the cop was watching."

With the young woman playing the clinging ivy to his oak Soapy walked past the policeman overcome with gloom. He seemed doomed to liberty.

At the next corner he shook off his companion and ran. He halted in the district where by night are found the lightest streets, hearts, vows and librettos. Women in furs and men in greatcoats moved gaily in the wintry air. A sudden fear seized Soapy that some dreadful enchantment had rendered him immune to arrest. The thought brought a little of panic upon it, and when he came upon another policeman lounging grandly in front of a transplendent theatre he caught at the immediate straw of "disorderly conduct."

On the sidewalk Soapy began to yell drunken gibberish at the top of his harsh voice. He danced, howled, raved, and otherwise disturbed the welkin.

The policeman twirled his club, turned his back to Soapy and remarked to a citizen.

" 'Tis one of them Yale lads celebratin' the goose egg they give to the Hartford College. Noisy; but no harm. We've instructions to lave them be."

Disconsolate, Soapy ceased his unavailing racket. Would never a policeman lay hands on him? In his fancy the Island seemed an unattainable Arcadia. He buttoned his thin coat against the chilling wind. In a cigar store he saw a well-dressed man lighting a cigar at a swinging light. His silk umbrella he had set by the door on entering. Soapy stepped inside, secured the umbrella and sauntered off with it slowly. The man at the cigar light followed hastily.

"My umbrella," he said, sternly.

"Oh, is it?" sneered Soapy, adding insult to petit larceny.

"Well, why don't you call a policeman? I took it. Your umbrella! Why don't you call a cop? There stands one on the corner."

The umbrella owner slowed his steps. Soapy did likewise, with a presentiment that luck would again run against him. The policeman looked at the two curiously.

"Of course," said the umbrella man—"that is—well, you know how these mistakes occur—I—if it's your umbrella I hope you'll excuse me—I picked it up this morning in a restaurant—If you recognize it as yours, why—I hope you'll—"

"Of course it's mine," said Soapy, viciously.

The ex-umbrella man retreated. The policeman hurried to assist a tall blonde in an opera cloak across the street in front of a street car that was approaching two blocks away.

Soapy walked eastward through a street damaged by improvements. He hurled the umbrella wrathfully into an excavation. He muttered against the men who wear helmets and carry clubs. Because he wanted to fall into their clutches, they seemed to regard him as a king who could do no wrong.

At length Soapy reached one of the avenues to the east where the glitter and turmoil was but faint. He set his face down this toward Madison Square, for the homing instinct survives even when the home is a park bench.

But on an unusually quiet corner Soapy came to a standstill. Here was an old church, quaint and rambling and gabled. Through one violet-stained window a soft light glowed, where, no doubt, the organist loitered over the keys, making sure of his mastery of the coming Sabbath anthem. For there drifted out to Soapy's ears sweet music that caught and held him transfixed against the convolutions of the iron fence.

The moon was above, lustrous and serene; vehicles and pedestrians were few; sparrows twittered sleepily in the eaves—for a little while the scene might have been a country churchyard. And the anthem that the organist played cemented Soapy to the iron fence, for he had known it well in the days when his life contained such things as mothers and roses and ambitions and friends and immaculate thoughts and collars.

The conjunction of Soapy's receptive state of mind and the influences about the old church wrought a sudden and wonderful change in his soul. He viewed with swift horror the pit into which he had tumbled, the degraded days, unworthy desires, dead hopes, wrecked faculties and base motives that made up his existence.

And also in a moment his heart responded thrillingly to this novel mood. An instantaneous and strong impulse moved him to battle with his desperate fate. He would pull himself out of the mire; he would make a man of himself again; he would conquer the evil that had taken possession of him. There was time; he was comparatively young yet; he would resurrect his old eager ambitions and pursue them without faltering. Those solemn but sweet organ notes had set up a revolution in him. To-morrow he would go into the roaring downtown district and find work. A fur importer had once offered him a place as driver. He would find him to-morrow and ask for the position. He would be somebody in the world. He would—

Soapy felt a hand laid on his arm. He looked quickly around into the broad face of a policeman.

"What are you doin' here?" asked the officer.

"Nothin'," said Soapy.

"Then come along," said the policeman.

"Three months on the Island," said the Magistrate in the Police Court the next morning.

THE IMPORTANCE OF LOAFING

Lin Yutang

Culture, as I understand it, is essentially a product of leisure. The art of culture is therefore essentially the art of loafing. From the Chinese point of view, the man who is wisely idle is the most cultured man. For there seems to be a philosophic contradiction between being busy and being wise. Those who are wise won't be busy, and those who are too busy can't be wise. The wisest man is therefore he who loafs most gracefully. Here I shall try to explain, not the technique and varieties of loafing as practised in China, but rather the philosophy which nourishes this divine desire for loafing in China and gives rise to that carefree, idle, happy-go-lucky—and often poetic—temperament in the Chinese scholars, and to a lesser extent, in the Chinese people in general. How did that Chinese temperament—that distrust of achievement and success and that intense love of living as such—arise?

In the first place, the Chinese theory of leisure, as expressed by a comparatively unknown author of the eighteenth century, Shu Paihsiang, who happily achieved oblivion, is as follows: time is useful because it is not being used. "Leisure in time is like unoccupied floor space in a room." Every working girl who rents a small room where every inch of space is fully utilized feels highly uncomfortable because she has no room to move about, and the moment she gets a raise in salary, she moves into a bigger room where there is a little more unused floor space, besides those strictly useful spaces occu-

pied by her single bed, her dressing table and her two-burner gas range. It is that unoccupied space which makes a room habitable, as it is our leisure hours which make life endurable. I understand there is a rich woman living on Park Avenue, who bought up a neighboring lot to prevent anybody from erecting a skyscraper next to her house. She is paying a big sum of money in order to have space fully and perfectly made useless, and it seems to me she never spent her money more wisely.

In this connection, I might mention a personal experience. I could never see the beauty of skyscrapers in New York, and it was not until I went to Chicago that I realized that a skyscraper could be very imposing and very beautiful to look at, if it had a good frontage and at least half a mile of unused space around it. Chicago is fortunate in this respect, because it has more space than Manhattan. The tall buildings are better spaced, and there is the possibility of obtaining an unobstructed view of them from a long distance. Figuratively speaking, we, too, are so cramped in our life that we cannot enjoy a free perspective of the beauties of our spiritual life. We lack spiritual frontage. . . .

To the Chinese, therefore, with the fine philosophy that "Nothing matters to a man who says nothing matters," Americans offer a strange contrast. Is life really worth all the bother, to the extent of making our soul a slave to the body? The high spirituality of the philosophy of loafing forbids it. The most characteristic advertisement I ever saw was one by an engineering firm with the big words: "Nearly Right Is Not Enough." The desire for one hundred per cent efficiency seems almost obscene. The trouble with Americans is that when a thing is nearly right, they want to make it still better, while for a Chinese, nearly right is good enough.

The three great American vices seem to be efficiency, punctuality and the desire for achievement and success. They are the things that make the Americans so unhappy and so nervous. They steal from them their inalienable right of loafing and cheat them of many a good, idle and beautiful afternoon. One must start out with a belief that there are no catastrophes in this world, and that besides the noble art of getting things done, there is a nobler art of leaving things undone. On the whole, if one answers letters promptly, the result is about as good or as bad as if he had never answered them at all. After all, nothing happens, and while one may have missed a few good appointments, one may have also avoided a few unpleasant ones. Most of the letters are not worth answering, if you keep them in your drawer for three months; reading them three months afterwards, one might realize how utterly futile and what a waste of time it would have been to answer them all. Writing letters really can become a vice. It turns our writers into fine promotion salesmen and our college professors into good efficient business executives. In this sense, I can understand Thoreau's contempt for the American who always goes to the post office.

Our quarrel is not that efficiency gets things done and very well done, too. I always rely on American water-taps, rather than on those made in China, because American water-taps do not leak. That is a consolation. Against the old contention, however, that we must all be useful, be efficient, become officials and have power, the old reply is that there are always enough fools left in the world who are willing to be useful, be busy and enjoy power, and so somehow the business of life can and will be carried on. The only point is who are the wise, the loafers or the hustlers? Our quarrel with efficiency is not that it gets things done, but that it is a thief of time when it leaves us no leisure to enjoy ourselves and that it frays our nerves in trying to get things done perfectly. An Ameri-

can editor worries his hair gray to see that no typographical mistakes appear on the pages of his magazine. The Chinese editor is wiser than that. He wants to leave his readers the supreme satisfaction of discovering a few typographical mistakes for themselves. More than that, a Chinese magazine can begin printing serial fiction and forget about it halfway. In America it might bring the roof down on the editors, but in China *it doesn't matter, simply because it doesn't matter.* American engineers in building bridges calculate so finely and exactly as to make the two ends come together within one-tenth of an inch. But when two Chinese begin to dig a tunnel from both sides of a mountain, both come out on the other side. The Chinese's firm conviction is that it doesn't matter so long as a tunnel is dug through, and if we have two instead of one, why, we have a double track to boot. Provided you are not in a hurry, two tunnels are as good as one, dug somehow, finished somehow and if the train can get through somehow. And the Chinese are extremely punctual, provided you give them plenty of time to do a thing. They always finish a thing on schedule, provided the schedule is long enough.

The tempo of modern industrial life forbids this kind of glorious and magnificent idling. But worse than that, it imposes upon us a different conception of time as measured by the clock, and eventually turns the human being into a clock himself. This sort of thing is bound to come to China, as is evident, for instance in a factory of twenty thousand workers. The luxurious prospect of twenty thousand workers coming in at their own sweet pleasure at all hours is, of course, somewhat terrifying. Nevertheless, this is what makes life so hard and hectic. A man who has to be punctually at a certain place at five o'clock has the whole afternoon from one to five ruined for him already. Every American adult is arranging his time on the pattern of the schoolboy—three o'clock for this, five o'clock for that, six-thirty for change of dress; six-fifty for entering the taxi and seven o'clock for emerging into a hotel room. It just makes life not worth living.

And Americans have now come to such a sad state that they are booked up not only for the following day, or the following week, but even for the following month. An appointment three weeks ahead of time is a thing unknown in China. And when a Chinese receives an invitation card, happily he never has to say whether he is going to be present or not. He can put down on the invitation list "coming" if he accepts, or "thanks" if he declines, but in the majority of cases the invited party merely writes the word "know," which is a statement of fact that he knows of the invitation and not a statement of intention. An American or a European leaving Shanghai can tell me that he is going to attend a committee meeting in Paris on April 19, 1938, at three o'clock and that he will be arriving in Vienna on May 21st by the seven o'clock train. If an afternoon is to be condemned and executed, must we announce its execution so early? Cannot a fellow travel and be lord of himself, arriving when he likes and taking departure when he likes?

But above all, the American's inability to loaf comes directly from his desire for doing things and in his placing action above being. We should demand that there be character in our lives as we demand there be character in all great art worthy of the name. Unfortunately, character is not a thing which can be manufactured overnight. Like the quality of mellowness in wine, it is acquired by standing still and by the passage of time. The desire of American old men and women for action, trying in this way to gain their self-respect and the respect of the younger generation, is what makes them look so ridiculous to an Oriental. Too much action in an old man is like a broadcast of jazz music from a megaphone on top of an old cathedral. Is it not sufficient that the old people *are* something? Is it necessary that they must be forever *doing* something? The loss of the capacity for loafing is bad enough in men of middle age, but the same loss in old age is a crime com-

mitted against human nature.

Character is always associated with something old and takes time to grow, like the beautiful facial lines of a man in middle age, lines that are the steady imprint of the man's evolving character. It is somewhat difficult to see character in a type of life where every man is throwing away his last year's car and trading it in for the new model. As are the things we make, so are we ourselves. In 1937 every man and woman looks 1937, and in 1938 every man and woman will look 1938. We love old cathedrals, old furniture, old silver, old dictionaries and old prints, but we have entirely forgotten about the beauty of old men. I think an appreciation of that kind of beauty is essential to our life, for beauty, it seems to me, is what is old and mellow and well-smoked.

Sometimes a prophetic vision comes to me, a beautiful vision of a millenium when Manhattan will go slow, and when the American "go-getter" will become an Oriental loafer. American gentlemen will float in skirts and slippers and amble on the sidewalks of Broadway with their hands in their pockets, if not with both hands stuck in their sleeves in the Chinese fashion. Policemen will exchange a word of greeting with the slow-devil at the crossings, and the drivers themselves will stop and accost each other and inquire after their grandmothers' health in the midst of traffic. Some one will be brushing his teeth outside his shopfront, talking the while placidly with his neighbors, and once in a while, an absent-minded scholar will sail by with a limp volume rolled up and tucked away in his sleeve. Lunch counters will be abolished, and people will be lolling and lounging in soft, low armchairs in an Automat, while others will have learned the art of killing a whole afternoon in some cafe. A glass of orange juice will last half an hour, and people will learn to sip wine by slow mouthfuls, punctuated by delightful, chatty remarks, instead of swallowing it at a gulp. Registration in a hospital will be abolished, "emergency wards" will be unknown, and patients will exchange their philosophy with their doctors. Fire engines will proceed at a snail's pace, their staff stopping on the way to gaze at and dispute over the number of passing wild geese in the sky. It is too bad that there is no hope of this kind of a millennium on Manhattan ever being realized. There might be so many more perfect idle afternoons.

THE SECOND COMING OF ARISTOTLE

Pierre Berton

In spite of scientific prognostications that the day is coming when there won't be enough work to go around, when machines will take over a good deal of the mind-destroying labours now performed by human automata, when the work week may be reduced to a few hours (or, more likely, the work year to a few weeks), when leisure may become a way of life, in its own way as difficult to cope with as some work—in spite of all these signs and portents a kind of luncheon-club Greek chorus continues to equate "work" with all that is fine and noble and leisure (which is confused with "idleness," "free time," and "laziness") with all that is sinful and debilitating.

The party line can generally be found in the pages of *Industry*, the official voice of the Canadian Manufacturers' Association, which succinctly summed up the prevailing attitude in 1948 when it clearly equated hard work and austerity with high morality.

"The more constructive form of austerity is a readiness to put in more hours of work and to work harder in those hours. . . . If austerity is demoralizing to all except the saints, then only a toughened sinner would be demoralized by a little hard work."

This Calvinist theme has been a continuing one with the C.M.A. In 1955 *Industry* editorialized that "a leisure economy with a resultant leisure market could conceivably send the nation sliding into bankruptcy. Hobbies are fine as long as work isn't one of them." The following year, the same publication asked rhetorically: "Just how much leisure can the ordinary individual use intelligently? . . . The thought of a pretty fair slice of the population living to loaf is terrifying. Actually it makes a mockery of commonsense."

The C.M.A., of course, supports a system of untrammeled free enterprise and it has specifically categorized those who oppose such a system as "too lazy . . . to pursue the opportunities it presents." Yet the real weakness in the system may be that the great mass of the people are not "lazy" enough.

A similar theme is to be found in the monthly letter published by the Royal Bank of Canada. Consider these clichés culled from *The Royal Bank Letter* during the mid-1950's:

"Work is not a curse. The law 'and by the sweat of thy brow shalt thou eat bread' may be read as one of the most beneficent laws of life. It was probably because they had nothing to do that Adam and Eve became such easy victims to the tempter. . . . As every thinking man and woman would admit, work is strengthening, satisfying, and a great blessing. It is essential to human happiness. . . . There is a kind of joy and rest after work. . . . The good life is not the idle life of a beachcomber who subsists on the bounty, the left-overs, and the wrecks of others. It is a strenuous life of responsibilities. . . . One mark of a man who is determined to achieve happiness in his work is that he doesn't ask, as a preliminary to taking a job, whether the seat is soft or the building air-conditioned. He is in too much of a hurry to get busy. . . . To be fully prepared for life you must learn to work. Someone has said that idleness is the nurse of naughtiness; at any rate it is the death of progress. Life is not a thing of ease . . . ."

One is tempted to ask the editors of *Industry* and of *The Royal Bank Letter* some specific questions: What do you mean exactly by that word "work"? Do you mean the kind of work you do or the kind a ditch-digger does? What do you mean by words like "idleness," "loafing," "leisure," and "progress"? Is a monk in a cloister idle? Is a yogi a loafer? And while we're on the subject, why on earth shouldn't a man—if he seeks "progress"—seek more comfortable working conditions? Why should he be condemned, to use your own analogy, to spend the major portion of his waking life on unnecessarily hard seats in unnecessarily fetid surroundings?

The air-conditioned office and the cushioned seat are marks of status in the executive suite; with these symbols go the responsibility of making speeches to conventions, luncheon meetings, and gatherings of the clan. One wonders, sometimes, if all the speeches are typed up by the same ghostwriter. Do major executives really enjoy listening to each other repeating the same old saws? Do they believe that, if the myths are parroted often enough, they will somehow become truths?

Consider these statements, culled over the past twenty years, from the speeches of big business executives on the subject of work and leisure:

"Work harder to produce more [the Chamber of Commerce slogan for 1951] because our survival may well depend on how fast we in con-

cert with our friends move to get the wheels of industry in highest gear. . . ." (*Frances G. Winspear, President, Canadian Chamber of Commerce*)

"The greatest present danger is one of mankind's greatest weaknesses—the disinclination to work. . . ." (*Edgar Andrew Collard, Editor, Montreal* Gazette)

"Let us recapture the splendid spirit of our pioneering forefathers, who by courage and hard work made this wilderness blossom like a rose. . . ." (*John Bassett Sr., Managing Director, Montreal* Gazette)

"A man will come to less harm from overworking than he will by overplaying. Loafing is not fun to the man of spirit." (*Lord Beaverbrook*)

"One may wonder whether there is a tendency not only by labour but also by management to like leisure too much, to prefer a less arduous life to one of unremitting attention to business, to be unwilling to sacrifice our relaxed hours on our golf courses, in our homes, or in our vacation environment. Do social attitudes approve an enervating, commonplace egalitarianism rather than accomplishment?" (*Neil J. McKinnon, President, Canadian Imperial Bank of Commerce*)

It is certainly no time to be resting on our oars or discarding those ancient Canadian virtues which are just as valid in my humble view as they ever were—the virtues of thrift and hard work. It is no time for us to be lax." (*Donald Fleming, Minister of Finance*)

"Hard work and struggle built backbone and character in our parents. And the parents by denying this just right to their children in many cases produce weaklings and loafers. Many of our outstanding leaders in city and national life today are boys from the farm who learned to do a hard day's work and still find time for study. Some of our leaders are city boys who came from humble homes, yes, and some tasted poverty; but they had the guidance of Christian parents who inspired them to work and get an education and to 'give' to society not 'take' from society. . . ." (*Hiram E. McCallum, Mayor of*

When all this jumble of fallacy, generalization, and cliché is assembled in cold print the nonsense surely becomes obvious. Yet I am willing to lay a modest wager that I can go to the nearest Canadian Club tomorrow, utter any or all of these statements in a solemn tone, pause expectantly, and get more than a smattering of enthusiastic applause. These are the slogans of our time and the fact that they are outmoded makes them no less effective.

Most of the industrialists, politicians, and editorialists who talk so glibly of "work" are only thinking of one kind of work. They mean the kind of work *they* do, *i.e.*, work that (*a*) they like and (*b*) makes money. It does not seem to occur to them that there are two other kinds of work.

First, there is the work that people do because they have to support themselves and their dependants, but which they generally hate. Much of this work is both demoralizing and mindless and some of it, happily, is being rendered unnecessary by modern technological progress. The idea that there should be more of it is truly monstrous.

Second, there is the "work" that people do for the joy of it, whether it pays or not. This runs all the way from tending your own garden to writing a poem or painting a picture you never intend to sell. This broader definition of work does not seem to be in Neil McKinnon's lexicon. When he talks of sacrificing one's relaxed hours on the golf course or home in favour of a life of "unremitting attention to business," he obviously equates human endeavour with making a profit. Anything else is "leisure" or, to use Lord Beaverbrook's word, "loafing."

For years my friend W. O. Mitchell has been wandering about the streets and fields of High River, Alberta, thinking about his work, which is creative writing. For a long time Mitchell puzzled and baffled his neighbours. "When are you going to work, Bill?" they'd ask him, and it was useless for him to try to explain that in his terms he *was* working. Work to them was a "job" and one of the problems we face in the automated world of the future is this dangerous confusion in terms.

For men without "jobs" may still be productive and creative members of society; indeed, in the future, they may be among the most productive and creative. If we manage to change our attitude toward the Gross National Product and realize that it ought to include health, brains, and creativity then we may begin to use these resources properly. Until now they have been wasted shamefully: the nation sickly because of the lack of a comprehensive medical scheme, its brainpower half used because of a university program that caters to the upper class, its creative artists stifled because of a narrow, bookkeeping attitude to what constitutes "work."

One of the basic attitudes inherent in this establishment acceptance of the work ethic is that what is good for one generation must obviously be good for the next. Both John Basset Sr. and Donald Fleming look back wistfully over their shoulders to a Puritan past when they speak about recapturing the splendid spirit of one's forefathers or retaining the ancient Canadian virtues of thrift and hard work. As *Executive* magazine wrote of Mr. Fleming, when he departed public life in 1963: "Hard work, genuine belief in the spiritual values of Canadian society established long ago in the crude homes and hard wildernesses of Upper Canada influenced Mr. Fleming's public and private life and are reflected in [his] political career."

Alas for Mr. Fleming and his generation, the values of Huguenot pioneers are not the values of an age which can perceive, if only dimly, a future in which the mass of the people will be loosed from the shackles of drudgery—freed, in the Greek sense, "from the necessity of labour." A true age of leisure is on the horizon. It is not the second coming of Christ that we await but the second coming of Aristotle. . . .

THE FLY

Katherine Mansfield

"Y'are very snug in here," piped old Mr. Woodifield, and he peered out of the great, green-leather armchair by his friend the boss's desk as a baby peers out of its pram. His talk was over; it was time for him to be off. But he did not want to go. Since he had retired, since his —— stroke, the wife and the girls kept him boxed up in the house every day of the week except Tuesday. On Tuesday he was dressed and brushed and allowed to cut back to the City for the day. Though what he did there the wife and girls couldn't imagine. Made a nuisance of himself to his friends, they supposed. —— Well, perhaps so. All the same, we cling to our last pleasures as the tree clings to its last leaves. So there sat old Woodifield, smoking a cigar and staring almost greedily at the boss, who rolled in his office chair, stout, rosy, five years older than he, and still going strong, still at the helm. It did one good to see him.

Wistfully, admiringly, the old voice added, "It's snug in here, upon my word!"

"Yes, it's comfortable enough," agreed the boss, and he flipped the *Financial Times* with a paper-knife. As a matter of fact he was proud of his room; he liked to have it admired, especially by old Woodifield. It gave him a feeling of deep, solid satisfaction to be planted there in the midst of it in full view of that frail old figure in the muffler.

"I've had it done up lately," he explained, as he had explained for the past—how many?—weeks. "New carpet," and he pointed to the bright red carpet with a pattern of large white rings. "New furniture," and he nodded towards the massive bookcase and the table with the legs like twisted treacle. "Electric heating!" He waved almost exultantly towards the five transparent, pearly sausages glowing so softly in the tilted copper pan.

But he did not draw old Woodifield's attention to the photograph over the table of a grave-looking boy in uniform standing in one of those spectral photographer's parks with photographer's storm-clouds behind him. It was not new. It had been there for over six years.

"There was something I wanted to tell you," said old Woodifield, and his eyes grew dim remembering. "Now what was it? I had it in my mind when I started out this morning." His hands began to tremble, and patches of red showed above his beard.

"Poor old chap, he's on his last pins," thought the boss. And, feeling kindly, he winked at the old man, and said jokingly, "I tell you what. I've got a little drop of something here that'll do you good before you go out into the cold again. It's beautiful stuff. It wouldn't hurt a child." He took a key off his watch-chain, unlocked a cupboard below his desk, and drew forth a dark, squat bottle. "That's the medicine," said he. "And the man from whom I got it told me on the strict Q.T. it came from the cellars at Windsor Castle."

Old Woodifield's mouth fell open at the sight. He couldn't have looked more surprised if the boss had produced a rabbit.

"It's whisky, aint it?" he piped, feebly.

The boss turned the bottle and lovingly showed him the label. Whisky it was.

"D'you know," said he, peering up at the boss wonderingly, "they won't let me touch it at

— "*The Fly*" by Katherine Mansfield, from *The Dove's Nest and other stories*, published by Alfred A. Knopf, Inc., New York, 1923; reprinted by permission of The Society of Authors, literary representative of the estate of the late Katherine Mansfield

home." And he looked as though he was going to cry.

"Ah, that's where we know a bit more than the ladies," cried the boss, swooping across for two tumblers that stood on the table with the water-bottle, and pouring a generous finger into each. "Drink it down. It'll do you good. And don't put any water with it. It's sacrilege to tamper with stuff like this. Ah!" He tossed off his, pulled out his handkerchief, hastily wiped his moustaches, and cocked an eye at old Woodifield, who was rolling his in his chaps.

The old man swallowed, was silent a moment, and then said faintly, "It's nutty!"

But it warmed him; it crept into his chill old brain—he remembered.

"That was it," he said, heaving himself out of his chair. "I thought you'd like to know. The girls were in Belgium last week having a look at poor Reggie's grave, and they happened to come across your boy's. They're quite near each other, it seems."

Old Woodifield paused, but the boss made no reply. Only a quiver in his eyelids showed that he heard.

"The girls were delighted with the way the place is kept," piped the old voice. "Beautifully looked after. Couldn't be better if they were at home. You've not been across, have yer?"

"No, no!" For various reasons the boss had not been across.

"There's miles of it," quavered old Woodifield, "and it's all as neat as a garden. Flowers growing on all the graves. Nice broad paths." It was plain from his voice how much he liked a nice broad path.

The pause came again. Then the old man brightened wonderfully.

"D'you know what the hotel made the girls pay for a pot of jam?" he piped. "Ten francs! Robbery, I call it. It was a little pot, so Gertrude says, no bigger than a half-crown. And she hadn't taken more than a spoonful when they charged her ten francs. Gertrude brought the pot away with her to teach 'em a lesson. Quite right, too; it's trading on our feelings. They

think because we're over there having a look around we're ready to pay anything. That's what it is." And he turned towards the door.

"Quite right, quite right!" cried the boss, though what was quite right he hadn't the least idea. He came round by his desk, followed the shuffling footsteps to the door, and saw the old fellow out. Woodifield was gone.

For a long moment the boss stayed, staring at nothing, while the gray-haired office messenger, watching him, dodged in and out of his cubby-hole like a dog that expects to be taken for a run. Then: "I'll see nobody for half an hour, Macey," said the boss. "Understand? Nobody at all."

"Very good, sir."

The door shut, the firm heavy steps recrossed the bright carpet, the fat body plumped down in the spring chair, and leaning forward, the boss covered his face with his hands. He wanted, he intended, he had arranged to weep. ——

It had been a terrible shock to him when old Woodifield sprang that remark upon him about the boy's grave. It was exactly as though the earth had opened and he had seen the boy lying there with Woodifield's girls staring down at him. For it was strange. Although over six years had passed away, the boss never thought of the boy except as lying unchanged, unblemished in his uniform, asleep for ever. "My son!" groaned the boss. But no tears came yet. In the past, in the first months and even years after the boy's death, he had only to say those words to be overcome by such grief that nothing short of a violent fit of weeping could relieve him. Time, he had declared then, he had told everybody, could make no difference. Other men perhaps might recover, might live their loss down, but not he. How was it possible? His boy was an only son. Ever since his birth the boss had worked at building up this business for him; it had no other meaning if it was not for the boy. Life itself had come to have no other meaning. How on earth could he have slaved, denied himself, kept going all those years without the promise for ever before him of the boy's stepping into his shoes and carrying on where he left off?

And that promise had been so near being fulfilled. The boy had been in the office learning the ropes for a year before the war. Every morning they had started off together; they had come back by the same train. And what congratulations he had received as the boy's father! No wonder; he had taken to it marvellously. As to his popularity with the staff, every man jack of them down to old Macey couldn't make enough of the boy. And he wasn't in the least spoilt. No, he was just his bright, natural self, with the right word for everybody, with that boyish look and his habit of saying, "Simply splendid!"

But all that was over and done with as though it never had been. The day had come when Macey had handed him the telegram that brought the whole place crashing about his head. "Deeply regret to inform you ——." And he had left the office a broken man with his life in ruins.

Six years ago, six years. —— How quickly time passed! It might have happened yesterday. The boss took his hands from his face; he was puzzled. Something seemed to be wrong with him. He wasn't feeling as he wanted to feel. He decided to get up and have a look at the boy's photograph. But it wasn't a favorite photograph of his; the expression was unnatural. It was cold, even stern-looking. The boy had never looked like that.

At that moment the boss noticed that a fly had fallen into his broad inkpot, and was trying feebly but desperately to clamber out again. Help! help! said those struggling legs. But the sides of the inkpot were wet and slippery; it fell back again and began to swim. The boss took up a pen, picked the fly out of the ink, and shook it on to a piece of blotting-paper. For a fraction of a second it lay still on the dark patch that oozed round it. Then the front legs waved, took hold, and, pulling its small, sodden body up, it began the immense task of cleaning the ink from its wings. Over and under, over and under, went a leg along a wing as the stone goes over

and under the scythe. Then there was a pause, while the fly, seeming to stand on the tip of its toes, tried to expand first one wing and then the other. It succeeded at last, and, sitting down, it began, like a minute cat, to clean its face. Now one could imagine that the little front legs rubbed against each other lightly, joyfully. The horrible danger was over; it had escaped; it was ready for life again.

But just then the boss had an idea. He plunged his pen back into the ink, leaned his thick wrist on the blotting-paper, and as the fly tried its wings down came a great heavy blot. What would it make of that? What indeed! The little beggar seemed absolutely cowed, stunned, and afraid to move because of what would happen next. But then, as if painfully, it dragged itself forward. The front legs waved, caught hold, and, more slowly this time, the task began from the beginning.

He's a plucky little devil, thought the boss, and he felt a real admiration for the fly's courage. That was the way to tackle things; that was the right spirit. Never say die; it was only a question of ——. But the fly had again finished its laborious task, and the boss had just time to refill his pen, to shake fair and square on the new-cleaned body yet another dark drop. What about it this time? A painful moment of suspense followed. But behold, the front legs were again waving; the boss felt a rush of relief. He leaned over the fly and said to it tenderly, "You artful little b———." And he actually had the brilliant notion of breathing on it to help the drying process. All the same, there was something timid and weak about its efforts now, and the boss decided that this time should be the last, as he dipped the pen into the inkpot.

It was. The last blot fell on the soaked blotting-paper, and the draggled fly lay in it and did not stir. The back legs were stuck to the body; the front legs were not to be seen.

"Come on," said the boss. "Look sharp!" And he stirred it with his pen—in vain. Nothing happened or was likely to happen. The fly was dead.

The boss lifted the corpse on the end of the paper-knife and flung it into the waste-paper basket. But such a grinding feeling of wretchedness seized him that he felt positively frightened. He started forward and pressed the bell for Macey.

"Bring me some fresh blotting-paper," he said, sternly, "and look sharp about it." And while the old dog padded away he fell to wondering what it was he had been thinking about before. What was it? It was ——. He took out his handkerchief and passed it inside his collar. For the life of him he could not remember.

WHAT I BELIEVE

E. M. Forster

I do not believe in Belief. But this is an age of faith, and there are so many militant creeds that, in self-defence, one has to formulate a creed of one's own. Tolerance, good temper and sympathy are no longer enough in a world which is rent by religious and racial persecution, in a world where ignorance rules, and science who ought to have ruled, plays the subservient pimp. Tolerance, good temper and sympathy— they are what matter really, and if the human race is not to collapse they must come to the front before long. But for the moment they are not enough, their action is no stronger than a flower, battered beneath a military jack-boot. They want stiffening, even if the process coarsens them. Faith, to my mind, is a stiffening process, a sort of mental starch, which ought to be applied as sparingly as possible. I dislike the stuff. I do not believe in it, for its own sake, at all. Herein I probably differ from most people, who believe in Belief, and are only sorry they cannot swallow even more than they do. My law-givers are Erasmus and Montaigne,

— "What I Believe" by E. M. Forster, from *Two Cheers for Democracy* by E. M. Forster, published by Edward Arnold & Co., London, 1951; reprinted by permission of the publishers

not Moses and St. Paul. My temple stands not upon Mount Moriah but in that Elysian Field where even the immoral are admitted. My motto is: "Lord, I disbelieve—help thou my unbelief."

I have, however, to live in an Age of Faith— the sort of epoch I used to hear praised when I was a boy. It is extremely unpleasant really. It is bloody in every sense of the word. And I have to keep my end up in it. Where do I start?

With personal relationships. Here is something comparatively solid in a world full of violence and cruelty. Not absolutely solid, for Psychology has split and shattered the idea of a "Person," and has shown that there is something incalculable in each of us, which may at any moment rise to the surface and destroy our normal balance. We don't know what we are like. We can't know what other people are like. How, then, can we put any trust in personal relationships, or cling to them in the gathering political storm? In theory we cannot. But in practice we can and do. Though A is not unchangeably A or B unchangeably B, there can still be love and loyalty between the two. For the purpose of living one has to assume that the personality is solid, and the "self" is an entity, and to ignore all contrary evidence. And since to ignore evidence is one of the characteristics of faith, I certainly can proclaim that I believe in personal relationships.

Starting from them, I get a little order into the contemporary chaos. One must be fond of people and trust them if one is not to make a mess of life, and it is therefore essential that they should not let one down. They often do. The moral of which is that I must, myself, be as reliable as possible, and this I try to be. But reliability is not a matter of contract— that is the main difference between the world of personal relationships and the world of business relationships. It is a matter for the heart, which signs no documents. In other words, reliability is impossible unless there is a natural warmth. Most men possess this warmth, though they often have bad luck and get chilled. Most of them, even when they are politicians, *want* to keep faith. And one can, at all events, show one's own little light here, one's own poor little trembling flame, with the knowledge that it is not the only light that is shining in the darkness, and not the only one which the darkness does not comprehend. Personal relations are despised to-day. They are regarded as bourgeois luxuries, as products of a time of fair weather which is now past, and we are urged to get rid of them, and to dedicate ourselves to some movement or cause instead. I hate the idea of causes, and if I had to choose between betraying my country and betraying my friend, I hope I should have the guts to betray my country. Such a choice may scandalise the modern reader, and he may stretch out his patriotic hand to the telephone at once and ring up the police. It would not have shocked Dante, though. Dante places Brutus and Cassius in the lowest circle of Hell because they had chosen to betray their friend Julius Caesar rather than their country Rome. Probably one will not be asked to make such an agonising choice. Still, there lies at the back of every creed something terrible and hard for which the worshipper may one day be required to suffer, and there is even a terror and a hardness in this creed of personal relationships,

urbane and mild though it sounds. Love and loyalty to an individual can run counter to the claims of the State. When they do—down with the State, say I, which means that the State would down me.

This brings me along to Democracy, "even Love, the Beloved Republic, which feeds upon Freedom and lives." Democracy is not a Beloved Republic really, and never will be. But it is less hateful than other contemporary forms of government, and to that extent it deserves our support. It does start from the assumption that the individual is important, and that all types are needed to make a civilisation. It does not divide its citizens into the bossers and the bossed—as an efficiency-regime tends to do. The people I admire most are those who are sensitive and want to create something or discover something, and do not see life in terms of power, and such people get more of a chance under a democracy than elsewhere. They found religions, great or small, or they produce literature and art, or they do disinterested scientific research, or they may be what is called "ordinary people," who are creative in their private lives, bring up their children decently, for instance, or help their neighbours. All these people need to express themselves; they cannot do so unless society allows them liberty to do so, and the society which allows them most liberty is a democracy.

Democracy has another merit. It allows criticism, and if there is not public criticism there are bound to be hushed-up scandals. That is why I believe in the Press, despite all its lies and vulgarity, and why I believe in Parliament. Parliament is often sneered at because it is a Talking Shop. I believe in it *because* it is a talking shop. I believe in the Private Member who makes himself a nuisance. He gets snubbed and is told that he is cranky or ill-informed, but he does expose abuses which would otherwise never have been mentioned, and very often an abuse gets put right just by being mentioned. Occasionally, too, a well-meaning public official starts losing his head in the cause of efficiency, and thinks himself God Almighty. Such officials are particularly frequent in the Home Office. Well, there will be questions about them in Parliament sooner or later, and then they will have to mind their steps. Whether Parliament is either a representative body or an efficient one is questionable, but I value it because it criticises and talks, and because its chatter gets widely reported.

So two cheers for Democracy: one because it admits variety and two because it permits criticism. Two cheers are quite enough: there is no occasion to give three. Only Love the Beloved Republic deserves that.

What about Force, though? While we are trying to be sensitive and advanced and affectionate and tolerant, an unpleasant question pops up: does not all society rest upon force? If a government cannot count upon the police and the army, how can it hope to rule? And if an individual gets knocked on the head or sent to a labour camp, of what significance are his opinions?

This dilemma does not worry me as much as it does some. I realise that all society rests upon force. But all the great creative actions, all the decent human relations, occur during the intervals when force has not managed to come to the front. These intervals are what matter. I want them to be as frequent and as lengthy as possible, and I call them "civilisation." Some people idealise force and pull it into the foreground and worship it, instead of keeping it in the background as long as possible. I think they make a mistake, and I think that their opposites, the mystics, err even more when they declare that force does not exist. I believe that it exists, and that one of our jobs is to prevent it from getting out of its box. It gets out sooner or later, and then it destroys us and all the lovely things which we have made. But it is not out all the time, for the fortunate reason that the strong are so stupid. Consider their conduct for a moment in the Niebelung's Ring. The giants there have the guns, or in other words the gold; but they do nothing with

it, they do not realise that they are all-powerful, with the result that the catastrophe is delayed and the castle of Walhalla, insecure but glorious, fronts the storms. Fafnir, coiled round his hoard, grumbles and grunts; we can hear him under Europe to-day; the leaves of the wood already tremble, and the Bird calls its warnings uselessly. Fafnir will destroy us, but by a blessed dispensation he is stupid and slow, and creation goes on just outside the poisonous blast of his breath. The Nietzschean would hurry the monster up, the mystic would say he did not exist, but Wotan, wiser than either, hastens to create warriors before doom declares itself. The Valkyries are symbols not only of courage but of intelligence; they represent the human spirit snatching its opportunity while the going is good, and one of them even finds time to love. Brünnhilde's last song hymns the recurrence of love, and since it is the privilege of art to exaggerate, she goes even further, and proclaims the love which is eternally triumphant and feeds upon freedom, and lives.

So that is what I feel about force and violence. It is, alas! the ultimate reality on this earth, but it does not always get to the front. Some people call its absences "decadence"; I call them "civilisation" and find in such interludes the chief justification for the human experiment. I look the other way until fate strikes me. Whether this is due to courage or to cowardice in my own case I cannot be sure. But I know that if men had not looked the other way in the past, nothing of any value would survive. The people I respect most behave as if they were immortal and as if society was eternal. Both assumptions are false: both of them must be accepted as true if we are to go on eating and working and loving, and are to keep open a few breathing holes for the human spirit. No millennium seems likely to descend upon humanity; no better and stronger League of Nations will be instituted; no form of Christianity and no alternative to Christianity will bring peace to the world or integrity to the individual; no "change of heart" will occur. And yet we need not despair, indeed, we cannot despair; the evidence of history shows us that men have always insisted on behaving creatively under the shadow of the sword; that they have done their artistic and scientific and domestic stuff for the sake of doing it, and that we had better follow their example under the shadow of the aeroplanes. Others, with more vision or courage than myself, see the salvation of humanity ahead, and will dismiss my conception of civilisation as paltry, a sort of tip-and-run game. Certainly it is presumptuous to say that we *cannot* improve, and that Man, who has only been in power for a few thousand years, will never learn to make use of his power. All I mean is that, if people continue to kill one another as they do, the world cannot get better than it is, and that since there are more people than formerly, and their means for destroying one another superior, the world may well get worse. What is good in people—and consequently in the world—is their insistence on creation, their belief in friendship and loyalty for their own sakes; and though Violence remains and is, indeed, the major partner in this muddled establishment, I believe that creativeness remains too, and will always assume direction when violence sleeps. So, though I am not an optimist, I cannot agree with Sophocles that it were better never to have been born. And although, like Horace, I see no evidence that each batch of births is superior to the last, I leave the field open for the more complacent view. This is such a difficult moment to live in, one cannot help getting gloomy and also a bit rattled, and perhaps short-sighted.

In search of a refuge, we may perhaps turn to hero-worship. But here we shall get no help, in my opinion. Hero-worship is a dangerous vice, and one of the minor merits of a democracy is that it does not encourage it, or produce that unmanageable type of citizen known as the Great Man. It produces instead different kinds of small men—a much finer achievement. But people who cannot get interested in the variety of life, and cannot make up their own minds, get discontented over this, and they long for a hero to bow down before and to follow blindly. It is significant that a hero is an integral part of the authoritarian stock-in-trade to-day. An efficiency-regime cannot be run without a few heroes stuck about it to carry off the dullness—much as plums have to be put into a bad pudding to make it palatable. One hero at the top and a smaller one each side of him is a favourite arrangement, and the timid and the bored are comforted by the trinity, and, bowing down, feel exalted and strengthened.

No, I distrust Great Men. They produce a desert of uniformity around them and often a pool of blood too, and I always feel a little man's pleasure when they come a cropper. Every now and then one reads in the newspapers some such statement as: "The coup d'etat appears to have failed, and Admiral Toma's whereabouts is at present unknown." Admiral Toma had probably every qualification for being a Great Man—an iron will, personal magnetism, dash, flair, sexlessness—but fate was against him, so he retires to unknown whereabouts instead of parading history with his peers. He fails with a completeness which no artist and no lover can experience, because with them the process of creation is itself an achievement, whereas with him the only possible achievement is success.

I believe in aristocracy, though—if that is the right word, and if a democrat may use it. Not an aristocracy of power, based upon rank and influence, but an aristocracy of the sensitive, the considerate and the plucky. Its members are to be found in all nations and classes, and all through the ages, and there is a secret understanding between them when they meet. They represent the true human tradition, the one permanent victory of our queer race over cruelty and chaos. Thousands of them perish in obscurity, a few are great names. They are sensitive for others as well as for themselves, they are considerate without being fussy, their pluck is not swankiness but the power to endure, and they can take a joke. I give no examples—it is risky to do that—but the reader may as well consider whether this is the type of person he would like to meet and to be, and whether (going farther with me) he would prefer that this type should *not* be an ascetic one. I am against asceticism myself. I am with the old Scotsman who wanted less chastity and more delicacy. I do not feel that my aristocrats are a real aristocracy if they thwart their bodies, since bodies are the instruments through which we register and enjoy the world. Still, I do not insist. This is not a major point. It is clearly possible to be sensitive, considerate and plucky and yet be an ascetic too, and if anyone possesses the first three qualities, I will let him in! On they go—an invincible army, yet not a victorious one. The aristocrats, the elect, the chosen, the Best People—all the words that describe them are false, and all attempts to organise them fail. Again and again Authority, seeing their value, has tried to net them and to utilise them as the Egyptian Priesthood or the Christian Church or the Chinese Civil Service or the Group Movement, or some other worthy stunt. But they slip through the net and are gone; when the door is shut, they are no longer in the room; their temple, as one of them remarked, is the Holiness of the Heart's Affection, and their kingdom, though they never possess it, is the wide-open world.

With this type of person knocking about, and constantly crossing one's path if one has eyes to see or hands to feel, the experiment of earthly life cannot be dismissed as a failure. But it may well be hailed as a tragedy, the tragedy being that no device has been found by which these private decencies can be transmitted to public affairs. As soon as people have power they go crooked and sometimes dotty as well, because the possession of power lifts them into a region where normal honesty never pays. For instance, the man who is selling newspapers outside the Houses of Parliament can safely leave his papers to go for a drink and his cap beside them: anyone who takes a paper is sure to drop a copper into the cap. But the men who are inside the Houses of Parliament—they cannot trust one another like that, still less can the Government they compose trust other governments. No caps upon the pavement here, but suspicion, treachery and armaments. The more highly public life is organised the lower does its morality sink; the nations of to-day behave to each other worse than they ever did in the past: they cheat, rob, bully and bluff, make war without notice, and kill as many women and children as possible; whereas primitive tribes were at all events restrained by taboos. It is a humiliating outlook—though the greater the darkness, the brighter shine the little lights, reassuring one another, signalling: "Well, at all events, I'm still here. I don't like it very much, but how are you?" Unquenchable lights of my aristocracy! Signals of the invincible army! "Come along—anyway, let's have a good time while we can." I think they signal that too.

The Saviour of the future—if ever he comes—will not preach a new Gospel. He will merely utilise my aristocracy, he will make effective the good will and the good temper which are already existing. In other words, he will introduce a new technique. In economics, we are told that if there was a new technique of distribution, there need be no poverty, and people would not starve in one place while crops were being ploughed under in another. A similar change is needed in the sphere of morals and politics. The desire for it is by no means new; it was expressed, for example, in theological terms by Jacopone da Todi over six hundred years ago. "*Ordina questo amore, O tu che m'ami*," he said; "O thou who lovest me—set this love in order." His prayer was not granted, and I do not myself believe that it ever will be, but here, and not through a change of heart, is our probable route. Not by becoming better, but by ordering and distributing his native goodness, will Man shut up Force into its box, and so gain time to explore the universe and to set his mark upon it worthily. At present he only explores it at odd moments, when Force is looking the other way, and his divine creativeness appears as a trivial by-product, to be scrapped as soon as the drums beat and the bombers hum.

Such a change, claim the orthodox, can only be made by Christianity, and will be made by it in God's good time: man always has failed and always will fail to organise his own goodness, and it is presumptuous of him to try. This claim—solemn as it is—leaves me cold. I cannot believe that Christianity will ever cope with the present world-wide mess, and I think that such influence as it retains in modern society is due to the money behind it, rather than to its spiritual appeal. It was a spiritual force once, but the indwelling spirit will have to be restated if it is to calm the waters again, and probably restated in a non-Christian form. Naturally a lot of people, and people who are not only good but able and intelligent, will disagree here; they will vehemently deny that Christianity has failed, or they will argue that its failure proceeds from the wickedness of men, and really proves its ultimate success. They have Faith, with a large F. My faith has a very small one, and I only intrude it because these are strenuous and serious days, and one likes to say what one thinks while speech is comparatively free: it may not be free much longer.

The above are the reflections of an individualist and a liberal who has found liberalism crumbling beneath him and at first felt ashamed. Then, looking around, he decided there was no special reason for shame, since other people, whatever they felt, were equally insecure. And as for individualism—there seems no way of getting off this, even if one wanted to. The dictator-hero can grind down his citizens till they are all alike, but he cannot melt them into a single man. That is beyond his power. He can order them to merge, he can incite them to mass-antics, but they are obliged to be born separately, and to die separately, and, owing to these unavoidable termini, will always be running off the totalitarian rails. The memory of birth and the expectation of death always lurk within the human being, making him separate from his fellows and consequently capable of intercourse with them. Naked I came into the world, naked I shall go out of it! And a very good thing too, for it reminds me that I am naked under my shirt, whatever its colour.

Man and society

In that condition [of humble and rustic life] the essential passions of the heart find soil in which they can attain their maturity, are less under restraint, and speak a plainer and more emphatic language; because in that condition of life, our elementary feelings coexist in a state of greater simplicity and, consequently, may be more accurately contemplated and more forcibly communicated.
— William Wordsworth

Western civilization, wherever it penetrates, brings with it watertaps, sewers, and police; but it brings also an ugliness, an insincerity, a vulgarity never before known in history, unless it be under the Roman Empire.
— G. Lowes Dickinson

We are held in the city neither by pleasure nor by economic necessity but by a hunger which transcends both practical and sensuous experience, a hunger seldom revealed by appearances, seldom acknowledged in our consciousness. We are held in the city by our need of a collective life; by our need of belonging and sharing; by our need of that direction and frame which our individual lives gain from a larger life lived together. . . . Our poets are too ready to give the city the devil. The city, I think, was the tool with which God made man. Perhaps it is the tool with which He is making man.
— Joseph Hudnut

The life history of the individual is first and foremost an accommodation to the patterns and standards traditionally handed down in his community. From the moment of his birth the customs into which he is born shape his experience and behaviour. By the time he can talk, he is the little creature of his culture, and by the time he is grown and able to take part in its activities, its habits are his habits, its beliefs his beliefs, its impossibilities his impossibilities.
— Ruth Benedict

HOLIDAY MEMORY

Dylan Thomas

August Bank Holiday. A tune on an ice-cream cornet. A slap of sea and a tickle of sand. A fanfare of sunshades opening. A wince and whinny of bathers dancing into deceptive water. A tuck of dresses. A rolling of trousers. A compromise of paddlers. A sunburn of girls and a lark of boys. A silent hullabaloo of balloons.

I remember the sea telling lies in a shell held to my ear for a whole harmonious, hollow minute by a small, wet girl in an enormous bathing-suit marked "Corporation Property."

I remember sharing the last of my moist buns with a boy and a lion. Tawny and savage, with cruel nails and capacious mouth, the little boy tore and devoured. Wild as seed-cake, ferocious as a hearth-rug, the depressed and verminous lion nibbled like a mouse at his half a bun, and hiccupped in the sad dusk of his cage.

I remember a man like an alderman or a bailiff, bowlered and collarless, with a bag of monkey-nuts in his hand, crying "Ride 'em, cowboy!" time and again as he whirled in his chairoplane giddily above the upturned laughing faces of the town girls bold as brass and the boys with padded shoulders and shoes sharp as knives; and the monkey-nuts flew through the air like salty hail.

Children all day capered or squealed by the glazed or bashing sea, and the steam-organ wheezed its waltzes in the threadbare playground and the waste lot, where the dodgems dodged, behind the pickle factory.

And mothers loudly warned their proud pink daughters or sons to put that jellyfish down; and fathers spread newspapers over their faces; and sand-fleas hopped on the picnic lettuce; and someone had forgotten the salt.

In those always radiant, rainless, lazily rowdy and sky-blue summers departed, I remember August Monday from the rising of the sun over the stained and royal town to the husky hushing of the roundabout music and the dowsing of the naphtha jets in the seaside fair: from bubble-and-squeak to the last of the sandy sandwiches.

There was no need, that holiday morning, for the sluggardly boys to be shouted down to breakfast; out of their jumbled beds they tumbled, scrambled into their rumpled clothes; quickly at the bath-room basin they catlicked their hands and faces, but never forgot to run the water loud and long as though they washed like colliers; in front of the cracked looking-glass bordered with cigarette-cards, in their treasure-trove bedrooms, they whisked a gap-tooth comb through their surly hair; and with shining cheeks and noses and tide-marked necks, they took the stairs three at a time.

But for all their scramble and scamper, clamour on the landing, catlick and toothbrush flick, hair-whisk and stair-jump, their sisters were always there before them. Up with the lady lark, they had prinked and frizzed and hot-ironed; and smug in their blossoming dresses, ribboned for the sun, in gym-shoes white as the blanco'd snow, neat and silly with doilies and tomatoes they helped in the higgledy kitchen. They were calm; they were virtuous; they had washed their necks; they did not romp, or fidget; and only the smallest sister put out her tongue

200

at the noisy boys.

And the woman who lived next door came into the kitchen and said that her mother, an ancient uncertain body who wore a hat with cherries, was having "one of her days" and had insisted, that very holiday morning, in carrying all the way to the tram-stop a photograph album and the cut-glass fruit-bowl from the front room.

This was the morning when father, mending one hole in the thermos-flask, made three; when the sun declared war on the butter, and the butter ran; when dogs, with all the sweet-binned backyards to wag and sniff and bicker in, chased their tails in the jostling kitchen, worried sand-shoes, snapped at flies, writhed between legs, scratched among towels, sat smiling on hampers.

And if you could have listened at some of the open doors of some of the houses in the street you might have heard:

"Uncle Owen says he can't find the bottle-opener ——"

"Has he looked under the hall-stand?"

"Willy's cut his finger ——"

"Got your spade?"

"If somebody doesn't kill that dog ——"

"Uncle Owen says why should the bottle-opener be under the hall-stand?"

"Never again, never again ——"

"I know I put the pepper somewhere ——"

"Willy's bleeding ——"

"Look, there's a bootlace in my bucket ——"

"Oh come *on*, come on ——"

"Let's have a look at the bootlace in your bucket ——"

"If I lay my hands on that dog ——"

"Uncle Owen's found the bottle-opener ——"

"Willy's bleeding over the cheese ——"

And the trams that hissed like ganders took us all to the beautiful beach.

There was cricket on the sand, and sand in the sponge cake, sand-flies in the watercress, and foolish, mulish, religious donkeys on the unwilling trot. Girls undressed in slipping tents of propriety; under invisible umbrellas, stout ladies dressed for the male and immoral sea.

Little naked navvies dug canals; children with spades and no ambition built fleeting castles; wispy young men, outside the bathing-huts, whistled at substantial young women and dogs who desired thrown stones more than the bones of elephants. Recalcitrant uncles huddled over luke ale in the tiger-striped marquees. Mothers in black, like wobbling mountains, gasped under the discarded dresses of daughters who shrilly braved the goblin waves. And fathers, in the once-a-year sun, took fifty winks. Oh, think of all the fifty winks along the paper-bagged sand.

Liquorice allsorts, and Welsh hearts, were melting, and the sticks of rock, that we all sucked, were like barbers' poles made of rhubarb.

In the distance, surrounded by disappointed theoreticians and an ironmonger with a drum, a cross man on an orange-box shouted that holidays were wrong.

And the waves rolled in, with rubber ducks and clerks upon them.

I remember the patient, laborious, and enamouring hobby, or profession, of burying relatives in sand.

I remember the princely pastime of pouring sand, from cupped hands or buckets, down collars and tops of dresses; the shriek, the shake, the slap.

I can remember the boy by himself, the beachcombing lone-wolf, hungrily waiting at the edge of family cricket; the friendless fielder, the boy uninvited to bat or to tea.

I remember the smell of sea and seaweed, wet flesh, wet hair, wet bathing-dresses, the warm smell as of a rabbity field after rain, the smell of pop and splashed sunshades and toffee, the stable-and-straw smell of hot, tossed, tumbled, dug, and trodden sand, the swill-and-gaslamp smell of Saturday night, though the sun shone strong, from the bellying beer-tents, the smell of the vinegar on shelled cockles, winkle-smell, shrimp-smell, the dripping-oily backstreet winter-smell of chips in newspapers, the smell of ships from the sun-dazed docks round the corner of the sand-hills, the smell of the known and paddled-in sea moving, full of the drowned and herrings, out and away and beyond and further still towards the antipodes that hung their koala-bears and Maoris, kangaroos, and boomerangs, upside down over the backs of the stars.

And the noise of pummelling Punch, and Judy falling, and a clock tolling or telling no time in the tenantless town; now and again a bell from a lost tower or a train on the lines behind us clearing its throat, and always the hopeless, ravenous swearing and pleading of the gulls, donkey-bray and hawker-cry, harmonicas and toy trumpets, shouting and laughing and singing, hooting of tugs and tramps, the clip of the chair-attendant's puncher, the motor-boat coughing in the bay, and the same hymn and washing of the sea that was heard in the Bible.

"If it could only just, if it could only just?" your lips said again and again as you scooped, in the hob-hot sand, dungeons, garages, torture-chambers, train tunnels, arsenals, hangars for zeppelins, witches' kitchens, vampires' parlours, smugglers' cellars, trolls' grogshops, sewers, under a ponderous and cracking castle, "If it could only just be like this for ever and ever amen." August Monday all over the earth, from Mumbles where the aunties grew like ladies on a seaside tree to brown, bear-hugging Henty-land and the turtled Ballantyne Islands.

"Could donkeys go on the ice?"

"Only if they got snowshoes."

We snowshoed a meek, complaining donkey and galloped him off in the wake of the ten-foot-tall and Atlas-muscled Mounties, rifled and pemmicanned, who always, in the white Gold Rush wastes, got their black-oathed-and-bearded Man.

"Are there donkeys on desert islands?"

"Only sort-of donkeys."

"What d'you mean, sort-of donkeys?"

"Native donkeys. They hunt things on them!"

"Sort-of walruses and seals and things?"

"Donkeys can't swim!"

"These donkeys can. They swim like whales, they swim like anything, they swim like ——"

"Liar."

"Liar yourself."

And two small boys fought fiercely and silently in the sand, rolling together in a ball of legs and bottoms.

Then they went and saw the pierrots, or bought vanilla ices.

Lolling or larriking that unsoiled, boiling beauty of a common day, great gods with their braces over their vests sang, spat pips, puffed smoke at wasps, gulped and ogled, forgot the rent, embraced, posed for the dickybird, were coarse, had rainbow-coloured armpits, winked, belched, blamed the radishes, looked at Ilfracombe, played hymns on paper-and-comb, peeled bananas, scratched, found seaweed in their panamas, blew up paper-bags and banged them, wished for nothing.

But over all the beautiful beach I remember most the children playing, boys and girls tumbling, moving jewels, who might never be happy again. And "happy as a sandboy" is true as the heat of the sun.

Dusk came down; or grew up out of the sands and the sea; or curled around us from the calling docks and the bloodily smoking sun. The day was done, the sands brushed and ruffled suddenly with a sea-broom of cold wind.

And we gathered together all the spades and buckets and towels, empty hampers and bottles, umbrellas and fish-frails, bats and balls and knitting, and went—oh, listen, Dad!—to the fair in the dusk on the bald seaside field.

Fairs were no good in the day; then they were shoddy and tired; the voices of hoop-la girls were crimped as elocutionists; no cannon-ball could shake the roosting coco-nuts; the gondolas mechanically repeated their sober lurch; the Wall of Death was safe as a governess cart; the wooden animals were waiting for the night.

But in the night, the hoop-la girls, like operatic crows, croaked at the coming moon; whizz, whirl, and ten for a tanner, the coco-nuts rained from their sawdust like grouse from the Highland sky; tipsy the griffin-prowed gondolas weaved on dizzy rails and the Wall of Death was a

202

spinning rim of ruin, and the neighing wooden horses took, to a haunting hunting tune, a thousand Beecher's Brooks as easily and breezily as hooved swallows.

Approaching, at dusk, the fair-field from the beach, we scorched and gritty boys heard above the belabouring of the batherless sea the siren voices of the raucous, horsy barkers.

"Roll up, roll up!"

In her tent and her rolls of flesh the Fattest Woman in the World sat sewing her winter frock, another tent, and fixed her little eyes, blackcurrants in blancmange, on the skeletons who filed and sniggered by.

"Roll up, roll up, roll up to see the Largest Rat on Earth, the Rover or Bonzo of vermin."

Here scampered the smallest pony, like a Shetland shrew. And here "The Most Intelligent Fleas," trained, reined, bridled, and bitted, minutely cavorted in their glass corral.

Round galleries and shies and stalls, pennies were burning holes in a hundred pockets.

Pale young men with larded hair and Valentino-black side-whiskers, fags stuck to their lower lips, squinted along their swivel-sighted rifles and aimed at ping-pong balls dancing on fountains.

In knife-creased, silver-grey, skirt-like Oxford bags, and a sleeveless, scarlet, zip-fastened shirt with yellow horizontal stripes, a collier at the strength-machine spat on his hands, raised the hammer, and brought it Thor-ing down. The bell rang for Blaina.

Outside his booth stood a bitten-eared and barndoor-chested pug with a nose like a twisted swede and hair that started from his eyebrows and three teeth yellow as a camel's inviting any sportsman to a sudden and sickening basting in the sandy ring or a quid if he lasted a round; and, wiry, cocky, bow-legged, coal-scarred, boozed, sportsmen by the dozen strutted in and reeled out; and still those three teeth remained, chipped and camel-yellow in the bored, teak face.

Draggled and stout-wanting mothers, with haphazard hats, hostile hatpins, buns awry, bursting bags, and children at their skirts like pop-filled and jam-smeared limpets, screamed before distorting mirrors, at their suddenly tapering or tubular bodies and huge ballooning heads, and the children gaily bellowed at their own reflected bogies withering and bulging in the glass.

Old men, smelling of Milford Haven in the rain, shuffled, badgering and cadging, round the edges of the swaggering crowd, their only wares a handful of damp confetti.

A daring dash of schoolboys, safely, shoulder to shoulder, with their father's trilbies cocked at a desperate angle over one eye, winked at and whistled after the procession past the swings of two girls arm-in-arm: always one pert and pretty, and always one with glasses.

Girls in skulled and cross-boned tunnels shrieked, and were comforted.

Young men, heroic after pints, stood up on the flying chairoplanes, tousled, crimson, and against the rules.

Jaunty girls gave sailors sauce.

All the fun of the fair in the hot, bubbling night. The Man in the sandy-yellow moon over the hurdy of gurdies. The swing-boats swimming to and fro like slices of the moon. Dragons and hippogriffs at the prows of the gondolas breathing fire and Sousa. Midnight roundabout riders tantivying under the fairy-lights, huntsmen on billygoats and zebras hallooing under a circle of glow-worms.

And as we climbed home, up the gas-lit hill, to the still homes over the mumbling bay, we heard the music die and the voices drift like sand. And we saw the lights of the fair fade. And, at the far end of the seaside field, they lit their lamps, one by one, in the caravans.

THE DUMP GROUND

Wallace Stegner   Descriptive Narration

One aspect of Whitemud's history, and only one, and a fragmentary one, we knew: the town dump. It lay in a draw at the southeast corner of town, just where the river left the hills and where the old Mounted Police patrol trail (I did not know that that was what it was) made a long, easy, willow-fringed traverse across the bottoms. That stretch of the river was a favorite campsite for passing teamsters, gypsies, sometimes Indians. The very straw scattered around those camps, the ashes of those strangers' campfires, the manure of their teams and saddle horses, were hot with adventurous possibilities. The camps made an extension, a living suburb, of the dump ground itself, and it was for this that we valued them. We scoured them for artifacts of their migrant tenants as if they had been archaeological sites potent with the secrets of ancient civilizations. I remember toting around for weeks a broken harness strap a few inches long. Somehow or other its buckle looked as if it had been fashioned in a far place, a place where they were accustomed to flatten the tongues of buckles for reasons that could only be exciting, and where they had a habit of plating the metal with some valuable alloy, probably silver. In places where the silver was worn away, the buckle underneath shone dull yellow: probably gold.

Excitement liked that end of town better than our end. Old Mrs. Gustafson, deeply religious and a little raddled in the head, went over there once with a buckboard full of trash, and as she was driving home along the river she saw a spent catfish, washed in from the Swift Current or some other part of the watershed in the spring flood. He was two feet long, his whiskers hung down, his fins and tail were limp—a kind of fish no one had seen in the Whitemud in the three or four years of the town's life, and a kind that none of us children had ever seen anywhere. Mrs. Gustafson had never seen one like him, either. She perceived at once that he was the devil, and she whipped up the team and reported him, pretty loudly, at Hoffman's elevator.

We could still hear her screeching as we legged it for the river to see for ourselves. Sure enough, there he was, drifting slowly on the surface. He looked very tired, and he made no great effort to get away when we rushed to get an old rowboat, and rowed it frantically down to where our scouts eased along shore beckoning and ducking willows, and sank the boat under him and brought him ashore in it. When he died we fed him experimentally to two half-wild cats, who seemed to suffer no ill effects.

Upstream from the draw that held the dump, the irrigation flume crossed the river. It always seemed to me giddily high when I hung my chin over its plank edge and looked down, but it probably walked no more than twenty feet above the water on its spidery legs. Ordinarily in summer it carried six or eight inches of smooth water, and under the glassy surface of the little boxed stream the planks were coated with deep sun-warmed moss as slick as frogs' eggs. A boy could sit in the flume with the water walling up against his back, and grab a cross-brace above him, and pull, shooting himself sledlike ahead until he could reach the next cross-brace for another pull, and so on across the river in four scoots.

After ten minutes in the flume he would come out wearing a dozen or more limber black leeches, and could sit in the green shade where darning needles flashed blue, and dragonflies hummed and stopped in the air, and skaters dimpled slack and eddy with their delicate transitory footprints, and there pull the leeches off one by one, while their sucking ends clung and clung, until at last, stretched far out, they let go with a tiny wet *puk* and snapped together like rubber bands. The smell of the flume and the low bars of that part of the river was the smell of wolf willow.

But nothing else in the east end of town was as good as the dump ground. Through a historical process that went back to the roots of community sanitation, and that in law dated from the Unincorporated Towns Ordinance of the territorial government, passed in 1888, the dump was the very first community enterprise, the town's first institution.

More than that, it contained relics of every individual who had ever lived there. The bedsprings on which Whitemud's first child was begotten might be out there; the skeleton of a boy's pet colt; books soaked with water and chemicals in a house fire, and thrown out to flap their stained eloquence in the prairie wind. Broken dishes, rusty tinware, spoons that had been used to mix paint; once a box of percussion caps, sign and symbol of the carelessness that most of us had in matters of personal or public safety. My brother and I put some of them on the railroad tracks and were anonymously denounced in the *leader* for nearly derailing the speeder of a section crew. There were also old iron, old brass, for which we hunted assiduously, by night conning junkmen's catalogs to find out how much wartime value there might be in the geared insides of clocks or in a pound of tea lead carefully wrapped in a ball whose weight astonished and delighted us.

Sometimes the unimaginable world reached out and laid a finger on us because of our activities on the dump. I recall that, aged about seven, I wrote a Toronto junk house asking if they preferred their tea lead and tinfoil wrapped in balls, or whether they would rather have it pressed flat in sheets, and I got back a typewritten letter in a window envelope advising me that they would be happy to have it any way that was convenient to me. They added that they valued my business and were mine very truly. Dazed, I carried that windowed grandeur around in my pocket until I wore it out.

We hunted old bottles in the dump, bottles caked with filth, half buried, full of cobwebs, and we washed them out at the horse trough by the elevators, putting in a handful of shot along with the water to knock the dirt loose; and when we had shaken them until our arms were tired, we hauled them down in somebody's coaster wagon and turned them in at Bill Christenson's pool hall, where the smell of lemon pop was so sweet on the dark pool-hall air that it sometimes awakens me in the night even yet.

Smashed wheels of wagons and buggies, tangles of rusty barbed wire, the collapsed perambulator that the French wife of one of the town's doctors had once pushed proudly up the plank sidewalks and along the ditchbank paths. A welter of foul-smelling feathers and coyote-scattered carrion, that was all that remained of somebody's dream of a chicken ranch. The chickens had all got some mysterious pip at the same time, and died as one, and the dream lay out there with the rest of the town's short history to rustle to the empty sky on the border of the hills.

There was melted glass in curious forms, and the half-melted office safe left from the burning of Joe Knight's hotel. On very lucky days we might find a piece of the lead casing that had enclosed the wires of the town's first telephone system. The casing was just the right size for rings, and so soft that it could be whittled with a jackknife. If we had been Indians of fifty years earlier, that bright soft metal could have enlisted our maximum patience and craft, and come out as ring and medal and amulet inscribed with the symbols of our observed world.

Perhaps there were too many ready-made alternatives in the local drug, hardware, and general stores; in any case our artistic response was feeble, and resulted in nothing better than crude seal rings with initials or pierced hearts carved in them. They served a purpose in juvenile courtship, but they stopped a good way short of art.

The dump held very little wood, for in that country anything burnable got burned. But it had plenty of old metal, furniture, papers, mattresses that were the delight of field mice, and jugs and demijohns that were sometimes their bane, for they crawled into the necks and drowned in the rainwater or redeye that was inside.

If the history of Whitemud was not exactly written, it was at least hinted, in the dump. I think I had a pretty sound notion even at eight or nine of how significant was that first institution of our forming Canadian civilization. For rummaging through its foul purlieus I had several times been surprised and shocked to find relics of my own life tossed out there to blow away or rot.

Some of the books were volumes of the set of Shakespeare that my father had bought, or been sold, before I was born. They had been carried from Dakota to Seattle, and Seattle to Bellingham, and Bellingham to Redmond, and Redmond back to Iowa, and Iowa to Saskatchewan. One of the Cratchet girls had borrowed them, a hatchet-faced, thin, eager, transplanted Cockney girl with a frenzy for reading. Stained in a fire, they had somehow found the dump rather than come back to us. The lesson they preached was how much is lost, how much thrown aside, how much carelessly or of necessity given up, in the making of a new country. We had so few books that I knew them all; finding those thrown away was like finding my own name on a gravestone.

And yet not the blow that something else was, something that impressed me even more with how closely the dump reflected the town's intimate life. The colt whose picked skeleton lay out there was mine. He had been incurably crippled when dogs chased our mare Daisy the morning after she foaled. I had worked for months to make him well, had fed him by hand, curried him, talked my father into having iron braces made for his front legs. And I had not known that he would have to be destroyed. One weekend I turned him over to the foreman of one of the ranches, presumably so that he could be better cared for. A few days later I found his skinned body, with the braces still on his crippled front legs, lying on the dump. I think I might eventually have accepted the colt's death, and forgiven his killer, if it had not been for that dirty little two-dollar meanness that skinned him.

Not even finding his body cured me of going to the dump, though our parents all forbade us on pain of cholera or worse to do so. The place fascinated us, as it should have. For this was the kitchen midden of all the civilization we knew. It gave us the most tantalizing glimpses into our neighbors' lives and our own; it provided an aesthetic distance from which to know ourselves.

The town dump was our poetry and our history. We took it home with us by the wagon load, bringing back into town the things the town had used and thrown away. Some little part of what we gathered, mainly bottles, we managed to bring back to usefulness, but most of our gleanings we left lying around barn or attic or cellar until in some renewed fury of spring cleanup our families carted them off to the dump again, to be rescued and briefly treasured by some other boy. Occasionally something we really valued with a passion was snatched from us in horror and returned at once. That happened to the mounted head of a white mountain goat, somebody's trophy from old times and the far Rocky Mountains, that I brought home one day. My mother took one look and discovered that his beard was full of moths.

I remember that goat; I regret him yet. Poetry is seldom useful, but always memorable. If I were a sociologist anxious to study in detail the life of any community I would go very early to its refuse piles. For a community may be as well judged by what it throws away—what it has to throw away and what it chooses to—as by any other evidence. For whole civilizations we sometimes have no more of the poetry and little more of the history than this.

It is all *we* had for the civilization we grew up in. Nevertheless there was more, much more. . . .

THE INVISIBLE CITY

Joseph Hudnut

Perhaps because I was born and brought up in the country I have always wanted to live near the heart of a great city. Even now I look forward to the day when I can live again in New York: in a little flat, say, at the corner of Broadway and Forty-second Street. I should like to be clothed again in the strength and space of that city; to taste again the diversity of its fashions and humors; to feel about me the encompassment and drift of its opinion. I am not alone in New York even when I am alone. The city furnishes and fortifies my mind.

I once owned a farm near Westport, Connecticut, and for twelve years I tried valiantly to simulate that compassion for rusticity which was and still is fashionable. I was not successful. I could not after the first careless rapture dissemble my boredom with a cottage which was as quaint as a daisy chain at a Vassar commencement and as full of Ye Spirit of Ye Olden Tyme as an eggnog at Christmas. It was all very well so long as I had the fun of adding things on; but when I had added on a loggia, a terrace, a garage, an outside stairway, a gazebo, and all

— *"The Invisible City" by Joseph Hudnut, reprinted by permission of the publishers from Architecture and the Spirit of Man by Joseph Hudnut, Cambridge, Mass.: Harvard University Press; copyright 1949 by the President and Fellows of Harvard College*

the money I could borrow my week-ends became something to be got through with. Every recollection of my "little place in the country" is filled with a definite vexation and ennui. My memory flies from it like a bird from its cage to those familiar symbols of urbanism which each Monday morning greeted my return to New York: the houses gathering ever more closely around me across the Bronx, the iron bridges over the Harlem River, the long tunnel expectant of the day's adventure, the sudden light-filled space of the Grand Central Station.

The literature of the world is filled with a poet's conspiracy against the city: with advertisements of the city's clamors and indecencies, with the illusion of the country's solace. Only God, we are reminded, can make a tree. As if He had no part in the making of poems and cities!

I am not of course speaking of holidays in the country or of traveling in the country. These are altogether different experiences from that of *living* in the country. Of course I take pleasure in meadows and woods, in mountains and in the gentle forms of New England villages, nor have I forgotten the taste of strawberries fresh from the vine. I am not speaking of recreation or of play, essential ingredients in every life, nor of reverie and the contemplation of sunsets, but of the notion that a rural environment is more congenial to human happiness than the environment of a city. I am thinking of that fantasy of feeling which projects a paramount virtue and health on the country way of life and especially I am thinking of that strange inconsistency of our minds which in spite of poetic sensibilities and discomforts innumerable holds us in the city. My friends in New York talk constantly of escape and yet do not escape. If they had to live there they wouldn't exchange the tip of the Woolworth Building for all that part of the continent which—doubtless through no fault of its own—lies westward of the Hudson River. There is a paradox here which ought to be resolved.

We say that we are imprisoned in cities by economic necessity. A casuistry, surely. There is nothing in the business of making a living, whether it be by way of manufacturing or merchandising or professional service, which absolutely demands a civic environment. Our enterprises grow to larger proportions amid huge concentrations of populations and yet taken as a whole they breed no richer or more numerous rewards than they would if population and place of work were both scattered over the countryside. We could break up our cities without serious consequence to our economy.

Leonardo, in 1486, laid at the feet of Ludovico Sforza a practical plan for dispersing the city of Milan into ten satellite towns so that the people "should not be packed together like goats and pollute the air for one another." Four hundred years later Ebenezer Howard offered London the same program; and today the British Ministry of Town and Country Planning is again flirting at no small expense with that seductive phantom. If we pay little attention to these physicians of our society it is because we do not wish to do so.

The city's pleasures, then? We are held here by crowds and neon lights, by the excitement and comedy of streets and shop windows, by theaters, spectator sports and places of recreation, by the arts which flourish only amid brick and asphalt landscapes?

These are the distant magnets for country-bred youth but they do not explain those acres of our interminable cities in which such pleasures exist in the merest shreds. The pale colorations woven into the tedious fabrics of Queens and the Bronx would seem to afford a dull recompense for mountain vistas and the voices of forest streams; and even if the delights which lie along the spine of Manhattan be considered sufficient to anchor a few thousand there we ought not to overlook the millions of New Yorkers who taste these delights infrequently or not at all. In Chicago there are tens of thousands who have never ventured within the enrapturing atmosphere of the Loop.

We are held in the city neither by pleasure nor by economic necessity but by a hunger which transcends both practical and sensuous experience, a hunger seldom revealed by appearances, seldom acknowledged in our consciousness. We are held in the city by our need of a collective life; by our need of belonging and sharing; by our need of that direction and frame which our individual lives gain from a larger life lived together.

There are city habits and city thoughts, city moralities and loyalties, city harmonies of valuations which surround us in cities with an authority and system which, whatever may be the turmoil in which they exist, are yet friendly to the human spirit and essential to its wellbeing. Beneath the visible city laid out in patterns of streets and houses there lies an invisible city laid out in patterns of idea and behavior which channels the citizen with silent persistent pressures and, beneath the confusion, noise, and struggle of the material and visible city, makes itself known and reconciles us to all of these.

We have lived in that invisible city a very long time and are patterned more comfortably than we suppose to its congenial mold. It was in the invisible city that we grew over centuries into what we are today, shaped less by forest, wind, and soil than by the social relationships and activities which are city-engendered. Our human nature was created, not as some imagine in treetops and caves, but in that invisible city.

It was there that we learned the art of living together, developed the shield of values and relationships which protect us, least armored of animals, from the hostile powers that array us, and it was there that we came to know the destiny which on earth we must share together. In the invisible city, frail crystallization of idea and habit of thought, we learned, circumscribed by forest, river, and the near horizon, to meet the recurrent crises of birth, adolescence, and death, of flood and famine and the malice of our gods. There we learned to organize ourselves with language, conference, magic, education, and law; to use tools, fire, animals, and seed; to possess property and women; to trade and manufacture; and out of all these to build that structure of meanings which reconciled our new-discovered spirit not merely to the non-human world which surrounds us but to the growing complexities of our economies and the tyrannies of our swift technologies.

Under the mechanizations and the new freedoms with which science has transformed the material and actual city, under steel, electricity, and machine, under subway, hospital, and grand hotel, under democracy, progressive education, and assembly-line manufacture lie the firm strata of experience gathered across the centuries in the invisible city. Mound above mound, a thousand Troys laid on Troy, these lift us above the arid plain of biological and economic existence. The roots of our minds reach deeply into these deposits and draw from them the law of our present vision and behavior. We are not always aware of that law, so light is its accustomed authority, so nice is our conformity to its channelings; nor do we always understand, wrapped in the business of living, how these give steadfastness and direction to our lives.

Every creature on this earth finds happiness in that setting which gives scope to his peculiar energies. Tigers are happy in the jungle, birds in the shade-bestowing trees, and men in the free air of cities. Each living thing attained its present attributes by adjustments long continued between itself and the world which encircled it. Each has its home having been fashioned by his home. Creature and environment are parts of a whole. Tigers, birds, and men do not always know that they are happy; but take them out of their familiar elements and they soon know what it is to be unhappy.

Our poets are too ready to give the city to the devil. The city, I think, was the tool with which God made man. Perhaps it is the tool with which He is making man.

Almost from the beginnings of human history the invisible city has been the theme of the social art of architecture. The musician, the dancer, the poet were the channels through which the experience and emotion of individuals were made known but the architect celebrated the intangible fabric of communal feeling discovered by him beneath street and wall, beneath family, ambition, and the market, beneath the tumult of politics and war—discovered by him and by him advertised in his many-voiced art.

There is a mode of that art having as its materials not buildings or gardens or public places merely, but the totalities of cities: a mode of architecture—sometimes anonymous, sometimes guided by genius—sometimes swift in process, sometimes operative over slow centuries—which sets forth in the language of form that civic consciousness without which cities are only biological conveniences; which seizes upon that consciousness and holds it before us in a thousand different interpretations, each universal in substance and yet specific to time and circumstance. The practitioner of that architecture is the collective soul, silent for a moment beneath our present turbulence of circumstance, but certain of renewal and regained authority. Our necessity paves a channel for that inevitable progress. Our hunger prepares the table which shall nourish it.

We are too apt nowadays to think of architecture as a minister of individual comfort and delight, and even when we remember that architecture may be an element in civic patterns it exists in our minds as decoration or ceremonial background. The design of cities has become a matter of traffic highways and housing projects —with here and there a splash of peristyle and ordered space to give dignity to a city hall. The idea of form in cities, of cities which exhibit in their aggregates of shelter, space, and tree an ideal and pattern of life, of cities which are works of art: this idea seems to be lost under the present urgencies of our mechanizations. In the great traditions of architecture this idea was not, as it is today, thus alien to our minds.

Architecture did not impose itself upon the practical activities of a city, was not an intruder into social or economic life, was not inconsistent with politics, war or individual ambition, but marched with all of these holding before all the shining symbols which revealed the direction and unity of the general life.

An invisible Athens existed beneath the visible Athens and was the deep source of its splendor. The Athenians were well aware of their city as commercial utility and political instrument, but their imaginations were not, happily, limited to that awareness. Themistocles planned the city with a regard for profit and empire not less strict than was Burnham's solicitude for the railroads of Chicago. The roads to Athenian supremacy were the trade routes which led to Egypt and the Black Sea and the great harbor of the Piraeus was laid out with the intent to keep open these freedom-freighted avenues. The quays were wide, straight, and well protected, the warehouses and arsenals were ordered and convenient for maritime trade, the exchanges for corn, wool, metals, dyes, and slaves were designed in accordance with the rigid and functional science developed in the technological schools of Miletus. The plan of the Piraeus, so far as it has been revealed under the foundations of the modern city, seems to have followed a practical and systematic geometry not unlike that which Le Corbusier proposed for modern Paris: the traffic regulated, the quarters clearly bounded, the public works set apart from the homes of the people. The art of civic design—

that art which Aristotle called a "sociological architecture"—was a useful art, appropriate and at home under the life-filled porticoes of the crowded *agorae*.

That art nevertheless was not limited by the technologies of enterprise. It was not the architecture of commerce—of the Piraeus whose arms embraced the sea-borne traffic of a hundred nations—nor the architecture of politics, nor yet the architecture of their homes, threaded with narrow and tortuous streets, which best served the Athenian people, but the shining temples built out of loyalties and memories, out of great deeds accomplished together, out of gratitudes never to be forgotten in the collective heart. This was the city the Persians could not destroy, the invisible city, proud, exultant, and eternal, which the people had guarded behind the wooden walls of Salamis. Symbol and sentinel of that city the Acropolis stood above the clash of party and of class, a harmony crowning a harmony, the white crest of a wave which had gathered strength across centuries. The Acropolis was not a political document or a civic decoration or an abstraction of art—still less a "cultural center," pale refuge such as we build for our besieged civilization—but a spiritual reality which kindled the collective life and yet was intimate also to the life of every Athenian.

I am sure that the Romans, whose lives were lived under stately porticoes and amid the pomp of great temples, found in that background an ever present dignity which must have followed them even into the poverty and confusions of the crowded, many-storied *insulae*. The wide forums and the glittering thermae did not arise merely from the vanity of emperors and the corruption of the people. These were the songs in which the Roman soul made itself known above the cries of the circus and the clash of civil swords. The Gothic cathedrals were, in part at least, prayers of thanksgiving for a joy discovered in the revival of cities, and the *piazze* into which Venice poured her compressed splendor are jubilant with that new enfranchisement. These are not each an ornament added to a city but summations of a city's spirit to which houses and streets, walls, canals, and the domes of public buildings are the harmonious counterparts. Florence, Padua, Cordoba; the Paris of Richelieu, the Philadelphia of Franklin: each of these might have been the work of a single architect, so consistent is the ordinance and expression of their streets and structures. With what persistence have they held their characters over the years in spite of political crisis and economic change! Because the men who lived in these cities lived also within the city's pattern of idea, from which no citizen could imagine himself apart, the pattern in which they clothed themselves became, even without their conscious consent, the mirror which revealed the city's anonymous heart. In that mirror the citizen recognized his own dignity and his faith. The architecture of the city— a term which included all of the city's structures and ordered space— confirmed that which men believed about themselves.

All things—even the suns—are subject to deformations. Trees are gnarled and twisted by the sea winds, green fields turn to dust under drought and sun, and peace-loving men become savages amid the frenzies of war. Through long progressions the million species of the earth reach each its characteristic form and yet none is invulnerable to accident. A sudden crisis may arrest any progress—a violent alteration in wind or sun, an invasion of new enemies, a storm too rough for accustomed measures of security—and distortion, blight, and adventitious growth may overcome the healthiest organism.

So it was with the city under the fierce impact of the Industrial Revolutions and of that explosive mercantilism which at the end of the eighteenth century scattered the European peoples over the earth. Cities, new and old, grew rapidly to unprecedented dimensions and as they grew shattered that humanity of texture and expression which had once been impressed upon them by collective thought and feeling long continued. No longer do our cities exhibit in their outward aspects that framework of social purpose, that cement of manners, conventions, and moralities, that *tradition* built by slow change and patient compromise which once gave character and beauty to the city's life.

The symbol and chief actor in this disintegration was the factory—the factory and its accomplice, the railroad, together with the thousand other children of iron and steam. We did not guess when we admitted the factory to our cities that it would destroy their patterns; destroy them utterly and with that destruction provoke the questionings and discontents which color our present judgments of cities. Servile and seemingly innocent utilities, born of windmill and mountain stream, growing slowly in the green forests beside their white waterfalls, their many windows caressed by sunshine and fresh winds, there was little in the first factories that was prescient of Birmingham and Chicago. No one was aware of crisis. Across the countryside, silently, unnoticed, factory and city began their unequal duel.

Nevertheless it was inevitable that the two should meet on closer ground. People must work where they live: the factory must invade the city, or the city come to the factory. The railroad and the steam engine were prompt to respond to that necessity; these united city and factory; united them but not as the elements of an art are united in a pattern, not as new functions are united by slow development to a growing organism, but as aliens forced together by outside pressure, as a foreign body is thrust into living tissue. The factory came into the city not as architecture but as machine. Unlike the temple and the theater, the house and the market place, the factory was built, not out of love and the commerce of society but out of calculation and economic necessities. A consequence, not of feeling but of ingenuity, a device by which men—and children—lent themselves to machines and machines to men, the factory was little else than pulley and wheel grown to vast proportions.

We know how that growth, once the factory was firmly planted within the city, eclipsed in speed and consequence all other growth in the long history of mankind. Within a single century pulley and wheel gathered the city within their giant shadows and gave the city a new law. Pulley and wheel raised new values for the city to live by; refashioned the city's manners, speech, and faith; recoined the city's time; remade in its own image the city's streets and squares. The people of the city must then arrange their lives in accordance with its uncongenial necessities; government must listen to its decrees; religion rewrite her mythologies to condone its tyrannies; and social custom, family life, recreation and the arts, the ambitions of men and their standards of right and wrong, must be made conformable to these mechanical rhythms, to these uniformities of process and product. The cathedral, once generator and guardian of cities, had cherished and consoled all who lived at its side. The palace, also a generator of cities, ennobled the citizens with an ordinance and art of living; the distant trading posts bound together with common enterprise and shared destiny those who gathered around them; and even the fortress inspired in those who must live beneath its walls a loyalty from which they drew a communal strength. The factory merely used the city. As if in response to some blind biological law the city transformed itself from home and commonwealth into storehouse and machine.

The giant lizards could not survive a sudden change of climate. It may be that man now confronts that peril also. Could that be one of the secret causes of the giant wars which now convulse the earth?

Please do not misunderstand me. I am not for imitations of Venice and Athens set down in Cleveland and San Francisco. Our cities are the homes of our great industries and they must take the way of industry. I am for mechanized cities and for every technological improvement in cities; nor would I hide these under cloaks of romance or academic decorums. Neither do I believe that we can restore the old and beautiful patterns of society by inviting our civic populations to enter shining new houses laid out for them by architects confident of their art to transform the universe. Our architecture, and especially the architecture of our cities, will be created by our society to whose mood and necessities the architect is instrument. I am for no Utopia.

Nevertheless I have faith in the power of man to shape his environment in accordance with his inward needs and I know that that reshaping is most essential for human happiness. Beneath these wheels and pulleys, these endless turnings and meaningless propulsions, there still lies that invisible city in which we must live or perish. That city has desperate need of architecture: of an architecture peculiar to itself, unlike any other architecture, and yet as constant as any other in its affirmation of purpose and dignity.

Sometimes when I am in Rockefeller Center, where skyscrapers, music halls, gardens, and shops innumerable crowd into an islanded harmony I imagine that I feel the promise of that new renaissance of our art. A city rises about me; I am in a theater prepared for me as if by ancient usage and rehearsal. At such times I like to believe that architecture may indeed reassume its forgotten importance as outward frame and envelope of a communal life, being shaped once more by the commerce of a society that is civilized, polite, and urbane.

Civilized, polite, and urbane—each word rooted in a word that means *the city*.

THE DOG THAT BIT PEOPLE

James Thurber

Probably no one man should have as many dogs in his life as I have had, but there was more pleasure than distress in them for me except in the case of an Airedale named Muggs. He gave me more trouble than all the other fifty-four or -five put together, although my moment of keenest embarrassment was the time a Scotch terrier named Jeannie, who had just had four puppies in the shoe closet of a fourth-floor apartment in New York, had the fifth and last at the corner of—but we shall get around to that later on. Then, too, there was the prize-winning French poodle, a great big black poodle—none of your little, untroublesome white miniatures—who got sick riding in the rumble seat of a car with me on her way to the Greenwich Dog Show. She had a red rubber bib tucked around her throat and, since a rainstorm came up when we were halfway through the Bronx, I had to hold over her a small green umbrella, really more of a parasol. The rain beat down fearfully, and suddenly the driver of the car drove into a big garage, filled with mechanics. It happened so quickly that I forgot to put the umbrella down, and I shall always remember the look of incredulity that came over the face of the garageman who came over to see what we wanted. "Get a load of this, Mac," he called to someone behind him.

But the Airedale, as I have said, was the worst of all my dogs. He really wasn't my dog, as a matter of fact; I came home from a vacation one summer to find that my brother Robert had bought him while I was away. A big, burly, choleric dog, he always acted as if he thought I wasn't one of the family. There was a slight advantage in being one of the family, for he didn't bite the family as often as he bit strangers. Still, in the years that we had him he bit everybody but Mother, and he made a pass at her once but missed. That was during the month when we suddenly had mice, and Muggs refused to do anything about them. Nobody ever had mice exactly like the mice we had that month. They acted like pet mice, almost like mice somebody had trained. They were so friendly that one night when Mother entertained at dinner the Friraliras, a club she and my father had belonged to for twenty years, she put down a lot of little dishes with food in them on the pantry floor so that the mice would be satisfied with that and wouldn't come into the dining room. Muggs stayed out in the pantry with the mice, lying on the floor, growling to himself—not at the mice, but about all the people in the next room that he would have liked to get at. Mother slipped out into the pantry once to see how everything was going. Everything was going fine. It made her so mad to see Muggs lying there, oblivious of the mice—they came running up to her—that she slapped him and he slashed at her, but didn't make it. He was sorry immediately, Mother said. He was always sorry, she said, after he bit someone, but we could not understand how she figured this out. He didn't act sorry.

Mother used to send a box of candy every Christmas to the people the Airedale bit. The list finally contained forty or more names. Nobody could understand why we didn't get rid of the dog. I didn't understand it very well myself, but we didn't get rid of him. I think that one or two people tried to poison Muggs—

---

he acted poisoned once in a while—and old Major Moberly fired at him once with his service revolver near the Seneca Hotel in East Broad Street—but Muggs lived to be almost eleven years old, and even when he could hardly get around, he bit a congressman who had called to see my father on business. My mother had never liked the congressman—she said the signs of his horoscope showed he couldn't be trusted (he was Saturn with the moon in Virgo) —but she sent him a box of candy that Christmas. He sent it right back, probably because he suspected it was trick candy. Mother persuaded herself it was all for the best that the dog had bitten him, even though father lost an important business association because of it. "I wouldn't be associated with such a man," Mother said. "Muggs could read him like a book."

We used to take turns feeding Muggs to be on his good side, but that didn't always work. He was never in a very good humor, even after a meal. Nobody knew exactly what was the matter with him, but whatever it was it made him irascible, especially in the mornings. Robert never felt very well in the morning, either, especially before breakfast, and once when he came downstairs and found that Muggs had moodily chewed up the morning paper he hit him in the face with a grapefruit and then jumped up on the dining-room table, scattering dishes and silverware and spilling the coffee. Mugg's first free leap carried him all the way across the table and into a brass fire screen in front of the gas grate, but he was back on his feet in a moment, and in the end he got Robert and gave him a pretty vicious bite in the leg. Then he was all over it; he never bit anyone more than once at a time. Mother always mentioned that as an argument in his favor; she said he had a quick temper but that he didn't hold a grudge. She was forever defending him. I think she liked him because he wasn't well. "He's not strong," she would say, pityingly, but that was inaccurate; he may not have been well but he was terribly strong.

One time my mother went to the Chittenden Hotel to call on a woman mental healer who was lecturing in Columbus on the subject of "Harmonious Vibrations." She wanted to find out if it was possible to get harmonious vibrations into a dog. "He's a large tan-colored Airedale," Mother explained. The woman said she had never treated a dog, but she advised my mother to hold the thought that he did not bite and would not bite. Mother was holding the thought the very next morning when Muggs got the iceman, but she blamed that slip-up on the iceman. "If you didn't think he would bite you, he wouldn't," Mother told him. He stomped out of the house in a terrible jangle of vibrations.

One morning when Muggs bit me slightly, more or less in passing, I reached down and grabbed his short stumpy tail and hoisted him into the air. It was a foolhardy thing to do and the last time I saw my mother, about six months ago, she said she didn't know what possessed me. I don't either, except that I was pretty mad. As long as I held the dog off the floor by his tail he couldn't get at me, but he twisted and jerked so, snarling all the time, that I realized I couldn't hold him that way very long. I carried him to the kitchen and flung him onto the floor and shut the door on him just as he crashed against it. But I forgot about the back stairs. Muggs went up the back stairs and down the front stairs and had me cornered in the living room. I managed to get up onto the mantelpiece above the fireplace, but it gave way and came down with a tremendous crash, throwing a large marble clock, several vases, and myself heavily to the floor. Muggs was so alarmed by the racket that when I picked myself up he had disappeared. We couldn't find him anywhere, although we whistled and shouted, until old Mrs. Detweiler called after dinner that night. Muggs had bitten her once, in the leg, and she came into the living room only after we assured her that Muggs had run away. She had just seated herself when, with a great growling and scratching of claws, Muggs emerged from under a davenport where he had been quietly hiding all the time, and bit her again. Mother examined the bite and put arnica on it and told Mrs. Detweiler that it was only a bruise. "He just bumped you," she said. But Mrs. Detweiler left the house in a nasty state of mind.

Lots of people reported our Airedale to the police, but my father held a municipal office at the time and was on friendly terms with the police. Even so, the cops had been out a couple of times—once when Muggs bit Mrs. Rufus Sturtevant and again when he bit Lieutenant-Governor Malloy—but Mother told them that it hadn't been Muggs' fault but the fault of the people who were bitten. "When he starts for them, they scream," she explained, "and that excites him." The cops suggested that it might be a good idea to tie the dog up, but Mother said that it mortified him to be tied up and that he wouldn't eat when he was tied up.

Muggs at his meals was an unusual sight. Because of the fact that if you reached toward the floor he would bite you, we usually put his food plate on top of an old kitchen table with a bench alongside the table. Muggs would stand on the bench and eat. I remember that my mother's Uncle Horatio, who boasted that he was the third man up Missionary Ridge, was splutteringly indignant when he found out that we fed the dog on a table because we were afraid to put his plate on the floor. He said he wasn't afraid of any dog that ever lived and that he would put the dog's plate on the floor if we would give it to him. Robert said that if Uncle Horatio had fed Muggs on the ground just before the battle he would have been the first man up Missionary Ridge. Uncle Horatio was furious. "Bring him in! Bring him in now!" he shouted. "I'll feed the ——— on the floor!" Robert was all for giving him a chance, but my father wouldn't hear of it. He said that Muggs had already been fed. "I'll feed him again!" bawled Uncle Horatio. We had quite a time quieting him.

In his last year Muggs used to spend practic-ally all of his time outdoors. He didn't like to stay in the house for some reason or other—perhaps it held too many unpleasant memories for him. Anyway, it was hard to get him to come in, and as a result the garbageman, the iceman, and the laundryman wouldn't come near the house. We had to haul the garbage down to the corner, take the laundry out and bring it back, and meet the iceman a block from home. After this had gone on for some time, we hit on an ingenious arrangement for getting the dog in the house so that we could lock him up while the gas meter was read, and so on. Muggs was afraid of only one thing, an electrical storm. Thunder and lightning frightened him out of his senses (I think he thought a storm had broken the day the mantelpiece fell). He would rush into the house and hide under a bed or in a clothes closet. So we fixed up a thunder machine out of a long narrow piece of sheet iron with a wooden handle on one end. Mother would shake this vigorously when she wanted to get Muggs into the house. It made an excellent imitation of thunder, but I suppose it was the most roundabout system for running a household that was ever devised. It took a lot out of Mother.

A few months before Muggs died, he got to "seeing things." He would rise slowly from the floor, growling low, and stalk stiff-legged and menacing toward nothing at all. Sometimes the Thing would be just a little to the right or left of a visitor. Once a Fuller Brush salesman got hysterics. Muggs came wandering into the room like Hamlet following his father's ghost. His eyes were fixed on a spot just to the left of the Fuller Brush man, who stood it until Muggs was about three slow, creeping paces from him. Then he shouted. Muggs wavered on past him into the hallway, grumbling to himself, but the Fuller Brush man went on shouting. I think Mother had to throw a pan of cold water on him before he stopped. That was the way she used to stop us boys when we got into fights.

Muggs died quite suddenly one night. Mother wanted to bury him in the family plot under a marble stone with some such inscription as "Flights of angels sing thee to thy rest" but we persuaded her it was against the law. In the end we just put up a smooth board above his grave along a lonely road. On the board I wrote with an indelible pencil "*Cave Canem.*" Mother was quite pleased with the simple, classic dignity of the old Latin epitaph.

from SAMUEL MARCHBANKS' ALMANACK

Robertson Davies

To Amyas Pilgarlic, Esq.

Dear Pil:

You know where I stand on dogs: I am not a person in whose life Man's Dumb Chum has played a leading role. But a day or so ago I had to attend a dog show, and as I watched the eager crowd I was visited, for perhaps the fiftieth time in my life, by the reflection that if people had to meet the rigorous standards of physical appearance which are set for dogs and other show animals it would go hardly with most of us.

The judges at the show, for instance, would have cut poor figures if the dogs had been judging them. The most important of them had a really shocking head—coarse muzzle, apple-domed skull and, so far as could be seen, a poor coat. The other judge had a narrow, splayed front, a snipey muzzle, and ears set far too high. The third judge was a woman and, though I hate to say it, a poor mover, being cow-hocked and badly spaced between her shoulders, hips and stifles. None of the judges had a bright eye nor, I should say, an affectionate nature. They did not answer readily to

words of command, and showed a strong tendency to turn right when it was necessary for them to turn left. Poor creatures, useless for breeding; it would have been better to drown them as puppies.

Have you observed that a miserable-looking dog is regarded, quite rightly, as a poor-spirited creature, probably in need of worming, whereas a miserable-looking man is usually taken to be a philosopher, or at the very least, an economist? There is food for profound reflection in this.

Yours,
Sam.

To Mrs. Morrigan.

My dear Mrs. Morrigan:

I was at a concert last night where a pianist played Handel's variations called *The Harmonious Blacksmith*. Of course Handel never called it anything of the kind and the name was not attached to the piece until long after Handel was dead. But the program note repeated the old story of how he received his inspiration for the piece while sheltering from a thunderstorm in a smithy. How good old George Frederick would have snorted! He loathed flapdoodle.

But this reminded me of that other legend, preserved in the old Ontario Third Reader, of how Beethoven, walking through the streets of

— excerpts from Samuel Marchbanks' Almanack by Robertson Davies; © 1967 by Robertson Davies; reprinted by permission of The Canadian Publishers, McClelland and Stewart Limited, Toronto

Vienna with a friend one night, heard a piano being played in a basement; peeping through the window, he saw that a blind girl was playing to her aged father. "Alas, papa," said she, "if only I could go to the concert tomorrow night, to hear the great Beethoven play, how happy I should be! But (sob) we have no money." Without a word the great composer rushed into the cellar, sat down at the piano and played a magnificent program, improvising the *Moonlight Sonata* at the conclusion, and wowing the simple music-lover. As a child I was much touched by this story.

What disillusion awaited me when I began to look through the private papers of my Viennese ancestor, Wolfgang Amadeus Marchbanks, who was a close friend of Beethoven. Indeed, he was the very friend who accompanied Beethoven on that memorable walk. And my great-great-great-uncle Wolfgang says that in reality Beethoven pushed his head through the window, and said, "Stop that row, woman; if you must play my stuff, stop vamping the bass." Beethoven was not an easy man to please.

Truth, alas, is sometimes even uglier than fiction.

Your humble servant,
Samuel Marchbanks.

To Raymond Cataplasm, M.D., F.R.C.P.

Dear Dr. Cataplasm:
Whenever I am near Death, I think of you. And I have been very near Death recently, for I have had a number of conversations with an Insurance Man, and he brought me very close to Death's door on a number of occasions.

Now I am perfectly ready to subscribe to the Scriptural admonitions that all flesh is grass, that the body is but clay, and that my soul may be required of me at any moment. But I cannot say that I like to have my nose rubbed in these indubitable truths by a man whose business it appears to be to guarantee that my survivors shall live the life of Riley after I am gone.

"We've all got to face it," says he; quite so, but I prefer to face Death in the company of a few learned and picturesque old clergymen, with an unaccompanied choir singing in the distance; I do not especially like to face Death in the company of a fellow with sport shoes on his feet, a decorative tack through his necktie and a staggering number of pens and pencils in his bosom pocket. But then, I am an eccentric in such matters.

People of my temperament, in the days of the first Queen Elizabeth, quite often kept a skull on their desks; occasionally, for added effect, the skull had a bone stuck in its jaws. This object was called a "memento mori" and its purpose was to keep its owner reminded of the fact that he too would die. But the modern memento mori is the insurance agent, with his pencils, and whenever I see one I mutter through the General Confession, just in case.

Your perennial patient,
Samuel Marchbanks.

P.S. Do you know why women, as a rule, outlive their husbands? It is because women have too much sense to let themselves be worried to death by insurance salesmen.

To Amyas Pilgarlic, Esq.

Dear Pil:
This is a world of rush and bustle, but I have found one point of calm in the maelstrom, one unfailing fountain of surcease. For some years I have subscribed to two or three English weekend papers, deceiving myself that I do so in order to keep up with what is doing abroad. I take the *New Statesman*, and the *Spectator*, and the *Sunday Times*, but I have long realized, at the back of my mind, that I do not read these to keep up with the news, but to put a brake on the news. When I get these journals—or I suppose they should be called hebdomadals—they are about a month old, and I have the delightful sensation of reading about the past,

laughing at the predictions which have been proved untrue, and the fears which have become groundless. It is a thoroughly god-like amusement.

Why they arrive so late I cannot really discover. In my grandfather's day it took about a month to get a paper from England, and it still does. The English attitude toward such things is leisurely. I imagine the Editor of the *New Statesman* saying to his secretary, "Oh, Elsie, have you sent the parcel to that Canadian chap—Matchbox or whatever his name is?" And Elsie says, "Not this week; the new ball of twine hasn't come yet; I shall attend to it first thing next week." Then the Editor says, "Oh, plenty of time; the mail-packets leave Tilbury every second Thursday." And thus it goes. I pray that modern efficiency may never reach the circulation departments of the radical journals, or I may lose this delicious sensation of repose.

Your crony,
Sam.

To Amyas Pilgarlic, Esq.

Dear Pil:
Since I wrote to you I have gone through what is widely believed to be one of the most moving spiritual experiences a Canadian can sustain— a jaunt through the Rocky Mountains. I enjoyed it, but spiritually I am exactly where I was before. I have seen them in full sunlight, which robs them of all mystery, and I have seen them in a rainy haze, which is much better. I have gaped at chunks of rock which are said to resemble the faces of Indians, though the likeness escaped me. I have looked shudderingly down into gorges over which the train was passing. I have been pleased, diverted and surprised, but I am not one of those who finds a sight of the Rockies an equivalent for getting religion at a revival meeting.

To make a shameful confession, the Rockies put me in mind of nothing so much as the first act of *Rose Marie*, a musical comedy of my younger days and the favourite theatre entertainment of his late Majesty, King George V. At any moment I expected a lovely French-Canadian girl to leap on the observation car, saying, "You make ze marriage wiz me, no?" Or an Indian girl, more lithe and beautiful than any Indian girl has ever been, to begin a totem dance on the track. The scenery was right: only the actors were missing.

Upon arrival in Vancouver, the first thing to meet my eye was a notice, signed by the Chief of Police, warning me against confidence tricksters. It told me in detail how I might expect them to work. I would be approached, first of all, by someone who would try to make friends: this would be "The Steerer" who would eventually steer me to "The Spieler," who would sell me Stanley Park or the harbour at a bargain price. Not long after I had read this I was approached by a crafty-looking woman carrying a handful of pasteboards. "Juwanna buy four chances on the Legion car?" she cried, blocking my way. "Madam, you are wasting your time," said I; "I know you for what you are—a Steerer." She shrank away, muttering unpleasantly. Never let it be said that Marchbanks failed to heed a warning.

Vancouver has much to recommend it as a city; indeed, if it were not on the other side of those pestilent mountains I should go there often. Among other attractions it has a large and interesting Chinese quarter, where I ate the best Chinese food I have ever tasted. There are times when I think that I shall give up Occidental cuisine altogether, and eat Chinese food for the rest of my life. After lunch I wandered among the Chinese shops, and found one which sold a scent called "Girl Brand Florida Water." There is a simplicity about that name which enchants me. In the same shop I saw the only piece of Chinese nude art that has ever come my way; the Chinese are believed not to care for representations of the nude: but this was plainly the result of Western influence; it was a Chinese girl, lightly draped, holding aloft a bunch of paper flowers. Her legs were short, her body long, and she seemed more amply endowed for sitting than Western standards of beauty permit. It was, I suppose, the kind of thing one finds in Chinese bachelor apartments, just as Occidental bachelors enrich their rooms with ash-trays held aloft by naked beauties in chrome, and drink beer from glasses into which libidinous pictures have been etched. East is East, and West is West, but bachelors are wistful rascals the world over.

Normally I do not mind cigars. I smoke them myself. But on a train—! Opposite me as I write sits a little bald man with a baby face and a head like a peeled onion who has, for the past 45 minutes, burned and sucked the most villainous stogie I have ever choked over. He has doused it with his drool, and re-lit it, five several times. He is just about to do so again and I must leave him to it, or strike him with the emergency axe, or be sick myself. If he made that stench by any other means, the sanitary inspector would condemn him.

Yours gaggingly,
Sam.

To Amyas Pilgarlic, Esq.

Dear Pil:

Last night I was at the movies, and as usual it was necessary to sit through a good deal of rather depressing stuff before we were allowed to see the film which had really brought us to the theatre. Among these shorts (why do you suppose they call them shorts? Surely shortness is a comparative thing? Judged by the anguish of spirit they induced, these affairs were immeasurably long)—but as I was saying, among these shorts was one in which the audience was asked to join in the singing of popular gems of modern minstrelsy. But the audience refrained from doing so, and sat in a glum and resentful silence until the short had dragged out its weary length.

This is a hopeful sign. Human beings are refusing to be cajoled into doing silly things by machines, and by celluloid shadows. For a group of people to sing because a movie machine asks them to do so is just nonsense, and they know it.

Mark my words, the revolution of Man against Machine is close at hand, and when it comes we shall see the end of that era which historians are already referring to in learned works as The Age of Boloney.

Adieu,
Sam.

To Chandos Fribble, Esq.

Learned Fribble:

I have been reading a good deal of Canadian Poetry lately, and it has disturbed me. But last Sunday I attempted to go for a country walk, and by the time I had reached home again I knew what was wrong with Canadian Poetry.

Canadian poets are not allowed to come into contact with Nature. The great English poets have, in most cases, refreshed themselves continually by spells of country life, or by excursions into the country. Canadian poets cannot do this. I walked about two miles in the country and although I did not count them I estimated that roughly 300 cars passed me in that time. I had no time for Nature; I was perpetually on the jump. So I decided to walk across country. A farmer chased me, and told me not to tramp on his Fall wheat, which I was not doing. However, I left his land and struck into the bush. This was a mistake, for a big dog came and pointed his nose at me, and did his best to look like a bronze dog on a book-end. Soon two men with guns came crashing through the undergrowth, and seemed astonished when they saw me. "Say, what's that bird doing here?" cried one, and I knew at once that they had mistaken me for a partridge. But as they seemed about to blast my tailfeathers off I had the presence of mind to shout "I'm a game-warden!" and they made off as fast as their legs would carry them. The dog was still pointing, and as stiff as a mackerel, so they snatched it up in one piece and bore it away with them.

That is what Nature means in Canada. Cars, grouchy landowners, people with guns. No wonder our poetry is of nervous, urban, over-bred elegance.

Yours for a less cluttered countryside,
Samuel Marchbanks.

To Dionysus Fishorn, Esq.

Dear Mr. Fishorn:
No, I will not support your application for a Canada Council grant to enable you to write your novel. I know nothing about you, but I know a good deal about novels, and you are on the wrong track.

You say you want money to be "free of care" for a year, so that you can "create," and you speak of going to Mexico, to live cheaply and avoid distraction. Fishorn, I fear that your fictional abilities have spilled over from your work into your life. You see yourself in some lovely, unspoiled part of Mexico, where you will stroll out of your study onto the patio after a day's "creation," to gaze at the sunset and get into the cheap booze; your wife will admire you extravagantly and marvel that you ever con-descended to marry such a workaday person as herself; the villagers will speak of you with awe as El Escritor, and will pump your beautiful servant Ramona for news of your wondrous doings; you will go down into the very depths of Hell in your creative frenzies, but you will emerge, scorched and ennobled, in time for publication, translation into all known lan-guages, and the Nobel Prize.

Ah, Fishorn, would that it were so! But take the advice of an old hand: you won't write any better in Mexico than in Tin Cup, B.C., and unless you are wafted into a small, specially favoured group of the insane, you will never be free from care. So get to work, toiling in the bank or wherever it is by day, and serving the Triple Goddess at night and on weekends. Art is long, and grants are but yearly, so forget about them. A writer should not take handouts from anybody, even his country.

Benevolently but uncompromisingly,
Samuel Marchbanks.

KILLING WITH KINDNESS

Richard Needham

If you can get a copy of John Collier's little collection *Fancies and Goodnights*, you will find in it an amusing short story about a young man who goes to a magician, seeking a potion which

---

— *"Killing with Kindness"* by Richard J. Needham, from *Needham's Inferno* by Richard J. Needham, published by The Macmillan Company of Canada Limited (*This article originally appeared in The Globe and Mail, Canadian national newspaper.*)

will make a certain cold-hearted young lady fall madly, totally, permanently, in love with him.

"Why, yes," says the magician. "Pop this into her coffee, and she will love you with all of her heart, all of the time. She will always be thinking about you and worrying about you." The young man is delighted, the more so when he learns that this remarkable elixir costs only a dollar.

He buys it, and while doing so, notices a bottle

tagged at $5,000. The magician explains to him that this is a deadly poison, which can never be traced; it removes people quickly, painlessly, and with no embarrassing questions from the police. The young man is astonished that anybody should want such a thing, and be willing to pay such a high price for it. Shaking his head, he wanders off with the love potion. "Goodbye," he says to the magician. The magician replies, "Au revoir."

I thought of this story when I read in the Toronto newspapers about a San Francisco divorce case. Mrs. Carl Jeske wanted to break things up, not because her husband was so terribly cold and cruel, but because he was so terribly loving and kind. He wouldn't let her make the morning coffee, insisted on doing the laundry, and always washed the dishes. He tucked her into bed every night. If she baked a cake, he insisted on taking it out of the oven, so she wouldn't risk getting burned. Mrs. Jeske said: "He certainly was attentive, but he treated me like a child."

Well, you can have too much of a good thing —including affection itself. All through the body of English literature runs the theme of killing with kindness, choking the cat with cream. Writers of the sixteenth century like John Lyly and Robert Greene make frequent references (which may or may not be zoologically correct) to apes which kill their young by hugging them too tightly.

In Shakespeare's *The Taming of the Shrew*, Petruchio does just this to Katharina—messing up the meal, the bed, everything, on the pretext of looking after her properly. "Aye, and amid this hurly I intend that all is done in reverend care of her —— This is a way to kill a wife with kindness!"

Let's never be against love, which makes the world go round, go sideways, go swooping up and down like the CNE roller-coaster. But doesn't it last longer when it is touched with a measure of coolness, of detachment, of respect for the other person's essential dignity and liberty and privacy? If I had just one word of advice for

people entering a male-female relationship (or a child-parent relationship, or indeed any other) it would be from the Austrian poet Rainer Maria Rilke: "Love consists in this—that two solitudes protect, and touch, and greet one another."

To put it in commonplace terms, you can't live in someone else's pocket; and you can't have them living in your pocket, either. Isn't this what a lot of men and women try to do to each other? Isn't this what a lot of parents do to their children, and some children at least to their parents? If you really love another person, you should respect them, too—keep your distance, let them be, don't be forever poking and prodding at them, demanding to know their thoughts, trying to get in under their skin. It's a pretty sure way to wreck any relationship.

Coming to home life, I should think it could stand less, not more, emotion; more, not fewer, separations and absences. Freya Stark's good on this, as she is on many other things. "Absence is one of the most useful ingredients of family life, and to dose it rightly is an art like any other." And Mignon McLaughlin chimes in: "One of life's few really reliable pleasures is to have a family you love, and to leave them for a week."

Too much togetherness seems to be a pretty good recipe for apartness. Marriage would work much better, I've often thought, if husband and wife got clean out of each other's sight one day a week, or one week a month, or one month a year. And children would get along better with their parents if there were some recognized age at which they became and were treated as adults—free, responsible, standing on their own feet and making their own decisions.

I'd put that age at 16, but when I suggest it to high-school students, I'm hooted down and told that in modern society 16-year-olds are babes and sucklings, yea verily. All right then, when *do* people grow up? When should they be sprung? When can they be treated as adults? I often wonder. And I wonder the more when I see in the paper that the University of

Guelph is to have a residence housing both men and women students, but that the blocks will be separated by walls of solid steel. Look, Dick, look, Jane, look and see.

THE TROUBLE WITH PEOPLE

Vance Packard

"IN VERY FEW INSTANCES DO PEOPLE REALLY KNOW WHAT THEY WANT, EVEN WHEN THEY SAY THEY DO." — *Advertising Age*

The trend in marketing to the depth approach was largely impelled by difficulties the marketers kept encountering in trying to persuade Americans to buy all the products their companies could fabricate.

One particularly disturbing difficulty was the apparent perversity and unpredictability of the prospective customers. Marketers repeatedly suffered grievous losses in campaigns that by all the rules of logic should have succeeded. The marketers felt increasing dissatisfaction with their conventional methods for sizing up a market. These methods were known in the trade most commonly as "nose-counting." Under nose-counting, statistic-minded interviewers would determine the percentage of married women, ages twenty-one to thirty-five, in Omaha, Nebraska, who said they wanted, and would buy a three-legged stove if it cost no more than $249.

The trouble with this approach, they found, was that what people might tell interviewers had only a remote bearing on how the people would actually behave in a buying situation when confronted with a three-legged stove or almost anything else.

Gradually, many perceptive marketers began becoming suspicious of three basic assumptions they had made, in their efforts to be logical, concerning the predictable behavior of human beings, especially customers.

First, they decided, you can't assume that people know what they want.

A major ketchup maker kept getting complaints about its bottle, so it made a survey. Most of the people interviewed said they would prefer another type the company was considering. When the company went to the expense of bringing out this other bottle in test markets, it was overwhelmingly rejected in favor of the old bottle, even by people who had favored it in interviews. In a survey of male beer drinkers the men expressed a strong preference for a "nice dry beer." When they were then asked how a beer could be dry they were stumped. Those who were able to offer any answers at all revealed widely different notions.

Second, some marketers concluded, you can't assume people will tell you the truth about their wants and dislikes even if they know them. What you are more likely to get, they decided, are answers that will protect the informants in their steadfast endeavor to appear to the world as really sensible, intelligent, rational beings. One management consulting firm has concluded that accepting the word of a customer as to what he wants is "the least reliable index the manufacturer can have on what he ought to do to win customers."

The Advertising Research Foundation took magazines to task for asking people what magazines they read frequently, and naïvely accepting the answers given as valid. The people, it contended, are likely to admit reading only magazines of high prestige value. One investigator suggests that if you seriously accepted people's answers you might assume that *Atlantic Monthly* is America's most-read magazine and some of the confession magazines the least read; whereas actually the confession magazines in question may have twenty times the readership of *Atlantic Monthly*.

A brewery making two kinds of beer made a survey to find what kind of people drank each beer, as a guide to its merchandisers. It asked people known to favor its general brand name: "Do you drink the light or the regular?" To its astonishment it found people reporting they drank light over the regular by better than three to one. The truth of the matter was that for years the company, to meet consumer demand, had been brewing nine times as much regular beer as light beer. It decided that in asking people that question it was in effect asking: Do you drink the kind preferred by people of refinement and discriminating taste, or do you just drink the regular stuff?

The Color Research Institute conducted an experiment after it began suspecting the reliability of people's comments. Women while waiting for a lecture had the choice of two waiting rooms. One was a functional modern chamber with gentle tones. It had been carefully designed for eye ease and to promote a relaxed feeling. The other room was a traditional room filled with period furniture, oriental rugs, expensive-looking wallpaper.

It was found that virtually all the women instinctively went into the Swedish modern room to do their waiting. Only when every chair was filled did the women start to overflow into the more ornate room. After the lecture the ladies were asked, "Which of those two rooms do you like the better?" They looked thoughtfully at the two rooms, and then 84 per cent of them said the period room was the nicer room.

In another case the institute asked a group of people if they borrowed money from personal-loan companies. Every person said no. Some of them virtually shouted their answer. The truth was that all those selected for interviewing were people who were listed in the records of a local loan company as borrowers.

Psychologists at the McCann-Erickson advertising agency asked a sampling of people why they didn't buy one client's product—kippered herring. The main reason the people gave under direct questioning was that they just didn't like the taste of kippers. More persistent probing however uncovered the fact that 40 per cent of the people who said they didn't like the taste of kippers had never, in their entire lives, tasted kippers!

Finally, the marketers decided it is dangerous to assume that people can be trusted to behave in a rational way.

The Color Research Institute had what it felt was a startling encounter with this proneness to irrationality when it tested package designs for a new detergent. It was testing to see if a woman is influenced more than she realizes, in her opinion of a product, by the package. It gave the housewives three different boxes filled with detergent and requested that they try them all out for a few weeks and then report which was the best for delicate clothing. The wives were given the impression that they had been given three different types of detergent. Actually only the boxes were different; the detergents inside were identical.

The design for one was predominantly yellow. The yellow in the test was used because some merchandisers were convinced that yellow was the best color for store shelves because it has very strong visual impact. Another box was predominantly blue without any yellow in it; and the third box was blue but with splashes of yellow.

In their reports the housewives stated that the detergent in the brilliant yellow box was too strong; it even allegedly ruined their clothes in some cases. As for the detergent in the predominantly blue box, the wives complained in many cases that it left their clothes dirty looking. The third box, which contained what the institute felt was an ideal balance of colors in the package design, overwhelmingly received favorable responses. The women used such words as "fine" and "wonderful" in describing the effect the detergent in that box had on their clothes.

A department store that had become skeptical of the rationality of its customers tried an experiment. One of its slowest-moving items was priced at fourteen cents. It changed the price to two for twenty-nine cents. Sales promptly increased 30 per cent when the item was offered at this "bargain" price.

One of the most costly blunders in the history of merchandising was the Chrysler Corporation's assumption that people buy automobiles on a rational basis. It decided back in the early 1950's, on the basis of direct consumer surveys and the reasoning of its eminently sensible and engineering-minded executives, that people wanted a car in tune with the times, a car without frills that would be sturdy and easy to park. With streets and parking spaces becoming increasingly packed with cars the times seemed obviously to call for a more compact car, a car with a shorter wheel base.

In 1953, *Tide*, a leading trade journal of marketing-management men, asked, "Is This the End of the 'Big Fat Car'?" and told of Chrysler's decision that such was the case, and its planned style revolution for all its makes. The company's styling director was quoted as saying, "The people no longer want to buy a big fat car. The public wants a slim car." The article also mentioned that Chrysler had recently mailed stockholders a pamphlet entitled "Leadership in Engines," an area where it felt it was supreme.

What happened? Chrysler's share of the auto market dropped from 26 per cent in 1952 to about 13 per cent in 1954. The company was desperate. It looked more deeply into what sells cars and completely overhauled its styling. The result is shown in another article in *Tide* two years later. It reported:

Chrysler, going downhill in 1954, makes a marketing comeback. Whole line suffered mostly from styling. . . . One look at this year's products tells the story. People want long, low cars today. So some of the new cars by Chrysler are as much as 16 inches longer and 3 inches lower. Plymouth is now the longest car in the low-price field. The Dodge is the first car with 3-color exteriors.

The happy result (for Chrysler) was that its share of the market bounced back very substantially in 1955. *Tide* called it one of the most remarkable turnabouts in marketing history.

Our toothbrushing habits offer a prime example of behavior that is at least seemingly irrational. If you ask people why they brush their teeth, most of them will tell you that their main purpose in doing so is to get particles of food out of the crevices of their teeth and thus combat decay germs. Tooth-paste producers accepted this explanation for many years and based their sales campaigns on it. Advertising men who made a study of our toothbrushing habits, however, came upon a puzzle. They found that most people brushed their teeth once a day, and at the most pointless moment possible in the entire twenty-four-hour day, from the dental hygiene standpoint. That was in the morning just before breakfast, after decay germs had had a whole night to work on their teeth from particles left from supper—and just before the consumption of breakfast would bring in a new host of bacteria.

One advertising agency puzzling over this seemingly irrational behavior made a more thorough study of the reasons why we brush our teeth. It concluded that we are motivated by differing reasons, based on our personality. Some people, particularly hypochondriacs, are really concerned about those germs and are swayed by a "decay" appeal. (The hammering in recent years on all the wondrous anti-decay pastes has swollen the size of this group.) Another group, mostly extroverts, brush their teeth in the hope they will be bright and shiny. The majority of people, however, brush their teeth primarily for a reason that has little to do with dental hygiene or even their teeth. They put the brush and paste into their mouth in order to give their mouth a thorough purging, to get rid of the bad taste that has accumulated overnight. In short, they are looking for a taste sensation, as a part of their ritual of starting the day afresh. At least two of the major paste merchandisers began hitting hard at this appeal in 1955 and 1956. One promised a "clean mouth taste" and the other proclaimed that its paste "cleans your breath while it guards your teeth." (More recently one of these products got itself a new ad agency, as often happens, and the new mentor began appealing to the extrovert in us through the slogan, "You'll wonder where the yellow went——." Good results are reported, which simply proves there is always more than one way to catch a customer.)

Business Week, in commenting on the often seemingly irrational behavior of consumers, said: "People don't seem to be reasonable." However, it made this further point: "But people do act with purpose. Their behavior makes sense if you think about it in terms of its goals, of people's needs and their motives. That seems to be the secret of understanding or manipulating people."

Another aspect of people's behavior that has troubled marketers is that they are too easily satisfied with what they already have. Most of the marketers' factories have ever-larger warehouses full of goods to move.

By the mid-fifties American goods producers were achieving a fabulous output, and the output with automation promised to keep getting more fabulous. Since 1940, gross national product had soared more than 400 per cent; and man-hour productivity was doubling about every quarter century.

One way of viewing this rich, full life the people were achieving was the glowing one that everyone could enjoy an ever-higher standard of living. That view was thoroughly publicized. But there was another way of viewing it: that we must consume more and more, whether we want to or not, for the good of our economy.

In late 1955 the church publication *Christianity and Crisis* commented grimly on America's "ever-expanding economy." It observed that the pressure was on Americans to "consume, consume and consume, whether we need or even desire the products almost forced upon us." It added that the dynamics of an ever-expanding system require that we be "persuaded to consume to meet the needs of the productive process."

With growing productivity and prosperity the average American had five times as many discretionary dollars as he had in 1940. (These are dollars we have after we take care of our basic, immediate needs.) But discretionary dollars are also deferrable dollars—we can defer spending them if we are satisfied with what we already have. This hazard posed by so many optional dollars in our pockets was summed up quite eloquently in the October 24, 1955, issue of *Advertising Age* by an executive of the publishing firm of McGraw-Hill. He stated:

As a nation we are already so rich that consumers are under no pressure of immediate necessity to buy a very large share—perhaps as much as 40%—of what is produced, and the pressure will get progressivly less in the years ahead. But if consumers exercise their option not to buy a large share of what is produced, a great depression is not far behind.

The view virtually all goods producers choose to take when confronted with a threat of overproduction was voiced in what might seem a comical way to non-natives of his state by Senator Alexander Wiley, of Wisconsin, sometimes known as "the cheese Senator." In the mid-fifties when America had such a glut of cheese that cheese was even being stored in old World War II vessels, thanks largely to the great outpouring of the product from his section, he said: "Our problem is not too much cheese produced, but rather too little cheese consumed."

In the early fifties, with overproduction threatening on many fronts, a fundamental shift occurred in the preoccupation of people in executive suites. Production now became a relatively secondary concern. Executive planners changed from being maker-minded to market-minded. The president of the National Sales Executives in fact exclaimed: "Capitalism is dead—consumerism is king!"

There was talk at management conventions of "the marketing revolution" and considerable pondering on how best to "stimulate" consumer buying, by creating wants in people that they still didn't realize existed. An auto maker talked of increasing his car sales by selling to "those who do not yet know what they need."

This urgently felt need to "stimulate" people brought new power, glory, and prosperity to the professional stimulators or persuaders of American industry, particularly the skilled gray-flanneled suiters of New York's Madison Avenue, known as "ad alley." In 1955, $9,000,000,000 was poured into United States advertising, up a billion from 1954 and up three billion from 1950. For each man, woman, and child in America in 1955 roughly $53 was spent to persuade him or her to buy products of industry. Some cosmetics firms began spending a fourth of all their income from sales on advertising and promotion. A cosmetics tycoon, probably mythical, was quoted as saying: "We don't sell lipstick, we buy customers."

One big and intimidating obstacle confronting the stimulators was the fact that most Americans already possessed perfectly usable stoves, cars, TV sets, clothes, etc. Waiting for those products to wear out or become physically obsolete before urging replacements upon the owner was intolerable. More and more, ad men began talking of the desirability of creating "psychological obsolescence."

At a conference of gas-range people the conferees were exhorted to emulate the more up-to-date car makers in this business of creating psychological obsolescence. They were reminded that auto merchandisers strive to make everyone ashamed to drive a car more than two or three years. The gas-range people were told bluntly by the director of American Color Trends: "Ladies and gentlemen, you know and I know that too many housekeepers have the attitude that "any old piece of equipment will do so long as it works at all." He described the recent trend to change the color of many products and explained: "All of these trends have a definite bearing on what you can do to step up the obsolescence of gas appliances."

By the mid-fifties merchandisers of many different products were being urged by psychological counselors to become "merchants of discontent." One ad executive exclaimed with fervor: "What makes this country great is the creation of wants and desires, the creation of dissatisfaction with the old and outmoded."

A third major dilemma that was forcing marketers to search for more powerful tools of persuasion was the growing sameness of their products, with increased standardization. Too many people were complacently saying that the gasoline brands were "all the same" and equally good. Pierre Martineau, director of research at *The Chicago Tribune*, frankly asked a group of ad men; "What difference really is there between brands of gasoline, tires, cigarette tobacco, orange juice, milk, and what have you?——What is the advertising direction going to be when the differences become trivial or nonexistent?"

How can you make a logical sales talk to a prospect to persuade him to swear by your brand when in truth the brands are essentially alike in physical characteristics? That was a real dilemma for ad men. Ad agency president David Ogilvy commented on this problem by stating:

"I am astonished to find how many advertising men, even among the new generation, believe that women can be persuaded by logic and argument to buy one brand in preference to another, even when the two brands concerned are technically identical. . . . The greater the similarity between products, the less part reason really plays in brand selection. There really isn't any significant difference between the various brands of whisky or the various cigarettes or the various brands of beer. They are all about the same. And so are the cake mixes and the detergents and the automobiles." (This was not to imply, of course, that *all* brands of a product are the same. In some lines substantial differentiations exist. And it is also true that most companies strive mightily to develop product differences.)

An annual conference of advertising-agency men heard an appeal for more "gifted artists" in persuasion to cope with this problem of the "rapidly diminishing product differences."

Thus it was that for several compelling reasons marketers began groping for new and more penetrating persuasion techniques, for deeper approaches, better hooks. They needed customer-catching techniques that would be powerful and still not get them in trouble with the Federal Trade Commission, which has been taking a sternly righteous and disapproving attitude toward overextravagant claims and promises, such as had often characterized some of the ad copy of yesteryear.

The search for more persuasive ways to sell was summed up colorfully by a car salesman in Atlanta who said of his problem in selling cars in a then-slack market: "If buyer shopping gets any worse, we'll have to hit the customer over the head and get him to sign while he's unconscious." . . .

CLASS REUNION

Sinclair Lewis

His march to greatness was not without disastrous stumbling.

Fame did not bring the social advancement which the Babbitts deserved. They were not asked to join the Tonawanda Country Club nor invited to the dances at the Union. Himself, Babbitt fretted, he didn't "care a fat hoot for all these highrollers, but the wife would kind of like to be Among Those Present." He nervously awaited his university class-dinner and an evening of furious intimacy with such social leaders as Charles McKelvey the millionaire contrac-

— Chapter 15 from *Babbitt* by Sinclair Lewis; copyright 1922, by Harcourt, Brace & World, Inc., renewed 1950 by Sinclair Lewis; reprinted by permission of the publisher

tor, Max Kruger the banker, Irving Tate the tool-manufacturer, and Adelbert Dobson the fashionable interior decorator. Theoretically he was their friend, as he had been in college, and when he encountered them they still called him "Georgie," but he didn't seem to encounter them often, and they never invited him to dinner (with champagne and a butler) at their houses on Royal Ridge.

All the week before the class-dinner he thought of them. "No reason why we shouldn't become real chummy now!"

II

Like all true American diversions and spiritual outpourings, the dinner of the men of the Class of 1896 was thoroughly organized. The dinner-committee hammered like a sales-corporation.

Once a week they sent out reminders:

Old man, are you going to be with us at the livest Friendship Feed the alumni of the good old U have ever known? The alumnae of '08 turned out 60% strong. Are we boys going to be beaten by a bunch of skirts? Come on, fellows, let's work up some real genuine enthusiasm and all boost together for the snappiest dinner yet! Elegant eats, short ginger-talks, and memories shared together of the brightest, gladdest days of life.

The dinner was held in a private room at the Union Club. The club was a dingy building, three pretentious old dwellings knocked together, and the entrance-hall resembled a potato cellar, yet the Babbitt who was free of the magnificence of the Athletic Club entered with embarrassment. He nodded to the doorman, an ancient proud negro with brass buttons and a blue tail-coat, and paraded through the hall, trying to look like a member.

Sixty men had come to the dinner. They made islands and eddies in the hall; they packed the elevator and the corners of the private dining-room. They tried to be intimate and enthusiastic. They appeared to one another exactly as they had in college—as raw youngsters whose present mustaches, baldnesses, paunches, and wrinkles were but jovial disguises put on for the evening. "You haven't changed a particle!" they marveled. The men whom they could not recall they addressed, "Well, well, great to see you again, old man. What are you— Still doing the same thing?"

Some one was always starting a cheer or a college song, and it was always thinning into silence. Despite their resolution to be democratic they divided into two sets: the men with dress-clothes and the men without. Babbitt (extremely in dress-clothes) went from one group to the other. Though he was, almost frankly, out for social conquest, he sought Paul Riesling first. He found him alone, neat and silent.

Paul sighed, "I'm no good at this handshaking and 'well, look who's here' bunk."

"Rats now, Paulibus, loosen up and be a mixer! Finest bunch of boys on earth! Say, you seem kind of glum. What's matter?"

"Oh, the usual. Run-in with Zilla."

"Come on! Let's wade in and forget our troubles."

He kept Paul beside him, but worked toward the spot where Charles McKelvey stood warming his admirers like a furnace.

McKelvey had been the hero of the Class of '96; not only football captain and hammer-thrower but debater, and passable in what the State University considered scholarship. He had gone on, had captured the construction-company once owned by the Dodsworths, best-known pioneer family of Zenith. He built state capitols, skyscrapers, railway terminals. He was a heavy-shouldered, big-chested man, but not sluggish. There was a quiet humor in his eyes, a syrup-smooth quickness in his speech, which intimidated politicians and warned reporters; and in his presence the most intelligent scientist or the most sensitive artist felt thin-blooded, unworldly, and a little shabby. He was, particularly when he was influencing legislature or hiring labor-spies, very easy and lovable and gorgeous. He was baronial; he was a peer in the rapidly crystallizing American aristocracy, inferior only to the haughty Old Families. (In Zenith, an Old Family is one which came to town before 1840.) His power was the greater because he was not hindered by scruples, by either the vice or the virtue of the older Puritan tradition.

McKelvey was being placidly merry now with the great, the manufacturers and bankers, the land-owners and lawyers and surgeons who had chauffeurs and went to Europe. Babbitt squeezed among them. He liked McKelvey's smile as much as the social advancement to be had from his favor. If in Paul's company he felt ponderous and protective, with McKelvey he felt slight and adoring.

He heard McKelvey say to Max Kruger, the banker, "Yes, we'll put up Sir Gerald Doak." Babbitt's democratic love for titles became a rich relish. "You know, he's one of the biggest iron-men in England, Max. Horribly well-off —— Why, hello, old Georgie! Say, Max, George Babbitt is getting fatter than I am!"

The chairman shouted, "Take your seats, fellows!"

"Shall we make a move, Charley?" Babbitt said casually to McKelvey.

"Right. Hello, Paul! How's the old fiddler? Planning to sit anywhere special, George? Come on, let's grab some seats. Come on, Max. Georgie, I read about your speeches in the campaign. Bully work!"

After that, Babbitt would have followed him through fire. He was enormously busy during the dinner, now bumblingly cheering Paul, now approaching McKelvey with "Hear you're going to build some piers in Brooklyn," now noting how enviously the failures of the class, sitting by themselves in a weedy group, looked up to him in his association with the nobility, now warming himself in the Society Talk of McKelvey and Max Kruger. They spoke of a "jungle dance" for which Mona Dodsworth had decorated her house with thousands of orchids. They spoke, with an excellent imitation of casualness, of a dinner in Washington at which McKelvey had met a Senator, a Balkan princess, and an English major-general. McKelvey called the princess "Jenny," and let it be known that he had danced with her.

Babbitt was thrilled, but not so weighted with awe as to be silent. If he was not invited by them to dinner, he was yet accustomed to talking with bank-presidents, congressmen, and club-women who entertained poets. He was bright and referential with McKelvey:

"Say, Charley, juh remember in Junior year how we chartered a sea-going hack and chased down to Riverdale, to the big show Madame Brown used to put on? Remember how you beat up that hick constabule that tried to run us in, and we pinched the pants-pressing sign and took and hung it on Prof. Morrison's door? Oh, gosh, those were the days!"

Those, McKelvey agreed, were the days.

Babbitt had reached "It isn't the books you study in college but the friendships you make that counts" when the men at head of the table broke into song. He attacked McKelvey:

"It's a shame, uh, shame to drift apart because our, uh, business activities lie in different fields. I've enjoyed talking over the good old days. You and Mrs. McKelvey must come to dinner some night."

Vaguely, "Yes, indeed—"

"Like to talk to you about the growth of real estate out beyond your Grantsville warehouse. I might be able to tip you off to a thing or two, possibly."

"Splendid! We must have dinner together, Georgie. Just let me know. And it will be a great pleasure to have your wife and you at the house," said McKelvey, much less vaguely.

Then the chairman's voice, the prodigious voice which once had roused them to cheer defiance at rooters from Ohio or Michigan or Indiana, whooped, "Come on, you wombats! All together in the long yell!" Babbitt felt that life would never be sweeter than now, when he joined with Paul Riesling and the newly recovered hero, McKelvey, in:

> Baaaaaattle-ax
> Get an ax,
> Bal-ax,
> Get-nax,
> Who, who? The U.!
> Hooroo!

III

The Babbitts invited the McKelveys to dinner, in early December, and the McKelveys not only accepted but, after changing the date once or twice, actually came.

The Babbitts somewhat thoroughly discussed the details of the dinner, from the purchase of a bottle of champagne to the number of salted almonds to be placed before each person. Especially did they mention the matter of the other guests. To the last Babbitt held out for giving Paul Riesling the benefit of being with the McKelveys. "Good old Charley would like

Paul and Verg Gunch better than some high-falutin' Willy boy," he insisted, but Mrs. Babbitt interrupted his observations with, "Yes—perhaps—I think I'll try to get some Lynnhaven oysters," and when she was quite ready she invited Dr. J. T. Angus, the oculist, and a dismally respectable lawyer named Maxwell, with their glittering wives.

Neither Angus nor Maxwell belonged to the Elks or to the Athletic Club; neither of them had ever called Babbitt "brother" or asked his opinions on carburetors. The only "human people" whom she invited, Babbitt raged, were the Littlefields; and Howard Littlefield at times became so statistical that Babbitt longed for the refreshment of Gunch's, "Well, old lemon-pie-face, what's the good word?"

Immediately after lunch Mrs. Babbitt began to set the table for the seven-thirty dinner to the McKelveys, and Babbitt was, by order, home at four. But they didn't find anything for him to do, and three times Mrs. Babbitt scolded, "Do please try to keep out of the way!" He stood in the door of the garage, his lips drooping, and wished that Littlefield or Sam Doppelbrau or somebody would come along and talk to him. He saw Ted sneaking about the corner of the house.

"What's the matter, old man?" said Babbitt.

"Is that you, thin, owld one? Gee, Ma certainly is on the warpath! I told her Rone and I would jus' soon not be let in on the fiesta to-night, and she bit me. She says I got to take a bath, too. But, say, the Babbitt men will be some lookers to-night! Little Theodore in a dress-suit!"

"The Babbitt men!" Babbitt liked the sound of it. He put his arm about the boy's shoulder. He wished that Paul Riesling had a daughter, so that Ted might marry her. "Yes, your mother is kind of rouncing round, all right," he said, and they laughed together, and sighed together, and dutifully went in to dress.

The McKelveys were less than fifteen minutes late.

Babbitt hoped that the Doppelbraus would see the McKelvey's limousine, and their uniformed chauffeur, waiting in front.

The dinner was well cooked and incredibly plentiful, and Mrs. Babbitt had brought out her grandmother's silver candlesticks. Babbitt worked hard. He was good. He told none of the jokes he wanted to tell. He listened to the others. He started Maxwell off with a resounding, "Let's hear about your trip to the Yellowstone." He was laudatory, extremely laudatory. He found opportunities to remark that Dr. Angus was a benefactor to humanity, Maxwell and Howard Littlefield profound scholars, Charles McKelvey an inspiration to ambitious youth, and Mrs. McKelvey an adornment to the social circles of Zenith, Washington, New York, Paris, and numbers of other places.

But he could not stir them. It was a dinner without a soul. For no reason that was clear to Babbitt, heaviness was over them and they spoke laboriously and unwillingly.

He concentrated on Lucile McKelvey, carefully not looking at her blanched lovely shoulder and the tawny silken band which supported her frock.

"I suppose you'll be going to Europe pretty soon again, won't you?" he invited.

"I'd like awfully to run over to Rome for a few weeks."

"I suppose you see a lot of pictures and music and curios and everything there."

"No, what I really go for is: there's a little *trattoria* on the Via della Scrofa where you get the best *fettuccine* in the world."

"Oh, I—Yes. That must be nice to try that. Yes."

At a quarter to ten McKelvey discovered with profound regret that his wife had a headache. He said blithely, as Babbitt helped him with his coat, "We must lunch together some time, and talk over the old days."

When the others had labored out, at half-past ten, Babbitt turned to his wife, pleading, "Charley said he had a corking time and we must lunch—said they wanted to have us up to the house for dinner before long."

She achieved, "Oh, it's just been one of those quiet evenings that are often so much more enjoyable than noisy parties where everybody talks at once and doesn't really settle down to —nice quiet enjoyment."

But from his cot on the sleeping-porch he heard her weeping, slowly, without hope.

IV

For a month they watched the social columns, and waited for a return dinner-invitation.

As the hosts of Sir Gerald Doak, the McKelveys were headlined all the week after the Babbitts' dinner. Zenith ardently received Sir Gerald (who had come to America to buy coal). The newspapers interviewed him on prohibition, Ireland, unemployment, naval aviation, the rate of exchange, tea-drinking *versus* whisky-drinking, the psychology of American women, and daily life as lived by English county families. Sir Gerald seemed to have heard of all those topics. The McKelveys gave him a Singhalese dinner, and Miss Elnora Pearl Bates, society editor of the *Advocate-Times*, rose to her highest lark note. Babbitt read aloud at breakfast-table:

'Twixt the original and Oriental decorations, the strange and delicious food, and the personalities both of the distinguished guests, the charming hostess and the noted host, never had Zenith seen a more recherche affair than the Ceylon dinner-dance given last evening by Mr. and Mrs. Charles McKelvey to Sir Gerald Doak. Methought as we —fortunate one! —were privileged to view that fairy and foreign scene, nothing at Monte Carlo or the choicest ambassadorial sets of foreign capitals could be more lovely. It is not for nothing that Zenith is in matters social rapidly becoming known as the choosiest inland city in the country.

Though he is too modest to admit it, Lord Doak gives a cachet to our smart quartier such as it has not received since the ever-memorable visit of the Earl of Sittingbourne. Not only is he of the British peerage, but he is also, on dit, a leader of the British metal industries. As he comes from Nottingham, a favorite haunt of Robin Hood, though now, we are informed by Lord Doak, a live modern city of 275,573 inhabitants, and important lace as well as other industries, we like to think, that perhaps through his veins runs some of the blood, both virile red and bonny blue, of that earlier lord o' the good greenwood, the roguish Robin.

The lovely Mrs. McKelvey never was more fascinating than last evening in her black net gown relieved by dainty bands of silver and at her exquisite waist a glowing cluster of Aaron Ward roses.

Babbitt said bravely, "I hope they don't invite us to meet this Lord Doak guy. Darn sight rather just have a nice quiet little dinner with Charley and the Missus."

At the Zenith Athletic Club they discussed it amply. "I s'pose we'll have to call McKelvey 'Lord Chaz' from now on," said Sidney Finkelstein.

"It beats all get-out," meditated that man of data, Howard Littlefield, "how hard it is for some people to get things straight. Here they call this fellow 'Lord Doak' when it ought to be 'Sir Gerald.' "

Babbitt marvelled, "Is that a fact! Well, well! 'Sir Gerald,' eh? That's what you call um, eh? Well, sir, I'm glad to know that."

Later he informed his salesmen, "It's funnier 'n a goat the way some folks that, just because they happen to lay up a big wad, go entertaining famous foreigners, don't have any more idea 'n a rabbit how to address 'em so's to make 'em feel at home!"

That evening, as he was driving home, he passed McKelvey's limousine and saw Sir Gerald, a large, ruddy, pop-eyed, Teutonic Englishman whose dribble of yellow mustache gave him an aspect sad and doubtful. Babbitt drove on slowly, oppressed by futility. He had a sudden, unexplained, and horrible conviction that the McKelveys were laughing at him.

He betrayed his depression by the violence with which he informed his wife, "Folks that really tend to business haven't got the time to waste on a bunch like the McKelveys. This society stuff is like any other hobby; if you devote yourself to it, you get on. But I like to have a chance to visit with you and the children instead of all this idiotic chasing round."

They did not speak of the McKelveys again.

V

It was a shame, at this worried time, to have to think about the Overbrooks.

Ed Overbrook was a classmate of Babbitt who had been a failure. He had a large family and a feeble insurance business out in the suburb of Dorchester. He was gray and thin and unimportant. He had always been gray and thin and unimportant. He was the person whom, in any group, you forgot to introduce, then introduced with extra enthusiasm. He had admired Babbitt's good-fellowship in college, had admired ever since his power in real estate, his beautiful house and wonderful clothes. It pleased Babbitt, though it bothered him with a sense of responsibility. At the class-dinner he had seen poor Overbrook, in a shiny blue serge business-suit, being diffident in a corner with three other failures. He had gone over and been cordial: "Why, hello, young Ed! I hear you're writing all the insurance in Dorchester now. Bully work!"

They recalled the good old days when Overbrook used to write poetry. Overbrook embarrassed him by blurting, "Say, Georgie, I hate to think of how we been drifting apart. I wish you and Mrs. Babbitt would come to dinner some night."

Babbitt boomed, "Fine! Sure! Just let me know. And the wife and I want to have you at the house." He forgot it, but unfortunately Ed Overbrook did not. Repeatedly he telephoned to Babbitt, inviting him to dinner. "Might as well go and get it over," Babbitt groaned to his wife. "But don't it simply amaze you the way the poor fish doesn't know the first thing about social etiquette? Think of him 'phoning me, instead of his wife sitting down and writing us a regular bid! Well, I guess we're stuck for it. That's the trouble with all this class-brother hooptedoodle."

He accepted Overbrook's next plaintive invitation, for an evening two weeks off. A dinner two weeks off, even a family dinner, never seems so appalling, till the two weeks have astoundingly disappeared and one comes dismayed to the ambushed hour. They had to change the date, because of their own dinner to the McKelveys, but at last they gloomily drove out to the Overbrooks' house in Dorchester.

It was miserable from the beginning. The Overbrooks had dinner at six-thirty, while the Babbitts never dined before seven. Babbitt permitted himself to be ten minutes late. "Let's make it as short as possible. I think we'll duck out quick. I'll say I have to be at the office extra early to-morrow," he planned.

The Overbrook house was depressing. It was the second story of a wooden two-family dwelling; a place of baby-carriages, old hats hung in the hall, cabbage-smell, and a Family Bible on the parlor table. Ed Overbrook and his wife were as awkward and threadbare as usual, and the other guests were two dreadful families whose names Babbitt never caught and never desired to catch. But he was touched, and disconcerted, by the tactless way in which Overbrook praised him: "We're mighty proud to have old George here to-night! Of course you've all read about his speeches and oratory in the papers—and the boy's good-looking, too, eh?— but what I always think of is back in college, and what a great old mixer he was, and one of the best swimmers in the class."

Babbitt tried to be jovial; he worked at it; but he could find nothing to interest him in Overbrook's timorousness, the blankness of the other guests, or the drained stupidity of Mrs. Overbrook, with her spectacles, drab skin, and tight-drawn hair. He told his best Irish story, but it sank like soggy cake. Most bleary moment of all was when Mrs. Overbrook, peering out of her fog of nursing eight children and cooking and scrubbing, tried to be conversational.

"I suppose you go to Chicago and New York right along, Mr. Babbitt," she prodded.

"Well, I get to Chicago fairly often."

"It must be awfully interesting. I suppose you take in all the theatres."

"Well, to tell the truth, Mrs. Overbrook, thing that hits me best is a great big beefsteak at a Dutch restaurant in the Loop!"

They had nothing more to say. Babbitt was sorry, but there was no hope; the dinner was a failure. At ten, rousing out of the stupor of meaningless talk, he said as cheerily as he could, "'Fraid we got to be starting, Ed. I've got a fellow coming to see me early to-morrow." As Overbrook helped him with his coat, Babbitt said, "Nice to rub up on the old days! We must have lunch together, P.D.Q."

Mrs. Babbitt sighed, on their drive home, "It was pretty terrible. But how Mr. Overbrook does admire you!"

"Yep. Poor cuss! Seems to think I'm a little tin archangel, and the best-looking man in Zenith."

"Well, you're certainly not that but— Oh, Georgie, you don't suppose we have to invite them to dinner at our house now, do we?"

"Ouch! Gaw, I hope not!"

"See here, now, George! You didn't say anything about it to Mr. Overbrook, did you?"

"No! Gee! No! Honest, I didn't! Just made a bluff about having him to lunch some time."

"Well. —— Oh, dear. —— I don't want to hurt their feelings. But I don't see how I could stand another evening like this one. And suppose somebody like Dr. and Mrs. Angus came in when we had the Overbrooks there, and thought they were friends of ours!"

For a week they worried, "We really ought to invite Ed and his wife, poor devils!" But as they never saw the Overbrooks, they forgot them, and after a month or two they said, "That really was the best way, just to let it slide. It wouldn't be kind to *them* to have them here. They'd feel so out of place and hard-up in our home."

They did not speak of the Overbrooks again.

THE GIRAFFE

Mauro Senesi

The giraffe entered our town in the morning and looked at us all from high above. It had been brought along to attract a crowd by one of those men who set themselves up in the squares to sell razor blades. It was taller than the steeple, seen in perspective, but its eyes seemed close to us just the same, and rosy and good like stars at dawn.

Not only the children fell under a spell watching it, but we boys too, even the men and the women at first. It was the most extraordinary thing that had ever been in our square. Slowly it would lower its head and then raise it again to a dizzying height. It must have seen over the houses the clotted red of the roofs and the horizon, who knows how far.

We boys made faces at it from below and shouted dirty words as if it were a girl with a long neck; it was only a way of distinguishing ourselves from the children, who admired it with their mouths wide open, but inside we felt still more joy and excitement than they did. By now we had discovered everything in our world, we knew the alleys, the houses of the town one by

— "*The Giraffe*" by Mauro Senesi, copyright © 1962, by Harper's Magazine, Inc.; reprinted from the January 1963 issue of *Harper's Magazine* by permission of the author

one, and the people, the words, the seasons, the days always the same: a reality full of limits that now the giraffe extended easily. We felt we were in Africa just to see it.

Every minute we had free—Flavio, Agostino, Boddo, the others and I—there we were in the square, making a circle around it. The peddler said, "Will you come, come and buy my blades?" But our beards hadn't grown yet enough for us to need them.

All at once we saw the man's face turn red and then white, we saw him fall to the ground and lie there, still. The giraffe swung its head down slowly and kept it low, immobile over him. Soon after, the doctor arrived and said, "He's dead, just like that."

When they had taken him away, the giraffe raised its head again in the middle of the square. It moved its jaws, and its eyes had suddenly become attentive. The people standing around said, "Poor animal, what will we do with it?"

No one knew, not even the policeman, and it was then that Rolandino jumped out and said, "I'll keep it, until someone comes to get it."

What will you do with it, Rolandino, with a giraffe?

Rolandino was a stubby boy, couldn't even reach high enough to touch its belly, so of course the people standing there had to laugh, but we boys told him, "We'll help you, or else it'll eat you alive."

Rolandino took it by the halter and we pushed it from behind, because at first it didn't want to budge. The people asked us, "Where will you take it? What will you do with it?"

What will we do with it, boys, with a giraffe?

At last it moved and from then on gently followed us. It was lovely and new, leading it through our narrow streets. The roofs couldn't imprison that high head, and it seemed they took on another aspect and we ourselves had another look about us too. It was as if the giraffe were our periscope, to see from up above who knows what, who knows where.

Meanwhile we studied every spot on its skin, every movement of its delicate muscles, its every

expression. By the time we were done, it seemed we had built it with our own hands.

A thing pure and agile amid the stumpy, blackened shapes of the houses; even the girls seemed homely in comparison, standing still at their doors and you could tell by their eyes how much they would have liked to come along after us. Whereas the old women crossed themselves as if it were a wild beast, our giraffe.

We didn't know what to give it to eat, but it took care of that itself, denuding the trees the Mayor had had planted in a little square to camouflage it as a public park. A giraffe, certainly, is more important than leaves (anyway the winter would have eaten them), and yet everyone put up a fuss, even to going and calling the policeman, who came and said, "If you don't take it away I'll kill it with my revolver."

Then it began to get dark and the eyes of our giraffe grew little by little larger and almost bloody, and we led it close to other people on purpose to give them a fright. Even most of the men, besides the old women, didn't know, right then and there, whether giraffes are fierce or not.

Rolandino especially was happy when the giraffe—letting its head droop low—made someone go running. It was a kind of revenge for him, so tiny and used to having to run away from everyone else. He felt tall and free, escaped from reality, when he had that absurd wonderful animal close by, as for that matter all of us did, even though we kept pretending we had taken it up as a game.

The darkness became so thick it swallowed up the giraffe's head, which was taller still than the street lamps; there remained only its gray and slender legs dancing among us, over the stones. For a while, we continued wandering through the town, by now deserted. Our town went to bed early nights. We took the giraffe in front of the windows, so that its head looked in from outside. No one had been expecting it, that glance, in the privacy of their homes, and cries of fear or of shame were heard. Who knows what our giraffe had discovered?

When all the shutters had been closed with a bang, a tremor seemed to pass down the animal's long legs. Rolandino said, "He's cold, he's used to the sun of Africa, where can we find a place for him to sleep?"

There wasn't a house or a stall high enough for it and we didn't know what to do. The cold came from every part of the horizon, squeezing us together into a tight circle. The giraffe's skin was icy as a stone and all at once we seemed to have a monument before us.

A funny giraffe monument, boys, pierces slender and long into the sky. What shall we do with it?

Rolandino had an idea and said, "It'd fit into the church."

We felt dismayed for a second, but then one of us said, "I'll go and rob the key from the sexton." Another said, "God will certainly be happy to have it as a guest."

It took some doing to make it lower its head enough—and it wasn't much—to enter the church. Then we had to light a candle or two and the giraffe looked smaller to us but its shadow immense over the nave. Motionless it remained all night in front of the altar while we dozed here and there among the pews and the confessionals. By morning however it had eaten the roses, the carnations, the lilies, the chrysanthemums, and the candles, too.

It was then that the little old women dressed in black arrived for the first Mass and they began to shout, to cry, to pray. The giraffe, frightened, withdrew to the front of the church, placing its head right next to that of Jesus.

The Priest arrived from the sacristy and at first buried his hands in his red hair but then we thought we saw him smile, even though he charged us to take that beast immediately out of the house of God.

The town had awakened early that morning; we found the square full of people who were angry with us and our giraffe, the women on account of the profaned church and the men perhaps on account of its glances at them through their windows the night before, sudden, merciless, and divine. But there must have been other reasons too for the hatred of the people: like the defense of an equilibrium, of a reality that we wanted to subvert with our giraffe. So many reasons there must have been, but we boys couldn't understand, we knew only that they had matured in a single night, like poisonous mushrooms.

Even the Mayor was there and furious because of his lovely little trees, now bare. He said, "We'll have to kill the giraffe." Everyone agreed. If they kill it, boys, shall we start the revolution?

Luckily Rolandino had another idea. He began to run all of a sudden, pulling the giraffe behind him, the Mayor and the people moved aside. We other boys slipped into the gap he had opened, without giving heed to our mothers and our bosses who were calling us, because it was time to return to everyday life.

Out of the square and beyond the town we ran, behind the sinuous giraffe, to look for hay-fields. Soon we were moving in harmony with it, a magical lightness in our limbs, until panting we stopped in a field on the side of a hill and Rolandino said happily, "We've made it."

Among ourselves we pretended it was a game, whereas it wasn't. We set to work pulling hay from the earth with our hands and the farmers looked at us grimly from the threshing floor but they didn't have the courage to come out. Who knows whether they're fierce, those giraffes?

Meanwhile we made plans for getting it back in the town, thinking of ways to force it on the Mayor and the people. Livio said, "We could build it a house next to the town walls and put a fence around it, make a zoo."

Rolandino said the giraffe had to stay free.

But our talk was useless, and it was slow, for we knew we were defeated. And the giraffe knew it, too; we held the hay up but it didn't want any. It kept its head high and immobile on its stiffened neck, its eyes had an opaque, anemic red in them, like the stars when they're on the point of dying out.

Rolandino said, "It's the cold, or maybe those leaves it ate have hurt it somehow." There were tears in his voice.

Our giraffe stood still, its head piercing the sky. We called it in vain, we punched it with sticks and climbed on one another's shoulders to carry the sweet-smelling hay to its mouth, which it didn't open.

Slowly, then, it folded its legs. Its neck alone remained erect for an instant, before flowing to the ground with a long desperate sob. Its eyes were at our feet and we saw that they were spent, solid, and smooth, like those of marble statues.

Our giraffe has died by itself, boys, there was no need for them to kill it. Damn this town anyway, where giraffes can't live, because there's room only for the things that are already here.

THERE WILL COME SOFT RAINS

Ray Bradbury

The house was a good house and had been planned and built by the people who were to live in it, in the year 1980. The house was like many another house in that year; it fed and slept and entertained its inhabitants, and made a good life for them. The man and wife and their two children lived at ease there, and lived happily, even while the world trembled. All of the fine things of living, the warm things, music and poetry, books that talked, beds that warmed and made themselves, fires that built themselves in the fireplaces of evenings, were in this house, and living there was a contentment.

And then one day the world shook and there was an explosion followed by ten thousand explosions and red fire in the sky and a rain of ashes and radioactivity, and the happy time was over.

In the living room the voice-clock sang, *Tick-tock, seven A.M. o'clock, time to get up!* as if it were afraid nobody would. The house lay empty. The clock talked on into the empty morning.

The kitchen stove sighed and ejected from its warm interior eight eggs, sunny side up, twelve bacon slices, two coffees, and two cups of hot cocoa. *Seven nine, breakfast time, seven nine.*

"Today is April 28th, 1985," said a phonograph voice in the kitchen ceiling. "Today, remember, is Mr. Featherstone's birthday. Insurance, gas, light, and water bills are due."

Somewhere in the walls, relays clicked, memory tapes glided under electric eyes. Recorded voices moved beneath steel needles:

Eight one, run, run, off to school, off to work, run, run, tick-tock, eight one o'clock!

But no doors slammed, no carpets took the quick tread of rubber heels. Outside, it was raining. The voice of the weather box on the front door sang quietly: "Rain, rain, go away, rubbers, raincoats for today." And the rain tapped on the roof.

At eight thirty the eggs were shriveled. An aluminum wedge scraped them into the sink, where hot water whirled them down a metal throat which digested and flushed them away to the distant sea.

— *"There will come soft rains" by Ray Bradbury, from* Adventures in Tomorrow, *Greenberg Publisher, New York, 1951; this story copyright 1950 by Ray Bradbury, reprinted by permission of the Harold Matson Company, Inc.*

236

Nine fifteen, sang the clock, *time to clean*.

Out of warrens in the wall, tiny mechanical mice darted. The rooms were acrawl with the small cleaning animals, all rubber and metal. They sucked up the hidden dust, and popped back in their burrows.

Ten o'clock. The sun came out from behind the rain. The house stood alone on a street where all the other houses were rubble and ashes. At night, the ruined town gave off a radioactive glow which could be seen for miles.

Ten fifteen. The garden sprinkler filled the soft morning air with golden fountains. The water tinkled over the charred west side of the house where it had been scorched evenly free of its white paint. The entire face of the house was black, save for five places. Here, the silhouette, in paint, of a man mowing a lawn. Here, a woman bent to pick flowers. Still farther over, their images burned on wood in one titanic instant, a small boy, hands flung in the air— higher up, the image of a thrown ball—and opposite him a girl, her hands raised to catch a ball which never came down.

The five spots of paint—the man, the woman, the boy, the girl, the ball—remained. The rest was a thin layer of charcoal.

The gentle rain of the sprinkler filled the garden with falling light.

Until this day, how well the house had kept its peace. How carefully it had asked, "Who goes there?" and getting no reply from rains and lonely foxes and whining cats, it had shut up its windows and drawn the shades. If a sparrow brushed a window, the shade snapped up. The bird, startled, flew off! No, not even an evil bird must touch the house.

And inside, the house was like an altar with nine thousand robot attendants, big and small, servicing, attending, singing in choirs, even though the gods had gone away and the ritual was meaningless.

A dog whined, shivering, on the front porch.

The front door recognized the dog's voice and opened. The dog padded in wearily, thinned to the bone, covered with sores. It tracked mud on the carpet. Behind it whirred the angry robot mice, angry at having to pick up mud and maple leaves, which, carried to the burrows, were dropped down cellar tubes into an incinerator which sat like an evil Baal in a dark corner.

The dog ran upstairs, hysterically yelping at each door. It pawed the kitchen door wildly.

Behind the door, the stove was making pancakes which filled the whole house with their odor.

The dog frothed, ran insanely, spun in a cricle, biting its tail, and died.

It lay in the living room for an hour.

One o'clock.

Delicately sensing decay, the regiments of mice hummed out of the walls, soft as blown leaves, their electric eyes blowing.

One fifteen.

The dog was gone.

The cellar incinerator glowed suddenly and a whirl of sparks leaped up the flue.

Two thirty-five.

Bridge tables sprouted from the patio walls. Playing cards fluttered onto pads in a shower of pips. Martinis appeared on an oaken bench.

But the tables were silent, the cards untouched.

At four thirty the tables folded back into the walls.

Five o'clock. The bathtubs filled with clear hot water. A safety razor dropped into a wall-mold, ready.

Six, seven, eight, nine o'clock.

Dinner made, ignored, and flushed away; dishes washed; and in the study, the tobacco stand produced a cigar, half an inch of gray ash on it, smoking, waiting. The hearth fire bloomed up all by itself, out of nothing.

Nine o'clock. The beds began to warm their hidden circuits, for the night was cool.

A gentle click in the study wall. A voice spoke from above the crackling fireplace:

"Mrs. McClellan, what poem would you like to hear this evening?"

The house was silent.

The voice said, "Since you express no preference, I'll pick a poem at random." Quiet music rose behind the voice. "Sara Teasdale. A favorite of yours, as I recall."

There will come soft rains and the smell of the
    ground,
And swallows circling with their shimmering sound;
And frogs in the pools singing at night,
And wild plum-trees in tremulous white.

Robins will wear their feathery fire
Whistling their whims on a low fence-wire;

And not one will know of the war, not one
Will care at last when it is done.

Not one would mind, neither bird nor tree,
If mankind perished utterly:

And Spring herself, when she woke at dawn,
Would scarcely know that we were gone.

The voice finished the poem. The empty chairs faced each other between the silent walls, and the music played.

At ten o'clock, the house began to die.

The wind blew. The bough of a falling tree smashed the kitchen window. Cleaning solvent, bottled, crashed on the stove.

"Fire!" screamed voices. "Fire!" Water pumps shot down water from the ceilings. But the solvent spread under the doors, making fire as it went, while other voices took up the alarm in chorus.

The windows broke with heat and the wind blew in to help the fire. Scurrying water rats, their copper wheels spinning, squeaked from the walls, squirted their water, ran for more.

Too late! Somewhere, a pump stopped. The ceiling sprays stopped raining. The reserve water supply, which had filled baths and washed dishes for many silent days, was gone.

The fire crackled upstairs, ate paintings, lay hungrily in the beds! It devoured every room.

The house was shuddering, oak bone on bone, the bared skeleton cringing from the heat, all the wires revealed as if a surgeon had torn the skin off to let the red veins quiver in scalded air. Voices screamed, "*Help, help, fire, run!*" Windows snapped open and shut, like mouths, undecided. *Fire, run!* the voices wailed a tragic nursery rhyme, and the silly Greek chorus faded as the sound-wires popped their sheathings. Ten dozen high, shrieking voices died, as emergency batteries melted.

In the other parts of the house, in the last instant under the fire avalanche, other choruses could be heard announcing the time, the weather, appointments, diets; playing music, reading poetry in the fiery study, while doors opened and slammed and umbrellas appeared at the doors and put themselves away—a thousand things happening, like the interior of a clockshop at midnight, all clocks striking, a merry-go-round of squeaking, whispering, rushing, until all the film spools were burned and fell, and all the wires withered and the circuits cracked.

In the kitchen, an instant before the final collapse, the stove, hysterically hissing, could be seen making breakfasts at a psychopathic rate, ten dozen pancakes, six dozen loaves of toast.

The crash! The attic smashing kitchen down into cellar and subcellar. Deep freeze, armchairs, film tapes, beds, were thrown in a cluttered mound deep under.

Smoke and silence.

Dawn shone faintly in the east. In the ruins, one wall stood alone. Within the wall, a voice said, over and over again and again, even as the sun rose to shine upon the heaped rubble and steam:

"Today is April 29th, 1985. Today is April 29th, 1985. Today is ——"

HOW PRINCES SHOULD KEEP FAITH

Niccolo Machiavelli

Every one understands how praiseworthy it is in a Prince to keep faith, and to live uprightly and not craftily. Nevertheless, we see from what has taken place in our own days that Princes who have set little store by their word, but have known how to overreach men by their cunning, have accomplished great things, and in the end got the better of those who trusted to honest dealing.

Be it known, then, that there are two ways of contending, one in accordance with the laws, the other by force; the first of which is proper to men, the second to beasts. But since the first method is often ineffectual, it becomes necessary to resort to the second. A Prince should, therefore, understand how to use well both the man and the beast. And this lesson has been covertly taught by the ancient writers, who relate how Achilles and many others of these old Princes were given over to be brought up and trained by Chiron the Centaur; since the only meaning of their having for instructor one who was half man and half beast is, that it is necessary for a Prince to know how to use both natures, and that the one without the other has no stability.

But since a Prince should know how to use the beast's nature wisely, he ought of beasts to choose both the lion and the fox; for the lion cannot guard himself from the toils, nor the fox from wolves. He must therefore be a fox to discern toils, and a lion to drive off wolves.

— *excerpts from* The Prince (*pages 59-62 and 78-79*) *by Niccolo Machiavelli, translated by N. H. Thomson, published as Vol. 31 in the Harvard Classics by P. F. Collier and Son, New York, 1910; this material reprinted with the kind permission of Crowell Collier and Macmillan, Inc.*

To rely wholly on the lion is unwise; and for this reason a prudent Prince neither can nor ought to keep his word when to keep it is hurtful to him and the causes which led him to pledge it are removed. If all men were good, this would not be good advice, but since they are dishonest and do not keep faith with you, you, in return, need not keep faith with them; and no prince was ever at a loss for plausible reasons to cloak a breach of faith. Of this numberless recent instances could be given, and it might be shown how many solemn treaties and engagements have been rendered inoperative and idle through want of faith in Princes, and that he who was best known to play the fox has had the best success.

It is necessary, indeed, to put a good colour on this nature, and to be skilful in simulating and dissembling. But men are so simple, and governed so absolutely by their present needs, that he who wishes to deceive will never fail in finding willing dupes. One recent example I will not omit. Pope Alexander VI had no care or thought but how to deceive, and always found material to work on. No man ever had a more effective manner of asseverating, or made promises with more solemn protestations, or observed them less. And yet, because he understood this side of human nature, his frauds always succeeded.

It is not essential, then, that a Prince should have all the good qualities which I have enumerated above, but it is most essential that he should seem to have them; I will even venture to affirm that if he has and invariably practises them all, they are hurtful, whereas the appearance of having them is useful. Thus, it is well to seem merciful, faithful, humane, religious, and upright, and also to be so; but the mind should remain so balanced that were it needful not to be so, you should be able and know how to change to the contrary.

And you are to understand that a Prince, and most of all a new Prince, cannot observe all those rules of conduct in respect whereof men are accounted good, being often forced, in order to preserve his Princedom, to act in opposition to good faith, charity, humanity, and religion. He must therefore keep his mind ready to shift as the winds and tides of Fortune turn, and, as I have already said, he ought not to quit good courses if he can help it, but should know how to follow evil courses if he must.

A Prince should therefore be very careful that nothing ever escapes his lips which is not replete with the five qualities above named, so that to see and hear him, one would think him the embodiment of mercy, good faith, integrity, humanity, and religion. And there is no virtue which it is more necessary for him to seem to possess than this last; because men in general judge rather by the eye than by the hand, for every one can see but few can touch. Every one sees what you seem, but few know what you are, and these few dare not oppose themselves to the opinion of the many who have the majesty of the State to back them up.

Moreover, in the actions of all men, and most of all of Princes, where there is no tribunal to which we can appeal, we look to results. Wherefore if a Prince succeeds in establishing and maintaining his authority, the means will always be judged honourable and be approved by every one. For the vulgar are always taken by appearances and by results, and the world is made up of the vulgar, the few only finding room when the many have no longer ground to stand on.

A certain Prince of our own days, whose name it is as well not to mention, is always preaching peace and good faith, although the mortal enemy of both; and both, had he practised them as he preaches them, would, oftener than once, have lost him his kingdom and authority.

Having now spoken of the chief of the qualities above referred to, the rest I shall dispose of briefly with these general remarks, that a Prince, as has already in part been said, should consider how he may avoid such courses as would make him hated or despised; and that whenever he succeeds in keeping clear of these, he has performed his part, and runs no risk though he incur other infamies.

A Prince, as I have said before, sooner becomes hated by being rapacious and by interfering with the property and with the women of his subjects, than in any other way. From these, therefore, he should abstain. For so long as neither their property nor their honour is touched, the mass of mankind live contentedly, and the Prince has only to cope with the ambition of a few, which can in many ways and easily be kept within bounds. . . .

Again, a Prince should show himself a patron of merit, and should honour those who excel in every art. He ought accordingly to encourage his subjects by enabling them to pursue their callings, whether mercantile, agricultural, or any other, in security, so that this man shall not be deterred from beautifying his possessions from the apprehension that they may be taken from him, or that other refrain from opening a trade through fear of taxes; and he should provide rewards for those who desire so to employ themselves, and for all who are disposed in any way to add to the greatness of his City or State.

He ought, moreover, at suitable seasons of the year to entertain the people with festivals and shows. And because all cities are divided into guilds and companies, he should show attention to these societies, and sometimes take part in their meetings; offering an example of courtesy and munificence, but always maintaining the dignity of his station, which must under no circumstances be compromised.

THE TWELVE MEN

G. K. Chesterton

The other day, while I was meditating on morality and Mr. H. Pitt, I was, so to speak, snatched up and put into a jury box to try people. The snatching took some weeks, but to me it seemed something sudden and arbitrary. I was put into this box because I lived in Battersea, and my name began with a C. Looking round me, I saw that there were also summoned and in attendance in the court whole crowds and processions of men, all of whom lived in Battersea, and all of whose names began with a C.

It seems that they always summon jurymen in this sweeping alphabetical way. At one official blow, so to speak, Battersea is denuded of all its C's, and left to get on as best it can with the rest of the alphabet. A Cumberpatch is missing from one street—a Chizzolpop from another—three Chucksterfields from Chucksterfield House; the children are crying out for an absent Cadgerboy; the woman at the street corner is weeping for her Coffintop, and will not be comforted. We settle down with a rollicking ease into our seats (for we are a bold, devil-may-care race, the C's of Battersea), and an oath is administered to us in a totally inaudible manner by an individual resembling an Army surgeon in his second childhood. We understand, however, that we are to well and truly try the case between our sovereign lord the King and the prisoner at the bar, neither of whom has put in an appearance as yet.

Just when I was wondering whether the King

and the prisoner were, perhaps, coming to an amicable understanding in some adjoining public-house, the prisoner's head appears above the barrier of the dock; he is accused of stealing bicycles, and he is the living image of a great friend of mine. We go into the matter of the stealing of the bicycles. We do well and truly try the case between the King and the prisoner in the affair of the bicycles. And we come to the conclusion, after a brief but reasonable discussion, that the King is not in any way implicated. Then we pass on to a woman who neglected her children, and who looks as if somebody or something had neglected her. And I am one of those who fancy that something had.

All the time that the eye took in these light appearances and the brain passed these light criticisms, there was in the heart a barbaric pity and fear which men have never been able to utter from the beginning, but which is the power behind half the poems of the world. The mood cannot even inadequately be suggested, except faintly by this statement that tragedy is the highest expression of the infinite value of human life. Never had I stood so close to pain; and never so far away from pessimism. Ordinarily, I should not have spoken of these dark emotions at all, for speech about them is too difficult; but I mention them now for a specific and particular reason to the statement of which I will proceed at once. I speak of these feelings because out of the furnace of them there came a curious realization of a political or social truth. I saw with a queer and indescribable kind of clearness what a jury really is, and why we must never let it go.

The trend of our epoch up to this time has been consistently towards specialism and professionalism. We tend to have trained soldiers because they fight better, trained singers because they sing better, trained dancers because

——"The Twelve Men" by G. K. Chesterton, from *Tremendous Trifles* by G. K. Chesterton, published by Methuen and Company, London, third edition, December 1909; reprinted by permission of the estate of G. K. Chesterton

they dance better, specially instructed laughers because they laugh better, and so on and so on. The principle has been applied to law and politics by innumerable modern writers. Many Fabians have insisted that a greater part of our political work should be performed by experts. Many legalists have declared that the untrained jury should be altogether supplanted by the trained judge.

Now, if this world of ours were really what is called reasonable, I do not know that there would be any fault to find with this. But the true result of all experience and the true foundation of all religion is this. That the four or five things that it is most practically essential that a man should know, are all of them what people call paradoxes. That is to say, that though we all find them in life to be mere plain truths, yet we cannot easily state them in words without being guilty of seeming verbal contradictions. One of them, for instance, is the unimpeachable platitude that the man who finds most pleasure for himself is often the man who least hunts for it. Another is the paradox of courage; the fact that the way to avoid death is not to have too much aversion to it. Whoever is careless enough of his bones to climb some hopeless cliff above the tide may save his bones by that carelessness. Whoever will lose his life, the same shall save it; an entirely practical and prosaic statement.

Now, one of these four or five paradoxes which should be taught to every infant prattling at his mother's knee is the following: That the more a man looks at a thing, the less he can see it, and the more a man learns a thing the less he knows it. The Fabian argument of the expert, that the man who is trained should be the man who is trusted would be absolutely unanswerable if it were really true that a man who studied a thing and practised it every day went on seeing more and more of its significance. But he does not. He goes on seeing less and less of its sig-

nificance. In the same way, alas! we all go on every day, unless we are continually goading ourselves into gratitude and humility, seeing less and less of the significance of the sky or the stones.

Now, it is a terrible business to mark a man out for the vengeance of men. But it is a thing to which a man can grow accustomed, as he can to other terrible things; he can even grow accustomed to the sun. And the horrible thing about all legal officials, even the best, about all judges, magistrates, barristers, detectives, and policemen, is not that they are wicked (some of them are good), not that they are stupid (several of them are quite intelligent), it is simply that they have got used to it.

Strictly they do not see the prisoner in the dock; all they see is the usual man in the usual place. They do not see the awful court of judgment; they only see their own workshop. Therefore, the instinct of Christian civilization has most wisely declared that into their judgments there shall upon every occasion be infused fresh blood and fresh thoughts from the streets. Men shall come in who can see the court and the crowd, and coarse faces of the policeman and the professional criminals, the wasted faces of the wastrels, the unreal faces of the gesticulating counsel, and see it all as one sees a new picture or a play hitherto unvisited.

Our civilization has decided, and very justly decided, that determining the guilt or innocence of men is a thing too important to be trusted to trained men. It wishes for light upon that awful matter, it asks men who know no more law than I know, but who can feel the things that I felt in the jury box. When it wants a library catalogued, or the solar system discovered, or any trifle of that kind, it uses up its specialists. But when it wishes anything done which is really serious, it collects twelve of the ordinary men standing round. The same thing was done, if I remember right, by the Founder of Christianity.

TWO FISHERMEN

Morley Callaghan

The only reporter on the town paper, the *Examiner*, was Michael Foster, a tall, long-legged, eager young fellow, who wanted to go to the city some day and work on an important newspaper.

The morning he went into Bagley's Hotel, he wasn't at all sure of himself. He went over to the desk and whispered to the proprietor, Ted Bagley, "Did he come here, Mr. Bagley?"

Bagley said slowly, "Two men came here from this morning's train. They're registered." He put his spatulate forefinger on the open book and said, "Two men. One of them's a drummer. This one here, T. Woodley. I know because he was through this way last year and just a minute ago he walked across the road to Molson's hardware store. The other one—here's his name, K. Smith."

"Who's K. Smith?" Michael asked.

"I don't know. A mild, harmless-looking little guy."

"Did he look like the hangman, Mr. Bagley."

"I couldn't say that, seeing as I never saw one. He was awfully polite and asked where he could get a boat so he could go fishing on the lake this evening, so I said likely down at Smollet's place by the power-house."

"Well, thanks. I guess if he was the hangman, he'd go over to the jail first," Michael said.

He went along the street, past the Baptist church to the old jail with the high brick fence around it. Two tall maple trees, with branches drooping low over the sidewalk, shaded one of the walls from the morning sunlight. Last night, behind those walls, three carpenters, working by lamplight, had nailed the timbers for the scaffold. In the morning, young Thomas Delaney, who had grown up in the town, was being hanged: he had killed old Mathew Rhinehart whom he had caught molesting his wife when she had been berry-picking in the hills behind the town. There had been a struggle and Thomas Delaney had taken a bad beating before he had killed Rhinehart. Last night a crowd had gathered on the sidewalk by the lamp-post, and while moths and smaller insects swarmed around the high blue carbon light, the crowd had thrown sticks and bottles and small stones at the out-of-town workmen in the jail yard. Billy Hilton, the town constable, had stood under the light with his head down, pretending not to notice anything. Thomas Delaney was only three years older than Michael Foster.

Michael went straight to the jail office, where Henry Steadman, the sheriff, a squat, heavy man, was sitting on the desk idly wetting his long moustaches with his tongue. "Hello, Michael, what do you want?" he asked.

"Hello, Mr. Steadman, the *Examiner* would like to know if the hangman arrived yet."

"Why ask me?"

"I thought he'd come here to test the gallows. Won't he?"

"My, you're a smart young fellow, Michael, thinking of that."

"Is he in there now, Mr. Steadman?"

"Don't ask me. I'm saying nothing. Say, Michael, do you think there's going to be trouble? You ought to know. Does anybody seem sore at me? I can't do nothing. You can see that."

"I don't think anybody blames you, Mr. Steadman. Look here, can't I see the hangman? Is his name K. Smith?"

"What does it matter to you, Michael? Be a

— *"Two Fishermen"* by *Morley Callaghan, from Morley Callaghan's Stories; reprinted by permission of the author and of the publisher, The Macmillan Company of Canada Limited, 1959*

sport, go on away and don't bother us any more."

"All right, Mr. Steadman," Michael said very competently, "just leave it to me."

Early that evening, when the sun was setting, Michael Foster walked south of the town on the dusty road leading to the power-house and Smollet's fishing pier. He knew that if Mr. K. Smith wanted to get a boat he would go down to the pier. Fine powdered road dust whitened Michael's shoes. Ahead of him he saw the power-plant, square and low, and the smooth lake water. Behind him the sun was hanging over the blue hills beyond the town and shining brilliantly on square patches of farm land. The air around the power-house smelt of steam.

Out on the jutting, tumbledown pier of rock and logs, Michael saw a little fellow without a hat, sitting down with his knees hunched up to his chin, a very small man with little gray baby curls on the back of his neck, who stared steadily far out over the water. In his hand he was holding a stick with a heavy fishing-line twined around it and a gleaming copper spoon bait, the hooks brightened with bits of feathers such as they used in the neighbourhood when trolling for lake trout. Apprehensively Michael walked out over the rocks toward the stranger and called, "Were you thinking of going fishing, mister?" Standing up, the man smiled. He had a large head, tapering down to a small chin, a birdlike neck and a very wistful smile. Puckering his mouth up, he said shyly to Michael, "Did you intend to go fishing?"

"That's what I came down here for. I was going to get a boat back at the boat-house there. How would you like if we went together?"

"I'd like it first rate," the shy little man said eagerly. "We could take turns rowing. Does that appeal to you?"

"Fine. Fine. You wait here and I'll go back to Smollet's place and ask for a row-boat and I'll row around here and get you."

"Thanks. Thanks very much," the mild little man said as he began to untie his line. He seemed very enthusiastic.

When Michael brought the boat around to the end of the old pier and invited the stranger to make himself comfortable so he could handle the line, the stranger protested comically that he ought to be allowed to row.

Pulling strong at the oars, Michael was soon out in the deep water and the little man was letting his line out slowly. In one furtive glance, he had noticed that the man's hair, gray at the temples, was inclined to curl to his ears. The line was out full length. It was twisted around the little man's forefinger, which he let drag in the water. And then Michael looked full at him and smiled because he thought he seemed so meek and quizzical. "He's a nice little guy," Michael assured himself and he said, "I work on the town paper, the *Examiner*."

"Is it a good paper? Do you like the work?"

"Yes, But it's nothing like a first-class city paper and I don't expect to be working on it long. I want to get a reporter's job on a city paper. My name's Michael Foster."

"Mine's Smith. Just call me Smitty."

"I was wondering if you'd been over to the jail yet."

Up to this time the little man had been smiling with the charming ease of a small boy who finds himself free, but now he became furtive and disappointed. Hesitating, he said, "Yes, I was over there first thing this morning."

"Oh, I just knew you'd go there," Michael said. They were a bit afraid of each other. By this time they were far out on the water which had a mill-pond smoothness. The town seemed to get smaller, with white houses in rows and streets forming geometric patterns, just as the blue hills behind the town seemed to get larger at sundown.

Finally Michael said, "Do you know this Thomas Delaney that's dying in the morning?" He knew his voice was slow and resentful.

"No. I don't know anything about him. I never read about them.

"Aren't there any fish at all in this old lake? I'd like to catch some fish," he said rapidly. "I told my wife I'd bring her home some fish." Glancing at Michael, he was appealing, without speaking, that they should do nothing to spoil an evening's fishing.

The little man began to talk eagerly about fishing as he pulled out a small flask from his hip pocket. "Scotch," he said, chuckling with delight. "Here, take a swig." Michael drank from the flask and passed it back. Tilting his head back and saying, "Here's to you, Michael," the little man took a long pull at the flask. "The only time I take a drink," he said still chuckling, "is when I go on a fishing trip by myself. I usually go by myself," he added apologetically as if he wanted the young fellow to see how much he appreciated his company.

They had gone far out on the water but they had caught nothing. It began to get dark. "No fish tonight, I guess, Smitty," Michael said.

"It's a crying shame," Smitty said. "I looked forward to coming up here when I found out the place was on the lake. I wanted to get some fishing in. I promised my wife I'd bring her back some fish. She'd often like to go fishing with me, but of course, she can't because she can't travel around from place to place like I do. Whenever I get a call to go some place, I always look at the map to see if it's by a lake or on a river, then I take my lines and hooks along."

"If you took another job, you and your wife could probably go fishing together," Michael suggested.

"I don't know about that. We sometimes go fishing together anyway." He looked away, waiting for Michael to be repelled and insist that he ought to give up the job. And he wasn't ashamed as he looked down at the water, but he knew that Michael thought he ought to be ashamed. "Somebody's got to do my job. There's got to be a hangman," he said.

"I just meant that if it was such disagreeable work, Smitty."

The little man did not answer for a long time. Michael rowed steadily with sweeping, tireless strokes. Huddled at the end of the boat, Smitty suddenly looked up with a kind of melancholy hopelessness and said mildly, "The job hasn't been so disagreeable."

"Good God, man, you don't mean you like it?"

"Oh, no," he said, to be obliging, as if he knew what Michael expected him to say. "I mean you get used to it, that's all." But he looked down again at the water, knowing he ought to be ashamed of himself.

"Have you got any children?"

"I sure have. Five. The oldest boy is fourteen. It's funny, but they're all a lot bigger and taller than I am. Isn't that funny?"

They started a conversation about fishing rivers that ran into the lake farther north. They felt friendly again. The little man, who had an extraordinary gift for story-telling, made many quaint faces, puckered up his lips, screwed up his eyes and moved around restlessly as if he wanted to get up in the boat and stride around for the sake of more expression. Again he brought out the whiskey flask and Michael stopped rowing. Grinning, they toasted each other and said together, "Happy days." The boat remained motionless on the placid water. Far out, the sun's last rays gleamed on the water-line. And then it got dark and they could only see the town lights. It was time to turn around and pull for the shore. The little man tried to take the oars from Michael, who shook his head resolutely and insisted that he would prefer to have his friend catch a fish on the way back to the shore.

"It's too late now, and we may have scared all the fish away," Smitty laughed happily. "But we're having a grand time, aren't we?"

When they reached the old pier by the power-house, it was full night and they hadn't caught a single fish. As the boat bumped against the rocks Michael said, "You can get out here. I'll take the boat around to Smollet's."

"Won't you be coming my way?"

"Not just now. I'll probably talk with Smollet a while."

The little man got out of the boat and stood on the pier looking down at Michael. "I was thinking dawn would be the best time to catch some fish," he said. "At about five o'clock. I'll have an hour and a half to spare anyway. How would you like that?" He was speaking with so much eagerness that Michael found himself saying, "I could try. But if I'm not here at dawn, you go on without me."

"All right. I'll walk back to the hotel now."

"Good night, Smitty."

"Good night, Michael. We had a fine neighbourly time, didn't we?"

As Michael rowed the boat around to the boat-house, he hoped that Smitty wouldn't realize he didn't want to be seen walking back to town with him. And later, when he was going slowly along the dusty road in the dark and hearing all the crickets chirping in the ditches, he couldn't figure out why he felt so ashamed of himself.

At seven o'clock next morning Thomas Delaney was hanged in the town jail yard. There was hardly a breeze on that leaden gray morning and there were no small whitecaps out over the lake. It would have been a fine morning for fishing. Michael went down to the jail, for he thought it his duty as a newspaperman to have all the facts, but he was afraid he might get sick. He hardly spoke to all the men and women who were crowded under the maple trees by the jail wall. Everybody he knew was staring at the wall and muttering angrily. Two of Thomas Delaney's brothers, big, strapping fellows with bearded faces, were there on the sidewalk. Three automobiles were at the front of the jail.

Michael, the town newspaperman, was admitted into the courtyard by old Willie Mathews, one of the guards, who said that two newspapermen from the city were at the gallows on the other side of the building. "I guess you can go around there, too, if you want to," Mathews said, as he sat down slowly on the step. White-faced, and afraid, Michael sat down on the step with Mathews and they waited and said nothing.

At last the old fellow said, "Those people outside there are pretty sore, ain't they?"

"They're pretty sullen, all right. I saw two of Delaney's brothers there."

"I wish they'd go," Mathews said. "I don't want to see anything. I didn't even look at

Delaney. I don't want to hear anything. I'm sick." He put his head back against the wall and closed his eyes.

The old fellow and Michael sat close together till a small procession came around the corner from the other side of the yard. First came Mr. Steadman, the sheriff, with his head down as though he were crying, then Dr. Parker, the physician, then two hard-looking young newspapermen from the city, walking with their hats on the backs of their heads, and behind them came the little hangman, erect, stepping out with military precision and carrying himself with a strange cocky dignity. He was dressed in a long black cut-away coat with gray striped trousers, a gates-ajar collar and a narrow red tie, as if he alone felt the formal importance of the occasion. He walked with brusque precision till he saw Michael, who was standing up, staring at him with his mouth open.

The little hangman grinned and as soon as the procession reached the doorstep, he shook hands with Michael. They were all looking at Michael. As though his work were over now, the hangman said eagerly to Michael, "I thought I'd see you here. You didn't get down to the pier at dawn?"

"No. I couldn't make it."

"That was tough, Michael. I looked for you," he said. "But never mind. I've got something for you." As they all went into the jail, Dr. Parker glanced angrily at Michael, then turned his back on him. In the office, where the doctor prepared to sign a certificate, Smitty was bending down over his fishing-basket which was in the corner. Then he pulled out two good-sized salmon-bellied trout, folded in a newspaper, and said, "I was saving these for you, Michael. I got four in an hour's fishing." Then he said, "I'll talk about that later, if you'll wait. We'll be busy here, and I've got to change my clothes."

Michael went out to the street with Dr. Parker and the two city newspapermen. Under his arm he was carrying the fish, folded in the newspaper. Outside, at the jail door, Michael thought that the doctor and the two newspapermen were standing a little apart from him. Then the small crowd, with their clothes all dust-soiled from the road, surged forward, and the doctor said to them, "You might as well go home, boys. It's all over."

"Where's old Steadman?" somebody demanded.

"We'll wait for the hangman," somebody else shouted.

The doctor walked away by himself. For a while Michael stood beside the two city newspapermen, and tried to look as nonchalant as they were looking, but he lost confidence in them when he smelled whiskey. They only talked to each other. Then they mingled with the crowd, and Michael stood alone. At last he could stand there no longer looking at all those people he knew so well, so he, too, moved out and joined the crowd.

When the sheriff came out with the hangman and two of the guards, they got half-way down to one of the automobiles before someone threw an old boot. Steadman ducked into one of the cars, as the boot hit him on the shoulder, and the two guards followed him. The hangman, dismayed, stood alone on the sidewalk. Those in the car must have thought at first that the hangman was with them for the car suddenly shot forward, leaving him alone on the sidewalk. The crowd threw small rocks and sticks, hooting at him as the automobile backed up slowly towards him. One small stone hit him on the head. Blood trickled from the side of his head as he looked around helplessly at all the angry people. He had the same expression on his face, Michael thought, as he had had last night when he had seemed ashamed and had looked down steadily at the water. Only now, he looked around wildly, looking for someone to help him as the crowd kept pelting him. Farther and farther

Michael backed into the crowd and all the time he felt dreadfully ashamed as though he were betraying Smitty, who last night had had such a good neighbourly time with him. "It's different now, it's different," he kept thinking, as he held the fish in the newspaper tight under his arm. Smitty started to run toward the automobile, but James Mortimer, a big fisherman, shot out his foot and tripped him and sent him sprawling on his face.

Mortimer, the big fisherman, looking for something to throw, said to Michael, "Sock him, sock him."

Michael shook his head and felt sick.

"What's the matter with you, Michael?"

"Nothing. I got nothing against him."

The big fisherman started pounding his fists up and down in the air. "He just doesn't mean anything to me at all," Michael said quickly. The fisherman, bending down, kicked a small rock loose from the road bed and heaved it at the hangman. Then he said, "What are you holding there, Michael, what's under your arm? Fish. Pitch them at him. Here, give them to me." Still in a fury, he snatched the fish, and threw them one at a time at the little man just as he was getting up from the road. The fish fell in the thick dust in front of him, sending up a little cloud. Smitty seemed to stare at the fish with his mouth hanging open, then he didn't even look at the crowd. That expression on Smitty's face as he saw the fish on the road made Michael hot with shame and he tried to get out of the crowd.

Smitty had his hands over his head, to shield his face as the crowd pelted him, yelling "Sock the little rat. Throw the runt in the lake." The sheriff pulled him into the automobile. The car shot forward in a cloud of dust.

MY OBJECT ALL SUBLIME . . .

Poul Anderson

We met in line of business. Michaels' firm wanted to start a subdivision on the far side of Evanston and discovered that I held title to some of the most promising acreage. They made me a good offer, but I was stubborn; they raised it and I stayed stubborn; finally the boss himself looked me up. He wasn't entirely what I'd expected. Aggressive, of course, but in so polite a way that it didn't offend, his manners so urbane you rarely noticed his lack of formal education. Which lack he was remedying quite fast, anyhow, via night classes and extension courses as well as omnivorous reading.

We went out for a drink while we talked the matter over. He led me to a bar that had little of Chicago about it: quiet, shabby, no jukebox, no television, a bookshelf and several chess sets, but none of the freaks and phonies who usually infest such places. Besides ourselves, there were only half a dozen customers—a professor-emeritus type among the books, some people arguing politics with a degree of factual relevancy, a young man debating with the bartender whether Bartok was more original than Schoenberg or vice versa. Michaels and I found a corner table and some Danish beer.

I explained that I didn't care about money one way or another, but objected to bulldozing some rather good-looking countryside in order to erect still another chrome-plated slum. Michaels stuffed his pipe before answering. He

---

— "*My Object All Sublime*" by Poul Anderson, reprinted from <u>12 Great Classics of Science Fiction</u>, edited by Groff Conklin, Gold Medal Books, Fawcett Publications, Inc., 1963; copyright © 1961 by Galaxy Publications, Inc.; reprinted by permission of the author and his agents, Scott Meredith Literary Agency, Inc., 580 Fifth Avenue, New York, New York 10036

was a lean, erect man, long-chinned and Roman-nosed, his hair grizzled, his eyes dark and luminous. "Didn't my representative explain?" he said. "We aren't planning a row of identical split-level sties. We have six basic designs in mind, with variations, to be located in a pattern —— so."

He took out pencil and paper and began to sketch. As he talked, his accent thickened, but the fluency remained. And he made his own case better than anyone had done for him. Like it or not, he said, this was the middle twentieth century and mass production was here to stay. A community need not be less attractive for being ready-made, could in fact gain an artistic unity. He proceeded to show me how.

He didn't press me too hard, and conversation wandered.

"Delightful spot, this," I remarked. "How'd you find it?"

He shrugged. "I often prowl about, especially at night. Exploring."

"Isn't that rather dangerous?"

"Not in comparison," he said with a touch of grimness.

"Uh —— I gather you weren't born over here?"

"No. I didn't arrive in the United States until 1946. What they called a DP, a displaced person. I became Thad Michaels because I got tired of spelling out Tadeusz Michalowski. Nor did I want any part of old-country sentimentalism; I'm a zealous assimilationist."

Otherwise he seldom talked much about himself. Later I got some details of his early rise in business, from admiring and envious competitors. Some of them didn't yet believe it was possible to sell a house with radiant heating for less than twenty thousand dollars and show a profit. Michaels had found ways to make it possible. Not bad for a penniless immigrant.

I checked up and found he'd been admitted on a special visa, in consideration of services rendered the U.S. Army in the last stages of the European war. Those services had taken nerve as well as quick-wittedness.

Meanwhile our acquaintance developed. I sold him the land he wanted, but we continued to see each other, sometimes in the tavern, sometimes at my bachelor apartment, most often in his lakeshore penthouse. He had a stunning blonde wife and a couple of bright, well-mannered boys. Nonetheless he was a lonely man, and I fulfilled his need for friendship.

A year or so after we first met, he told me the story.

I'd been invited over for Thanksgiving dinner. Afterwards we sat around and talked. And talked. And talked. When we had ranged from the chances of an upset in the next city election to the chances of other planets following the same general course of history as our own, Amalie excused herself and went to bed. This was long past midnight. Michaels and I kept on talking. I had not seen him so excited before. It was as if that last subject, or some particular word, had opened a door for him. Finally he got up, refilled our whisky glasses with a motion not altogether steady, and walked across the living room (noiseless on that deep green carpet) to the picture window.

The night was clear and sharp. We overlooked the city, streaks and webs and coils of glittering color, ruby, amethyst, emerald, topaz, and the dark sheet of Lake Michigan; almost it seemed we could glimpse endless white plains beyond. But overhead arched the sky, crystal black, where the Great Bear stood on his tail and Orion went striding along the Milky Way. I had not often seen so big and frosty a view.

"After all," he said, "I know what I'm talking about."

I stirred, deep in my armchair. The fire on the hearth spat tiny blue flames. Besides this, only one shaded lamp lit the room, so that the star swarms had also been visible to me when I passed by the window earlier. I gibed a little. "Personally?"

He glanced back toward me. His face was stiff. "What would you say if I answered yes?"

I sipped my drink. King's Ransom is a noble and comforting brew, most especially when the Earth itself seems to tone with a deepening chill. "I'd suppose you had your reasons and wait to see what they were."

He grinned one-sidedly. "Oh, well, I'm from this planet too," he said. "And yet—yet the sky is so wide and strange, don't you think the strangeness would affect men who went there? Wouldn't it seep into them, so they carried it back in their bones, and Earth was never quite the same afterward?"

"Go on. You know I like fantasies."

He stared outward, and then back again, and suddenly he tossed off his drink. The violent gesture was unlike him. But so had his hesitation been.

He said in a harsh tone, with all the former accent: "Okay, then, I shall tell you a fantasy. It is a story for winter, though, a cold story, that you are best advised not to take so serious."

I drew on the excellent cigar he had given me and waited in the silence he needed.

He paced a few times back and forth before the window, eyes to the floor, until he filled his glass anew and sat down near me. He didn't look at me but at a picture on the wall, a somber, unintelligible thing which no one else liked. He seemed to get strength from it, for he began talking, fast and softly.

"Once upon a time, a very, very long time in the future, there was a civilization. I shall not describe it to you, for that would not be possible. Could you go back to the time of the Egyptian pyramid builders and tell them about this city below us? I don't mean they wouldn't believe you; of course they wouldn't, but that hardly matters. I mean they would not understand. Nothing you said could make sense to them.

And the way people work and think and believe would be less comprehensible than those lights and towers and machines. Not so? If I spoke to you of people in the future living among great blinding energies, and of genetic changelings, and imaginary wars, and talking stones, and a certain blind hunter, you might feel anything at all, but you would not understand.

"So I ask you only to imagine how many thousands of times this planet has circled the sun, how deeply buried and forgotten we are; and then also to imagine that this other civilization thinks in patterns so foreign that it has ignored every limitation of logic and natural law, to discover means of traveling in time. So, while the ordinary dweller in that age (I can't exactly call him a citizen, or anything else for which we have a word, because it would be too misleading)—the average educated dweller knows in a vague, uninterested way that millenia ago some semi-savages were the first to split the atom—only one or two men have actually been here, walked among us, studied and mapped us and returned with a file of information for the central brain, if I may call it by such a name. No one else is concerned with us, any more than you are concerned with early Mesopotamian archeology. You see?"

He dropped his gaze to the tumbler in his hand and held it there, as if the whisky was an oracular pool. The silence grew. At last I said, "Very well. For the sake of the story, I'll accept the premise. I imagine time travelers would be unnoticeable. They'd have techniques of disguise and so on. Wouldn't want to change their own past."

"Oh, no danger of that," he said. "It's only that they couldn't learn much if they went around insisting they were from the future. Just imagine."

I chuckled.

Michaels gave me a shadowed look. "Apart from the scientific," he said, "can you guess what use there might be for time travel?"

"Well," I suggested, "trade in objects of art or natural resources. Go back to the dinosaur age and dig up iron before man appeared to strip the richest mines."

He shook his head. "Think again. They'd only want a limited number of Minoan statuettes, Ming vases, or Third World Hegemony dwarfs, chiefly for their museums. If 'museum' isn't too inaccurate a word. I tell you, they are *not* like us. As for natural resources, they're beyond the point of needing any; they make their own."

He paused, as if before a final plunge. Then: "What was this penal colony the French abandoned?"

"Devil's Island?"

"Yes, that was it. Can you imagine a better revenge on a condemned criminal than to maroon him in the past?"

"Why, I should think they'd be above any concept of revenge, or even of deterrence by horrible examples. Even in this century, we're aware that that doesn't work."

"Are you sure?" he asked quietly. "Side by side with the growth of today's enlightened penology, haven't we a corresponding growth of crime itself? You were wondering, some time ago, how I dared walk the night streets alone. Furthermore, punishment is a catharsis of society as a whole. Up in the future they'd tell you that public hangings did reduce the crime rate, which would otherwise have been still higher. Somewhat more important, these spectacles made possible the eighteenth century birth of real humanitarianism." He raised a sardonic brow. "Or so they claim in the future. It doesn't matter whether they are right, or merely rationalizing a degraded element in their own civilization. All you need assume is that they do send their very worst criminals back into the past."

"Rather rough on the past," I said.

"No, not really. For a number of reasons, including the fact that everything they cause to happen has already happened. —— Damn! English isn't built for talking about these paradoxes. Mainly, though, you must remember that they don't waste all this effort on ordinary miscreants. One has to be a very rare criminal to deserve exile in time. And the worst crime in the world depends on the particular year of the world's history. Murder, brigandage, treason, heresy, narcotics peddling, slaving, patriotism, the whole catalogue, all have rated capital punishment in some epochs, and been lightly regarded in others, and positively commended in still others. Think back and see if I'm not right."

I regarded him for a while, observing how deep the lines were in his face and recalling that at his age he shouldn't be so gray. "Very well," I said. "Agreed. But would not a man from the future, possessing all its knowledge—"

He set his glass down with audible force. "*What* knowledge?" he rapped. "Use your brains! Imagine yourself left naked and alone in Babylon. How much Babylonian language or history do you know? Who's the present king, how much longer will he reign, who'll succeed him? What are the laws and customs you must obey? You remember that eventually the Assyrians or the Persians or someone will conquer Babylon and there'll be hell to pay. But when? How? Is the current war a mere border skirmish or an all-out struggle? If the latter, is Babylon going to win? If not, what peace terms will be imposed? Why, there wouldn't be twenty men today who could answer those questions without looking up the answers in a book. And you're not one of them; nor have you been given a book."

"I think," I said slowly, "I'd head for the nearest temple, once I'd picked up enough of the language. I'd tell the priest I could make —— oh —— fireworks—"

He laughed, with small merriment. "How? You're in Babylon, remember. Where do you find sulfur and saltpeter? If you can get across to the priest what you want, and somehow persuade him to obtain the stuff for you, how do you compound a powder that'll actually go off instead of just fizzing? For your information,

that's quite an art. Hell, you couldn't even get a berth as a deckhand. You'd be lucky if you ended up scrubbing floors. A slave in the fields is a likelier career. Isn't it?"

The fire sank low.

"All right," I conceded. "True."

"They pick the era with care, you know." He looked back toward the window. Seen from our chairs, reflection on the glass blotted out the stars, so that we were only aware of the night itself.

"When a man is sentenced to banishment," he said, "all the experts confer, pointing out what the periods of their specialties would be like for this particular individual. You can see how a squeamish, intellectual type, dropped into Homeric Greece, would find it a living nightmare, whereas a rowdy type might get along fairly well—might even end up as a respected warrior. If the rowdy was not the blackest of criminals, they might actually leave him near the hall of Agamemnon, condemning him to no more than danger, discomfort, and homesickness.

"Oh, God," he whispered. "The homesickness!"

So much darkness rose in him as he spoke that I sought to steady him with a dry remark: "They must immunize the convict to every ancient disease. Otherwise this'd only be an elaborate death sentence."

His eyes focused on me again. "Yes," he said. "And of course the longevity serum is still active in his veins. That's all, however. He's dropped in an unfrequented spot after dark, the machine vanishes, he's cut off for the rest of his life. All he knows is that they've chosen an era for him with —— such characteristics —— that they expect the punishment will fit his crime."

Stillness fell once more upon us, until the clock on the mantel became the loudest thing in the world, as if all other sound had frozen to death outside. I glanced at its dial. The night was old; soon the east would be turning pale.

When I looked back, he was still watching me,

disconcertingly intent. "What was your crime?" I asked.

He didn't seem taken aback, only said wearily, "What does it matter? I told you the crimes of one age are the heroisms of another. If my attempt had succeeded, the centuries to come would have adored my name. But I failed."

"A lot of people must have got hurt," I said. "A whole world must have hated you."

"Well, yes," he said. And after a minute: "This is a fantasy I'm telling you, of course. To pass the time."

"I'm playing along with you," I smiled.

His tension eased a trifle. He leaned back, his legs stretched across that glorious carpet. "So. Given as much of the fantasy as I've related, how did you deduce the extent of my alleged guilt?"

"Your past life. When and where were you left?"

He said, in as bleak a voice as I've ever heard, "Near Warsaw, in August, 1939."

"I don't imagine you care to talk about the war years."

"No, I don't."

However, he went on when enough defiance had accumulated: "My enemies blundered. The confusion following the German attack gave me a chance to escape from police custody before I could be stuck in a concentration camp. Gradually I learned what the situation was. Of course, I couldn't predict anything. I still can't; only specialists know, or care, what happened in the twentieth century. But by the time I'd become a Polish conscript in the German forces, I realized this was the losing side. So I slipped across to the Americans, told them what I'd observed, became a scout for them. Risky—but if I'd stopped a bullet, what the hell? I didn't; and I ended up with plenty of sponsors to get me over here; and the rest of the story is conventional."

My cigar had gone out. I relit it, for Michaels' cigars were not to be taken casually. He had them especially flown from Amsterdam.

"The alien corn," I said.

"What?"

"You know. Ruth in exile. She wasn't badly treated, but she stood weeping for her homeland."

"No, I don't know that story."

"It's in the Bible."

"Ah, yes. I really must read the Bible sometime." His mood was changing by the moment, toward the assurance I had first encountered. He swallowed his whisky with a gesture almost debonair. His expression was alert and confident.

"Yes," he said, "that aspect was pretty bad. Not so much the physical conditions of life. You've doubtless gone camping and noticed how soon you stop missing hot running water, electric lights, all the gadgets that their manufacturers assure us are absolute necessities. I'd be glad of a gravity reducer or a cell stimulater if I had one, but I get along fine without. The homesickness, though, that's what eats you. Little things you never noticed, some particular food, the way people walk, the games played, the small-talk topics. Even the constellations. They're different in the future. The sun has traveled that far in its galactic orbit.

"But, voluntary or forced, people have always been emigrating. We're all descended from those who could stand the shock. I adapted."

A scowl crossed his brows. "I wouldn't go back now even if I were given a free pardon," he said, "the way those traitors are running things."

I finished my own drink, tasting it with my whole tongue and palate, for it was a marvelous whisky, and listened to him with only half an ear. "You like it here?"

"Yes," he said. "By now I do. I'm over the emotional hump. Being so busy the first few years just staying alive, and then so busy establishing myself after I came to this country, that helped. I never had much time for self-pity. Now my business interests me more and more, a fascinating game, and pleasantly free of extreme penalties for wrong moves. I've discovered qualities here that the future has lost —— I'll bet you have no idea how exotic this city is. Think. At this moment, within five miles of us, there's a soldier on guard at an atomic laboratory, a bum freezing in a doorway, an orgy in a millionaire's apartment, a priest making ready for sunrise rites, a merchant from Araby, a spy from Muscovy, a ship from the Indies ——"

His excitement softened. He looked from the window and the night, inward, toward the bedrooms. "And my wife and kids," he finished, most gently. "No, I wouldn't go back, no matter what happened."

I took a final breath of my cigar. "You *have* done rather well."

Liberated from his gray mood, he grinned at me. "You know, I think you believe that yarn."

"Oh, I do." I stubbed out the cigar, rose, and stretched. "The hour is late. We'd better be going."

He didn't notice at once. When he did, he came out of his chair like a big cat. "*We?*"

"Of course." I drew a nerve gun from my pocket. He stopped in his tracks. "This sort of thing isn't left to chance. We check up. Come along, now."

The blood drained from his face. "No," he mouthed, "no, no, no, you can't, it isn't fair, not to Amalie, the children—"

"That," I told him, "is part of the punishment."

I left him in Damascus, the year before Tamerlane sacked it.

THE CASK OF AMONTILLADO

Edgar Allan Poe

The thousand injuries of Fortunato I had borne as I best could, but when he ventured upon insult I vowed revenge. You, who so well know the nature of my soul, will not suppose, however, that I gave utterance to a threat. *At length* I would be avenged; this was a point definitely settled—but the very definitiveness with which it was resolved precluded the idea of risk. I must not only punish but punish with impunity. A wrong is unredressed when retribution overtakes its redresser. It is equally unredressed when the avenger fails to make himself felt as such to him who has done the wrong.

It must be understood that neither by word nor deed had I given Fortunato cause to doubt my good will. I continued, as was my wont, to smile in his face, and he did not perceive that my smile *now* was at the thought of his immolation.

He had a weak point—this Fortunato—although in other regards he was a man to be respected and even feared. He prided himself on his connoisseurship in wine. Few Italians have the true virtuoso spirit. For the most part their enthusiasm is adopted to suit the time and opportunity, to practise imposture upon the British and Austrian *millionaires*. In painting and gemmary, Fortunato, like his countrymen, was a quack, but in the matter of old wines he was sincere. In this respect I did not differ

— "*The Cask of Amontillado*" by Edgar Allan Poe, reprinted from *Selected Writings of Edgar Allan Poe*, edited by Edward H. Davidson and published by Houghton Mifflin Company, Boston, The Riverside Press, Cambridge; reprinted with the kind permission of the publisher

from him materially; —I was skilful in the Italian vintages myself, and bought largely whenever I could.

It was about dusk, one evening during the supreme madness of the carnival season, that I encountered my friend. He accosted me with excessive warmth, for he had been drinking much. The man wore motley. He had on a tight-fitting parti-striped dress, and his head was surmounted by the conical cap and bells. I was so pleased to see him that I thought I should never have done wringing his hand.

I said to him—"My dear Fortunato, you are luckily met. How remarkably well you are looking to-day. But I have received a pipe of what passes for Amontillado, and I have my doubts."

"How?" said he. "Amontillado? A pipe? Impossible! And in the middle of the carnival!"

"I have my doubts," I replied; "and I was silly enough to pay the full Amontillado price without consulting you in the matter. You were not to be found, and I was fearful of losing a bargain."

"Amontillado!"

"I have my doubts."

"Amontillado!"

"And I must satisfy them."

"Amontillado!"

"As you are engaged, I am on my way to Luchresi. If any one has a critical turn, it is he. He will tell me ——"

"Luchresi cannot tell Amontillado from Sherry."

"And yet some fools will have it that his taste is a match for your own."

"Come, let us go."

"Whither?"

"To your vaults."

"My friend, no; I will not impose upon your good nature. I perceive you have an engagement. Luchresi ——"

"I have no engagement;—come."

"My friend, no. It is not the engagement, but the severe cold with which I perceive you are afflicted. The vaults are insufferably damp. They are encrusted with nitre."

"Let us go, nevertheless. The cold is merely nothing. Amontillado! You have been imposed upon. And as for Luchresi, he cannot distinguish Sherry from Amontillado."

Thus speaking, Fortunato possessed himself of my arm; and putting on a mask of black silk and drawing a *roquelaire* closely about my person, I suffered him to hurry me to my palazzo.

There were no attendants at home; they had absconded to make merry in honour of the time. I had told them that I should not return until the morning, and had given them explicit orders not to stir from the house. These orders were sufficient, I well knew, to insure their immediate disappearance, one and all, as soon as my back was turned.

I took from their sconces two flambeaux, and giving one to Fortunato, bowed him through several suites of rooms to the archway that led into the vaults. I passed down a long and winding staircase, requesting him to be cautious as he followed. We came at length to the foot of the descent, and stood together on the damp ground of the catacombs of the Montresors.

The gait of my friend was unsteady, and the bells upon his cap jingled as he strode.

"The pipe?" said he.

"It is farther on," said I; "but observe the white web-work which gleams from these cavern walls."

He turned towards me, and looked into my eyes with two filmy orbs that distilled the rheum of intoxication.

"Nitre?" he asked, at length.

"Nitre," I replied. "How long have you had that cough?"

"Ugh! ugh! ugh!—ugh! ugh! ugh!—ugh! ugh! ugh! ugh! ugh!—ugh! ugh! ugh!"

My poor friend found it impossible to reply for many minutes.

"It is nothing," he said, at last.

"Come," I said, with decision, "we will go back; your health is precious. You are rich, respected, admired, beloved; you are happy, as once I was. You are a man to be missed. For

254

me it is no matter. We will go back; you will be ill, and I cannot be responsible. Besides, there is Luchresi ———"

"Enough," he said; "the cough is a mere nothing; it will not kill me. I shall not die of a cough." *Understatement (irony)*

"True—true," I replied; "and, indeed, I had no intention of alarming you unnecessarily— but you should use all proper caution. A draught of this Medoc will defend us from the damps."

Here I knocked off the neck of a bottle which I drew from a long row of its fellows that lay upon the mould.

"Drink," I said, presenting him the wine.

He raised it to his lips with a leer. He paused and nodded to me familiarly, while his bells jingled.

"I drink," he said, "to the buried that repose around us."

"And I to your long life."

He again took my arm, and we proceeded.

"These vaults," he said, "are extensive."

"The Montresors," I replied, "were a great and numerous family."

"I forget your arms."

"A huge human foot d'or, in a field azure; the foot crushes a serpent rampant whose fangs are imbedded in the heel."

"And the motto?"

"*Nemo me impune lacessit.*"

"Good!" he said.

The wine sparkled in his eyes and the bells jingled. My own fancy grew warm with the Medoc. We had passed through long walls of piled skeletons, with casks and puncheons inter- mingling, into the inmost recesses of the cata- combs. I paused again, and this time I made bold to seize Fortunato by an arm above the elbow.

"The nitre!" I said; "see, it increases. It hangs like moss upon the vaults. We are below the river's bed. The drops of moisture trickle among the bones. Come, we will go back ere it is too late. Your cough ———"

"It is nothing," he said; "let us go on. But first, another draught of the Medoc."

I broke and reached him a flagon of De Grâve. He emptied it at a breath. His eyes flashed with a fierce light. He laughed and threw the bottle upward with a gesticulation I did not understand.

I looked at him in surprise. He repeated the movement—a grotesque one.

"You do not comprehend?" he said.

"Not I," I replied.

"Then you are not of the brotherhood."

"How?"

"You are not of the masons."

"Yes, yes," I said; "yes, yes."

"You? Impossible! A mason?"

"A mason," I replied.

"A sign," he said, "a sign."

"It is this," I answered, producing from be- neath the folds of my *roquelaire* a trowel.

"You jest," he exclaimed, recoiling a few paces. "But let us proceed to the Amontillado."

"Be it so," I said, replacing the tool beneath the cloak and again offering him my arm. He leaned upon it heavily. We continued our route in search of the Amontillado. We passed through a range of low arches, descended, passed on, and descending again, arrived at a deep crypt, in which the foulness of the air caused our flam- beaux rather to glow than flame.

At the most remote end of the crypt there appeared another less spacious. Its walls had been lined with human remains, piled to the vault overhead, in the fashion of the great cata- combs of Paris. Three sides of this interior crypt were still ornamented in this manner. From the fourth the bones had been thrown down, and lay promiscuously upon the earth, forming at one point a mound of some size. Within the wall thus exposed by the displacing of the bones, we perceived a still interior crypt or recess, in depth about four feet, in width three, in height six or seven. It seemed to have been constructed for no especial use within it- self, but formed merely the interval between two of the colossal supports of the roof of the cata- combs, and was backed by one of their circum- scribing walls of solid granite.

It was in vain that Fortunato, uplifting his dull torch, endeavoured to pry into the depth of the recess. Its termination the feeble light did not enable us to see.

"Proceed," I said; "herein is the Amontillado. As for Luchresi ——"

"He is an ignoramus," interrupted my friend, as he stepped unsteadily forward, while I followed immediately at his heels. In an instant he had reached the extremity of the niche, and finding his progress arrested by the rock, stood stupidly bewildered. A moment more and I had fettered him to the granite. In its surface were two iron staples, distant from each other about two feet, horizontally. From one of these depended a short chain, from the other a padlock. Throwing the links about his waist, it was but the work of a few seconds to secure it. He was too much astounded to resist. Withdrawing the key I stepped back from the recess.

"Pass your hand," I said, "over the wall; you cannot help feeling the nitre. Indeed it is *very* damp. Once more let me *implore* you to return. No? Then I must positively leave you. But I must first render you all the little attentions in my power."

"The Amontillado!" ejaculated my friend, not yet recovered from his astonishment.

"True," I replied; "the Amontillado."

As I said these words I busied myself among the pile of bones of which I have before spoken. Throwing them aside, I soon uncovered a quantity of building stone and mortar. With these materials and with the aid of my trowel, I began vigorously to wall up the entrance of the niche.

I had scarcely laid the first tier of the masonry when I discovered that the intoxication of Fortunato had in a great measure worn off. The earliest indication I had of this was a low moaning cry from the depth of the recess. It was *not* the cry of a drunken man. There was then a long and obstinate silence. I laid the second tier, and the third, and the fourth; and then I heard the furious vibrations of the chain. The noise lasted for several minutes, during which, that I might hearken to it with the more

satisfaction, I ceased my labours and sat down upon the bones. When at last the clanking subsided, I resumed the trowel, and finished without interruption the fifth, the sixth, and the seventh tier. The wall was now nearly upon a level with my breast. I again paused, and holding the flambeaux over the mason-work, threw a few feeble rays upon the figure within.

A succession of loud and shrill screams, bursting suddenly from the throat of the chained form, seemed to thrust me violently back. For a brief moment I hesitated, I trembled. Unsheathing my rapier, I began to grope with it about the recess; but the thought of an instant reassured me. I placed my hand upon the solid fabric of the catacombs, and felt satisfied. I reapproached the wall. I replied to the yells of him who clamoured. I re-echoed, I aided, I surpassed them in volume and in strength. I did this, and the clamourer grew still.

It was now midnight, and my task was drawing to a close. I had completed the eighth, the ninth, and the tenth tier. I had finished a portion of the last and the eleventh; there remained but a single stone to be fitted and plastered in. I struggled with its weight; I placed it partially in its destined position. But now there came from out the niche a low laugh that erected the hairs upon my head. It was succeeded by a sad voice, which I had difficulty in recognizing as that of the noble Fortunato. The voice said—

"Ha! ha! ha!—he! he! he!—a very good joke, indeed—an excellent jest. We will have many a rich laugh about it at the palazzo—he! he! he!—over our wine—he! he! he!"

"The Amontillado!" I said.

"He! he! he!—he! he! he!—yes, the Amontillado. But is it not getting late? Will not they be awaiting us at the palazzo, the Lady Fortunato and the rest? Let us be gone."

"Yes," I said, "let us be gone."

"*For the love of God, Montresor!*"

"Yes," I said, "for the love of God!"

But to these words I hearkened in vain for a reply. I grew impatient. I called aloud—

"Fortunato!"

No answer. I called again—

"Fortunato!"

No answer still. I thrust a torch through the remaining aperture and let it fall within. There came forth in return only a jingling of the bells. My heart grew sick; it was the dampness of the catacombs that made it so. I hastened to make an end of my labour. I forced the last stone into its position; I plastered it up. Against the new masonry I re-erected the old rampart of bones. For the half of a century no mortal has disturbed them. *In pace requiescat!*

THE KILLERS

Ernest Hemingway

The door of Henry's lunch-room opened and two men came in. They sat down at the counter.

"What's yours?" George asked them.

"I don't know," one of the men said. "What do you want to eat, Al?"

"I don't know," said Al. "I don't know what I want to eat."

Outside it was getting dark. The street-light came on outside the window. The two men at the counter read the menu. From the other end of the counter Nick Adams watched them. He had been talking to George when they came in.

"I'll have a roast pork tenderloin with apple sauce and mashed potatoes," the first man said.

"It isn't ready yet."

"What the hell do you put it on the card for?"

"That's the dinner," George explained. "You can get that at six o'clock."

George looked at the clock on the wall behind the counter.

"It's five o'clock."

"The clock says twenty minutes past five," the second man said.

"It's twenty minutes fast."

"Oh, to hell with the clock," the first man said. "What have you got to eat?"

"I can give you any kind of sandwiches," George said. "You can have ham and eggs, bacon and eggs, liver and bacon, or a steak."

"Give me chicken croquettes with green peas and cream sauce and mashed potatoes."

"That's the dinner."

"Everything we want's the dinner, eh? That's the way you work it."

"I can give you ham and eggs, bacon and eggs, liver——"

"I'll take ham and eggs," the man called Al said. He wore a derby hat and a black overcoat buttoned across the chest. His face was small and white and he had tight lips. He wore a silk muffler and gloves.

"Give me bacon and eggs," said the other man. He was about the same size as Al. Their faces were different, but they were dressed like twins. Both wore overcoats too tight for them. They sat leaning forward, their elbows on the counter.

"Got anything to drink?" Al asked.

"Silver beer, bevo, ginger-ale," George said.

"I mean you got anything to *drink*?"

"Just those I said."

"This is a hot town," said the other. "What do they call it?"

"Summit."

"Ever hear of it?" Al asked his friend.

"No," said the friend.

"What do you do here nights?" Al asked.

"They eat the dinner," his friend said. "They all come here and eat the big dinner."

"That's right," George said.

"So you think that's right?" Al asked George.

"Sure."

"You're a pretty bright boy, aren't you?"

"Sure," said George.

"Well, you're not," said the other little man. "Is he, Al?"

"He's dumb," said Al. He turned to Nick. "What's your name?"

"Adams."

"Another bright boy," Al said. "Ain't he a bright boy, Max?"

"The town's full of bright boys," Max said.

George put the two platters, one of ham and eggs, the other of bacon and eggs, on the counter. He set down two side-dishes of fried potatoes and closed the wicket into the kitchen.

"Which is yours?" he asked Al.

"Don't you remember?"

"Ham and eggs."

"Just a bright boy," Max said. He leaned forward and took the ham and eggs. Both men ate with their gloves on. George watched them eat.

"What are *you* looking at?" Max looked at George.

"Nothing."

"The hell you were. You were looking at me."

"Maybe the boy meant it for a joke, Max," Al said.

George laughed.

"*You* don't have to laugh," Max said to him. "*You* don't have to laugh at all, see?"

"All right," said George.

"So he thinks it's all right." Max turned to Al. "He thinks it's all right. That's a good one."

"Oh, he's a thinker," Al said. They went on eating.

"What's the bright boy's name down the counter?" Al asked Max.

"Hey, bright boy," Max said to Nick. "You go around on the other side of the counter with your boy friend."

"What's the idea?" Nick asked.

"There isn't any idea."

"You better go around, bright boy," Al said. Nick went around behind the counter.

"What's the idea?" George asked.

"None of your damn business," Al said. "Who's out in the kitchen?"

"The nigger."

"What do you mean the nigger?"

"The nigger that cooks."

"Tell him to come in."

"What's the idea?"

"Tell him to come in."

"Where do you think you are?"

"We know damn well where we are," the man called Max said. "Do we look silly?"

"You talk silly," Al said to him. "What the hell do you argue with this kid for? Listen," he said to George, "tell the nigger to come out here."

"What are you going to do to him?"

"Nothing. Use your head, bright boy. What would we do to a nigger?"

George opened the slit that opened back into the kitchen. "Sam," he called. "Come in here a minute."

The door to the kitchen opened and the nigger came in. "What was it?" he asked. The two men at the counter took a look at him.

"All right, nigger. You stand right there," Al said.

Sam, the nigger, standing in his apron, looked at the two men sitting at the counter. "Yes, sir," he said. Al got down from his stool.

"I'm going back to the kitchen with the nigger and bright boy," he said. "Go on back to the kitchen, nigger. You go with him, bright boy." The little man walked after Nick and Sam, the cook, back into the kitchen. The door shut after them. The man called Max sat at the counter opposite George. He didn't look at George but looked in the mirror that ran along back of the counter. Henry's had been made over from a saloon into a lunch-counter.

"Well, bright boy," Max said, looking into the mirror, "why don't you say something?"

"What's it all about?"

"Hey, Al," Max called, "bright boy wants to know what it's all about."

"Why don't you tell him?" Al's voice came from the kitchen.

"What do you think it's all about?"

"I don't know."

"What do you think?"

Max looked into the mirror all the time he was talking.

"I wouldn't say."

"Hey, Al, bright boy says he wouldn't say what he thinks it's all about."

"I can hear you, all right," Al said from the kitchen. He had propped open the slit that dishes passed through into the kitchen with a catsup bottle. "Listen, bright boy," he said from the kitchen to George. "Stand a little further along the bar. You move a little to the left, Max." He was like a photographer arranging for a group picture.

"Talk to me, bright boy," Max said. "What do you think's going to happen?"

George did not say anything.

"I'll tell you," Max said. "We're going to kill a Swede. Do you know a big Swede named Ole Andreson?"

"Yes."

"He comes here to eat every night, don't he?"

"Sometimes he comes here."

"He comes here at six o'clock, don't he?"

"If he comes."

"We know all that, bright boy," Max said. "Talk about something else. Ever go to the movies?"

"Once in a while."

"You ought to go to the movies more. The movies are fine for a bright boy like you."

"What are you going to kill Ole Andreson for? What did he ever do to you?"

"He never had a chance to do anything to us. He never even seen us."

"And he's only going to see us once," Al said from the kitchen.

"What are you going to kill him for, then?" George asked.

"We're killing him for a friend. Just to oblige a friend, bright boy."

"Shut up," said Al from the kitchen. "You talk too goddam much."

"Well, I got to keep bright boy amused. Don't I, bright boy?"

"You talk too damn much," Al said. "The nigger and my bright boy are amused by themselves. I got them tied up like a couple of girl-friends in the convent."

"I suppose you were in a convent?"

"You never know."

"You were in a kosher convent. That's where you were."

George looked up at the clock.

"If anybody comes in you tell them the cook is off, and if they keep after it, you tell them you'll go back and cook yourself. Do you get that, bright boy?"

"All right," George said. "What you going to do with us afterward?"

"That'll depend," Max said. "That's one of those things you never know at the time."

George looked up at the clock. It was a quarter past six. The door from the street opened. A street-car motorman came in.

"Hello, George," he said. "Can I get supper?"

"Sam's gone out," George said. "He'll be back in about half an hour."

"I'd better go up the street," the motorman said. George looked at the clock. It was twenty minutes past six.

"That was nice, bright boy," Max said. "You're a regular little gentleman."

"He knew I'd blow his head off," Al said from the kitchen.

"No," said Max. "It ain't that. Bright boy is nice. He's a nice boy. I like him."

At six-fifty-five George said: "He's not coming."

Two other people had been in the lunch-room. Once George had gone out to the kitchen and made a ham-and-egg sandwich "to go" that a man wanted to take with him. Inside the kitchen he saw Al, his derby hat tipped back, sitting on a stool beside the wicket with the muzzle of a sawed-off shotgun resting on the ledge. Nick and the cook were back to back in the corner, a towel tied in each of their mouths. George had cooked the sandwich, wrapped it up in oiled paper, put it in a bag, brought it in, and the man had paid for it and gone out.

"Bright boy can do everything," Max said. "He can cook and everything. You'd make some girl a nice wife, bright boy."

"Yes?" George said. "Your friend, Ole Andreson, isn't going to come."

"We'll give him ten minutes," Max said.

Max watched the mirror and the clock. The hands of the clock marked seven o'clock, and then five minutes past seven.

"Come on, Al," said Max. "We better go. He's not coming."

"Better give him five minutes," Al said from the kitchen.

In the five minutes a man came in, and George explained that the cook was sick.

"Why the hell don't you get another cook?" the man asked. "Aren't you running a lunch-counter?" He went out.

"Come on, Al," Max said.

"What about the two bright boys and the nigger?"

"They're all right."

"You think so?"

"Sure. We're through with it."

"I don't like it," said Al. "It's sloppy. You talk too much."

"Oh, what the hell," said Max. "We got to keep amused, haven't we?"

"You talk too much, all the same," Al said. He came out from the kitchen. The cut-off barrels of the shotgun made a slight bulge under the waist of his too tight-fitting overcoat. He straightened his coat with his gloved hands.

"So long, bright boy," he said to George. "You got a lot of luck."

"That's the truth," Max said. "You ought to play the races, bright boy."

The two of them went out the door. George watched them, through the window, pass under the arc-light and cross the street. In their tight overcoats and derby hats they looked like a vaudeville team. George went back through the swinging-door into the kitchen and untied Nick and the cook.

"I don't want any more of that," said Sam, the cook. "I don't want any more of that."

Nick stood up. He had never had a towel in his mouth before.

"Say," he said. "What the hell?" He was trying to swagger it off.

"They were going to kill Ole Andreson," George said. "They were going to shoot him when he came in to eat."

"Ole Andreson?"

"Sure."

The cook felt the corners of his mouth with his thumbs.

"They all gone?" he asked.

"Yeah," said George. "They're gone now."

"I don't like it," said the cook. "I don't like any of it at all."

"Listen," George said to Nick. "You better go see Ole Andreson."

"All right."

"You better not have anything to do with it at all," Sam, the cook, said. "You better stay way out of it."

"Don't go if you don't want to," George said.

"Mixing up in this ain't going to get you anywhere," the cook said. "You stay out of it."

"I'll go see him," Nick said to George. "Where does he live?"

The cook turned away.

"Little boys always know what they want to do," he said.

"He lives up at Hirsch's rooming-house," George said to Nick.

"I'll go up there."

Outside the arc-light shone through the bare branches of a tree. Nick walked up the street beside the car-tracks and turned at the next arc-light down a side-street. Three houses up the street was Hirsch's rooming-house. Nick walked up the two steps and pushed the bell. A woman came to the door.

"Is Ole Andreson here?"

"Do you want to see him?"

"Yes, if he's in."

Nick followed the woman up a flight of stairs and back to the end of a corridor. She knocked on the door.

"Who is it?"

"It's somebody to see you, Mr. Andreson," the woman said.

"It's Nick Adams."

"Come in."

Nick opened the door and went into the room. Ole Andreson was lying on the bed with all his clothes on. He had been a heavyweight prizefighter and he was too long for the bed. He lay with his head on two pillows. He did not look at Nick.

"What was it?" he asked.

"I was up at Henry's," Nick said, "and two fellows came in and tied up me and the cook, and they said they were going to kill you."

It sounded silly when he said it. Ole Andreson said nothing.

"They put us out in the kitchen," Nick went on. "They were going to shoot you when you came in to supper."

Ole Andreson looked at the wall and did not say anything.

"George thought I better come and tell you about it."

"There isn't anything I can do about it," Ole Andreson said.

"I'll tell you what they were like."

"I don't want to know what they were like," Ole Andreson said. He looked at the wall. "Thanks for coming to tell me about it."

"That's all right."

Nick looked at the big man lying on the bed.

"Don't you want me to go and see the police?"

"No," Ole Andreson said. "That wouldn't do any good."

"Isn't there something I could do?"

"No. There ain't anything to do."

"Maybe it was just a bluff."

"No. It ain't just a bluff."

Ole Andreson rolled over toward the wall.

"The only thing is," he said, talking toward the wall, "I just can't make up my mind to go out. I been in here all day."

"Couldn't you get out of town?"

"No," Ole Andreson said. "I'm through with all that running around."

He looked at the wall.

"There ain't anything to do now."

"Couldn't you fix it up some way?"

"No. I got in wrong." He talked in the same flat voice. "There ain't anything to do. After a while I'll make up my mind to go out."

"I better go back and see George," Nick said.

"So long," said Ole Andreson. He did not look toward Nick. "Thanks for coming around."

Nick went out. As he shut the door he saw Ole Andreson with all his clothes on, lying on the bed looking at the wall.

"He's been in his room all day," the land-lady said down-stairs. "I guess he don't feel well. I said to him: 'Mr. Andreson, you ought to go out and take a walk on a nice fall day like this,' but he didn't feel like it."

"He doesn't want to go out."

"I'm sorry he don't feel well," the woman said. "He's an awfully nice man. He was in the ring, you know."

"I know it."

"You'd never know it except from the way his face is," the woman said. They stood talking just inside the street door. "He's just as gentle."

"Well, good-night, Mrs. Hirsch," Nick said.

"I'm not Mrs. Hirsch," the woman said. "She owns the place. I just look after it for her. I'm Mrs. Bell."

"Well, good-night, Mrs. Bell," Nick said.

"Good-night," the woman said.

Nick walked up the dark street to the corner under the arc-light, and then along the car-tracks to Henry's eating-house. George was inside, back of the counter.

"Did you see Ole?"

"Yes," said Nick. "He's in his room and he won't go out."

The cook opened the door from the kitchen when he heard Nick's voice.

"I don't even listen to it," he said and shut the door.

"Did you tell him about it?" George asked.

"Sure. I told him but he knows what it's all about."

"What's he going to do?"

"Nothing."

"They'll kill him."

"I guess they will."

"He must have got mixed up in something in Chicago."

"I guess so," said Nick.

"It's a hell of a thing."

"It's an awful thing," Nick said.

They did not say anything. George reached down for a towel and wiped the counter.

"I wonder what he did?" Nick said.

"Double-crossed somebody. That's what they kill them for."

"I'm going to get out of this town," Nick said.

"Yes," said George. "That's a good thing to do."

"I can't stand to think about him waiting in the room and knowing he's going to get it. It's too damned awful."

"Well," said George, "you better not think about it."

THE INTERLOPERS

Saki

In a forest of mixed growth somewhere on the eastern spurs of the Carpathians, a man stood one winter night watching and listening, as though he waited for some beast of the woods to come within the range of his vision, and, later, of his rifle. But the game for whose presence he kept so keen an outlook was none that figured in the sportsman's calendar as lawful and proper for the chase; Ulrich von Gradwitz patrolled the dark forest in quest of a human enemy.

The forest lands of Gradwitz were of wide extent and well stocked with game; the narrow strip of precipitous woodland that lay on its outskirt was not remarkable for the game it harboured or the shooting it afforded, but it was the most jealously guarded of all its owner's territorial possessions. A famous lawsuit, in the days of his grandfather, had wrested it from the illegal possession of a neighbouring family of petty landowners; the dispossessed party had never acquiesced in the judgment of the Courts, and a long series of poaching affrays and similar scandals had embittered the relationships between the families for three generations. The neighbour feud had grown into a personal one since Ulrich had come to be head of his family; if there was a man in the world whom he detested and wished ill to it was Georg Znaeym, the inheritor of the quarrel and the tireless game-snatcher and raider of the disputed border-forest. The feud might, perhaps, have died down or been compromised if the personal ill-will of the two men had not stood in the way; as boys they had thirsted for one another's blood, as men each prayed that misfortune

— *"The Interlopers" by Saki (H. H. Munro), from The Short Stories of Saki; copyright 1930 by The Viking Press, Inc.*

262

might fall on the other, and this wind-scourged winter night Ulrich had banded together his foresters to watch the dark forest, not in quest of four-footed quarry, but to keep a look-out for the prowling thieves whom he suspected of being afoot from across the land boundary. The roe-buck, which usually kept in the sheltered hollows during a storm-wind, were running like driven things tonight, and there was movement and unrest among the creatures that were wont to sleep through the dark hours. Assuredly there was a disturbing element in the forest, and Ulrich could guess the quarter from whence it came.

He strayed away by himself from the watchers whom he had placed in ambush on the crest of the hill, and wandered far down the steep slopes amid the wild tangle of undergrowth, peering through the tree-trunks and listening through the whistling and skirling of the wind and the restless beating of the branches for sight or sound of the marauders. If only on this wild night, in this dark, lone spot, he might come across Georg Znaeym, man to man, with none to witness— that was the wish that was uppermost in his thoughts. And as he stepped round the trunk of a huge beech he came face to face with the man he sought.

The two enemies stood glaring at one another for a long silent moment. Each had a rifle in his hand, each had hate in his heart and murder uppermost in his mind. The chance had come to give full play to the passions of a lifetime. But a man who has been brought up under the code of a restraining civilization cannot easily nerve himself to shoot down his neighbour in cold blood and without word spoken, except for an offence against his hearth and honour. And before the moment of hesitation had given way to action a deed of Nature's own violence over-whelmed them both. A fierce shriek of the storm had been answered by a splitting crash over their heads, and ere they could leap aside a mass of falling beech tree had thundered down on them. Ulrich von Gradwitz found himself stretched on the ground, one arm numb beneath

him and the other held almost as helplessly in a tight tangle of forked branches, while both legs were pinned beneath the fallen mass. His heavy shooting-boots had saved his feet from being crushed to pieces, but if his fractures were not as serious as they might have been, at least it was evident that he could not move from his present position till someone came to release him. The descending twigs had slashed the skin of his face, and he had to wink away some drops of blood from his eyelashes before he could take in a general view of the disaster. At his side, so near that under ordinary circum-stances he could almost have touched him, lay Georg Znaeym, alive and struggling, but ob-viously as helplessly pinioned down as himself. All round them lay a thick-strewn wreckage of splintered branches and broken twigs.

Relief at being alive and exasperation at his captive plight brought a strange medley of pious thank-offerings and sharp curses to Ulrich's lips. Georg, who was nearly blinded with the blood which trickled across his eyes, stopped his struggling for a moment to listen, and then gave a short, snarling laugh.

"So you're not killed, as you ought to be, but you're caught, anyway," he cried; "caught fast. Ho, what a jest, Ulrich von Gradwitz snared in his stolen forest. There's real justice for you!"

And he laughed again, mockingly and sa-vagely.

"I'm caught in my own forest-land," retorted Ulrich. "When my men come to release us you will wish, perhaps, that you were in a better plight than caught poaching on a neighbour's land, shame on you."

Georg was silent for a moment; then he answered quietly:

"Are you sure that your men will find much to release? I have men, too, in the forest tonight, close behind me, and *they* will be here first and do the releasing. When they drag me out from under these damned branches it won't need much clumsiness on their part to roll this mass of trunk right over on the top of you. Your men will find you dead under a fallen beech tree. For form's sake I shall send my condolences to your family."

"It is a useful hint," said Ulrich fiercely. "My men had orders to follow in ten minutes' time, seven of which must have gone by already, and when they get me out—I will remember the hint. Only as you will have met your death poaching on my lands, I don't think I can decently send any message of condolence to your family."

"Good," snarled Georg, "good. We fight this quarrel out to the death, you and I and our foresters, with no cursed interlopers to come between us. Death and damnation to you, Ulrich von Gradwitz."

"The same to you, Georg Znaeym, forest-thief, game-snatcher."

Both men spoke with the bitterness of possible defeat before them, for each knew that it might be long before his men would seek him out or find him; it was a bare matter of chance which party would arrive first on the scene.

Both had now given up the useless struggle to free themselves from the mass of wood that held them down. Ulrich limited his endeavours to an effort to bring his one partially free arm near enough to his outer coat-pocket to draw out his wine-flask. Even when he had accomplished that operation it was long before he could manage the unscrewing of the stopper or get any of the liquid down his throat. But what a Heaven-sent draught it seemed! It was an open winter, and little snow had fallen as yet, hence the captives suffered less from the cold than might have been the case at that season of the year; nevertheless, the wine was warming and reviving to the wounded man, and he looked across with something like a throb of pity to where his enemy lay, just keeping the groans of pain and weariness from crossing his lips.

"Could you reach this flask if I threw it over to you?" asked Ulrich suddenly; "there is good wine in it, and one may as well be as comfortable as one can. Let us drink, even if tonight one of us dies."

"No, I can scarcely see anything; there is so much blood caked round my eyes," said Georg, "and in any case I don't drink wine with an enemy."

Ulrich was silent for a few minutes, and lay listening to the weary screeching of the wind. An idea was slowly forming and growing in his brain, an idea that gained strength every time that he looked across at the man who was fighting so grimly against pain and exhaustion. In the pain and languor that Ulrich himself was feeling the old fierce hatred seemed to be dying down.

"Neighbour," he said presently, "do as you please if your men come first. It was a fair compact. But as for me, I've changed my mind. If my men are the first to come you shall be the first to be helped, as though you were my guest. We have quarrelled like devils all our lives over this stupid strip of forest, where the trees can't even stand upright in a breath of wind. Lying here tonight, thinking, I've come to think we've been rather fools; there are better things in life than getting the better of a boundary dispute. Neighbour, if you will help me to bury the old quarrel I—I will ask you to be my friend."

Georg Znaeym was silent for so long that Ulrich thought, perhaps, he had fainted with the pain of his injuries. Then he spoke slowly and in jerks.

"How the whole region would stare and gabble if we rode into the market-square together. No one living can remember seeing a Znaeym and a Von Gradwitz talking to one another in friendship. And what peace there would be among the forester folk if we ended our feud tonight. And if we choose to make peace among our people there is none other to interfere, no interlopers from outside. ——You would come and keep the Sylvester night beneath my roof, and I would come and feast on some high day at your castle. ——I would never fire a shot on your land, save when you invited me as a guest; and you should come and shoot with me down in the marshes where the wildfowl are. In all the countryside there are none that could hinder if we willed to make peace. I never thought to have wanted to do other than hate you all my life, but I think I have changed my mind about things too, this last half-hour. And you offered me your wine-flask. ——Ulrich von Gradwitz, I will be your friend."

For a space both men were silent, turning over in their minds the wonderful changes that this dramatic reconciliation would bring about. In the cold, gloomy forest, with the wind tearing in fitful gusts through the naked branches and whistling round the tree-trunks, they lay and waited for the help that would now bring release and succour to both parties. And each prayed a private prayer that his men might be the first to arrive, so that he might be the first to show honourable attention to the enemy that had become a friend.

Presently, as the wind dropped for a moment, Ulrich broke silence.

"Let's shout for help," he said; "in this lull our voices may carry a little way."

"They won't carry far through the trees and undergrowth," said Georg, "but we can try. Together, then."

The two raised their voices in a prolonged hunting call.

"Together again," said Ulrich a few minutes later, after listening in vain for an answering halloo.

"I heard something that time, I think," said Ulrich.

"I heard nothing but the pestilential wind," said Georg hoarsely.

There was silence again for some minutes, and then Ulrich gave a joyful cry.

"I can see figures coming through the wood. They are following in the way I came down the hillside."

Both men raised their voices in as loud a shout as they could muster.

"They hear us! They've stopped. Now they see us. They're running down the hill towards us," cried Ulrich.

"How many of them are there?" asked Georg.

"I can't see distinctly," said Ulrich; "nine or ten."

"Then they are yours," said Georg; "I had only seven out with me."

"They are making all the speed they can, brave lads," said Ulrich gladly.

"Are they your men?" asked Georg. "Are they your men?" he repeated impatiently as Ulrich did not answer.

"No," said Ulrich with a laugh, the idiotic chattering laugh of a man unstrung with hideous fear.

"Who are they?" asked Georg quickly, straining his eyes to see what the other would gladly not have seen.

"*Wolves.*"

LETTER FROM UPPER CANADA

From Thomas W. Magrath, Esq., Upper Canada, to the Rev. Thomas Radcliff, Dublin.

Erindale, Toronto, Jan. 1832.

My dear Sir,

It may be interesting to you, and useful to your friends, to have some information relative to our first agricultural attempts, and subsequent operations on our new land. My last letter, being confined to one object, omitted some details on these subjects, which I now hasten to furnish.

After having purchased our lot of seven hundred acres[1] from Government, for fifteen hundred and seventy dollars, (about £325 British,) my father, during the period of his residence in York, sent my brothers and myself to erect a log-house on our farm, of which we all took possession immediately after its completion; and when fairly lodged in that, we undertook the building of our present residence, which is a frame-house.

This dwelling is 44 feet by 33, containing

three stories; *that* under ground is 12 feet high, and built with stone and lime.

The mode of forming such a house is as follows: —

A framer, on receiving the dimensions and plan, cuts out the mortices and prepares the frame. A *Bee*, which means an assemblage of the neighbours, is then called; and a person well skilled in the business, and termed a *Boss*, takes the leadership of the active party, who, with the mere mechanical aid of a *following*, or *raising*, pole, gradually elevates the mighty bents,[2] until the tenants (connected with each other by tie beams,[3]) drop into their mortices in the sill, to which, as well as to each other, they are immediately afterwards secured by pins, and in a few hours the skeleton of the house, with its rafters, &c. is ready for shingles and clap boards.[4]

It will appear strange to you that a house could be covered in before the sides are finished; and still more so, that the cellar, or basement story, should not be excavated, nor the foundation-walls built up to the sill until the upper works are completed; but such was our course of proceeding.

At the raising of my father's house, seventy kind neighbours assisted, and worked extremely hard for an entire day, without any recompense whatever, except a plentiful dinner *al fresco*.

In a few months my brothers and I, who are tolerably handy, with the aid of two carpenters, had the *inside* finished; and we have now been nearly three years inhabiting a truly comfortable house, quite in the home fashion, except that it has the advantage of a verandah, (not

---

[1] From its local advantages, being within 18 miles of York, by the river Credit, Mr. Magrath preferred the *purchase* of this farm to the occupation of 2,000 acres *granted* to him by Government, in a wilder district. He found that the lands contiguous to roads, markets, and rivers, had been long settled; and he did not wish to go into the remote Bush. Besides, the fees on patent and settlement duties, would have amounted to *three-fourths* of the purchase money of the property he preferred. —Editor.

— *"Letter from Upper Canada" by Thomas Magrath, reprinted from* Authentic Letters from Upper Canada *edited by Thomas Radcliff and published by The Macmillan Company of Canada Limited (1953)*

[2] Bents. — Perpendicular parts of the frame.
[3] Tie Beams are those that connect the Bents.
[4] Clap Boards are those that over-lap, and form the outer covering of the frame-work. Scantling of Frame, 15 inches by 12. —Editor.

very common in Ireland,) on three sides, (supported by pillars and secured by railing,) into which we can walk from our bed-rooms, and enjoy the delightful air of the summer and autumn mornings.

This verandah is 12 feet in breadth. We pass our leisure hours in it during the fine weather, choosing the shady, and sheltered side, according to the sun, or wind; and frequently sitting there with candles until bed time; with the occasional annoyance, however, of the troublesome moskitoes;—but where can we expect to find perfect enjoyment?

When we had completed the house, we raised a barn, sixty feet by thirty-six, and eighteen feet in height, with an ice-house, root house, and summer dairy beneath it, which cost us, in cash for hired labour, only twelve dollars to a framer, and the price of some nails, worth about 2s. 10d.

We had a second *Bee* for the raising of this, which was effected in five hours, and on this occasion were able to supply our obliging neighbours, who again volunteered their valuable services, with an abundant dinner and supper in the dwelling house; and to gratify them with a little music.

The floor of this barn would surprize you, it is supported by twenty-three beams of wood, eighteen inches square—with two courses of three-inch plank over them. There is in fact as much timber in the floor alone, as would cost *you* more than a hundred pounds.

With us it is a *cheap* commodity, and it is less expensive to draw and use it in great bulk, than to send it to the saw mill to be reduced to smaller scantlings. The cause of the double flooring of thick plank is that (the timber being fresh) the grain, which would be lost through the opening joints of a single floor, may be saved, by having those joints covered by a second tier of boards.

My two brothers, James and Charles, unassisted, cut eighteen thousand shingles for the roof and laid them on, besides siding and flooring the barn—no idle hours here!

Before the house was ready for our reception, we had cleared twenty[5] acres of the land for wheat, and during the successive operations of brushing, chopping, logging, burning and fencing—my father was obliged to hire workmen.

The land has a miserable appearance when first cleared, the surface and stumps being as black as fire can render them, and these latter standing three feet high, to facilitate their being drawn out by two yoke of oxen when their roots decay, which does not take effect for seven or eight years, (according to the kind of timber) and is more tedious if the land be laid down for grass.

Our first agricultural proceedings are as rude and simple as can well be imagined. A triangular harrow, the teeth of which weigh 7 lbs. each, is dragged over the newly prepared ground; its irregular and jumping passage over the roots and loose vegetable earth, scatters the ashes of the burned timber over the entire surface; the wheat is then sown, about one bushel to the acre, and another scrape of the harrow completes the process.

On some portion of his land thus cleared, the new settler plants potatoes, turnips, pumpkins and Indian corn, merely laying the seed upon the ground, and, with a hoe, scratching a sufficient portion of earth and ashes to cover it—a luxuriant crop generally succeeds; in this district from twenty to thirty bushels of wheat per acre—the land is sown with Timothy grass and clover in the following spring, while the snow is on the ground, that it may be easily ascertained whether the seed is sown correctly.

After wheat, no other crop is taken (generally speaking) except hay, until after the removal of the roots, when the ploughs can work.

The weight of hay seldom exceeds two tons per acre, because mowing on such land is a work of difficulty; with all our care we leave much of it uncut, and frequently break our scythes.

---

[5]They have subsequently cleared about 20 acres every year, and now have for cropping 150 acres. —Editor.

To reduce the expense in harvest time, we use cradle scythes to cut *all* the grain, although they do not make quite as clean work as the sickles.

A good cradler will take down from two to three acres of wheat in a day. Gleaning is not worth the attention of even a child; the scattered grains go to the sustenance of the wild pigeons of which the flocks are sometimes *miles* in length.

By the way, I must ask you to account for a curious circumstance which results from sowing wheat on a swamp, or wherever wet lodges.

The purest seed wheat that can be procured, in such soil, becomes a kind of grain called *chesse*. Some dry land of ours produces fine *wheat*; but where there is a tendency to swamp the chesse grows, and in one spot, with us there was last year half an acre of it with very little wheat among it. Some farmers maintain that it does not proceed from wheat, but from a dormant seed; others, of whom my father is one, are of opinion that the wheat degenerates from the constant moisture and becomes what we term *chesse*, and, what tends to confirm this very natural hypothesis is that chesse did not grow in any part of the field where wheat is not sown, and the adjoining patches which were purposely left unsown produced only rank grass and weeds.

This chesse looks exactly like wheat, whilst growing, but when beginning to shoot or spindle —the head opens.

I will send you a specimen of it cut in harvest time.

It is an advantageous circumstance for the clearing of this country, that the settler finds it his advantage to bring in fresh land every year. Some emigrants, who are without capital or assistance, exhaust their first clearance; and others prepare their land by *girdling*[6] the trees, which though it kills them, and allows vegetation under and around them, is an injudicious mode, as they frequently fall either on the fences or on the crops, or, what is worse, on the cattle, and occasion annual and often very inconvenient labour to remove them.

We had a very spirited manager for the Canada company in this neighbourhood—Mr. Galt—whose various publications bear strong evidence of his literary powers, and whose foresight and perseverence, acting upon a great scale, would eventually have produced a wonderful improvement in advancing the most important interests of this country.

The London merchants, however, composing the Canada company, did not approve of the expenditure of too much of their cash on general improvements, without an *immediate return*, and recalled him, placing in his room the Hon. William Allen and Messrs. Thomas Mercer Jones, and Dunlop, better known by the name of Tiger Dunlop—the last, though not least, of whom, is Warden of the woods and forests— all excellent and honourable men, who will conscientiously do their duty, and may, perhaps, eventually reap the advantage of Mr. Galt's wisdom and exertions.

An *individual* emigrant must expend capital and toil before he can have an overplus for market; why then should immediate profit be expected by the company from a *number* of colonists, within a shorter period?

I believe you will not be sorry that I close my letter here.

My next shall treat of various unconnected matters that may be interesting and useful to settlers.

Your's, my dear Sir,
Faithfully,
T. W. MAGRATH.

---

[6]This is done by cutting through the bark in rings, by which the communication of the sap being interrupted—the trunk perishes. —Editor.

[The footnotes were added by the Rev. Thomas Radcliffe in his edition of the collected letters.]

LIFE AMONG THE QALLUNAAT

Minnie Aodla Freeman

(*As a young Inuit woman, the author came to Ottawa from James Bay to work as a translator for the federal government.*)

Stranger; how odd is the meaning of that word and yet that is what I was in my own country. It is a word I never heard used in my own language. Even white people have a beautiful Inuit name, *qallunaat*—"people who pamper their eyebrows." After two months I decided that the *qallunaat* were the saddest, most worried and most hurried, never-smiling people. It seemed that my parents wasted their time telling me, "If you have nothing to say, smile." I could neither speak nor smile in the South.

I began to meet a lot of people. My first visit to a *qallunaat* family and first long ride by car were exhausting. While in the car I did not know what to look at. There were other cars, buildings and stores. And there were people standing about, others walking as if they had big loads on their backs, though they carried only small bags in their hands. The man who was driving told me that he had just learned to drive. This surprised me; I thought he had known how to drive since childhood, just as I knew how to hitch a dog team at the age of five.

The home of the *qallunaat* family held more surprises. I noticed the children at once. They were not allowed to be normal, free to move, free to ask questions, or free to think aloud. In my culture children are encouraged to speak. As they grow older, questioning becomes a boring habit;

they have gained wisdom and eventually become more intelligent. The more intelligent they become, the quieter they are. That is the reason Inuit children are allowed to be children. *Qallunaat* who have gone north and lived in the settlements, who do not understand Inuit home life or believe in our way of child-rearing, think that Inuit children are spoiled.

When I entered this *qallunaat* home, I could not help but notice the treatment of the children by the parents. One child asked, "Who is that girl?" She was answered with whispers and told to leave. Instead of being proud that the child was curious, instead of considering the way the child used her words, the parents silenced her immediately. To my people, such discipline can prevent a child from growing mentally, killing the child's sense of interest. "Is it very cold where she comes from? Did she live in an igloo before she came here?" Shhhh! the mother was cautioning. "Go outside! Don't do that! Move away!" How I wanted to pick up the child and say, "It is not very cold where I come from because we wear warm clothes." But words like "don't," "no," "move" were to me like talking to a dog who was eating from some other dog's dish or who did not obey commands given during sled travel. My culture tells me that the word no leads to disobedient children who become very hard to handle later on. My visit that day was an event, though I could not express my thoughts and feelings. Being very shy, all I said was yes, no and thank you.

Many Reasons for Loneliness

My weekends and evenings were often lonely. At times I would just lie on my bed, wishing I was with my family, and out of nowhere tears would come down my cheeks. I missed friends, open air, howling dogs, even the chores I had had to do—washing, cleaning, cutting wood, filling the water pails. I missed the sound of the sea just a few feet from our home, gathering twigs from the shore, welcoming a dog team just back from a hunting trip and most of all joking, laughing and smiling through these everyday events. I missed my food, especially frozen seal liver with seal fat. I missed going out on canoe trips to pick berries and the smell of tea brewed on an open fire.

I missed my brother, with whom I shared all these chores. His letters would make me cry. "I do all the work alone now. Today I put up snares; I am still allowed to use one dog but I miss your help pushing the sled." I could just picture him. He had to get up as soon as he opened his eyes because of our culture's tradition that we not lie around. That can lead to difficulty in bringing up children, and for a girl it means that she will have hard times while giving birth. We were never allowed to eat before we went outside. Grandmother would remind us, "Go out, look at the world, greet and admire your outdoor surroundings." Having to do this every day in our childhood became a joke to me and my brother. We would burst out laughing. What were we looking for? Grandmother always knew that we were laughing at something that we were not supposed to, and she would warn us that we would bear unhealthy children. Naturally we would be scared and try not to laugh at anything again.

I Knew Him and Yet Did Not

I joined the church's young people's association. My first meeting with the group was very happy. The minister who lead the group looked familiar and I guess he felt the same about me. Upon repeating my name and asking if I had ever been to Moose Factory, he realized who I was and I too began to remember. As we talked, I discovered that he had been my teacher at St. Thomas School in Moose Factory in 1941-2 and 1942-3. I had been too young to say that I knew him well. I knew him and yet did not, and he too knew me

and yet not the young woman I had become.

I sat through the whole meeting and observed everything that was said and done. Various people were invited to speak about other countries. When my turn came I could not believe that I would stand up in front of all those people to speak. I put my hands in my shirt pockets, my legs swayed back and forth, and I stared at the floor. I spoke about Christmas, that we did not give gifts at Christmas, but on New Year's Day. They began to ask questions when I only wished it were over. Whenever anybody asked me about home, I just wanted to cry, missing it so much. They asked me to speak longer than I wanted to, and this was when my image of the *qallunaat* collapsed. I used to think they knew everything, were capable of anything, could change all things from bad to good. And most of all, I thought they knew all about the Inuit. All of the *qallunaat* who had come to my land had that attitude. But here all they knew was that it was cold in the North, that Inuit rub noses—and even then they thought that we caress with our noses like they caress with their lips. Sooner or later came the question I had learned to expect: "How do you like the weather?"

My Clothes Were Valuable

Washing my clothes taught me that nothing was free in the South. I remember going down to the basement with my *qallunaaq* friend. I expected to see a washing board; instead, I saw a square, white box. I watched my *qallunaaq* friend but asked no questions. She took it for granted that I knew how to operate the machine. Not a word was spoken as I copied her actions. I put in my clothes, added soap, inserted a quarter and away it went. I expected never to see my clothes again. While we waited my friend said that she wished they had a dryer. What is a dryer? All this time I thought they had a wash line outside. I even pictured myself standing out in a breeze and my washing shaking gently in the fresh air. Later, when we went to get our clothes, she showed me the wash line—in another room in the basement!

The thought of smelling like musty, grey cement hung in my mind. I was told to be careful not to leave my clothes there too long or they would be stolen. Who would want to steal my clothes? At home I was taught never to steal, and surely *qallunaat* would not do that either. But in the evening, when I went for my clothes, two pairs of my panties, two pairs of nylons and a slip were missing. Nothing is impossible. Missionaries themselves stressed that stealing was a sin, and I was given the impression that *qallunaat* do not commit sins. To this day my friend does not know that I had never run an automatic washing machine before that day. And I often wonder why her underwear was not valued highly enough to be stolen.

So Close Together and Yet So Far Apart

My first ride on a bus during rush hour made me wonder how the bus could move with all its passengers. When I travelled with my family, the sled would not move if it was too full; the dogs could not budge it without help. But the bus, run by a motor, was something else. I was with a man and we were on our way to visit his family. I sat while he stood, but felt rather awkward as I was taught to let my elders sit, man or woman. Much later I learned that it was his custom to be a gentleman to a female, young or old.

No one spoke. Now and then I would hear a little bell and I learned that the bell meant that somebody was getting off. (I decided I would never ride the bus alone, because I would be too shy to ring the bell.) It occurred to me that people can be close together and yet far apart. No one seemed to know any other. I could not understand how people could ignore each other when they were sharing a bus, let alone one seat. While the bus lulled me into daydreams, making my mind drunk with the smell of gasoline, I thought of big gatherings at home. When a whale or seal was divided among the families, children laughed and threw stones into the water, dogs yapped and everybody enjoyed the food. I could hear the water at the shore and the merriment down the banks.

Exciting for a Qallunaat Girl

One day I stopped off at the mail office (another routine I had to get used to), and I picked up a strange looking envelope. Its contents told me to vote. What is vote? Why am I to vote? I did not understand it; I had never heard of it. My *qallunaaq*, who was younger than I, said to me that I was lucky, that she had to wait another four years before she could vote. She was very excited about it but I could not see any reason why. What is vote? What do I do? Who is the person I have to vote for? My *qallunaaq* told me where I had to go, that there were two men whose names would be written on a piece of paper, and that I should try to put an X on the right line or it would not count. What would not count? If I put it below or above the line? Who were these two men? What were they? I went to vote but still did not understand. Putting an X on a piece of paper was something I did not find exciting.

Keep Your Houses Clean

I began to take walks by myself, and my favourite spot was behind Parliament Hill, near the water. There all the memories of home would come to mind. Many times I would sit on a stone and tears would fall. I pictured a tent near the shore and heard waves smacking against canoes. I yearned to get pails and pails of water for drinking or for next day's wash. But the water I gazed at did not look normal at all. I would wonder why *qallunaat* stressed to Inuit people that they keep their houses clean, when the water right in their backyard looked so filthy. When I returned my *qallunaaq* would ask me where I had been and why. What did I see there? Somehow I could never explain. I had no words to tell her that somehow it made me feel at home to hear water smacking against the shore.

I Would Like to See to Whom I Am Talking

When I was first shown the telephone at Laurentian Terrace I had wondered who would call me. I had never really thought much about this machine and it took me ages to think of using it. At the office where I worked, I was often alone during lunch hours. Occasionally the phone, which sat next to my desk, would ring—always when I was alone it seemed. I ignored it. I would not know what to say if I picked it up. In fact I felt awkward about talking to someone I could not see.

It was one of those days when I was alone and the telephone started to ring. This time it would not stop. It got to the point that I could not ignore it. I thought of leaving the office, but on leaving I would have to pass it. I felt a bit ridiculous about my plan. Finally, I decided to answer and told myself that whoever was wanted was not there; I would simply say so and hang up fast. I do not know how I sounded from the other end, but the voice said, "Speak up, Minnie, I cannot hear you." The voice I recognized! "I thought you would never answer," it said. "Minnie, it is only me. Wait, I will hang up and come over. I am just across the hall."

It was the lady who had been taking me various places for civil service tests. It was one of her tests. She explained to me how to answer, take messages and so on. Why can't the caller just call back?

My *qallunaaq* worked in another building. I asked her if I could phone her the next day. I discovered that it was not so scary after all, and it was rather fun to feel that I had mastered another machine. But each time, when I did learn something new, I felt a little change in me. Somehow I seemed braver and braver, but still very shy.

To Please a Friend

There were things that I was willing to try, but others I did not care for. Bicycling was one of the things I did not care for. There were things imposed on me that I could refuse, but to please a friend one day I agreed to go bicycling. We started off from Rideau Street and planned to cycle up to Sussex Drive. I got on; in that instant I had to summon all the senses that had not been used since I left home, my eyes, my ears, my sense of direction, my balance and most of all my nerves. All these things I had been taught to use in order to survive. A car screeched behind me. I looked, and all I could see was the driver shouting with a mad look on his face. And there was my friend yelling, "Minnie! Stop! Stop!" My nerves went all tense and my heart seemed to beat all over my body. My friend was right behind me, reminding me to stay on the right side, making me all the more fearful. When we finally got home, my friend was able to relax casually on her bed, while I was still shaking. And all I whispered to myself was peace, Minnie, peace, peace, peace.

Out of the Box

Television was something I could not get over. Even now, if I had the freedom to watch it day and night I would. Commercials fascinated me the most, not because of what they advertised, but because of the way they came on—everything seemed to flash quickly and disappear just as quickly, as if they didn't really want people to see what it was. It made me wonder how it happened. Where does the picture come from? How do people that are on television get inside? How do they know what to say? I found out quite by accident one black day.

A man came to me and said that I had to be televised. I was given fifteen minutes to get ready. Will I be boxed in? My imagination began to take over. My second worst enemy, other than shyness, began to work within me: I will not be able to breathe! Whenever there is no light or daylight, I feel I am being smothered.

I was told to tell the taxi driver where to go. Me? Tell him where to go? He should know where it is, he is from around here. But I relayed the instructions politely to the driver, and to my relief he did not seem to mind being told by a person who was younger than himself. Not long after I saw a sign with red lights, so pretty against the blue sky. The sign said CBC. When I entered the building everyone I saw had a beautiful smile and seemed very friendly. A man came over and shook my hand and introduced himself. His name was Percy Saltzman. He asked me questions. "What do you miss most from home? What can you not get used to here?" I was amazed by him. He was the first *qallunaaq* who asked human questions. For a long time he stood out in my memory. I told myself that somewhere in this world of the *qallunaat* lived people with sensitive minds.

The next day people kept coming to tell me that they had seen me on television. I felt shy and awkward that I was seen by so many people and that my very private thoughts were known by them all. But I stopped worrying about how television works after that. I know now that people on television are not boxed in.

I Did Not Hear Him Arrive

I had been a year in the South before I saw another Inuk. The man, just returned from Greenland, was on his way home to Cornwallis Island, Northwest Territories. I wanted to hug him. I wanted to welcome him the way I would have in my own home, to make tea and talk about his trip. But I could not. My surroundings did not allow me to be me at all. The steel desks seemed to say, you are part of us, do not act like a human being. There was a lump in my throat and my tears were hard to keep back.

I was so happy to see him, not only because he was Inuk but because he knew Inuk ways. His reawakening of the Inuit in me made me realize how alone I was. He told me about his family; he had a daughter almost the same age as me and he said that I would meet her one day. He made me wish that I had an Inuk girl to chum with, someone who saw things in the Inuit way. No matter how hard I tried to communicate with my *qallunaaq,* my comments never seemed to hit her right. He also made me realize that I was losing the sense of humour that my parents had con-

sidered so important to survival on unfamiliar ground. My "Inukism" was slowly disappearing, being buried deeper and deeper. With an effort, I tried to bring out my normal reaction to his arrival and said, "I did not hear you arrive, where did you park your dogs?" That hit him right on the Inuk funny spot and he laughed. My welcoming instincts slowly began to come back.

Grandmother's Quillik was Very Bright

I have known about electricity since I was five years old, but its power was not known to me until I saw electric lights. In school I was taught that electricity came from thunder and lightning. To me, it meant danger, and I was brought up to be very cautious of lightning and thunder at home. When there was a thunderstorm, my brother and I were always reminded to put our hands on our ears as the sound could injure the nerves inside us, even kill us. We were never allowed to handle anything shiny, such as iron or metal cans, while it stormed. We were told that such objects attracted thunder and lightning.

I learned that electricity is dangerous but also very wonderful, and useful, and I compared it to the *quillik*—the seal oil lamp, which was also wonderful, useful and a comfort to us. Every evening women would sit down on the floor or ground, catching the last speck of daylight, to clean and fix the wick of the *quillik*. Watching my grandmother, it never occurred to me that there was another such light, brighter than what I thought was so bright. To my thinking, that is what the *qallunaat* woman has as a source of comfort. Here in the South, she has light merely by flicking a most innocent looking gadget on the wall. The Inuit woman has first of all to make sure the seal oil is ready to be poured into a pot, the oil having been rendered from the fats of the seal. The wick has to be cut neatly and even, so it will not give smoke or cause any odor. The burned part of the wick has to be trimmed off, so it will give an even flame. The oil has to be poured into another pan from the original processing pan in order that the saturated parts of cooked fat may be removed. Doing this was a comfort to an Inuk woman.

Sometimes these lamps were lit early in the morning, before the sun came up, so the women could finish sewing the garments to be worn by the men that same morning. The *quillik* was her only light during the early darkness of winter. Who can say who enjoys more comfort? It is me who is comfortable today because I can reach up and switch on a gadget, because I do not have to reach down and put in all that work in order to enjoy a single flame. Though I realize how lucky I am, I will never cease to believe that my ancestors were smart and resourceful. But I do have a reason to be afraid of thunderstorms, because I can see now what it can do in the hands of the *qallunaat.* I have been told by *qallunaat* individuals that thunderstorms cannot hurt me. But I still will not stay close to shiny objects. If it storms while I am at home, I cover everything that shines.

Almost Lost an Arm for a Stamp

Sooner or later I had to write letters to my family and friends. I had known for a long time that a letter had to have a stamp in order to be mailed, but I had never quite understood what it was for. I knew neither where the stamps came from nor where to buy them. One day I found out where these little stickers were available. It was one of those days when my *qallunaaq* and I met after work; she said that she had to get stamps from the post office. I just followed her until we arrived at an enormous building.

The first thing I noticed were the odd-looking doors. I was afraid to enter through them but my *qallunaaq* did not seem bothered. I was right behind her and did not notice that when she pushed it, it began to revolve. I was so busy trying to figure out what made it go around that I forgot myself. The next thing I knew my arm was caught. A woman behind me was screaming, "She's caught!" over and over. I panicked; nothing was coming out of me but little aching sounds. By this time a crowd had gathered, and someone

managed to pull the revolving door backwards. My arm was so sore that I was in tears. This made me feel all the more awkward as I was taught never to shed a tear in public. I learned two things on this occasion: that someone in pain is very exciting to people, and that this was the place where stamps came from.

I felt a bit afraid to handle the stamps I bought, and many questions began to pour into my mind. Why does a letter have to have a stamp? Is there something that has to be done to it? Not quite knowing anything about it I handled them very carefully, with high respect, as if I might break some law if I did not take care of them. The image of the Queen on the stamp also made me feel afraid, as if she would know how I was handling her. After sixteen years in the South I know why stamps are necessary. Everything has its own place in the South, it seems.

Dog Meat in the South?

It was one of those days when my *qallunaaq* and I met after work. She suggested that we eat at a restaurant. I had no idea just what to do there. As usual I followed my *qallunaaq* without question. A lady came over and handed us a folded sheet of paper. "Menu," it read. Do we sit here and figure out what to cook for ourselves? I felt lost; it was not at all like the place where we ate at the Terrace.

Finally I became aware of the other people in this restaurant. They were not doing anything but eating. The lady was passing food around. Ah! I have to tell the lady what I want and she will go and cook it.

I had discovered that there was nothing free in the South, so I had to think about the cost of what I was about to ask the lady to cook for me. For the first time I had a good look at the sheet of paper. There it showed the prices. Anything that sounded good was beyond the amount in my purse. Finally, my *qallunaaq* said that she would have a hot dog. I burst out laughing and could not stop. What is a hot dog? Do not tell me people in the South eat dog meat! I felt a bit sick. Which one is that? She pointed: wiener on a bun, twenty-five cents. I asked the lady to cook one for me as well; in fact, I asked for everything my *qallunaaq* asked for—cola, jello and a hot dog. When the dog was brought to our table I stared at it. I was very hungry at that moment and began to picture nice fresh seal meat, but the aroma of the dog killed it. I did not like it. I washed the taste down with cola. Unfortunately, cola became a habit of mine; I drank so much that my face broke into a million pimples!

Did They Really Pamper Their Eyebrows?

I said at the beginning that *qallunaat* means "people who pamper their eyebrows." It was never explained to me by any of my ancestors why the *quallunaat* were named that. I know for sure that it does not mean white man—there is no meaning in it at all pertaining to colour or white or man. I know for sure, too, that it was the *qallunaat* who named themselves white men, to distinguish themselves from other colours, for it is they who have always been aware of different racial colours. Inuit are aware of different races, but not of colour. I have never known or been taught to identify another race by skin colour.

Qallunaat; I have turned the word inside out to try and find the meaning. First of all the word *qallu* can mean eyebrow; by adding an ending one has *qallu-naaq*, one; two *qallunaaq* is *qallunaat*—many *qallunaaq*. The word implies humans who pamper or fuss with nature, of materialistic habit. Avaricious people. *Qallu* is also the beginning of the word *qallunartak,* material or fabric or anything that is manufactured or store-bought. It can also mean a rag made of material or fabric, or any material other than a material from nature.

Somehow I cannot see how the Inuit would have been impressed if the *qallunaat* pampered their eyebrows. I cannot imagine the *qallunaat* pampering their eyebrows when they did not care how they looked in the middle of the Arctic; even today, they do not seem to care how they look. They are so busy making money, they don't seem to have time to pamper themselves, let alone their eyebrows. Furthermore, when I see pictures of the first *qallunaat* who came to the Arctic, they always look so dishevelled in overalls, plaid shirts and heavy-looking sweaters, their faces covered with beard and their hair uncombed. For those reasons, I do not understand why the *qallunaat* would be called people who pamper their eyebrows. I believe it is the other meaning that is significant—*qallunaaraaluit*, very respectable, avaricious, materialistic, who could do anything with material, or those who fear for their ability to manufacture material. All those meanings are in that one word: *qallu*, material or fabric (manmade); *naa*, avaricious, who is proud to show his material, who lures with material; *raa*, respectable, fearing, magical; *luit,* many, human. (*Luit* can also mean they or them rather than us.) I was born too late to witness the naming of the first *qallunaat* arrivals to the Arctic; possibly they pampered their eyebrows, more likely they were *qallunaaraaluit*. Over time the word has been shortened and the literal meaning changed.

The Inuit, too, gave themselves an identity. To me the word "Eskimo" means nothing. It is an Indian word—*escheemau*—that the *qallunaat* tried to say at one time. It is a Cree word: *Escee*, sickening, can't stand it; *mau*, human. At first encounter Cree Indians were sickened by the sight of the Inuit eating raw meat. Today, the Inuit still eat raw meat and it's still *yam yam* as far as I am concerned. When we lived in Old Factory amongst Indians, we had to be very careful that we did not eat raw meat in front of them, not because we were ashamed but because we did not want to upset them. The Inuit differentiated themselves from the animals of nature, not from other races. *Inuk* means one human; *Inuuk* means two humans; *Inuit* means many humans. *Inuk* can also mean alive as opposed to dead. Today, of course, the Inuk identifies himself as *Inuk*, different from any other race he has encountered since the days when just he and the animals of his land lived in the north.

ONE VOTE FOR THIS AGE OF ANXIETY

Margaret Mead

When critics wish to repudiate the world in which we live today, one of their familiar ways of doing it is to castigate modern man because anxiety is his chief problem. This, they say, in W. H. Auden's phrase, is the age of anxiety. This is what we have arrived at with all our vaunted progress, our great technological advances, our great wealth—everyone goes about with a burden of anxiety so enormous that, in the end, our stomachs and our arteries and our skins express the tension under which we live. Americans who have lived in Europe come back to comment on our favorite farewell which, instead of the old goodbye (God be with you), is now "Take it easy," each American admonishing the other not to break down from the tension and strain of modern life.

Whenever an age is characterized by a phrase, it is presumably in contrast to other ages. If we are the age of anxiety, what were other ages? And here the critics and carpers do a very amusing thing. First, they give us lists of the opposites of anxiety: security, trust, self-confidence, self-direction. Then, without much further discussion, they let us assume that other ages, other periods of history, were somehow the ages of trust or confident direction.

The savage who, on his South Sea island, simply sat and let bread fruit fall into his lap, the simple peasant, at one with the fields he ploughed and the beasts he tended, the craftsman busy with his tools and lost in the fulfilment of the instinct of workmanship—these are the counter-images conjured up by descriptions of the strain under which men live today. But no one who lived in those days has returned to testify how paradisiacal they really were.

Certainly if we observe and question the savages or simple peasants in the world today, we find something quite different. The untouched savage in the middle of New Guinea isn't anxious; he is seriously and continually *frightened*—of black magic, of enemies with spears who may kill him or his wives and children at any moment, while they stoop to drink from a spring, or climb a palm tree for a coconut. He goes warily, day and night, taut and fearful.

As for the peasant populations of a great part of the world, they aren't so much anxious as hungry. They aren't anxious about whether they will get a salary raise, or which of the three colleges of their choice they will be admitted to, or whether to buy a Ford or Cadillac, or whether the kind of TV set they want is too expensive. They are hungry, cold and, in many parts of the world, they dread that local warfare, bandits, political coups may endanger their homes, their meager livelihoods and their lives. But surely they are not anxious.

For anxiety, as we have come to use it to describe our characteristic state of mind, can be contrasted with the active fear of hunger, loss, violence and death. Anxiety is the appropriate emotion when the immediate personal terror—of a volcano, an arrow, the sorcerer's spell, a stab in the back and other calamities, all directed against one's self—disappears.

This is not to say that there isn't plenty to worry about in our world of today. The explosion of a bomb in the streets of a city whose name no one had ever heard before may set in motion forces which end up by ruining one's carefully planned education in law school, half

— "One Vote for this Age of Anxiety" by Margaret Mead, from the New York Times Magazine, May 20, 1956; reprinted by permission of the author (also available in Dell Paperback, The Edge of Awareness)

276

a world away. But there is still not the personal, immediate, active sense of impending disaster that the savage knows. There is rather the vague anxiety, the sense that the future is unmanageable.

The kind of world that produces anxiety is actually a world of relative safety, a world in which no one feels that he himself is facing sudden death. Possibly sudden death may strike a certain number of unidentified other people—but not him. The anxiety exists as an uneasy state of mind, in which one has a feeling that something unspecified and undeterminable may go wrong. If the world seems to be going well, this produces anxiety—for good times may end. If the world is going badly—it may get worse. Anxiety tends to be without locus; the anxious person doesn't know whether to blame himself or other people. He isn't sure whether it is the current year or the Administration or a change in climate or the atom bomb that is to blame for this undefined sense of unease.

It is clear that we have developed a society which depends on having the *right* amount of anxiety to make it work. Psychiatrists have been heard to say, "He didn't have enough anxiety to get well," indicating that, while we agree that too much anxiety is inimical to mental health, we have come to rely on anxiety to push and prod us into seeing a doctor about a symptom which may indicate cancer, into checking up on that old life insurance policy which may have out-of-date clauses in it, into having a conference with Billy's teacher even though his report card looks all right.

People who are anxious enough keep their car insurance up, have the brakes checked, don't take a second drink when they have to drive, are careful where they go and with whom they drive on holidays. People who are too anxious either refuse to go into cars at all—and so complicate the ordinary course of life—or drive so tensely and overcautiously that they help cause accidents. People who aren't anxious enough take chance after chance, which increases the terrible death toll of the roads.

On balance, our age of anxiety represents a large advance over savage and peasant cultures. Out of a productive system of technology drawing upon enormous resources, we have created a nation in which anxiety has replaced terror and despair, for all except the severely disturbed. The specter of hunger means something only to those Americans who can identify themselves with the millions of hungry people on other continents. The specter of terror may still be roused in some by a knock at the door in a few parts of the South, or in those who have just escaped from a totalitarian regime or who have kin still behind the Curtains.

But in this twilight world which is neither at peace nor at war, and where there is insurance against certain immediate, downright, personal disasters, for most Americans there remains only anxiety over what may happen, might happen, could happen.

This is the world out of which grows the hope, for the first time in history, of a society where there will be freedom from want and freedom from fear. Our very anxiety is born of our knowledge of what is now possible for each and for all. The number of people who consult psychiatrists today is not, as is sometimes felt, a symptom of increasing mental ill health, but rather the precursor of a world in which the hope of genuine mental health will be open to everyone, a world in which no individual feels that he need be hopelessly brokenhearted, a failure, a menace to others or a traitor to himself.

But if, then, our anxieties are actually signs of hope, why is there such a voice of discontent abroad in the land? I think this comes perhaps because our anxiety exists without an accompanying recognition of the tragedy which will always be inherent in human life, however well we build our world. We may banish hunger, and fear of sorcery, violence or secret police; we may bring up children who have learned to trust life and who have the spontaneity and curiosity necessary to devise ways of making trips to the moon; we cannot—as we have tried to do—banish death itself.

Americans who stem from generations which left their old people behind and never closed their parents' eyelids in death, and who have experienced the additional distance from death provided by two world wars fought far from our shores are today pushing away from them both a recognition of death and a recognition of the tremendous significance—for the future—of the way we live our lives. Acceptance of the inevitability of death, which, when faced, can give dignity to life, and acceptance of our inescapable role in the modern world, might transmute our anxiety about making the right choices, taking the right precautions, and the right risks into the sterner stuff of responsibility, which ennobles the whole face rather than furrowing the forehead with the little anxious wrinkles of worry.

Worry in an empty context means that men die daily little deaths. But good anxiety—not about the things that were left undone long ago that return to haunt and harry men's minds, but active, vivid anxiety about what must be done and that quickly—binds men to life with an intense concern.

This is still a world in which too many of the wrong things happen somewhere. But this is a world in which we now have the means to make a great many more of the right things happen everywhere. For Americans, the generalization which a Swedish social scientist made about our attitudes on race relations is true in many other fields: anticipated change which we feel is right and necessary but difficult makes us unduly anxious and apprehensive, but such change, once consummated, brings a glow of relief. We are still a people who—in the literal sense—believe in making good.

Science, technology, and the arts

All that can be seen or heard or felt or smelled, directly or indirectly, is brought to the scientist's loom, and only insofar as our senses themselves are limited is the raw material selected or restricted.
— *N. J. Berrill*

We have more moral, political, and historical wisdom than we know how to reduce into practice; we have more scientific and economical knowledge than can be accommodated to the just distribution of the produce which it multiplies . . . we want the creative faculty to imagine what we know; we want the generous impulse to act that which we imagine; we want the poetry of life. . . .
— *Percy Bysshe Shelley*

Art gives us a tongue with which to speak in more than a stammer; an ear with which to hear what is not a mere noise; an eye with which to see the glory of a mountain top or of the sea in a storm.
— *Frederick Philip Grove*

Critics who argue that the subject-matter of modern art is proof of the decadence of modern society don't really understand what they are talking about. Art has always been a reflection of the aspirations and obsessions of its time and the art of today is no exception. If it is haunted and distracted, if it is often ugly and even horrifying, it does not mean that the artists themselves are worse men than Haydn was. It means only that they have not refused, as Haydn did, to accept responsibility for Captain Bligh. For all its horrors, the twentieth century is better than the eighteenth; no politician or dictator who has tried to defy its conscience has been able, in the end, to succeed.
— *Hugh MacLennan*

THE UGLY AMERICAN
AND THE UGLY SARKHANESE

William J. Lederer and Eugene Burdick

Two weeks later Atkins and his wife left by plane for Sarkhan. Emma, a stout woman with freckles across her nose was, in her way, quite as ugly as her husband. She was hopelessly in love with Atkins, but had never been able to tell him why adequately.

She did not blink when Atkins told her they were going to Sarkhan. She told Homer that she'd be pleased to move into a smaller house where she could manage things with her own hands, and where she wouldn't need servants.

Two weeks later the Atkins were living in a small cottage in a suburb of Haidho. They were the only Caucasians in the community. Their house had pressed earth floors, one spigot of cold water, a charcoal fire, two very comfortable hammocks, a horde of small, harmless insects, and a small, dark-eyed Sarkhanese boy about nine years old who apparently came with the house. The boy's name was Ong. He appeared promptly at six each morning and spent the entire day following Emma around.

Emma Atkins enjoyed herself in Sarkhan. She learned enough of the language so that she could discuss with her neighbors the best places to buy chickens, ducks, and fresh vegetables. She learned how to prepare beautifully fluffy rice seasoned with saffron. She liked working in her house, and it was a matter of some pride to her that she was as good a housekeeper as most of her neighbors.

Homer Atkins kept busy with his man-powered water pump. The idea had developed

very slowly in his mind. What was needed was some kind of efficient pump to raise the water from one terraced paddy to another. Lifting water in the hilly sections consumed enormous amounts of energy. It was usually done by a pail, or by a cloth sack, attached to the end of a long pole. One man would lower the pail and swing it up to the next terrace where another man would empty it. It was a slow and cumbersome method, but the Sarkhanese had been doing it for generations and saw no reason to change. Atkins had decided that there was no sense in trying to talk them out of an obviously inefficient method unless he could offer them a more efficient method to replace it.

He solved two-thirds of his problem. A simple pump needed three things. First, it needed cheap and readily available piping. He had decided that the pipes could be made out of bamboo, which was abundant. Second, the pump needed a cheap and efficient pump mechanism. This had taken longer to find, but in the end Atkins had succeeded. Outside many Sarkhanese villages were piled the remains of jeeps which had been discarded by the military authorities. Atkins had taken pistons from one of these jeeps and had replaced the rings with bands of cheap felt to make a piston for his pump. He then cut the block of the jeep in two; he used one of the cylinders as a suction chamber, and the other cylinder as a discharge chamber. With a simple mechanical linkage the piston could be agitated up and down, and would suck water as high as thirty feet. The third problem, which Atkins had not yet solved, was the question of what power could be applied to the linkage.

In the end Emma gave him the answer.

"Why don't you just send off to the States for a lot of hand pumps like they use on those little cars men run up and down the railroads?" she asked one day.

"Now, look, dammit, I've explained to you before," Atkins said. "It's got to be something they use out here. It's no good if I go spending a hundred thousand dollars bringing in something. It has to be something right here, something the natives understand."

"Why, Homer," Emma said, "with all that money you've got in the bank back at Pittsburgh, why don't you give some of it to these nice Sarkhanese?"

Atkins looked up sharply, but saw at once that she was teasing him. He grunted.

"You know why. Whenever you give a man something for nothing the first person he comes to dislike is you. If the pump is going to work at all, it has to be their pump, not mine."

Emma smiled fondly at Homer Atkins. She turned and looked out the window. A group of Sarkhanese on bicycles, as usual, were moving in toward the market places at Haidho. She watched them for a few moments, and then spun around, excitement in her eyes.

"Why don't you use bicycles? There are millions of them in this country and they must wear out. Maybe you could use the drive mechanism of an old bicycle to move the pump."

Atkins looked at Emma and slowly sat up straight. He slapped his hand against his knee.

"By God, I think you've got it, girl," he said softly. "We could take the wheels off an old bike, link the chain of the bike to one large reduction gear, and then drive the piston up and down with an eccentric."

Atkins began to walk around the room. Emma, a slight grin on her face, returned to her charcoal fire over which she had a fragrant pot of chicken cooking. In a few moments she heard the rustle of paper and knew that Atkins was bent over his drawing board. Two hours later he was still drawing furiously. An hour after that he went to a footlocker, took out a half-dozen bottles of beer, and brought them back to his work table. By dinner time he had drunk them all and was whistling under his

breath. When Emma tapped him on the shoulder and told him that dinner was ready, he swung around excitedly.

"Look, baby, I think I've got it," he said, and began to explain it to her rapidly, interrupting himself to make quick calculations on a piece of paper. When she finally got him to sit down, he ate so fast that the chicken gravy ran down his chin. He wiped his chin with his shirt sleeve and made sure none of the gravy got on his precious drawings. Emma Atkins watched her husband fondly. She was proud of him, and she was happy when he was happy. Today she felt very happy, indeed.

"Stop drinking beer, Homer Atkins," Emma said, grinning. "You'll get drunk. And then you'll forget that it was my idea about the bicycle."

"Your idea?" he yelled in astonishment. "Woman, you're crazy. I was thinking about that all along. You just reminded me of it."

But then he went back to the locker, brought back two bottles of beer, and blew suds at her when he filled her glass.

Two days later Atkins had a working model. Not a single item in the crude pump would have to be imported. He had calculated that there was probably enough scrap around the countryside to make a couple of thousand pumps. What he had to do now was to get a couple of pumps actually in operation, to see how they worked. At this point Emma Atkins demonstrated her diplomatic skills.

"Now look, Homer, don't go running off like a wild man," Emma said softly. "You've got a good machine there. I'm proud of you. But don't think that just because it's good the Sarkhanese are going to start using it right away. Remember the awful time that you had getting trade unions in America to accept earth-moving equipment. These people here are no different. You have to let them use the machine themselves and in their own way. If you try to jam it down their throats, they'll never use it."

"All right, Mrs. Foster Dulles, you tell me what to do," Atkins said. He knew she was right and he was grateful to her. "You tell me how I ought to approach the Sarkhanese."

Emma calmly explained her plan to Homer. He realized that she had been thinking of this for some time. It was an intricate, beautiful plan, and he wished that some of the stuffed-shirts in the American Embassy could hear his wife talking.

The next day he put into operation Emma Atkins' grand strategy.

He drove in his used jeep to the tiny village of Chang 'Dong, a community of one hundred souls, living in fifteen or twenty houses. The village was set precariously on a steep hill sixty miles outside of Haidho. The soil there was rich; but the backbreaking, time-consuming process of lifting water up seven or eight levels —even though the differentials were small— had always made Chang 'Dong a poor village.

Atkins politely asked the first person he met in Chang 'Dong where the home of the head-man was. He talked to the headman, a vener-able man of seventy-five, without an interpreter. It was not easy, but he could tell that the head-man was pleased that Atkins was making the effort to talk his language. With infinite courtesy the old man sensed what words Atkins was searching for, and politely supplied them. The conversation moved along more rapidly than Homer had expected it would.

Atkins explained that he was an American and that he was an inventor. He had an idea for a pump to lift water. He, Atkins, wanted to develop and patent this pump and sell it at a profit. What Atkins wanted the headman to find was a Sarkhanese worker with mechanical skill. Atkins said he would pay well for this man's time and skill; if he was able to help with the pump, he would become half-owner of the patent. The old man nodded gravely. They then began a long, complicated, and delicate negotiation over the matter of how much the native mechanic should be paid. Atkins under-stood all of this quite well—it was just like negotiating with a trade union organizer in the States. Each man knew that he would eventu-

ally have to compromise; and each took pleasure in talking the whole thing out. In the end Atkins got the services of a mechanic for a price which he knew was just slightly higher than the going rate. Both the headman and Atkins were satisfied. They shook hands, and the headman left to bring in the mechanic. Atkins reached in his shirt pocket, took out a cigar, and lit it with pleasure. This would, he thought, be fun.

When the headman returned he brought with him a small, stocky, heavily-muscled man whom he introduced as Jeepo. The headman ex-plained that the name was not a native name. He was called Jeepo because of his reputation as a famous mechanic in the maintenance and repair of jeeps. Atkins didn't listen too closely to what the headman was saying. He was study-ing Jeepo, and he liked what he saw.

Jeepo looked like a craftsman. His finger-nails were as dirty as Atkins', and his hands were also covered with dozens of little scars. Jeepo looked back steadily at Atkins without humility or apology, and Atkins felt that in the mechanic's world of bolts and nuts, pistons and leathers, and good black grease he and Jeepo would understand one another.

And Jeepo was ugly. He was ugly in a rowdy, bruised, carefree way that pleased Atkins. The two men smiled at one another.

"The headman says you are a good me-chanic," Atkins said. "He says that you're an expert on repairing jeeps. But I must have a man who is expert at other things as well. Have you ever worked on anything besides jeeps?"

Jeepo smiled.

"I've worked on winches, pumps, Citroëns, American and French tanks, windmills, bicycles, the toilets of wealthy white people, and a few airplanes."

"Did you understand everything that you were working on?" Atkins asked.

"Who understands everything that he works on?" Jeepo said. "I feel that I can work with anything that is mechanical. But that is only my opinion. Try me."

"We'll start this afternoon," Atkins said. "In my jeep outside is a heap of equipment. You and I will unload it and we'll start at once."

By the middle of the afternoon they had assembled most of Atkins' equipment on the edge of a paddy on the second level of the village of Chang 'Dong. Twenty-five feet of bamboo pipe had been fastened together; the bottom of the pipe was put into a backwater of the river that flowed by the village. The top piece of the pipe was fitted by a rubber gasket to the crude pump which Atkins had designed. Above the pump was the frame of a used bicycle with both of its wheels removed. Jeepo had done the assembly entirely by himself. Atkins had made one attempt to help, but Jeepo had gone ahead on his own, and Atkins realized that he wanted to demonstrate his virtuosity. By late afternoon the assembly was ready.

Atkins squatted calmly in the mud waiting for Jeepo to finish. The headman and two or three of the elders of the village were squatting beside him. Although they were externally as passive as Atkins, he was aware that they were very excited. They understood perfectly what the machine was intended for; they were not sure it would work.

"Sir, the mechanism is ready to operate," Jeepo finally said quietly. "I'm not sure we can get suction at so great a height; but I'd be pleased to turn the bicycle pedals for the first few minutes to test it."

Atkins nodded. Jeepo climbed aboard the bicycle and began to pump slowly. The chain-drive of the bicycle turned with increasing speed. The crude pipes made a sucking noise. For several seconds there was no other sound except this gurgle. Then, suddenly, from the outflow end of the pump, a jet of dirty brown water gushed forth. Jeepo did not stop peddling nor did he smile; but the headman and the other elders could not restrain their excitement about the size of the jet of water that was being lifted to the second rice terrace.

"This is a very clever machine," the headman said to Atkins. "In a few minutes you have lifted more water than we could lift by our old methods in five hours of work."

Atkins did not respond to the man's delight. He was waiting to see how Jeepo reacted. He sensed that Jeepo was not entirely happy or convinced.

Jeepo continued to pump at the machine. He looked down at the machinery, noted some tiny adjustments that had to be made, and called them out to Atkins. When the small paddy was full of water he stopped, and swung down out of the bicycle seat.

"It is a very clever machine, Mr. Atkins," Jeepo said quietly. "But it will not be a sensible machine for this country."

Atkins looked steadily at Jeepo for a long moment, and then nodded.

"Why not?" he asked.

Jeepo did not respond at once. He moved silently around the mechanism, twisting a bolt here, adjusting a lever there; then he stood up and faced Atkins.

"The machine works very, very well," Jeepo said. "But to make it work a person would have to have a second bicycle. In this country, Mr. Atkins, very few people have enough money to afford two bicycles. Unless you can find another way to drive the pump, or unless your government is prepared to give us thousands of bicycles, your very clever device is a waste of time."

For a moment Atkins felt a flush of anger. It was a hard thing to be criticised so bluntly. For a hot, short moment, Atkins calculated how many bicycles his three million dollars would buy; then, with the memory of Emma's tact in his mind, he put the thought aside. He turned back to Jeepo.

"What happens to old bicycles in this country?" he asked. "Aren't there enough of them to serve as power machines for the pumps?"

"There are no old or discarded bicycles in this country," Jeepo said. "We ride bicycles until they are no good. When a man throws his bicycle away, it's too old to be used for one of these pumps."

For a moment the ugly American faced the ugly Sarkhanese. When he was younger, Atkins would have turned on his heel and walked away. Now he grinned at Jeepo.

"All right, Jeepo, you say you're an expert mechanic. What would you do? Am I simply to give up my idea—or can we find some other way to give power to the pump?"

Jeepo did not answer at once. He squatted in the shallow rice-field, his khaki shorts resting in three inches of mud. He stared fixedly at the improbable machine. For ten minutes he said nothing. Then he stood up and walked slowly to the machine. He turned the pedal and held his finger over the rear-drive sprocket of the wheel as if to test its strength. Then he walked back and squatted again.

The headman looked once at Atkins and then talked in a sharp voice to the elders. The headman was embarrassed at Jeepo's arrogance, and he was saying that the entire village of Chang 'Dong would lose face by this ridiculous performance. Jeepo's ears became slightly red at the criticism, but he did not turn his head or acknowledge that he heard the headman's words.

Atkins felt like laughing. The headman and the elders reminded him very much of the diplomats to whom he had talked for so many months in Phnom Penh. He was quite sure that Jeepo had an answer for these comments, and he was also sure that it was not a political or personal answer, but technical. Atkins squatted down beside Jeepo, and for fifteen minutes the two men sat quietly on their heels studying the machine. Atkins was the first to speak.

"Perhaps we could make the frame of the bicycle out of wood and then we'd only have to buy the sprocket mechanism," Atkins said in a tentative voice.

"But that's the part of the bicycle which is most expensive," Jeepo said.

For perhaps another ten minutes they squatted motionless. Behind him Atkins could hear the shrill voices of the headman and the elders. Although they were attempting to maintain

their dignity and manners, it was clear to Atkins that they were trying to find a way to apologize to him and to smooth the whole thing over. It never occurred to Atkins to talk to them. He and Jeepo were hard at work.

Once Atkins walked to the mechanism, turned the pedals rapidly, held his finger on the sprocket gear, and looked at Jeepo. Jeepo shook his head. He understood the mechanical question that Atkins had asked and was giving his answer. Without exchanging a word they demonstrated six or eight alternative ways of making the pump work, and discarded them all. Each shake of the head upset the headman and elders profoundly.

It was dusk before they solved the problem, and it was Jeepo who came up with the solution. He suddenly stood bolt upright, walked over to the bicycle, remounted, and began to pedal furiously. Water gushed out of the outflow of the pump. Jeepo looked back over his shoulder at the lower level of the pump, then started to shout at Atkins in a loud and highly disrespectful voice in which there was the sound of discovery. It took Atkins another five minutes to understand fully what Jeepo was proposing.

It was the height of simplicity. What he proposed was that a treadmill be built which could be turned by the rear wheel of an ordinary bicycle fitted into a light bamboo frame. What this meant was that a family with a single bicycle could put the bicycle in the bamboo rack, mount it, and pedal. The rear wheel would drive the treadmill which in turn would drive the pump with an efficiency almost as great as Atkin's original model. When anyone needed to use the bike, he could simply pick it up from the rack and ride away.

"This man has made a very great discovery," Atkins said solemnly to the headman and the elders. "He has developed a way in which a bicycle can be used to drive the pump and still be used for transportation. Without Jeepo's help my idea would have been useless. What I propose is that we draw up a document giving Jeepo one-half of the profits which might come from this invention."

The headman looked at Jeepo and then at the elders. He commenced talking to the elders in a solemn voice. Atkins grasped that the headman had never heard of a binding legal document between a white man and a Sarkhanese. It became clear to him, also, that the headman was determined to drive a hard bargain. After several minutes of consultation he turned to Atkins.

"Do you propose that you and Jeepo will begin to build such pumps?" the headman asked.

"Yes. I would like to enter into business with Jeepo. We will open a shop to build this kind of a pump, and we will sell it to whoever will buy. If the customer does not have the money, we will agree that he can pay off the cost of the pump over a three-year period. But don't get the idea that Jeepo will be paid by me for doing nothing. He must work as the foreman of the shop, and he will have to work hard. Not any harder than I work, but as hard as I do."

One of the elders broke in excitedly. He pointed out that it was very unlikely that a white man would work as hard as Jeepo. He had never seen a white man work with his hands before, and what guarantee could they have that Atkins would work as hard. Another of the elders agreed, pointing out that this looked like the trick of a white man to get cheap labor from a Sarkhanese artisan. Both of the elders were firmly opposed to Jeepo entering into the partnership.

During all of this discussion, Jeepo did not speak. He tinkered with the pump and bicycle mechanism, tightening gears, checking valves, and tightening the bicycle chain. When the two elders had finished talking, he turned around and came through the mud of the rice paddy to where the group was talking.

"I have listened without speaking to what you foolish old men have been saying," Jeepo said, his voice harsh with anger. "This American is different from other white men. He knows how to work with his hands. He built this machine with his own fingers and his own brain. You

people do not understand such things. But men that work with their hands and muscles understand one another. Regardless of what you say, I will enter into business with this man if he will have me."

There was a quick flush of shame on the headman's face. "I think that Jeepo is correct," he said. "This man can be trusted. I will now write up the document which will assure that he and Jeepo share the profits and the work equally."

"And the document should say that neither I nor the American shall license or patent the idea of the pump," Jeepo said. "We will make the idea available to anyone else who can make it. But on the ones we make, we deserve the profit. That is the way of working men."

Jeepo looked at Atkins. Atkins was pleased, and he nodded.

"Also, when we have made some pumps and sold them we will print little books and it will show others how to do it," Atkins said. "We will send it around the whole of Sarkhan, and the village of Chang 'Dong will become famous for its mechanical skills."

Jeepo and Atkins did not wait for the headman to complete their contract before beginning work. Two days later they had rented a large old rice warehouse on the edge of Chang 'Dong. In another day they had hired twelve workers. Jeepo and Atkins drove into Haidho, bought used tools and supplies, and carted them back to the warehouse. In a week the plant was in full operation. Over the entrance to the warehouse a small sign written in Sarkhanese said: "The Jeepo-Atkins Company, Limited." Inside the warehouse was a scene of incredible and frantic effort. Jeepo and Atkins worked eighteen to twenty hours a day. They trained the Sarkhanese; they installed a small forge which glowed red-hot most of the day; they tested materials; they hammered; they swore; and several times a day they lost their tempers and ranted at one another. Their arguments, for some reason, caused the Sarkhanese workmen a great deal of pleasure, and it was not until several months had passed that Atkins realized why—they were the only times that the Sarkhanese had ever seen one of their own kind arguing fairly and honestly, and with a chance of success, against a white man.

Emma Atkins did not stay long in the suburb outside of Haidho. Within a week she had moved their belongings to a small house in Chang 'Dong. She bustled about her home and through the village, buying chickens and vegetables, and making huge casseroles of rice and chicken. Every day at noon she and several of the village women brought two of the casseroles to the warehouse and all of the men ate from them. Emma seemed to find it not at all unusual that her husband should be in a tiny hillside village constructing something as outlandish as bicycle water pumps.

Once a technical advisor from the American Embassy called at the warehouse and watched quietly for several hours. The next day the counsellor of the Embassy called. Taking Atkins to one side, he pointed out to him that for white men to work with their hands, and especially in the countryside, lowered the reputation of all white men. He appealed to Atkins' pride to give up this project. Moreover, he pointed out that the French, most experienced of colonizers, had never allowed natives to handle machinery. Atkins' reply was brief, but it was pointed, and the counsellor drove away in anger. Atkins returned joyfully to his work in the warehouse.

At the end of six weeks they had manufactured twenty-three pumps. When the twenty-fourth pump was finished, Atkins called all of the men together. He and Jeepo then faced the group and between them outlined what now had to be done. Jeepo did most of the talking.

"This is the difficult part," Jeepo started quietly. "You have worked hard and well to build these pumps—now you must sell them. Our friend Atkins here says that in America one of the best things that can happen to engineers like yourself is to be allowed to sell what they make. So each of you will now take two of these pumps as samples, and go out and take orders for more. For each pump that you sell you will get a ten per cent commission."

One of the men interrupted. He did not understand what a commission was. There was a confused five minutes while Atkins and Jeepo explained, and when they were finished the prospective engineer-salesmen were smiling cheerfully. They had never heard of such a proposal before, but it struck them as both attractive and ingenious. When the discussion was over, twelve contracts were laid out on a table; and each of the Sarkhanese signed a contract between himself and The Jeepo-Atkins Company, Limited.

The next morning twelve oxcarts were lined up outside the warehouse. Two of the pumps were carefully laid out on beds of straw on each of these carts. By noon the twelve salesmen had left for all parts of the province.

Now the waiting began. Jeepo, the headman, the elders, and everyone else in the village realized that everything rested on the persuasiveness of the engineer-salesmen and the performance of the bicycle-powered pump. If no orders were placed, Atkins would have to leave, and the excitement of the factory would disappear. In only a few weeks all of this activity had become very important to the people of Chang 'Dong. The people drifted into the warehouse, and watched Jeepo and Atkins at work, and many of them began to help. The tension grew steadily; and when four days had passed and not one of the salesmen had returned, a blanket of gloom as thick as a morning mist settled over the village.

Then on the morning of the fifth day one of the salesmen returned. He drove at a speed which, for an oxcart, is rare. The ox stumbled and splashed mud in the air, and the salesman beat the animal with gusto and enthusiasm. As the ox labored up the hill, everyone in the village came to the warehouse to learn what would happen. When the cart, covered with mud, drew to a halt, there was a low murmur. They could all see that the cart was empty. The driver got down from the cart slowly, fully

286

aware of his importance. He walked over calmly and stood before his two employers.

"I have the pleasure to inform you, sirs, that I have done wrong," he began, a grin on his face. "You told me that I should bring back the two samples, but I was unable to do it. I have taken orders for eight pumps. But two of my customers insisted that I deliver the pumps at once. Because their paddies were in desperate need of water and the crops might have been ruined, I reluctantly gave them the pumps. I hope I have not made a mistake."

There was a deep sigh from the crowd and everyone turned and looked at Jeepo and Atkins. These two squat, ugly, grease-splattered men stared at one another for a moment, and then let out shouts of joy. Jeepo hugged Atkins. Atkins hugged Jeepo, and then Jeepo hugged Mrs. Atkins. Then everyone in the village hugged everyone else. For several hours an improvised party involved the entire village.

The next morning the village was up early, but not as early as Atkins and Jeepo. As the people went down to the warehouse, they heard the clank of hammers and wrenches. They peered into the dim interior of the warehouse and smiled at one another. Atkins and Jeepo were in the midst of a terrible argument over a modification of the pump. Emma Atkins was laying out a huge breakfast in front of the two men, and they were ignoring it as they continued their argument.

TIN LIZZIE

John Dos Passos

For twenty years or more,
    ever since he'd left his father's farm when he was sixteen to get a job in a Detroit machineshop, Henry Ford had been nuts about machinery. First it was watches, then he designed a steamtractor, then he built a horseless carriage with an engine adapted from the Otto gasengine he'd read about in *The World of Science*, then a mechanical buggy with a onecylinder fourcycle motor, that would run forward but not back;
    at last, in nineteight, he felt he was far enough along to risk throwing up his job with the Detroit Edison Company, where he'd worked his way up from night fireman to chief engineer, to put all his time into working on a new gasoline engine,

---

(in the late eighties he'd met Edison at a meeting of electriclight employees in Atlantic City. He'd gone up to Edison after Edison had delivered an address and asked him if he thought gasoline was practical as a motor fuel. Edison had said yes. If Edison said it, it was true. Edison was the great admiration of Henry Ford's life);
    and in driving his mechanical buggy, sitting there at the lever jauntily dressed in a tightbuttoned jacket and a high collar and a derby hat, back and forth over the level illpaved streets of Detroit,
    scaring the big brewery horses and the skinny trotting horses and the sleekrumped pacers with the motor's loud explosions,
    looking for men scatterbrained enough to invest money in a factory for building automobiles.

He was the eldest son of an Irish immigrant who during the Civil War had married the daughter of a prosperous Pennsylvania Dutch farmer and settled down to farming near Dearborn in Wayne County, Michigan;

like plenty of other Americans, young Henry grew up hating the endless sogging through the mud about the chores, the hauling and pitching manure, the kerosene lamps to clean, the irk and sweat and solitude of the farm.

He was a slender, active youngster, a good skater, clever with his hands; what he liked was to tend the machinery and let the others do the heavy work. His mother had told him not to drink, smoke, gamble, or go into debt, and he never did.

When he was in his early twenties his father tried to get him back from Detroit, where he was working as mechanic and repairman for the Drydock Engine Company that built engines for steamboats, by giving him forty acres of land.

Young Henry built himself an uptodate square white dwellinghouse with a false mansard roof and married and settled down on the farm,

but he let the hired men do the farming;

he bought himself a buzzsaw and rented a stationery engine and cut the timber off the woodlots.

He was a thrifty young man who never drank or smoked or gambled or coveted his neighbor's wife, but he couldn't stand living on the farm.

He moved to Detroit, and in the brick barn behind his house tinkered for years in his spare time with a mechanical buggy that would be light enough to run over the clayey wagonroads of Wayne County, Michigan.

By 1900 he had a practicable car to promote.

He was forty years old before the Ford Motor Company was started and production began to move.

Speed was the first thing the early automobile manufacturers went after. Races advertised the makes of cars.

Henry Ford himself hung up several records at the track at Grosse Pointe and on the ice on Lake St. Clair. In his .999 he did the mile in thirtynine and fourfifths seconds.

But it had always been his custom to hire others to do the heavy work. The speed he was busy with was speed in production, the records, records in efficient output. He hired Barney Oldfield, a stunt bicyclerider from Salt Lake City, to do the racing for him.

Henry Ford had ideas about other things than the designing of motors, carburetors, magnetos, jigs and fixtures, punches and dies; he had ideas about sales;

that the big money was in economical quantity production, quick turnover, cheap interchangeable easilyreplaced standardized parts;

it wasn't until 1909, after years of arguing with his partners, that Ford put out the first Model T.

Henry Ford was right.

That season he sold more than ten thousand tin lizzies, ten years later he was selling almost a million a year.

In these years the Taylor Plan was stirring up plantmanagers and manufacturers all over the country. Efficiency was the word. The same ingenuity that went into improving the performance of a machine could go into improving the performance of the workmen producing the machine.

In 1913 they established the assemblyline at Ford's. That season the profits were something like twenty-five million dollars, but they had trouble in keeping the men on the job, machinists didn't seem to like it at Ford's.

Henry Ford had ideas about other things than production.

He was the largest automobile manufacturer in the world; he paid high wages; maybe if the steady workers thought they were getting a cut (a very small cut) in the profits, it would give trained men an inducement to stick to their jobs,

wellpaid workers might save enough money to buy a tin lizzie; the first day Ford's announced that cleancut properlymarried American workers who wanted jobs had a chance to make five bucks a day (of course it turned out that there were strings to it; always there were strings to it)

such an enormous crowd waited outside the Highland Park plant

all through the zero January night

that there was a riot when the gates were opened; cops broke heads, jobhunters threw bricks; property, Henry Ford's own property, was destroyed. The company dicks had to turn on the firehose to beat back the crowd.

The American Plan; automotive prosperity seeping down from above; it turned out there were strings to it.

But that five dollars a day
paid to good, clean American workmen
who didn't drink or smoke cigarettes or read or think,
and who didn't commit adultery
and whose wives didn't take in boarders,
made America once more the Yukon of the sweated workers of the world;
made all the tin lizzies and the automotive age, and incidentally,
made Henry Ford the automobileer, the admirer of Edison, the birdlover,
the great American of his time.

FAREWELL, MY LOVELY!

Lee Strout White

I see by the new Sears Roebuck catalogue that it is still possible to buy an axle for a 1909 Model T Ford, but I am not deceived. The great days have faded, the end is in sight. Only one page in the current catalogue is devoted to parts and accessories for the Model T; yet everyone remembers springtimes when the Ford gadget section was larger than men's clothing, almost as large as household furnishings. The last Model T was built in 1927, and the car is fading from what scholars call the American scene— which is an understatement, because to a few million people who grew up with it, the old Ford practically *was* the American scene.

— *"Farewell, My Lovely!"* originally appeared in The New Yorker over the pseudonym Lee Strout White. It was suggested by a manuscript submitted to the magazine by Richard Lee Strout and was written by E. B. White (reprinted by permission; copyright © 1936, 1964 The New Yorker Magazine, Inc.; published in book form by G. P. Putnam's Sons under the title "Farewell to Model T" in 1936; reprinted under its original title in The Second Tree From the Corner, by E. B. White, Harper & Row, Publishers, 1954)

It was the miracle God had wrought. And it was patently the sort of thing that could only happen once. Mechanically uncanny, it was like nothing that had ever come to the world before. Flourishing industries rose and fell with it. As a vehicle, it was hardworking, commonplace, heroic; and it often seemed to transmit those qualities to the persons who rode in it. My own generation identifies it with Youth, with its gaudy, irretrievable excitements; before it fades into the mist, I would like to pay it the tribute of the sigh that is not a sob, and set down random entries in a shape somewhat less cumbersome than a Sears Roebuck catalogue.

The Model T was distinguished from all other makes of cars by the fact that its transmission was of a type known as planetary—which was half metaphysics, half sheer friction. Engineers accepted the word "planetary" in its epicyclic sense, but I was always conscious that it also meant "wandering," "erratic." Because of the peculiar nature of this planetary element, there was always, in Model T, a certain dull rapport between engine and wheels, and even when the car was in a state known as neutral, it trembled with a deep imperative and tended to inch forward. There was never a moment when the bands were not faintly egging the machine on. In this respect it was like a horse, rolling the bit on its tongue, and country people brought to it the same technique they used with draft animals.

Its most remarkable quality was its rate of acceleration. In its palmy days the Model T could take off faster than anything on the road. The reason was simple. To get under way, you simply hooked the third finger of the right hand around a lever on the steering column, pulled down hard, and shoved your left foot forcibly against the low-speed pedal. These were simple, positive motions; the car responded by lunging forward with a roar. After a few seconds of this turmoil, you took your toe off the pedal, eased up a mite on the throttle, and the car, possessed of only two forward speeds, catapulted directly into high with a series of ugly jerks and was off on its glorious errand. The abruptness of this departure was never equalled in other cars of the period. The human leg was (and still is) incapable of letting in a clutch with anything like the forthright abandon that used to send Model T on its way. Letting in a clutch is a negative, hesitant motion, depending on delicate nervous control; pushing down the Ford pedal was a simple, country motion—an expansive act, which came as natural as kicking an old door to make it budge.

The driver of the old Model T was a man enthroned. The car, with top up, stood seven feet high. The driver sat on top of the gas tank, brooding it with his own body. When he wanted gasoline, he alighted, along with everything else in the front seat; the seat was pulled off, the metal cap unscrewed, and a wooden stick thrust down to sound the liquid in the well. There were always a couple of these sounding sticks kicking around in the ratty sub-cushion regions of a flivver. Refuelling was more of a social function then, because the driver had to unbend, whether he wanted to or not. Directly in front of the driver was the windshield—high,

uncompromisingly erect. Nobody talked about air resistance, and the four cylinders pushed the car through the atmosphere with a simple disregard of physical law.

There was this about a Model T: the purchaser never regarded his purchase as a complete, finished product. When you bought a Ford, you figured you had a start—a vibrant, spirited framework to which could be screwed an almost limitless assortment of decorative and functional hardware. Driving away from the agency, hugging the new wheel between your knees, you were already full of creative worry. A Ford was born naked as a baby, and a flourishing industry grew up out of correcting its rare deficiencies and combatting its fascinating diseases. Those were the great days of lily-painting. I have been looking at some old Sears Roebuck catalogues, and they bring everything back so clear.

First you bought a Ruby Safety Reflector for the rear, so that your posterior would glow in another's car's brilliance. Then you invested thirty-nine cents in some radiator Moto Wings, a popular ornament which gave the Pegasus touch to the machine and did something godlike to the owner. For nine cents you bought a fanbelt guide to keep the belt from slipping off the pulley.

You bought a radiator compound to stop leaks. This was as much a part of everybody's equipment as aspirin tablets are of a medicine cabinet. You bought special oil to prevent chattering, a clamp-on dash light, a patching outfit, a tool box which you bolted to the running board, a sun visor, a steering-column brace to keep the column rigid, and a set of emergency containers for gas, oil, and water—three thin, disc-like cans which reposed in a case on the running board during long, important journeys —red for gas, gray for water, green for oil. It was only a beginning. After the car was about a year old, steps were taken to check the alarming disintegration. (Model T was full of tumors, but they were benign.) A set of anti-rattlers (ninety-eight cents) was a popular panacea.

You hooked them on to the gas and spark rods, to the brake pull rod, and to the steering-rod connections. Hood silencers, of black rubber, were applied to the fluttering hood. Shock-absorbers and snubbers gave "complete relaxation." Some people bought rubber pedal pads, to fit over the standard metal pedals. (I didn't like these, I remember.) Persons of a suspicious or pugnacious turn of mind bought a rear-view mirror; but most Model T owners weren't worried by what was coming from behind because they would soon enough see it out in front. They rode in a state of cheerful catalepsy. Quite a large mutinous clique among Ford owners went over to a foot accelerator (you could buy one and screw it to the floor board), but there was a certain madness in these people, because the Model T, just as she stood, had a choice of three foot pedals to push, and there were plenty of moments when both feet were occupied in the routine performance of duty and when the only way to speed up the engine was with the hand throttle.

Gadget bred gadget. Owners not only bought ready-made gadgets, they invented gadgets to meet their special needs. I myself drove my car directly from the agency to the blacksmith's, and had the smith affix two enormous iron brackets to the port running board to support an army trunk.

People who owned closed models builded along different lines: they bought ball grip handles for opening doors, window anti-rattlers, and de-luxe flower vases of the cut-glass anti-splash type. People with delicate sensibilities garnished their car with a device called the Donna Lee Automobile Disseminator—a porous vase guaranteed, according to Sears, to fill the car with a "faint clean odor of lavender." The gap between open cars and closed cars was not as great then as it is now: for $11.95, Sears Roebuck converted your touring car into a sedan and you went forth renewed. One agreeable quality of the old Fords was that they had no bumpers, and their fenders softened and wilted with the years and permitted the driver to squeeze in and out of tight places.

Tires were 30 x 3½, cost about twelve dollars, and punctured readily. Everybody carried a Jiffy patching set, with a nutmeg grater to roughen the tube before the goo was spread on. Everybody was capable of putting on a patch, expected to have to, and did have to.

During my association with Model T's, self-starters were not a prevalent accessory. They were expensive and under suspicion. Your car came equipped with a serviceable crank, and the first thing you learned was how to Get Results. It was a special trick, and until you learned it (usually from another Ford owner, but sometimes by a period of appalling experimentation) you might as well have been winding up an awning. The trick was to leave the ignition switch off, proceed to the animal's head, pull the choke (which was a little wire protruding through the radiator) and give the crank two or three nonchalant upward lifts. Then, whistling as though thinking about something else, you would saunter back to the driver's cabin, turn the ignition on, return to the crank, and this time, catching it on the down stroke, give it a quick spin with plenty of That. If this procedure was followed, the engine almost always responded—first with a few scattered explosions, then with a tumultuous gunfire, which you checked by racing around to the driver's seat and retarding the throttle. Often, if the emergency brake hadn't been pulled all the way back, the car advanced on you the instant the first explosion occurred and you would hold it back by leaning your weight against it. I can still feel my old Ford nuzzling me at the curb, as though looking for an apple in my pocket.

In zero weather, ordinary cranking became an impossibility, except for giants. The oil thickened, and it became necessary to jack up the rear wheels, which, for some planetary reason, eased the throw.

The lore and legend that governed the Ford were boundless. Owners had their own theories about everything; they discussed mutual problems in that wise, infinitely resourceful way old women discuss rheumatism. Exact knowledge was pretty scarce, and often proved less effective than superstition. Dropping a camphor ball into the gas tank was a popular expedient; it seemed to have a tonic effect on both man and machine. There wasn't much to base exact knowledge on. The Ford driver flew blind. He didn't know the temperature of his engine, the speed of his car, the amount of his fuel, or the pressure of his oil (the old Ford lubricated itself by what was amiably described as the "splash system"). A speedometer cost money and was an extra, like a windshield-wiper. The dashboard of the early models was bare save for an ignition key; later models, grown effete, boasted an ammeter which pulsated alarmingly with the throbbing of the car. Under the dash was a box of coils, with vibrators which you adjusted, or thought you adjusted. Whatever the driver learned of his motor, he learned not through instruments but through sudden developments. I remember that the timer was one of the vital organs about which there was ample doctrine. When everything else had been checked, you "had a look" at the timer. It was an extravagantly odd little device, simple in construction, mysterious in function. It contained a roller, held by a spring, and there were four contact points on the inside of the case against which, many people believed, the roller rolled. I have had a timer apart on a sick Ford many times. But I never really knew what I was up to—I was just showing off before God. There were almost as many schools of thought as there were timers. Some people, when things went wrong, just clenched their teeth and gave the timer a smart crack with a wrench. Other people opened it up and blew on it. There was a school that held that the timer needed large amounts of oil; they fixed it by frequent baptism. And there was a school that was positive it was meant to run dry as a bone; these people were continually taking it off and wiping it. I remember once spitting into a timer; not in anger, but in a spirit of research. You see, the Model T driver moved in the realm of metaphysics. He believed his car could be hexed.

One reason the Ford anatomy was never reduced to an exact science was that, having "fixed" it, the owner couldn't honestly claim that the treatment had brought about the cure. There were too many authenticated cases of Fords fixing themselves—restored naturally to health after a short rest. Farmers soon discovered this, and it fitted nicely with their draft-horse philosophy: "Let 'er cool off and she'll snap into it again."

A Ford owner had Number One Bearing constantly in mind. This bearing, being at the front end of the motor, was the one that always burned out, because the oil didn't reach it when the car was climbing hills. (That's what I was always told, anyway.) The oil used to recede and leave Number One dry as a clam flat; you had to watch that bearing like a hawk. It was like a weak heart—you could hear it start knocking, and that was when you stopped to let her cool off. Try as you would to keep the oil supply right, in the end Number One always went out. "Number One Bearing burned out on me and I had to have her replaced," you would say, wisely; and your companions always had a lot to tell about how to protect and pamper Number One to keep her alive.

Sprinkled not too liberally among the millions of amateur witch doctors who drove Fords and applied their own abominable cures were the heaven-sent mechanics who could really make the car talk. These professionals turned up in undreamed-of spots. One time, on the banks of the Columbia River in Washington, I heard the rear end go out of my Model T when I was trying to whip it up a steep incline onto the deck of a ferry. Something snapped; the car slid backward into the mud. It seemed to me like the end of the trail. But the captain of the ferry, observing the withered remnant, spoke up.

"What's got her?" he asked.

"I guess it's the rear end," I replied, listlessly. The captain leaned over the rail and stared.

Then I saw that there was a hunger in his eyes that set him off from other men.

"Tell you what," he said, carelessly, trying to cover up his eagerness, "let's pull the son of a bitch up onto the boat, and I'll help you fix her while we're going back and forth on the river."

We did just this. All that day I plied between the towns of Pasco and Kennewick, while the skipper (who had once worked in a Ford garage) directed the amazing work of resetting the bones of my car.

Springtime in the heyday of the Model T was a delirious season. Owning a car was still a major excitement, roads were still wonderful and bad. The Fords were obviously conceived in madness: any car which was capable of going from forward into reverse without any perceptible mechanical hiatus was bound to be a mighty challenging thing to the human imagination. Boys used to veer them off the highway into a level pasture and run wild with them, as though they were cutting up with a girl. Most everybody used the reverse pedal quite as much as the regular foot brake—it distributed the wear over the bands and wore them all down evenly. That was the big trick, to wear all the bands down evenly, so that the final chattering would be total and the whole unit scream for renewal.

The days were golden, the nights were dim and strange. I still recall with trembling those loud, nocturnal crises when you drew up to a signpost and raced the engine so the lights would be bright enough to read destinations by. I have never been really planetary since. I suppose it's time to say goodbye. Farewell, my lovely!

CLEAN FUN AT RIVERHEAD

Tom Wolfe

The inspiration for the demolition derby came to Lawrence Mendelsohn one night in 1958 when he was nothing but a spare-ribbed twenty-eight-year-old stock car driver halfway through his 10th lap around the Islip, L.I., Speedway and taking a curve too wide. A lubberly young man with a Chicago boxcar haircut came up on the inside in a 1949 Ford and caromed him 12 rows up into the grandstand, but Lawrence Mendelsohn and his entire car did not hit one spectator.

"That was what got me," he said. "I remember I was hanging upside down from my seat belt like a side of Jersey bacon and wondering why no one was sitting where I hit. 'Lousy promotion,' I said to myself.

"Not only that, but everybody who *was* in the stands forgot about the race and came running over to look at me gift-wrapped upside down in a fresh pile of junk."

At that moment occurred the transformation of Lawrence Mendelsohn, racing driver, into Lawrence Mendelsohn, promoter, and, a few transactions later, owner of the Islip Speedway, where he kept seeing more of this same underside of stock car racing that everyone in the industry avoids putting into words. Namely, that for every purist who comes to see the fine points of the race, such as who is going to win, there are probably five waiting for the wrecks to which stock car racing is so gloriously prone.

The pack will be going into a curve when suddenly two cars, three cars, four cars tangle, spinning and splattering all over each other and

— "*Clean Fun at Riverhead*" by *Tom Wolfe, reprinted with permission of Farrar, Straus & Giroux, Inc. from The Kandy-Kolored Tangerine-Flake Streamline Baby by Tom Wolfe; copyright © 1963 by The New York Herald Tribune Inc.*

the retaining walls, upside down, right side up, inside out and in pieces, with the seams bursting open and discs, rods, wires and gasoline spewing out and yards of sheet metal shearing off like Reynolds Wrap and crumpling into the most baroque shapes, after which an ash-blue smoke starts seeping up from the ruins and a thrill begins to spread over the stands like Newburg sauce.

So why put up with the monotony between crashes?

Such, in brief, is the early history of what is culturally the most important sport ever originated in the United States, a sport that ranks with the gladiatorial games of Rome as a piece of national symbolism. Lawrence Mendelsohn had a vision of an automobile sport that would be all crashes. Not two cars, not three cars, not four cars, but 100 cars would be out in an arena doing nothing but smashing each other into shrapnel. The car that outrammed and outdodged all the rest, the last car that could still move amid the smoking heap, would take the prize money.

So at 8:15 at night at the Riverhead Raceway, just west of Riverhead, L.I., on Route 25, amid the quaint tranquility of the duck and turkey farm flatlands of eastern Long Island, Lawrence Mendelsohn stood up on the back of a flat truck in his red neon warmup jacket and lectured his 100 drivers on the rules and niceties of the new game, the "demolition derby." And so at 8:30 the first 25 cars moved out onto the raceway's quarter-mile stock car track. There was not enough room for 100 cars to mangle each other. Lawrence Mendelsohn's dream would require four heats. Now the 25 cars were placed at intervals all about the circumference of the track, making flatulent revving noises, all headed not around the track but toward a point in the center of the infield.

Then the entire crowd, about 4,000, started chanting a countdown, "Ten, nine, eight, seven, six, five, four, three, two," but it was impossible to hear the rest, because right after "two" half the crowd went into a strange whinnying wail.

The starter's flag went up, and the 25 cars took off, roaring into second gear with no mufflers, all headed toward that same point in the center of the infield, converging nose on nose.

The effect was exactly what one expects that many simultaneous crashes to produce: the unmistakable tympany of automobiles colliding and cheap-gauge sheet metal buckling; front ends folding together at the same cockeyed angles police photographs of night-time wreck scenes capture so well on grainy paper; smoke pouring from under the hoods and hanging over the infield like a howitzer cloud; a few of the surviving cars lurching eccentrically on bent axles. At last, after four heats, there were only two cars moving through the junk, a 1953 Chrysler and a 1958 Cadillac. In the Chrysler a small fascia of muscles named Spider Ligon, who smoked a cigar while he drove, had the Cadillac cornered up against a guard rail in front of the main grandstand. He dispatched it by swinging around and backing full throttle through the left side of its grille and radiator.

By now the crowd was quite beside itself. Spectators broke through a gate in the retaining screen. Some rushed to Spider Ligon's car, hoisted him to their shoulders and marched off the field, howling. Others clambered over the stricken cars of the defeated, enjoying the details of their ruin, and howling. The good, full cry of triumph and annihilation rose from Riverhead Raceway, and the demolition derby was over.

That was the 154th demolition derby in two years. Since Lawrence Mendelsohn staged the first one at Islip Speedway in 1961, they have been held throughout the United States at the rate of one every five days, resulting in the destruction of about 15,000 cars. The figures alone indicate a gluttonous appetite for the sport. Sports writers, of course, have managed to ignore demolition derbies even more successfully than they have ignored stock car racing and drag racing. All in all, the new automobile sports have shown that the sports pages, which on the surface appear to hum with life and earthiness, are at bottom pillars of gentility. This drag racing and demolition derbies and things, well, there are too many kids in it with sideburns, tight Levis and winklepicker boots.

Yet the demolition derbies keep growing on word-of-mouth publicity. The "nationals" were held last month at Langhorne, Pa., with 50 cars in the finals, and demolition derby fans everywhere know that Don McTavish, of Dover, Mass., is the new world's champion. About 1,250,000 spectators have come to the 154 contests held so far. More than 75 per cent of the derbies have drawn full houses.

The nature of their appeal is clear enough. Since the onset of the Christian era, i.e., since about 500 A.D., no game has come along to fill the gap left by the abolition of the purest of all sports, gladiatorial combat. As late as 300 A.D. these bloody duels, usually between men but sometimes between women and dwarfs, were enormously popular not only in Rome but throughout the Roman Empire. Since then no game, not even boxing, has successfully acted out the underlying motifs of most sport, that is, aggression and destruction.

Boxing, of course, is an aggressive sport, but one contestant has actually destroyed the other in a relatively small percentage of matches. Other games are progressively more sublimated forms of sport. Often, as in the case of football, they are encrusted with oddments of passive theology and metaphysics to the effect that the real purpose of the game is to foster character, teamwork, stamina, physical fitness and the ability to "give-and-take."

But not even those wonderful clergymen who pray in behalf of Congress, expressway ribbon-cuttings, urban renewal projects and testimonial dinners for ethnic aldermen would pray for a demolition derby. The demolition derby is, pure and simple, a form of gladiatorial combat for our times.

As hand-to-hand combat has gradually disappeared from our civilization, even in wartime, and competition has become more and more sophisticated and abstract, Americans have turned to the automobile to satisfy their love of direct aggression. The mild-mannered man who turns into a bear behind the wheel of a car—i.e., who finds in the power of the automobile a vehicle for the release of his inhibitions— is part of American folklore. Among teen-agers the automobile has become the symbol, and in part the physical means, of triumph over family and community restrictions. Seventy-five per cent of all car thefts in the United States are by teen-agers out for "joy rides."

The symbolic meaning of the automobile tones down but by no means vanishes in adulthood. Police traffic investigators have long been convinced that far more accidents are purposeful crashes by belligerent drivers than they could ever prove. One of the heroes of the era was the Middle Eastern diplomat who rammed a magazine writer's car from behind in the Kalorama embassy district of Washington two years ago. When the American bellowed out the window at him, he backed up and smashed his car again. When the fellow leaped out of his car to pick a fight, he backed up and smashed his car a third time, then drove off. He was recalled home for having "gone native."

The unabashed, undisguised, quite purposeful sense of destruction of the demolition derby is its unique contribution. The aggression, the battering, the ruination are there to be enjoyed. The crowd at a demolition derby seldom gasps and often laughs. It enjoys the same full-throated participation as Romans at the Colosseum. After each trial or heat at a demolition derby, two drivers go into the finals. One is the driver whose car was still going at the end. The other is the driver the crowd selects from among the 24 vanquished on the basis of his courage, showmanship or simply the awesomeness of his crashes. The numbers of the cars are read over loudspeakers, and the crowd chooses one with its cheers. By the same token, the crowd may force a driver out of competition if he appears cowardly or merely cunning. This is the sort of driver who drifts around the edge of the battle avoiding crashes with the hope that the other cars will eliminate one another. The umpire waves a yellow flag at him and he must crash into someone within 30 seconds or run the risk of being booed off the field in dishonor and disgrace.

The frank relish of the crowd is nothing, however, compared to the kick the contestants get out of the game. It costs a man an average of $50 to retrieve a car from a junk yard and get it running for a derby. He will only get his money back—$50—for winning a heat. The chances of being smashed up in the madhouse first 30 seconds of a round are so great, even the best of drivers faces long odds in his shot at the $500 first prize. None of that matters to them.

Tommy Fox, who is nineteen, said he entered the demolition derby because, "You know, it's fun. I like it. You know what I mean?" What was fun about it? Tommy Fox had a way of speaking that was much like the early Marlon Brando. Much of what he had to say came from the trapezii, which he rolled quite a bit, and the forehead, which he cocked, and the eyebrows, which he could bring together expressively from time to time. "Well," he said, "you know, like when you hit 'em, and all that. It's fun."

Tommy Fox had a lot of fun in the first heat. Nobody was bashing around quite like he was in his old green Hudson. He did not win, chiefly because he took too many chances, but the crowd voted him into the finals as the best showman.

"I got my brother," said Tommy. "I came in from the side and he didn't even see me."

His brother is Don Fox, thirty-two, who owns the junk yard where they both got their cars. Don likes to hit them, too, only he likes it almost too much. Don drives with such abandon, smashing into the first car he can get a shot at and leaving himself wide open, he does not stand much chance of finishing the first three minutes.

For years now sociologists have been calling upon one another to undertake a serious study of America's "car culture." No small part of it is the way the automobile has, for one very large segment of the population, become the focus of the same sort of quasi-religious dedication as art is currently for another large segment of a higher social order. Tommy Fox is unemployed, Don Fox runs a junk yard, Spider Ligon is a maintenance man for Brookhaven Naval Laboratory, but to categorize them as such is getting no closer to the truth than to have categorized William Faulkner in 1926 as a clerk at Lord & Taylor, although he was.

Tommy Fox, Don Fox and Spider Ligon are acolytes of the car culture, an often esoteric world of arts and sciences that came into its own after World War II and now has believers of two generations. Charlie Turbush, thirty-five, and his son, Buddy, seventeen, were two more contestants, and by no stretch of the imagination can they be characterized as bizarre figures or cultists of the death wish. As for the dangers of driving in a demolition derby, they are quite real by all physical laws. The drivers are protected only by crash helmets, seat belts and the fact that all glass, interior handles, knobs and fixtures have been removed. Yet Lawrence Mendelsohn claims that there have been no serious injuries in 154 demolition derbies and now gets his insurance at a rate below that of stock car racing.

The sport's future may depend in part on word getting around about its relative safety. Already it is beginning to draw contestants here and there from social levels that could give the demolition derby the cachet of respectability. In eastern derbies so far two doctors and three young men of more than passable connections in eastern society have entered under whimsical *noms de combat* and emerged neither scarred nor victorious. Bull fighting had to win the same social combat.

All of which brings to mind that fine afternoon when some high-born Roman women were out in Nero's box at the Colosseum watching this sexy Thracian carve an ugly little Samnite up into prime cuts, and one said, darling, she had an inspiration, and Nero, needless to say, was all for it. Thus began the new vogue of Roman socialites fighting as gladiators themselves, for kicks. By the second century A.D. even the Emperor Commodus was out there with a tiger's head as a helmet hacking away at some poor dazed fall guy. He did a lot for the sport.

Arenas sprang up all over the empire like shopping center bowling alleys.

The future of the demolition derby, then, stretches out over the face of America. The sport draws no lines of gender, and post-debs may reach Lawrence Mendelsohn at his office in Deer Park.

THE DOOR

E. B. White

Everything (he kept saying) is something it isn't. And everybody is always somewhere else. Maybe it was the city, being in the city, that made him feel how queer everything was and that it was something else. Maybe (he kept thinking) it was the names of the things. The names were tex and frequently koid. Or they were flex and oid or they were duroid (sani) or flexsan (duro), but everything was glass (but not quite glass) and the thing that you touched (the surface, washable, crease-resistant) was rubber, only it wasn't quite rubber and you didn't quite touch it but almost. The wall, which was glass but thrutex, turned out on being approached not to be a wall, it was something else, it was an opening or doorway—and the doorway (through which he saw himself approaching) turned out to be something else, it was a wall. And what he had eaten not having agreed with him.

He was in a washable house, but he wasn't sure. Now about those rats, he kept saying to himself. He meant the rats that the Professor had driven crazy by forcing them to deal with problems which were beyond the scope of rats, the insoluble problems. He meant the rats that had been trained to jump at the square card with the circle in the middle, and the card (because it was something it wasn't) would give way and let the rat into a place where the food was, but then one day it would be a trick played on the rat, and the card would be changed, and the rat would jump but the card wouldn't give way, and it was an impossible situation (for a rat) and the rat would go insane and into its eyes would come the unspeakably bright imploring look of the frustrated, and after the convulsions were over and the frantic racing around, then the passive stage would set in and the willingness to let anything be done to it, even if it was something else.

He didn't know which door (or wall) or opening in the house to jump at, to get through, because one was an opening that wasn't a door (it was a void, or koid) and the other was a wall that wasn't an opening, it was a sanitary cupboard of the same color. He caught a glimpse of his eyes staring into his eyes, in the thrutex, and in them was the expression he had seen in the picture of the rats—weary after convulsions and the frantic racing around, when they were willing and did not mind having anything done to them. More and more (he kept saying) I am confronted by a problem which is incapable of solution (for this time even if he chose the right door, there would be no food behind it) and that is what madness is, and things seeming different from what they are. He heard, in the house where he was, in the city to which he had gone (as toward a door which might, or might not, give way), a noise—not a loud noise but more of a low prefabricated humming. It came from a place in the base of the wall (or stat) where the flue carrying the filterable air was, and not far from the Minipiano, which was made of the same material nailbrushes are made of, and which was under the stairs. "This, too, has been tested," she said, pointing, but not at it, "and found viable." It wasn't a loud noise, he kept thinking, sorry that he had seen his eyes, even though it was through his own eyes that he had seen them.

First will come the convulsions (he said), then the exhaustion, then the willingness to let anything be done. "And you better believe it *will* be."

All his life he had been confronted by situations which were incapable of being solved, and there was a deliberateness behind all this, behind this changing of the card (or door), because they would always wait till you had learned to jump at the certain card (or door)—the one with the circle—and then they would change it on you. There have been so many doors changed on me, he said, in the last twenty years, but it is now becoming clear that it is an impossible situation, and the question is whether to jump again, even though they ruffle you in the rump with a blast of air—to make you jump. He wished he wasn't standing by the Minipiano. First they would teach you the prayers and the Psalms, and that would be the right door (the one with the circle), and the long sweet words with the holy sound, and that would be the one to jump at to get where the food was. Then one day you jumped and it didn't give way, so that all you got was the bump on the nose, and the first bewilderment, the first young bewilderment.

I don't know whether to tell her about the door they substituted or not, he said, the one with the equation on it and the picture of the amoeba reproducing itself by division. Or the one with the photostatic copy of the check for thirty-two dollars and fifty cents. But the jumping was so long ago, although the bump is ——— how those old wounds hurt! Being crazy this way wouldn't be so bad if only, if only. If only when you put your foot forward to take a step, the ground wouldn't come up to meet your foot the way it does. And the same way in the street (only I may never get back to the street unless I jump at the right door), the curb coming up to meet your foot, anticipating ever so delicately the weight of the body, which is somewhere else. "We could take your name," she said, "and send it to you." And it wouldn't be so bad if only you could read a sentence all the way through without jumping (your eye) to something else on the same page; and then (he kept thinking) there was that man out in Jersey, the one who started to chop his trees down, one by one, the man who began talking about how he would take his house to pieces, brick by brick, because he faced a problem incapable of solution, probably, so he began to hack at the trees in the yard, began to pluck with trembling fingers at the bricks in the house. Even if a house is not washable, it is worth taking down. It is not till later that the exhaustion sets in.

But it is inevitable that they will keep changing the doors on you, he said, because that is what they are for; and the thing is to get used to it and not let it unsettle the mind. But that would mean not jumping, and you can't. Nobody can not jump. There will be no not-jumping. Among rats, perhaps, but among people never. Everybody has to keep jumping at a door (the one with the circle on it) because that is the way everybody is, especially some people. You wouldn't want me, standing here, to tell you, would you, about my friend the poet (deceased) who said, "My heart has followed all my days something I cannot name"? (It had the circle on it.) And like many poets, although few so beloved, he is gone. It killed him, the jumping. First, of course, there were the preliminary bouts, the convulsions, and the calm and the willingness.

I remember the door with the picture of the girl on it (only it was spring), her arms outstretched in loveliness, her dress (it was the one with the circle on it) uncaught, beginning the slow, clear, blinding cascade—and I guess we would all like to try that door again, for it seemed like the way and for a while it was the way, the door would open and you would go through winged and exalted (like any rat) and the food would be there, the way the Professor had it arranged, everything o.k., and you had chosen the right door, for the world was young. The time they changed that door on me, my nose bled for a hundred hours—how do you like that, Madam? Or would you prefer to show me further through this so strange house, or you could take my name and send it to me, for although my heart has followed all my days something I cannot name, I am tired of the jumping and I do not know which way to go, Madam, and I am not even sure that I am not tried beyond the endurance of man (rat, if you will) and have taken leave of sanity. What are you following these days, old friend, after your recovery from the last bump? What is the name, or is it something you cannot name? The rats have a name for it by this time, perhaps, but I don't know what they call it. I call it plexikoid and it comes in sheets, something like insulating board, unattainable and ugli-proof.

And there was the man out in Jersey, because I keep thinking about his terrible necessity and the passion and trouble he had gone to all those years in the indescribable abundance of a householder's detail, building the estate and the planting of the trees and in spring the lawn-dressing and in fall the bulbs for the spring burgeoning, and the watering of the grass on the long light evenings in summer and the gravel for the driveway (all had to be thought out, planned) and the decorative borders, probably, the perennials and the bug spray, and the building of the house from plans of the architect, first the sills, then the studs, then the full corn in the ear, the floors laid on the floor timbers, smoothed, and then the carpets upon the smooth floors and the curtains and the rods therefor. And then, almost without warning, he would be jumping at the same old door and it wouldn't give: they had changed it on him, making life no longer supportable under the elms in the elm shade, under the maples in the maple shade.

"Here you have the maximum of openness in a small room."

It was impossible to say (maybe it was the city) what made him feel the way he did, and I am not the only one either, he kept thinking—ask any doctor if I am. The doctors, they know how many there are, they even know where the trouble is only they don't like to tell you about the prefrontal lobe because that means making a hole in your skull and removing the work of centuries. It took so long coming, this lobe, so many, many years. (Is it something you read in the paper, perhaps?) And now, the strain being so great, the door having been changed by the Professor once too often —— but it only means a whiff of ether, a few deft strokes, and the higher animal becomes a little easier in his mind and more like the lower one. From now on, you see, that's the way it will be, the ones with the small prefrontal lobes will win because the other ones are hurt too much by this incessant bumping. They can stand just so much, eh, Doctor? (And what is that, pray, that you have in your hand?) Still, you never can tell, eh, Madam?

He crossed (carefully) the room, the thick carpet under him softly, and went toward the door carefully, which was glass and he could see himself in it, and which, at his approach, opened to allow him to pass through; and beyond he half expected to find one of the old doors that he had known, perhaps the one with the circle, the one with the girl, her arms outstretched in loveliness and beauty before him. But he saw instead a moving stairway, and descended in light (he kept thinking) to the street below and to the other people. As he stepped off, the ground came up slightly, to meet his foot.

FLOWERS FOR ALGERNON

Daniel Keyes

progris riport 1 — Martch 5, 1965

Dr. Strauss says I shud rite down what I think
and evrey thing that happins to me from now on.
I dont know why but he says its importint so
they will see if they will use me. I hope they
use me. Miss Kinnian says maybe they can
make me smart. I want to be smart. My name
is Charlie Gordon. I am 37 years old. I have
nuthing more to rite now so I will close for today.

progris riport 2 — martch 6

I had a test today. I think I faled it. And I
think maybe now they wont use me. What
happind is a nice young man was in the room
and he had some white cards and ink spilled
over them. He sed Charlie what do you see on
this card. I was very skared even tho I had my
rabits foot in my pockit because when I was a
kid I always faled tests in school and I spillled
ink to.

I told him I saw a inkblot. He said yes and
it made me feel good, I thot that was all but
when I got up to go he said Charlie we are not
thru yet. Then I dont rcmember so good but
he wantid me to say what was in the ink. I
dint see nuthing in the ink but he said there was
picturs. I reely tryed. I held the card close up
and then far away. Then I said if I had my
glases I could see better I usally only ware my
glases in the movies or TV but I said they are
in the closit in the hall. I got them. Then I
said let me see that card agen I bett Ill find
it now.

I tryed hard but I only saw the ink. I told
him maybe I need new glases. He rote something down on a paper and I got skared of faling
the test. I told him it was a very nice inkblot
with littel points all around the edges. He looked
very sad so that wasnt it. I said please let me
try agen. Ill get it in a few minits because Im
not so fast sometimes. Im a slow reeder too in
Miss Kinnians class for slow adults but I'm
trying very hard.

He gave me a chance with another card that
had 2 kinds of ink spilled on it red and blue.

He was very nice and talked slow like Miss
Kinnian does and he explaned it to me that it
was a *raw shok*. He said pepul see things in the
ink. I said show me where. He said think. I
told him I think a inkblot but that wasn't rite
eather. He said what does it remind you—
pretend something. I closed my eyes for a long
time to pretend. I told him I pretend a fowntan
pen with ink leeking all over a table cloth.

I dont think I passed the *raw shok* test

progris riport 3 — martch 7

Dr Strauss and Dr Nemur say it dont matter
about the inkblots. They said that maybe they
will still use me. I said Miss Kinnian never gave
me tests like that one only spelling and reading.
They said Miss Kinnian told that I was her
bestist pupil in the adult nite scool becaus I
tryed the hardist and I reely wantid to lern.
They said how come you went to the adult nite
scool all by yourself Charlie. How did you
find it. I said I asked pepul and sumbody told
me where I shud go to lern to read and spell
good. They said why did you want to. I told
them becaus all my life I wanted to be smart and
not dumb. But its very hard to be smart. They
said you know it will probly be tempirery. I
said yes. Miss Kinnian told me. I dont care
if it herts.

Later I had more crazy tests today. The nice
lady who gave it to me told me the name and
I asked her how do you spellit so I can rite it
my progris riport. THEMATIC APPERCEPTION

TEST. I dont know the frist 2 words but I know what *test* means. You got to pass it or you get bad marks. This test looked easy because I coud see the picturs. Only this time she dint want me to tell her the picturs. That mixed me up. She said make up storys about the pepul in the picturs.

I told her how can you tell storys about pepul you never met. I said why shud I make up lies. I never tell lies any more because I always get caut.

She told me this test and the other one the raw-shok was for getting personality. I laffed so hard. I said how can you get that thing from inkblots and fotos. She got sore and put her picturs away. I don't care. It was sily. I gess I faled that test too.

Later some men in white coats took me to a difernt part of the hospitil and gave me a game to play. It was like a race with a white mouse. They called the mouse Algernon. Algernon was in a box with a lot of twists and turns like all kinds of walls and they gave me a pencil and a paper with lines and lots of boxes. On one side it said START and on the other end it said FINISH. They said it was *amazed* and that Algernon and me had the same *amazed* to do. I dint see how we could have the same *amazed* if Algernon had a box and I had a paper but I dint say nothing. Anyway there wasnt time because the race started.

One of the men had a watch he was trying to hide so I wouldnt see it so I tryed not to look and that made me nervus.

Anyway that test made me feel worser than all the others because they did it over 10 times with different *amazeds* and Algernon won every time. I dint know that mice were so smart. Maybe thats because Algernon is a white mouse. Maybe white mice are smarter than other mice.

progris riport 4 — Mar 8

Their going to use me! Im so exited I can hardly write. Dr Nemur and Dr Strauss had a argament about it first. Dr Nemur was in the office when Dr Strauss brot me in. Dr Nemur was worryed about using me but Dr Strauss told him Miss Kinnian rekemmended me the best from all the people who she was teaching. I like Miss Kinnian becaus shes a very smart teacher. And she said Charlie your going to have a second chance. If you volenteer for this experament you mite get smart. They dont know if it will be perminint but theirs a chance. Thats why I said ok even when I was scared because she said it was an operashun. She said dont be scared Charlie you done so much with so little I think you deserv it most of all.

So I got scaird when Dr. Nemur and Dr. Strauss argud about it. Dr. Strauss said I had something that was very good. He said I had a good *motorvation*. I never even knew I had that. I felt proud when he said that not every body with an eye-q of 68 had that thing. I dont know what it is or where I got it but he said Algernon had it too. Algernons *motor-vation* is the cheese they put in his box. But it cant be that because I dint eat any cheese this week.

Then he told Dr Nemur something I dint understand so while they were talking I wrote down some of the words.

He said Dr. Nemur I know Charlie is not what you had in mind as the first of your new brede of intelek** (coudnt get the word) super-man. But most people of his low ment** are host** and uncoop** they are usually dull apath** and hard to reach. He has a good natcher hes intristed and eager to please.

Dr Nemur said remember he will be the first human beeng ever to have his intelijence tripled by surgicle meens.

Dr. Strauss said exakly. Look at how well hes lerned to read and write for his low mentel age its as grate an acheve** as you and I lerning einstines therey of **vity without help. That shows the inteness motor-vation. Its comparat** a tremen** achiev** I say we use Charlie.

I dint get all the words but it sounded like Dr Strauss was on my side and like the other one wasnt.

Then Dr Nemur nodded he said all right maybe your right. We will use Charlie. When he said that I got so exited I jumped up and shook his hand for being so good to me. I told him thank you doc you wont be sorry for giving me a second chance. And I mean it like I told him. After the operashun Im gonna try to be smart. Im gonna try awful hard.

progris riport 5 — Mar 10

Im skared. Lots of the nurses and the people who gave me the tests came to bring me candy and wish me luck. I hope I have luck. I got my rabits foot and my lucky penny. Only a black cat crossed me when I was comming to the hospitil. Dr Strauss says dont be superstitis Charlie this is science. Anyway Im keeping my rabits foot with me.

I asked Dr Strauss if Ill beat Algernon in the race after the operashun and he said maybe. If the operashun works Ill show that mouse I can be as smart as he is. Maybe smarter. Then Ill be abel to read better and spell the words good and know lots of things and be like other people. I want to be smart like other people. If it works perminint they will make everybody smart all over the wurld.

They dint give me anything to eat this morning. I don't know what eating has to do with getting smart. Im very hungry and Dr. Nemur took away my box of candy. That Dr Nemur is a grouch. Dr Strauss says I can have it back after the operashun. You cant eat befor a operation ——

progress report 6 — Mar 15

The operashun dint hurt. He did it while I was sleeping. They took off the bandijis from my head today so I can make a PROGRESS REPORT. Dr. Nemur who looked at some of my other ones says I spell PROGRESS wrong and told me how to spell it and REPORT too. I got to try and remember that.

I have a very bad memary for spelling. Dr Strauss says its ok to tell about all the things that happin to me but he says I should tell more about what I feel and what I think. When I told him I dont know how to think he said try.

All the time when the bandijis were on my eyes I tryed to think. Nothing happened. I dont know what to think about. Maybe if I ask him he will tell me how I can think now that Im suppose to get smart. What do smart people think about. Fancy things I suppose. I wish I knew some fancy things already.

progress report 7 — mar 19

Nothing is happining. I had lots of tests and different kinds of races with Algernon. I hate that mouse. He always beats me. Dr. Strauss said I got to play those games. And he said some time I got to take those tests over again. Those inkblots are stupid. And those pictures are stupid too. I like to draw a picture of a man and a woman but I wont make up lies about people.

I got a headache from trying to think so much. I thot Dr Strauss was my friend but he dont help me. He dont tell me what to think or when Ill get smart. Miss Kinnian dint come to see me. I think writing these progress reports are stupid too.

progress report 8 — Mar 23

Im going back to work at the factery. They said it was better I shud go back to work but I cant tell anyone what the operashun was for and I have to come to the hospitil for an hour evry night after work. They are gonna pay me mony every month for learning to be smart.

Im glad Im going back to work because I miss my job and all my friends and all the fun we have there.

Dr Strauss says I shud keep writing things down but I dont have to do it every day just when I think of something or something speshul happins. He says dont get discoridged because it takes time and it happins slow. He says it took a long time with Algernon before he got 3 times smarter than he was before. Thats why Algernon beats me all the time because he had that operashun too. That makes me feel better. I could probly do that *amazed* faster than a reglar mouse. Maybe some day Ill beat him.

302

That would be something. So far Algernon looks smart perminent.

MAR 25 (I dont have to write PROGRESS REPORT on top any more just when I hand it in once a week for Dr Nemur. I just have to put the date on. That saves time)

We had a lot of fun at the factery today. Joe Carp said hey look where Charlie had his operashun what did they do Charlie put some brains in. I was going to tell him but I remembered Dr Strauss said no. Then Frank Reilly said what did you do Charlie forget your key and open your door the hard way. That made me laff. Their really my friends and they like me.

Sometimes somebody will say hey look at Joe or Frank or George he really pulled a Charlie Gordon. I dont know why they say that but they always laff. This morning Amos Borg who is the 4 man at Donnegans used my name when he shouted at Ernie the office boy. Ernie lost a packige. He said Ernie for godsake what are you trying to be a Charlie Gordon. I dont understand why he said that.

MAR 28 Dr Strauss came to my room tonight to see why I dint come in like I was suppose to. I told him I dont like to race with Algernon any more. He said I dont have to for a while but I shud come in. He had a present for me. I thot it was a little television but it wasnt. He said I got to turn it on when I go to sleep. I said your kidding why shud I turn it on when Im going to sleep. Who ever herd of a thing like that But he said if I want to get smart I got to do what he says. I told him I dint think I was going to get smart and he puts his hand on my sholder and said Charlie you dont know it yet but your getting smarter all the time. You wont notice for a while. I think he was just being nice to make me feel good because I dont look any smarter.

Oh yes I almost forgot. I asked him when I can go back to the class at Miss Kinnians school. He said I wont go their. He said that soon Miss Kinnian will come to the hospitil to start and teach me speshul.

MAR 29 That crazy TV kept up all night. How can I sleep with something yelling crazy things all night in my ears. And the nutty pictures. Wow. I don't know what it says when Im up so how am I going to know when Im sleeping.

Dr Strauss says its ok. He says my brains are lerning when I sleep and that will help me when Miss Kinnian starts my lessons in the hospitl (only I found out it isn't a hospitil its a labatory.) I think its all crazy. If you can get smart when your sleeping why do people go to school. That thing I don't think will work. I use to watch the late show and the late late shown on TV all the time and it never made me smart. Maybe you have to sleep while you watch it.

progress report 9 — April 3

Dr Strauss showed me how to keep the TV turned low so now I can sleep. I don't hear a thing. And I still dont understand what it says. A few times I play it over in the morning to find out what I lerned when I was sleeping and I don't think so. Miss Kinnian says Maybe its another langwidge. But most times it sounds american. It talks faster than even Miss Gold who was my teacher in 6 grade.

I told Dr. Strauss what good is it to get smart in my sleep. I want to be smart when Im awake. He says its the same thing and I have two minds. Theres the *subconscious* and the *conscious* (thats how you spell it). And one dont tell the other one what its doing. They don't even talk to each other. Thats why I dream. And boy have I been having crazy dreams. Wow. Ever since that night TV. The late late late show.

I forgot to ask him if it was only me or if everybody had those two minds.

(I just looked up the word in the dictionary Dr Strauss gave me. The word is *subsconscious. adj. Of the nature of mental operations yet not present in consciousness; as, subconscious conflict of desires.*) There's more but I still dont know what it means. This isnt a very good dictionary for dumb people like me.

Anyway the headache is from the party. My friends from the factory Joe Carp and Frank

Reilly invited me to go to Muggsys Saloon for some drinks. I don't like to drink but they said we will have lots of fun. I had a good time.

Joe Carp said I should show the girls how I mop out the toilet in the factory and he got me a mop. I showed them and everyone laffed when I told that Mr. Donnegan said I was the best janiter he ever had because I like my job and do it good and never miss a day except for my operashun.

I said Miss Kinnian always said Charlie be proud of your job because you do it good.

Everybody laffed and we had a good time and they gave me lots of drinks and Joe said Charlie is a card when hes potted. I dont know what that means but everybody likes me and we have fun. I cant wait to be smart like my best friends Joe Carp and Frank Reilly.

I dont remember how the party was over but I think I went out to buy a newspaper and coffee for Joe and Frank and when I came back there was no one their. I looked for them all over till late. Then I dont remember so good but I think I got sleepy or sick. A nice cop brot me back home. Thats what my landlady Mrs Flynn says.

But I got a headache and a big lump on my head. I think maybe I fell but Joe Carp says it was the cops they beat up drunks some times. I don't think so. Miss Kinnian says cops are to help people. Anyway I got a bad headache and Im sick and hurt all over. I dont think Ill drink anymore.

APRIL 6 I beat Algernon! I dint even know I beat him until Burt the tester told me. Then the second time I lost because I got so exited I fell off the chair before I finished. But after that I beat him 8 more times. I must be getting smart to beat a smart mouse like Algernon. But I dont *feel* smarter.

I wanted to race Algernon some more but Burt said thats enough for one day. They let me hold him for a minit. Hes not so bad. Hes soft like a ball of cotton. He blinks and when he opens his eyes their black and pink on the eges.

I said can I feed him because I felt bad to beat him and I wanted to be nice and make friends. Burt said no Algernon is a very specshul mouse with an operashun like mine, and he was the first of all the animals to stay smart so long. He told me Algernon is so smart that every day he has to solve a test to get his food. Its a thing like a lock on a door that changes every time Algernon goes in to eat so he has to learn something new to get his food. That made me sad because if he coudnt lern he would be hungry.

I don't think its right to make you pass a test to eat. How woud Dr Nemur like it to have to pass a test every time he wants to eat. I think Ill be friends with Algernon.

APRIL 9 Tonight after work Miss Kinnian was at the laboratory. She looked like she was glad to see me but scared. I told her dont worry Miss Kinnian Im not smart yet and she laffed. She said I have confidence in you Charlie the way you struggled so hard to read and right better than all the others. At werst you will have it for a littel wile and your doing something for science.

We are reading a very hard book. Its called *Robinson Crusoe* about a man who gets merooned on a dessert Iland. Hes smart and figers out all kinds of things so he can have a house and food and hes a good swimmer. Only I feel sorry because hes all alone and has no friends. But I think their must be somebody else on the iland because theres a picture with his funny umbrella looking at footprints. I hope he gets a frend and not be lonly.

APRIL 10 Miss Kinnian teaches me to spell better. She says look at a word and close your eyes and say it over and over until you remember. I have lots of truble with *through* that you say *threw* and *enough* and *tough* that you dont say *enew* and *tew*. You got to say *enuff* and *tuff*. Thats how I use to write it before I started to get smart. Im confused but Miss Kinnian says theres no reason in spelling.

APR 14 Finished *Robinson Crusoe*. I want to find out more about what happens to him but Miss Kinnian says thats all there is. *Why*.

APR 15   Miss Kinnian says Im lerning fast. She read some of the Progress Reports and she looked at me kind of funny. She says Im a fine person and Ill show them all. I asked her why. She said never mind but I shouldnt feel bad if I find out everybody isnt nice like I think. She said for a person who god gave so little to you done more then a lot of people with brains they never even used. I said all my friends are smart people but there good. They like me and they never did anything that wasnt nice. Then she got something in her eye and she had to run out to the ladys room.

APR 16   Today, I lerned, the *comma*, this is a comma (,) a period, with a tail, Miss Kinnian, says its important, because, it makes writing, better, she said, somebody, coud lose, a lot of money, if a comma, isnt, in the, right place, I don't have, any money, and I dont see, how a comma, keeps you, from losing it,

APR 17   I used the comma wrong. Its punctuation. Miss Kinnian told me to look up long words in the dictionary to lern to spell them. I said whats the difference if you can read it anyway. She said its part of your education so now on Ill look up all the words Im not sure how to spell. It takes a long time to write that way but I only have to look up once and after that I get it right.

You got to mix them up. she showed? me" how. to mix! them (and now; I can! mix up all kinds" of punctuation, in! my writing? There, are lots! of rules? to lern; but In gettin'g them in my head.

One thing I like about, Dear Miss Kinnian: (thats the way it goes in a business letter if I ever go into business) is she, always gives me' a reason" when—I ask. She's a gen'ius! I wish I cou'd be smart" like, her;

(Punctuation, is; fun!)

APRIL 18   What a dope I am! I didn't even understand what she was talking about. I read the grammar book last night and it explanes the whole thing. Then I saw it was the same way as Miss Kinnian was trying to tell me, but I didn't get it.

Miss Kinnian said that the TV working in my sleep helped out. She said I reached a plateau. That's a flat hill.

After I figured out how punctuation worked, I read over all my old Progress Reports from the beginning. Boy, did I have crazy spelling and punctuation! I told Miss Kinnian I ought to go over the pages and fix all the mistakes but she said, "No, Charlie, Dr. Nemur wants them just as they are. That's why he let you keep them after they were photostated, to see your own progress. You're coming along fast, Charlie."

That made me feel good. After the lesson I went down and played with Algernon. We don't race any more.

APRIL 20   I feel sick inside. Not sick like for a doctor, but inside my chest it feels empty like getting punched and a heartburn at the same time. I wasn't going to write about it, but I guess I got to, because it's important. Today was the first time I ever stayed home from work.

Last night Joe Carp and Frank Reilly invited me to a party. There were lots of girls and some men from the factory. I remembered how sick I got the last time I drank too much, so I told Joe I didn't want anything to drink. He gave me a plain coke instead.

We had a lot of fun for a while. Joe said I should dance with Ellen and she would teach me the steps. I fell a few times and I couldn't understand why because no one else was dancing besides Ellen and me. And all the time I was tripping because somebody's foot was always sticking out.

Then when I got up I saw the look on Joe's face and it gave me a funny feeling in my stomack. "He's a scream," one of the girls said. Everybody was laughing.

"Look at him. He's blushing. Charlie is blushing."

"Hey, Ellen, what'd you do to Charlie? I never saw him act like that before."

I didn't know what to do or where to turn. Everyone was looking at me and laughing and I felt naked. I wanted to hide. I ran outside and I threw up. Then I walked home. It's a funny thing I never knew that Joe and Frank and the others liked to have me around all the time to make fun of me.

Now I know what it means when they say "to pull a Charlie Gordon." I'm ashamed.

progress report 11

APRIL 21   Still didn't go into the factory. I told Mrs. Flynn my landlady to call and tell Mr. Donnegan I was sick. Mrs. Flynn looks at me very funny lately like she's scared.

I think it's a good thing about finding out how everybody laughs at me. I thought about it a lot. It's because I'm so dumb and I don't even know when I'm doing something dumb. People think it's funny when a dumb person can't do things the same way they can.

Anyway, now I know I'm getting smarter every day. I know punctuation and I can spell good. I like to look up all the hard words in the dictionary and I remember them. I'm reading a lot now, and Miss Kinnian says I read very fast. Sometimes I even understand what I'm reading about, and it stays in my mind. There are times when I can close my eyes and think of a page and it all comes back like a picture.

Besides history, geography and arithmetic, Miss Kinnian said I should start to learn foreign languages. Dr. Strauss gave me some more tapes to play while I sleep. I still don't understand how that conscious and unconscious mind works, but Dr. Strauss says not to worry yet. He asked me to promise that when I start learning college subjects next week I wouldn't read any books on psychology—that is, until he gives me permission.

I feel a lot better today, but I guess I'm still a little angry that all the time people were laughing and making fun of me because I wasn't so smart. When I become intelligent like Dr. Strauss says, with three times my I.Q. of 68, then maybe I'll be like everyone else and people will like me.

I'm not sure what an I.Q. is. Dr. Nemur said it was something that measured how intelligent you were—like a scale in the drugstore weighs pounds. But Dr. Strauss had a big argument with him and said an I.Q. didn't weigh intelligence at all. He said an I.Q. showed how much intelligence you could get, like the numbers on the outside of a measuring cup. You still had to fill the cup up with stuff.

Then when I asked Burt, who gives me my intelligence tests and works with Algernon, he said that both of them were wrong (only I had to promise not to tell them he said so). Burt says that the I.Q. measures a lot of different things including some of the things you learned already, and it really isn't any good at all.

So I still don't know what I.Q. is except that mine is going to be over 200 soon. I didn't want to say anything, but I don't see how if they don't know *what* it is, or *where* it is—I don't see how they know *how much* of it you've got.

Dr. Nemur says I have to take a *Rorshach Test* tomorrow. wonder what *that* is.

APRIL 22   I found out what a Rorshach is. It's the test I took before the operation—the one with the inkblots on the pieces of cardboard.

I was scared to death of those inkblots. I knew the man was going to ask me to find the pictures and I knew I couldn't. I was thinking to myself, if only there was some way of knowing what kind of pictures were hidden there. Maybe there weren't any pictures at all. Maybe it was just a trick to see if I was dumb enough to look for something that wasn't there. Just thinking about that made me sore at him.

"All right, Charlie," he said, "you've seen these cards before, remember?"

"Of course I remember."

The way I said it, he knew I was angry, and he looked surprised. "Yes, of course. Now I want you to look at this. What might this be? What do you see on this card? People see all sorts of things in these inkblots. Tell me what it might be for you—what it makes you think of."

I was shocked. That wasn't what I had expected him to say. "You mean there are no pictures hidden in those inkblots?"

He frowned and took off his glasses. "What?"

"Pictures. Hidden in the inkblots. Last time

you told me everyone could see them and you wanted me to find them too."

He explained to me that the last time he had used almost the exact same words he was using now. I didn't believe it, and I still have the suspicion that he misled me at the time just for the fun of it. Unless—I don't know any more—could I have been *that* feeble-minded?

We went through the cards slowly. One looked like a pair of bats tugging at something. Another one looked like two men fencing with swords. I imagined all sort of things. I guess I got carried away. But I didn't trust him any more, and I kept turning them around, even looking on the back to see if there was anything there I was supposed to catch. While he was making his notes, I peeked out of the corner of my eye to read it. But it was all in code that looked like this:

WF+A   DdF— Ad orig.   WF —A
         SF+obj.

The test still doesn't make sense to me. It seems to me that anyone could make up lies about things that they didn't really imagine. Maybe I'll understand it when Dr. Strauss lets me read up on psychology.

APRIL 25 I figured out a new way to line up the machines in the factory, and Mr. Donnegan says it will save him ten thousand dollars a year in labor and increased production. He gave me a $25 bonus.

I wanted to take Joe Carp and Frank Reilly out to lunch to celebrate but Joe said he had to buy some things for his wife, and Frank said he was meeting his cousin for lunch. I guess it'll take a little time for them to get used to the changes in me. Everybody seems to be frightened of me. When I went over to Amos Borg and tapped him, he jumped up in the air.

People don't talk to me much any more or kid around they way they used to. It makes the job kind of lonely.

APRIL 27 I got up the nerve today to ask Miss Kinnian to have dinner with me tomorrow night to celebrate my bonus.

At first she wasn't sure it was right, but I asked Dr. Strauss and he said it was okay. Dr. Strauss and Dr. Nemur don't seem to be getting along so well. They're arguing all the time. This evening I heard them shouting. Dr. Nemur was saying that it was *his* experiment and *his* research, and Dr. Strauss shouted back that he contributed just as much, because he found me through Miss Kinnian and he performed the operation. Dr. Strauss said that someday thousands of neurosurgeons might be using his technique all over the world.

Dr. Nemur wanted to publish the results of the experiment at the end of this month. Dr. Strauss wanted to wait a while to be sure. Dr. Strauss said Dr. Nemur was more interested in the Chair of Psychology at Princeton than he was in the experiment. Dr. Nemur said Dr. Strauss was nothing but an opportunist trying to ride to glory on *his* coattails.

When I left afterwards I found myself trembling. I don't know why for sure, but it was as if I'd seen both men clearly for the first time. I remember hearing Burt say Dr. Nemur had a shrew of a wife who was pushing him all the time to get things published so he could become famous. Burt said that the dream of her life was to have a big shot husband.

APRIL 28 I don't understand why I never noticed how beautiful Miss Kinnian really is. She has brown eyes and feathery brown hair that comes to the top of her neck. She's only thirty-four! I think from the beginning I had the feeling that she was an unreachable genius—and very, very old. Now, every time I see her she grows younger and more lovely.

We had dinner and a long talk. When she said I was coming along so fast I'd be leaving her behind, I laughed.

"It's true, Charlie. You're already a better reader than I am. You can read a whole page at a glance while I can take in only a few lines at a time. And you remember every single thing you read. I'm lucky if I can recall the main thoughts and the general meaning."

"I don't feel intelligent. There are so many

things I don't understand."

She took out a cigarette and I lit it for her. "You've got to be a *little* patient. You're accomplishing in days and weeks what it takes normal people a lifetime to do in. That's what makes it so amazing. You're like a giant sponge now, soaking things in. Facts, figures, general knowledge. And soon you'll begin to connect them, too. You'll see how different branches of learning are related. There are many levels, Charlie, like steps on a giant ladder that take you up higher and higher to see more and more of the world around you.

"I can see only a little bit of that, Charlie, and I won't go much higher than I am now, but you'll keep climbing up and up, and see more and more, and each step will open new worlds that you never even knew existed." She frowned. "I hope —— I just hope to God ——"

"What?"

"Never mind, Charles. I just hope I wasn't wrong to advise you to go into this in the first place."

I laughed. "How could that be? It worked, didn't it? Even Algernon is still smart."

We sat there silently for a while and I knew what she was thinking about as she watched me toying with the chain of my rabbit's foot and my keys. I didn't want to think of that possibility any more than elderly people want to think of death. I *knew* that this was only the beginning. I knew what she meant about levels because I'd seen some of them already. The thought of leaving her behind made me sad.

I'm in love with Miss Kinnian.

progress report 12

APRIL 30 I've quit my job with Donnegan's Plastic Box Company. Mr. Donnegan insisted it would be better for all concerned if I left. What did I do to make them hate me so?

The first I knew of it was when Mr. Donnegan showed me the petition. Eight hundred names, everyone in the factory, except Fanny Girden. Scanning the list quickly, I saw at once that hers was the only missing name. All the rest demanded that I be fired.

Joe Carp and Frank Reilly wouldn't talk to me about it. No one else would either, except Fanny. She was one of the few people I'd known who set her mind to something and believed it no matter what the rest of the world proved, said or did—and Fanny did not believe that I should have been fired. She had been against the petition on principle and despite the pressure and threats she'd held out.

"Which don't mean to say," she remarked, "that I don't think there's something mighty strange about you, Charlie. Them changes. I don't know. You used to be a good, dependable, ordinary man—not too bright maybe, but honest. Who knows what you done to yourself to get so smart all of a sudden. Like everybody around here's been saying, Charlie, it's not right."

"But how can you say that, Fanny? What's wrong with a man becoming intelligent and wanting to acquire knowledge and understanding of the world around him?"

She stared down at her work and I turned to leave. Without looking at me, she said: "It was evil when Eve listened to the snake and ate from the tree of knowledge. It was evil when she saw that she was naked. If not for that none of us would ever have to grow old and sick and die."

Once again now, I have the feeling of shame burning inside me. This intelligence has driven a wedge between me and all the people I once knew and loved. Before, they laughed at me and despised me for my ignorance and dullness; now, they hate me for my knowledge and understanding. What in God's name do they want of me?

They've driven me out of the factory. Now I'm more alone than ever before ——

MAY 15 Dr. Strauss is very angry at me for not having written any progress reports in two weeks. He's justified because the lab is now paying me a regular salary. I told him I was too busy thinking and reading. When I pointed out that writing was such a slow process that it made me impatient with my poor handwriting, he suggested I learn to type. It's much easier to write now because I can type seventy-five words a minute. Dr. Strauss continually reminds me of the need to speak and write simply so people will be able to understand me.

I'll try to review all the things that happened to me during the last two weeks. Algernon and I were presented to the *American Psychological Association* sitting in convention with the *World Psychological Association*. We created quite a sensation. Dr. Nemur and Dr. Strauss were proud of us.

I suspect that Dr. Nemur, who is sixty—ten years older than Dr. Strauss—finds it necessary to see tangible results of his work. Undoubtedly the result of pressure by Mrs. Nemur.

Contrary to my earlier impressions of him, I realize that Dr. Nemur is not at all a genius. He has a very good mind, but it struggles under the spectre of self-doubt. He wants people to take him for a genius. Therefore it is important for him to feel that his work is accepted by the world. I believe that Dr. Nemur was afraid of further delay because he worried that someone else might make a discovery along these lines and take the credit from him.

Dr. Strauss on the other hand might be called a genius, although I feel his areas of knowledge are too limited. He was educated in the tradition of narrow specialization; the broader aspects of background were neglected far more than necessary—even for a neurosurgeon.

I was shocked to learn the only ancient languages he could read were Latin, Greek and Hebrew, and that he knows almost nothing of mathematics beyond the elementary levels of the calculus of variations. When he admitted this to me, I found myself almost annoyed. It was as if he'd hidden this part of himself in order to deceive me, pretending—as do many people I've discovered—to be what he is not. No one I've ever known is what he appears to be on the surface.

Dr. Nemur appears to be uncomfortable around me. Sometimes when I try to talk to him, he just looks at me strangely and turns away. I was angry at first when Dr. Strauss told me I was giving Dr. Nemur an inferiority complex. I thought he was mocking me and I'm oversensitive at being made fun of.

How was I to know that a highly respected psychoexperimentalist like Nemur was unacquainted with Hindustani and Chinese? It's absurd when you consider the work that is being done in India and China today in the very field of his study.

I asked Dr. Strauss how Nemur could refute Rahajamati's attack on his method if Nemur couldn't even read them in the first place. That strange look on Strauss' face can mean only one of two things. Either he doesn't want to tell Nemur what they're saying in India, or else—and this worries me—Dr. Strauss doesn't know either. I must be careful to speak and write clearly and simply so people won't laugh.

MAY 18 I am very disturbed. I saw Miss Kinnian last night for the first time in over a week. I tried to avoid all discussions of intellectual concepts and to keep the conversation on a simple, everyday level, but she just stared at me blankly and asked me what I meant about the mathematical variance equivalent in Dobermann's *Fifth Concerto*.

When I tried to explain she stopped me and laughed. I guess I got angry, but I suspect I'm approaching her on the wrong level. No matter what I try to discuss with her, I am unable to communicate. I must review Vrostadt's equations on *Levels of Semantic Progression*. I find I don't communicate with people much any more. Thank God for books and music and things I can think about. I am alone at Mrs. Flynn's boarding house most of the time and seldom speak to anyone.

MAY 20 I would not have noticed the new dishwasher, a boy of about sixteen, at the corner diner where I take my evening meals if not for the incident of the broken dishes.

They crashed to the floor, sending bits of white china under the tables. The boy stood there, dazed and frightened, holding the empty tray in his hand. The catcalls from the customers (the cries of "Hey, there go the profits!" ——"*Mazeltov*!"—— and "Well, he didn't work here very long——" which invariably seem to follow the breaking of glass or dishware in a public restaurant) all seemed to confuse him.

When the owner came to see what the excitement was about, the boy cowered as if he expected to be struck. "All right! All right, you dope," shouted the owner, "don't just stand there! Get the broom and sweep that mess up. A broom——a broom, you idiot! It's in the kitchen!"

The boy saw he was not going to be punished. His frightened expression disappeared and he smiled as he came back with the broom to sweep the floor. A few of the rowdier customers kept up the remarks, amusing themselves at his expense.

"Here, sonny, over here there's a nice piece behind you ——"

"He's not so dumb. It's easier to break 'em than wash 'em!"

As his vacant eyes moved across the crowd of onlookers, he slowly mirrored their smiles and finally broke into an uncertain grin at the joke he obviously did not understand.

I felt sick inside as I looked at his dull, vacuous smile, the wide, bright eyes of a child, uncertain but eager to please. They were laughing at him because he was mentally retarded.

And I had been laughing at him too.

Suddenly I was furious at myself and all those who were smirking at him. I jumped up and shouted, "Shut up! Leave him alone! It's not his fault he can't understand! He can't help what he is! But he's still a human being!"

The room grew silent. I cursed myself for losing control. I tried not to look at the boy as I walked out without touching my food. I felt ashamed for both of us.

How strange that people of honest feelings and sensibility, who would not take advantage of a man born without arms or eyes—how such people think nothing of abusing a man born with low intelligence. It infuriated me to think

that not too long ago I had foolishly played the clown.

And I had almost forgotten.

I'd hidden the picture of the old Charlie Gordon from myself because now that I was intelligent it was something that had to be pushed out of my mind. But today in looking at that boy, for the first time I saw what I had been. *I was just like him!*

Only a short time ago, I learned that people laughed at me. Now I can see that unknowingly I joined with them in laughing at myself. That hurts most of all.

I have often reread my progress reports and seen the illiteracy, the childish naïveté, the mind of low intelligence peering from a dark room, through the keyhole at the dazzling light outside. I see that even in my dullness I knew I was inferior, and that other people had something I lacked—something denied me. In my mental blindness, I thought it was somehow connected with the ability to read and write, and I was sure that if I could get those skills I would automatically have intelligence too.

Even a feeble-minded man wants to be like other men.

A child may not know how to feed itself, or what to eat, yet it knows of hunger.

This then is what I was like. I never knew. Even with my gift of intellectual awareness, I never really knew.

This day was good for me. Seeing the past more clearly, I've decided to use my knowledge and skills to work in the field of increasing human intelligence levels. Who is better equipped for this work? Who else has lived in both worlds? These are my people. Let me use my gift to do something for them.

Tomorrow, I will discuss with Dr. Strauss how I can work in this area. I may be able to help him work out the problems of widespread use of the technique which was used on me. I have several good ideas of my own.

There is so much that might be done with this technique. If I could be made into a genius, what about thousands of others like myself? What fantastic levels might be achieved by using this technique on normal people? On *geniuses?*

There are so many doors to open. I am impatient to begin.

progress report 13

MAY 23 It happened today. Algernon bit me. I visited the lab to see him as I do occasionally, and when I took him out of his cage, he snapped at my hand. I put him back and watched him for a while. He was unusually disturbed and vicious.

MAY 24 Burt, who is in charge of the experimental animals, tells me that Algernon is changing. He is less cooperative; he refuses to run the maze any more; general motivation has decreased. And he hasn't been eating. Everyone is upset about what this may mean.

MAY 25 They've been feeding Algernon, who now refuses to work the shifting-lock problem. Everyone identifies me with Algernon. In a way we're both the first of our kind. They're all pretending that Algernon's behavior is not necessarily significant for me. But it's hard to hide the fact that some of the other animals who were used in this experiment are showing strange behavior.

Dr. Strauss and Dr. Nemur have asked me not to come to the lab any more. I know what they're thinking but I can't accept it. I am going ahead with my plans to carry their research forward. With all due respect to both these fine scientists. I am well aware of their limitations. If there is an answer, I'll have to find it out for myself. Suddenly, time has become very important to me.

MAY 29 I have been given a lab of my own and permission to go ahead with the research. I'm onto something. Working day and night. I've had a cot moved into the lab. Most of my writing time is spent on the notes which I keep in a separate folder, but from time to time I feel it necessary to put down my moods and thoughts from sheer habit.

I find the *calculus of intelligence* to be a fascinating study. Here is the place for the application of all the knowledge I have acquired.

MAY 31 Dr. Strauss thinks I'm working too hard. Dr. Nemur says I'm trying to cram a lifetime of research and thought into a few weeks. I know I should rest, but I'm driven on by something inside that won't let me stop. I've got to find the reason for the sharp regression in Algernon. I've got to know *if* and *when* it will happen to me.

June 4 LETTER TO DR. STRAUSS (*copy*)

Dear Dr. Strauss:

Under separate cover I am sending you a copy of my report entitled, "The Algernon-Gordon Effect: A Study of Structure and Function of Increased Intelligence," which I would like to have published.

As you see, my experiments are completed. I have included in my report all of my formulae, as well as mathematical analysis in the appendix. Of course, these should be verified.

Because of its importance to both you and Dr. Nemur (and need I say to myself, too?) I have checked and rechecked my results a dozen times in the hope of finding an error. I am sorry to say the results must stand. Yet for the sake of science, I am grateful for the little bit that I here add to the knowledge of the function of the human mind and of the laws governing the artificial increase of human intelligence.

I recall your once saying to me that an experimental *failure* or the *disproving* of a theory was as important to the advancement of learning as a success would be. I know now that this is true. I am sorry, however, that my own contribution to the field must rest upon the ashes of the work of two men I regard so highly.

Yours truly,

Charles Gordon

JUNE 5 I must not become emotional. The facts and the results of my experiments are clear, and the more sensational aspects of my own rapid climb cannot obscure the fact that the tripling of intelligence by the surgical technique developed by Drs. Strauss and Nemur must be viewed as having little or no practical applicability (at the present time) to the increase of human intelligence.

As I review the records and data on Algernon, I see that although he is still in his physical infancy, he has regressed mentally. Motor activity is impaired; there is a general reduction of glandular activity; there is an accelerated loss of coordination.

There are also strong indications of progressive amnesia.

As will be seen by my report, these and other physical and mental deterioration syndromes can be predicted with significant results by the application of my formula.

The surgical stimulus to which we were both subjected has resulted in an intensification and acceleration of all mental processes. The unforeseen development, which I have taken the liberty of calling the *Algernon-Gordon Effect*, is the logical extension of the entire intelligence speed-up. The hypothesis here proven may be described simply in the following terms: Artificially increased intelligence deteriorates at a rate of time directly proportional to the quantity of the increase.

I feel that this, in itself, is an important discovery.

As long as I am able to write, I will continue to record my thoughts in these progress reports. It is one of my few pleasures. However, by all indications, my own mental deterioration will be very rapid.

I have already begun to notice signs of emotional instability and forgetfulness, the first symptoms of the burnout.

JUNE 10 Deterioration progressing. I have become absent-minded. Algernon died two days ago. Dissection shows my predictions were right. His brain had decreased in weight and there was a general smoothing out of cerebral convolutions, as well as a deepening and broadening of brain fissures.

I guess the same thing is or will soon be happening in me. Now that it's definite, I don't want it to happen.

I put Algernon's body in a cheese box and buried him in the back yard. I cried.

JUNE 15 Dr. Strauss came to see me again. I wouldn't open the door and I told him to go away. I want to be left to myself. I am touchy and irritable. I feel the darkness closing in. It's hard to throw off thoughts of suicide. I keep telling myself how important this journal will be.

It's a strange sensation to pick up a book you enjoyed just a few months ago and discover you don't remember it. I remembered how great I thought John Milton was, but when I picked up *Paradise Lost* I couldn't understand it at all. I got so angry I threw the book across the room.

I've got to try to hold on to some of it. Some of the things I've learned. Oh, God, please don't take it all away.

JUNE 19 Sometimes, at night, I go out for a walk. Last night, I couldn't remember where I lived. A policeman took me home. I have the strange feeling that this has all happened to me before—a long time ago. I keep telling myself I'm the only person in the world who can describe what's happening to me.

JUNE 21 Why can't I remember? I've got to fight. I lie in bed for days and I don't know who or where I am. Then it all comes back to me in a flash. Fugues of amnesia. Symptoms of senility—second childhood. I can watch them coming on. It's so cruelly logical. I learned so much and so fast. Now my mind is deteriorating rapidly. I won't let it happen. I'll fight it. I can't help thinking of the boy in the restaurant, the blank expression, the silly smile, the people laughing at him. No—please—not that again. ——

JUNE 22 I'm forgetting things that I learned recently. It seems to be following the classic pattern—the last things learned are the first things forgotten. Or is that the pattern? I'd better look it up again. ——

I reread my paper on the *Algernon-Gordon Effect* and I get the strange feeling that it was written by someone else. There are parts I don't even understand.

Motor activity impaired. I keep tripping over

things, and it becomes increasingly difficult to

JUNE 23   I've given up using the typewriter. My coordination is bad. I feel I'm moving slower and slower. Had a terrible shock today. I picked up a copy of an article I used in my research, Krueger's *Uber psychische Ganzheit*, to see if it would help me understand what I had done. First I thought there was something wrong with my eyes. Then I realized I could no longer read German. I tested myself in other languages. All gone.

JUNE 30   A week since I dared to write again. It's slipping away like sand through my fingers. Most of the books I have are too hard for me now. I get angry with them because I know that I read and understood them just a few weeks ago.

I keep telling myself I must keep writing these reports so that somebody will know what is happening to me. But it gets harder to form the words and remember spellings. I have to look up even simple words in the dictionary now and it makes me impatient with myself.

Dr. Strauss comes around almost every day, but I told him I wouldn't see or speak to anybody. He feels guilty. They all do. But I don't blame anyone. I knew what might happen. But how it hurts.

JUNE 7   I don't know where the week went. Todays Sunday I know because I can see through my window people going to church. I think I stayed in bed all week but I remember Mrs. Flynn bringing food to me a few times. I keep saying over and over I've got to do something but then I forget or maybe its just easier not to do what I say I'm going to do.

I think of my mother and father a lot these days. I found a picture of them with me taken at a beach. My father has a big ball under his arm and my mother is holding me by the hand. I dont remember them the way they are in the picture. All I remember is my father drunk most of the time and arguing with mom about money.

He never shaved much and he used to scratch my face when he hugged me. My Mother said he died but Cousin Miltie said he heard his dad say that my father ran away with another woman. When I asked my mother she slapped me and said my father was dead. I dont think I ever found out the truth but I dont care much. (He said he was going to take me to see cows on a farm once but he never did. He never kept his promises. ——)

JULY 10   My landlady Mrs. Flynn is very worried about me. She says the way I lay around all day and dont do anything I remind her of her son before she threw him out of the house. She said she doesn't like loafers. If Im sick its one thing, but if Im a loafer thats another thing and she won't have it. I told her I think Im sick.

I try to read a little bit every day, mostly stories, but sometimes I have to read the same thing over and over again because I don't know what it means. And its hard to write. I know I should look up all the words in the dictionary but its so hard and Im so tired all the time.

Then I got the idea that I would only use the easy words instead of the long hard ones. That saves time. I put flowers on Algernons grave about once a week. Mrs. Flynn thinks Im crazy to put flowers on a mouses grave but I told her that Algernon was special.

JULY 14   Its sunday again. I dont have anything to do to keep me busy now because my television set is broke and I dont have any money to get it fixed. (I think I lost this months check from the lab. I dont remember)

I get awful headaches and asperin doesnt help me much. Mrs. Flynn knows Im really sick and she feels very sorry for me. Shes a wonderful woman whenever someone is sick.

JULY 22   Mrs. Flynn called a strange doctor to see me. She was afraid I was going to die. I told the doctor I wasnt too sick and I only forget sometimes. He asked me did I have any friends or relatives and I said no I dont have any. I told him I had a friend called Algernon once but he was a mouse and we used to run races together. He looked at me kind of funny like he thought I was crazy. He smiled when I told him I used to be a genius. He talked to me like I was a baby and he winked at Mrs. Flynn. I got mad and chased him out because he was making fun of me the way they all used to.

JULY 24 I have no more money and Mrs Flynn says I got to go to work somewhere and pay the rent because I havent paid for two months. I dont know any work but the job I used to have at Donnegans Box Company. I dont want to go back because they all knew me when I was smart and maybe they'll laugh at me. But I dont know what else to do to get money.

JULY 25 I was looking at some of my old progress reports and its very funny but I cant read what I wrote. I can make out some of the words but they dont make sense.

Miss Kinnian came to the door but I said go away I dont want to see you. She cried and I cried too but I wouldnt let her in because I didn't want her to laugh at me. I told her I didnt like her any more. I told her I didnt want to be smart any more. Thats not true. I still love her and I still want to be smart but I had to say that so shed go away. She gave Mrs. Flynn money to pay the rent. I dont want that. I got to get a job.

Please —— please let me not forget how to read and write. ——

JULY 27 Mr. Donnegan was very nice when I came back and asked him for my old job of janitor. First he was very suspicious but I told him what happened to me then he looked very sad and put his hand on my shoulder and said Charlie Gordon you got guts.

Everybody looked at me when I came downstairs and started working in the toilet sweeping it out like I used to. I told myself Charlie if they make fun of you dont get sore because you remember their not so smart as you once thot they were. And besides they were once your friends and if they laughed at you that doesnt mean anything because they liked you too.

One of the new men who came to work there after I went away made a nasty crack he said hey Charlie I hear your a very smart fella a real quiz kid. Say something intelligent. I felt bad but Joe Carp came over and grabbed him by the shirt and said leave him alone you lousy cracker or I'll break your neck. I didnt expect Joe to take my part so I guess hes really my friend.

Later Frank Reilly came over and said Charlie if anybody bothers you or trys to take advantage you call me or Joe and we will set em straight. I said thanks Frank and I got choked up so I had to turn around and go into the supply room so he wouldnt see me cry. Its good to have friends.

JULY 28 I did a dumb thing today I forgot I wasnt in Miss Kinnians class at the adult center any more like I use to be. I went in and sat down in my old seat in the back of the room and she looked at me funny and she said Charles. I dint remember she ever called me that before only Charlie so I said hello Miss Kinnian Im redy for my lesin today only I lost my reader that we was using. She startid to cry and run out of the room and everybody looked at me and I saw they wasnt the same pepul who use to be in my class.

Then all of a suddin I remembered some things about the operashun and me getting smart and I said holy smoke I reely pulled a Charlie Gordon that time. I went away before she come back to the room.

Thats why Im going away from New York for good. I dont want to do nothing like that agen. I dont want Miss Kinnian to feel sorry for me. Evry body feels sorry at the factery and I dont want that eather so Im going someplace where nobody knows that Charlie Gordon was once a genus and now he cant even reed a book or rite good.

Im taking a cuple of books along and even if I cant reed them Ill practise hard and maybe I wont forget every thing I lerned. If I try reel hard maybe Ill be a littel bit smarter than I was before the operashun. I got my rabits foot and my luky penny and maybe they will help me.

If you ever reed this Miss Kinnian dont be sorry for me Im glad I got a second chanse to be smart becaus I lerned a lot of things that I never even new were in this world and Im grateful that I saw it all for a littel bit. I dont know why Im dumb agen or what I did wrong maybe its because I dint try hard enuff. But if I try and practis very hard maybe Ill get a littl smarter and know what all the words are. I remember a littel bit how nice I had a feeling with the blue book that has the torn cover when I red it. Thats why Im gonna keep trying to get smart so I can have that feeling agen. Its a good feeling to know things and be smart. I wish I had it rite now if I did I would sit down and reed all the time. Anyway I bet Im the first dumb person in the world who ever found out somthing importent for science. I remember I did somthing but I dont remember what. So I gess its like I did it for all the dumb pepul like me.

Goodbye Miss Kinnian and Dr. Strauss and everybody. And P.S. please tell Dr. Nemur not to be such a grouch when pepul laff at him and he would have more frends. Its easy to make frends if you let pepul laff at you. Im going to have lots of frends where I go. P.P.S. Please if you get a chanse put some flowrs on Algernons grave in the back yard. ——

ON LIVING IN A COLD COUNTRY

Hugh MacLennan

I was twenty-one before I met a live writer; before I met, one might say, my fate. It was on my first voyage to England, where I was going to study: I had never been away from home before.

It is difficult for me to remember now how naïve I was then. I had worked and played hard, and had been equipping myself for twentieth-century life by studying Latin and Greek. I had never been outside the little province of Nova Scotia since the cessation of the period known to the psychologists as childhood amnesia (in my infancy, I'm told, I was in England for several months), and the polyglot passengers aboard that ship fascinated me, for the ship had sailed from New York and her ultimate destination was Antwerp. At Halifax, where I lived, she had stopped for half a day to take on two thousand barrels of apples, two elderly ladies, and myself.

——"On Living in a Cold Country" from *The Other Side of Hugh MacLennan* by Hugh MacLennan. Reprinted by permission of The Macmillan Company of Canada Limited

Prowling about the ship after we got to sea, I had observed a sloppily dressed man of indeterminate age lounging in the smoke-room or brooding over the ocean with his elbows on the railing. I could not imagine what his profession was, but the cut of his suit was American—in those days even I could distinguish an American suit from an English one—and his face looked as though some things I had never heard of had sunk into it and stayed there. When he told me he was a writer, I was impressed. When he later informed me that he was engaged on a three-hundred-thousand-word novel about Lincoln, in three sections of equal length, and in three different styles, I was reverent.

"The first section will be in the style of Mark Twain," he explained. "Why? Because that is the only style that fits the mood of Lincoln's youth. The second section"—he paused and assessed me with give-away, spaniel's eyes—"will be in the style of Henry James."

In those days I had heard of Henry James, but only barely.

"You see, Lincoln's middle period was one of doubts, hesitations, and parentheses. He was a Hamlet in Illinois. Shakespeare would have made a success of *Hamlet* if he had written it in novel form in the style of Henry James."

The third section was to be written in the style of a writer I had not even heard about barely; it was to be written in the style of the last chapter of James Joyce's *Ulysses*.

"The choice is obvious," the writer explained. "Lincoln's third period was the presidency, and presidents, by the very nature of their jobs, can't think. They haven't the time. The stuff just pours through them."

I had never heard of this ship-met writer before, and perhaps I have already said enough to explain why I have never heard of him since. Yet he abides with me. I learned more from him about the trade of writing than I learned from any other teacher except Experience herself.

One night over his sixth drink he said that writing would be easy if it weren't for what he called "all the other things that went along with it", and that the chief of these other things were three insoluble problems. "Money," he said, "Women, and Liquor," and he pronounced each word as though a capital letter stood before it.

Much of what he had been saying had sounded strange to me, but this rang a familiar note. I admitted that my father had told me much the same thing the day before I sailed, but had not limited the three problems to writers. According to him, Money, Women, and Liquor were the three problems of every man who ever lived, nor were they (according to him) insoluble. With the first I was to be thrifty; the other two I was entirely to avoid.

The writer observed me gloomily: "If you take that advice, your Oedipus will be screaming before you're thirty."

I told him I had an *Oedipus* in my stateroom, and added guiltily that I ought to be studying it at that particular moment.

"My God," he said, "do you still think Oedipus is a play? But to get back—money you must have for obvious reasons, but too much is worse than too little. A high standard of living invariably produces a low standard of prose. But women and liquor, these are even more essential than money. They're necessary food for your subconscious. You need them to awaken your guilts." After ordering another drink, he sighed: "But the trouble with liquor is it's apt to leave you with nothing else *but* your subconscious. And alcoholic remorse, I'm sorry to say, is an uncreative remorse."

The next morning on deck he was obviously suffering from alcoholic remorse, and as we leaned on the railing and stared down at the yard-wide band of white brine seething along the vessel's flank, he told me he was feeling sorry for me.

"Because you want to be a writer," he said, "and you haven't a chance."

I felt myself flushing, for in those days I never told my love. I pretended that all I wished to be was a scholar.

"What gives you the idea I want to write?" I asked.

"When I meet a man I know will be no good for anything else, I always know he's going to get the bug sooner or later, and probably sooner."

"Well, supposing I do? Why do you say I haven't a chance?"

"You aren't decadent enough. In fact, you're not decadent at all, and as you're twenty-one already, I doubt if you'll become decadent in time for it to matter. Frankly, your country has ruined any chance you might ever have had of becoming a writer."

"What's my country to do with it?"

"It's a cold country. In the entire history of the human race, no important art has ever come out of a cold country."

"But Canada can also get very hot," I protested.

He shook his head. "No. Canada is a cold country because that's what the world believes it is. Wait till you begin talking to editors and you'll remember that I told you so."

Some twenty years later I was talking with an editor and I did remember that he had told me so. By that time I had been writing long enough to be acutely aware of the first of the Three Problems, and this editor belonged to a super-colossal magazine that paid super-colossal fees. I wanted one of those fees to finance six months' work on a novel. While we ate lunch, with a tableful of bilingual lawyers across the aisle discussing a case with Gallic gestures, the editor informed me that what he wanted was "a real, true-to-life piece on Canada". For a subject I could take my pick of Eskimos, trappers, Mounties, or husky dogs, and if I could manage to work all four of them into the same piece, it would be perfect, providing it met the literary standards of his magazine. While we talked, the temperature was ninety degrees, and the editor was feeling it, for he had come north clad in heavy worsteds. Mopping his forehead, he explained that this would be what he called a "duty-piece". His magazine sold several hundred thousand copies in Canada every month, and occasionally the management felt it a duty to print some Canadian material. I must have made a comment about there being no Eskimos, trappers, or husky dogs within fifteen hundred miles of where we were sitting, for he cut me short with a gesture.

"No, they're imperative. In an African duty-piece you stress the heat and the jungle. In an English duty-piece you stress how old everything is. A French duty-piece has got to be romantic, but at the same time we like an angle showing the French are also practical and getting themselves orientated to the up-to-date. But in a Canadian duty-piece you simply have to go heavy on the snow and the cold."

But to return to that morning at sea—for some reason my newly met American writer had taken an interest in me. After saying that he believed in Voltaire's way of dealing with aspiring young authors ("If I had a son who wanted to write, I'd strangle him out of sheer good nature"), he asked me how I'd been living "up there", his notion of Canada being a red-painted roof on top of the North American house.

"Well actually," I told him, "and so much for your idea of my living in a cold country, for the past eleven years I've been living in a tent."

"In a *what*?"

"The first time in eleven years that I've slept between four walls was my first night aboard this ship. Well yes, I suppose it does sound a little odd."

"It sounds *very* odd." His eyes opened wide at me. "Indeed, it sounds so odd that it may indicate possibilities for you. Continue. Tell me about it."

So I told him.

In those days in Halifax the life was not much different from life in a village, even though we had the harbour, the university, the hospitals, the Government House, the curfew gun on the Citadel, and the memory of the explosion which had smashed a third of the town a few years before. Behind every house was some sort of back yard—the word "yard" had probably reached us from New England Loyalists—and most of these had a kitchen garden, a few fruit trees, and a one-horse stable which might or might not have been converted into a one-car garage. In the early 1920s there was still a faint smell of stable behind the houses and a reasonably strong smell of it in the streets. Each yard was separated from its neighbours by a rough board fence on the top of which prowling tom cats sat in the nights and howled at the female cats they knew were inside the houses.

In the summer of my eleventh year I went to a boys' camp where we slept under canvas, and when I returned to Halifax, the weather was so hot I could not sleep well indoors. Heat waves are rare in Nova Scotia, but when they come, the salt humidity sticks to your skin. My father reminded me of a little tent in the basement he had used years ago for fishing trips and he said it was probably mouldy in spots. It was, but I got it out, pitched it in the back yard, installed a battered old hospital cot and a packing case to hold a saucer with a candle in it, and that night I slept beautifully. The next day I told my parents I intended to stay out in the tent until school began.

But when school began on the first of September it was still warm, so I decided to stay out until it got cold. Then in the first week of October the mornings were cool enough, but there was dew on the ripe apples and pears, and waking up in such air was a sensual experience as delicious as any I can remember. I told my parents I intended staying out until it got really cold. Three weeks later I woke to see the tent walls sagging and a foot of snow on the ground. Presumably this was really cold, but I told my parents I had slept so well I would stay out until it got impossibly cold.

It never did. The Canadian climate in the early 1920s had a mean average temperature three to four degrees lower than it has now, and this, meteorologists tell me, represents a substantial differential. Nowadays the temperature seldom drops below zero in Halifax, though the salt humidity of a Maritime climate makes zero feel as cold as twenty-five below on the prairies. But it often got below zero in Halifax when I was a boy, and one night in my first January in the tent the thermometer fell to seventeen below, and the trees cracked like guns in the frost. Once more I slept beautifully, and after that night I decided to remain outside indefinitely.

It seemed perfectly natural to do this. I used to wear in the winters two pairs of flannel pajamas, a pair of woollen socks, and a red beret. When I emerged from the back door in this regalia I carried a hot-water bottle (it was bad the night it broke) to warm the blankets before my own body-heat sustained a modest furnace inside of them. The only part of me that ever got cold in the tent was my nose. And here is an item for anyone who does not already know it: a cold nose is a better sedative than a quarter-grain Seconal.

Phenomena belonging to the science of physics became high poetry on the really cold nights. My breath made snow, real snow. As it issued warm from my nose and mouth, it mounted to the canvas under the ridge-pole and turned into a delicate cloud in the still, frigid air. When it congealed, it was converted into a filmy snow-mist, which descended and settled on top of the bed. Once I woke with a bright orange sun flaring into the tent and found myself warm under a quarter-inch layer of the softest snow I ever saw, each crystal dancing in the eye of that Austerlitz sunrise.

But congealed breath made another problem, an uncomfortable chin. In the vicinity of the mouth, when you sleep out in sub-zero weather, your breath does not turn into snow but into ice, and ice irritates the skin. Having been helpless all my adulthood in the presence of the most elementary technical problem, it gives me a certain satisfaction to relate how I dealt with this one when I was ten years old and resourceful. I asked my mother for an old sheet, cut it crosswise into strips a foot wide, and each night when I tucked myself in by candle light I laid this length of sheeting under my jaw. Whenever I woke with ice irritating me, I shifted the sheeting to a dry place. After a while this routine became so automatic that I was unconscious of it.

A more serious problem was the one of waking up in the morning.

In those days my family kept a maid from Newfoundland called Sadie, a fisherman's daughter from the little island of Ramea off the southern coast of the Ancient Colony. Ramea is barren, but the water surrounding it is so abundant in codfish that in Cabot's time the density of the cod impeded the motion of his ships. Ramea's climate is a little milder than Labrador's, but some of Sadie's tales of *her* experience of living in a cold country made Halifax seem like a sultry port in a sugar island. Sometimes the salt sea froze out a distance of two miles from the shore of Ramea, and when this happened, if the fishermen wanted food, they had to haul their dories over the treacherous, spongy, salt-water ice to deep water, and then haul them back in the evening with the catch. More than one man Sadie knew was drowned doing things like this. So to her, warmth was a thing you hoarded. When her Newfoundland friends, seamen all, visited her kitchen, the fug was so thick you could barely see through it, for while the men smoked shag in cutty pipes, the stove glowed cherry-red as it brewed the gallons of tea they drank. Happy in a hundred-degree temperature, the Newfoundlanders conversed in a dialect I could hardly understand, for the speech of their outports is the speech that was used by common folk in western England in

Shakespeare's time.

Newfoundlanders are polite people, and Sadie never said straight out that I was crazy. But she did say it was no part of her duty to wade through the snow of a zero morning in order to waken a small boy who had a perfectly comfortable room indoors. My mother agreed with her; indeed, I suspect her of hoping that this would settle the matter, for she knew I would never wake up in time for school if left to myself.

However, there was a chandler's shop along the Halifax waterfront which boasted that it sold everything from a needle to an anchor, and displayed in its window an anchor and a sail-maker's needle to prove it. Thither I repaired one afternoon when school was out, and came home lugging a four-pound gong of the kind they used to place on the outside of school walls to ring in the children from recess. This gong I installed inside the tent, and ran a cord from its clapper through a row of pulleys to the kitchen window. After boring a hole through the window-frame, I thrust the cord inside for Sadie to pull. And at seven-thirty the next morning, pull she did—with the vigour of a fisher girl heaving on a halyard.

The noise was appalling, for this was a gong which was meant to be audible for a quarter of a mile. I was out of the tent and inside the house before I was even awake. My father feared the police would intervene if the gong was used again. My mother, ever hopeful, telephoned the neighbours to apologize and to ask if they had been disturbed. She was told by all of them that they were delighted with the gong. They all got up at seven-thirty, and if they could be assured the gong would always ring, they would not have to worry about setting their own alarm clocks.

Now all the problems about sleeping in the tent were solved and I settled in for the years and the seasons that lay ahead. The little bells on the horses pulling milkmen's sleighs, jingling past on the street beyond the fence at six o'clock in the morning, used to reach through the walls of sleep like the bells of elfland. In the foggy springtimes I fell asleep with my ears filled with the groans, snores, and musical clangs of the fog signals and bell-buoys of Halifax harbour. When summer came, I often read by candlelight before falling asleep, and with the passage of seasons and years moved the passage of education and even of history.

I was sleeping in the tent when I learned how to translate the invaluable information that on the second day before the Kalends of June, Caesar moved his camp and marched his legions a distance of ten miles to a place where he made another camp. I was sleeping in the tent when, years later, I made my first acquaintance with communism in the form of Plato's *Republic*. I was in the tent the night when Lindbergh, after having spent the previous day flying over Nova Scotia, was dodging the ice-making clouds over the Atlantic. To the tent I returned at two o'clock in the morning the night Tunney beat Dempsey in Philadelphia, which also happened to be the first night I ever wore a dinner jacket or went to a Government House Ball.

Such was the story I told my writer-friend, and when I had finished I said: "So you see—it wasn't such a cold country after all."

He was silent a while, possibly engrossed in thoughts of Lincoln, probably worrying about his liver, and I felt embarrassed to have spoken so much about myself. But he seemed to have heard, for finally he turned and spoke.

"You'll never go back to that again, of course."

"I don't see why not."

"You must have slept without movement to have gotten away with it. If you'd moved in your sleep, you'd have disturbed the blankets and let in the cold."

"I did sleep without movement."

The spaniel eyes were prophetic: "Well, you have given me clear proof that your days of sleeping without movement are numbered. This avoidance of the house where your parents were sleeping, this compulsive crawling away from their vicinity and *into* that little tent in the back yard—if that doesn't indicate an Oedipus complex of magnitude I don't know what else it indicates. A little while—and remember I told you so—and it will burst out. A little while, and your guilts will make you thrash and writhe in your sleep, and the last thing you'll ever think of doing will be to sleep in the tent with your lost innocence."

He stared out over the sea: "No, I can't help you. You're going to be a writer, all right."

THE OBSOLESCENCE OF MAN

Arthur C. Clarke

About a million years ago, an unprepossessing primate discovered that his forelimbs could be used for other purposes besides locomotion. Objects like sticks and stones could be grasped —and, once grasped, were useful for killing game, digging up roots, defending or attacking, and a hundred other jobs. On the third planet of the Sun, tools had appeared; and the place would never be the same again.

The first users of tools were *not* men—a fact appreciated only in the last year or two—but prehuman anthropoids; and by their discovery they doomed themselves. For even the most primitive of tools, such as a naturally pointed stone that happens to fit the hand, provides a tremendous physical and mental stimulus to the user. He has to walk erect; he no longer needs huge canine teeth—since sharp flints can do a better job—and he must develop manual dexterity of a high order. These are the specifications of Homo sapiens; as soon as they start to be filled, all earlier models are headed for rapid obsolescence. To quote Professor Sherwood Washburn of the University of California's anthropology department: "It was the success of the simplest tools that started the whole trend of human evolution and led to the civilizations of today."

Note that phrase—"the whole trend of human evolution." The old idea that man invented tools is therefore a misleading half-truth; it would be more accurate to say that *tools invented man.* They were very primitive tools, in the hands of creatures who were little more than apes. Yet they led to us—and to the eventual extinction of the ape-men who first wielded them.

Now the cycle is about to begin again; but neither history nor prehistory ever exactly repeats itself, and this time there will be a fascinating twist in the plot. The tools the ape-men invented caused them to evolve into their successor, Homo sapiens. The tool we have invented *is* our successor. Biological evolution has given way to a far more rapid process—technological evolution. To put it bluntly and brutally, the machine is going to take over.

This, of course, is hardly an original idea. That the creations of man's brain might one day threaten and perhaps destroy him is such a tired old *cliché* that no self-respecting science-fiction writer would dare to use it. It goes back, through Capek's R.U.R., Samuel Butler's *Erewhon,* Mary Shelley's *Frankenstein* and the Faust legend to the mysterious but perhaps not wholly mythical figure of Daedalus, King Minos' one-man office of scientific research. For at least three thousand years, therefore, a vocal

— *"The Obsolescence of Man"* by Arthur C. Clarke, *from Playboy Magazine; copyright © 1961 by H.M.H. Publications; reprinted by permission of the author and the author's agent, David Higham in London*

minority of mankind has had grave doubts about the ultimate outcome of technology. From the self-centered, human point of view, these doubts are justified. But that, I submit, will not be the only—or even the most important—point of view for much longer.

When the first large-scale electronic computers appeared some fifteen years ago, they were promptly nick-named "Giant Brains"—and the scientific community, as a whole, took a poor view of the designation. But the scientists objected to the wrong word. The electronic computers were not *giant* brains; they were dwarf brains, and they still are, though they have grown a hundredfold within less than one generation of mankind. Yet even in their present flint-ax stage of evolution, they have done things which not long ago almost everyone would have claimed to be impossible—such as translating from one language to another, composing music, and playing a fair game of chess. And much more important than any of these infant *jeux d'esprit* is the fact that they have breached the barrier between brain and machine.

This is one of the greatest—and perhaps one of the last—breakthroughs in the history of human thought, like the discovery that the Earth moves round the Sun, or that man is part of the animal kingdom, or that $E = mc^2$. All these ideas took time to sink in, and were frantically denied when first put forward. In the same way it will take a little while for men to realize that machines can not only think, but may one day think them off the face of the Earth.

At this point you may reasonably ask: "Yes—but what do you mean by *think*?" I propose to sidestep that question, using a neat device for which I am indebted to the English mathematician A. M. Turing. Turing imagined a game played by two teleprinter operators in separate rooms—this impersonal link being used to remove all clues given by voice, appearance, and so forth. Suppose one operator was able to ask the other any questions he wished, and the other had to make suitable replies. If, after some hours or days of this conversation, the questioner could not decide whether his telegraph acquaintance was human or purely mechanical, then he could hardly deny that he/it was capable of thought. An electronic brain that passed this test would, surely, have to be regarded as an intelligent entity. Anyone who argued otherwise would merely prove that he was less intelligent than the machine; he would be a splitter of nonexistent hairs, like the scholar who proved that the *Odyssey* was not written by Homer, but by another man of the same name.

We are still decades—but not centuries—from building such a machine, yet already we are sure that it could be done. If Turing's experiment is never carried out, it will merely be because the intelligent machines of the future will have better things to do with their time than conduct extended conversations with men. I often talk with my dog, but I don't keep it up for long.

The fact that the great computers of today are still high-speed morons, capable of doing nothing beyond the scope of the instructions carefully programmed into them, has given many people a spurious sense of security. No machine, they argue, can possibly be more intelligent than its makers—the men who designed it, and planned its functions. It may be a million times faster in operation, but that is quite irrelevant. Anything and everything that an electronic brain can do must also be within the scope of a human brain, if it had sufficient time and patience. Above all, it is maintained, no machine can show originality or creative power or the other attributes which are fondly labeled "human."

The argument is wholly fallacious; those who still bring it forth are like the buggy-whip makers who used to poke fun at stranded Model T's. Even if it were true, it could give no comfort, as a careful reading of these remarks by Dr. Norbert Wiener will show:

"This attitude (the assumption that machines cannot possess any degree of originality) in my opinion should be rejected entirely. . . . It is my thesis that machines can and do transcend some of the limitations of their designers. . . . It may well be that in principle we cannot make any machine, the elements of whose behaviour we cannot comprehend sooner or later. This does not mean in any way that we shall be able to comprehend them in substantially less time than the operation of the machine, nor even within any given number of years or generations. . . . This means that though they are theoretically subject to human criticism, such criticism may be ineffective until a time long after it is relevant."

In other words, even machines *less* intelligent than men might escape from our control by sheer speed of operation. And in fact, there is every reason to suppose that machines will become much more intelligent than their builders, as well as incomparably faster.

There are still a few authorities who refuse to grant any degree of intelligence to machines, now or in the future. This attitude shows a striking parallel to that adopted by the chemists of the early nineteenth century. It was known then that all living organisms are formed from a few common elements—mostly carbon, hydrogen, oxygen, and nitrogen—but it was firmly believed that the materials of life could not be made from "mere" chemicals alone. There must be some other ingredient—some essence or vital principle, forever unknowable to man. No chemist could ever take carbon, hydrogen, and so forth and combine them to form any of the substances upon which life was based. There was an impassable barrier between the worlds of "inorganic" and "organic" chemistry.

This *mystique* was destroyed in 1828, when Wöhler synthesized urea, and showed that there was no difference at all between the chemical reactions taking place in the body, and those taking place inside a retort. It was a terrible shock to those pious souls who believed that the mechanics of life must always be beyond human understanding or imitation. Many people are equally shocked today by the suggestion that machines can think, but their dislike of the situation will not alter it in the least.

Since this is not a treatise on computer design,

you will not expect me to explain how to build a thinking machine. In fact, it is doubtful if any human being will ever be able to do this in detail, but one can indicate the sequence of events that will lead from H. sapiens to M. sapiens. The first two or three steps on the road have already been taken; machines now exist that can learn by experience, profiting from their mistakes and—unlike human beings—never repeating them. Machines have been built which do not sit passively waiting for instructions, but which explore the world around them in a manner which can only be called inquisitive. Others look for proofs of theorems in mathematics or logic, and sometimes come up with surprising solutions that had never occurred to their makers.

These faint glimmerings of original intelligence are confined at the moment to a few laboratory models; they are wholly lacking in the giant computers that can now be bought by anyone who happens to have a few hundred thousand dollars to spare. But machine intelligence will grow, and it will start to range beyond the bounds of human thought as soon as the second generation of computers appears—the generation that has been designed, not by men, but by other, "almost intelligent" computers. And not only designed, but also built—for they will have far too many components for manual assembly.

It is even possible that the first genuine thinking machines may be *grown* rather than constructed; already some crude but very stimulating experiments have been carried out along these lines. Several artificial organisms have been built which are capable of rewiring themselves to adapt to changing circumstances. Beyond this there is the possibility of computers which will start from relatively simple beginnings, be programmed to aim at specific goals, and search for them by constructing their own circuits, perhaps by growing networks of threads in a conducting medium. Such a growth may be no more than a mechanical analogy of what happens to every one of us in the first nine months of our existence.

All speculations about intelligent machines are inevitably conditioned—indeed, inspired—by our knowledge of the human brain, the only thinking device currently on the market. No one, of course, pretends to understand the full workings of the brain, or expects that such knowledge will be available in any forseeable future. (It is a nice philosophical point as to whether the brain can ever, even in principle, understand itself.) But we do know enough about its physical structure to draw many conclusions about the limitations of "brains"—whether organic or inorganic.

There are approximately ten billion separate switches—or neurons—inside your skull, "wired" together in circuits of unimaginable complexity. Ten billion is such a large number that, until recently, it could be used as an argument against the achievement of mechanical intelligence. About ten years ago a famous neurophysiologist made a statement (still produced like some protective incantation by the advocates of cerebral supremacy) to the effect that an electronic model of the human brain would have to be as large as the Empire State Building, and would need Niagara Falls to keep it cool when it was running.

This must now be classed with such interesting pronouncements as, "No heavier than air machine will ever be able to fly." For the calculation was made in the days of the vacuum tube (remember it?), and the transistor has now completely altered the picture. Indeed—such is the rate of technological progress today—the transistor itself is being replaced by still smaller and faster devices, based upon abstruse principles of quantum physics. If the problem was merely one of space, today's electronic techniques would allow us to pack a computor as complex as the human brain on to a single floor of the Empire State Building.

Interlude for agonizing reappraisal. It's a tough job keeping up with science, and since I wrote that last paragraph the Marquardt Corporation's Astro Division has announced a new memory device which could store inside a six-foot cube *all information recorded during the last 10,000 years.* This means, of course, not only every book ever printed, but *everything* ever written in *any* language on paper, papyrus, parchment, or stone. It represents a capacity untold millions of times greater than that of a single human memory, and though there is a mighty gulf between merely storing information and thinking creatively—the Library of Congress has never written a book—it does indicate that mechanical brains of enormous power could be quite small in physical size.

This should not surprise anyone who remembers how radios have shrunk from the bulky cabinet models of the thirties to the vest-pocket (yet much more sophisticated) transistor sets of today. And the shrinkage is just gaining momentum, if I may employ such a mind-boggling phrase. Radio receivers the size of lumps of sugar have now been built; before long, they will be the size not of lumps but of grains, for the slogan of the microminiaturization experts is "If you can see it, it's too big."

Just to prove that I am not exaggerating, here are some statistics you can use on the next hi-fi fanatic who takes you on a tour of his wall-to-wall installation. During the 1950's, the electronic engineers learned to pack up to a hundred thousand components into one cubic foot. (To give a basis of comparison, a good hi-fi set may contain two or three hundred components, a domestic radio about a hundred.) Here at the beginning of the sixties, the attainable figure is around a million components per cubic foot; by 1970, when to-day's experimental techniques of microscopic engineering have begun to pay off, it may reach a hundred million.

Fantastic though this last figure is, the human brain surpasses it by a thousandfold, packing its ten billion neurons into a *tenth* of a cubic foot. And although smallness is not necessarily a virtue, even this may be nowhere near the limit of possible compactness.

For the cells composing our brains are slow-acting, bulky, and wasteful of energy—compared with the scarcely more than atom-sized computer elements that are theoretically possible. The mathematician John von Neumann once calculated that electronic cells could be ten billion times more efficient than protoplasmic ones; already they are a million times swifter in operation, and speed can often be traded for size. If we take these ideas to their ultimate conclusion, it appears that a computer equivalent in power to one human brain need be no bigger than a matchbox.

This slightly shattering thought becomes more reasonable when we take a critical look at flesh and blood and bone as engineering materials. All living creatures are marvelous, but let us keep our sense of proportion. Perhaps the most wonderful thing about Life is that it works at all, when it has to employ such extraordinary materials, and has to tackle its problems in such roundabout ways.

As a perfect example of this, consider the eye. Suppose *you* were given the problem of designing a camera—for that, of course, is what the eye is —which *has to be constructed entirely of water and jelly*, without using a scrap of glass, metal, or plastic. Obviously, it can't be done.

You're quite right; the feat is impossible. The eye is an evolutionary miracle, but it's a lousy camera. You can prove this while you're reading the next sentence.

Here's a medium-length word:—photography. Close one eye and keep the other fixed—repeat, *fixed*—on that center "g." You may be surprised to discover that—unless you cheat by altering the direction of your gaze—you cannot see the whole word clearly. It fades out three or four letters to the right and left.

No camera ever built—even the cheapest— has as poor an optical performance as this. For color vision also, the human eye is nothing to boast about; it can operate only over a small band of the spectrum. To the worlds of the infrared and ultraviolet, visible to bees and other insects, it is completely blind.

We are not conscious of these limitations because we have grown up with them, and indeed if they were corrected the brain would be quite unable to handle the vastly increased flood of information. But let us not make a virtue of a necessity; if our eyes had the optical performance of even the cheapest miniature camera we would live in an unimaginably richer and more colorful world.

These defects are due to the fact that precision scientific instruments simply cannot be manufactured from living materials. With the eye, the ear, the nose—indeed, all the sense organs— evolution has performed a truly incredible job against fantastic odds. But it will not be good enough for the future; indeed, it is not good enough for the present.

There are some senses that do not exist, that can probably never be provided by living structures, and that we need in a hurry. On this planet, to the best of our knowledge, no creature has ever developed organs that can detect radio waves or radioactivity. Though I would hate to lay down the law and claim that nowhere in the universe can there be organic Geiger counters or living TV sets, I think it highly improbable. There are some jobs that can be done only by vacuum tubes or magnetic fields or electron beams, and are therefore beyond the capability of purely organic structures.

There is another fundamental reason living machines such as you and I cannot hope to compete with non-living ones. Quite apart from our poor materials, we are handicapped by one of the toughest engineering specifications ever issued. What sort of performance would you expect from a machine which has to grow several billionfold during the course of manufacture—and which has to be completely and continuously rebuilt, molecule by molecule, every few weeks? This is what happens to all of us, all the time; you are not the man you were last year, in the most literal sense of the expression.

Most of the energy and effort required to run the body goes into its perpetual tearing down and rebuilding—a cycle completed every few weeks. New York City, which is a very much simpler structure than a man, takes hundreds of times longer to remake itself. When one tries to picture the body's myriads of building contractors and utility companies all furiously at work, tearing up arteries and nerves and even bones, it is astonishing that there is any energy left over for the business of thinking.

Now I am perfectly well aware that many of the "limitations" and "defects" just mentioned are nothing of the sort, looked at from another point of view. Living creatures, because of their very nature, can evolve from simple to complex organisms. They may well be the only path by which intelligence can be obtained, for it is a little difficult to see how a lifeless planet can progress directly from metal ores and mineral deposits to electronic computers by its own un-aided efforts.

Though intelligence can arise only from life, it may then discard it. Perhaps at a later stage, as the mystics have suggested, it may also discard matter; but this leads us in realms of speculations which an unimaginative person like myself would prefer to avoid.

One often-stressed advantage of living creatures is that they are self-repairing and reproduce themselves with ease—indeed, with enthusiasm. This superiority over machines will be short-lived; the general principles underlying the construction of self-repairing and self-reproducing machines have already been worked out. There is, incidentally, something ironically appropriate in the fact that A. M. Turing, the brilliant mathematician who pioneered in this field and first indicated how thinking machines might be built, shot himself a few years after publishing his results. It is very hard not to draw a moral from this.

The greatest single stimulus to the evolution of mechanical—as opposed to organic—intelligence is the challenge of space. Only a vanishingly small fraction of the universe is directly accessible to mankind, in the sense that we can live there without elaborate protection or mechanical aids. If we generously assume that humanity's potential *Lebensraum* extends from sea level to a height of three miles, over the whole Earth, that gives us a total of some half billion cubic miles. At first sight this is an im-

pressive figure, especially when you remember that the entire human race could be packaged into a one-mile cube. But it is absolutely nothing, when set against Space with a capital "S." Our present telescopes, which are certainly not the last word on the subject, sweep a volume at least a million million million million million million million million million million times greater.

Though such a number is, of course, utterly beyond conception, it can be given a vivid meaning. If we reduced the known universe to the size of the Earth, then the portion in which *we* can live without space suits and pressure cabins is about the size of a single atom.

It is true that, one day, we are going to explore and colonize many other atoms in this Earth-sized volume, but it will be at the cost of tremendous technical efforts, for most of our energies will be devoted to protecting our frail and sensitive bodies against the extremes of temperature, pressure, or gravity found in space and on other worlds. Within very wide limits, machines are indifferent to these extremes. Even more important, they can wait patiently through the years and the centuries that will be needed for travel to the far reaches of the universe.

Creatures of flesh and blood such as ourselves can explore space and win control over infinitesimal fractions of it. But only creatures of metal and plastic can ever really conquer it, as indeed they have already started to do. The tiny brains of our Prospectors and Rangers barely hint at the mechanical intelligence that will one day be launched at the stars.

It may well be that only in space, confronted with environments fiercer and more complex than any to be found upon this planet, will intelligence be able to reach its fullest stature. Like other qualities, intelligence is developed by struggle and conflict; in the ages to come, the dullards may remain on placid Earth, and real genius will flourish only in space—the realm of the machine, not of flesh and blood.

A striking parallel to this situation can already be found on our planet. Some millions of years ago, the most intelligent of the mammals withdrew from the battle of the dry land and returned to their ancestral home, the sea. They are still there, with brains larger and potentially more powerful than ours. But (as far as we know) they do not use them; the static environment of the sea makes little call upon intelligence. The porpoises and whales, which might have been our equals and perhaps our superiors had they remained on land, now race in simpleminded and innocent ecstasy beside the new sea monsters carrying sixteen megatons of death. Perhaps they, not we, made the right choice; but it is too late to join them now.

If you have followed me so far, the protoplasmic computer inside your skull should now be programmed to accept the idea—at least for the sake of argument—that machines can be both more intelligent and more versatile than men, and may well be so in the very near future. So it is time to face the question: Where does that leave man?

I suspect that this is not a question of very great importance—except, of course, to man. Perhaps the Neanderthalers made similar plaintive noises, around 100,000 B.C., when H. sapiens appeared on the scene, with his ugly vertical forehead and ridiculous protruding chin. Any Paleolithic philosopher who gave his colleagues the right answer would probably have ended up in the cooking pot; I am prepared to take that risk.

The short-term answer may indeed be cheerful rather than depressing. There may be a brief golden age when men will glory in the power and range of their new partners. Barring war, this age lies directly ahead of us. As Dr. Simon Remo put it recently: "The extension of the human intellect by electronics will become our greatest occupation within a decade." That is undoubtedly true, if we bear in mind that at a somewhat later date the word "extension" may be replaced by "extinction."

One of the ways in which thinking machines will be able to help us is by taking over the humbler tasks of life, leaving the human brain free to concentrate on higher things. (Not, of course, that this is any guarantee that it will do so.) For a few generations, perhaps, every man will go through life with an electronic companion, which may be no bigger than today's transistor radios. It will "grow up" with him from infancy, learning his habits, his business affairs, taking over all the minor chores like routine correspondence and income-tax returns and engagements. On occasion it could even take its master's place, keeping appointments he preferred to miss, and then reporting back in as much detail as he desired. It could substitute for him over the telephone so completely that no one would be able to tell whether man or machine was speaking; a century from now, Turing's "game" may be an integral part of our social lives, with complications and possibilities which I leave to the imagination.

You may remember that delightful robot, Robbie, from the movie *Forbidden Planet*. (One of the three or four movies so far made that anyone interested in science fiction can point to without blushing; the fact that the plot was Shakespeare's doubtless helped.) I submit, in all seriousness, that most of Robbie's abilities—together with those of a better known character, Jeeves—will one day be incorporated in a kind of electronic companion-secretary-valet. It will be much smaller and neater than the walking jukeboxes or mechanized suits of armor which Hollywood presents, with typical lack of imagination, when it wants to portray a robot. And it will be extremely talented, with quick-release connectors allowing it to be coupled to an unlimited variety of sense organs and limbs. It would, in fact, be a kind of general purpose, disembodied intelligence that could attach itself to whatever tools were needed for any particular occasion. One day it might be using microphones or electric typewriters or TV cameras; on another, automobiles or airplanes—or the bodies of men and animals.

And this is, perhaps, the moment to deal with a conception which many people find even more horrifying than the idea that machines will replace or supersede us. It is the idea that they may combine with us.

I do not know who first thought of this; probably the physicist J. D. Bernal, who in 1929 published an extraordinary book of scientific predictions called *The World, the Flesh and the Devil*. In this slim and long out-of-print volume (I sometimes wonder what the sixty-year-old Fellow of the Royal Society now thinks of his youthful indiscretion, if he ever remembers it), Bernal decided that the numerous limitations of the human body could be overcome only by the use of mechanical attachments or substitutes—until, eventually, all that might be left of man's original organic body would be the brain.

This idea is already far more plausible than when Bernal advanced it, for in the last few decades we have seen the development of mechanical hearts, kidneys, lungs, and other organs, and the wiring of electronic devices directly into the human nervous system.

Olaf Stapledon developed this theme in his wonderful history of the future, *Last and First Men*, imagining an age of immortal "giant brains," many yards across, living in beehive-shaded cells, sustained by pumps and chemical plants. Though completely immobile, their sense organs could be wherever they wished, so their center of awareness—or consciousness, if you like—could be anywhere on Earth or in the space above it. This is an important point which we—who carry our brains around in the same fragile structure as our eyes, ears, and other sense organs, often with disastrous results—may easily fail to appreciate. Given perfected tele-communications, a fixed brain is no handicap, but rather the reverse. Your present brain, totally imprisoned behind its walls of bone, communicates with the outer world and receives its impressions of it over the telephone wires of the central nervous system—wires varying in length from a fraction of an inch to several feet. *You would never know the difference if those "wires" were actually hundreds or thousands of miles long, or included mobile radio links, and your brain never moved at all.*

In a crude way—yet one that may accurately foreshadow the future—we have already extended our visual and tactile senses away from our bodies. The men who now work with radio isotopes, handling them with remotely-controlled mechanical fingers and observing them by television, have achieved a partial separation between brain and sense organs. They are in one place, their minds effectively in another.

Recently the word "Cyborg" (cybernetic organism) has been coined to describe the machine-animal of the type we have been discussing. Doctors Manfred Clynes and Nathan Kline of Rockland State Hospital, Orangeburg, New York, who invented the name, define a Cyborg in these stirring words: "an exogenously extended organizational complex functioning as a homeostatic system." To translate, this means a body which has machines hitched to it, or built into it, to take over or modify some of its functions.

I suppose one could call a man in an iron lung a Cyborg, but the concept has far wider implications than this. One day we may be able to enter into temporary unions with any sufficiently sophisticated machines, thus being able not merely to control but to *become* a spaceship or a submarine or a TV network. This would give far more than purely intellectual satisfaction; the thrill that can be obtained from driving a racing car or flying an airplane may be only a pale ghost of the excitement our great-grandchildren may know, when the individual human consciousness is free to roam at will from machine to machine, through all the reaches of sea and sky and space.

But how long will this partnership last? Can the synthesis of man and machine ever be stable, or will the purely organic component become such a hindrance that it has to be discarded? If this eventually happens—and I have given good reasons for thinking that it must—we have nothing to regret, and certainly nothing to fear.

The popular idea, fostered by comic strips and the cheaper forms of science fiction, that intelligent machines must be malevolent entities hostile to man, is so absurd that it is hardly worth wasting energy to refute it. I am almost tempted to argue that only *un*intelligent machines can be malevolent; anyone who has tried to start a balky outboard will probably agree. Those who picture machines as active enemies are merely projecting their own aggressive instincts, inherited from the jungle, into a world where such things do not exist. The higher the intelligence, the greater the degree of cooperativeness. If there is ever a war between men and machines, it is easy to guess who will start it.

Yet however friendly and helpful the machines of the future may be, most people will feel that it is a rather bleak prospect for humanity if it ends up as a pampered specimen in some biological museum—even if that museum is the whole planet Earth. This, however, is an attitude I find impossible to share.

No individual exists forever; why should we expect our species to be immortal? Man, said Nietzsche, is a rope stretched between the animal and the superhuman—a rope across the abyss. That will be a noble purpose to have served.

THE PORTABLE PHONOGRAPH

Walter Van Tilburg Clark

The red sunset, with narrow, black cloud strips like threats across it, lay on the curved horizon of the prairie. The air was still and cold, and in it settled the mute darkness and greater cold of night. High in the air there was wind, for through the veil of the dusk the clouds could be seen gliding rapidly south and changing shapes. A queer sensation of torment, of two-sided, unpredictable nature, arose from the stillness of the earth air beneath the violence of the upper air. Out of the sunset, through the dead, matted grass and isolated weed stalks of the prairie, crept the narrow and deeply rutted remains of a road. In the road, in places, there were crusts of shallow, brittle ice. There were little islands of an old oiled pavement in the road, too, but most of it was mud, now frozen rigid. The frozen mud still bore the toothed impress of great tanks, and a wanderer on the neighboring undulations might have stumbled, in this light,

into large, partially filled-in and weed-grown cavities, their banks channelled and beginning to spread into badlands. These pits were such as might have been made by falling meteors, but they were not. They were the scars of gigantic bombs, their rawness already made a little natural by rain, seed, and time. Along the road, there were rakish remnants of fence. There was also, just visible, one portion of tangled and multiple barbed wire still erect, behind which was a shelving ditch with small caves, now very quiet and empty, at intervals in its back wall. Otherwise there was no structure or remnant of a structure visible over the dome of the darkling earth, but only, in sheltered hollows, the darker shadows of young trees trying again.

Under the wuthering arch of the high wind a V of wild geese fled south. The rush of their pinions sounded briefly, and the faint, plaintive notes of their expeditionary talk. Then they left a still greater vacancy. There was the smell and expectation of snow, as there is likely to be when the wild geese fly south. From the remote distance, towards the red sky, came faintly the protracted howl and quick yap-yap of a prairie wolf.

North of the road perhaps a hundred yards,

— *"The Portable Phonograph"* by Walter Van Tilburg Clark, from *The Watchful Gods and other stories* by Walter Van Tilburg Clark, published by Random House, Inc., 1950; reprinted by permission of the publisher

lay the parallel and deeply intrenched course of a small creek, lined with leafless alders and willows. The creek was already silent under ice. In the bank above it was dug a sort of cell, with a single opening, like the mouth of a mine tunnel. Within the cell there was a little red of fire, which showed dully through the opening, like a reflection or a deception of the imagination. The light came from the chary burning of four blocks of poorly aged peat, which gave off a petty warmth and much acrid smoke. But the precious remnants of wood, old fence posts and timbers from the long-deserted dugouts, had to be saved for the real cold, for the time when a man's breath blew white, the moisture in his nostrils stiffened at once when he stepped out, and the expansive blizzards paraded for days over the vast open, swirling and settling and thickening, till the dawn of the cleared day when the sky was thin blue-green and the terrible cold, in which a man could not live for three hours unwarmed, lay over the uniformly drifted swell of the plain.

Around the smoldering peat, four men were seated cross-legged. Behind them, traversed by their shadows, was the earth bench, with two old and dirty army blankets, where the owner of the cell slept. In a niche in the opposite wall were a few tin utensils which caught the glint of the coals. The host was re-wrapping in a piece of daubed burlap four fine, leather-bound books. He worked slowly and very carefully, and at last tied the bundle securely with a piece of grass-woven cord. The other three looked intently upon the process, as if a great significance lay in it. As the host tied the cord, he spoke. He was an old man, his long, matted beard and hair gray to nearly white. The shadows made his brows and cheekbones appear gnarled, his eyes and cheeks deeply sunken. His big hands, rough with frost and swollen by rheumatism, were awkward but gentle at their task. He was like a prehistoric priest performing a fateful ceremonial rite. Also his voice had in it a suitable quality of deep, reverent despair, yet perhaps at the moment, a sharpness of selfish satisfaction.

"When I perceived what was happening," he said, "I told myself, 'It is the end. I cannot take much; I will take these.'

"Perhaps I was impractical," he continued. "But for myself, I do not regret, and what do we know of those who will come after us? We are the doddering remnant of a race of mechanical fools. I have saved what I love; the soul of what was good in us is here; perhaps the new ones will make a strong enough beginning not to fall behind when they become clever."

He rose with slow pain and placed the wrapped volumes in the niche with his utensils. The others watched him with the same ritualistic gaze.

"Shakespeare, the Bible, 'Moby Dick,' the 'Divine Comedy'," one of them said softly. "You might have done worse, much worse."

"You will have a little soul left until you die," said another harshly. "That is more than is true of us. My brain becomes thick, like my hands." He held the big, battered hands, with their black nails, in the glow to be seen.

"I want paper to write on," he said. "And there is none."

The fourth man said nothing. He sat in the shadow farthest from the fire, and sometimes his body jerked in its rags from the cold. Although he was still young, he was sick and coughed often. Writing implied a greater future than he now felt able to consider.

The old man seated himself laboriously, and reached out, groaning at the movement, to put another block of peat on the fire. With bowed heads and averted eyes, his three guests acknowledged his magnanimity.

"We thank you, Dr. Jenkins, for the reading," said the man who had named the books.

They seemed then to be waiting for something. Dr. Jenkins understood, but was loathe to comply. In an ordinary moment he would have said nothing. But the words of "The Tempest" which he had been reading, and the religious attention of the three, made this an unusual occasion.

"You wish to hear the phonograph," he said grudgingly.

The two middle-aged men stared into the fire, unable to formulate and expose the enormity of their desire.

The young man, however, said anxiously, between suppressed coughs, "Oh, please," like an excited child.

The old man rose again in his difficult way, and went to the back of the cell. He returned and placed tenderly upon the packed floor, where the firelight might fall upon it, an old portable phonograph in a black case. He smoothed the top with his hand, and then opened it. The lovely green-felt-covered disk became visible.

"I have been using thorns as needles," he said. "But tonight, because we have a musician among us," he bent his head to the young man, almost invisible in the shadow, "I will use a steel needle. There are only three left."

The two middle-aged men stared at him in speechless adoration. The one with the big hands, who wanted to write, moved his lips, but the whisper was not audible.

"Oh, don't!" cried the young man, as if he were hurt. "The thorns will do beautifully."

"No," the old man said. "I have become accustomed to the thorns, but they are not really good. For you, my young friend, we will have good music tonight.

"After all," he added generously, and beginning to wind the phonograph, which creaked, "they can't last forever."

"No, nor we," the man who needed to write said harshly. "The needle, by all means."

"Oh, thanks," said the young man. "Thanks," he said again in a low, excited voice, and then stifled his coughing with a bowed head.

"The records, though," said the old man when he had finished winding, "are a different matter. Already they are very worn. I do not play them more than once a week. One, once a week, that is what I allow myself.

"More than a week I cannot stand it; not to hear them," he apologized.

"No, how could you?" cried the young man. "And with them here like this."

"A man can stand anything," said the man who wanted to write, in his harsh, antagonistic voice.

"Please, the music," said the young man.

"Only the one," said the old man. "In the long run, we will remember more that way."

He had a dozen records with luxuriant gold and red seals. Even in that light the others could see that the threads of the records were becoming worn. Slowly he read out the titles, and the tremendous, dead names of the composers and the artists and the orchestras. The three worked upon the names in their minds, carefully. It was difficult to select from such a wealth what they would at once most like to remember. Finally, the man who wanted to write named Gershwin's "New York."

"Oh, no!" cried the sick young man, and then could say nothing more because he had to cough. The others understood him, and the harsh man withdrew his selection and waited for the musician to choose.

The musician begged Dr. Jenkins to read the titles again, very slowly, so that he could remember the sounds. While they were read, he lay back against the wall, his eyes closed, his thin, horny hand pulling at his light beard, and listened to the voices and the orchestras and the single instruments in his mind.

When the reading was done he spoke despairingly. "I have forgotten," he complained; "I cannot hear them clearly.

"There are things missing," he explained.

"I know," said Dr. Jenkins. "I thought that I knew all of Shelley by heart. I should have brought Shelley."

"That's more soul than we can use," said the harsh man. " 'Moby Dick' is better.

"By God, we can understand that," he emphasized.

The Doctor nodded.

"Still," said the man who had admired the books, "we need the absolute if we are to keep a grasp on anything.

"Anything but these sticks and peat clods and rabbit snares," he said bitterly.

"Shelley desired an ultimate absolute," said the harsh man. "It's too much," he said. "It's no good; no earthly good."

The musician selected a Debussy nocturne. The others considered and approved. They rose to their knees to watch the Doctor prepare for the playing, so that they appeared to be actually in an attitude of worship. The peat glow showed the thinness of their bearded faces, and the deep lines in them, and revealed the condition of their garments. The other two continued to kneel as the old man carefully lowered the needle onto the spinning disk, but the musician suddenly drew back against the wall again, with his knees up, and buried his face in his hands.

At the first notes of the piano the listeners were startled. They stared at each other. Even the musician lifted his head in amazement, but then quickly bowed it again, strainingly, as if he were suffering from a pain he might not be able to endure. They were all listening deeply, without movement. The wet, blue-green notes tinkled forth from the old machine, and were individual, delectable presences in the cell. The individual, delectable presences swept into a sudden tide of unbearably beautiful dissonance, and then continued fully the swelling and ebbing of that tide, the dissonant inpourings, and the resolutions, and the diminishings, and the little, quiet wavelets of interlude lapping between. Every sound was piercing and singularly sweet. In all the men except the musician, there occurred rapid sequences of tragically heightened recollection. He heard nothing but what was there. At the final, whispering disappearance, but moving quietly so that the others would not hear him and look at him, he let his head fall back in agony, as if it were drawn there by the hair, and clenched the fingers of one hand over his teeth. He sat that way while the others were silent, and until they began to breathe again normally. His drawn-up legs were trembling violently.

Quickly Dr. Jenkins lifted the needle off, to save it and not to spoil the recollection with scraping. When he had stopped the whirling of the sacred disk, he courteously left the phonograph open and by the fire, in sight.

The others, however, understood. The musician rose last, but then abruptly, and went quickly out at the door without saying anything. The others stopped at the door and gave their thanks in low voices. The Doctor nodded magnificently.

"Come again," he invited, "in a week. We will have the 'New York'."

When the two had gone together, out towards the rimed road, he stood in the entrance, peering and listening. At first, there was only the resonant boom of the wind overhead, and then far over the dome of the dead, dark plain, the wolf cry lamenting. In the rifts of clouds the Doctor saw four stars flying. It impressed the Doctor that one of them had just been obscured by the beginning of a flying cloud at the very moment he heard what he had been listening for, a sound of suppressed coughing. It was not nearby, however. He believed that down against the pale alders he could see the moving shadow.

With nervous hands he lowered the piece of canvas which served as a door, and pegged it at the bottom. Then quickly and quietly, looking at the piece of canvas frequently, he slipped the records into the case, snapped the lid shut, and carried the phonograph to his couch. There, pausing often to stare at the canvas and listen, he dug earth from the wall and disclosed a piece of board. Behind this there was a deep hole in the wall, into which he put the phonograph. After a moment's consideration, he went over and reached down his bundle of books and inserted it also. Then, guardedly, he once more sealed up the hole with the board and the earth. He also changed his blankets, and the grass-stuffed sack which served as a pillow, so that he could lie facing the entrance. After carefully placing two more blocks of peat upon the fire, he stood for a long time watching the stretched canvas, but it seemed to billow naturally with the first gusts of a lowering wind. At last he prayed, and got in under his blankets, and closed his smoke-smarting eyes. On the inside of the bed, next the wall, he could feel with his hands, the comfortable piece of lead pipe.

WHATEVER HAPPENED TO PLAIN ENGLISH?

Doris Anderson

Much as we would all like to be fluent in at least one other language, I find it more and more difficult to cope with plain English—because English isn't plain anymore. As with so many other things in our complex world, English tends to be used in such a specialized and peculiar way by each particular group or profession, that sometimes we seem to be in danger of becoming a modern-day Tower of Babel.

For example, why can't we talk about "poor people" anymore? We know we have them by the millions. We call them "underprivileged," or "culturally deprived." In the days when I was poor, I would have been insulted to be called "culturally deprived." I was poor. No money.

And why can't we come flat out and say people are trying to get ahead instead of saying they have "upward mobility"? And when conditions are getting worse, what's the matter with stating this fact instead of saying they are "escalating downward"?

Why is it we never have discussions anymore? Why do we always have "seminars"? And why can't we just do things instead of "effect" them? When people don't want to do something, why can't they say "no" instead of "opting out"? And when someone doesn't like a situation, does it help to say he's "alienated"?

And while we're on the subject of people— what happened to them? When did they become "human resources" or "human factors"?

On the other hand, it's easy to understand why we talk of the "credibility gap" instead of "how much will the public swallow"? But instead of saying "at this point in time" wouldn't it be easier just to say "now"? And if something doesn't come off, isn't it simpler just to call it a flop instead of an "abortive attempt"?

In speaking of children the verbiage is even thicker. We never say a child is bad or naughty. He is "aggressive" or "displaying his aggressions." He is never spanked or punished. He is "adjusted" (like a little machine). If he's behaving, he's never called a good child (heavens, no!). He's "well adjusted." When he is learning something, he is being "oriented." And when he can't learn something, he has a "learning disability." He doesn't even sit in a schoolroom anymore. He's in a "learning laboratory." When he goes to look something up, he goes, not to an old-fashioned library, but to a "resources centre."

It's true and trite to say every limp and worn cliché in our language laundry bag such as "bright as a new penny," "clean as the driven snow" was once a new verbal invention. But even the most clever language creations, in our age of rapid communication, become rapidly crushed and soiled.

And I don't mind that. What I do mind is the gimmickry that we load on the way we talk and write. Our infatuation with jargon builds no bridge of better understanding between people. It builds little walled-in societies where you need a special language key to participate. And that isn't what language is for, is it?

— *"Whatever happened to plain English?"*, *editorial, Doris Anderson, Chatelaine, June 1967*

BUCK FANSHAW'S FUNERAL

Mark Twain

Somebody has said that in order to know a community, one must observe the style of its funerals and know what manner of men they bury with most ceremony. I cannot say which class we buried with most éclat in our "flush times," the distinguished public benefactor or the distinguished rough—possibly the two chief grades or grand divisions of society honored their illustrious dead about equally; and hence, no doubt, the philosopher I have quoted from would have needed to see two representative funerals in Virginia before forming his estimate of the people.

There was a grand time over Buck Fanshaw when he died. He was a representative citizen. He had "killed his man"—not in his own quarrel, it is true, but in defence of a stranger unfairly beset by numbers. He had kept a sumptuous saloon. He had been the proprietor of a dashing helpmeet whom he could have discarded without the formality of a divorce. He had held a high position in the fire department and been a very Warwick in politics. When he died there was great lamentation throughout the town, but especially in the vast bottom-stratum of society.

On the inquest it was shown that Buck Fanshaw, in the delirium of a wasting typhoid fever, had taken arsenic, shot himself through the body, cut his throat, and jumped out of a four-story window and broken his neck—and after due deliberation, the jury, sad and tearful, but with intelligence unblinded by its sorrow, brought in a verdict of death "by the visitation of God." What could the world do without juries?

Prodigious preparations were made for the funeral. All the vehicles in town were hired, all the saloons put in mourning, all the municipal and fire-company flags hung at half-mast, and all the firemen ordered to muster in uniform and bring their machines duly draped in black. Now—let us remark in parenthesis—as all the peoples of the earth had representative adventurers in the Silverland, and as each adventurer had brought the slang of his nation or his locality with him, the combination made the slang of Nevada the richest and the most infinitely varied and copious that had ever existed anywhere in the world, perhaps, except in the mines of California in the "early days." Slang was the language of Nevada. It was hard to preach a sermon without it, and be understood. Such phrases as "You bet!" "Oh, no, I reckon not!" "No Irish need apply," and a hundred others, became so common as to fall from the lips of a speaker unconsciously—and very often when they did not touch the subject under discussion and consequently failed to mean anything.

After Buck Fanshaw's inquest, a meeting of the short-haired brotherhood was held, for nothing can be done on the Pacific coast without a public meeting and an expression of sentiment. Regretful resolutions were passed and various committees appointed; among others, a committee of one was deputed to call on the minister, a fragile, gentle, spirituel new fledgling from an Eastern theological seminary, and as yet unacquainted with the ways of the mines. The committeeman, "Scotty" Briggs, made his visit; and in after days it was worth something to hear the minister tell about it. Scotty was a stalwart rough, whose customary suit, when on weighty official business, like committe work, was a fire helmet, flaming red flannel shirt, patent-leather belt with spanner and revolver attached, coat hung over arm, and pants stuffed into boot-

— *Chapter 47 from Roughing It by Mark Twain; reprinted from The Complete Travel Books of Mark Twain, Garden City, Doubleday and Company, Inc., 1966; reprinted by permission of Harper & Row, Publishers; the title "Buck Fanshaw's Funeral" is not in the original*

tops. He formed something of a contrast to the pale theological student. It is fair to say of Scotty, however, in passing, that he had a warm heart, and a strong love for his friends, and never entered into a quarrel when he could reasonably keep out of it. Indeed, it was commonly said that whenever one of Scotty's fights was investigated, it always turned out that it had originally been no affair of his, but that out of native goodheartedness he had dropped in of his own accord to help the man who was getting the worst of it. He and Buck Fanshaw were bosom friends, for years, and had often taken adventurous "pot-luck" together. On one occasion, they had thrown off their coats and taken the weaker side in a fight among strangers, and after gaining a hard-earned victory, turned and found that the men they were helping had deserted early, and not only that, but had stolen their coats and made off with them. But to return to Scotty's visit to the minister. He was on a sorrowful mission, now, and his face was the picture of woe. Being admitted to the presence he sat down before the clergyman, placed his fire-hat on an unfinished manuscript sermon under the minister's nose, took from it a red silk handkerchief, wiped his brow and heaved a sigh of dismal impressiveness, explanatory of his business. He choked, and even shed tears; but with an effort he mastered his voice and said in lugubrious tones:

"Are you the duck that runs the gospel-mill next door?"

"Am I the—pardon me, I believe I do not understand?"

With another sigh and a half-sob, Scotty rejoined:

"Why you see we are in a bit of trouble, and the boys thought maybe you would give us a lift, if we'd tackle you—that is, if I've got the rights of it and you are the head clerk of the doxology-works next door."

"I am the shepherd in charge of the flock whose fold is next door."

"The which?"

"The spiritual adviser of the little company

of believers whose sanctuary adjoins these premises."

Scotty scratched his head, reflected a moment, and then said:

"You ruther hold over me, pard. I reckon I can't call that hand. Ante and pass the buck."

"How? I beg pardon. What did I understand you to say?"

"Well, you've ruther got the bulge on me. Or maybe we've both got the bulge, somehow. You don't smoke me and I don't smoke you. You see, one of the boys has passed in his checks, and we want to give him a good send-off, and so the thing I'm on now is to roust out somebody to jerk a little chin-music for us and waltz him through handsome."

"My friend, I seem to grow more and more bewildered. Your observations are wholly incomprehensible to me. Cannot you simplify them in some way? At first I thought perhaps I understood you, but I grope now. Would it not expedite matters if you restricted yourself to categorical statements of fact unencumbered with obstructing accumulations of metaphor and allegory?"

Another pause, and more reflection. Then, said Scotty:

"I'll have to pass, I judge."

"How?"

"You've raised me out, pard."

"I still fail to catch your meaning."

"Why, that last lead of yourn is too many for me—that's the idea. I can't neither trump nor follow suit."

The clergyman sank back in his chair perplexed. Scotty leaned his head on his hand and gave himself up to thought. Presently his face came up, sorrowful but confident.

"I've got it now, so's you can savvy," he said. "What we want is a gospel-sharp. See?"

"A what?"

"Gospel-sharp. Parson."

"Oh! Why did you not say so before? I am a clergyman—a parson."

"Now you talk! You see my blind and straddle it like a man. Put it there!"—extending a brawny paw, which closed over the minister's small hand and gave it a shake indicative of fraternal sympathy and fervent gratification.

"Now we're all right, pard. Let's start fresh. Don't you mind my snuffling a little—becuz we're in a power of trouble. You see, one of the boys has gone up the flume—"

"Gone where?"

"Up the flume—throwed up the sponge, you understand."

"Thrown up the sponge?"

"Yes—kicked the bucket—"

"Ah—has departed to that mysterious country from whose bourne no traveler returns."

"Return! I reckon not. Why, pard, he's *dead!*"

"Yes, I understand."

"Oh, you do? Well I thought maybe you might be getting tangled some more. Yes, you see he's dead again—"

"*Again!* Why, has he ever been dead before?"

"Dead before? No! Do you reckon a man has got as many lives as a cat? But you bet you he's awful dead now, poor old boy, and I wish I'd never seen this day. I don't want no better friend than Buck Fanshaw. I knowed him by the back; and when I know a man and like him, I freeze to him—you hear *me*. Take him all round, pard, there never was a bullier man in the mines. No man ever knowed Buck Fanshaw to go back on a friend. But it's all up, you know, it's all up. It ain't no use. They've scooped him."

"Scooped him?"

"Yes—death has. Well, well, well, we've got to give him up. Yes, indeed. It's a kind of a hard world, after all, *ain't* it? But pard, he was a rustler! You ought to seen him get started once. He was a bully boy with a glass eye! Just spit in his face and give him room according to his strength, and it was just beautiful to see him peel and go in. He was the worst son of a thief that ever drawed breath. Pard, he was *on* it! He was on it bigger than an Injun!"

"On it? On what?"

"On the shoot. On the shoulder. On the fight, you understand. *He* didn't give a continental for *any*body. *Beg* your pardon, friend, for coming so near a cuss-word—but you see I'm on an awful strain, in this palaver, on account of having to cramp down and draw everything so mild. But we've got to give him up. There ain't any getting around that, I don't reckon. Now if we can get you to help plant him—"

"Preach the funeral discourse? Assist at the obsequies?"

"Obs'quies is good. Yes. That's it—that's our little game. We are going to get the thing up regardless, you know. He was always nifty himself, and so you bet you his funeral ain't going to be no slouch—solid-silver door-plate on his coffin, six plumes on the hearse, and a nigger on the box in a biled shirt and a plug hat—how's that for high? And we'll take care of *you*, pard. We'll fix you all right. There'll be a Kerridge for you; and whatever you want, you just 'scape out and we'll 'tend to it. We've got a shebang fixed up for you to stand behind, in No. 1's house, and don't you be afraid. Just go in and toot your horn, if you don't sell a clam. Put Buck through as bully as you can, pard, for anybody that knowed him will tell you that he was one of the whitest men that was ever in the mines. You can't draw it too strong. He never could stand it to see things going wrong. He's done more to make this town quiet and peaceable than any man in it. I've seen him lick four Greasers in eleven minutes, myself. If a thing wanted regulating, *he* warn't a man to go browsing around after somebody to do it, but he would prance in and regulate it himself. He warn't a Catholic. Scasely. He was down on 'em. His word was, 'No Irish need apply!' But it didn't make no difference about that when it came down to what a man's rights was—and so, when some roughs jumped the Catholic bone-yard and started in to stake out town lots in it he *went* for 'em! And he *cleaned* 'em, too! I was there, pard, and I seen it myself."

"That was very well indeed—at least the impulse was—whether the act was strictly defensible or not. Had deceased any religious convictions?

That is to say, did he feel a dependence upon, or acknowledge allegiance to a higher power?"

More reflection.

"I reckon you've stumped me again, pard. Could you say it over once more, and say it slow?"

"Well, to simplify it somewhat, was he, or rather had he ever been connected with any organization sequestered from secular concerns and devoted to self-sacrifice in the interests of morality?"

"All down but nine—set 'em up on the other alley, pard."

"What did I understand you to say?"

"Why, you're most too many for me, you know. When you get in with your left I hunt grass every time. Every time you draw, you fill; but I don't seem to have any luck. Let's have a new deal."

"How? Begin again?"

"That's it."

"Very well. Was he a good man, and—"

"There—I see that; don't put up another chip till I look at my hand. A good man, says you? Pard, it ain't no name for it. He was the best man that ever—pard, you would have doted on that man. He could lam any galoot of his inches in America. It was him that put down the riot last election before it got a start; and everybody said he was the only man that could have done it. He waltzed in with a spanner in one hand and a trumpet in the other, and sent fourteen men home on a shutter in less than three minutes. He had that riot all broke up and prevented nice before anybody ever got a chance to strike a blow. He was always for peace, and he would *have* peace—he could not stand disturbances. Pard, he was a great loss to this town. It would please the boys if you could chip in something like that and do him justice. Here once when the Micks got to throwing stones through the Methodis' Sunday-school windows, Buck Fanshaw, all of his own notion, shut up his saloon and took a couple of six-shooters and mounted guard over the Sunday-school. Says he, 'No Irish need apply!' And they didn't. He was the bulliest man in the mountains, pard! He could run faster, jump higher, hit harder, and hold more tanglefoot whisky without spilling it than any man in seventeen counties. Put that in, pard—it'll please the boys more than anything you could say. And you can say, pard, that he never shook his mother."

"Never shook his mother?"

"That's it—any of the boys will tell you so."

"Well, but why *should* he shake her?"

"That's what *I* say—but some people does."

"Not people of any repute?"

"Well, some that averages pretty so-so."

"In my opinion the man that would offer personal violence to his own mother, ought to—"

"Cheese it, pard; you've banked your ball clean outside the string. What I was a drivin' at, was, that he never *throwed off* on his mother—don't you see? No indeedy. He give her a house to live in, and town lots, and plenty of money; and he looked after her and took care of her all the time; and when she was down with the smallpox I'm d——d if he didn't set up nights and nuss her himself! *Beg* your pardon for saying it, but it hopped out too quick for yours truly. You've treated me like a gentleman, pard, and I ain't the man to hurt your feelings intentional. I think you're white. I think you're a square man, pard. I like you, and I'll lick any man that don't. I'll lick him till he can't tell himself from a last year's corpse! Put it *there*!" Another fraternal handshake—and exit.

The obsequies were all that "the boys" could desire. Such a marvel of funeral pomp had never been seen in Virginia. The plumed hearse, the dirge-breathing brass-bands, the closed marts of business, the flags drooping at half-mast, the long, plodding procession of uniformed secret societies, military battalions and fire companies, draped engines, carriages of officials, and citizens in vehicles and on foot, attracted multitudes of spectators to the sidewalks, roofs, and windows; and for years afterward, the degree of grandeur attained by any civic display in Virginia was determined by comparison with Buck Fanshaw's funeral.

Scotty Briggs, as a pall-bearer and a mourner, occupied a prominent place at the funeral, and when the sermon was finished and the last sentence of the prayer for the dead man's soul ascended, he responded, in a low voice, but with feeling:

"AMEN. No Irish need apply."

As the bulk of the response was without apparent relevancy, it was probably nothing more than a humble tribute to the memory of the friend that was gone; for, as Scotty had once said, it was "his word."

Scotty Briggs, in after days, achieved the distinction of becoming the only convert to religion that was ever gathered from the Virginia roughs; and it transpired that the man who had it in him to espouse the quarrel of the weak out of inborn nobility of spirit was no mean timber whereof to construct a Christian. The making him one did not warp his generosity or diminish his courage; on the contrary it gave intelligent direction to the one and a broader field to the other. If his Sunday-school class progressed faster than the other classes, was it matter for wonder? I think not. He talked to his pioneer small-fry in a language they understood! It was my large privilege, a month before he died, to hear him tell the beautiful story of Joseph and his brethren to his class "without looking at the book." I leave it to the reader to fancy what it was like, as it fell, riddled with slang, from the lips of that grave, earnest teacher, and was listened to by his little learners with a consuming interest that showed that they were as unconscious as he was that any violence was being done to the sacred proprieties!

MR. KAPLAN AND SHAKESPEARE

Leonard Q. Ross

It was Miss Higby's idea in the first place. She had suggested to Mr. Parkhill that the students came to her class unaware of the *finer* side of English, of its beauty and, as she put it, "the glorious heritage of our literature." She suggested that perhaps poetry might be worked into the exercises of Mr. Parkhill's class. The beginners' grade had, after all, been subjected to almost a year of English and might be presumed to have achieved some linguistic sophistication. Poetry would make the students conscious of precise enunciation; it would make them read with greater care and an ear for sounds. Miss Higby, who had once begun a master's thesis on

— "*Mr. Kaplan and Shakespeare*" by Leonard Q. Ross, from *The Education of Hyman Kaplan* by Leonard Q. Ross; copyright, 1937, by Harcourt, Brace & World, Inc.; renewed, 1965, by Leo Rosten; reprinted by permission of the publisher

Coventry Patmore, *loved* poetry. And, it should be said in all justice, she argued her cause with considerable logic. Poetry *would* be excellent for the enunciation of students, thought Mr. Parkhill.

So it was that when he faced the class the following Tuesday night, Mr. Parkhill had a volume of Shakespeare on his desk, and an eager, almost an expectant, look in his eye. The love that Miss Higby bore for poetry in general was as nothing compared to the love that Mr. Parkhill bore for Shakespeare in particular. To Mr. Parkhill, poetry meant Shakespeare. Many years ago he had played Polonius in his senior class play.

"Tonight, class," said Mr. Parkhill, "I am going to try an experiment."

The class looked up dutifully. They had come to regard Mr. Parkhill's pedagogical innovations as part of the natural order.

"I am going to introduce you to poetry— great poetry. You see—" Mr. Parkhill delivered a modest lecture on the beauty of poetry, its expression of the loftier thoughts of men, its economy of statement. He hoped it would be a relief from spelling and composition exercises to use poetry as the subject matter of the regular Recitation and Speech period. "I shall write a passage on the board and read it for you. Then, for Recitation and Speech, you will give short addresses, using the passage as the general topic, telling us what it has brought to your minds, what thoughts and ideas.

The class seemed quite pleased by the announcement. Miss Mitnick blushed happily. (This blush was different from most of Miss Mitnick's blushes; there was aspiration and idealism in it.) Mr. Norman Bloom sighed with a business-like air: you could tell that for him poetry was merely another assignment, like a speech on "What I Like to Eat Best" or a composition on "A Day at a Picnic." Mrs. Moskowitz, to whom any public performance was unpleasant, tried to look enthusiastic, without much success. And Mr. Hyman Kaplan, the heroic smile on his face as indelibly as ever, looked at Mr. Parkhill with admiration and whispered to himself: "Poyetry! Now is poyetry! My! Mus' be progriss ve makink awreddy!"

"The passage will be from Shakespeare," Mr. Parkhill announced, opening the volume.

An excited buzz ran through the class as the magic of that name fell upon them.

"Imachine!" murmured Mr. Kaplan. "Jakesbeer!"

"*Shake*speare, Mr. Kaplan!"

Mr. Parkhill took a piece of chalk and, with care and evident love, wrote the following passage on the board in large, clear letters:

Tomorrow, and tomorrow, and tomorrow
Creeps in this petty pace from day to day,
To the last syllable of recorded time;
And all our yesterdays have lighted fools
The way to dusty death. Out, out, brief candle!
Life's but a walking shadow, a poor player
That struts and frets his hour upon the stage,
And then is heard no more; it is a tale

Told by an idiot, full of sound and fury,
Signifying nothing.

A reverent hush filled the classroom, as eyes gazed with wonder on this passage from the Bard. Mr. Parkhill was pleased at this.

"I shall read the passage first," he said. "Listen carefully to my enunciation—and—er—let Shakespeare's thoughts sink into your minds."

Mr. Parkhill read: " 'Tomorrow, and tomorrow, and tomorrow. . . .' " Mr. Parkhill read very well and this night, as if some special fire burned in him, he read with rare eloquence. "Out, out, brief candle!" In Miss Mitnick's eyes there was inspiration and wonder. "Life's but a walking shadow. . . ." Mrs. Moskowitz sat with a heavy frown, indicating cerebration. "It is a tale told by an idiot. . . ." Mr. Kaplan's smile had taken on something luminous; but his eyes were closed: it was not clear whether Mr. Kaplan had surrendered to the spell of the Immortal Bard or to that of Morpheus.

"I shall—er—read the passage again," said Mr. Parkhill, clearing his throat vociferously until he saw Mr. Kaplan's eyes open. " 'Tomorrow, and tomorrow, and tomorrow. . . .' "

When Mr. Parkhill had read the passage for the second time, he said: "That should be quite clear now. Are there any questions?"

There were a few questions. Mr. Scymzak wanted to know whether "frets" was only "a little kind excitement." Miss Schneiderman asked about "struts." Mr. Kaplan wasn't sure about "cripps." Mr. Parkhill explained the words carefully, with several illustrative uses of each word. "No more questions? Well, I shall allow a few minutes for you all to—er—think over the meaning of the passage. Then we shall begin Recitation and Speech."

Mr. Kaplan promptly closed his eyes again, his smile beatific. The students sank into that revery miscalled thought, searching their souls for the symbols evoked by Shakespeare's immortal words.

"Miss Caravello, will you begin?" asked Mr. Parkhill at last.

Miss Caravello went to the front of the room.

"Da poem isa gooda," she said slowly. "Itsa have—"

"It *has*."

"It hasa beautiful wordsa. Itsa lak Dante, Italian poet—"

"Ha!" cried Mr. Kaplan scornfully. "Shaksbeer you metchink mit Tante? *Shaksbeer?* Mein Gott!"

It was obvious that Mr. Kaplan had identified himself with Shakespeare and would tolerate no disparagement of his *alter ego*.

"Miss Caravello is merely expressing her own ideas," said Mr. Parkhill pacifically. (Actually, he felt completely sympathetic to Mr. Kaplan's point of view.)

"Hau Kay," agreed Mr. Kaplan, with a generous wave of the hand. "But to me is no comparink a high-cless man like Shaksbeer mit a Tante, dat's all."

Miss Caravello, her poise shattered, said a few more words and sat down.

Mrs. Yampolsky's contribution was brief. "This is full deep meanings," she said, her eyes on the floor. "Is hard for a person not so good in English to understand. But I like."

"'*Like*!'" cried Mr. Kaplan with a fine impatience. "'*Like?*' Batter *love*, Yampolsky. Mit Shaksbeer mus' be *love*!"

Mr. Parkhill had to suggest that Mr. Kaplan control his aesthetic passions. He did understand how Mr. Kaplan felt, however, and sensed a new bond between them. Mrs. Yampolsky staggered through several more nervous comments and retired.

Mr. Bloom was next. He gave a long declamation, ending: "So is passimistic ideas in the poem, and I am optimist. Life should be happy —so we should remember this is only a poem. Maybe is Shakespeare too passimistic."

"You wronk, Bloom!" cried Mr. Kaplan with prompt indignation. "Shaksbeer is passimist because is de *life* passimist also!"

Mr. Parkhill, impressed by this philosophical stroke, realized that Mr. Kaplan, afire with the glory of the Swan of Avon, could not be suppressed. Mr. Kaplan was the kind of man who

brooked no criticism of his gods. The only solution was to call on Mr. Kaplan for his recitation at once. Mr. Parkhill was, indeed, curious about what fresh thoughts Mr. Kaplan would utter after his passionate defences of the Bard. When Mr. Parkhill had corrected certain parts of Mr. Bloom's speech, emphasizing Mr. Bloom's failure to use the indefinite article, he said: "Mr. Kaplan, will *you* speak next?"

Mr. Kaplan's face broke into a glow; his smile was like a rainbow. "Soitinly," he said, walking to the front of the room. Never had he seemed so dignified, so eager, so conscious of a great destiny.

"Er—Mr. Kaplan," added Mr. Parkhill, suddenly aware of the possibilities which the situation (Kaplan on Shakespeare) involved: "Speak *carefully*."

"*Spacially* careful vill I be," Mr. Kaplan reassured him. He cleared his throat, adjusted his tie, and began: "Ladies an' gantleman, you hoid all kinds minninks abot dis piece poyetry, an'—"

"*Po*etry."

"—abot dis piece *po*etry. But to me is a difference minnink altogadder. Ve mus' tink abot Julius Scissor an' how *he* falt!"

Mr. Parkhill moved nervously, puzzled.

"In dese exact voids is Julius Scissor sayink—"

"Er—Mr. Kaplan," said Mr. Parkhill once he grasped the full import of Mr. Kaplan's error. "The passage is from 'Macbeth.'"

Mr. Kaplan looked at Mr. Parkhill with injured surprise. "*Not* fromm 'Julius Scissor'?" There was pain in his voice.

"No. And it's—er—'Julius *Cae*sar.'"

Mr. Kaplan waited until the last echo of the name had permeated his soul. "Podden me, Mr. Pockheel. Isn't '*seezor*' vat you cottink somting op mit?"

"That," said Mr. Parkhill quickly, "is 'scissor.' You have used 'Caesar' for 'scissor' and 'scissor' for 'Caesar.'"

Mr. Kaplan nodded, marvelling at his own virtuosity.

"But go on with your speech, please." Mr.

Parkhill, to tell the truth, felt a little guilty that he had not announced at the very beginning that the passage was from "Macbeth." Tell us *why* you thought the lines were from 'Julius Caesar.' "

"Vell," said Mr. Kaplan to the class, his smile assuming its normal serenity. "I vas positif, becawss I can *see* de whole ting." He paused, debating how to explain this cryptic remark. Then his eyes filled with a strange enchantment. "I see de whole scinn. It's in a tant, on de night bafore dey makink Julius de Kink fromm Rome. So he is axcited an' ken't slip. He is layink in bad, tinking: 'Tomorrow an' tomorrow an' tomorrow. How slow dey movink! Almost cripps! Soch a pity de pace!' "

Before Mr. Parkhill could explain that "petty pace" did not mean "Soch a pity de pace!" Mr. Kaplan had soared on.

"De days go slow, fromm day to day, like leetle tsyllables on phonograph racords fromm time."

Anxiety and bewilderment invaded Mr. Parkhill's eyes.

" 'An' vat abot yestidday?' tinks Julius Scissor. Ha! 'All our yestiddays are only makink a good light for fools to die in de dost!' "

" 'Dusty death' doesn't mean—" There was no interrupting Mr. Kaplan.

"An' Julius Scissor is so tired, an' he vants to fallink aslip. So he hollers, mit fillink, 'Go ot! Go ot! Short candle!' So it goes ot."

Mr. Kaplan's voice dropped to a whisper. "But he ken't slip. Now is bodderink him de idea fromm life. 'Vat is de life altogadder?' tinks Julius Scissor. An' he gives enswer, de pot I like de bast. 'Life is like a bum actor, strottink an' hollerink arond de stage for only vun hour bafore he's kicked ot. Life is a tale told by idjots, dat's all, full of fonny sonds an' phooey!' "

Mr. Parkhill could be silent no longer. " 'Full of sound and fury!' " he cried desperately. But inspiration, like an irresistible force, swept Mr. Kaplan on.

" 'Life is monkey business! It don' minn a ting. It signifies nottink!' An' den Julius Scissor closes his ice fest—" Mr. Kaplan demonstrated the Consul's exact ocular process in closing his "ice"— "—an' falls dad!"

The class was hushed as Mr. Kaplan stopped. In the silence, a tribute to the fertility of Mr. Kaplan's imagination and the power of his oratory, Mr. Kaplan went to his seat. But just before he sat down, as if adding a postscript, he sighed: "Dat vas mine idea. But ufcawss is all wronk, becawss Mr. Pockheel said de voids ain't abot Julius Scissor altogadder. It's all abot an Irishman by de name Macbat."

Then Mr. Kaplan sat down.

It was some time before Mr. Parkhill could bring himself to criticize Mr. Kaplan's pronunciation, enunciation, diction, grammar, idiom, and sentence structure. For Mr. Parkhill discovered that he could not easily return to the world of reality. He was still trying to tear himself away from that tent outside Rome, where "Julius Scissor," cursed with insomnia, had thought of time and life—and philosophized himself to a strange and sudden death.

Mr. Parkhill was distinctly annoyed with Miss Higby.

COMPOSITION: DOUBLE EXPOSURE

Silver Donald Cameron

I find this type of photography very difficult.

One wants to be creative, of course. You may have noticed my modest library of reference books here in the darkroom. *Creative Photography. Creative Darkroom Techniques. The ABC of Creative Lighting.* To be creative is evidently the secret of good photography. All the authorities agree on the point.

I believe creativity would be much easier if one had the proper equipment. I cannot wait, however, to buy proper equipment. The child's birthday is next week. Mind you, I do not say that my equipment is improper. Quite the contrary. My equipment is quite good of its kind. I have two Asahi Pentax Spotmatic II bodies, and a wide range of accessories, including six lenses. This case contains nothing but filters. There is a light meter built into the cameras, but I have another here for precise metering of localized areas. If the illumination is inadequate, I can fill it in with photofloods or electronic flash, which I carry in that silver-coloured case. I utilize both a tripod and a monopod. In the same case are stored my cable release and my extension tubes for close-up work.

Those are lens hoods. I have a hood for each of the six lenses. The hood looks like a funnel protruding from the front of the lens; it prevents accidental light from reaching the aperture from the side. I plan my photographs carefully. Nothing strikes me as more distasteful than accidental light. I have never understood why some photographers value it. My lens hoods exclude it absolutely.

——"*Composition: Double Exposure*" by Silver Donald Cameron from *New Canadian Stories '76*, published by Oberon Press; by permission of the author

Some people also consider a Nikon superior to a Pentax, but I have always found the Pentax line quite satisfactory within the limitations of 35-millimetre photography in general. Those limitations, however, are what appear to be the impediment to creativity in this particular technique.

The technique is known as in-camera double exposure. Normally one takes a picture, exposing the film once, and then advances the roll of film to the next unexposed frame. Interesting effects, however, may be attained by taking a *second* exposure in the same frame. With the old box cameras on which most people my age began doing photography, accidental double exposures were quite common. The cameras had no fail-safe mechanism which would prevent firing the shutter again without winding the film. That fail-safe mechanism is a simple enough contrivance which is now a feature of almost any camera on the market. The accidental double exposure is virtually a thing of the past. I am grateful for that. Nothing disgusted me more than those accidental double exposures.

A deliberate double exposure is quite a different matter. It provides a means of revealing two images at once, and the juxtaposition of the two may express a meaning different from that of either alone.

Here is an annual of photography which contains a few examples. In this first one, the photographer has taken a black-and-white photograph of a New England farm. He has noted carefully the position of this black tree in the foreground. On a film, complete blackness is registered as an *absence* of light; if you were to process an unexposed frame it would come out completely black.

A black area in a photograph, therefore, is until it is processed simply an area of unexposed film. If one now exposes the film again, the second image will be registered on any dark areas of the first photograph. In this example, the photographer has taken a second photograph of a tombstone, making sure that the tombstone was located in the frame precisely where the black tree trunk was located in the initial exposure. You see the result: a picture of a New England farm with a hazy impression here and there of a cemetery, but with that one tombstone standing in a kind of halo inside the trunk of the tree. No doubt the image as a whole communicates something about the age of the farm and the fate of the people who have lived there. So it seems to me. I notice that the editor of the annual has singled out the photographer as one of the most creative exponents of the intentional double exposure as an in-camera technique.

Here is another, in which the face of a horse has been superimposed on the front of a locomotive. I am told it is quite witty. I have not myself been struck by its humour, though I do not consider myself deficient in humour. Some of my colleages at the Bureau claim I am very droll, though I admit I do not invariably appreciate the full humour of what I have apparently said.

Perhaps the difficulty I am having with the equipment will become clearer if you see the nature of my present project. I am trying to combine these two photographs in a single image, in the camera. It might be possible to combine them in the processing, by making use of the enlarger, but I have not attempted that technique yet. I doubt that I have time enough to learn. The child's birthday is next week. That fact is important. It constitutes a limitation as severe as those imposed by the equipment itself.

This first photograph is of the child. A girl, ten years old, quite beautiful in an ethereal mode. Her hair is long, blond, and light enough to have been lifted from her shoulders by a passing current of air. You might think I was fortunate to have fired the shutter at that particular instant, but that would be incorrect. The current of air is provided by an electric fan. It took over an hour to position the fan correctly. One difficulty was posed by the child, who insisted on minutely changing her position from time to time. I re-member thinking that though I never became angry myself, such behaviour would no doubt have angered the average person. Perhaps that is one of the average person's problems: he is far too emotional. I pride myself on having my own emotions under complete control. I believe that is why I have attained my present rank in the civil service. I make decisions entirely on a rational basis.

The same is true in my hobby, of course. Some photographers and commentators on photography consider the genius of the art to lie in its capability to capture the immediate, the fleeting, and the arbitrary. I find such an attitude distasteful, and the photographs it produces seem to me disorderly.

I do have some right to an opinion, after all. I am an amateur, but I have won a number of prizes in contests and exhibitions, even at the national level. No first prize has ever been awarded to me, admittedly, but I attribute that fact to the widespread misapprehension about the nature of the art which I have already described. No adjudicator who subscribes to such romantic foolishness can be expected to find my work entirely satisfying. Nevertheless I propose to continue doing what I believe to be right.

If you notice a physical similarity between my own features and those of the child, the cause is almost certainly genetic. She is my daughter, or she was: I am unsure which form of words is correct.

This second photograph shows a horse galloping more or less toward the camera. He appears quite close, but in fact I used a two-hundred-millimetre lens, which allowed me to shoot from some distance in perfect safety. Such a long lens, of course, tends to flatten out the perspective, so that the horse appears somewhat shorter in the body than in fact he was. If you look, you will notice that he is running at a slight angle to the camera in any case. His left front shoulder is quite evident, while his right front shoulder is concealed. He appears a very dark grey in colour, almost black. In life he was chestnut.

I work almost entirely in black and white.

Admittedly my photographs are consequently rather austere, but colour adds another element of the arbitrary which I find difficult to control. Black and white also means that the idea of the photograph, its design and composition, become its dominant quality. I admire austerity and restraint. Surely that is obvious.

The horse belonged to the child. I have many photographs of each, but these are the best. I have a photograph of the child with the horse on the occasion of her tenth birthday, when she received the horse, but it does not have the significance I am attempting to achieve in this double exposure. She is quite pleased, and that fact shows in her face. The horse is not moving, but standing still; he therefore expresses not power and speed but training and docility. These are not the implications I have chosen for the present composition.

It is entirely impossible to make the photograph from life. Quite aside from the virtually insuperable difficulty of knowing the precise position in the frame of a moving horse, and the difficulty of seeing precisely the range, neither the horse nor the child is presently alive. Next week would have marked her eleventh birthday, but she has in fact been dead six months. The horse died at the same time.

Now, perhaps, you are in position to appreciate my difficulty. I seek to expose the child's face in a halo of light within the left front shoulder of the horse, so that the child seems implied by the horse. The difficulty, however, is in locating in the frame the precise location of his left shoulder, so that I may focus that point on the child's face and make the second exposure.

I believe I have been scrupulous about winding the film tight before the initial exposure, and then holding the rewind crank utterly still while I pressed the film release button and cocked the shutter. Normally, of course, the very act of cocking the shutter on a Pentax advances the film. These precautions are necessary to prevent the exposed film from moving inside the camera. The slightest movement would destroy not only the composition but the actual *possibility* of the composition. One would have no notion whatever of the precise location of the horse's left shoulder; one could not therefore hope to superimpose the child's face.

Ideally such a composition should be made on a camera with a ground-glass image finder rather than a viewfinder such as this. With a ground glass one can draw the outline of the first image on the actual glass, and the second image can be stationed very accurately within the outline. Unfortunately in the low-price range the only available cameras with ground-glass image finders are double-lens reflexes, the cameras which appear from the front like a pair of binoculars turned on their side, the two lenses aligned above one another. Such a camera exposes a large area of film, two and a quarter inches square compared with the inch by inch and a half one has in a Pentax or other 35-millimetre camera, and that large area of film yields a much sharper definition if one attempts to make very large enlargements.

The double-lens reflex camera, unfortunately, poses difficulties which are fatal when one works in extreme proximity to the subject. Looking at the ground glass, one sees an image which has been transmitted through the upper lens. The camera, however, takes the actual photograph through the lower lens. In other words, the film sees the image from a viewpoint an inch or two below that of the photographer. If the image is distant from the camera, the difference between the two views is insignificant, but if one were photographing the child's image, say, at a range of two inches, her face when within the frame of the upper lens would appear in the frame of the lower lens only partially or not at all. The viewfinder might show her face and the camera photograph her waist. This phenomenon is known as parallax. One of the great advantages of a single-lens reflex camera such as the Pentax is that there can be no parallax, since the viewfinder through a system of mirrors observes the image through the same lens the camera utilizes in taking the picture. In the slang expression, what you see is indeed what you get. I have often wondered whether that expression was coined by a photographer explaining this problem of parallax.

The point is that the precise alignment of the images is essential to the in-camera double exposure. A double-lens reflex does not align the two images properly in the first place, and a single-lens reflex does not permit one to be precise, because one only has the memory of the location of the first image to aid one in positioning the second.

I began using the Pentax system some years ago, when I first joined the Department. Through the years I have added components as the money became available. In our family budget I have allocated a small amount for this purpose. It seems to me unreasonable to permit family life to obliterate one's personal interests, a fact I was eventually able to make clear to my wife. It was her wish to live in the country. I find no charm in these animals; for myself I would have preferred an apartment near the office. I did point out, however, that we could not afford to buy this little farm, maintain such interests as photography and have a large family. Any close scrutiny of our finances made that fact abundantly clear. That is one of the chief reasons we had no further children after our daughter.

Even now—and I am now Director of a Bureau—I cannot afford a Hasselblad. I do not complain, but I do note that only a Hasselblad, to the best of my knowledge, is really suitable for the in-camera double exposure. It is a single-lens reflex which takes two-and-a-quarter square negative and utilizes a ground-glass image finder, the perfect combination of qualities. I suspect that this present composition, when I complete it, will reveal considerable grain when it is enlarged to a size suitable for framing. That graininess is a direct consequence of the very small size of the negative itself. I will point this out to my wife when she unwraps the picture, making it clear that though the work is technically imperfect it is the best that can be done within the limitations of my equipment. I hope she will not be in a state of such emotion that she cannot attend to what I tell her. She is still extremely emotional about the accident, even though I have told her repeatedly that I do not blame her for her carelessness.

Ideally, I suppose, one might have photographed the actual accident or more properly its aftermath. It occured, however, during office hours, and I was not notified until much later. But this present composition, if I can resolve the technical difficulties, should provide a fitting memorial. I expect it will touch my wife very deeply, despite its imperfections.

THE CATASTROPHE OF SUCCESS

Tennessee Williams

This winter marked the third anniversary of the Chicago opening of "The Glass Menagerie," an

event which terminated one part of my life and began another about as different in all external circumstances as could well be imagined. I was snatched out of virtual oblivion and thrust into sudden prominence, and from the precarious tenancy of furnished rooms about the country I was removed to a suite in a first-class Manhattan hotel. My experience was not unique. Success has often come that abruptly into the lives of Americans. The Cinderella story is our favorite national myth, the cornerstone of the film industry if not of the Democracy itself. I have seen it enacted on the screen so often that I was now inclined to yawn at it, not with disbelief but with an attitude of Who Cares! Anyone with such beautiful teeth and hair as the screen protagonist of such a story was bound to have a good time one way or another, and you could bet your bottom dollar and all the tea in China that that one would not be caught dead or alive at any meeting involving a social conscience.

No, my experience was not exceptional, but neither was it quite ordinary, and if you are willing to accept the somewhat eclectic proposition that I had not been writing with such an experience in mind—and many people are not willing to believe that a playwright is interested in anything but popular success—there may be some point in comparing the two estates.

The sort of life which I had had previous to this popular success was one that required endurance, a life of clawing and scratching along a sheer surface and holding on tight with raw fingers to every inch of rock higher than the one caught hold of before, but it was a good life because it was the sort of life for which the human organism is created.

I was not aware of how much vital energy had gone into this struggle until the struggle was removed. I was out on a level plateau with my arms still thrashing and my lungs still grabbing at air that no longer resisted. This was security at last.

I sat down and looked about me and was suddenly very depressed. I thought to myself, this is just a period of adjustment. Tomorrow morning I will wake up in this first-class hotel suite above the discreet hum of an East Side boulevard and I will appreciate its elegance and luxuriate in its comforts and know that I have arrived at our American plan of Olympus. Tomorrow morning when I look at the green satin sofa I will fall in love with it. It is only temporarily that the green satin looks like slime on stagnant water.

But in the morning the inoffensive little sofa looked more revolting than the night before and I was already getting too fat for the $125 suit which a fashionable acquaintance had selected for me. In the suite things began to break accidentally. An arm came off the sofa. Cigarette burns appeared on the polished surface of the furniture. Windows were left open and a rain storm flooded the suite. But the maid always put it straight and the patience of the management was inexhaustible. Late parties could not offend them seriously. Nothing short of a demolition bomb seemed to bother my neighbors.

I lived on room service. But in this, too, there was a disenchantment. Some time between the moment when I ordered dinner over the phone and when it was rolled into my living room like a corpse on a rubber-wheeled table, I lost all interest in it. Once I ordered a sirloin steak and a chocolate sundae, but everything was so cunningly disguised on the table that I mistook the chocolate sauce for gravy and poured it over the sirloin steak.

Of course all this was the more trivial aspect of a spiritual dislocation that began to manifest itself in far more disturbing ways. I soon found myself becoming indifferent to people. A well of cynicism rose in me. Conversations all sounded as if they had been recorded years ago and were being played back on a turntable. Sincerity and kindliness seemed to have gone out of my friends' voices. I suspected them of hypocrisy. I stopped calling them, stopped seeing them. I was impatient of what I took to be inane flattery.

I got so sick of hearing people say, "I loved your play!" that I could not say thank you any more. I choked on the words and turned rudely away from the usually sincere person. I no longer felt any pride in the play itself but began to dislike it, probably because I felt too lifeless inside ever to create another. I was walking around dead in my shoes and I knew it but there were no friends I knew or trusted sufficiently, at that time, to take them aside and tell them what was the matter.

This curious condition persisted about three months, till late spring, when I decided to have another eye operation mainly because of the excuse it gave me to withdraw from the world behind a gauze mask. It was my fourth eye operation, and perhaps I should explain that I had been afflicted for about five years with a cataract on my left eye which required a series of needling operations and finally an operation on the muscle of the eye. (The eye is still in my head. So much for that.)

Well, the gauze mask served a purpose. While I was resting in the hospital the friends whom I had neglected or affronted in one way or another began to call on me and now that I was in pain and darkness, their voices seemed to have changed, or rather that unpleasant mutation which I had suspected earlier in the season had now disappeared and they sounded now as they had used to sound in the lamented days of my obscurity. Once more they were sincere and kindly voices with the ring of truth in them and that quality of understanding for which I had originally sought them out.

As far as my physical vision was concerned, this last operation was only relatively successful (although it left me with an apparently clear black pupil in the right position, or nearly so) but in another, figurative way, it had served a much deeper purpose.

When the gauze mask was removed I found myself in a readjusted world. I checked out of the handsome suite at the first-class hotel, packed my papers and a few incidental belongings and left for Mexico, an elemental country where you can quickly forget the false dignities and conceits imposed by success, a country where vagrants innocent as children curl up to sleep on the pavements and human voices, especially when their language is not familiar to the ear, are soft as birds'. My public self, that artifice of mirrors, did not exist here and so my natural being was resumed.

Then, as a final act of restoration, I settled for a while at Chapala to work on a play called "The Poker Night," which later became "A Streetcar Named Desire." It is only in his work that an artist can find reality and satisfaction, for the actual world is less intense than the world of his invention and consequently his life, without recourse to violent disorder, does not seem very substantial. The right condition for him is that in which his work is not only convenient but unavoidable.

For me a convenient place to work is a remote place among strangers where there is good swimming. But life should require a certain minimal effort. You should not have too many people waiting on you, you should have to do most things for yourself. Hotel service is embarrassing. Maids, waiters, bell-hops, porters and so forth are the most embarrassing people in the world for they continually remind you of inequities which we accept as the proper thing. The sight of an ancient woman, gasping and wheezing as she drags a heavy pail of water down a hotel corridor to mop up the mess of some drunken over-privileged guest, is one that sickens and weighs upon the heart and withers it with shame for this world in which it is not only tolerated but regarded as proof positive that the wheels of Democracy are functioning as they should without interference from above or below. Nobody should have to clean up anybody else's mess in this world. It is terribly bad for both parties, but probably worse for the one receiving the service.

I have been corrupted as much as anyone else by the vast number of menial services which our society has grown to expect and depend on. We should do for ourselves or let the machines do for us, the glorious technology that is supposed to be the new light of the world. We are like a man who has bought a great amount of equipment for a camping trip, who has the canoe and the tent and the fishing lines and the axe and the guns, the mackinaw and the blankets, but who now, when all the preparations and the provisions are piled expertly together, is suddenly too timid to set out on the journey but remains where he was yesterday and the day before and the day before that, looking suspiciously through white lace curtains at the clear sky he distrusts. Our great technology is a God-given chance for adventure and for progress which we are afraid to attempt. Our ideas and our ideals remain exactly what they were and where they were three centuries ago. No. I beg your pardon. It is no longer safe for a man to even declare them!

This is a long excursion from a small theme into a large one which I did not intend to make, so let me go back to what I was saying before.

This is an over-simplification. One does not escape that easily from the seduction of an effete way of life. You cannot arbitrarily say to yourself, I will now continue my life as it was before this thing, Success, happened to me. But once you fully apprehend the vacuity of a life without struggle you are equipped with the basic means of salvation. Once you know this is true, that the heart of man, his body and his brain, are forged in a white-hot furnace for the purpose of conflict (the struggle of creation) and that with the conflict removed, the man is a sword cutting daisies, that not privation but luxury is the wolf at the door and that the fangs of this wolf are all the little vanities and conceits and laxities that Success is heir to—why, then with this knowledge you are at least in a position of knowing where danger lies.

You know, then, that the public Somebody you are when you "have a name" is a fiction created with mirrors and that the only somebody worth being is the solitary and unseen you that existed from your first breath and which is the sum of your actions and so is constantly

in a state of becoming under your own volition —and knowing these things, you can even survive the catastrophe of Success!

It is never altogether too late, unless you embrace the Bitch Goddess, as William James called her, with both arms and find in her smothering caresses exactly what the homesick little boy in you always wanted, absolute protection and utter effortlessness. Security is a kind of death, I think, and it can come to you in a storm of royalty checks beside a kidney-shaped pool in Beverly Hills or anywhere at all that is removed from the conditions that made you an artist, if that's what you are or were or intended to be. Ask anyone who has experienced the kind of success I am talking about—What good is it? Perhaps to get an honest answer you will have to give him a shot of truth-serum but the word he will finally groan is unprintable in genteel publications.

Then what is good? The obsessive interest in human affairs, plus a certain amount of compassion and moral conviction, that first made the experience of living something that must be translated into pigment or music or bodily movement or poetry or prose or anything that's dynamic and expressive—that's what's good for you if you're at all serious in your aims. William Saroyan wrote a great play on this theme, that purity of heart is the one success worth having. "In the time of your life—live!" That time is short and it doesn't return again. It is slipping away while I write this and while you read it, and the monosyllable of the clock is Loss, loss, loss, unless you devote your heart to its opposition.

KAUFMAN AND HART

Moss Hart

I was asleep when the telephone rang the next morning, but contrary to my usual custom of putting the pillow over my head and turning over, I got out of bed and answered it myself.

"Is this the young author?" the voice of Max Siegel came cheerfully over the telephone.

"Yes," I answered, thoroughly wide awake in a moment and shaking a little with excitement.

"Can you meet George Kaufman here at the Music Box at three o'clock?" he went on.

"You mean he read it?" I asked incredulously.

"Certainly he read it," said Max Siegel. "That's what he wants the meeting for this afternoon. He likes it very much—I told you he would. What's the matter?" He laughed. "You sound like you don't believe it! It's true. You'll be here at three o'clock then?"

"Yes," I managed to reply. "Three o'clock, the Music Box."

I hung up, and startled my mother, who had just come into the room, by throwing my arms around her and kissing her three or four times soundly.

"We're going to be rich," I said gleefully. "This time next year we may not even be living in Brooklyn." She smiled, pleased at my good spirits, but refrained from asking if they were once again based upon my "homework." She had been through six years of varying forms and degrees of enthusiasm every time I finished a play, and I have no doubt she had heard a version of the same speech before.

"I'm going to work with George Kaufman, *that's* the difference *this* time," I said. "George

— an excerpt from <u>Act One</u>, <u>An Autobiography</u>, by Moss Hart, published by Random House, Inc., New York, 1959; copyright © 1959, by Catharine Carlisle Hart and Joseph M. Hyman, Trustees ; reprinted by permission

S. Kaufman," I repeated, rolling out the name luxuriously.

She stared at me blankly, the name having registered nothing at all, and then added hastily, "That's very nice." It was the tone of voice and the expression she reserved, I remembered, for such moments as when I would rush to show her a new stamp I had garnered by barter in my stamp-collecting days.

"You go ahead and do your shopping." I laughed. "I'll make my own breakfast." She smiled encouragingly, obviously pleased that she had not deflated my good spirits by her unawareness of who George Kaufman was.

"If you're going to bring him home to work with you," she said politely, "I hope you won't do it until after next week. We're having the painters next week."

"I'll explain that to him," I said carefully as I made my way toward the kitchen.

While the eggs fried, I composed in my mind a graceful little speech of gratitude I intended to deliver to Mr. Kaufman at the right moment after all the business details were out of the way. It sounded a shade too reverential even to my own ears, I decided, as I tried speaking it aloud while I waited for the coffee to boil, but there was no time to polish it up now. That could be done on the subway on the way into town.

I hurried through breakfast as quickly as possible and got to the telephone to acquaint Lester and Miss Fishbein with the happy trend of events, but more particularly to insist that for this first meeting I wanted to meet with George Kaufman alone. As I suspected, this did not sit any too well with either one of them, but I was firm, and at three o'clock I walked alone up the stairs of the Music Box Theatre to the mezzanine and knocked on the door of Sam Harris' office.

Max Siegel, smiling as usual, stood in the doorway, and behind him, slumped down in one of the large armchairs, I caught a glimpse of George Kaufman. That first glimpse of George

Kaufman caught fleetingly over Max Siegel's shoulder made all the caricatures I had seen of him in the Sunday drama sections through the years come instantly alive. The bushy hair brushed straight up from the forehead into an orderly but somehow unruly pompadour, the tortoiseshell glasses placed low on the bridge of the rather large nose, the quick, darting eyes searching incisively over the rims, the full sensuous mouth set at a humorously twisted tilt in the descending angularity of the long face—each single feature was a caricaturist's delight. It was easy to understand why he had been caricatured so often. It was not a handsome face in the way the word handsome is generally used to describe men's looks, but it was an immensely attractive one. He had the kind of good looks that men as well as women find attractive.

Though it was rather a mild October day, he sat in the chair in his overcoat, and around his neck was wrapped a long blue woolen scarf that hung outside the coat and came almost to his knees. His legs were twisted or, rather, entwined one under the other in the most intricate fashion, so that one wondered how he would ever get out of the chair if he had to do so quickly, and one arm was stretched clear around the back of his neck to the opposite side of his head where it was busily engaged in the business of scratching the back of his ear.

"This is the young author, George," said Max Siegel, ushering me to the center of the room

"Hi," said Mr. Kaufman wearily. He lifted in greeting one finger of the hand that was not engaged in scratching his ear, but he did not move otherwise. Even the one finger was lifted slowly and with infinite lassitude.

"Sit down," said Max Siegel, and smiled reassuringly at me. I retreated to the sofa at the other end of the room, but my eyes remained fastened and expectant on the figure slumped in the armchair.

"You want me to do the talking, George?" said Max Siegel after what seemed to me an unconscionably long time. Again the one finger

of the disengaged hand rose slowly in assent. "Mr. Kaufman is willing to work with you on the play and he has suggested some terms for a division of the royalties," said Max Siegel, consulting a typewritten slip of paper on the desk "Would you prefer to go over them with your agent?" he asked, coming over and handing me the paper. "I think you'll find they're very generous terms," he added.

"I'm sure there will be no difficulty," I said. I took the slip of paper from him and put it in my pocket without looking at it. My eyes were still riveted on the unmoving figure in the armchair. There was another long silence, and a long drawn-out and mournful sigh came from the depths of the chair, followed by a slight but unmistakable belch. It was a somewhat surprising sound—a cross between a prodigious yawn, a distant train whistle hooting over a lonely countryside, and the satisfied grunt of a large dog settling down in front of the fireplace. It was followed by still another silence while Mr. Kaufman's eyes restlessly searched for something they seemed to find missing on the ceiling. He had a perfect view of the ceiling, for he was now sunk so low in the chair that only the top of his head was visible from where I sat. The long legs wrapped one around the other in a tight sailor's knot obscured most of his face, but now the legs moved slightly and his voice issued clearly from behind them.

"When can we have a working session?" he said

"Whenever you want to," I answered quickly. "Right away—any time—now." The words came out in too great a rush, but there was nothing I could do to stem my eagerness. Behind the legs the arms rose slowly and one hand reached into an inside pocket and withdrew an envelope, while the other hand found a pencil in the handkerchief pocket. I could not see his face, but he was holding up the envelope and evidently regarding some notations on the back of it.

"Would eleven o'clock tomorrow morning be all right?" he asked tiredly.

"Fine," I replied.

"My house," he said, "158 East 63rd Street." The envelope and pencil were moving down and going back into his pocket and one arm was going around the back of his neck again to scratch his ear. I waited and looked inquiringly across the room to where Max Siegel sat behind the desk.

Max Siegel winked at me and addressed the armchair. "Is that all you want of the young author now, George?" he said.

"That's all," came the answer, "except a second act."

Max Siegel made a slight gesture back to me, which seemed to say, Well, that's it, I guess. I cleared my throat and took a deep breath. It seemed that the moment for my graceful little speech had arrived. I had polished it up rather well in the subway, I thought smugly, and I knew it by heart. I rose from the sofa and stood in front of the armchair.

"Mr. Kaufman," I said, "I would like you to know how very much it means to me to —— " and that was all I said. To my horror, the legs unwound themselves with an acrobatic rapidity I would not have believed possible, and the figure in the chair leaped up and out of it in one astonishing movement like a large bird frightened out of its solitude in the marshes. He was out of the chair, across the room, had opened the door and was flying down the stairs, the blue scarf whipping out behind him.

I stared dazedly after the retreating figure until it disappeared down the stairway. "What have I done?" I stammered. "What did I do?"

Max Siegel, to my intense relief, was shaking with laughter. "You haven't done anything," he answered. "Maybe I should have warned you. Mr. Kaufman hates any kind of sentimentality—can't stand it!" He started to laugh again, but controlled himself. "Maybe I should have told you about George over the phone, but it never occurred to me that you were going to make a speech at him. Did you actually prepare a speech of thanks?"

I nodded sheepishly.

"Well, no great harm done," he said. "He had a barber's appointment that he had to get to, and you saw to it that he got there on time." He handed me a sheet of paper with a check attached. "I'm certain Miss Fishbein will agree these are very generous terms, so you can just fill in the contracts and sign them. That's a check for five hundred dollars for your advance royalty. Congratulations." He held out his hand and smiled. "If you want to, you can make the speech to me so it won't be a total loss."

I smiled back and shook my head. "Is there anything else I ought to know about Mr. Kaufman?" I asked.

He hesitated and laughed again. "There is, but if I started you'd never make that eleven o'clock appointment tomorrow morning. Anyway, it's like marriage—nothing anybody tells you about it is really any help. You've got to live it out for yourself; and if I know George, you'll be living it out every day from now on. Get a good night's sleep—that's the best advice I can give you." We shook hands warmly and I walked out into the bright October afternoon.

I stood for a moment outside the Music Box and looked up at its columned façade with a new and proprietary interest, the contracts and the check rustling importantly in my pocket. There could be no doubt of it now; at last I was on my way. . . .

The next morning at five minutes of eleven, I rang the bell of 158 East 63rd Street. The rather modest brownstone house was a little disappointing to my fancy of how a famous playwright should live, but the street was fashionable and the maid who opened the door was a reassuring sight. She was in uniform, a starched white cap perched correctly on her head. More like it, I thought, as she held the door open for me to pass her. I walked in and glanced quickly down the hall at a dining room leading out into a little garden. There was a bowl of flowers on the polished table flanked by silver candlesticks. Just right, I told myself satisfactorily and looked inquiringly at the stairway.

"Mr. Kaufman is waiting for you," said the maid. "The top floor, just go right up."

I walked up the stairs and stopped briefly at the second landing to look at a drawing room and library divided by the stairwell. Both rooms might have come straight out of the movies as far as my innocent eyes were concerned. I knew at once that my first goal the moment the money began to roll in, beyond the taking of taxicabs wherever and whenever I wanted to, would be to live like this. It was an illuminating and expensive moment.

The doors on the third floor—evidently bedrooms—were all tightly closed, and as I reached the fourth-floor landing, Mr. Kaufman stood awaiting me in the doorway of what turned out to be his own bedroom and study combined. After the elegance and style of the drawing room and library, this room was a great blow. It was a small, rather dark room, furnished sparsely with a studio couch, a quite ugly typewriter desk and one easy chair. It was hard for me to believe that a stream of brilliant plays had come out of this monk-like interior. I am not certain what I expected the atelier of Kaufman and Connelly would be like, but it most certainly was the opposite of this. There was no hint of any kind that this room was in any way concerned with the theatre. Not a framed photograph or program hung on its walls, and except for an excellent etching of Mark Twain, it might well have been, I thought regretfully, the bedroom and workroom of a certified public accountant. My initial disappointment was to deepen into an active loathing of that room, but at the moment, my eyes after the first quick look were focused on its occupant.

Mr. Kaufman was in the process of greeting me with what turned out to be his daily supply of enthusiasm so far as the social amenities were concerned; that is to say, one finger was being wearily lifted and his voice was managing a tired "Hi." He had moved to the window after this display of cordiality and now stood with his back to the room and to me, staring out at the gardens of the houses on 62nd Street. I had not been asked to sit down, but I was too uncomfortable to remain standing and after a moment of waiting I sat down in the armchair and stared at his back. His arm now reached around his neck to scratch his ear, a gesture I was to come to recognize as a prelude to a rearrangement of a scene or the emergence of a new line; now he remained for a few moments engrossed in the movements of a large cat slowly moving along the garden fence as it contemplated a sparrow on one of the leafless trees. This backyard spectacle seemed to hold him in deep fascination until the cat leaped up into the tree and the bird flew off, whereupon he turned from the window with a large sigh.

I looked at him, eager and alert, but there were still other things of moment that caught and held his attention before he addressed me directly. As he turned from the window, he spied two or three pieces of lint on the floor, and these he carefully removed from the carpet with all the deftness of an expert botanist gathering specimens for the Museum of Natural History. This task completed, he turned his eye toward a mound of sharpened pencils on the desk, found two whose points were not razor-sharp or to his liking, and ground them down in a pencil sharpener attached to the wall. In the process of doing so, he discovered some more lint at the side of the desk and this, too, was carefully picked up, after which he held up and inspected a few sheets of carbon paper, found them still usable, and placed them neatly beside a pile of typewriter paper, which he neatly patted until all its edges were perfectly aligned. His eyes darted dolefully around the room again, seeming to be looking for something else—anything at all, it seemed to me! —to engage his attention, but the carpet being quite free of lint, his gaze finally came to rest on the armchair in which I sat, and he addressed me at last.

"Er ——" he said, and began to pace rapidly up and down the room. This, too—the word "Er" used as a form of address and followed by a rapid pacing—I was to come to recognize as the actual start of a working session: a signal that lint-picking, cat-watching and pencil-sharpening time was over and that he wanted my attention. During all the time we were engaged together on *Once in a Lifetime*, he never once addressed me by any other name but "Er," even in moments of stress or actual crisis. Perhaps he felt, being the innately shy and private person he was, that "Moss" was too intimate a name to call me; and to address me as "Mr. Hart" seemed a little silly, considering the difference in our ages and positions. But somehow or other I recognized at this first meeting that "Er" meant me and not a clearing of the throat, and I waited attentively until Mr. Kaufman stopped his pacing and stood in front of the armchair looking down at me.

"The trouble begins in the third scene of the first act," he said. "It's messy and unclear and goes off in the wrong direction. Suppose we start with that."

I nodded, trying to look agreeable and knowing at the same time; but this, like my disappointments with the workshop of the master, was my second blow of the morning. After the brilliant peroration on satire in the modern theatre that I had heard from Jed Harris, I had been looking forward with great eagerness to that first talk on play-writing by the celebrated Mr. Kaufman. I had expected to make mental notes on everything he said each day and put it all down every evening in a loose-leaf folder I had bought expressly for that purpose. But this flat, unvarnished statement that something was wrong with the third scene of the first act seemed to be all I was going to get, for Mr. Kaufman was already moving past me now on his way to the bathroom. I turned in my chair and looked at him as he stood by the washbasin and slowly and meticulously washed his hands, and I was struck then and forever afterward by the fact that his hands were what one imagines the hands of a great surgeon to be like.

This impression was further implemented by the odd circumstance that he invariably began the day's work by first washing his hands—a ritual that was, of course, unconscious on his part, but which he would sometimes perform two or three times more during each working session, usually at the beginning of attacking a new scene, as though the anatomy of a play were a living thing whose internal organs were to be explored surgically. I watched him dry his hands and forearms carefully—he took the trouble, I noticed, to undo the cuffs of his shirt and roll them up—and as he came back into the room, walked briskly toward the desk and selected a pencil with just the right pointed sharpness, I was again startled by the inescapable impression that the pencil held poised over the manuscript in those long tensile fingers was a scalpel.

The pencil suddenly darted down onto the paper and moved swiftly along the edge, crossing out a line here and there, making a large X through a solid speech, fusing two long sentences into one short one, indicating by an arrow or a question mark the condensation or transference of a section of dialogue so that its point was highlighted and its emphasis sharpened; the operation was repeated with lightning-like precision on the next page and the next, until the end of the scene. Then he picked up the manuscript from the desk and brought it over to me.

"Just cutting away the underbrush," he said. "See what you think." I took the manuscript and read with astonishment. The content of the scene remained the same, but its point was unmuddied by repetition, and the economy and clarity with which everything necessary was now said gave the scene a new urgency. The effect of what he had done seemed to me so magical that I could hardly believe I had been so downright repetitive and verbose. I looked up from the manuscript and stared admiringly at the waiting figure by the desk.

Mr. Kaufman evidently mistook my chagrined and admiring silence for pique. "I may have cut too deeply, of course," he said apologetically. "Is there something you want to have go back?"

"Oh, no," I replied hastily, "not a word. It's just wonderful now. Just great! I don't understand how I could have been so stupid. The scene really works now, doesn't it?"

It was Mr. Kaufman's turn to stare at me in silence for a moment, and he looked at me quizzically over the rims of his glasses before he spoke again. "No, it doesn't work at all," he said gently. "I thought the cuts would show you why it *wouldn't* work." He sighed and scratched his ear. "Perhaps the trouble starts earlier than I thought."

He took the play from my lap and placed it on the desk again. "All right. Page one—Scene One. I guess we might as well face it." He picked up a pencil and held it poised over the manuscript, and I watched fascinated and awestruck as the pencil swooped down on page after page.

If it is possible for a book of this sort to have a hero, then that hero is George S. Kaufman. In the months that followed that first day's work, however, my waking nightmare was of a glittering steel pencil suspended over my head that sometimes turned into a scalpel, or a baleful stare over the rims of a huge pair of disembodied tortoise-shell glasses. I do not think it far-fetched to say that such success as I have had in the theatre is due in large part to George Kaufman. I cannot pretend that I was without talent, but such gifts as I possessed were raw and undisciplined. It is one thing to have a flair for play-writing or even a ready wit with dialogue. It is quite another to apply these gifts in the strict and demanding terms of a fully articulated play so that they emerge with explicitness, precision and form. All of this and a great deal more I learned from George Kaufman. . . .

RODIN, AND PARIS

Malvina Hoffman

. . . To any one who has had the good fortune of being an art student in Paris and who has been poor enough to know the joys of a Sunday lunch on the Boulevard Montparnasse, after a week of home cooking and dishwashing, when *dessert et café* were added to the menu as a real spree, it would be unnecessary to state that there were no obstacles ominous enough to dim the promise of even a distant horizon. Reading the menus from right to left during the lean years made everything edible seem precious and worth fighting for. Many were the laughs indulged in, when the inevitable *gateau de riz* would be suggested as a means of satisfying any stray hunger pangs that might still be lurking in the mind or body of a passionate young art student.

It was my determined intention to become a pupil of Rodin. While still in America I had studied his work from books and photographs, and from the varied and interesting collection of his clay studies, bronzes, and marbles owned by Mrs. John Simpson in New York.

When I had tried five times in vain to present a letter of introduction at Rodin's studio, Rue de l'Université, my hopes were almost frustrated and the situation had become pretty desperate for me. His concierge gave me little encouragement, but some last grain of hope drove me to extreme action on my fifth visit, and I said:

"Tell Monsieur Rodin that if he does not see me today I must return to America, but that I came to Paris to study with him, and that I must deliver a message to him from his friend Madame Simpson. I shall not leave, he must admit me today."

The surprised guardian seemed to sense my adamant determination, and in a few moments came back smiling.

"Well, at last I have permission to admit you," she said, and I followed her past the many studios until she knocked at Rodin's door.

I found myself in a room crowded with marbles and covered clay models on stands. There were four or five Frenchmen with black coats and red rosettes in their lapels, talking to Rodin, who looked me over with a hooded searching gaze that made me feel rooted to the spot and unable to move. He came forward slowly, and put out his hand. As I gave him the messages, in my unconjugated French, from his friend across the seas, his grip tightened and he asked me why I had not mentioned her name at my first visit. I began to feel my blood move again in my veins. "So you were determined not to leave without seeing me," he said. I nodded. "What have you under your arm in that envelope?" he asked. "Oh, just two photographs of the only sculpture I have ever done —I am just a beginner but I find I cannot escape it. Sculpture seems to have taken possession of me and my desire is to be your pupil if you will be willing to guide me and criticize my work."

"Let me see the photographs," he said. "Who are these two men?"

"Well, the marble is of my father," I replied. "He was a musician who, after a long life, was serenely meditative. The other is of a young violinist who is just making his début in America as a soloist."

Rodin looked at the photographs for some minutes, put them back into the envelope, and handed them to me. "Character seems to interest you. You have studied these men well. One is the mature artist with his life battles behind him, the other is the young dreamer with his battles ahead of him. Wait here a few moments. I am just describing this marble of mine to these gentlemen and then I am lunching

— "*Rodin, and Paris*," an excerpt from *Heads and Tales* by Malvina Hoffman, published by Charles Scribner's Sons, New York, 1936; copyright © 1936 by Malvina Hoffman; reprinted by permission of the author's estate

with them." Rodin went back to the visitors and started to tell them that the figure represented a fallen angel that had broken his wings on a rock and that the idea had been conceived after reading a certain poem. He began reciting the lines in a deep monotone, but his memory failed him and he grew violent trying to recall the ending of the sonnet. He strode up and down before the great marble group.

By some extraordinary coincidence, I happened to know the poem, and when I saw that he could not recall the lines, I walked towards him. "Maître," I ventured, "I know that poem, shall I recite it?" He turned on me almost savagely—"What—*you* know it?—let me see if you do—recite it!" My blood was pounding, but I began the lines in a slow, quavering voice:

"*J'ai perdu ma force et ma vie,*
Et mes amis et ma gaîté;
J'ai perdu jusqu'à la fierté
Qui faisait croire à mon génie.

"*Quand j'ai connu la Vérité,*
J'ai cru que c'était une amie;
Quand je l'ai comprise et sentie,
J'en étais déjà dégoûté.

"*Et pourtant elle est éternelle,*
Et ceux qui se sont passés d'elle
Ici-bas ont tout ignoré.

"*Dieu parle, il faut qu'on lui réponde.*
Le seul bien qui me reste au monde
Est d'avoir quelquefois pleuré."

I stepped back once more to my place at the door, not daring to raise my eyes.

There was a murmur of surprise from the group of men. Rodin's voice suddenly rose in a tone of almost brutal abruptness—"*Allons, au déjeuner, mes amis—it est tard.*" He showed his friends out of the door, turned towards me—"Here," he said. "This is where my keys hang," and he lifted an old rag from a nail on the wall, on which hung two keys. "You may use them to open the other studios. Uncover all the work

and examine the trays of plaster studies and I will see you when I return." He went out, closed the door and locked it from the outside. I had certainly not only been admitted at last to his studio, I was locked into it—for better or worse—and I wasted no time wondering what it all meant, but started in at once to pull the linen shrouds off the marbles. A new world seemed suddenly to engulf my imagination. When I had examined one room I went to the next and then to another and finally returned to where I had started and began making drawings of the small plaster hands of which there were thirty or forty in various positions lying in wooden trays. I worked so intently that I did not notice that the fire in the stove had gone out and that the studio had grown icy cold. I did realize quite definitely, however, that I was very hungry, for I had not had anything to eat since my cup of coffee at 7:30 A.M. and I suddenly noticed that it must be well into the afternoon as the winter light had begun to fade. I re-covered all the marbles, and as I went over to try the door, hoping to be able to open it from the inside, I heard a knock. Wondering what I should do, I made no response—for if it were some visitor what would he think if I said I could not open the door? The knocking became louder and then a key turned in the lock and the door opened. Rodin came in and looked about. He caught sight of me behind one of the marble blocks. "Well," he said. "What have you done all this time? Why is everything covered over? Did you not examine the work or did you not like it, that you have covered everything again?"

I explained hastily that the sight of so many of his groups was too much for me to cope with at one time, and that although I had examined them all, I had re-covered them carefully and had concentrated my attention on the little plaster hand which seemed to be more my size. I had made a few drawings of this and he examined my sketch book. After looking through it he said, "My child, do you think these are all drawings?"

"Why, yes," I answered naïvely, "I *did* think so, what are they?" for I could see he was not of my opinion.

"They are sketches," he said. "Michelangelo *never* made sketches, everything he drew was a study, a real drawing. See that you never make any more sketches. Beware of the weakness of your American artists," pointing his finger at me very threateningly.

"What is their weakness?" I asked.

"*C'est leur sacrée facilité,*" he said, and then, going over to the stove, he realized how cold it had grown. The fire was out, and we were in semi-darkness. He came back and felt my hands; they were cold. He took off his heavy cloth cape and wrapped it about me and went to work remaking the fire. "Why did you let it go out?" he asked, and "Why do you look so pale and tired? By the way, did you have any lunch before coming to me at noon?"

"No, I had my coffee early but did not expect to be able to stay here so long today—it has been a great feast for a hungry artist, I shall never forget it."

He sat down beside me, drawing the little stools near the stove. "You forgot the fire, my child, because of the inner fire that burns you, but you cannot neglect hunger—nature is a stern mistress, and if you play tricks with her she will punish you every time. When I locked you in today, I never thought about food, I just wanted to make sure that you would be alone with my work, and that I would find you on my return." He rubbed my hands and held them near the glowing stove. "Now you must go home and take the little hand with you and make careful drawings for a week. Every day you must go to the Louvre and study and make copies of the old masters—Leonardo da Vinci and Michelangelo and Raphael—not to copy their technique only but to understand it, and develop a technique of your own, and each week come back here and bring me what you have done—and be sure to eat plenty of beefsteak and potatoes"—at this point he encircled my absurdly small wrist with his strong sensitive fingers—"you are too thin and sculpture needs plenty of fuel for the fires of art burn fiercely. When you come back, I may be drawing from a model, if so you may draw with me. You know where the keys hang, from now on you may feel at home in my studio." . . .

RAILWAY ACCIDENT

Thomas Mann

Tell you a story? But I don't know any. Well, yes, after all, here is something I might tell.

Once, two years ago now it is, I was in a railway accident; all the details are clear in my memory.

It was not really a first-class one—no wholesale telescoping or "heaps of unidentifiable dead"—not that sort of thing. Still, it was a proper accident, with all the trimmings, and on top of that it was at night. Not everybody has been through one, so I will describe it the best I can.

I was on my way to Dresden, whither I had been invited by some friends of letters: it was a literary and artistic pilgrimage, in short, such as, from time to time, I undertake not unwillingly. You make appearances, you attend functions, you show yourself to admiring crowds—not for nothing is one a subject of William II. And certainly Dresden is beautiful, especially the Zwinger; and afterwards I intended to go for ten days or a fortnight to the White Hart to rest, and if, thanks to the treatments, the spirit should come upon me, I might do a little work as well. To this end I had put my manuscript at the bottom of my trunk, together with my notes—a good stout bundle done up in brown paper and tied with string in the Bavarian colours. I like to travel in comfort, especially when my expenses are paid. So I patronized the sleeping-cars, reserving a place days ahead in a first-class compartment. All was in order; nevertheless I was excited, as I always am on such occasions, for a journey is still an adventure to me, and where travelling is concerned I shall

— *"Railway Accident" by Thomas Mann, from Stories of Three Decades (translated from the German by H. T. Lowe-Porter), published by Alfred A. Knopf Inc., New York, 1936; reprinted by permission of the publisher*

never manage to feel properly blasé. I perfectly well know that the night train for Dresden leaves the central station at Munich regularly every evening, and every morning is in Dresden. But when I am travelling with it, and linking my momentous destiny to its own, the matter assumes importance. I cannot rid myself of the notion that it is making a special trip today, just on my account, and the unreasoning and mistaken conviction sets up in me a deep and speechless unrest, which does not subside until all the formalities of departure are behind me—the packing, the drive in the loaded cab to the station, the arrival there, and the registration of luggage—and I can feel myself finally and securely bestowed. Then, indeed, a pleasing relaxation takes place, the mind turns to fresh concerns, the unknown unfolds itself beyond the expanse of window-pane, and I am consumed with joyful anticipations.

And so on this occasion. I had tipped my porter so liberally that he pulled his cap and gave me a pleasant journey; and I stood at the corridor window of my sleeping-car smoking my evening cigar and watching the bustle on the platform. There were whistlings and rumblings, hurryings and farewells, and the singsong of newspaper and refreshment vendors, and over all the great electric moons glowed through the mist of the October evening. Two stout fellows pulled a hand-cart of large trunks along the platform to the baggage car in front of the train. I easily identified, by certain unmistakable features, my own trunk; one among many there it lay, and at the bottom of it reposed my precious package. "There," thought I, "no need to worry, it is in good hands. Look at that guard with the leather cartridge-belt, the prodigious sergeant-major's moustache, and the inhospitable eye. Watch him rebuking the old woman in the threadbare black cape—for two pins she would have got into a second-class carriage. He is security, he is authority, he is our parent, he is the State. He is strict, not to say gruff, you would not care to mingle with him; but reliability is writ large upon his brow, and in his care your trunk reposes as in the bosom of Abraham."

A man was strolling up and down the platform in spats and a yellow autumn coat, with a dog on a leash. Never have I seen a handsomer dog: a small, stocky bull, smooth-coated, muscular, with black spots; as well groomed and amusing as the dogs one sees in circuses, who make the audience laugh by dashing round and round the ring with all the energy of their small bodies. This dog had a silver collar, with a plaited leather leash. But all this was not surprising, considering his master, the gentleman in spats, who had beyond a doubt the noblest origins. He wore a monocle, which accentuated without distorting his general air; the defiant perch of his moustache bore out the proud and stubborn expression of his chin and the corners of his mouth. He addressed a question to the martial guard, who knew perfectly well with whom he was dealing and answered hand to cap. My gentleman strolled on, gratified with the impression he had made. He strutted in his spats, his gaze was cold, he regarded men and affairs with penetrating eye. Certainly he was far above feeling journey-proud; travel by train was no novelty to him. He was at home in life, without fear of authority or regulations; he was an authority himself—in short, a nob. I could not look at him enough. When he thought the time had come, he got into the train (the guard had just turned his back). He came along the corridor behind me, bumped into me, and did not apologize. What a man! But that was nothing to what followed. Without turning a hair he took his dog with him into the sleeping-compartment! Surely it was forbidden to do that. When should I presume to take a dog with me into a sleeping-compartment? But he did it, on the strength of his prescriptive rights as a nob, and shut the door behind him.

There came a whistle outside, the locomotive whistled in response, gently the train began to move. I stayed awhile by the window watching the hand-waving and the shifting lights.——— I retired inside the carriage.

The sleeping-car was not very full, a compartment next to mine was empty and had not been got ready for the night; I decided to make myself comfortable there for an hour's peaceful reading. I fetched my book and settled in. The sofa had a silky salmon-pink covering, an ash-tray stood on the folding table, the light burned bright. I read and smoked.

The sleeping-car attendant entered in pursuance of his duties and asked for my ticket for the night. I delivered it into his grimy hands. He was polite but entirely official, did not even vouchsafe me a good-night as from one human being to another, but went out at once and knocked on the door of the next compartment. He would better have left it alone, for my gentleman of the spats was inside; and perhaps because he did not wish anyone to discover his dog, but possibly because he had really gone to bed, he got furious at anyone daring to disturb him. Above the rumbling of the train I heard his immediate and elemental burst of rage. "What do you want?" he roared. "Leave me alone, you swine." He said "swine." It was a lordly epithet, the epithet of a cavalry officer—it did my heart good to hear it. But the sleeping-car attendant must have resorted to diplomacy—of course he had to have the man's ticket—for just as I stepped into the corridor to get a better view the door of the compartment abruptly opened a little way and the ticket flew out into the attendant's face; yes, it was flung with violence straight in his face. He picked it up with both hands, and though he had got the corner of it in one eye, so that the tears came, he thanked the man, saluting and clicking his heels together. Quite overcome, I returned to my book.

I considered whether there was anything against my smoking another cigar and concluded that there was little or nothing. So I did it, rolling onward and reading; I felt full of contentment and good ideas. Time passed, it was ten o'clock, half past ten, all my fellow-travellers had gone to bed, at last I decided to follow them. I got up and went into my own compartment. A real little bedroom, most luxurious, with stamped leather wall hangings, clothes-hooks, a nickel-plated wash-basin. The lower berth was snowily prepared, the covers invitingly turned back. Oh, triumph of modern times! I thought. One lies in this bed as though at home, it rocks a little all night, and the result is that next morning one is in Dresden. I took my suitcase out of the rack to get ready for bed; I was holding it above my head, with my arms stretched up.

It was at this moment that the railway accident occurred. I remember it like yesterday.

We gave a jerk—but jerk is a poor word for it. It was a jerk of deliberately foul intent, a jerk with a horrid reverberating crash, and so violent that my suitcase leaped out of my hands I knew not whither, while I was flung forcibly with my shoulder against the wall. I had no time to stop and think. But now followed a frightful rocking of the carriage, and while that went on, one had plenty of leisure to be frightened. A railway carriage rocks going over switches or on sharp curves, that we know; but this rocking would not let me stand up, I was thrown from one wall to the other as the carriage careened. I had only one simple thought, but I thought it with concentration, exclusively. I thought: "Something is the matter, something is the matter, something is *very much* the matter!" Just in those words. But later I thought: "Stop, stop, stop!" For I knew that it would be a great help if only the train could be brought to a halt. And lo, at this my unuttered but fervent behest, the train did stop.

Up to now a deathlike stillness had reigned in the carriage, but at this point terror found tongue. Shrill feminine screams mingled with deeper masculine cries of alarm. Next door someone was shouting "Help!" No doubt about it, this was the very same voice which, just

previously, had uttered the lordly epithet—the voice of the man in spats, his very voice, though distorted by fear. "Help!" it cried; and just as I stepped into the corridor, where the passengers were collecting, he burst out of his compartment in a silk sleeping-suit and halted, looking wildly round him. "Great God!" he exclaimed, "Almighty God!" and then, as though to abase himself utterly, perhaps in hope to avert destruction, he added in a deprecating tone: "*Dear God!*" But suddenly he thought of something else, of trying to help himself. He threw himself upon the case on the wall where an axe and saw are kept for emergencies, and broke the glass with his fist. But finding that he could not release the tools at once, he abandoned them, buffeted his way through the crowd of passengers, so that the half-dressed women screamed afresh, and leaped out of the carriage.

All that was the work of a moment only. And then for the first time I began to feel the shock: in a certain weakness of the spine, a passing inability to swallow. The sleeping-car attendant, red-eyed, grimy-handed, had just come up; we all pressed round him; the women, with bare arms and shoulders, stood wringing their hands.

The train, he explained, had been derailed, we had run off the track. That, as it afterwards turned out, was not true. But behold, the man in his excitement had become voluble, he abandoned his official neutrality; events had loosened his tongue and he spoke to us in confidence, about his wife. "I told her today, I did. 'Wife,' I said, 'I feel in my bones somethin's goin' to happen.'" And sure enough, hadn't something happened? We all felt how right he had been. The carriage had begun to fill with smoke, a thick smudge; nobody knew where it came from, but we all thought it best to get out into the night.

That could only be done by quite a big jump from the footboard onto the line, for there was no platform of course, and besides our carriage was canted a good deal towards the opposite side. But the ladies—they had hastily covered their nakedness—jumped in desperation and soon we were all standing there between the lines.

It was nearly dark, but from where we were we could see that no damage had been done at the rear of the train, though all the carriages stood at a slant. But further forward—fifteen or twenty paces further forward! Not for nothing had the jerk we felt made such a horrid crash. There lay a waste of wreckage; we could see the margins of it, with the little lights of the guards' lanterns flickering across and to and fro.

Excited people came towards us, bringing reports of the situation. We were close by a small station not far beyond Regensburg, and as the result of a defective point our express had run onto the wrong line, had crashed at full speed into a stationary freight train, hurling it out of the station, annihilating its rear carriages, and itself sustaining serious damage. The great express engine from Maffei's in Munich lay smashed up and done for. Price seventy thousand marks. And in the forward coaches, themselves lying almost on one side, many of the seats were telescoped. No, thank goodness, there were no lives lost. There was talk of an old woman having been "taken out," but nobody had seen her. At least, people had been thrown in all directions, children buried under luggage, the shock had been great. The baggage car was demolished. Demolished—the baggage car? Demolished.

There I stood.

A bareheaded official came running along the track. The station-master. He issued wild and tearful commands to the passengers, to make them behave themselves and get back into the coaches. But nobody took any notice of him, he had no cap and no self-control. Poor wretch! Probably the responsibility was his. Perhaps this was the end of his career, the wreck of his prospects. I could not ask him about the baggage car—it would have been tactless.

Another official came up—he *limped* up. I recognized him by the sergeant-major's moustache: it was the stern and vigilant guard of the early evening—our Father, the State. He limped along, bent over with his hand on his knee, thinking about nothing else. "Oh, dear!" he said, "oh, dear, oh, dear me!" I asked him what was the matter. "I got stuck, sir, jammed me in the chest, I made my escape through the roof." This "made my escape through the roof" sounded like a newspaper report. Certainly the man would not have used the phrase in everyday life; he had experienced not so much an accident as a newspaper account of it—but what was that to me? He was in no state to give me news of my manuscript. So I accosted a young man who came up bustling and self-important from the waste of wreckage, and asked him about the heavy luggage.

"Well, sir, nobody can say anything as to that"—his tone implied that I ought to be grateful to have escaped unhurt. "Everything is all over the place. Women's shoes—" he said with a sweeping gesture to indicate the devastation, and wrinkled his nose. "When they start the clearing operations we shall see. —— Women's shoes. ——"

There I stood. All alone I stood there in the night and searched my heart. Clearing operations. Clearing operations were to be undertaken with my manuscript. Probably it was destroyed, then, torn up, demolished. My honeycomb, my spider-web, my nest, my earth, my pride and pain, my all, the best of me—what should I do if it were gone? I had no copy of what had been welded and forged, of what already was a living, speaking thing—to say nothing of my notes and drafts, all that I had saved and stored up and overheard and sweated over for years—my squirrel's hoard. What should I do? I inquired of my own soul and I knew that I should begin over again from the beginning. Yes, with animal patience, with the tenacity of a primitive creature the curious and complex product of whose little ingenuity and industry has been destroyed; after a moment of helpless bewilderment I should set to work again—and perhaps this time it would come easier!

But meanwhile a fire brigade had come up, their torches cast a red light over the wreck; when I went forward and looked for the baggage car, behold it was almost intact, the luggage quite unharmed. All the things that lay strewn about came out of the freight train: among the rest a quantity of balls of string—a perfect sea of string covered the ground far and wide.

A load was lifted from my heart. I mingled with the people who stood talking and fraternizing in misfortune—also showing off and being important. So much seemed clear, that the engine-driver had acted with great presence of mind. He had averted a great catastrophe by pulling the emergency brake at the last moment. Otherwise, it was said, there would have been a general smash and the whole train would have gone over the steep embankment on the left. Oh, praiseworthy engine-driver! He was not about, nobody had seen him, but his fame spread down the whole length of the train and we all lauded him in his absence. "That chap," said one man, and pointed with one hand somewhere off into the night, "that chap saved our lives." We all agreed.

But our train was standing on a track where it did not belong, and it behoved those in charge to guard it from behind so that another one did not run into it. Firemen perched on the rear carriage with torches of flaming pitch, and the excited young man who had given me such a fright with his "women's shoes" seized upon a torch too and began signalling with it, though no train was anywhere in sight.

Slowly and by degrees something like order was produced, the State our Father regained poise and presence. Steps had been taken, wires sent, presently a breakdown train from Regensburg steamed cautiously into the station and great gas flares with reflectors were set up about the wreck. We passengers were now turned off and told to go into the little station building to wait for our new conveyance. Laden with our hand luggage, some of the party with bandaged heads, we passed through a lane of inquisitive natives into the tiny waiting-room, where we herded together as best we could. And inside of an hour we were all stowed higgledy-piggledy into a special train.

I had my first-class ticket—my journey being paid for—but it availed me nothing, for everybody wanted to ride first and my carriage was more crowded than the others. But just as I found me a little niche, whom do I see diagonally opposite to me, huddled in the corner? My hero, the gentleman with the spats and the vocabulary of a cavalry officer. He did not have his dog, it had been taken away from him in defiance of his rights as a nob and now sat howling in a gloomy prison just behind the engine. His master, like myself, held a yellow ticket which was no good to him, and he was grumbling, he was trying to make head against this communistic levelling of rank in the face of general misfortune. But another man answered him in a virtuous tone: "You ought to be thankful that you can sit down." And with a sour smile my gentleman resigned himself to the crazy situation.

And now who got in, supported by two firemen? A wee little old grandmother in a tattered black cape, the very same who in Munich would for two pins have got into a second-class carriage. "Is this the first class?" she kept asking. And when we made room and assured her that it was, she sank down with a "God be praised!" onto the plush cushions as though only now was she safe and sound.

By Hof it was already five o'clock and light. There we breakfasted; an express train picked me up and deposited me with my belongings, three hours late, in Dresden.

Well, that was the railway accident I went through. I suppose it had to happen once; but whatever mathematicians may say, I feel that I now have every chance of escaping another.

A NOVELIST'S ALLEGORY

John Galsworthy

Once upon a time the Prince of Felicitas had occasion to set forth on a journey. It was a late autumn evening with few pale stars and a moon no larger than the paring of a finger-nail. And as he rode through the purlieus of his city, the white mane of his amber-colored steed was all that he could clearly see in the dusk of the high streets. His way led through a quarter but little known to him, and he was surprised to find that his horse, instead of ambling forward with his customary gentle vigor, stepped carefully from side to side, stopping now and then to curve his neck and prick his ears—as though at some thing of fear unseen in the darkness; while on either hand creatures could be heard rustling and scuttling, and little cold draughts as of wings fanned the rider's cheeks.

The Prince at last turned in his saddle, but so great was the darkness that he could not even see his escort.

"What is the name of this street?" he said.

"Sire, it is called the Vita Publica."

"It is very dark." Even as he spoke his horse staggered, but, recovering its foothold with an effort, stood trembling violently. Nor could all the incitements of its master induce the beast again to move forward.

"Is there no one with a lanthorn in this street?" asked the Prince.

His attendants began forthwith to call out loudly for any one who had a lanthorn. Now, it chanced that an old man sleeping in a hovel on a pallet of straw was awakened by these cries. When he heard that it was the Prince of Felicitas himself, he came hastily, carrying his lanthorn, and stood trembling beside the Prince's horse.

— "*A Novelist's Allegory*" by *John Galsworthy*, reprinted from *The Inn of Tranquility* by *John Galsworthy*, published by *William Heinemann Ltd.*, *London, 1912; reprinted by permission of the publisher*

It was so dark that the Prince could not see him.

"Light your lanthorn, old man," he said.

The old man laboriously lit his lanthorn. Its pale rays fled out on either hand; beautiful but grim was the vision they disclosed. Tall houses, fair courtyards, and a palm-grown garden; in front of the Prince's horse a deep cesspool, on whose jagged edges the good beast's hoofs were planted; and, as far as the glimmer of the lanthorn stretched, both ways down the rutted street, paving stones displaced, and smooth tesselated marble; pools of mud, the hanging fruit of an orange-tree, and dark, scurrying shapes of monstrous rats bolting across from house to house. The old man held the lanthorn higher; and instantly bats flying against it would have beaten out the light but for the thin protection of its horn sides.

The Prince sat still upon his horse, looking first at the rutted space that he had traversed and then at the rutted space before him.

"Without a light," he said, "this thoroughfare is dangerous. What is your name, old man?"

"My name is Cethru," replied the aged churl.

"Cethru!" said the Prince. "Let it be your duty henceforth to walk with your lanthorn up and down this street all night and every night," —and he looked at Cethru: "Do you understand, old man, what it is you have to do?"

The old man answered in a voice that trembled like a rusty flute:

"Aye, aye!—to walk up and down and hold my lanthorn so that folk can see where they be goin'."

The Prince gathered up his reins; but the old man, lurching forward, touched his stirrup.

"How long be I to go on wi' thiccy job?"

"Until you die!"

Cethru held up his lanthorn, and they could see his long, thin face, like a sandwich of dried leather, jerk and quiver, and his thin gray hairs flutter in the draught of the bats' wings circling round the light.

"'Twill be main hard!" he groaned; "an' my lanthorn's nowt but a poor thing."

With a high look, the Prince of Felicitas bent and touched the old man's forehead.

"Until you die, old man," he repeated; and bidding his followers to light torches from Cethru's lanthorn, he rode on down the twisting street. The clatter of the horse's hoofs died out in the night, and the scuttling and the rustling of the rats and the whispers of the bats' wings were heard again.

Cethru, left alone in the dark thoroughfare, sighed heavily; then, spitting on his hands, he tightened the old girdle round his loins, and slinging the lanthorn on his staff, held it up to the level of his waist, and began to make his way along the street. His progress was but slow, for he had many times to stop and rekindle the flame within his lanthorn, which the bats' wings, his own stumbles, and the jostlings of footpads or of revellers returning home, were forever extinguishing. In traversing that long street he spent half the night, and half the night in traversing it back again. The saffron swan of dawn, slow swimming up the sky-river between the high roofbanks, bent her neck down through the dark air-water to look at him staggering below her, with his still smoking wick. No sooner did Cethru see the sunlit bird, than with a deep sigh of joy he sat him down, and at once fell asleep.

Now when the dwellers in the houses of the Vita Publica first gained knowledge that this old man passed every night with his lanthorn up and down their street, and when they marked those pallid gleams gliding over the motley prospect of cesspools and garden gates, over the sightless hovels and the rich-carved frontages of their palaces; or saw them stay their journey and remain suspended like a handful of daffodils held up against the black stuffs of secrecy— they said:

"It is good that the old man should pass like this—we shall see better where we're going; and if the Watch have any job on hand, or want to put the pavements in order, his lanthorn will serve their purpose well enough." And they would call out of their doors and windows to him passing:

"Hola! old man Cethru! All's well with our house, and with the street before it?"

But, for answer, the old man only held his lanthorn up, so that in the ring of its pale light they saw some sight or other in the street. And his silence troubled them, one by one, for each had expected that he would reply:

"Aye, aye! All's well with *your house*, Sirs, and with the street before it!"

Thus they grew irritated with this old man who did not seem able to do anything but just hold his lanthorn up. And gradually they began to dislike his passing by their doors with his pale light, by which they could not fail to see, not only the rich-carved frontages and scrolled gates of courtyards and fair gardens, but things that were not pleasing to the eye. And they murmured amongst themselves: "What is the good of this old man and his silly lanthorn. We can see all we want to see without him; in fact, we got on very well before he came."

So, as he passed, rich folk who were supping would pelt him with orange-peel and empty the dregs of their wine over his head; and poor folk, sleeping in their hutches, turned over, as the rays of the lanthorn fell on them, and cursed him for that disturbance. Nor did revellers or footpads treat the old man civilly, but tied him to the wall, where he was constrained to stay until a kind passer-by released him. And ever the bats darkened his lanthorn with their wings and tried to beat the flame out. And the old man thought: "This be a terrible hard job; I don't seem to please nobody." But because the Prince of Felicitas had so commanded him, he continued nightly to pass with his lanthorn up and down the street; and every morning as the saffron swan came swimming overhead, to fall asleep. But his sleep did not last long, for he was compelled to pass many hours each day in gathering rushes and melting down tallow for his lanthorn; so that his lean face grew more then ever like a sandwich of dried leather.

Now it came to pass that the Town Watch having had certain complaints made to them that persons had been bitten in the Vita Publica by rats, doubted of their duty to destroy these ferocious creatures; and they held investigation, summoning the persons bitten and inquiring of them how it was that in so dark a street they could tell that the animals which had bitten them were indeed rats. Howbeit for some time no one could be found who could say more than what he had been told, and since this was not evidence, the Town Watch had good hopes that they would not after all be forced to undertake this tedious enterprise. But presently there came before them one who said that he had himself seen the rat which had bitten him, by the light of an old man's lanthorn. When the Town Watch heard this they were vexed, for they knew that if this were true they would now be forced to prosecute the arduous undertaking, and they said:

"Bring in this old man!"

Cethru was brought before them trembling.

"What is this we hear, old man, about your lanthorn and the rat? And in the first place, what were you doing in the Vita Publica at that time of night?"

Cethru answered: "I were just passin' with my lanthorn!"

"Tell us—did *you* see the rat?"

Cethru shook his head: "My lanthorn seed the rat, maybe!" he muttered.

"Old owl!" said the Captain of the Watch: "Be careful what you say! If you saw the rat, why did you then not aid this unhappy citizen who was bitten by it—first, to avoid that rodent, and subsequently to slay it, thereby relieving the public of a pestilential danger?"

Cethru looked at him, and for some seconds did not reply; then he said slowly: "I were just passin' with my lanthorn."

"That you have already told us," said the Captain of the Watch; "it is no answer."

Cethru's leathern cheeks became wine-col-ored, so desirous was he to speak, and so unable. And the Watch sneered and laughed, saying: "This is a fine witness."

But of a sudden Cethru spoke:

"What would I be duin'—killin' rats; tidden my business to kill rats."

The Captain of the Watch caressed his beard, and looking at the old man with contempt, said:

"It seems to me, brothers, that this is an idle old vagabond, who does no good to anyone. We should be well advised, I think, to prosecute him for vagrancy. But that is not at this moment the matter in hand. Owing to the accident— scarcely fortunate—of this old man's passing with his lanthorn, it would certainly appear that citizens have been bitten by rodents. It is then, I fear, our duty to institute proceedings against those poisonous and violent animals."

And amidst the sighing of the Watch, it was so resolved.

Cethru was glad to shuffle away, unnoticed, from the Court, and sitting down under a camel-date tree outside the City Wall, he thus reflected:

"They were rough with me! I done nothin', so far's I can see!"

And a long time he sat there with the bunches of the camel-dates above him, golden as the sunlight. Then, as the scent of the lyrio flowers, released by evening, warned him of the night dropping like a flight of dark birds on the plain, he rose stiffly, and made his way as usual toward the Vita Publica.

He had traversed but little of that black thoroughfare, holding his lanthorn at the level of his breast, when the sound of a splash and cries for help smote his long, thin ears. Remembering how the Captain of the Watch had admonished him, he stopped and peered about, but owing to his proximity to the light of his own lanthorn he saw nothing. Presently he heard another splash and the sound of blowings and of puffings, but still unable to see clearly whence they came, he was forced in bewilderment to resume his march. But he had no sooner entered the next bend of that obscure and winding avenue then the most lamentable, lusty cries assailed him. Again he stood still, blinded by his own light. Somewhere at hand a citizen was being beaten, for vague, quick-moving forms emerged into the radiance of his lanthorn out of the deep violet of the night air. The cries swelled, and died away, and swelled; and the mazed Cethru moved forward on his way. But very near the end of his first traversage, the sound of a long, deep sighing, as of a fat man in spiritual pain, once more arrested him.

"Drat me!" he thought, "this time I *will* see what 'tis," and he spun round and round, holding his lanthorn now high, now low, and to both sides.

"The devil an' all's in it to-night," he murmured to himself; "there's some 'at here fetchin' of his breath awful loud." But for his life he could see nothing, only that the higher he held his lanthorn the more painful grew the sound of the fat but spiritual sighing. And desperately, he at last resumed his progress.

On the morrow, while he still slept stretched on his straw pallet, there came to him a member of the Watch.

"Old man, you are wanted at the Court House; rouse up, and bring your lanthorn."

Stiffly Cethru rose.

"What be they wantin' me fur now, mester?"

"Ah!" replied the Watchman, "they are about to see if they can't put an end to your goings-on."

Cethru shivered, and was silent.

Now when they reached the Court House it was patent that a great affair was forward; for the Judges were in their robes, and a crowd of advocates, burgesses, and common folk thronged the carven, lofty hall of justice.

When Cethru saw that all eyes were turned on him, he shivered still more violently, fixing his fascinated gaze on the three Judges in their emerald robes.

"This then is the prisoner," said the oldest of the Judges; "proceed with the indictment!"

A little advocate in snuff-colored clothes rose on little legs, and commenced to read:

"Forasmuch as on the seventeenth night of August fifteen hundred years since the Messiah's death, one Celestine, a maiden of this city, fell into a cesspool in the Vita Publica, and while being quietly drowned, was espied of the burgess Pardonix by the light of a lanthorn held by the old man Cethru; and, forasmuch as, plunging in, the said Pardonix rescued her, not without grave risk of life and the ruin of his clothes, and to-day lies ill of fever; and forasmuch as the old man Cethru was the cause of these misfortunes to the burgess Pardonix, by reason of his wandering lanthorn's showing the drowning maiden, the watch do hereby indict, accuse, and otherwise place charge upon this Cethru of 'Vagabondage without serious occupation.'

"And, forasmuch as on this same night the Watchman Filepo, made aware, by the light of this said Cethru's lanthorn, of three sturdy footpads, went to arrest them, and was set on by the rogues and well nigh slain, the Watch do hereby indict, accuse, and otherwise charge upon Cethru complicity in this assault, by reasons, namely, first, that he discovered the footpads to the Watchman and the Watchman to the footpads by the light of his lanthorn; and, second, that, having thus discovered them, he stood idly by and gave no assistance to the law.

"And, forasmuch as on this same night the wealthy burgess Pranzo, who, having prepared a banquet, was standing in his doorway awaiting the arrival of his guests, did see, by the light of the said Cethru's lanthorn, a beggar woman and her children grovelling in the gutter for garbage, whereby his appetite was lost completely; and, forasmuch as he, Pranzo, has lodged a complaint against the Constitution for permitting women and children to go starved, the Watch do hereby indict, accuse, and otherwise make charge on Cethru of rebellion and of anarchy, in that wilfully he doth disturb good citizens by showing to them without provocation disagreeable sights, and doth moreover endanger the laws by causing persons to desire to change them.

"These be the charges, reverend Judges, so please you!"

And having thus spoken, the little advocate resumed his seat.

Then said the oldest of the Judges: "Cethru, you have heard; what answer do you make?"

But no word, only the chattering of teeth, came from Cethru.

"Have you no defence?" said the Judge: "these are grave accusations!"

Then Cethru spoke.

"So please your Highnesses," he said, "can I help what my lanthorn sees?"

And having spoken these words, to all further questions he remained more silent than a headless man.

The Judges took counsel of each other, and the oldest of them thus addressed himself to Cethru:

"If you have no defence, old man, and there is no one will say a word for you, we can but proceed to judgment."

Then in the main aisle of the Court there rose a youthful advocate.

"Most reverend Judges," he said in a mellifluous voice, clearer than the fluting of a bellbird, "it is useless to look for words from this old man, for it is manifest that he himself is nothing, and that his lanthorn is alone concerned in this affair. But, reverend Judges, bethink you well: Would you have a lanthorn ply a trade or be concerned with a profession, or do ought indeed but pervade the streets at night, shedding its light, which, if you will, is vagabondage? And, Sirs, upon the second count of this indictment: Would you have a lanthorn dive into cesspools to rescue maidens? Would you have a lanthorn to beat footpads? Or, indeed, to be any sort of partisan either of the Law or of them that break the Law? Sure, Sirs, I think not. And as to this third charge of fostering anarchy —let me but describe the trick of this lanthorn's flame. It is distilled, most reverend Judges, of oil and wick, together with that sweet secret heat of whose birth no words of mine can tell. And when, Sirs, this pale flame has sprung into the air swaying to every wind, it brings vision to the human eye. And, if it be charged on this old

man Cethru that he and his lanthorn by reason of their showing not only the good but the evil bring no pleasure into the world, I ask, Sirs, what in the world is so dear as this power to see —whether it be the beautiful or the foul that is disclosed? Need I, indeed, tell you of the way this flame spreads its feelers, and delicately darts and hovers in the darkness, conjuring things from nothing? This mechanical summoning, Sirs, of visions out of blackness is benign, by no means of malevolent intent; no more than if a man, passing two donkeys in the road, one lean and the other fat, could justly be arraigned for malignancy because they were not both fat. This, reverend Judges, is the essence of the matter concerning the rich burgess, Pranzo, who, on account of the sight he saw by Cethru's lanthorn, has lost the equilibrium of his stomach. For, Sirs, the lanthorn did but show that which was there, both fair and foul, no more, no less; and though it is indeed true that Pranzo is upset, it was not because the lanthorn maliciously produced distorted images, but merely caused to be seen, in due proportions, things which Pranzo had not seen before. And surely, reverend Judges, being just men, you would not have this lanthorn turn its light away from what is ragged and ugly because there are also fair things on which its light may fall; how, indeed, being a lanthorn, could it, if it would? And I would have you note this, Sirs, that by this impartial discovery of the proportions of one thing to another, this lanthorn must indeed perpetually seem to cloud and sadden those things which are fair, because of the deep instincts of harmony and justice planted in the human breast. However unfair and cruel, then, this lanthorn may seem to those who, deficient in these instincts, desire all their lives to see naught but what is pleasant, lest they, like Pranzo should lose their appetites—it is not consonant with equity that this lanthorn should, even if it could, be prevented from thus mechanically buffeting the holiday cheek of life. I would think, Sirs, that you should rather blame the queazy state of Pranzo's stomach. The old man has said that he cannot help what his lanthorn sees. This is a just saying. But if, reverend Judges, you deem this equipoised, indifferent lanthorn to be indeed blameworthy for having shown in the same moment, side by side, the skull and the fair face, the burdock and the tiger-lily, the butterfly and the toad, then, most reverend Judges, punish it, but do not punish this old man, for he himself is but a flume of smoke, thistledown dispersed—nothing!"

So saying, the young advocate ceased.

Again the three Judges took counsel of each other, and after much talk had passed between them, the oldest spoke:

"What this young advocate has said seems to us to be the truth. We cannot punish a lanthorn. Let the old man go!"

And Cethru went out into the sunshine. ——

Now it came to pass that the Prince of Felicitas, returning from his journey, rode once more on his amber-colored steed down the Vita Publica.

The night was dark as a rook's wing, but far away down the street burned a little light, like a red star truant from heaven. The Prince riding by descried it for a lanthorn, with an old man sleeping beside it.

"How is this, Friend?" said the Prince. "You are not walking as I bade you, carrying your lanthorn."

But Cethru neither moved nor answered.

"Lift him up!" said the Prince.

They lifted up his head and held the lanthorn to his closed eyes. So lean was that brown face that the beams from the lanthorn would not rest on it, but slipped past on either side into the night. His eyes did not open. He was dead. And the Prince touched him, saying: "Farewell, old man! The lanthorn is still alight. Go, fetch me another one, and let him carry it!" ——

A PIECE OF CHALK

G. K. Chesterton

I remember one splendid morning, all blue and silver, in the summer holidays, when I reluctantly tore myself away from the task of doing nothing in particular, and put on a hat of some sort and picked up a walking-stick, and put six very bright-coloured chalks in my pocket. I then went into the kitchen (which, along with the rest of the house, belonged to a very square and sensible old woman in a Sussex village), and asked the owner and occupant of the kitchen if she had any brown paper. She had a great deal; in fact, she had too much; and she mistook

—— "A Piece of Chalk" by G. K. Chesterton, from Tremendous Trifles by G. K. Chesterton, published by Methuen and Company, London, third edition, December 1909; reprinted by permission of the estate of G. K. Chesterton

the purpose and the rationale of the existence of brown paper. She seemed to have an idea that if a person wanted brown paper he must be wanting to tie up parcels; which was the last thing I wanted to do; indeed, it is a thing which I have found to be beyond my mental capacity. Hence she dwelt very much on the varying qualities of toughness and endurance in the material. I explained to her that I only wanted to draw pictures on it, and that I did not want them to endure in the least; and that from my point of view, therefore, it was a question not of tough consistency, but of responsive surface, a thing comparatively irrelevant in a parcel. When she understood that I wanted to draw she offered to overwhelm me with note-paper, apparently supposing that I did my notes and correspondence on old brown paper wrappers from motives of economy.

I then tried to explain the rather delicate logical shade, that I not only liked brown paper, but liked the quality of brownness in paper, just as I liked the quality of brownness in October woods, or in beer, or in the peat-streams of the North. Brown paper represents the primal twilight of the first toil of creation, and with a bright-coloured chalk or two you can pick out points of fire in it, sparks of gold, and blood-red, and sea-green, like the first fierce stars that sprang out of divine darkness. All this I said (in an off-hand way) to the old woman; and I put the brown paper in my pocket along with the chalks, and possibly other things. I suppose every one must have reflected how primeval and how poetical are the things that one carries in one's pocket; the pocket-knife, for instance, the type of all human tools, the infant of the sword. Once I planned to write a book of poems entirely about the things in my pocket. But I found it would be too long; and the age of the great epics is past.

With my stick and my knife, my chalks and my brown paper, I went out on to the great downs. I crawled across those colossal contours that express the best quality of England, because they are at the same time soft and strong. The smoothness of them has the same meaning as the smoothness of great cart-horses, or the smoothness of the beech-tree; it declares in the teeth of our timid and cruel theories that the mighty are merciful. As my eye swept the landscape, the landscape was as kindly as any of its cottages, but for power it was like an earthquake. The villages in the immense valley were safe, one could see, for centuries; yet the lifting of the whole land was like the lifting of one enormous wave to wash them all away.

I crossed one swell of living turf after another, looking for a place to sit down and draw. Do not, for heaven's sake, imagine I was going to sketch from Nature. I was going to draw devils and seraphim, and blind old gods that men worshipped before the dawn of right, and saints in robes of angry crimson, and seas of strange green, and all the sacred or monstrous symbols that look so well in bright colours on brown paper. They are much better worth drawing than Nature; also they are much easier to draw. When a cow came slouching by in the field next to me, a mere artist might have drawn it; but I always get wrong in the hind legs of quadrupeds. So I drew the soul of the cow; which I saw there plainly walking before me in the sunlight; and the soul was all purple and silver, and had seven horns and the mystery that belongs to all the beasts. But though I could not with a crayon get the best out of the landscape, it does not follow that the landscape was not getting the best out of me. And this, I think, is the mistake that people make about the old poets who lived before Wordsworth, and were supposed not to care very much about Nature because they did not describe it much.

They preferred writing about great men to writing about great hills; but they sat on the great hills to write it. They gave out much less about Nature, but they drank in, perhaps, much more. They painted the white robes of their holy virgins with the blinding snow, at which they had stared all day. They blazoned the shields of their paladins with the purple and gold of many heraldic sunsets. The greenness of a thousand green leaves clustered into the live green figure of Robin Hood. The blueness of a score of forgotten skies became the blue robes of the Virgin. The inspiration went in like sunbeams and came out like Apollo.

But as I sat scrawling these silly figures on the brown paper, it began to dawn on me, to my great disgust, that I had left one chalk, and that a most exquisite and essential chalk, behind. I searched all my pockets, but I could not find any white chalk. Now, those who are acquainted with all the philosophy (nay, religion) which is typified in the art of drawing on brown paper, know that white is positive and essential. I cannot avoid remarking here upon a moral significance. One of the wise and awful truths which this brown-paper art reveals, is this, that white is a colour. It is not a mere absence of colour; it is a shining and affirmative thing, as fierce as red, as definite as black. When (so to speak) your pencil grows red-hot, it draws roses; when it grows white-hot, it draws stars. And one of the two or three defiant verities of the best religious morality, of real Christianity for example, is exactly this same thing; the chief assertion of religious morality is that white is a colour. Virtue is not the absence of vices or the avoidance of moral dangers; virtue is a vivid and separate thing, like pain or a particular smell. Mercy does not mean not being cruel or sparing people revenge or punishment; it means a plain and positive thing like the sun, which one has either seen or not seen. Chastity does not mean abstention from sexual wrong; it means something flaming, like Joan of Arc. In a word, God paints in many colours; but He never paints so gorgeously, I had almost said so gaudily, as when He paints in white. In a sense our age has realized this fact, and expressed it in our sullen costume. For if it were really true that white was a blank and colourless thing, negative and non-committal, then white would be used instead of black and grey for the funeral dress of this pessimistic period. We should see city gentlemen in frock coats of spotless silver satin, with top hats as white as wonderful arum lilies. Which is not the case.

Meanwhile, I could not find my chalk.

I sat on the hill in a sort of despair. There was no town nearer than Chichester at which it was even remotely probable that there would be such a thing as an artist's colourman. And yet, without white, my absurd little pictures would be as pointless as the world would be if there were no good people in it. I stared stupidly round, racking my brain for expedients. Then I suddenly stood up and roared with laughter, again and again, so that the cows stared at me and called a committee. Imagine a man in the Sahara regretting that he had no sand for his hour-glass. Imagine a gentleman in mid-ocean wishing that he had brought some salt with him for his chemical experiments. I was sitting on an immense warehouse of white chalk. The landscape was made entirely out of white chalk. White chalk was piled mere miles until it met the sky. I stooped and broke a piece off the rock I sat on: it did not mark so well as the shop chalks do; but it gave the effect. And I stood there in a trance of pleasure, realizing that this Southern England is not only a grand peninsula, and a tradition and a civilization; it is something even more admirable. It is a piece of chalk.

THE SINGING SILENCE

Eva-Lis Wuorio

Old Vincente of Formentera was perhaps the happiest man I've ever known. And also, perhaps, the poorest.

He was a cadaverous, bent juniper of a man, brown and lined, and he owned not one piece of clothing that was not patched. He lived at Cala Pujol, in a lean-to made of stone and driftwood and brush, with a rusty iron brazier for his kitchen and a couple of cracked iron pots, discarded by the fishermen, from which to eat. But he owned also an excellent snorkel and a pair of rubber flippers and a diver's mask, and, as I say, I don't believe there was a happier man.

I had been coming to Formentera for several years before Vicente stood out in my eyes from the old fishermen who drew their boats up under the brush and the bamboo shelters at the end of the beach where the rocks begin. At last I realized he was not a fisherman. He had no time to fish.

I had some Ibicenco, his dialect, a language quite different from the Castilian Spanish, so I could tell, that day I first saw him, that he was asking with dignity, not pleading, for the loan of a fisherman's small boat. I could not understand, thinking him a fisherman, how he got along without a boat, but I offered to lend him the one I always rent in Formentera. I do not use it often anyhow. He thanked me, and again his dignity impressed me.

I watched him load the boat with the snorkel and the flippers and the face mask, an earthen jug of water, and a small parcel of provisions. There was no fishing gear, no underwater gun to go with his other equipment. I wondered

— *"The Singing Silence" by Eva-Lis Wuorio, from the magazine* Saturday Evening Post, *March 23, 1963; reprinted by permission of Monica McCall, Inc., literary agent; copyright © 1963 by Eva-Lis Wuorio*

what he intended to catch and how. I watched him row out, facing the horizon, a small man, intent.

I watched until he was but a speck on the horizon, and then I forgot about him. At Cala Pujol it is easy to forget. The turquoise waters are deep and clear to the bottom, the sand is untrodden, there is a long sweep of white-silver shore—the year I speak of, it was still that way—and the sun is a constant benediction. In peace, one forgets.

There came a day when the wind blew from Africa and the sea was sultry and the fishermen did not go out. They sat in the bamboo-roofed little bar on the beach and drank red wine and talked. "Vicente got in?"

"Not yet."

"He is *loco, este hombre*, a little crazy."

"Not at all, not so much. He has the good intention."

"You think so? You, too, are *loco*."

"Me? Not at all. I see the point. I understand very well."

"Vicente?" I asked. "He is the old man with the underwater equipment?"

"Ah," they said, "aha. Ah."

I asked for another bottle of the wine of the island, for only that is drunk there. We do not try to be smart by taking better-known wines.

And so, sitting there, with the wind from Africa blowing and stirring up the sea until it was muddy below and racing, sheep-white, above, I heard the story of Vicente.

He had been an ambitious boy 60 years ago, and he had left Formentera, the little island of the past. But 60 years ago there was not much for a Spaniard to do in his country of Spain. So Vicente went to sea in foreign ships, and after a time he came back. He walked the country, trying all sorts of jobs, but he ended where better men than he had ended, as a porter

370

on the quays of Barcelona—a *mozo*.

He had had a dream, but dreams fail a man sometimes. So he carried the luggage of others: the rich Spaniards, the visitors, the tourists. Until ten years ago he stood there at the quay, a number on his hat, waving his hand at the passengers from the boats, pointing to himself and shouting, "Me? Me! Number Seventy-three!"

One day a rich American from a Palma boat saw his frantic wave and beckoned. Vicente got in line with the other porters and pushed his way up the gangplank to the white boat. There this rich American said to him, "Here are six suitcases, and *that* thing. Be careful with it; it's an antique."

Vicente recognized the earthen vessel. It was an amphora, a Phoenician one, a fine, rare specimen of the big jugs used for transporting wine or grain. In the old days fishermen sometimes caught them in their nets. They had often thrown them back into the sea, but this they did no longer, not since the *senores* from the town came to buy them for their museums.

Vicente hoisted the bags on his back, picked up the big, pinkish, sea-encrusted jug and started down the gangplank. The people were pushing and pulling, getting off the boat, coming on board, and he shouted as they shouted. He came to the quay, and another porter, stumbling on a mooring rope, fell against him and he dropped the amphora.

Two thousand years went down in a dusty sound of earth falling. Well.

Ten years before there were still amphorae and other relics of the Greeks and Phoenicians and Romans in the shallow coves of the islands of Ibiza, but now there were mostly only almost valueless objects of more recent times; valuable specimens were very rare. The American had paid $500 for this water jug of a Phoenician sailor, having had it verified as authentic by the authorities. Naturally he was angry.

But he was also a sensible man and knew that never in a lifetime could the porter Vicente make $500, so he was resigned and ready to forget his loss.

Not so Vicente. He knew the value men set now on these useless old jugs and pots; he had seen the disappointment on the face of the American. Vicente was an honorable man and he wanted to make amends.

He followed the American to his hotel, pleaded for his name and address, and promised to pay him back. A ragged piece of paper torn from a diary and scribbled with Abraham Lincoln Smith, 72 Hudson Avenue, Milwaukee, Wisconsin, U.S.A. became his most valuable possession. It was to him the ultimate milepost on the long road of his search.

I believe that somehow, in his dreams, Vicente saw himself at last arriving in Milwaukee, Wisconsin, U.S.A., with the ancient Phoenician amphora under his arm, receiving with joy the praise that would greet him there.

Vicente knew that he would never have the money to buy an amphora, but what was to prevent his finding one? Others had, dozens of them in the time of his boyhood. Why not he?

He had no family, so it did not take him long to bid farewell to his life in Barcelona, that bustling, busy city by the sea, where he had carried bags for the price of a small glass of wine in a smoky wineshop, and a windowless room to roof his nights.

When he had sold his few possessions he had the deck fare to Ibiza, and a little more. From the stern of the boat he looked back and saw the city sink into the sea, and for the first time he knew that his years there had been a prison of his own making. He had never, there, lifted up his eyes from the narrow streets to the wide sky.

And once again, as when he was a boy, the sea sang to him.

Back on the islands he set about the task he had chosen. He learned where the last amphora had been found, and he realized, as had others before him, that since the ancient pieces were valuable, all the inshore places must have been searched and emptied of their treasure.

Young Sandik, of Santa Eulalia del Rio, the carpenter's son, had made himself a reputation as an undersea swimmer. He had found a cannon at the bottom of the sea—but that's another story. To consult him, Vicente traveled by bus to Santa Eulalia del Rio, and Sandik's advice was brief. Get a mask, get flippers, go far out into the sea. There, way out, were still unknown shallows, no deeper than the height of a man, or twice or thrice the height of a man, and caught in the caves of the sea bottom, treasures might still be.

Now Vicente, like many of the island-born, had never learned to swim. But he spent the rest of his money, as Sandik advised, on a good snorkel and flippers and a mask. Then he took the little mail boat *Manolito* back to his island of Formentera. There, camping on the beach, scrounging his meals, intent as are all men with a singleness of purpose to urge them on, he set about teaching himself to swim.

He was over 60 then. An old man, as time makes men like Vicente old. Yet he was young in his urgency to learn and go on toward the far horizon of his purpose.

He learned to swim, and he learned to dive with the snorkel and the flippers and the mask, a froglike, crablike figure in the clear shallows about the beaches of Cala Pujol. He ventured farther and farther, to where the water turned purple, where the deeps began. This was the most talkative time of his life, after his first dives, for he could not contain his wonder at the unexpected beauty of the deep sea. The gardens of starfish, the varicolored, bug-eyed gentle fish that followed him, the slant of translucent sunlight on the mysterious caves and rocks—these he recounted to the fisherman who toiled upon the surface of the sea. And his tales were touched with wonder and awe. Never, he swore, had he known such freedom as at the bottom of the sea.

"But you can't breathe there!"

"One breathes with one's eyes, one's pores." Never had he heard such music.

"But there is only silence under the sea!"

"It is a singing silence. Like many instruments sending their purest sounds up to the sky."

There is that to the Spanish language. The plowman often speaks the language of poetry. It is the way the words arrange themselves.

Day by day, week by week, month by month, and so on into the years, Vicente, searching for the amphora which in honor he felt he must find to replace the one he had broken, grew happier. Each day was a new delight, a new adventure. No longer were his days imprisoned by the needs of the hours. Somehow there was always something for those needs, a fish to grill, a glass of wine, a piece of bread, a box of matches. To the fishermen his search had become a part of their life on the beach and the sea, and their generosity was quick, unthinking.

They told me the story of Vicente, that day the wind blew from Africa and stirred up the depths of the sea and sent the high green waves scurrying, and I, too, searched the horizon for the little boat. Then I turned to Father Pedro, the curé of San Fernando, who had joined us.

"What do you think, Father?" I said. "Will old Vicente find his amphora?"

The fat little priest joined his fingers. His eyes, too, were on the horizon, but he seemed undisturbed. The wind from Africa swayed the bamboo shelter over us.

"Well, now, you see," he said, "Vicente has the search. It is not what one finds, you know, but the search itself that is important. Only the search."

Last year, on another day, when the sea rose suddenly, stirred to tumult by the wind, the little boat Vicente had borrowed was tossed back to the beach.

No one saw the old man again.

The seas had been heavy.

But tied securely, wrapped in seaweed at the bottom of the boat, was an amphora, an ancient Phoenician vessel salvaged from the centuries and the sea.

Father Pedro and the fisherman who had been Vicente's friends asked me, since I knew English, to write to Abraham Lincoln Smith of Milwaukee, Wisconsin, U.S.A. I did. I wrote a number of times to the address we had and finally to the mayor of the city.

No one had heard of him.

Annoyed by the foolish old man who had dropped his souvenir, the American had fabricated a name to get rid of him. Perhaps, however, he did come from Milwaukee. We do not know.

The sources of quotations used on the opening pages of the four units in this text are as follows:
— *page 1, top to bottom: Plato, from <u>The Republic</u> (Penguin edition); Ralph Waldo Emerson, from "Self-Reliance" in <u>Selected Prose and Poetry</u> (Rinehart edition); Arthur Joyce Cary, from "The Mass Mind," reprinted by permission of Curtis Brown Ltd.; Joseph Conrad, from <u>Youth: A Narrative, and Two Other Stories</u> (William Blackwood & Sons, 1902)*
— *page 99, top to bottom: Edmund Fuller, from <u>Men in Modern Fiction</u> (Vintage Books, a division of Random House, Inc. and Alfred A. Knopf, Inc., 1955), pp. 11, 23; Bernard DeVoto, from "Homily for a Troubled Time," first printed in <u>Woman's Day</u> (January 1951), reprinted by permission of Mrs. Bernard DeVoto; Henrik Ibsen, from <u>An Enemy of the People</u> (Modern Library edition, Random House, Inc.)*
— *page 199, top to bottom: William Wordsworth, from the "Preface to Lyrical Ballads (1800)" in <u>The</u>*

<u>Prelude: Selected Poems and Sonnets</u> (Rinehart edition); G. Lowes Dickinson, from "A Sacred Mountain" in <u>Letters from a Chinese Official</u> (1903), reprinted by permission of George Allen & Unwin; Joseph Hudnut, from "The Invisible City" in <u>Architecture and the Spirit of Man</u> (found in this text on pp. 207 ff.); Ruth Benedict, from <u>Patterns of Culture</u> (Houghton Mifflin Co., 1934), reprinted by permission of the publisher
— *page 279, top to bottom: N. J. Berrill, from "The Shape of Wonder" in <u>Man's Emerging Mind</u> (Dodd, Mead & Co., 1957), copyright © 1955 by N. J. Berrill; Percy Bysshe Shelley, from "Defence of Poetry" in <u>Selected Poetry and Prose</u> (Rinehart edition); Frederick Philip Grove, from "The Value of Art" in <u>It Needs to be Said</u> (The Macmillan Company of Canada Limited, 1929); Hugh MacLennan, from "The Shadow of Captain Bligh" in <u>Thirty and Three</u> (The Macmillan Company of Canada Ltd., 1954), reprinted by permission of the author and the publisher*

Index of authors and titles